APR 2 7 2005

Publisher
Jim Scheikofer
The Family Handyman®

Director, Publication Services
Sue Baalman-Pohlman
Home Design Alternatives, Inc.

Editor
Kimberly King
Home Design Alternatives, Inc.

Newsstand Sales
David Algire
Reader's Digest Association, Inc.

John Crouse
Reader's Digest Association, Inc.

Marketing Manager
Andrea Vecchio
The Family Handyman

Production Manager
Judy Rodriguez
The Family Handyman

Plans Administrator
Curtis Cadenhead
Home Design Alternatives, Inc.

Copyright 2004 by Home Service Publications, Inc., publishers of *The Family Handyman* Magazine, 2915 Commers Drive, Suite 700, Eagan, MN 55121. Plan copyrights held by home designer/architect.

The Family Handyman is a registered trademark of RD Publications, Inc.

RD Publications, Inc. is a subsidiary of The Reader's Digest Association, Inc.

Reader's Digest and The Family Handyman logo are registered trademarks of The Reader's Digest Association, Inc. All rights reserved. Unauthorized reproduction, in any manner is prohibited.

Artist drawings and photos shown in this publication may vary slightly from the actual working drawings. Some photos are shown in mirror reverse. Please refer to the floor plan for accurate layout. All plans appearing in this publication are protected under copyright law.

Reproduction of the illustrations or working drawings by any means is strictly prohibited. The right of building only one structure from the plans purchased is licensed exclusively to the buyer and the plans may not be resold unless by express written authorization.

Reader's Digest

The Family Handyman®

Vol. 18, No. 5

Contents

Featured Homes

Plan #708-0184 is featured on page 66.
Photo courtesy of HDA, Inc.

Plan #708-0322 is featured on page 193.
Photo courtesy of HDA, Inc.

Sections

The Family Handyman magazine and Home Design Alternatives (HDA, Inc.) are pleased to join together to bring you this collection of timeless and traditional home plans from some of the nation's leading designers and architects.

Technical Specifications - At the time the construction drawings were prepared, every effort was made to ensure that these plan and specifications meet nationally recognized building codes (BOCA, Southern Building Code Congress and others). Because national building codes change or vary from area to area some drawing modifications and/or the assistance of a professional designer or architect may be necessary to comply with your local codes or to accommodate specific building conditions. We advise you to consult with your local building official for information regarding codes governing your area.

D1567944

On The Cover . . .

Plan #708-0298 is featured on page 294.
Photo courtesy of HDA, Inc.

DISCARDED
BRADFORD WG PUBLIC LIBRARY

BRADFORD WG LIBRARY
100 HOLLAND COURT, BOX 130
BRADFORD, ONT. L3Z 2A7

Plan #708-0708

Stately Front Entrance With Style

2,615 total square feet of living area

Price Code E

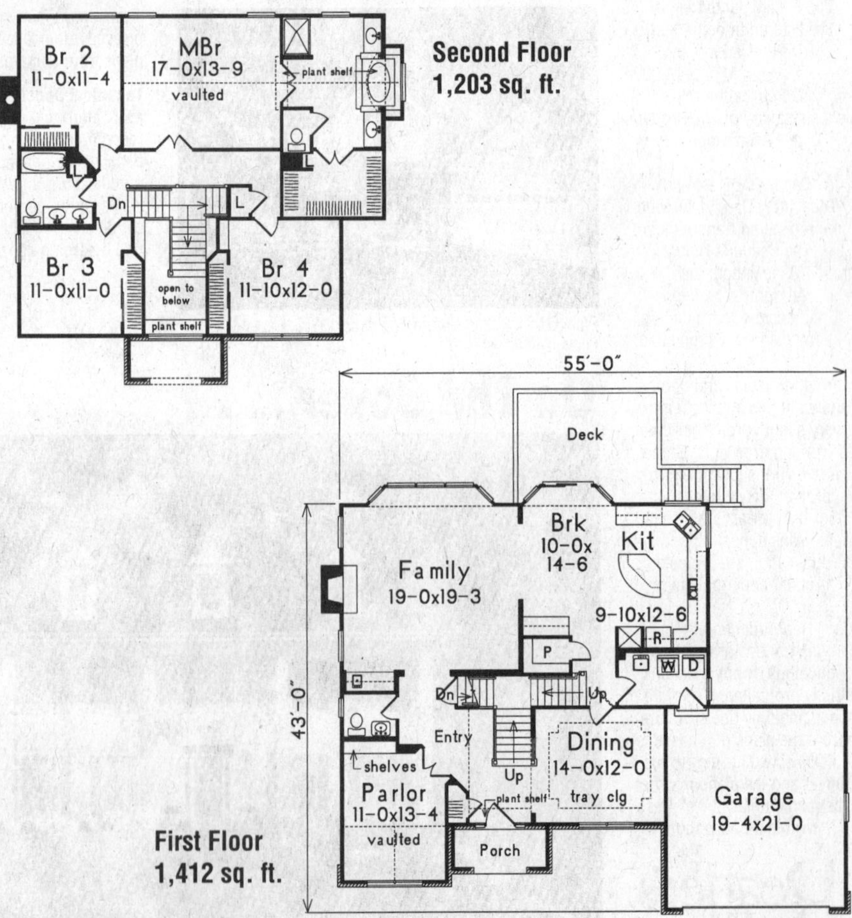
Br 2
11-0x11-4
MBr
17-0x13-9
vaulted
plant shelf
Dn
L
Br 3
11-0x11-0
open to below
plant shelf
Br 4
11-10x12-0
Second Floor
1,203 sq. ft.
55'-0"
Deck
Brk
10-0x
14-6
Kit
9-10x12-6
Family
19-0x19-3
P
R
W
D
Dn
Up
Entry
Dining
14-0x12-0
tray clg
shelves
Parlor
11-0x13-4
vaulted
Up
plant shelf
Porch
Garage
19-4x21-0
43'-0"
First Floor
1,412 sq. ft.

Special features

- Grand two-story entry features majestic palladian window, double French doors to parlor and access to powder room
- State-of-the-art kitchen has corner sink with two large archtop windows, island snack bar, menu desk and walk-in pantry
- Master bath is vaulted and offers a luxurious step-up tub, palladian window, built-in shelves and columns with plant shelf
- 4 bedrooms, 2 1/2 baths, 2-car garage
- Basement foundation

TO ORDER BLUEPRINTS USE THE FORM ON PAGE 15 OR CALL TOLL-FREE 1-877-671-6036

View thousands more home plans online at www.familyhandyman.com/homeplans

He's turned out to be quite
the expert in heating and cooling.

We're such good role models.

At Carrier, our products stand for unmatched expertise. But that's only half the story. We also have the professionals with unmatched expertise to install them — our Factory Authorized Dealers. They provide customized solutions and give 100% guaranteed satisfaction.* What a perfect combination.

Turn to your local Carrier expert at 1-800-Carrier or www.carrier.com

Carrier
Turn to the Experts.

©CARRIER CORPORATION 2004. A member of the United Technologies Corporation family. Stock symbol UT

The Family
Handyman

Plan #708-0690

Classic Ranch Has Grand Appeal With Expansive Porch

1,400 total square feet of living area **Price Code B**

Special features

- Master bedroom is secluded for privacy
- Large utility room with additional cabinet space
- Covered porch provides an outdoor seating area
- Roof dormers add great curb appeal
- Vaulted ceilings in living room and master bedroom
- Oversized two-car garage with storage
- 3 bedrooms, 2 baths, 2-car garage
- Basement foundation, drawings also include crawl space foundation

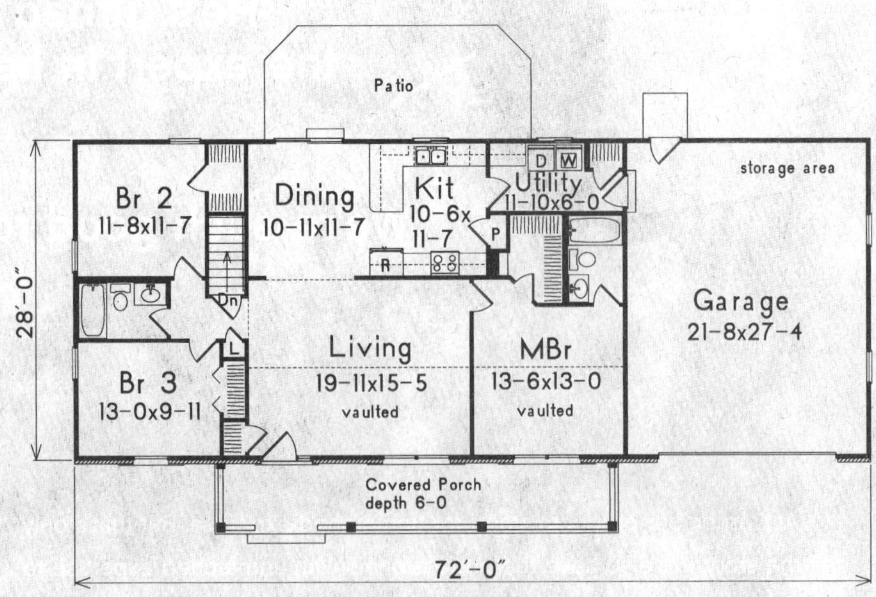
Patio
Br 2
11-8x11-7
Dining
10-11x11-7
Kit
10-6x
11-7
D W
Utility
11-10x6-0
storage area
P
R
Dn
L
Garage
21-8x27-4
28'-0"
Br 3
13-0x9-11
Living
19-11x15-5
vaulted
MBr
13-6x13-0
vaulted
Covered Porch
depth 6-0
72'-0"

TO ORDER BLUEPRINTS USE THE FORM ON PAGE 15 OR CALL TOLL-FREE 1-877-671-6036

View thousands more home plans online at www.familyhandyman.com/homeplans

NEW! Power Sand®

THE ULTIMATE ABRASIVE BLOCK.

TRY ME FREE!

IT SANDS WOOD!
4X FASTER THAN SANDPAPER*

IT STRIPS PAINT!
NEVER CLOGS OR GOES DULL

IT REMOVES RUST!
ONE BLOCK EQUALS UP TO 25 SHEETS OF SANDPAPER*

REVOLUTIONARY, NEW POWERSAND® IS THE NEXT GENERATION IN ABRASIVES

TACKLE TOUGH SURFACE PREP WITH POWERSAND SUPER STRIPPING BLOCKS. EACH BLOCK WORKS FOUR TIMES FASTER THAN SANDPAPER AND LASTS AS LONG AS TWENTY-FIVE SHEETS*. POWERSAND WILL NOT CLOG, TEAR OR GO DULL AND ELIMINATES THE NEED FOR CHEMICAL STRIPPERS.

TRY ME FREE! OFFER EXPIRES: 8/31/04

TO RECEIVE YOUR FULL REFUND ON THE PURCHASE OF POWERSAND, PLEASE FOLLOW THE INSTRUCTIONS BELOW.

1. COMPLETE THE INFORMATION BELOW:
   NAME ____________
   ADDRESS ____________
   CITY ________ STATE ____ ZIP ________
   EMAIL ADDRESS ____________
2. ENCLOSE A COPY OF STORE RECEIPT DATED BETWEEN MARCH 1, 2004 AND AUGUST 31, 2004
3. ENCLOSE A COPY OF THE ENTIRE UPC BAR CODE LABEL FROM POWERSAND PACKAGE
4. MAIL ALL 3 ITEMS, POSTMARKED WITHIN 30 DAYS, TO :
   EARTHSTONE INTERNATIONAL
   DEPARTMENT 353
   P.O. BOX 981123
   EL PASO, TX 79998-1123

OFFER VALID ON THE PURCHASE OF ANY POWERSAND PRODUCT. LIMIT 1 PER HOUSEHOLD – NOT TO EXCEED $5.00. OFFER EXPIRES AUGUST 31, 2004. SUBMISSIONS MUST BE POSTMARKED NO LATER THAN 30 DAYS AFTER DATE OF PURCHASE. PLEASE ALLOW 6-8 WEEKS FOR CHECK DELIVERY.

AVAILABLE AT LEADING HOME CENTERS AND OTHER PAINT & HARDWARE RETAILERS
www.earthstoneintl.com

** When compared to 60-grit sandpaper on latex paint.*

The Family
Handyman

Plan #708-0716

Grandscale Elegance

3,169 total square feet of living area **Price Code F**

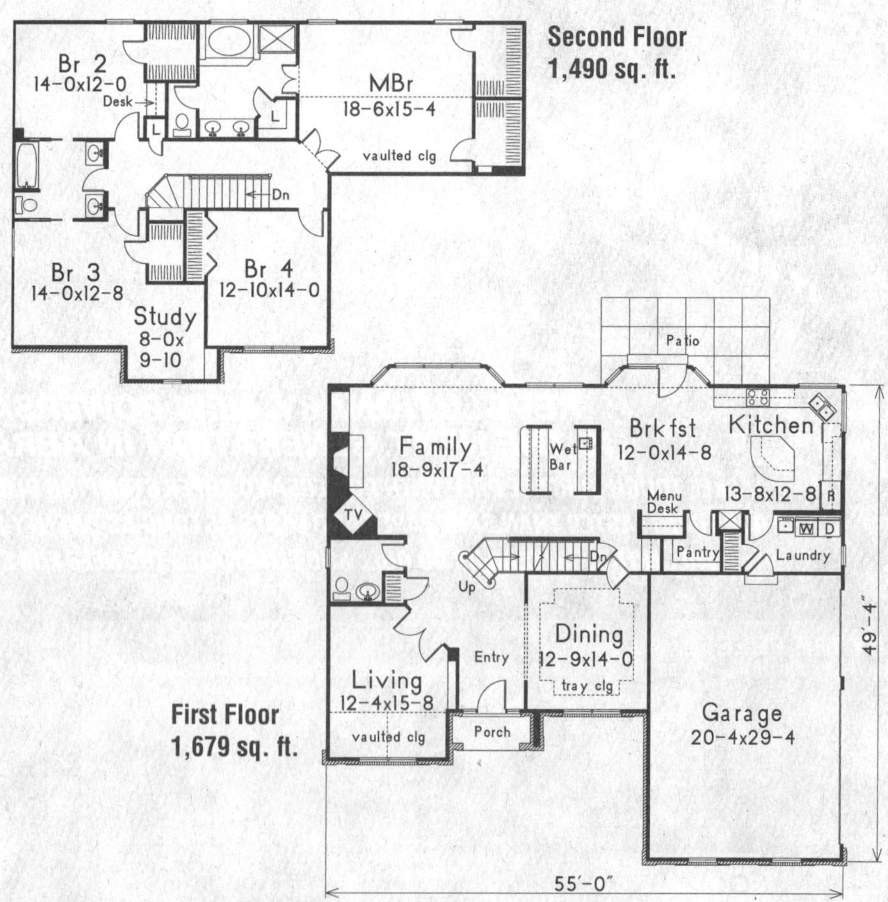
Second Floor
1,490 sq. ft.
Br 2
14-0x12-0
Desk
MBr
18-6x15-4
vaulted clg
Dn
Br 3
14-0x12-8
Br 4
12-10x14-0
Study
8-0x
9-10
Patio
Family
18-9x17-4
Wet Bar
Brkfst
12-0x14-8
Kitchen
13-8x12-8
Menu Desk
TV
Pantry
Laundry
Up
Dn
Dining
12-9x14-0
tray clg
Entry
Living
12-4x15-8
vaulted clg
Porch
Garage
20-4x29-4
49'-4"
55'-0"
First Floor
1,679 sq. ft.

Special features

- Formal areas include enormous entry with handcrafted stairway and powder room, French doors to living room and open dining area with tray ceiling
- Informal areas consist of a large family room with bay window, fireplace, walk-in wet bar and kitchen open to breakfast room
- Stylish master suite is located on second floor for privacy
- Front secondary bedroom includes a private study
- 4 bedrooms, 2 1/2 baths, 3-car side entry garage
- Basement foundation

TO ORDER BLUEPRINTS USE THE FORM ON PAGE 15 OR CALL TOLL-FREE 1-877-671-6036

View thousands more home plans online at www.familyhandyman.com/homeplans

Workshop Breakthrough!

You've GOT to see this!

Interchangeable workstation design lets you customize your shop for the type of work you'll be doing.

- Tools mount onto quick-change inserts. When you're ready to work, set the tool in place and lock it down. Changing tools takes just seconds!
- Save space. Store multiple benchtop tools in the Tool Rack.
- Tool accessories are within easy reach with blade and bit holders, built-in drawers, shelves and more.
- Rock-solid 18-gauge steel construction with 1-1/4" thick wood tops – designed to withstand hard use.
- Pick and choose the units that work best for your needs, and add on units as your workshop grows.

"Tool Dock is a GREAT product. I'm impressed with the quality. I really like the versatility of having my power tools mounted on changeable inserts, and being able to roll my projects into an open area."

Jim Marteney
Tool Dock owner
Loves Park, IL

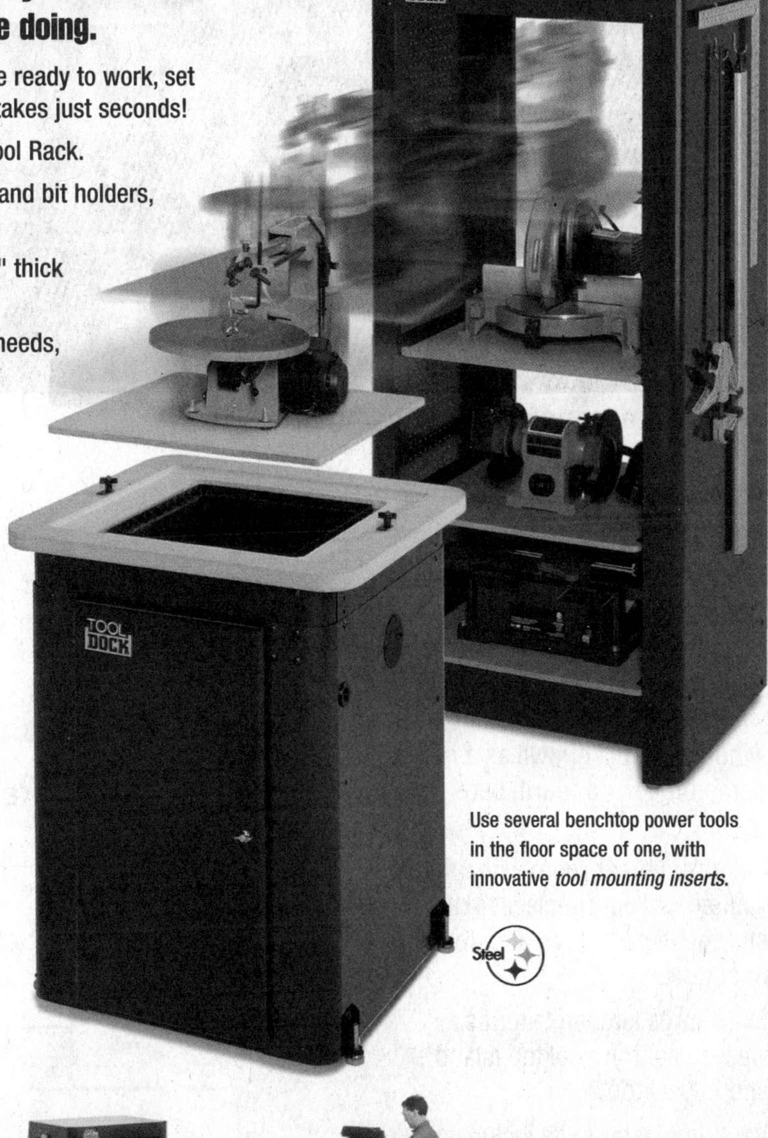

TOOL DOCK
TOOL DOCK

Use several benchtop power tools in the floor space of one, with innovative *tool mounting inserts.*

Steel

For complete details and an outlet near you:

www.tooldock.com

Or call toll-free: **1-866-866-5362**

TOOL
DOCK
TM

The Modular Workshop

Tools not included.

©2003 Waterloo Industries, Inc. Tool Dock™ is a trademark of Waterloo Industries, Inc.

The Family
Handyman

Plan #708-0368

Charming Design Features Home Office

2,452 total square feet of living area **Price Code D**

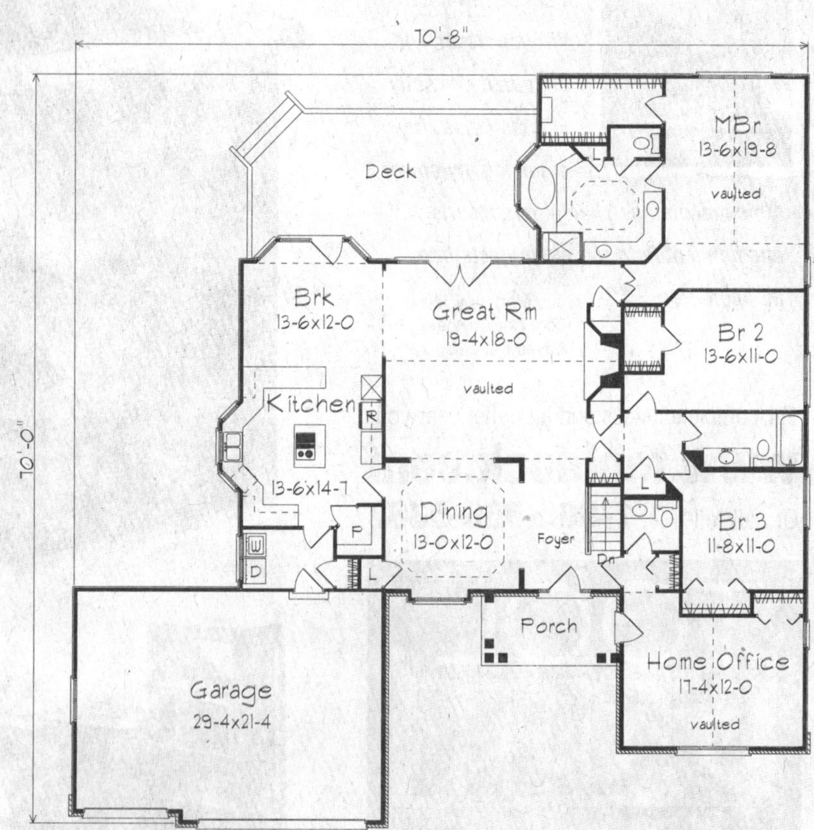
70'-8"
70'-0"
Deck
MBr
13-6x19-8
vaulted
Brk
13-6x12-0
Great Rm
19-4x18-0
vaulted
Br 2
13-6x11-0
Kitchen
13-6x14-7
Dining
13-0x12-0
Foyer
Br 3
11-8x11-0
Porch
Home Office
17-4x12-0
vaulted
Garage
29-4x21-4

Special features

- Cheery and spacious home office room with private entrance and bath, two closets, vaulted ceiling and transomed window perfect shown as a home office or a fourth bedroom
- Delightful great room with vaulted ceiling, fireplace, extra storage closets and patio doors to sundeck
- Extra-large kitchen features walk-in pantry, cooktop island and bay window
- Vaulted master suite includes transomed windows, walk-in closet and luxurious bath
- 4 bedrooms, 2 1/2 baths, 3-car garage
- Basement foundation

TO ORDER BLUEPRINTS USE THE FORM ON PAGE 15 OR CALL TOLL-FREE 1-877-671-6036

View thousands more home plans online at www.familyhandyman.com/homeplans

THE BLINDS WILL NEVER GET DIRTY. THE REST OF THE HOUSE IS ANOTHER STORY.

Between-the-Glass Blinds from Pella. It's a small miracle for parents everywhere.
1-800-54-PELLA www.pella.com

Pella

VIEWED TO BE THE BEST.™

© 2004 Pella Corporation

The Family
Handyman

Plan #708-0352

Two-Story Foyer With Grand Curved Stairway

3,144 total square feet of living area

Price Code E

Special features

- 9' ceilings on first floor
- Kitchen offers large pantry, island cooktop and close proximity to laundry and dining rooms
- Expansive family room includes wet bar, fireplace and attractive bay window
- 4 bedrooms, 4 1/2 baths, 3-car side entry garage
- Basement foundation

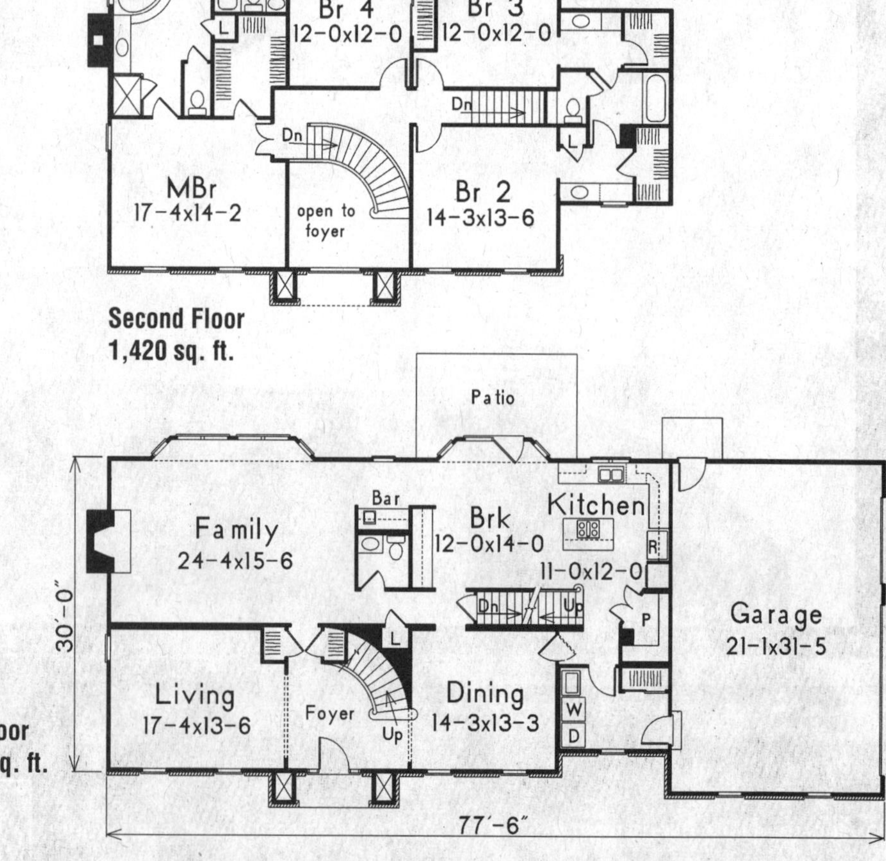
Br 4
12-0x12-0
Br 3
12-0x12-0
Dn
Dn
MBr
17-4x14-2
open to foyer
Br 2
14-3x13-6
Patio
Bar
Family
24-4x15-6
Brk
12-0x14-0
Kitchen
11-0x12-0
R
Dn
Up
P
Garage
21-1x31-5
30'-0"
Living
17-4x13-6
Foyer
Up
Dining
14-3x13-3
W
D
L
77'-6"

Second Floor
1,420 sq. ft.

First Floor
1,724 sq. ft.

TO ORDER BLUEPRINTS USE THE FORM ON PAGE 15 OR CALL TOLL-FREE 1-877-671-6036

View thousands more home plans online at www.familyhandyman.com/homeplans

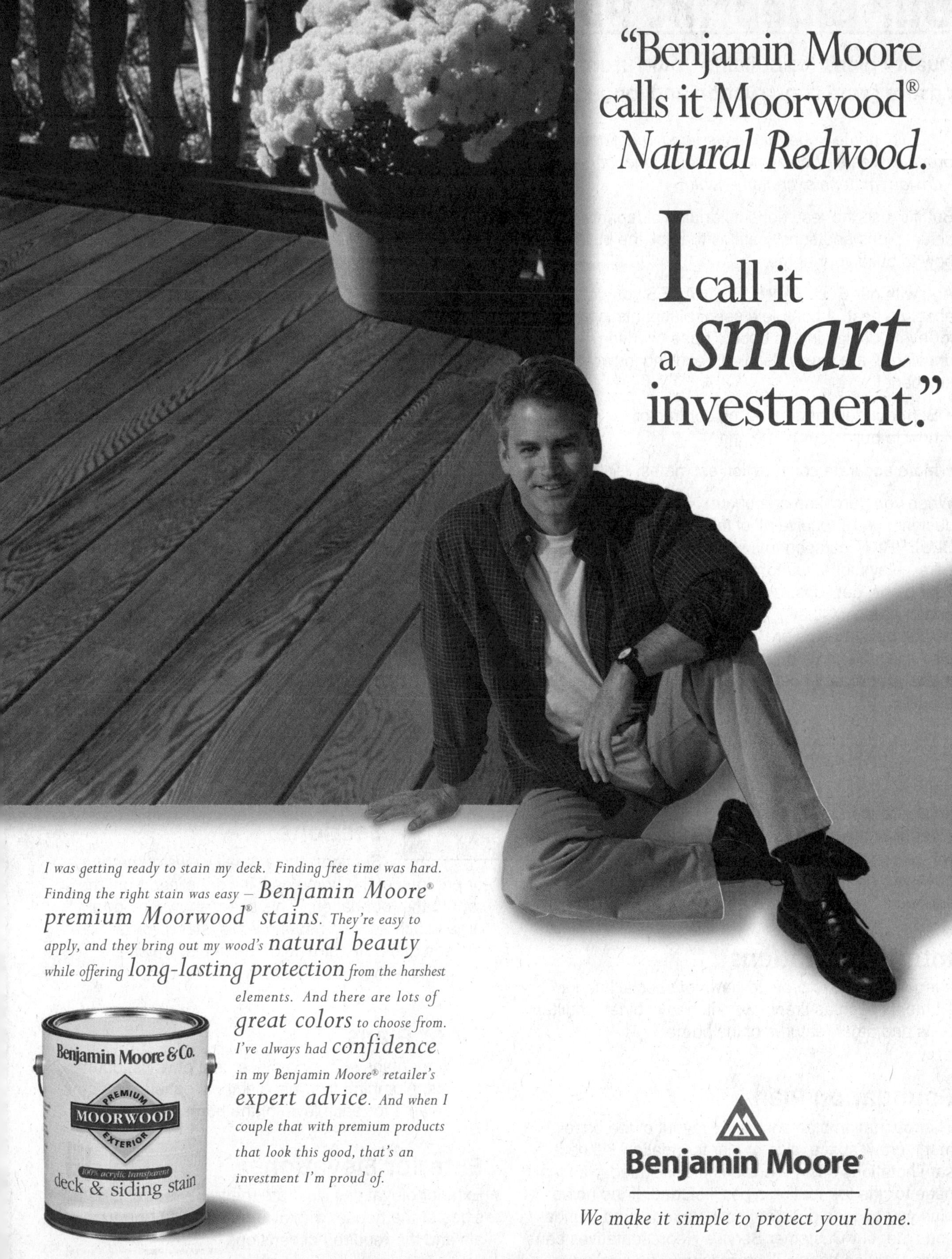
"Benjamin Moore calls it Moorwood® *Natural Redwood.*
I call it a *smart* investment."
I was getting ready to stain my deck. Finding free time was hard. Finding the right stain was easy – Benjamin Moore® premium Moorwood® stains. They're easy to apply, and they bring out my wood's natural beauty while offering long-lasting protection from the harshest elements. And there are lots of great colors to choose from. I've always had confidence in my Benjamin Moore® retailer's expert advice. And when I couple that with premium products that look this good, that's an investment I'm proud of.
Benjamin Moore & Co.
PREMIUM
MOORWOOD
EXTERIOR
100% acrylic transparent
deck & siding stain
Benjamin Moore®
We make it simple to protect your home.
For a retailer near you call 1-800-6-PAINT-6 or visit www.benjaminmoore.com
©2004 Benjamin Moore & Co. Benjamin Moore and Moorwood are registered trademarks and the triangle "M" symbol is a trademark, licensed to Benjamin Moore & Co.

Our Blueprint Packages Offer...

Quality plans for building your future, with extras that provide unsurpassed value, ensure good construction and long-term enjoyment.

A quality home - one that looks good, functions well, and provides years of enjoyment - is a product of many things - design, materials, craftsmanship.

But it's also the result of outstanding blueprints - the actual plans and specifications that tell the builder exactly how to build your home.

And with our BLUEPRINT PACKAGES you get the absolute best. A complete set of blueprints is available for every design in this book. These "working drawings," are highly detailed, resulting in two key benefits:

- Better understanding by the contractor of how to build your home and...
- More accurate construction estimates.

When you purchase one of our designs, you'll receive all of the BLUEPRINT components shown here - elevations, foundation plan, floor plans, sections, and/or details. Other helpful building aids are also available to help make your dream home a reality.

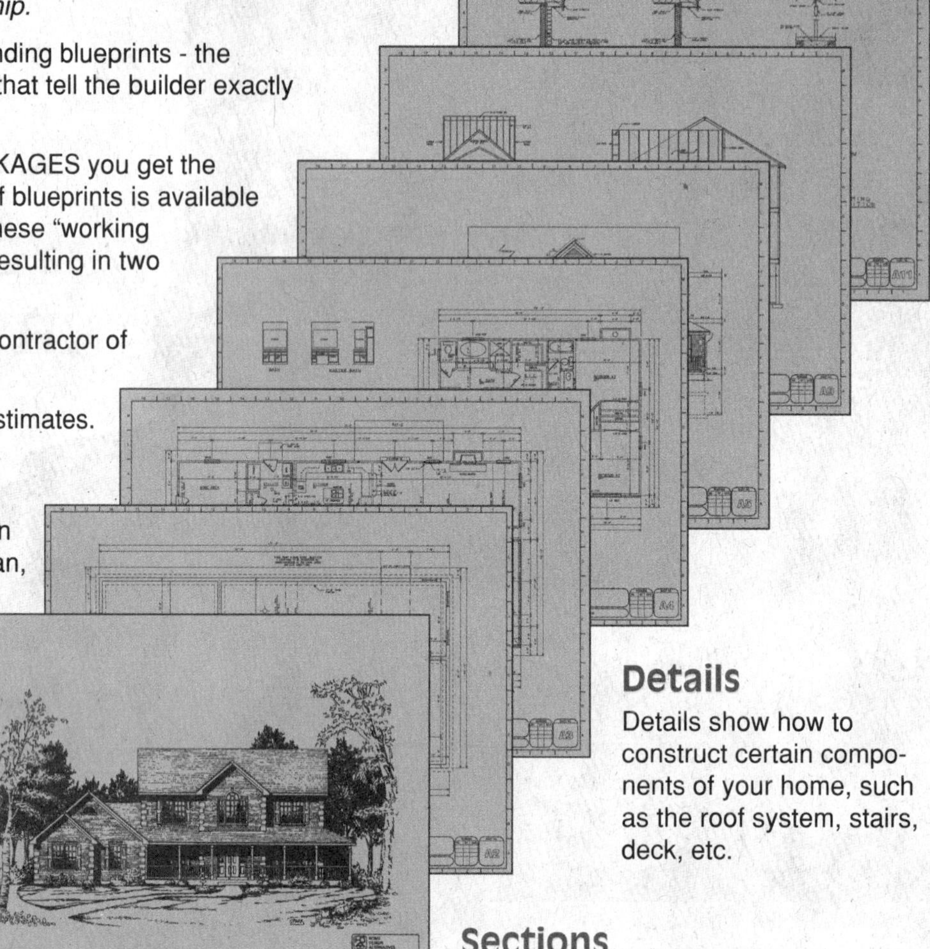

Cover Sheet

The cover sheet is the artist's rendering of the exterior of the home. It will give you an idea of how your home will look when completed and landscaped.

Interior Elevations

Interior elevations provide views of special interior elements such as fireplaces, kitchen cabinets, built-in units and other features of the home.

Foundation Plan

The foundation plan shows the layout of the basement, crawl space, slab or pier foundation. All necessary notations and dimensions are included. See plan page for the foundation types included. If the home plan you choose does not have your desired foundation type, our Customer Service Representatives can advise you on how to customize your foundation to suit your specific needs or site conditions.

Details

Details show how to construct certain components of your home, such as the roof system, stairs, deck, etc.

Sections

Sections show detail views of the home or portions of the home as if it were sliced from the roof to the foundation. This sheet shows important areas such as load-bearing walls, stairs, joists, trusses and other structural elements, which are critical for proper construction.

Floor Plans

The floor plans show the placement of walls, doors, closets, plumbing fixtures, electrical outlets, columns, and beams for each level of the home.

Exterior Elevations

Exterior elevations illustrate the front, rear and both sides of the house, with all details of exterior materials and the required dimensions.

What Kind Of Plan Package Do You Need?

Now that you've found the home you've been looking for, here are some suggestions on how to make your Dream Home a reality. To get started, order the type of plans that fit your particular situation.

YOUR CHOICES

- **THE 1-SET STUDY PACKAGE -** We offer a 1-set plan package so you can study your home in detail. This one set is considered a study set and is marked "not for construction". It is a copyright violation to reproduce blueprints.
- **THE MINIMUM 5-SET PACKAGE -** If you're ready to start the construction process, this 5-set package is the minimum number of blueprint sets you will need. It will require keeping close track of each set so they can be used by multiple subcontractors and tradespeople.
- **THE STANDARD 8-SET PACKAGE -** For best results in terms of cost, schedule and quality of construction, we recommend you order eight (or more) sets of blueprints. Besides one set for yourself, additional sets of blueprints will be required by your mortgage lender, local building department, general contractor and all subcontractors working on foundation, electrical, plumbing, heating/air conditioning, carpentry work, etc.
- **REPRODUCIBLE MASTERS -** If you wish to make some minor design changes, you'll want to order reproducible masters. These drawings contain the same information as the blueprints but are printed on erasable and reproducible paper which clearly indicates your right to copy or reproduce. This will allow your builder or a local design professional to make the necessary drawing changes without the major expense of redrawing the plans. This package also allows you to print copies of the modified plans as needed. The right of building only one structure from these plans is licensed exclusively to the buyer. You may not use this design to build a second or multiple dwelling(s) without purchasing another blueprint. Each violation of the Copyright Law is punishable in a fine.
- **MIRROR REVERSE SETS -** Plans can be printed in mirror reverse. These plans are useful when the house would fit your site better if all the rooms were on the opposite side than shown. They are simply a mirror image of the original drawings causing the lettering and dimensions to read backwards. Therefore, when ordering mirror reverse drawings, you must purchase at least one set of right reading plans.

COPYRIGHT

These plans are protected under Copyright Law. Reproduction by any means is strictly prohibited. The right of building only one structure from these plans is licensed exclusively to the buyer and these plans may not be resold unless by express written authorization from home designer/architect. You may not use this design to build a second or multiple dwelling(s) without purchasing another blueprint or blueprints or paying additional design fees. Each violation of the Copyright Law is punishable in a fine.

Other Helpful Building Aids...

Your Blueprint Package will contain the necessary construction information to build your home. We also offer the following products and services to save you time and money in the building process.

- **MATERIAL LIST -** Material lists are available for many of the plans in this book. Each list gives you the quantity, dimensions and description of the building materials necessary to construct your home. You'll get faster and more accurate bids from your contractor while saving money by paying for only the materials you need. See the Home Plans Index on page 14 for availability. Refer to the order form on page 15 for pricing.
- **DETAIL PLAN PACKAGES:** Framing, Plumbing & Electrical Plan Packages - Three separate packages offer homebuilders details for constructing various foundations; numerous floor, wall and roof framing techniques; simple to complex residential wiring; sump and water softener hookups; plumbing connection methods; installation of septic systems and more. Each package includes three-dimensional illustrations and a glossary of terms. Purchase one or all three. Cost: $20.00 each or all three for $40.00. Note: These drawings do not pertain to a specific home plan.
- **THE LEGAL KIT™ -** Our Legal Kit provides contracts and legal forms to help protect you from the potential pitfalls inherent in the building process. The Kit supplies commonly used forms and contracts suitable for homeowners and builders. It can save you a considerable amount of time and help protect you and your assets during and after construction. Cost: $35.00
- **EXPRESS DELIVERY -** Most orders are processed within 24 hours of receipt. Please allow 7-10 business days for delivery. If you need to place a rush order, please call us by 11:00 a.m. Monday-Friday CST and ask for express service (allow 1-2 business days).
- **TECHNICAL ASSISTANCE-** If you have questions, call our technical support line at 1-314-770-2228 between 8:00 a.m. and 5:00 p.m. Monday-Friday CST. Whether it involves design modifications or field assistance, our designers are extremely familiar with all of our designs and will be happy to help you. We want your home to be everything you expect it to be.

HOME DESIGN ALTERNATIVES, INC.

Home Plans Index

Plan Number	Sq. Ft.	Price Code	Page	Mat. List
708-0105	1,360	A	156	X
708-0110	1,605	B	320	X
708-0112	1,668	C	201	X
708-0135	2,529	E	318	X
708-0138	2,286	E	24	X
708-0147	2,820	E	314	X
708-0152	2,935	E	310	X
708-0159	3,368	F	112	X
708-0160	4,120	G	140	X
708-0161	1,630	B	87	X
708-0162	1,882	D	46	X
708-0170	2,618	E	164	X
708-0171	2,058	C	290	X
708-0173	1,220	A	189	X
708-0178	2,846	E	137	X
708-0184	2,411	D	66	X
708-0187	3,035	E	169	X
708-0200	1,343	A	286	X
708-0203	1,475	B	74	X
708-0217	1,360	A	70	X
708-0219	3,222	F	207	X
708-0223	2,328	D	185	X
708-0224	2,461	D	303	X
708-0225	1,260	A	244	X
708-0227	1,674	B	121	X
708-0228	1,996	C	85	X
708-0229	1,676	B	208	X
708-0230	2,073	D	20	X
708-0236	3,357	F	297	X
708-0244	1,994	D	265	X
708-0249	1,501	B	31	X
708-0253	1,458	A	157	X
708-0265	1,314	A	89	X
708-0267	1,453	A	272	X
708-0279	1,993	D	241	X
708-0280	1,847	C	175	X
708-0291	1,600	B	174	X
708-0295	1,609	B	145	X
708-0296	1,396	A	309	X
708-0297	1,320	A	129	X
708-0298	3,216	F	294	X
708-0302	1,854	D	247	X
708-0303	2,024	C	238	X
708-0306	2,360	D	113	X
708-0312	1,921	D	233	X
708-0318	2,147	C	96	X
708-0319	3,796	F	287	X
708-0320	2,061	D	159	X
708-0322	2,135	D	193	X
708-0335	1,865	D	91	X
708-0348	2,003	D	225	X
708-0349	2,204	D	177	X
708-0352	3,144	E	10	X
708-0356	2,806	E	196	X
708-0357	1,550	B	187	X
708-0364	2,531	D	273	X
708-0365	2,336	D	106	X
708-0366	2,624	E	112	X
708-0368	2,452	D	8	X
708-0370	1,721	C	99	X
708-0372	1,859	D	279	X
708-0374	2,213	E	161	X
708-0382	1,546	C	59	X
708-0387	1,958	C	252	X
708-0389	1,777	B	223	X
708-0393	1,684	B	127	X
708-0405	3,494	F	152	X
708-0407	2,517	D	268	X
708-0413	2,182	D	178	X
708-0418	3,850	F	199	X
708-0419	1,882	C	230	X
708-0425	2,076	C	191	X
708-0426	2,444	D	214	X
708-0427	3,411	F	307	X
708-0429	3,149	E	282	X
708-0437	2,333	D	147	X
708-0449	2,505	D	109	X

Plan Number	Sq. Ft.	Price Code	Page	Mat. List
708-0450	1,708	B	23	X
708-0477	1,140	AA	80	X
708-0478	1,092	AA	73	X
708-0479	1,294	A	280	X
708-0484	1,403	A	67	X
708-0485	1,195	AA	305	X
708-0487	1,189	AA	172	X
708-0491	1,808	C	277	X
708-0493	976	AA	117	X
708-0494	1,085	AA	75	X
708-0495	987	AA	65	X
708-0498	954	AA	71	X
708-0503	1,000	AA	95	X
708-0505	1,104	AA	131	X
708-0510	1,400	A	275	X
708-0515	1,344	A	236	X
708-0520	1,720	B	125	X
708-0529	1,285	B	63	X
708-0585	1,344	A	284	X
708-0600	3,025	E	209	X
708-0652	1,524	B	26	X
708-0656	1,700	B	154	X
708-0668	1,617	B	269	X
708-0670	1,170	AA	195	X
708-0671	1,427	A	257	X
708-0676	1,367	B	263	X
708-0678	1,567	C	139	X
708-0690	1,400	B	4	X
708-0691	2,730	E	267	X
708-0701	2,308	D	248	X
708-0702	1,558	B	115	X
708-0706	1,791	C	29	X
708-0707	2,723	E	48	X
708-0708	2,615	E	2	X
708-0709	2,521	D	205	X
708-0710	2,334	D	76	X
708-0711	1,575	B	25	X
708-0712	2,029	D	171	X
708-0716	3,169	F	6	X
708-0719	2,483	D	202	X
708-0720	3,138	E	296	X
708-0721	2,437	D	239	X
708-0725	1,977	C	259	X
708-0729	2,218	D	53	X
708-0731	1,761	B	18	X
708-0735	3,657	F	292	X
708-0736	2,900	E	289	X
708-0739	1,684	B	229	X
708-0741	1,578	B	211	X
708-0744	2,164	C	149	X
708-0747	1,977	C	103	X
708-0748	2,514	D	221	X
708-0754	3,420	F	300	X
708-0759	2,125	C	135	X
708-0774	1,680	B	119	X
708-0775	2,240	D	57	X
708-0778	2,356	D	49	X
708-0783	3,035	E	235	X
708-0793	2,384	D	45	X
708-0794	1,433	A	51	X
708-0796	1,599	B	227	X
708-0797	2,651	E	213	X
708-0798	2,128	C	43	X
708-0799	1,849	C	83	X
708-0809	1,084	AA	93	X
708-0811	1,161	AA	61	X
708-0813	888	AAA	79	X
708-0817	2,547	D	304	X
708-0821	2,695	E	298	X
708-0823	1,621	B	97	X
708-0827	1,308	A	301	X
708-1117	1,440	A	217	
708-1248	1,574	B	219	
708-1336	1,364	A	141	
708-AMD-1111AC	1,275	C	155	
708-AMD-1112	1,557	C	192	
708-AMD-1213	2,197	C	36	

Plan Number	Sq. Ft.	Price Code	Page	Mat. List
708-AMD-22120	3,231	G	243	
708-AP-1516	1,593	C	203	
708-AP-1717	1,787	B	105	
708-AP-1908	1,998	C	312	
708-AP-1911	1,992	C	126	
708-AP-2020	2,097	C	132	
708-AP-2520	2,564	D	220	
708-AX-301	1,783	D	317	
708-AX-93304	1,860	D	278	
708-AX-93305	2,567	F	27	
708-AX-93308	1,793	B	165	
708-AX-93311	1,945	D	100	
708-BF-2107	2,123	E	144	
708-BF-2108	2,194	C	215	
708-BF-2610	2,684	E	306	
708-BF-3007	3,012	E	111	
708-BF-DR1819-	2,424	D	54	
708-CHD-16-3	1,660	B	299	
708-CHD-16-41	1,634	B	212	
708-CHD-16-33	1,699	B	86	
708-CHD-28-39	2,526	D	266	
708-CHD-29-58	3,369	F	173	
708-CHP-1633-A-25	1,609	B	308	
708-CHP-2233-B-21	2,697	E	197	
708-CHP-2333-A-29	2,279	D	94	
708-CHP-2343-B-36	2,360	D	50	
708-CHP-2543-A-42	2,500	D	246	
708-DBI-1748-19	1,911	C	114	
708-DBI-2408	2,270	D	160	
708-DBI-2461	1,850	C	107	
708-DBI-2619	1,998	C	316	
708-DBI-2701	2,340	D	234	
708-DBI-9120	3,312	F	206	
708-DDI-93-102	1,288	A	311	
708-DDI-95-234	1,649	B	168	
708-DDI-98-106	1,588	B	116	
708-DDI-100-218	2,995	E	255	
708-DDI-101-102	2,148	C	60	
708-DH-1786	1,785	B	22	
708-DH-2005	1,700	B	218	
708-DH-2214	2,214	D	274	
708-DH-2323	2,293	D	158	
708-DH-2600	2,669	E	40	
708-DL-19603L2	1,960	C	56	
708-DL-23804L2	2,380	D	313	
708-DL-25454L1	2,545	D	90	
708-DL-35355LS2	3,535	F	182	
708-DR-2615	2,889	E	226	
708-DR-2891	2,310	D	295	
708-DR-2940	1,482	A	143	
708-DR-3812	2,129	C	52	
708-FB-845	1,779	B	228	
708-FB-930	2,322	D	146	
708-FB-933	2,193	C	253	
708-FB-963	2,126	C	251	
708-FB1119	1,915	C	102	
708-FB-1224	2,246	D	120	
708-FDG-7773	1,653	B	101	
708-FDG-7963-L	1,830	C	150	
708-FDG-8526	2,370	D	232	
708-FDG-8729-L	2,529	D	162	
708-FDG-9035	1,760	B	285	
708-GH-24326	1,505	B	82	
708-GH-24594	2,957	E	136	
708-GH-24701	1,625	B	245	
708-GH-24714	1,771	B	42	
708-GM-1550	1,550	B	110	
708-GM-1842	1,842	C	281	
708-GM-1849	1,849	C	64	
708-GM-2009	2,009	C	264	
708-GM-2361	2,361	D	138	
708-GSD-1023-C	1,890	C	33	
708-GSD-1123	1,734	B	186	
708-GSD-1260	2,788	E	128	
708-GSD-1748	1,496	A	231	
708-HDS-1571	1,571	B	39	
708-HDS-1670	1,670	B	210	

Plan Number	Sq. Ft.	Price Code	Page	Mat. List
708-HDS-1806	1,806	C	78	
708-HDS-1993	1,993	C	134	
708-HDS-2077	2,077	C	222	
708-HP-C460	1,389	A	34	
708-HP-C659	1,118	AA	123	
708-HP-C662	1,937	C	179	
708-HP-C689	1,295	A	250	
708-JA-62401	2,034	F	319	
708-JA-66096	1,495	A	72	
708-JA-73897	1,794	B	240	
708-JA-79298	2,229	D	77	
708-JA-81098	1,537	B	148	
708-JA-91099	3,246	F	276	
708-JFD-10-1436-1	1,436	A	98	
708-JFD-10-2178-2	2,178	C	262	
708-JFD-20-1868-1	1,868	C	124	
708-JFD-20-2097-1	2,097	C	256	
708-JFD-20-2121-1	2,121	C	170	
708-JV-1268-A	1,268	A	37	
708-JV-1325-B	1,325	A	118	
708-JV-1772-A-SJ	1,772	B	216	
708-JV-2012-A-SJ	2,012	C	184	
708-JV-2221-A	2,221	D	84	
708-JV-2726-A	2,726	E	271	
708-LBD-15-4A	1,575	B	190	
708-LBD-17-14A	1,725	B	176	
708-LBD-18-11A	1,890	C	28	
708-LBD-19-23A	1,932	C	153	
708-LBD-25-22A	2,586	D	261	
708-MG-02120	2,111	H	302	
708-MG-02236	1,985	G	108	
708-MG-9305	1,606	B	88	
708-MG-96132	2,450	D	270	
708-MG-96183	2,737	E	180	
708-MG-97162	3,304	F	58	
708-NDG-113-1	1,525	B	44	
708-NDG-148	1,538	B	291	
708-NDG-190	2,107	C	130	
708-NDG-517	1,989	C	283	
708-NDG-663	2,716	E	69	
708-NDG-700	2,217	C	237	
708-NDG-707	1,635	B	30	
708-RDD-1374-9	1,374	A	104	
708-RDD-1791-9	1,791	B	258	
708-RDD-1896-9	1,896	C	166	
708-RDD-2050-7A	2,050	C	92	
708-RJ-A19-36	1,945	C	41	
708-RJ-A20-24	2,079	C	188	
708-RJ-A22-27	2,281	D	242	
708-RJ-A26-15	2,600	E	254	
708-SH-SEA-058	2,170	C	315	
708-SH-SEA-091	1,541	B	38	
708-SH-SEA-100	2,582	D	194	
708-SH-SEA-242	1,408	A	204	
708-SH-SEA-245	1,578	B	151	
708-SH-SEA-400	1,568	B	183	
708-SRD-123	1,782	B	68	
708-SRD-147	2,320	D	163	
708-SRD-150	1,508	B	133	
708-SRD-214	1,856	C	249	
708-SRD-224	2,603	E	35	
708-SRD-307	1,860	C	224	
708-UD-C142	1,698	B	47	
708-UD-D162	2,198	C	198	
708-UD-D164	2,431	D	293	
708-UD-E141	3,272	F	181	
708-UDG-97008	2,086	C	62	
708-UDG-97010	2,900	E	167	
708-UDG-99003	1,425	A	260	
708-VL-1594	1,594	B	122	
708-VL-1815	1,815	C	200	
708-VL-1925	1,925	C	55	
708-VL-1926	1,926	C	288	
708-VL2069	2,069	C	142	
708-VL2162	2,162	C	81	

IMPORTANT INFORMATION TO KNOW BEFORE YOU ORDER

- **Exchange Policies -** Since blueprints are printed in response to your order, we cannot honor requests for refunds. However, if for some reason you find that the plan you have purchased does not meet your requirements, you may exchange that plan for another plan in our collection. At the time of the exchange, you will be charged a processing fee of 25% of your original plan package price, plus the difference in price between the plan packages (if applicable) and the cost to ship the new plans to you.
- **Building Codes & Requirements -** At the time the construction drawings were prepared, every effort was made to ensure that these plans and specifications meet nationally recognized codes. Our plans conform to most national building codes. Because building codes vary from area to area, some drawing modifications and/or the assistance of a professional designer or architect may be necessary to comply with your local codes or to accommodate specific building site conditions. We advise you to consult with your local building official for information regarding codes governing your area.

Please note: Reproducible drawings can only be exchanged if the package is unopened, and exchanges are allowed only within 90 days of purchase.

Questions? Call Our Customer Service Number 1-877-671-6036

BLUEPRINT PRICE SCHEDULE

BEST VALUE

Price Code	1-Set*	SAVE $110 5-Sets	SAVE $200 8-Sets	Material List**	Reproducible Masters
AAA	$225	$295	$340	$50	$440
AA	$275	$345	$390	$55	$490
A	$325	$395	$440	$60	$540
B	$375	$445	$490	$60	$590
C	$425	$495	$540	$65	$640
D	$475	$545	$590	$65	$690
E	$525	$595	$640	$70	$740
F	$575	$645	$690	$70	$790
G	$650	$720	$765	$75	$865
H	$755	$825	$870	$80	$970

Plan prices guaranteed through December 31, 2004.
Please note that plans are not refundable.

- **Additional Sets -** Additional sets of the plan ordered are available for $45.00 each. Five-set, eight-set, and reproducible packages offer considerable savings.
- **Mirror Reverse Plans -** Available for an additional $15.00 per set, these plans are simply a mirror image of the original drawings causing the dimensions and lettering to read backwards. Therefore, when ordering mirror reverse plans, you must purchase at least one set of right reading plans.
- **One-Set Study Package -** We offer a one-set plan package so you can study your home in detail. This one set is considered a study set and is marked "not for construction". It is a copyright violation to reproduce blueprints.

***1-Set Study Packages are not available for all plans.**
****Available only within 90 days after purchase of plan package or reproducible masters of same plan.**

SHIPPING & HANDLING CHARGES

U.S. SHIPPING	1-4 Sets	5-7 Sets	8 Sets or Reproducibles
Regular *(allow 7-10 business days)*	$15.00	$17.50	$25.00
Priority *(allow 3-5 business days)*	$25.00	$30.00	$35.00
Express* *(allow 1-2 business days)*	$35.00	$40.00	$45.00

CANADA SHIPPING (to/from) - Plans with suffix DR & SH	1-4 Sets	5-7 Sets	8 Sets or Reproducibles
Standard *(allow 8-12 business days)*	$25.00	$30.00	$35.00
Express* *(allow 3-5 business days)*	$40.00	$40.00	$45.00

Overseas Shipping/International - Call, fax, or e-mail (plans@hdainc.com) for shipping costs.

* For express delivery please call us by 11:00 a.m. Monday-Friday CST

How To Order

For fastest service, Call Toll-Free
1-877-671-6036
24 HOURS A DAY

Three Easy Ways To Order

1. CALL toll-free 1-877-671-6036 for credit card orders. MasterCard, Visa, Discover and American Express are accepted.
2. FAX your order to 1-314-770-2226.
3. MAIL the Order Form to:

HDA, Inc.
4390 Green Ash Drive
St. Louis, MO 63045

ORDER FORM

Please send me -

PLAN NUMBER 708BT - ____________

PRICE CODE ______ (see Plan Index)

Specify Foundation Type - see plan page for availability
☐ Slab ☐ Crawl space ☐ Pier
☐ Basement ☐ Walk-out basement

☐ Reproducible Masters $ ______
☐ Eight-Set Plan Package $ ______
☐ Five-Set Plan Package $ ______
☐ One-Set Study Package (no mirror reverse) $ ______
☐ Additional Plan Sets
______ (Qty.) at $45.00 each $ ______
☐ Print in Mirror Reverse
______ (Qty.) add $15.00 per set $ ______
☐ Material List $ ______
☐ Legal Kit (see page 13) $ ______
Detail Plan Packages: (see page 13)
☐ Framing ☐ Electrical ☐ Plumbing $ ______
SUBTOTAL $ ______
SALES TAX (MO residents add 6%) $ ______
☐ Shipping / Handling (see chart at left) $ ______
TOTAL ENCLOSED (US funds only) $ ______
(Sorry no CODs)

I hereby authorize HDA, Inc. to charge this purchase to my credit card account (check one):

☐ MasterCard ☐ VISA ☐ DISCOVER NOVUS ☐ AMERICAN EXPRESS Cards

Credit Card number ______________

Expiration date ______________

Signature ______________

Name ______________
(Please print or type)

Street Address ______________
(Please **do not** use PO Box)

City ______________

State ______ Zip ______________

Daytime phone number (____) - ______________

I'm a ☐ Builder/Contractor ☐ Homeowner ☐ Renter

I ☐ have ☐ have not selected my general contractor

Thank you for your order!

QUICK AND EASY CUSTOMIZING

MAKE CHANGES TO YOUR HOME PLAN IN 4 STEPS

HERE'S AN AFFORDABLE AND EFFICIENT WAY TO MAKE CHANGES TO YOUR PLAN.

1 Select the house plan that most closely meets your needs. Purchase of a reproducible master is necessary in order to make changes to a plan.

2 Call 1-877-671-6036 to place your order. Tell the sales representative you're interested in customizing a plan. A $50 refundable consultation fee will be charged. You will then be instructed to complete a customization checklist indicating all the changes you wish to make to your plan. You may attach sketches if necessary. If you proceed with the custom changes the $50 will be credited to the total amount charged.

3 FAX the completed customization checklist to our design consultant at 1-866-477-5173 or e-mail custom@drummonddesigns.com. Within *24-48 business hours you will be provided with a written cost estimate to modify your plan. Our design consultant will contact you by phone if you wish to discuss any of your changes in greater detail.

4 Once you approve the estimate, a 75% retainer fee is collected and customization work gets underway. Preliminary drawings can usually be completed within *5-10 business days. Following approval of the preliminary drawings your design changes are completed within *5-10 business days. Your remaining 25% balance due is collected prior to shipment of your completed drawings. You will be shipped five sets of revised blueprints or a reproducible master, plus a customized materials list if required.

*Terms are subject to change without notice.

BEFORE
Plan 2829

Customized Version of Plan 2829

AFTER

MODIFICATION PRICING GUIDE

CATEGORIES	Average Cost from...	to
Adding or removing living space (square footage)	Quote required	
Adding or removing a garage	$400	$680
Garage: Front entry to side load or vice versa	Starting at $300	
Adding a screened porch	$280	$600
Adding a bonus room in the attic	$450	$780
Changing full basement to crawl space or vice versa	Starting at $220	
Changing full basement to slab or vice versa	Starting at $260	
Changing exterior building material	Starting at $200	
Changing roof lines	$360	$630
Adjusting ceiling height	$280	$500
Adding, moving or removing an exterior opening	$55 per opening	
Adding or removing a fireplace	$90	$200
Modifying a non-bearing wall or room	$55 per room	
Changing exterior walls from 2"x4" to 2"x6"	Starting at $200	
Redesigning a bathroom or a kitchen	$120	$280
Reverse plan right reading	Quote required	
Adapting plans for local building code requirements	Quote required	
Engineering stamping only	Quote required	
Any other engineering services	Quote required	
Adjust plan for handicapped accessibility	Quote required	
Interactive illustrations (choices of exterior materials)	Quote required	
Metric conversion of home plan	$400	

Note: Any home plan can be customized to accommodate your desired changes. The average prices specified above are provided only as examples for the most commonly requested changes, and are subject to change without notice. Prices for changes will vary according to the number of modifications requested, plan size, style, and method of design used by the original designer. To obtain a detailed cost estimate, please contact us.

Home.
The way nature
intended it to be.

Ask Sherwin-Williams.®

SHERWIN-WILLIAMS

1-800-4-SHERWIN sherwin-williams.com

Intense Teal SW 6943, Lime Rickey SW 6717, and Morning Fog SW 6255 are part of the Natural Habitat Collection.
©2004 The Sherwin-Williams Company.

Plan #708-0731

Small Ranch For A Perfect Country Haven

1,761 total square feet of living area

Price Code B

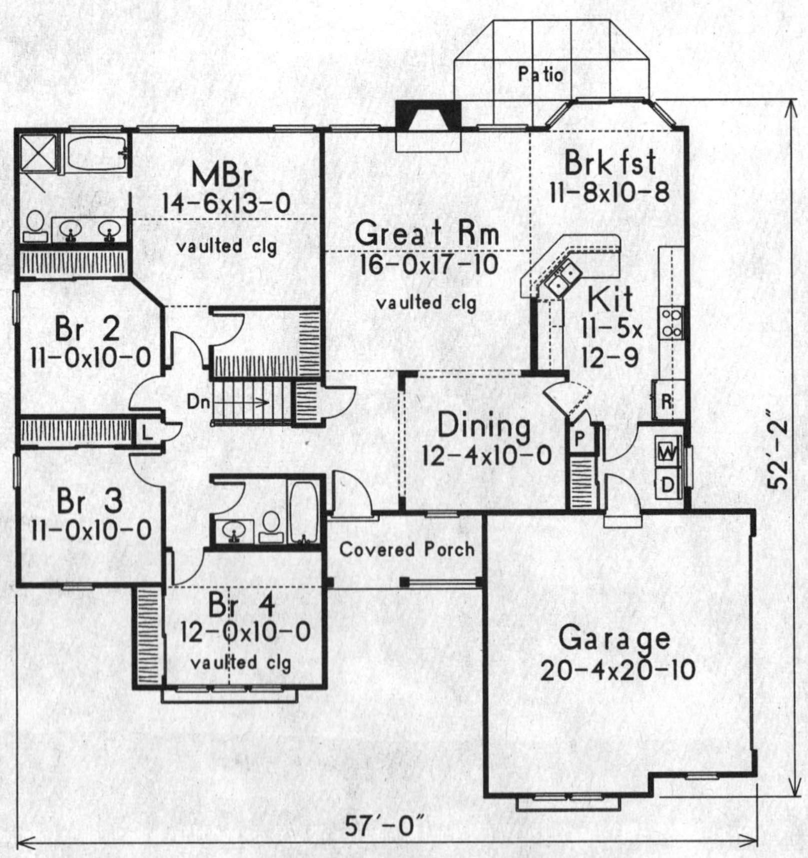
Patio
MBr
14-6x13-0
vaulted clg
Brkfst
11-8x10-8
Great Rm
16-0x17-10
vaulted clg
Kit
11-5x
12-9
Br 2
11-0x10-0
Dn
L
R
Dining
12-4x10-0
P
W
D
Br 3
11-0x10-0
Covered Porch
Br 4
12-0x10-0
vaulted clg
Garage
20-4x20-10
57'-0"
52'-2"

Special features

- Exterior window dressing, roof dormers and planter boxes provide visual warmth and charm
- Great room boasts a vaulted ceiling, fireplace and opens to a pass-through kitchen
- Master bedroom is vaulted with luxury bath and walk-in closet
- Home features eight separate closets with an abundance of storage
- 4 bedrooms, 2 baths, 2-car side entry garage
- Basement foundation

RESULTS VARY FROM BEAUTIFUL TO SPECTACULAR!

Wolman® makes it easy to keep outdoor wood looking beautiful, longer.

Beautiful stains and protective finishes. Superior surface prep products. A complete professional quality wood care system that simplifies deck care—and restores, beautifies and protects outdoor wood for spectacular results!

RainCoat® Tinted Water Repellent—Natural Hickory

RainCoat® Clear Water Repellent

F&P® Finish And Preservative—Redwood

DuraStain® Semi-Transparent Stain—Natural Oak

Professional Quality... Guaranteed Performance!

Wolman

Wolman Wood Care Products
A Division of ZINSSER Co., Inc.
173 Belmont Drive • Somerset, NJ 08875

Contact us at **1-800-556-7737** for a Wolman dealer near you. Or, visit **www.wolman.com** for product information, helpful wood care "tips" or to find a Wolman dealer in your area.

Plan #708-0230

Vaulted Ceilings Enhance Spacious Home

2,073 total square feet of living area **Price Code D**

Special features

- Family room provides ideal gathering area with a fireplace, large windows and vaulted ceiling
- Private first floor master bedroom suite with a vaulted ceiling and luxury bath
- Kitchen features angled bar connecting kitchen and breakfast area
- 4 bedrooms, 2 1/2 baths, 2-car side entry garage
- Basement foundation

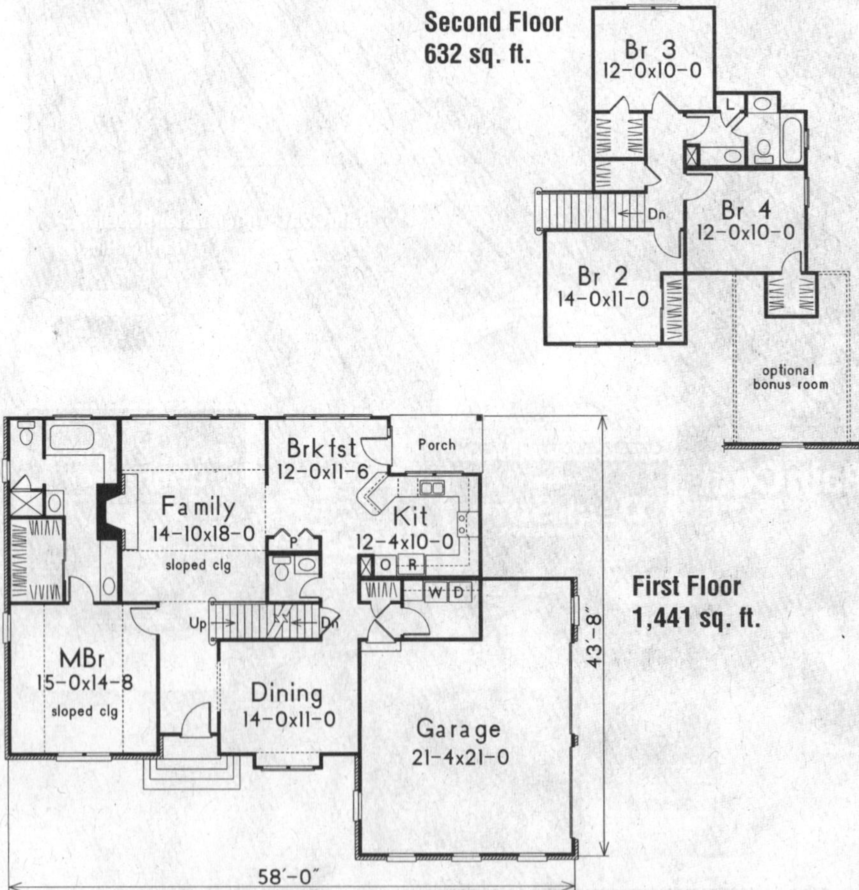
Second Floor
632 sq. ft.
Br 3
12-0x10-0
L
Dn
Br 4
12-0x10-0
Br 2
14-0x11-0
optional
bonus room
Brkfst
12-0x11-6
Porch
Family
14-10x18-0
sloped clg
Kit
12-4x10-0
P
O
R
W
D
Up
Dn
MBr
15-0x14-8
sloped clg
Dining
14-0x11-0
Garage
21-4x21-0
43'-8"
58'-0"
First Floor
1,441 sq. ft.

TO ORDER BLUEPRINTS USE THE FORM ON PAGE 15 OR CALL TOLL-FREE 1-877-671-6036

View thousands more home plans online at www.familyhandyman.com/homeplans

Get More Out of Your basement

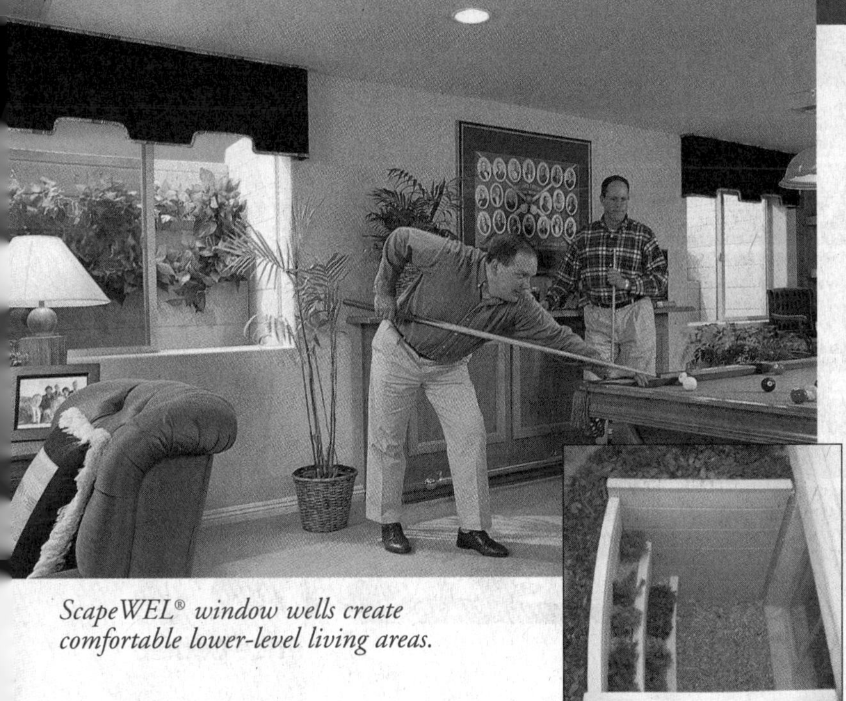

ScapeWEL® window wells create comfortable lower-level living areas.

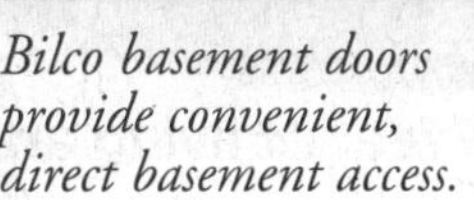

Bilco basement doors provide convenient, direct basement access.

Bilco Basement products will provide your home with comfort, convenience and enhanced value.

ScapeWEL® window wells create desirable new living space by adding unprecedented beauty and natural daylight to basement areas while providing safe emergency egress.

Create a lower-level family room, bedroom, home office or other living area to enhance the comfort and value of your home.

ScapeWEL window wells do not require pouring like concrete wells, are less expensive than site-built wells, and unlike metal wells, do not require unsightly ladders to meet emergency egress codes.

Available in a variety of sizes and with optional grates or clear domes, ScapeWEL window wells are landscape-ready and virtually maintenance-free.

Bilco basement doors, featuring counter-balanced lifting mechanisms, automatic safety latches, and weather-proof steel construction have been the first choice of homeowners, architects and contractors since 1926.

Bulky items are easily moved in and out without damage to first-floor walls or woodwork, trades people have easy access to basement-located mechanical systems, and security is enhanced by the positive action slide-lock or the optional keyed entry system.

Bilco doors are available in a variety of sizes, and can be supplied complete with precast concrete steps for new home construction.

ScapeWEL® Window wells and Bilco Basement doors are IRC 2000 compliant.

Bilco®

Since 1926

For more information call **(203)934-6363**
or log on to www.bilco.com

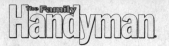

Traditional Southern Style Home

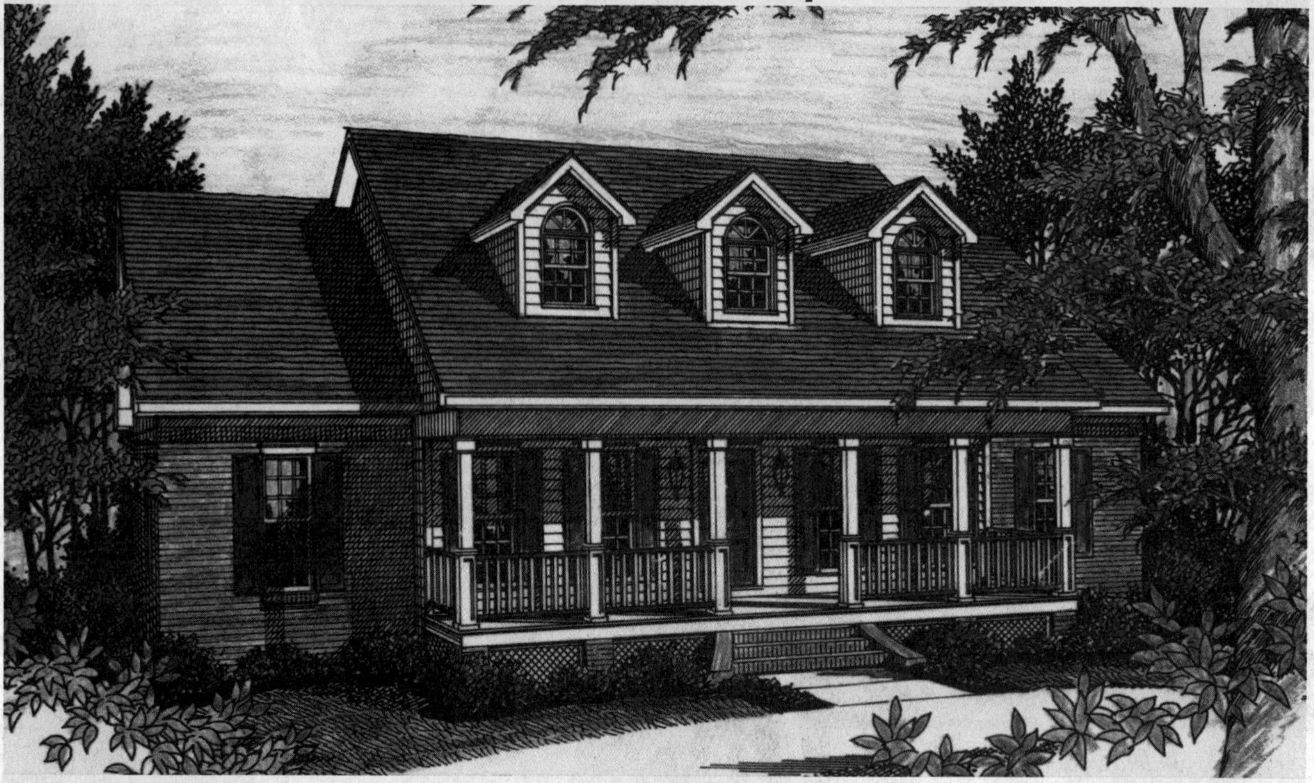

1,785 total square feet of living area

Price Code B

Special features

- 9' ceilings throughout home
- Luxurious master bath includes whirlpool tub and separate shower
- Cozy breakfast area is convenient to kitchen
- 3 bedrooms, 3 baths, 2-car detached garage
- Basement, crawl space or slab foundation, please specify when ordering

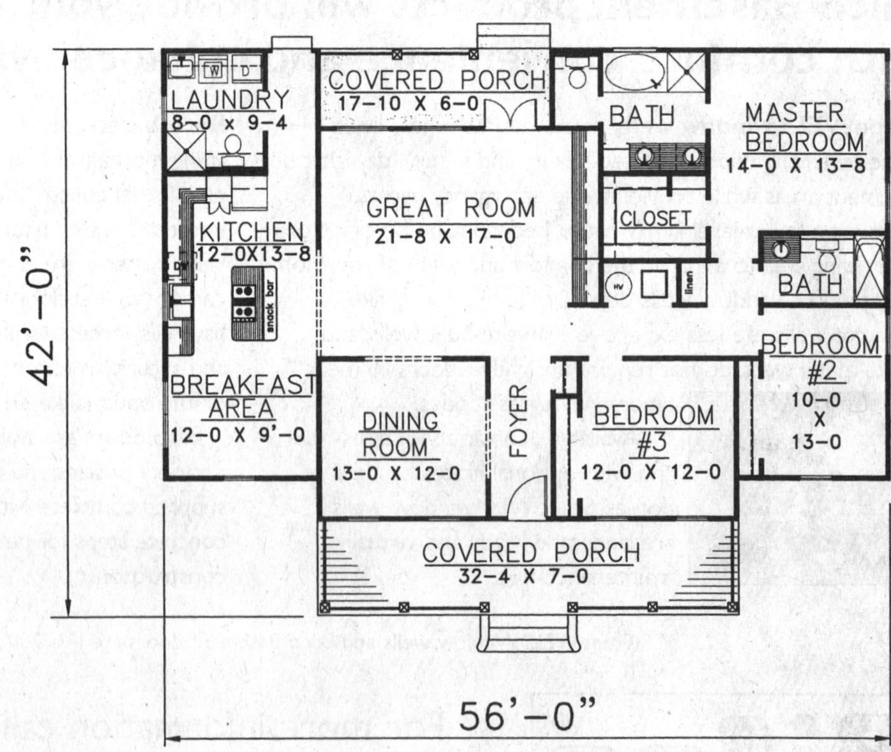
LAUNDRY
8-0 x 9-4
COVERED PORCH
17-10 X 6-0
BATH
MASTER BEDROOM
14-0 X 13-8
KITCHEN
12-0X13-8
GREAT ROOM
21-8 X 17-0
CLOSET
BATH
snack bar
BREAKFAST AREA
12-0 X 9'-0
DINING ROOM
13-0 X 12-0
FOYER
BEDROOM #3
12-0 X 12-0
BEDROOM #2
10-0 X 13-0
COVERED PORCH
32-4 X 7-0
42'-0"
56'-0"

TO ORDER BLUEPRINTS USE THE FORM ON PAGE 15 OR CALL TOLL-FREE 1-877-671-6036

View thousands more home plans online at www.familyhandyman.com/homeplans

Private Breakfast Room Provides Casual Dining

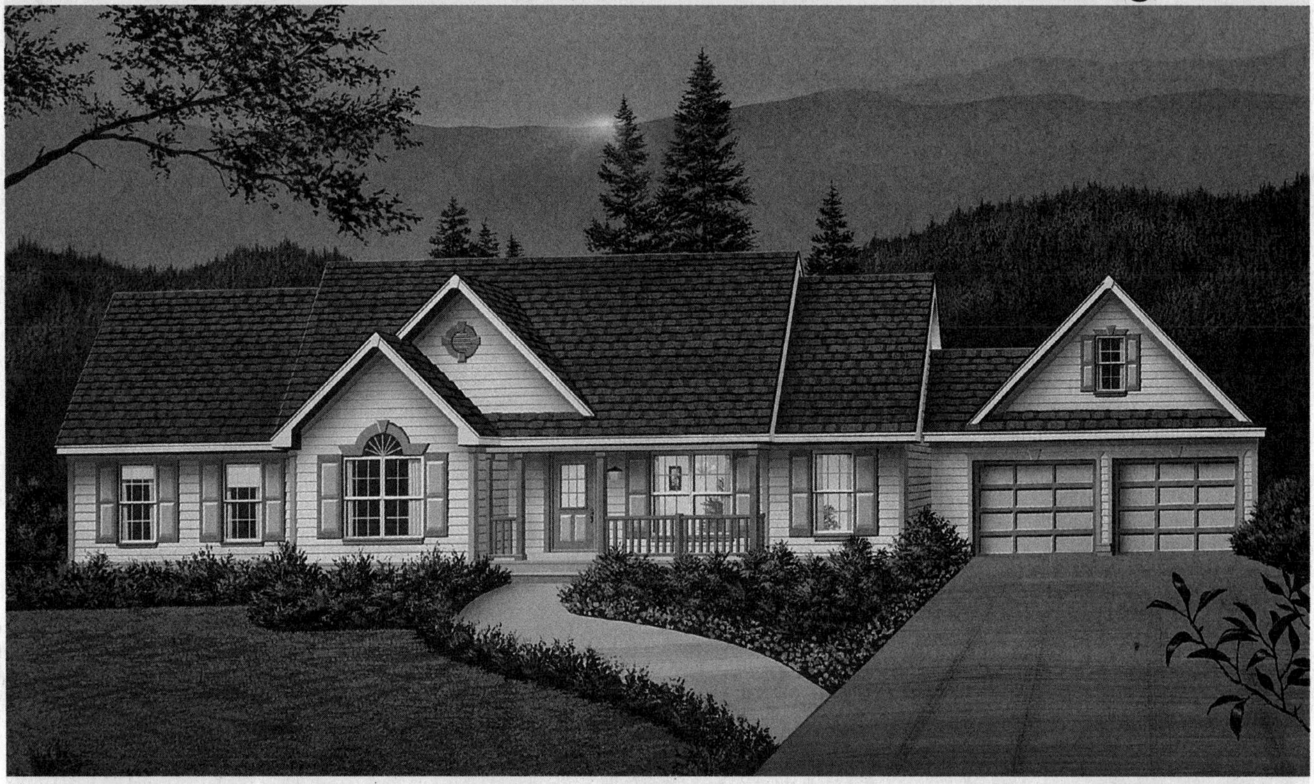

1,708 total square feet of living area

Price Code B

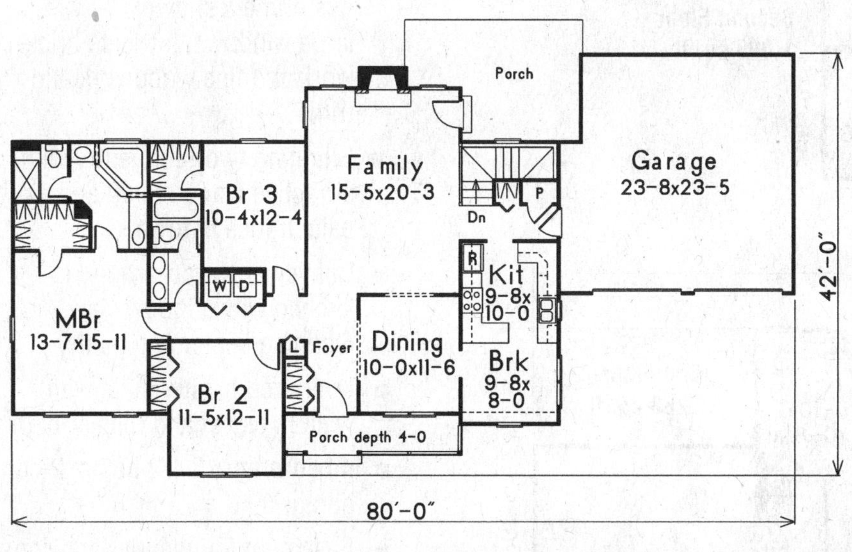
Porch
Family
15-5x20-3
Garage
23-8x23-5
Br 3
10-4x12-4
Dn
P
R
Kit
9-8x
10-0
W D
MBr
13-7x15-11
L
Foyer
Dining
10-0x11-6
Brk
9-8x
8-0
Br 2
11-5x12-11
Porch depth 4-0
42'-0"
80'-0"

Special features

- Massive family room enhanced with several windows, fireplace and access to porch
- Deluxe master bath accented by step-up corner tub flanked by double vanities
- Closets throughout maintain organized living
- Bedrooms isolated from living areas
- 3 bedrooms, 2 baths, 2-car garage
- Basement foundation, drawings also include crawl space foundation

The Family
Handyman

Plan #708-0138

Impressive Victorian Blends Charm And Efficiency

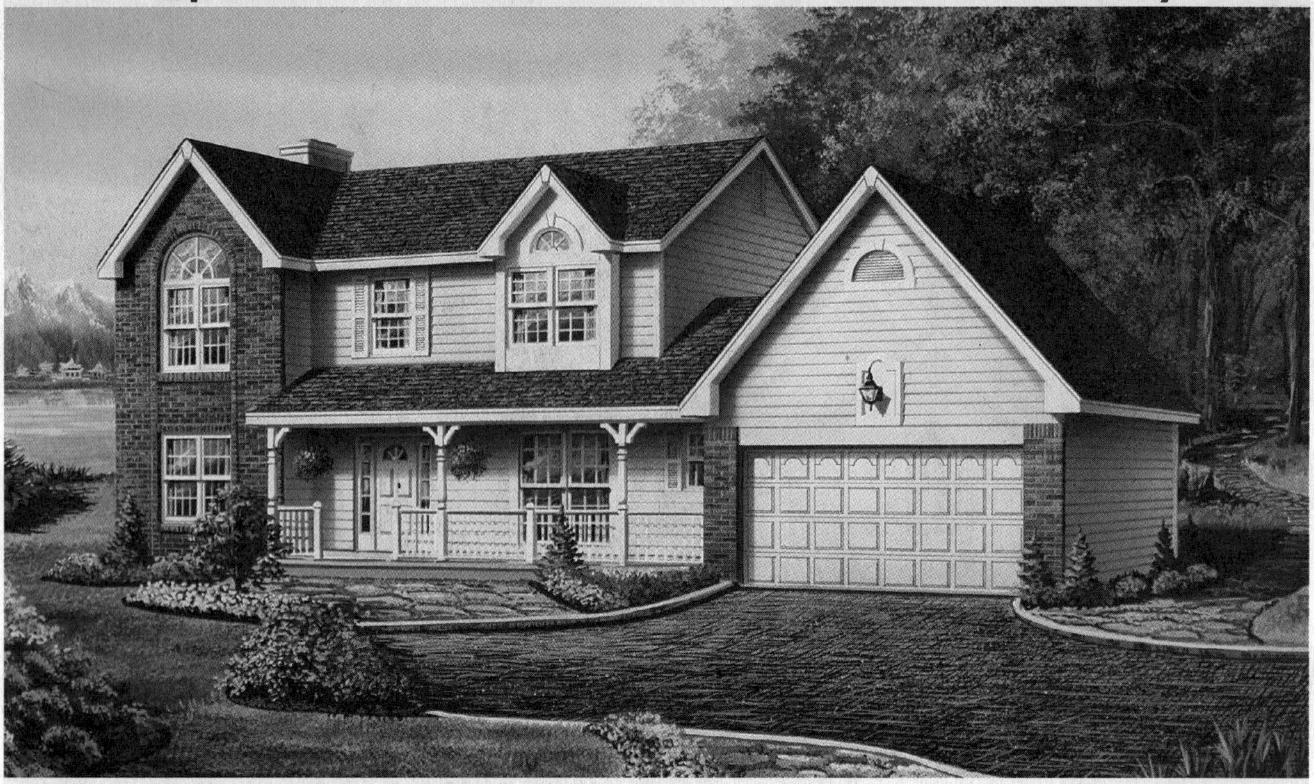

2,286 total square feet of living area **Price Code E**

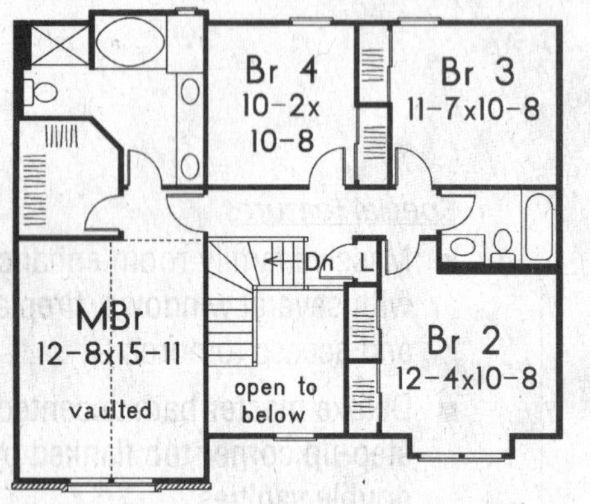
Br 4
10-2x
10-8
Br 3
11-7x10-8
Dn
L
MBr
12-8x15-11
vaulted
open to
below
Br 2
12-4x10-8

Second Floor
1,003 sq. ft.

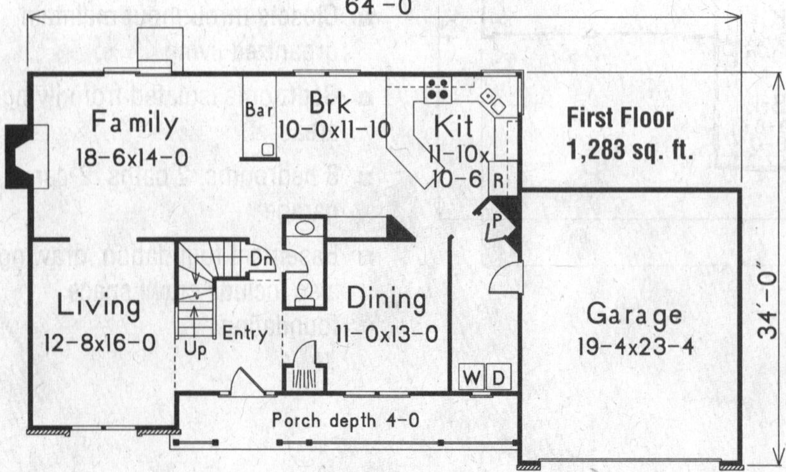
64'-0"
Family
18-6x14-0
Bar
Brk
10-0x11-10
Kit
11-10x
10-6
R
P
First Floor
1,283 sq. ft.
Dn
Living
12-8x16-0
Up
Entry
Dining
11-0x13-0
W
D
Garage
19-4x23-4
34'-0"
Porch depth 4-0

Special features

- Fine architectural detail makes this home a showplace with its large windows, intricate brick-work and fine woodwork and trim
- Stunning two-story entry with attractive wood railing and balustrades in foyer
- Convenient wrap-around kitchen with window view, planning center and pantry
- Oversized master suite with walk-in closet and master bath
- 4 bedrooms, 2 1/2 baths, 2-car garage
- Basement foundation, drawings also include crawl space and slab foundations

The Family
Handyman

Plan #708-0711

Stylish Living For A Narrow Lot

1,575 total square feet of living area **Price Code B**

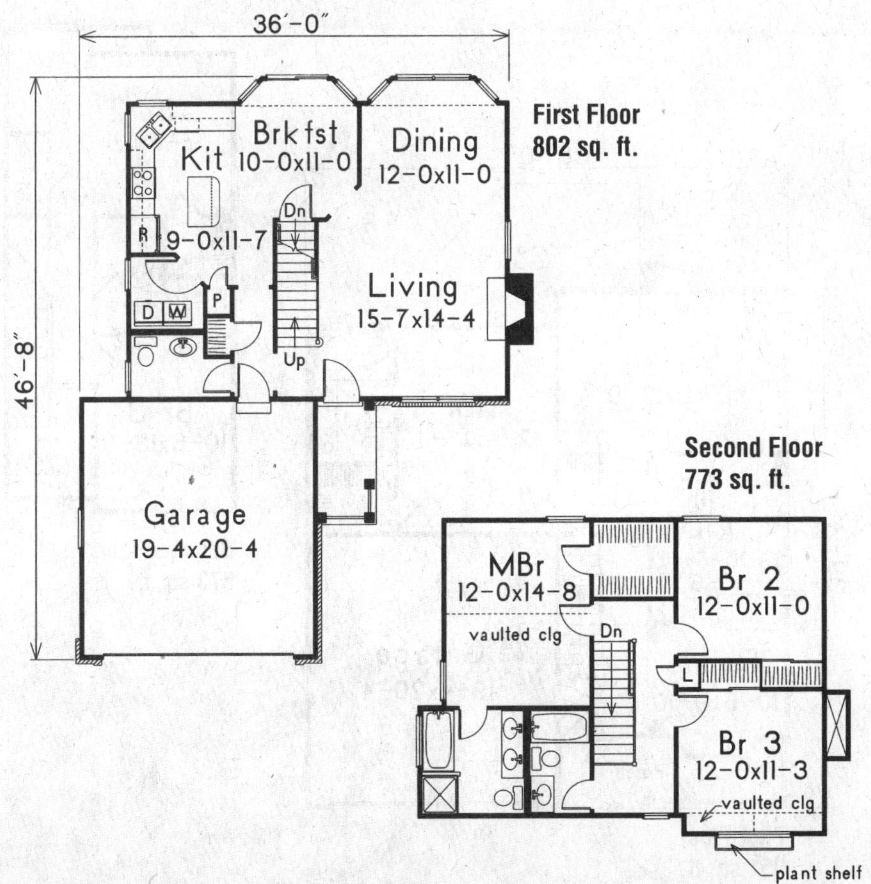
36'-0"
46'-8"
Brk fst
10-0x11-0
Kit
9-0x11-7
Dining
12-0x11-0
R
Dn
Living
15-7x14-4
D W
P
Up
Garage
19-4x20-4
MBr
12-0x14-8
vaulted clg
Dn
Br 2
12-0x11-0
L
Br 3
12-0x11-3
vaulted clg
plant shelf

First Floor
802 sq. ft.

Second Floor
773 sq. ft.

Special features

- Inviting porch leads to spacious living and dining rooms
- Kitchen with corner windows features an island snack bar, attractive breakfast room bay, convenient laundry and built-in pantry
- A luxury bath and walk-in closet adorn master bedroom suite
- 3 bedrooms, 2 1/2 baths, 2-car garage
- Basement foundation

TO ORDER BLUEPRINTS USE THE FORM ON PAGE 15 OR CALL TOLL-FREE 1-877-671-6

View thousands more home plans online at www.familyhandyman.com/homeplans

The Family
Handyman

Plan #708-0652

Dining With A View

1,524 total square feet of living area

Price Code B

Special features

- Delightful balcony overlooks two-story entry illuminated by oval window
- Roomy first floor master bedroom offers quiet privacy
- All bedrooms feature one or more walk-in closets
- 3 bedrooms, 2 1/2 baths, 2-car garage
- Basement foundation

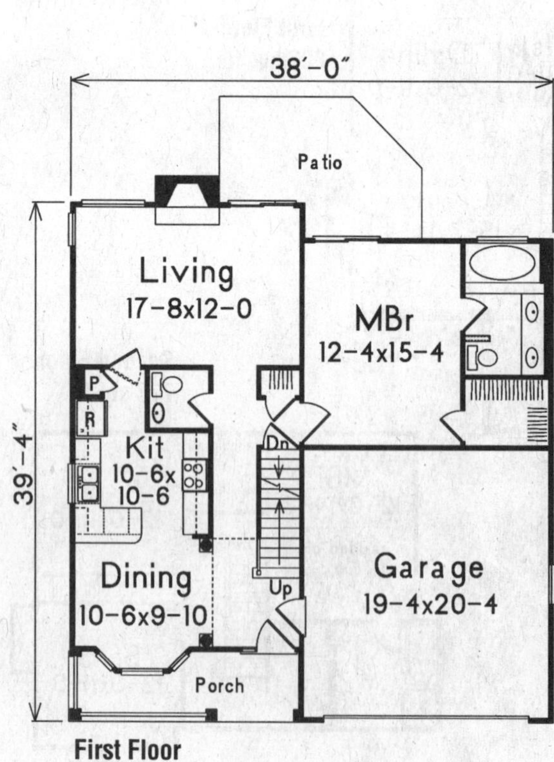
38′-0″
39′-4″
Patio
Living
17-8x12-0
MBr
12-4x15-4
P
R
Kit
10-6x
10-6
Dn
Dining
10-6x9-10
Up
Garage
19-4x20-4
Porch

First Floor
951 sq. ft.

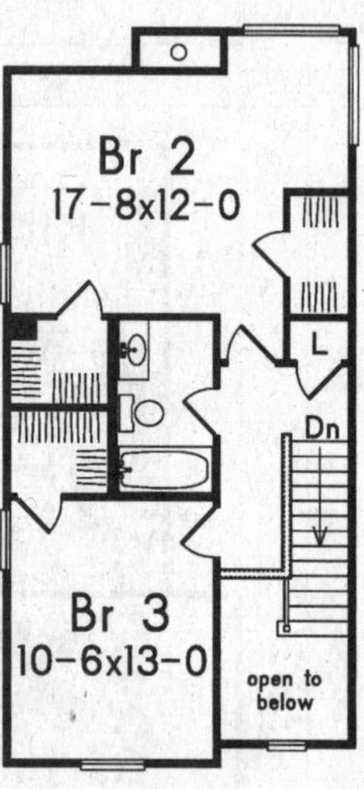
Br 2
17-8x12-0
L
Dn
Br 3
10-6x13-0
open to
below

Second Floor
573 sq. ft.

TO ORDER BLUEPRINTS USE THE FORM ON PAGE 15 OR CALL TOLL-FREE 1-877-671-6036

View thousands more home plans online at www.familyhandyman.com/homeplans

The Family
Handyman

Plan #708-AX-93305

Inviting Covered Porch

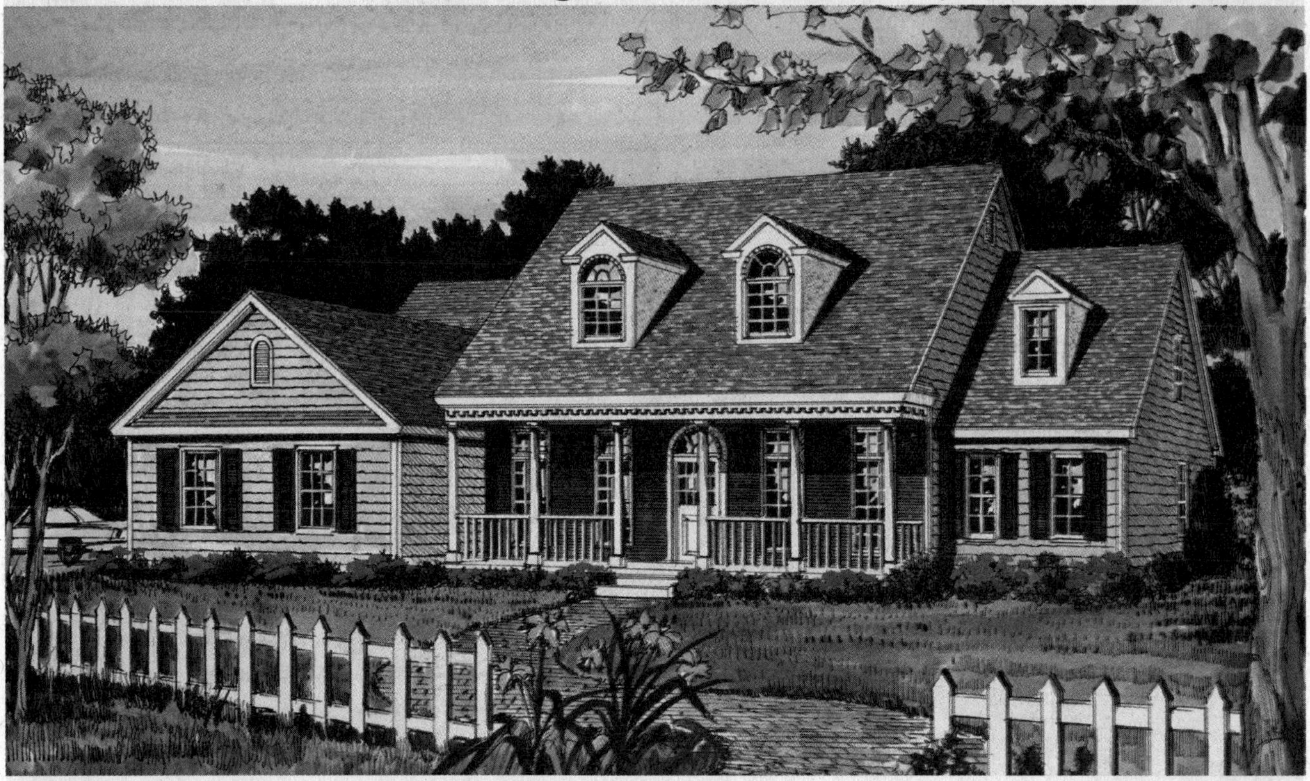

2,567 total square feet of living area **Price Code F**

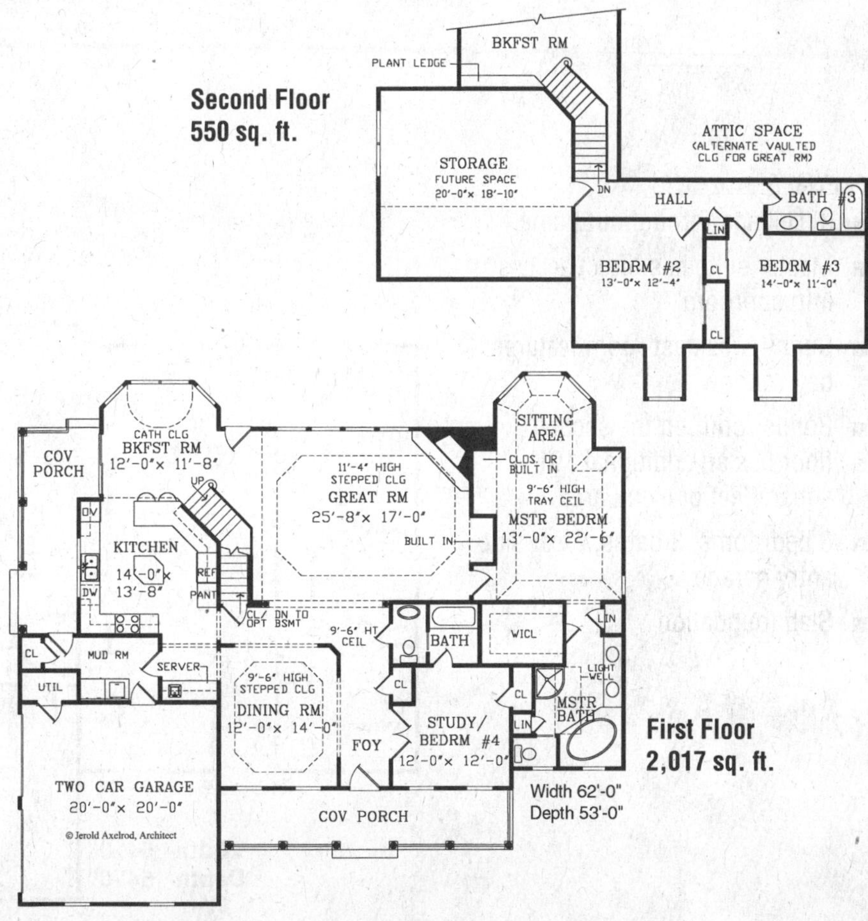
Second Floor
550 sq. ft.
BKFST RM
PLANT LEDGE
STORAGE
FUTURE SPACE
20'-0"x 18'-10"
DN
ATTIC SPACE
(ALTERNATE VAULTED CLG FOR GREAT RM)
HALL
BATH #3
LIN
BEDRM #2
13'-0"x 12'-4"
CL
BEDRM #3
14'-0"x 11'-0"
CL
COV PORCH
CATH CLG
BKFST RM
12'-0"x 11'-8"
UP
11'-4" HIGH STEPPED CLG
GREAT RM
25'-8"x 17'-0"
BUILT IN
SITTING AREA
CLOS. OR BUILT IN
9'-6" HIGH TRAY CEIL
MSTR BEDRM
13'-0"x 22'-6"
DW
KITCHEN
14'-0"x 13'-8"
REF
PANT
DW
CL/ DN TO OPT BSMT
9'-6" HT CEIL
BATH
WICL
LIN
CL
MUD RM
SERVER
UTIL
9'-6" HIGH STEPPED CLG
DINING RM
12'-0"x 14'-0"
CL
CL
LIGHT WELL
LIN
MSTR BATH
FOY
STUDY/ BEDRM #4
12'-0"x 12'-0"
First Floor
2,017 sq. ft.
TWO CAR GARAGE
20'-0"x 20'-0"
© Jerold Axelrod, Architect
COV PORCH
Width 62'-0"
Depth 53'-0"

Special features

- Breakfast room has a 12' cathedral ceiling and a bayed area full of windows
- Great room has a stepped ceiling, built-in media center and a corner fireplace
- Bonus room on the second floor has an additional 300 square feet of living area
- 4 bedrooms, 3 baths, 2-car side entry garage
- Basement, crawl space or slab foundation, please specify when ordering

Plan #708-MG-02236

Ranch With Traditional Feel

© 2003, Garrell Associates, Inc.

1,985 total square feet of living area

Price Code G

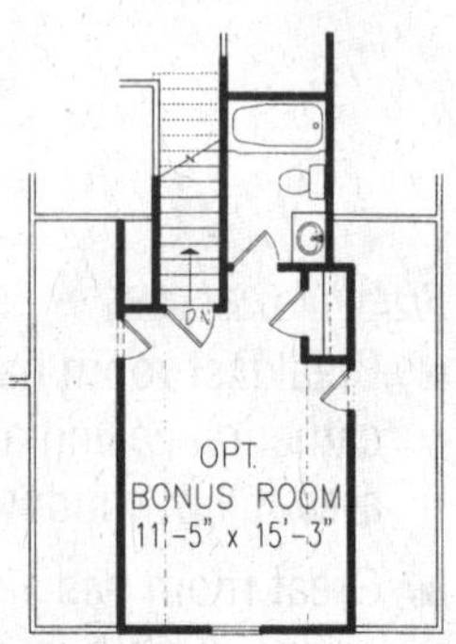

DN
OPT.
BONUS ROOM
11'-5" x 15'-3"

Optional Second Floor

Special features

- 9' ceilings throughout home
- Master suite has direct access into sunroom
- Sunny breakfast room features bay window
- Bonus room on the second floor has an additional 191 square feet of living area
- 3 bedrooms, 3 baths, 2-car side entry garage
- Slab foundation

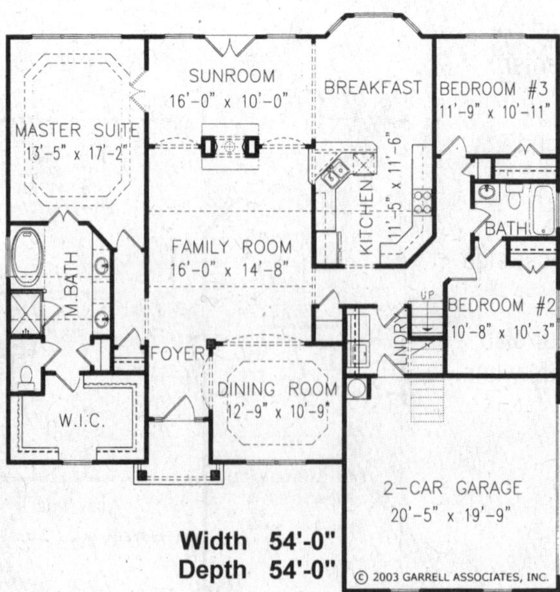

SUNROOM
16'-0" x 10'-0"
BREAKFAST
BEDROOM #3
11'-9" x 10'-11"
MASTER SUITE
13'-5" x 17'-2"
KITCHEN
11'-5" x 11'-6"
BATH
FAMILY ROOM
16'-0" x 14'-8"
M.BATH
UP
BEDROOM #2
10'-8" x 10'-3"
LNDRY
FOYER
DINING ROOM
12'-9" x 10'-9"
W.I.C.
2-CAR GARAGE
20'-5" x 19'-9"
© 2003 GARRELL ASSOCIATES, INC.

Width 54'-0"
Depth 54'-0"

First Floor
1,985 sq. ft.

TO ORDER BLUEPRINTS USE THE FORM ON PAGE 15 OR CALL TOLL-FREE 1-877-671-6036

View thousands more home plans online at www.familyhandyman.com/homeplans

The Family
Handyman

Plan #708-0706

Classic Exterior Employs Innovative Planning

1,791 total square feet of living area **Price Code C**

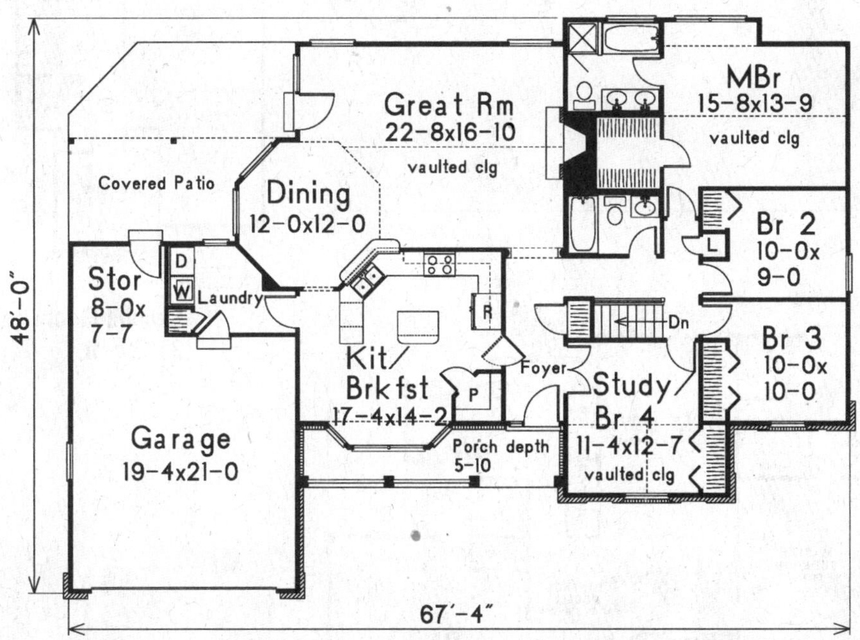
Great Rm
22-8x16-10
vaulted clg
MBr
15-8x13-9
vaulted clg
Covered Patio
Dining
12-0x12-0
Stor
8-0x
7-7
D
W
Laundry
Br 2
10-0x
9-0
L
R
Dn
Br 3
10-0x
10-0
Kit/
Brkfst
17-4x14-2
P
Foyer
Study/
Br 4
11-4x12-7
vaulted clg
Porch depth
5-10
Garage
19-4x21-0
48'-0"
67'-4"

Special features

- Vaulted great room and octagon-shaped dining area enjoy views of covered patio
- Kitchen features a pass-through to dining area, center island, large walk-in pantry and breakfast room with large bay window
- Master bedroom is vaulted with sitting area
- 4 bedrooms, 2 baths, 2-car garage with storage
- Basement foundation

TO ORDER BLUEPRINTS USE THE FORM ON PAGE 15 OR CALL TOLL-FREE 1-877-671-6036
View thousands more home plans online at www.familyhandyman.com/homeplans

Plan #708-NDG-707

Well-Designed Traditional

1,635 total square feet of living area **Price Code B**

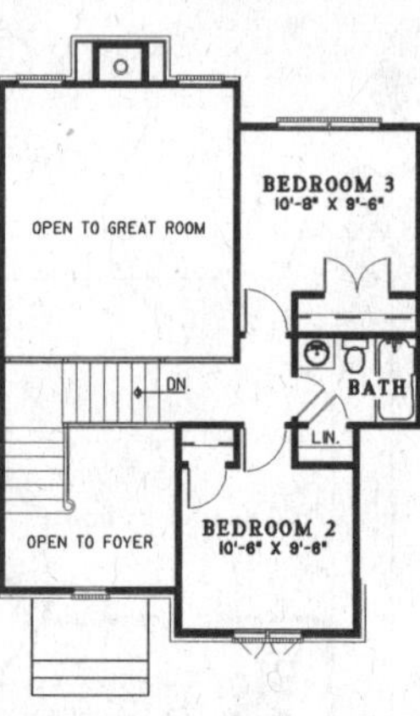
OPEN TO GREAT ROOM
BEDROOM 3
10'-8" X 9'-6"
DN.
BATH
LIN.
OPEN TO FOYER
BEDROOM 2
10'-6" X 9'-8"

Second Floor
355 sq. ft.

Special features

- Kitchen has a large counter dining area perfect for additional guests
- Corner whirlpool tub in the master bath is a great way to relax
- Convenient grilling porch adjacent to the breakfast room
- 3 bedrooms, 2 1/2 baths, 2-car garage
- Crawl space or slab foundation, please specify when ordering

56'-6"
49'-2"
GRILLING PORCH
11'-4" X 8'-0"
WHP TUB
GLASS SHWR
M.BATH
GREAT ROOM
14'-0" X 15'-10"
OPEN TO ABOVE
BREAKFAST ROOM
10'-8" X 9'-6"
KITCHEN
8'-8" X 14'-8"
RG.
REF
PAN
LAU
LIN
OPTIONAL BASEMENT STAIRS
MASTER BEDROOM
13'-0" X 16'-2"
FOYER
10'-4" X 9'-4"
OPEN TO ABOVE
UP
DINING ROOM
10'-8" X 11'-10"
GARAGE
20'-0" X 23'-0"
© 1991 NELSON DESIGN GROUP, LLC.

First Floor
1,280 sq. ft.

TO ORDER BLUEPRINTS USE THE FORM ON PAGE 15 OR CALL TOLL-FREE 1-877-671-6036

View thousands more home plans online at www.familyhandyman.com/homeplans

Plan #708-0249

Country-Style Home With Large Front Porch

1,501 total square feet of living area **Price Code B**

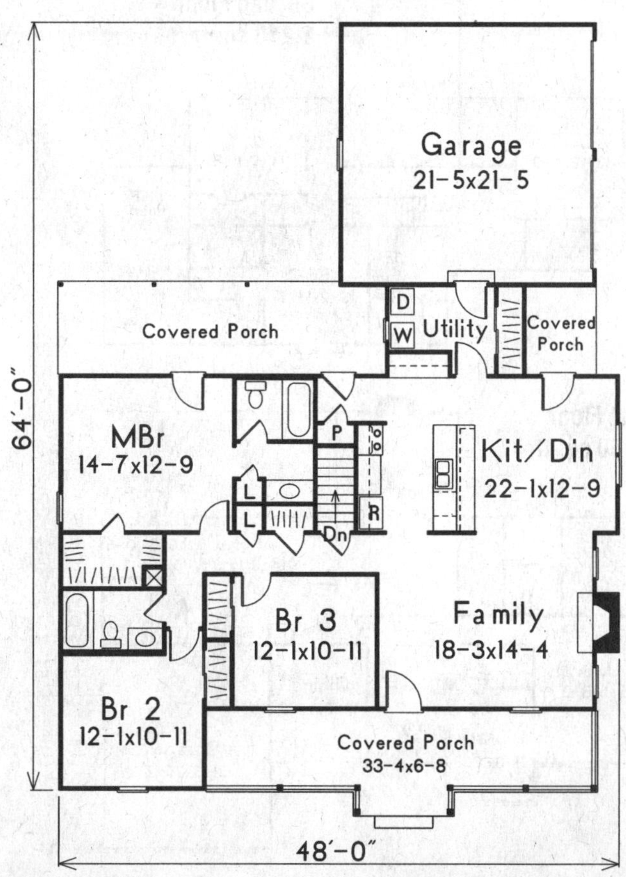

Garage
21-5x21-5
Covered Porch
D
W
Utility
Covered Porch
MBr
14-7x12-9
P
Kit/Din
22-1x12-9
L
L
R
Dn
Br 3
12-1x10-11
Family
18-3x14-4
Br 2
12-1x10-11
Covered Porch
33-4x6-8
64'-0"
48'-0"

Special features

- Spacious kitchen with dining area is open to the outdoors
- Convenient utility room is adjacent to garage
- Master suite with private bath, dressing area and access to large covered porch
- Large family room creates openness
- 3 bedrooms, 2 baths, 2-car side entry garage
- Basement foundation, drawings also include crawl space and slab foundations

TO ORDER BLUEPRINTS USE THE FORM ON PAGE 15 OR CALL TOLL-FREE 1-877-671-6036
View thousands more home plans online at www.familyhandyman.com/homeplans

The Family
Handyman

Plan #708-0159

A Great Manor House, Spacious Inside And Out

159

3,368 total square feet of living area

Price Code F

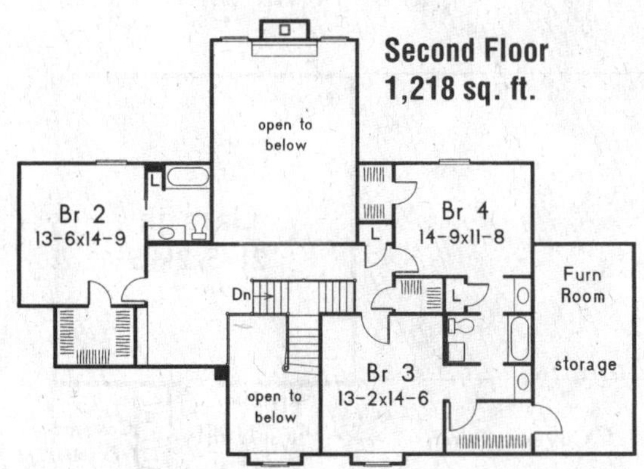
Second Floor
1,218 sq. ft.
open to below
Br 2
13-6x14-9
Br 4
14-9x11-8
Furn Room
storage
Dn
open to below
Br 3
13-2x14-6

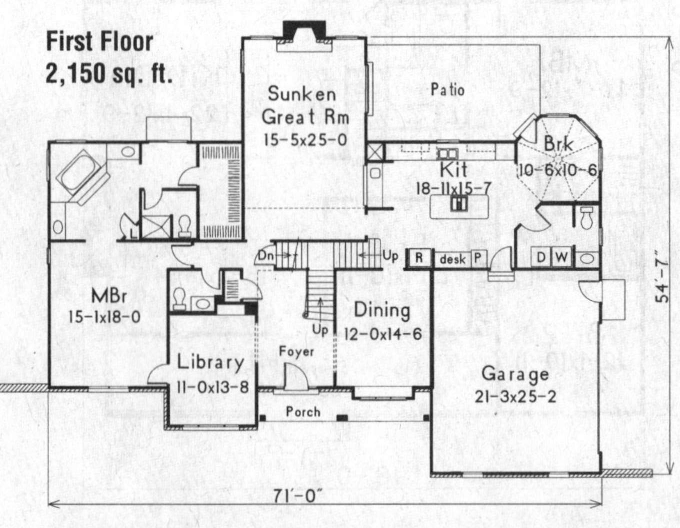
First Floor
2,150 sq. ft.
Sunken Great Rm
15-5x25-0
Patio
Brk
10-6x10-6
Kit
18-11x15-7
Dn
Up
R
desk
P
D
W
MBr
15-1x18-0
Dining
12-0x14-6
Up
Library
11-0x13-8
Foyer
Porch
Garage
21-3x25-2
54'-7"
71'-0"

Special features

- Sunken great room with cathedral ceiling, wooden beams, skylights and a masonry fireplace
- Octagon-shaped breakfast room has domed ceiling with beams, large windows and door to patio
- Master bedroom in a private wing with deluxe bath and dressing area
- Oversized walk-in closets and storage areas in each bedroom
- 4 bedrooms, 3 full baths, 2 half baths, 2-car side entry garage
- Basement foundation

TO ORDER BLUEPRINTS USE THE FORM ON PAGE 15 OR CALL TOLL-FREE 1-877-671-6036

View thousands more home plans online at www.familyhandyman.com/homeplans

Formal Living And Dining Rooms

1,890 total square feet of living area

Price Code C

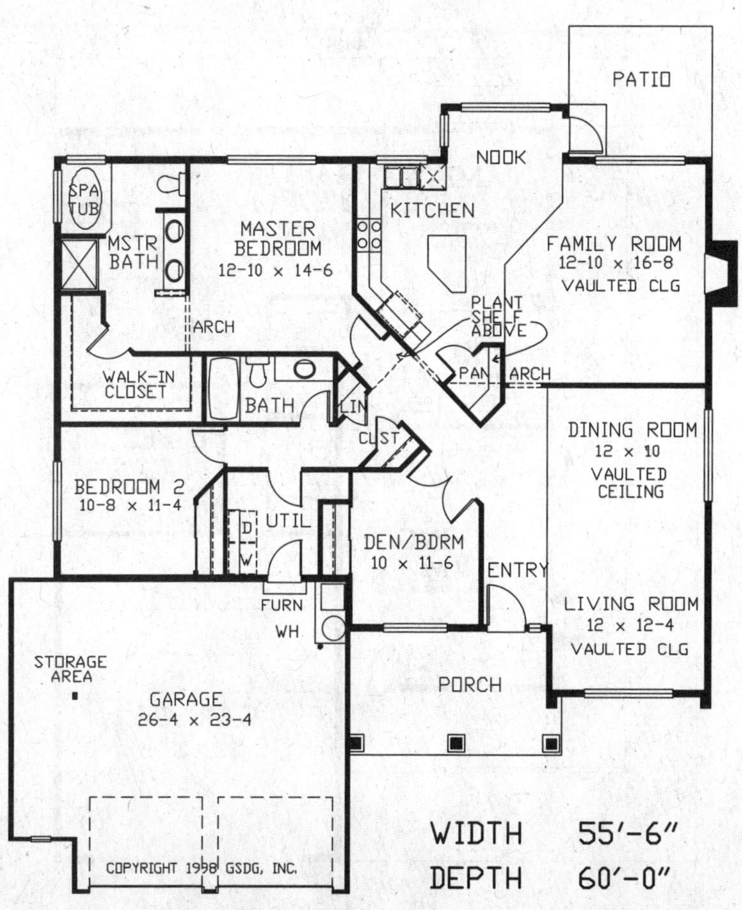
PATIO
NOOK
SPA TUB
MSTR BATH
MASTER BEDROOM
12-10 x 14-6
KITCHEN
FAMILY ROOM
12-10 x 16-8
VAULTED CLG
PLANT SHELF ABOVE
ARCH
WALK-IN CLOSET
BATH
LIN
PAN
ARCH
CLST
DINING ROOM
12 x 10
VAULTED CEILING
BEDROOM 2
10-8 x 11-4
UTIL
D
W
DEN/BDRM
10 x 11-6
ENTRY
LIVING ROOM
12 x 12-4
VAULTED CLG
FURN
WH
PORCH
STORAGE AREA
GARAGE
26-4 x 23-4
COPYRIGHT 1998 GSDG, INC.
WIDTH 55'-6"
DEPTH 60'-0"

Special features

- Inviting covered porch
- Vaulted ceilings in living, dining and family rooms
- Kitchen is open to family room and nook
- Large walk-in pantry in kitchen
- Arch accented master bath has spa tub, dual sinks and walk-in closet
- 3 bedrooms, 2 baths, 2-car garage
- Crawl space foundation

Plan #708-HP-C460

Simple Rooflines And Inviting Porch

1,389 total square feet of living area **Price Code A**

Special features

- Formal living room has warming fireplace and a delightful bay window
- U-shaped kitchen shares a snack bar with the bayed family room
- Lovely master bedroom has its own private bath
- 3 bedrooms, 2 baths, 2-car garage
- Slab foundation

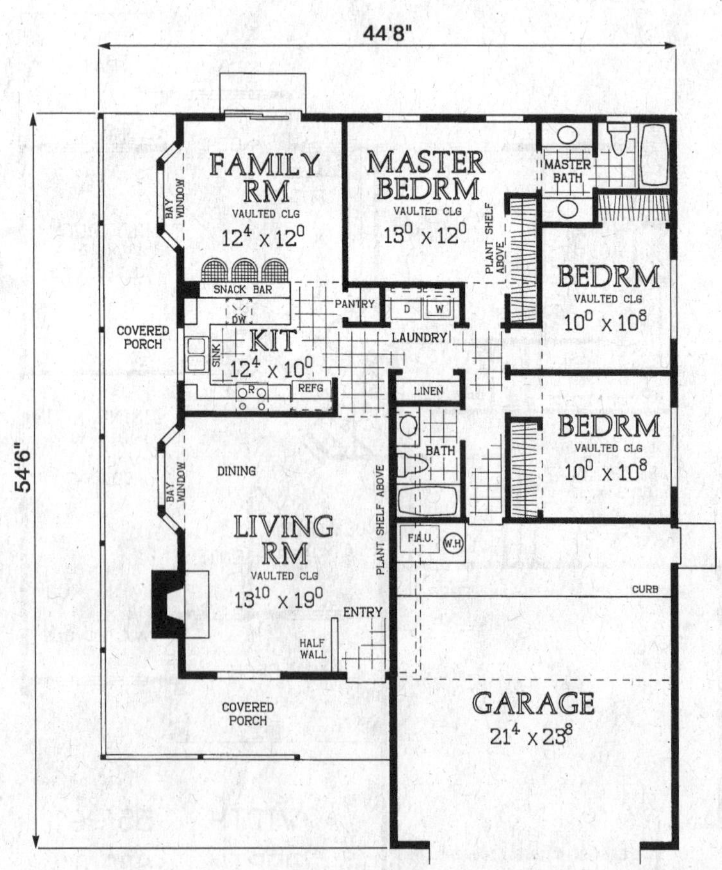
44'8"
54'6"
FAMILY RM
BAY WINDOW
VAULTED CLG
$12^4 \times 12^0$
MASTER BEDRM
VAULTED CLG
$13^0 \times 12^0$
PLANT SHELF ABOVE
MASTER BATH
BEDRM
VAULTED CLG
$10^0 \times 10^8$
SNACK BAR
PANTRY
D
W
DW
LAUNDRY
COVERED PORCH
SINK
KIT
$12^4 \times 10^0$
REFG
LINEN
BATH
BEDRM
VAULTED CLG
$10^0 \times 10^8$
DINING
BAY WINDOW
PLANT SHELF ABOVE
LIVING RM
VAULTED CLG
$13^{10} \times 19^0$
F.A.U.
W.H.
CURB
ENTRY
HALF WALL
COVERED PORCH
GARAGE
$21^4 \times 23^8$

TO ORDER BLUEPRINTS USE THE FORM ON PAGE 15 OR CALL TOLL-FREE 1-877-671-6036

View thousands more home plans online at www.familyhandyman.com/homeplans

Private Library Has Sloped Ceiling

2,603 total square feet of living area — Price Code E

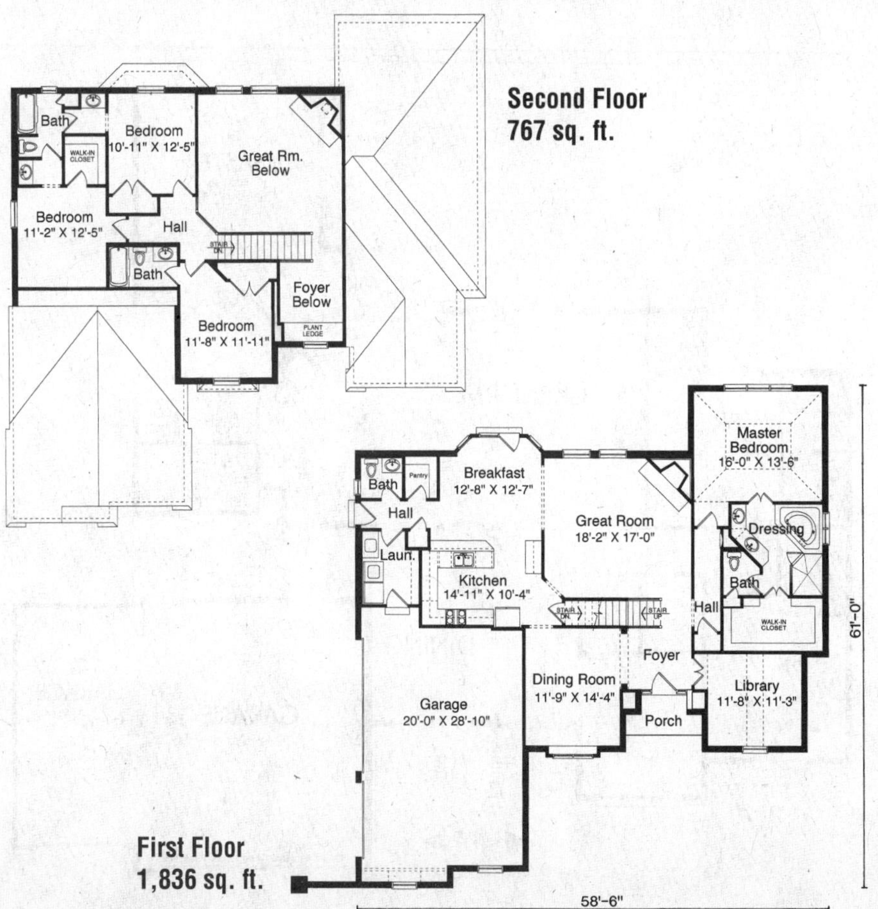
Bath
Bedroom
10'-11" X 12'-5"
Great Rm. Below
WALK-IN CLOSET
Bedroom
11'-2" X 12'-5"
Hall
Bath
Foyer Below
Bedroom
11'-8" X 11'-11"
PLANT LEDGE
Bath
Pantry
Breakfast
12'-8" X 12'-7"
Master Bedroom
16'-0" X 13'-6"
Hall
Great Room
18'-2" X 17'-0"
Laun.
Dressing
Kitchen
14'-11" X 10'-4"
Bath
Hall
WALK-IN CLOSET
Foyer
61'-0"
Dining Room
11'-9" X 14'-4"
Library
11'-8" X 11'-3"
Garage
20'-0" X 28'-10"
Porch
58'-6"

Second Floor
767 sq. ft.

First Floor
1,836 sq. ft.

Special features

- U-shaped kitchen offers a peninsula with bar and is lighted by windows in the breakfast room
- An open staircase leads to a second floor featuring three bedrooms
- The balcony provides a dramatic view to the great room and foyer
- 4 bedrooms, 3 1/2 baths, 3-car side entry garage
- Basement foundation

Plan #708-AMD-1213

Great Views At Rear Of Home

2,197 total square feet of living area | **Price Code C**

Special features

- Centrally located great room opens to kitchen, breakfast nook and private backyard
- Den located off entry ideal for home office
- Vaulted master bath has spa tub, shower and double vanity
- 3 bedrooms, 2 1/2 baths, 3-car garage
- Crawl space foundation

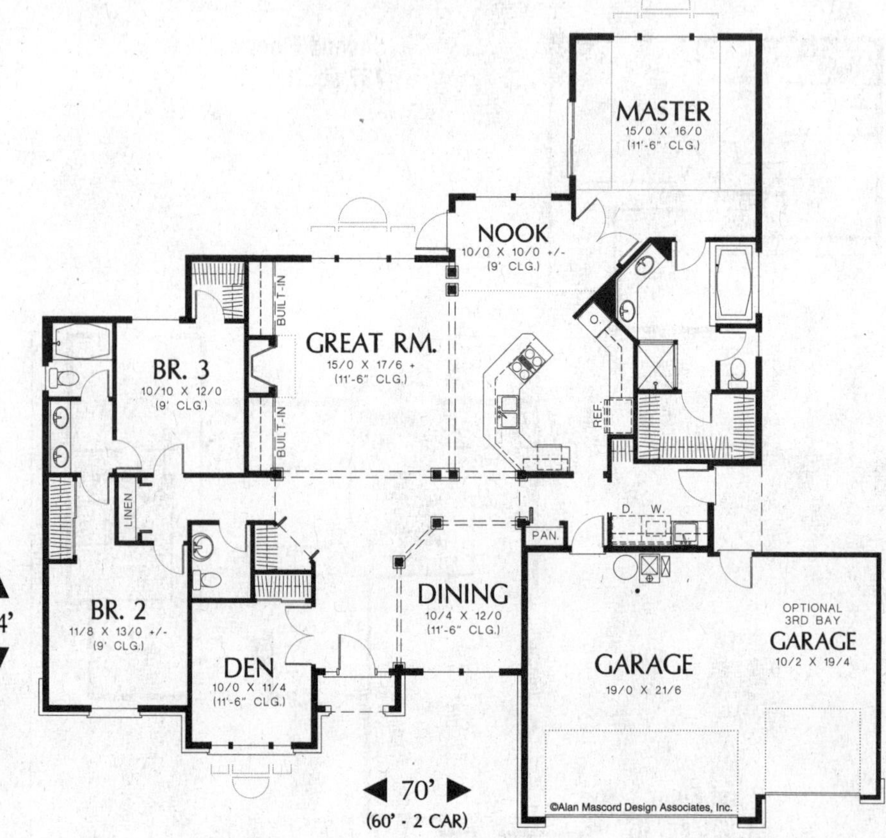
MASTER
15/0 X 16/0
(11'-6" CLG.)
NOOK
10/0 X 10/0 +/-
(9' CLG.)
GREAT RM.
15/0 X 17/6 +
(11'-6" CLG.)
BUILT-IN
BUILT-IN
BR. 3
10/10 X 12/0
(9' CLG.)
O.
REF.
LINEN
D. W.
PAN.
BR. 2
11/8 X 13/0 +/-
(9' CLG.)
64'
DINING
10/4 X 12/0
(11'-6" CLG.)
OPTIONAL
3RD BAY
GARAGE
10/2 X 19/4
GARAGE
19/0 X 21/6
DEN
10/0 X 11/4
(11'-6" CLG.)
70'
(60' - 2 CAR)
©Alan Mascord Design Associates, Inc.

TO ORDER BLUEPRINTS USE THE FORM ON PAGE 15 OR CALL TOLL-FREE 1-877-671-6036

View thousands more home plans online at www.familyhandyman.com/homeplans

Split Bedroom, Drive Under Garage Design

1,268 total square feet of living area **Price Code A**

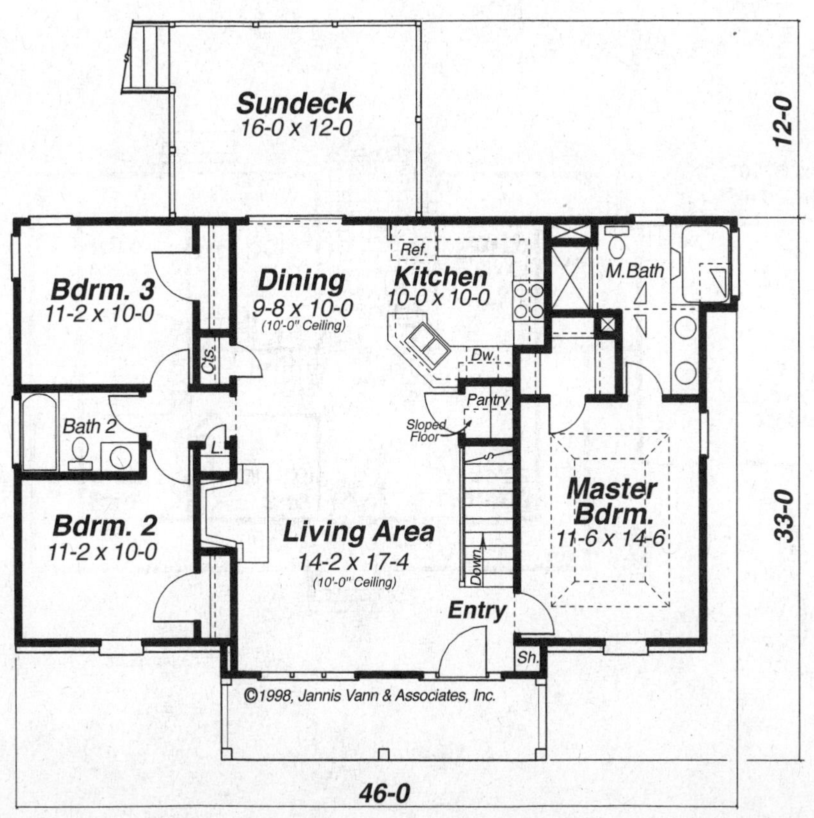
Sundeck
16-0 x 12-0
12-0
Bdrm. 3
11-2 x 10-0
Dining
9-8 x 10-0
(10'-0" Ceiling)
Ref.
Kitchen
10-0 x 10-0
Dw.
Pantry
Sloped Floor
M.Bath
Clo.
Bath 2
L.
Bdrm. 2
11-2 x 10-0
Living Area
14-2 x 17-4
(10'-0" Ceiling)
Down
Master Bdrm.
11-6 x 14-6
33-0
Entry
Sh.
©1998, Jannis Vann & Associates, Inc.
46-0

Special features

- Raised gable porch is a focal point creating a dramatic look
- 10' ceilings throughout living and dining areas
- Open kitchen is well-designed
- Master suite offers tray ceiling and private bath with both a garden tub and a 4' shower
- 3 bedrooms, 2 baths, 2-car drive under garage
- Basement foundation

Country Ranch With Spacious Wrap-Around Porch

1,541 total square feet of living area **Price Code B**

Special features

- Dining area offers access to a screened porch for outdoor dining and entertaining
- Country kitchen features a center island and a breakfast bay for casual meals
- Great room is warmed by a woodstove
- 3 bedrooms, 2 baths, 2-car garage
- Basement or crawl space foundation, please specify when ordering

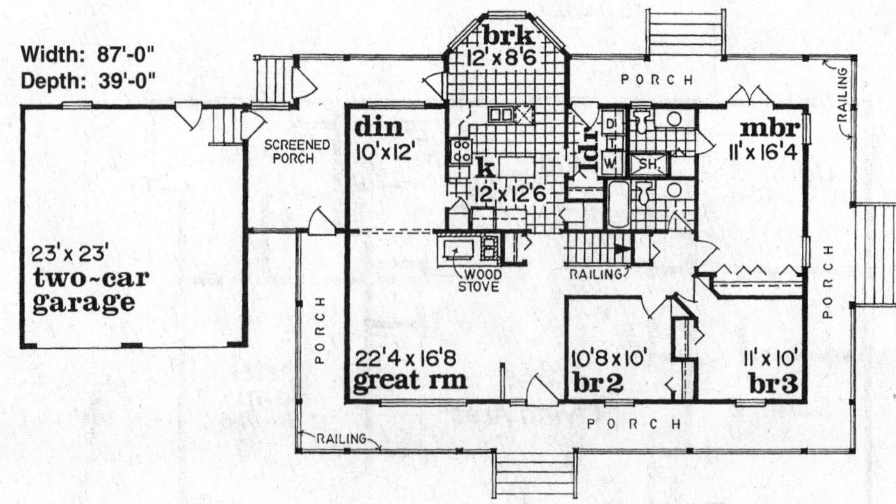
Width: 87'-0"
Depth: 39'-0"
brk
12'x8'6
PORCH
RAILING
din
10'x12'
SCREENED PORCH
k
12'x12'6
ldr
mbr
11'x16'4
SH
23'x23'
two-car garage
WOOD STOVE
RAILING
PORCH
PORCH
22'4 x 16'8
great rm
10'8 x 10'
br2
11'x 10'
br3
PORCH
RAILING

TO ORDER BLUEPRINTS USE THE FORM ON PAGE 15 OR CALL TOLL-FREE 1-877-671-6036

View thousands more home plans online at www.familyhandyman.com/homeplans

The Family
Handyman

Plan #708-HDS-1571

Whirlpool Tub In Master Bath

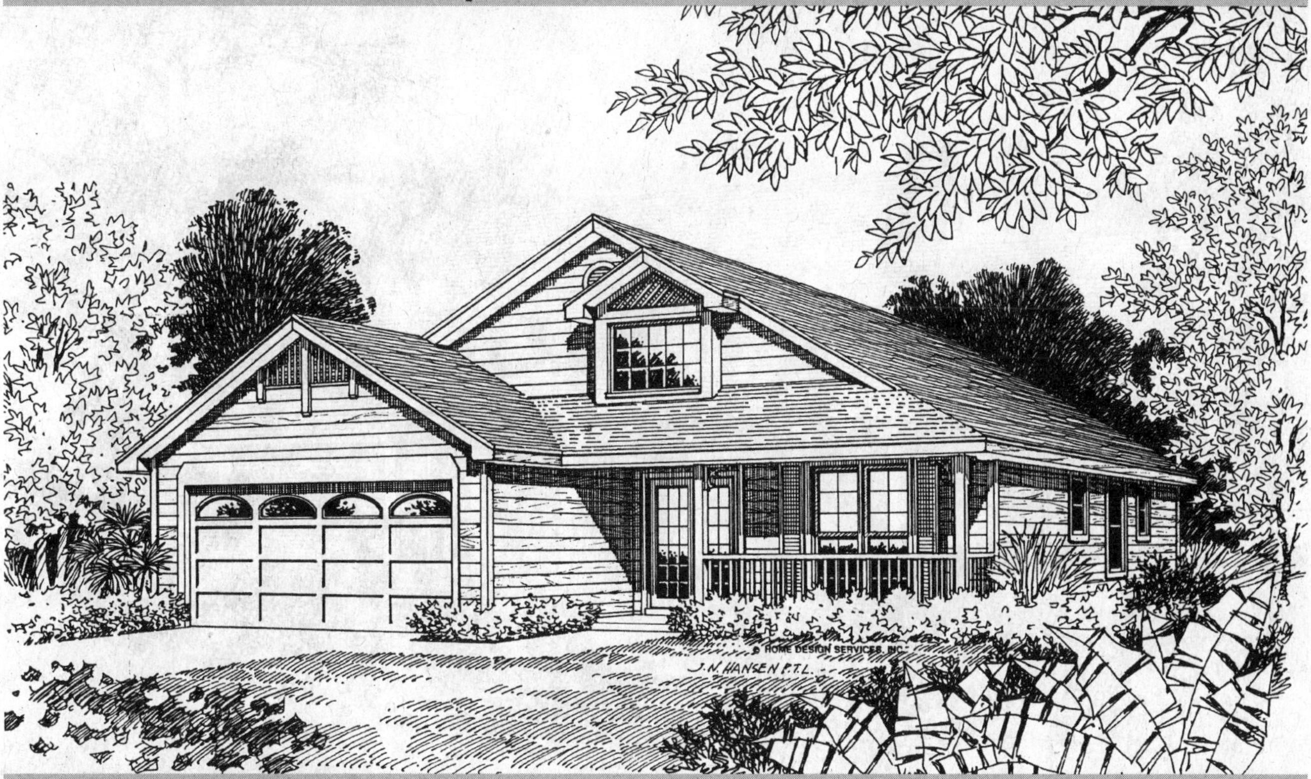

1,571 total square feet of living area **Price Code B**

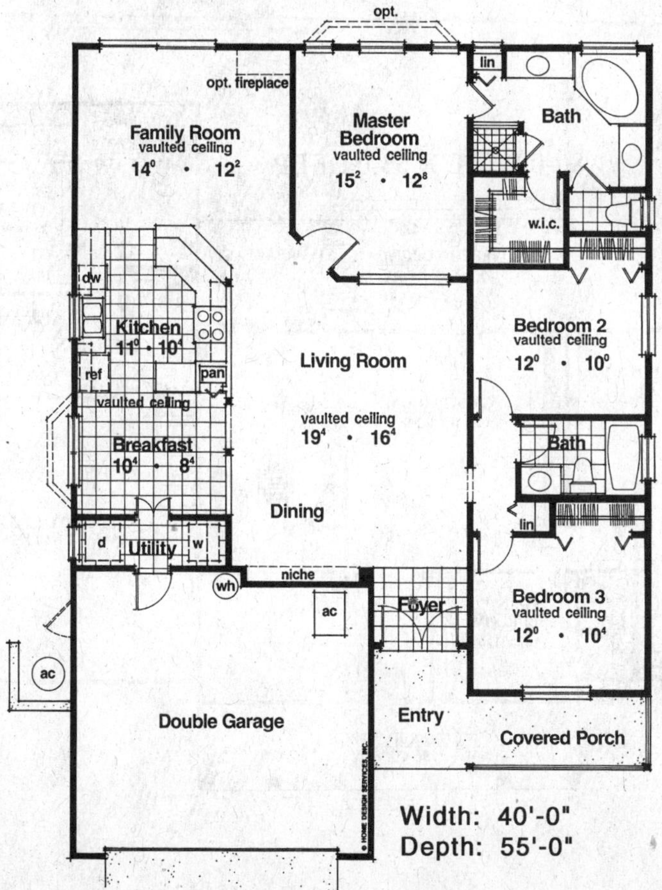
opt.
lin
opt. fireplace
Family Room
vaulted ceiling
$14^{0} \cdot 12^{2}$
Master Bedroom
vaulted ceiling
$15^{2} \cdot 12^{8}$
Bath
w.i.c.
dw
Kitchen
$11^{0} \cdot 10^{4}$
ref
pan
vaulted ceiling
Breakfast
$10^{4} \cdot 8^{4}$
Living Room
vaulted ceiling
$19^{4} \cdot 16^{4}$
Dining
Bedroom 2
vaulted ceiling
$12^{0} \cdot 10^{0}$
Bath
lin
d
Utility
w
wh
niche
ac
Foyer
Bedroom 3
vaulted ceiling
$12^{0} \cdot 10^{4}$
ac
Double Garage
Entry
Covered Porch
Width: 40'-0"
Depth: 55'-0"

Special features

- Bedrooms #2 and #3 share a bath in their own private hall
- Kitchen counter overlooks family room
- Open living area adds appeal with vaulted ceiling and display niche
- 3 bedrooms, 2 baths, 2-car garage
- Slab foundation

TO ORDER BLUEPRINTS USE THE FORM ON PAGE 15 OR CALL TOLL-FREE 1-877-671-6036

The Family
Handyman

Plan #708-DH-2600

Southern Elegance

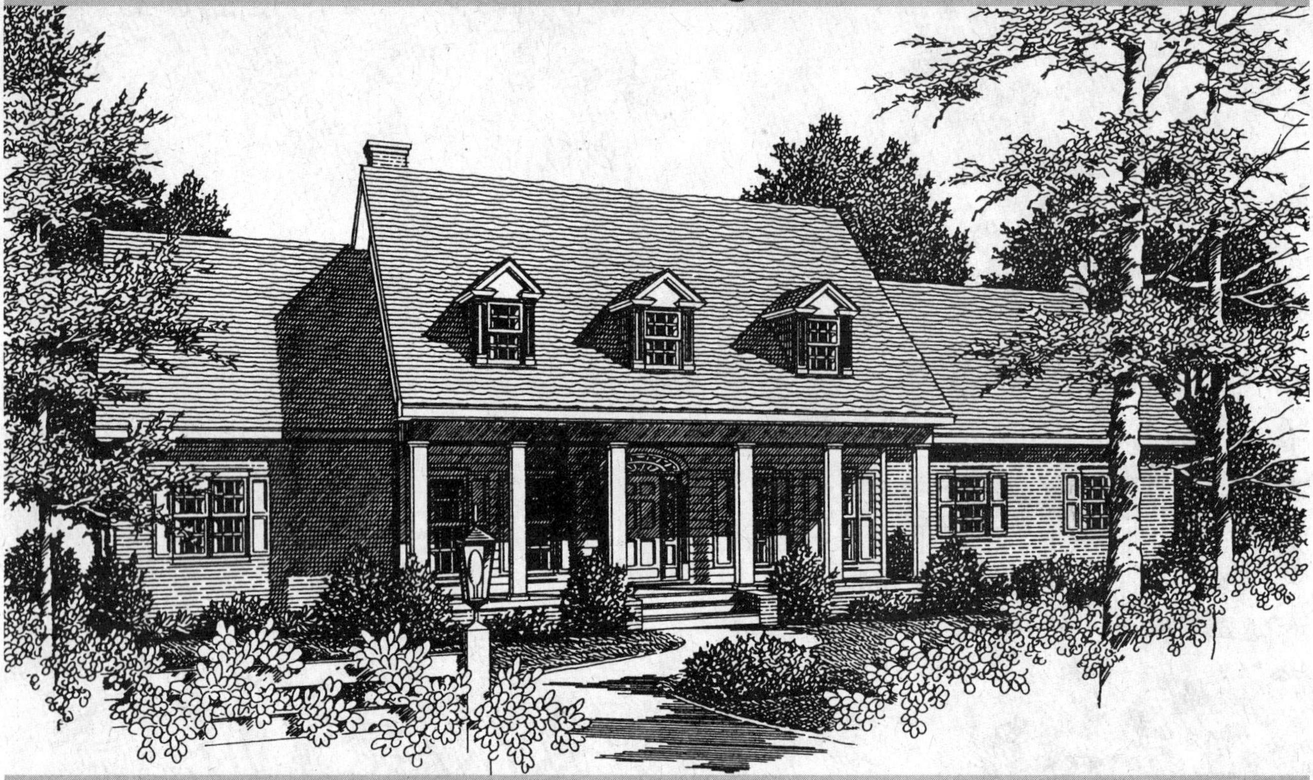

2,669 total square feet of living area **Price Code E**

Special features

- Nice-sized corner pantry in kitchen
- Guest bedroom located off the great room with a full bath would make an excellent office
- Master bath has double walk-in closets, whirlpool bath and a large shower
- 3 bedrooms, 3 1/2 baths, 2-car side entry garage
- Basement or slab foundation, please specify when ordering

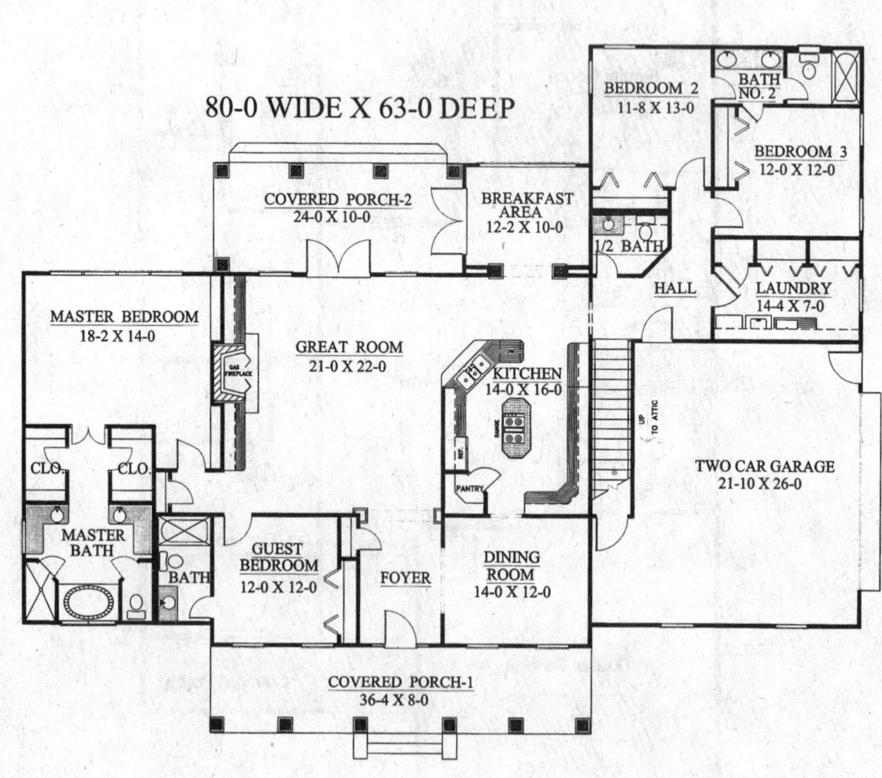
80-0 WIDE X 63-0 DEEP
BEDROOM 2
11-8 X 13-0
BATH NO. 2
BEDROOM 3
12-0 X 12-0
COVERED PORCH-2
24-0 X 10-0
BREAKFAST AREA
12-2 X 10-0
1/2 BATH
HALL
LAUNDRY
14-4 X 7-0
MASTER BEDROOM
18-2 X 14-0
GREAT ROOM
21-0 X 22-0
KITCHEN
14-0 X 16-0
CLO.
CLO.
PANTRY
TWO CAR GARAGE
21-10 X 26-0
MASTER BATH
BATH
GUEST BEDROOM
12-0 X 12-0
FOYER
DINING ROOM
14-0 X 12-0
COVERED PORCH-1
36-4 X 8-0

Plan #708-RJ-A19-36

Traditional Elegance

©Copyright 1988 Ralph Jones

1,945 total square feet of living area **Price Code C**

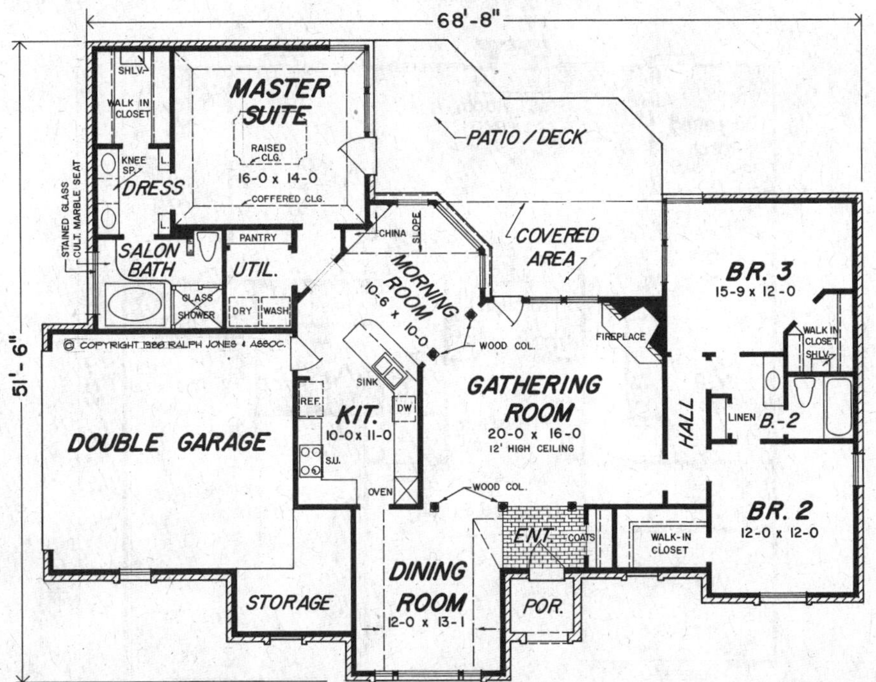
68'-8"
51'-6"
MASTER SUITE
RAISED CLG.
16-0 x 14-0
COFFERED CLG.
SHLV.
WALK IN CLOSET
KNEE SP.
DRESS
STAINED GLASS
CULT. MARBLE SEAT
SALON BATH
GLASS SHOWER
PANTRY
UTIL.
DRY
WASH
PATIO / DECK
CHINA
SLOPE
MORNING ROOM
10-6 x 10-0
COVERED AREA
WOOD COL.
FIREPLACE
BR. 3
15-9 x 12-0
WALK IN CLOSET
SHLV.
© COPYRIGHT 1988 RALPH JONES & ASSOC.
SINK
REF.
KIT.
10-0 x 11-0
DW
S.U.
OVEN
GATHERING ROOM
20-0 x 16-0
12' HIGH CEILING
HALL
LINEN
B.-2
DOUBLE GARAGE
WOOD COL.
ENT.
COATS
WALK-IN CLOSET
BR. 2
12-0 x 12-0
STORAGE
DINING ROOM
12-0 x 13-1
POR.

Special features

- Large gathering room with corner fireplace and 12' high ceiling
- Master suite with a coffered ceiling and French door leading to the patio/deck
- Master bath has a cultured marble seat, separate shower and tub
- All bedrooms have walk-in closets
- 3 bedrooms, 2 baths, 2-car side entry garage
- Slab or crawl space foundation, please specify when ordering

TO ORDER BLUEPRINTS USE THE FORM ON PAGE 15 OR CALL TOLL-FREE 1-877-671-6036

View thousands more home plans online at www.familyhandyman.com/homeplans

Plan #708-GH-24714

Traditional Ranch With Extras

1,771 total square feet of living area

Price Code B

Special features

- Den has sloped ceiling and charming window seat
- Private master bedroom has access outdoors
- Central kitchen allows for convenient access when entertaining
- 2 bedrooms, 2 baths, 2-car garage
- Basement, crawl space or slab foundation, please specify when ordering

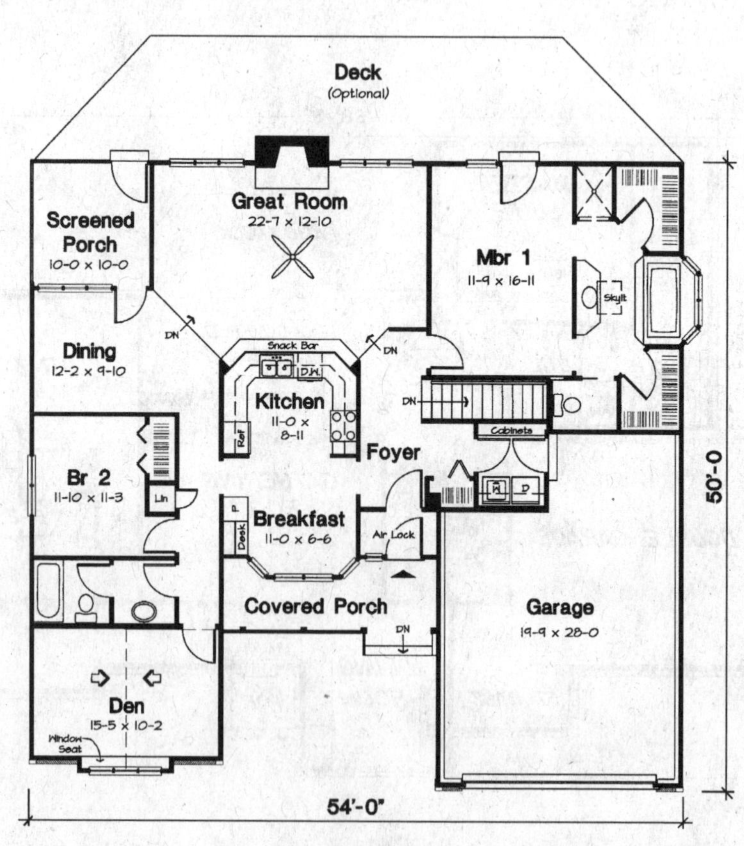
Deck
(Optional)
Great Room
22-7 x 12-10
Screened Porch
10-0 x 10-0
Mbr 1
11-9 x 16-11
Skylt
Dining
12-2 x 9-10
Snack Bar
Kitchen
11-0 x 8-11
Ref
DN
Foyer
Cabinets
Br 2
11-10 x 11-3
Lin
Breakfast
11-0 x 6-6
Desk
Air Lock
Covered Porch
Garage
19-9 x 28-0
Den
15-5 x 10-2
Window Seat
54'-0"
50'-0

TO ORDER BLUEPRINTS USE THE FORM ON PAGE 15 OR CALL TOLL-FREE 1-877-671-6036

View thousands more home plans online at www.familyhandyman.com/homeplans

The Family
Handyman

Plan #708-0798

Inviting Gabled Entry

2,128 total square feet of living area **Price Code C**

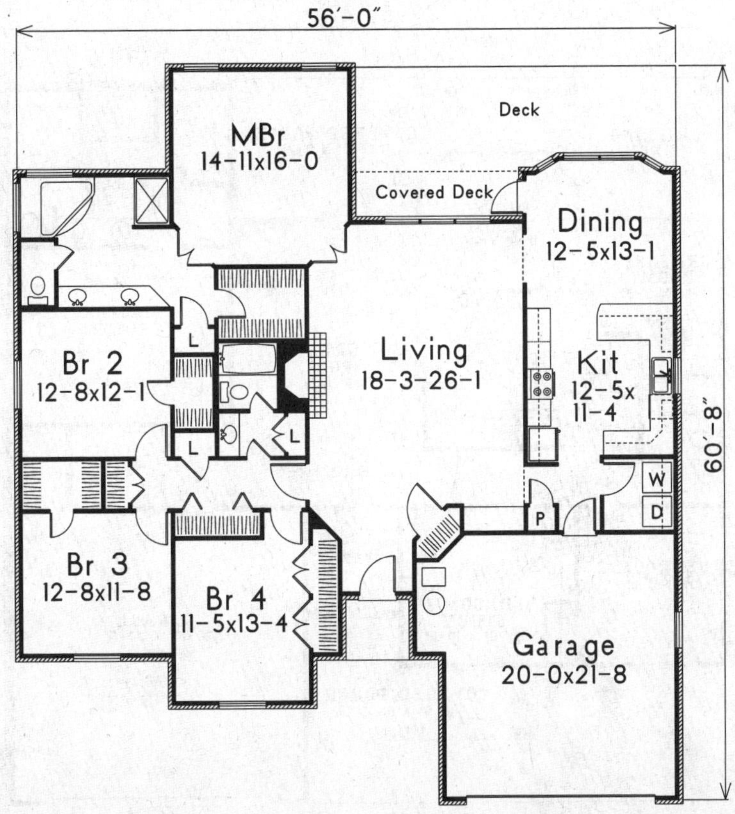
56'-0"
Deck
MBr
14-11x16-0
Covered Deck
Dining
12-5x13-1
L
Br 2
12-8x12-1
Living
18-3-26-1
Kit
12-5x
11-4
L
L
W
D
P
Br 3
12-8x11-8
Br 4
11-5x13-4
Garage
20-0x21-8
60'-8"

Special features

- Versatile kitchen has plenty of space for entertaining with large dining area and counter seating
- Luxurious master bedroom has double-door entry and private bath with jacuzzi tub, double sinks and large walk-in closet
- Secondary bedrooms include spacious walk-in closets
- Coat closet in front entry is a nice added feature
- 4 bedrooms, 2 baths, 2-car garage
- Slab foundation, drawings also include crawl space foundation

The Family
Handyman

Plan #708-NDG-113-1

Built-In Computer Desk

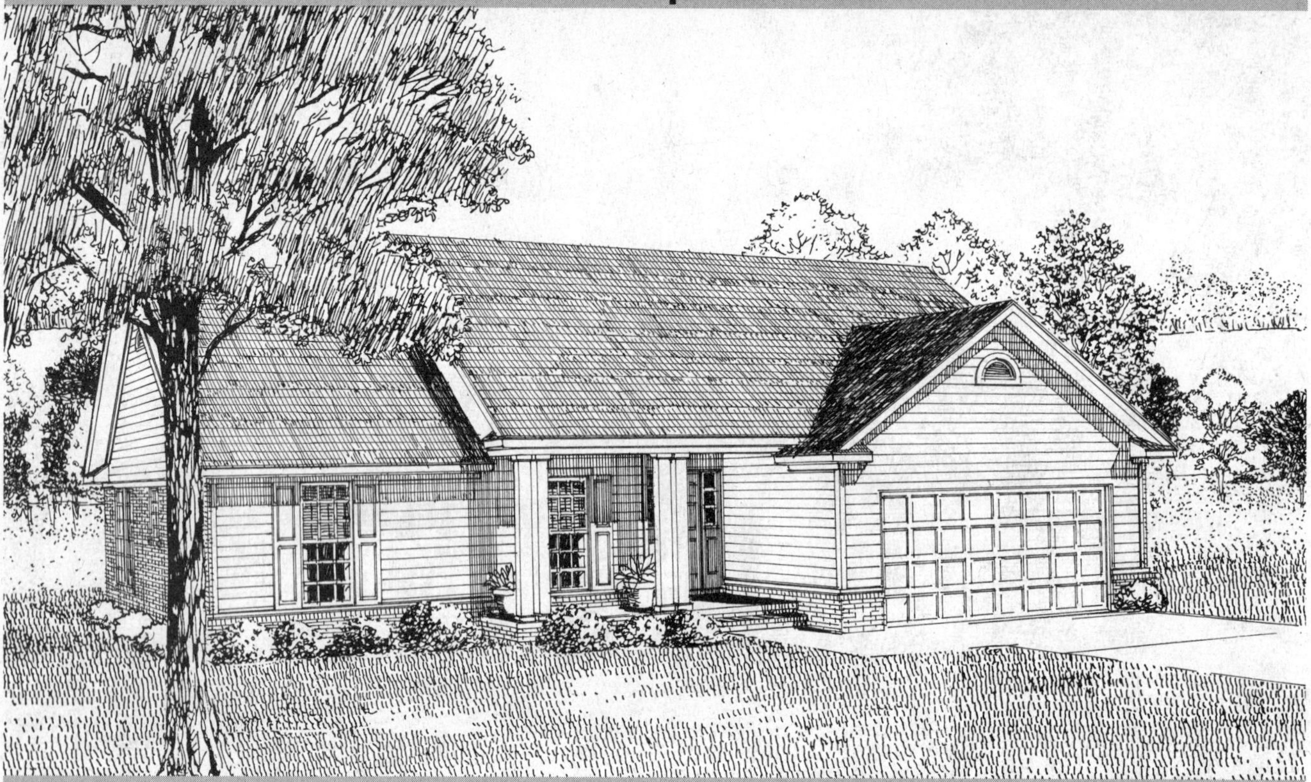

1,525 total square feet of living area

Price Code B

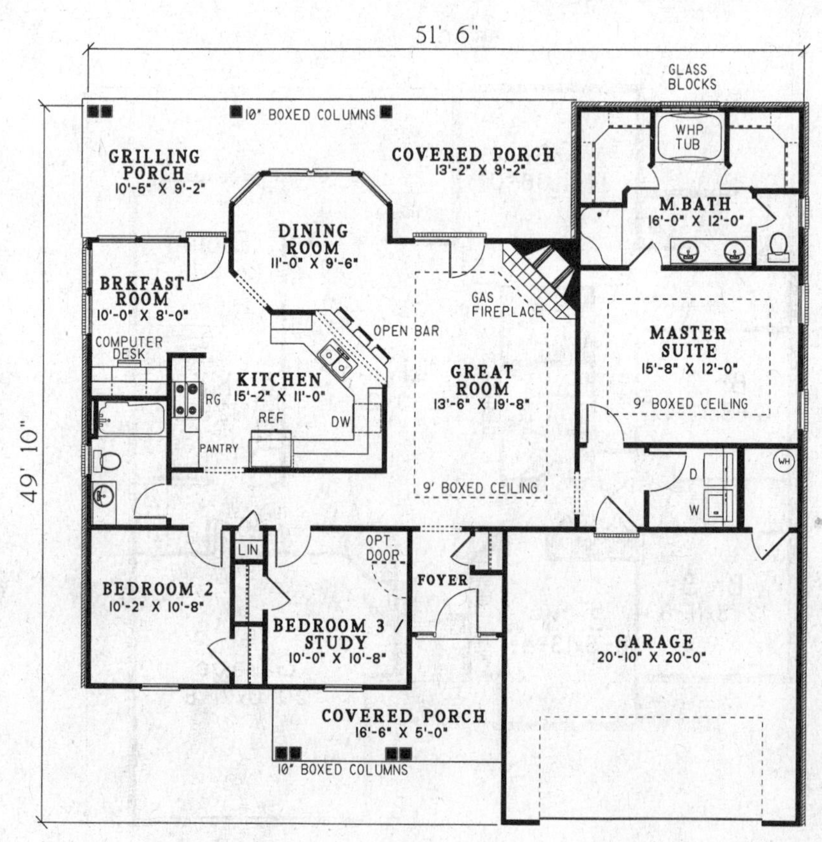
51' 6"
49' 10"
GLASS BLOCKS
10" BOXED COLUMNS
GRILLING PORCH
10'-5" X 9'-2"
COVERED PORCH
13'-2" X 9'-2"
WHP TUB
M.BATH
16'-0" X 12'-0"
DINING ROOM
11'-0" X 9'-6"
BRKFAST ROOM
10'-0" X 8'-0"
GAS FIREPLACE
OPEN BAR
MASTER SUITE
15'-8" X 12'-0"
COMPUTER DESK
KITCHEN
15'-2" X 11'-0"
RG
REF
DW
PANTRY
GREAT ROOM
13'-6" X 19'-8"
9' BOXED CEILING
9' BOXED CEILING
WH
D
W
LIN
OPT. DOOR
FOYER
BEDROOM 2
10'-2" X 10'-8"
BEDROOM 3 / STUDY
10'-0" X 10'-8"
GARAGE
20'-10" X 20'-0"
COVERED PORCH
16'-6" X 5'-0"
10" BOXED COLUMNS

Special features

- Corner fireplace highlighted in great room
- Unique glass block window over whirlpool tub in master bath
- Open bar overlooks both the kitchen and great room
- Breakfast room leads to an outdoor grilling and covered porch
- 3 bedrooms, 2 baths, 2-car garage
- Basement, walk-out basement, crawl space or slab foundation, please specify when ordering

TO ORDER BLUEPRINTS USE THE FORM ON PAGE 15 OR CALL TOLL-FREE 1-877-671-6036

The Family
Handyman

Plan #708-0793

Country Flavor With Atrium

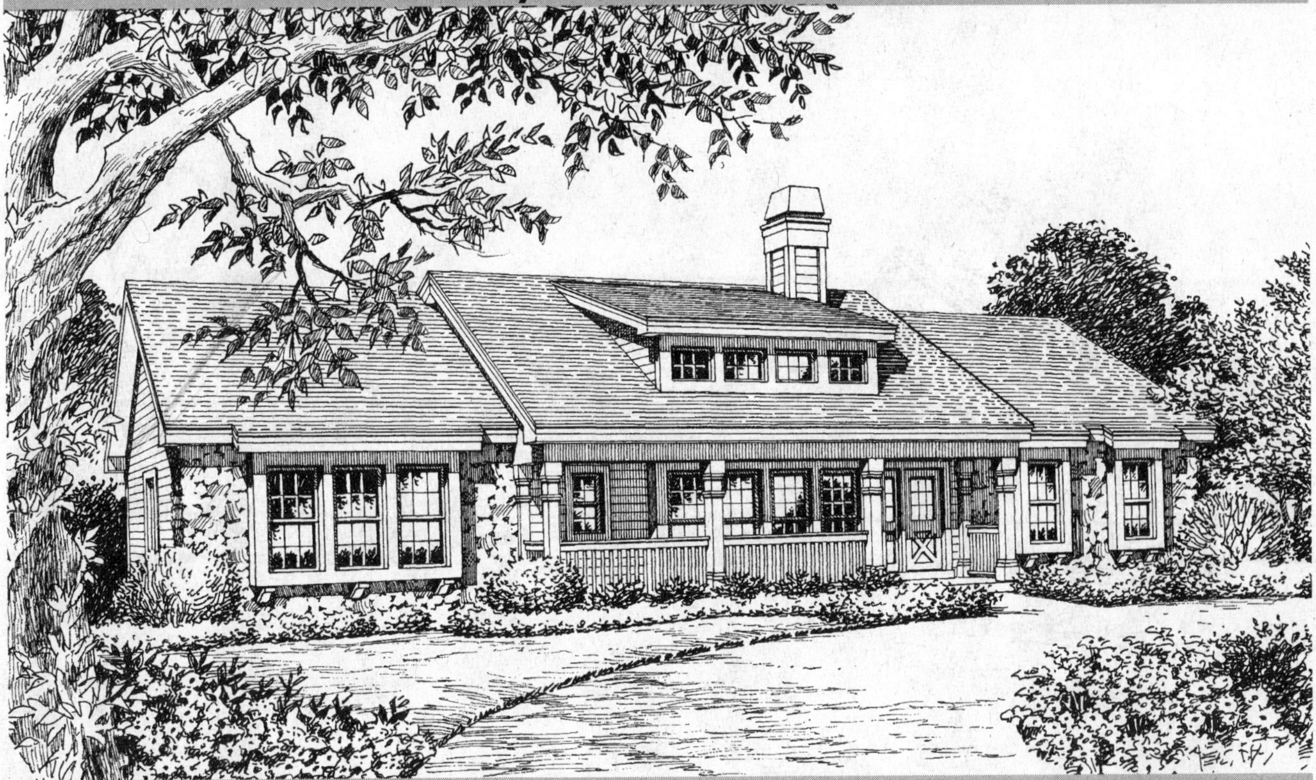

2,384 total square feet of living area

Price Code D

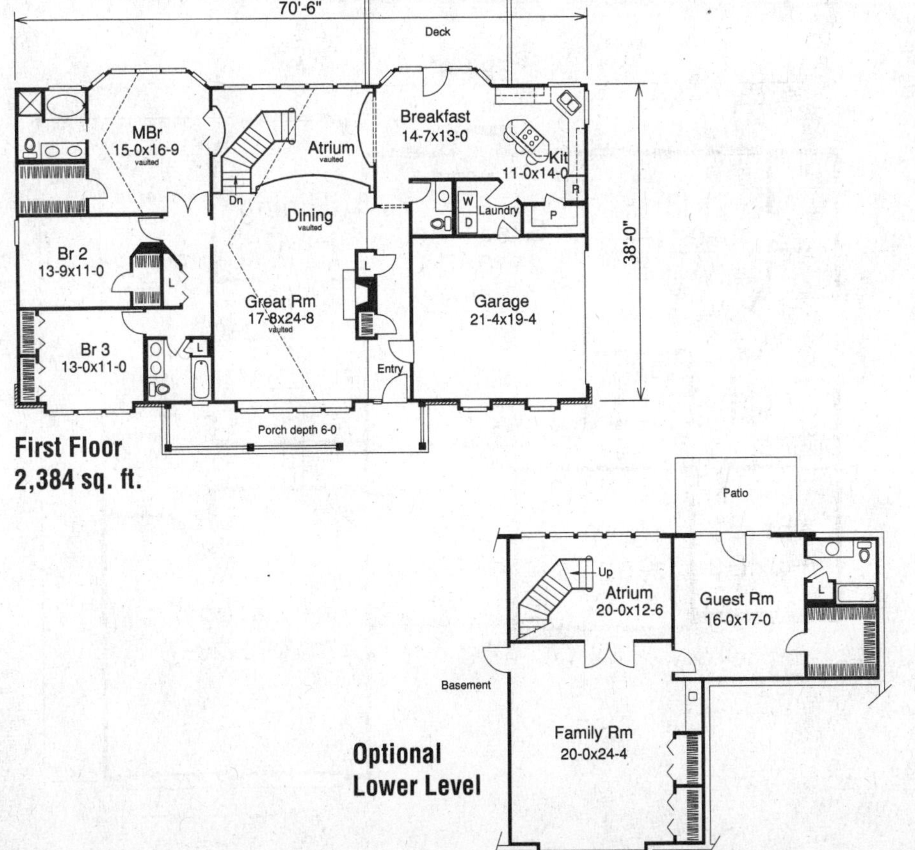
70'-6"
Deck
MBr
15-0x16-9
vaulted
Atrium
vaulted
Breakfast
14-7x13-0
Kit
11-0x14-0
Dn
Dining
vaulted
W
D
Laundry
P
R
Br 2
13-9x11-0
L
Great Rm
17-8x24-8
vaulted
Garage
21-4x19-4
38'-0"
Br 3
13-0x11-0
L
Entry
Porch depth 6-0
Patio
Up
Atrium
20-0x12-6
Guest Rm
16-0x17-0
L
Basement
Family Rm
20-0x24-4

First Floor
2,384 sq. ft.

Optional Lower Level

Special features

- Bracketed box windows create an exterior with country charm
- Massive-sized great room features a majestic atrium, fireplace, box window wall, dining balcony and vaulted ceilings
- An atrium balcony with large bay window off sundeck is enjoyed by the spacious breakfast room
- 1,038 square feet of optional living area below with family room, wet bar, bedroom #4 and bath
- 3 bedrooms, 2 1/2 baths, 2-car side entry garage
- Walk-out basement foundation

The Family Handyman

Plan #708-0162

Traditional Exterior, Handsome Accents

FOURNIER INC.

1,882 total square feet of living area **Price Code D**

Special features

- Wide, handsome entrance opens to the vaulted great room with fireplace
- Living and dining areas are conveniently joined but still allow privacy
- Private covered porch extends breakfast area
- Practical passageway runs through laundry and mud room from garage to kitchen
- Vaulted ceiling in master bedroom
- 3 bedrooms, 2 baths, 2-car garage
- Basement foundation

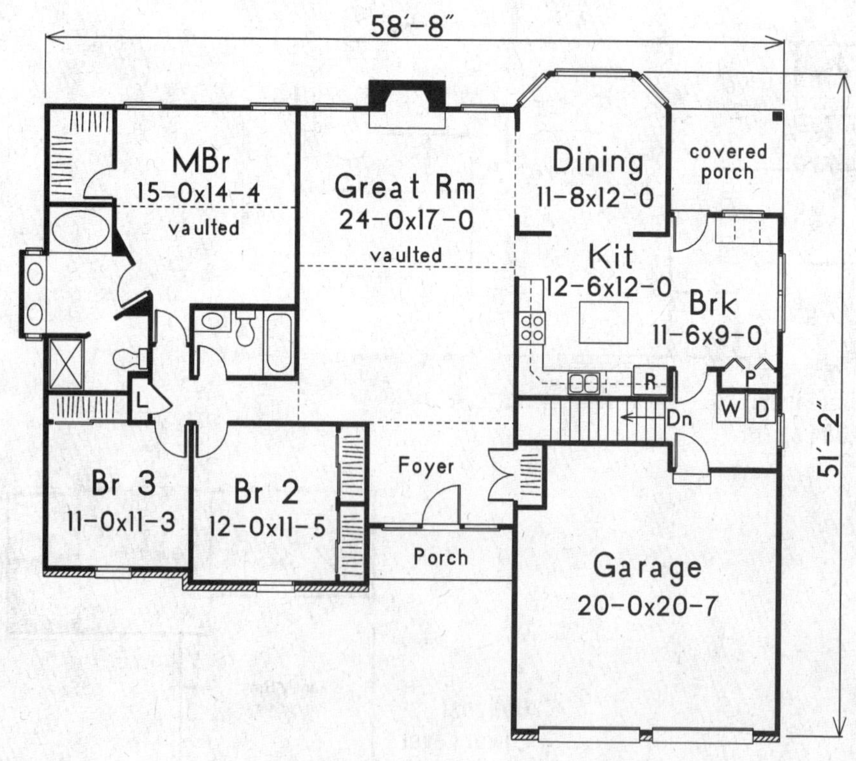

58'-8"
51'-2"
MBr
15-0x14-4
vaulted
Great Rm
24-0x17-0
vaulted
Dining
11-8x12-0
covered
porch
Kit
12-6x12-0
Brk
11-6x9-0
R
P
W
D
Dn
L
Foyer
Porch
Br 3
11-0x11-3
Br 2
12-0x11-5
Garage
20-0x20-7

TO ORDER BLUEPRINTS USE THE FORM ON PAGE 15 OR CALL TOLL-FREE 1-877-671-6036

View thousands more home plans online at www.familyhandyman.com/homeplans

Plan #708-UD-C142

Stunning Triple Dormers And Arches

1,698 total square feet of living area **Price Code B**

16' OVERHEAD DOOR
WORK BENCH/STORAGE
GARAGE
21'-0"x22'-0"
(CARPORT OR NO GARAGE OPTIONAL)
PATIO
20'-0"x12'-0"
WALK-IN CLOSET
W
D
LIN
PANTRY
DW
KITCHEN
13'-0"x10'-0"
DINING
11'-0"x10'-0"
DESK
BEDROOM #3
13'-0"x11'-10"
H A L L
MSTR BATH
PWDR
TUB/SHWR
COAT
FRIG
COLUMNS
LINEN
BATH
TUB/SHWR
OPTIONAL PRIVACY DOOR (POCKET)
8' CLG.
SITTING AREA
BUILT-IN
FP
GREAT ROOM
24'-0"x20'-0"
(10' CLG)
COAT
RIDGE OF VAULT
MASTER BEDROOM
15'-5"x16'-0"
(VAULTED CLG)
BEDROOM #2
13'-0"x11'-10"
OPTIONAL ROOM DIVIDER
DESK
COVERED PORCH
25'-0"x8'-0"
(10' CLG)

Width 59'-0"
Depth 61'-0"

Special features

- Vaulted master bedroom has a private bath and a walk-in closet
- Decorative columns flank the entrance to the dining room
- Open great room is perfect for gathering family together
- 3 bedrooms, 2 1/2 baths, 2-car side entry garage with storage
- Basement, crawl space or slab foundation, please specify when ordering

Plan #708-0707

Prestige Abounds In A Classic Ranch

2,723 total square feet of living area **Price Code E**

Special features

- Large porch invites you into an elegant foyer which accesses a vaulted study with private hall and coat closet
- Great room is second to none, comprised of fireplace, built-in shelves, vaulted ceiling and a 1 1/2 story window wall
- A spectacular hearth room with vaulted ceiling and masonry fireplace opens to an elaborate kitchen featuring two snack bars, cooking island and walk-in pantry
- 3 bedrooms, 2 1/2 baths, 3-car side entry garage
- Basement foundation

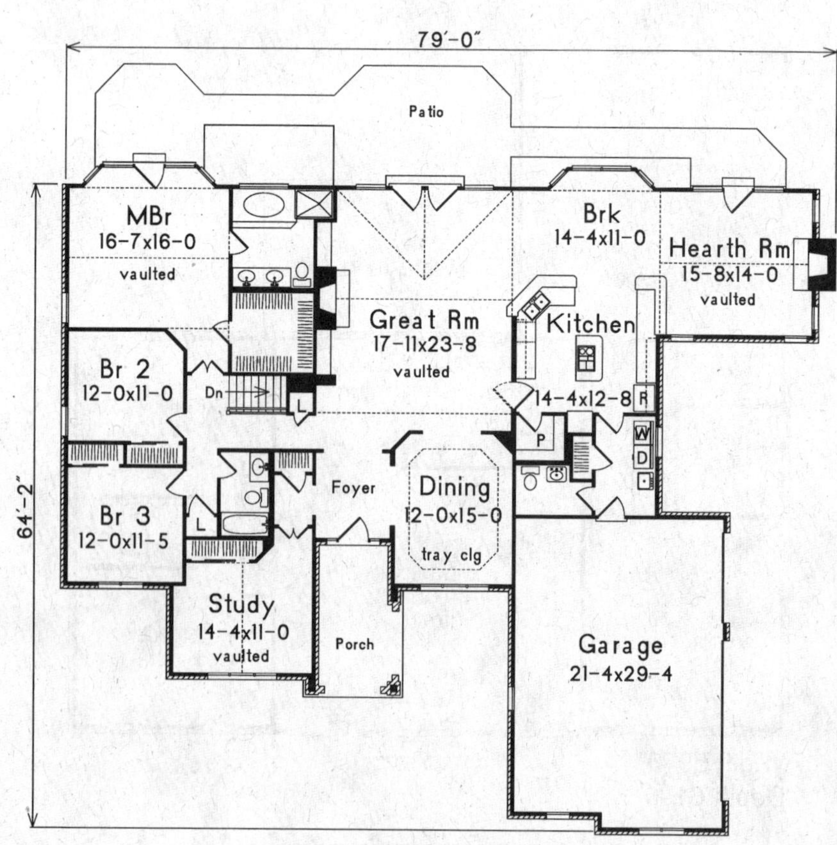
79′-0″
Patio
MBr
16-7x16-0
vaulted
Brk
14-4x11-0
Hearth Rm
15-8x14-0
vaulted
Great Rm
17-11x23-8
vaulted
Kitchen
14-4x12-8
Br 2
12-0x11-0
Dn
Br 3
12-0x11-5
Foyer
Dining
12-0x15-0
tray clg
Study
14-4x11-0
vaulted
Porch
Garage
21-4x29-4
64′-2″

TO ORDER BLUEPRINTS USE THE FORM ON PAGE 15 OR CALL TOLL-FREE 1-877-671-6036

View thousands more home plans online at www.familyhandyman.com/homeplans

1 1/2 Story Has Traditional Home Appeal

2,356 total square feet of living area

Price Code D

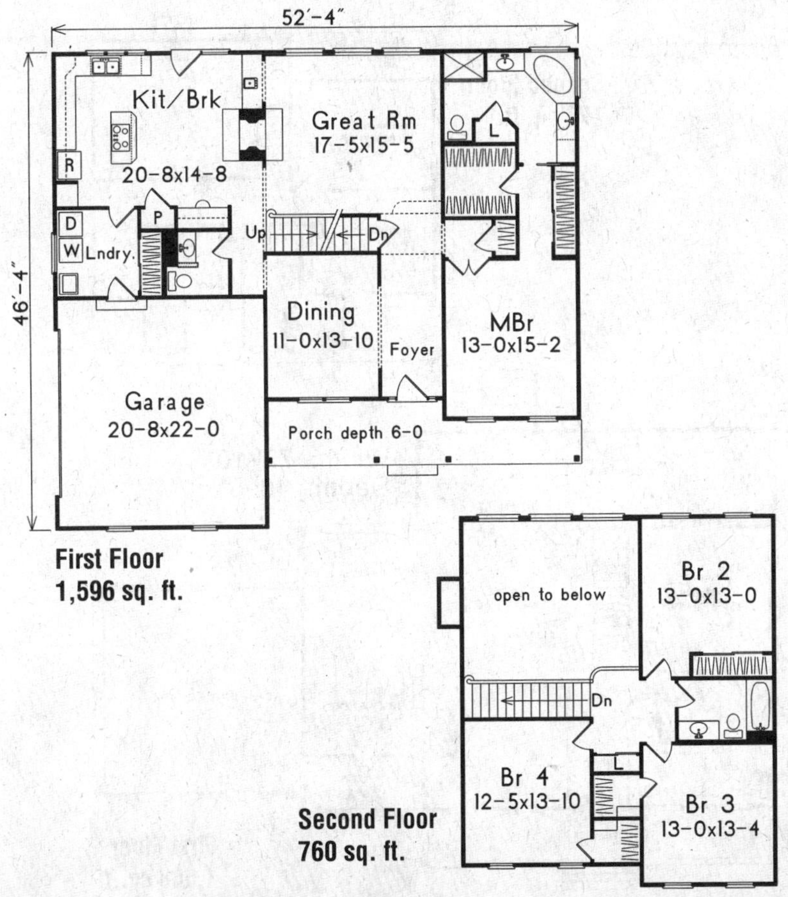
52'-4"
46'-4"
Kit/Brk
20-8x14-8
Great Rm
17-5x15-5
R
D
W
P
L
Lndry.
Up
Dn
Dining
11-0x13-10
Foyer
MBr
13-0x15-2
Garage
20-8x22-0
Porch depth 6-0
open to below
Br 2
13-0x13-0
Dn
Br 4
12-5x13-10
Br 3
13-0x13-4

First Floor
1,596 sq. ft.

Second Floor
760 sq. ft.

Special features

- Master suite is located on the first floor and features lots of closetspace and a luxury bath
- Plenty of extras throughout including a planning desk, large pantry, wet bar and a two-story great room
- Second floor boasts three bedrooms and a lovely view to the great room below
- 4 bedrooms, 2 1/2 baths, 2-car garage
- Basement foundation

TO ORDER BLUEPRINTS USE THE FORM ON PAGE 15 OR CALL TOLL-FREE 1-877-671-6036

View thousands more home plans online at www.familyhandyman.com/homeplans

The Family
Handyman

Plan #708-CHP-2343-B-36

Triple Dormers

2,360 total square feet of living area **Price Code D**

Special features

- First floor master bedroom has private bath with step-up tub
- Living area fireplace is flanked by double French doors that lead to a spacious deck
- Dormers accentuate upstairs bedrooms and bath
- 4 bedrooms, 2 1/2 baths, 2-car side entry garage
- Slab foundation

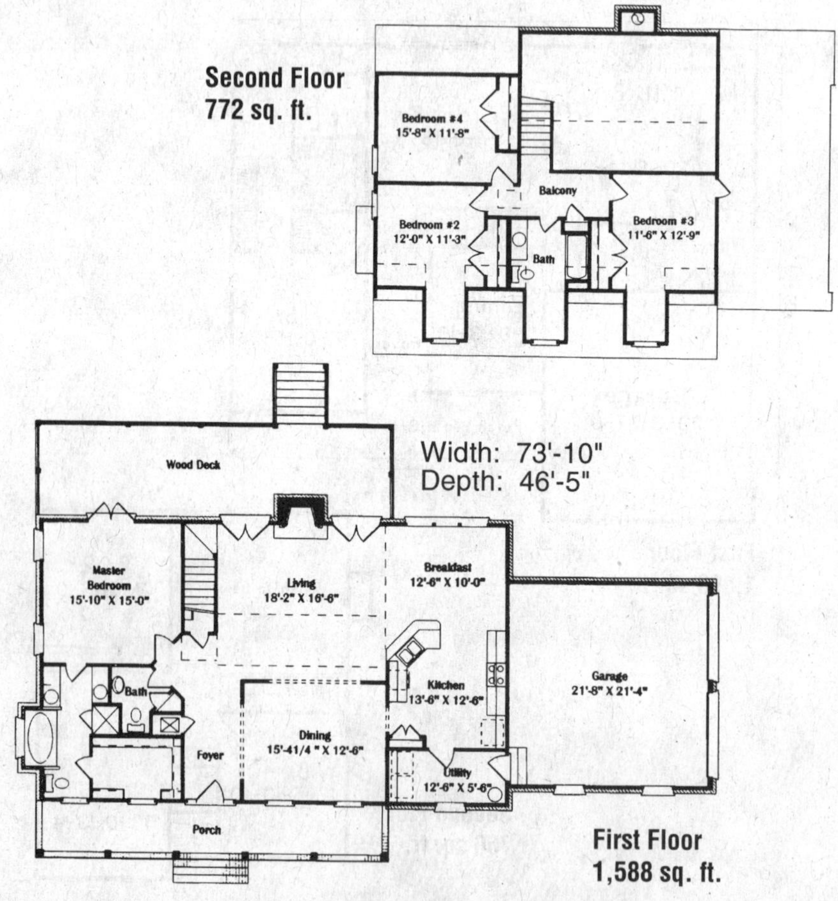
Second Floor
772 sq. ft.
Bedroom #4
15'-8" X 11'-8"
Balcony
Bedroom #2
12'-0" X 11'-3"
Bath
Bedroom #3
11'-6" X 12'-9"
Width: 73'-10"
Depth: 46'-5"
Wood Deck
Master Bedroom
15'-10" X 15'-0"
Living
18'-2" X 16'-6"
Breakfast
12'-6" X 10'-0"
Kitchen
13'-6" X 12'-6"
Garage
21'-8" X 21'-4"
Bath
Foyer
Dining
15'-41/4 " X 12'-6"
Utility
12'-6" X 5'-6"
Porch
First Floor
1,588 sq. ft.

The Family
Handyman

Plan #708-0794

Spacious Living In This Ranch

1,433 total square feet of living area

Price Code A

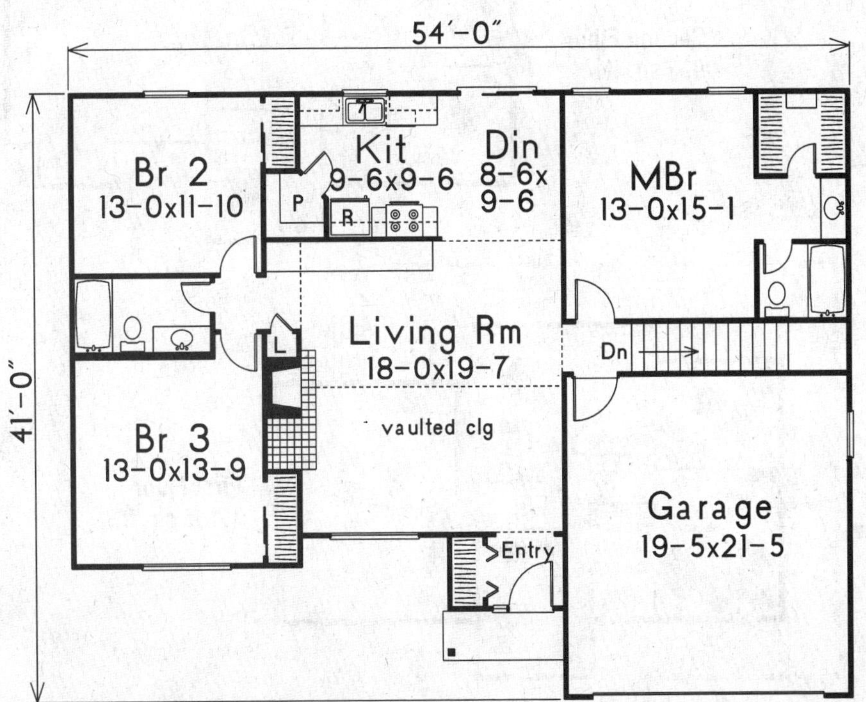
54'-0"
41'-0"
Br 2
13-0x11-10
Kit
9-6x9-6
Din
8-6x
9-6
P
R
MBr
13-0x15-1
Living Rm
18-0x19-7
vaulted clg
L
Dn
Br 3
13-0x13-9
Garage
19-5x21-5
Entry

Special features

- Vaulted living room includes cozy fireplace and an oversized entertainment center
- Bedrooms #2 and #3 share a full bath
- Master bedroom has a full bath and large walk-in closet
- 3 bedrooms, 2 baths, 2-car garage
- Basement foundation, drawings also include crawl space and slab foundations

The Family
Handyman

Plan #708-DR-3812

Perfect Farmhouse For Family Living

2,129 total square feet of living area

Price Code C

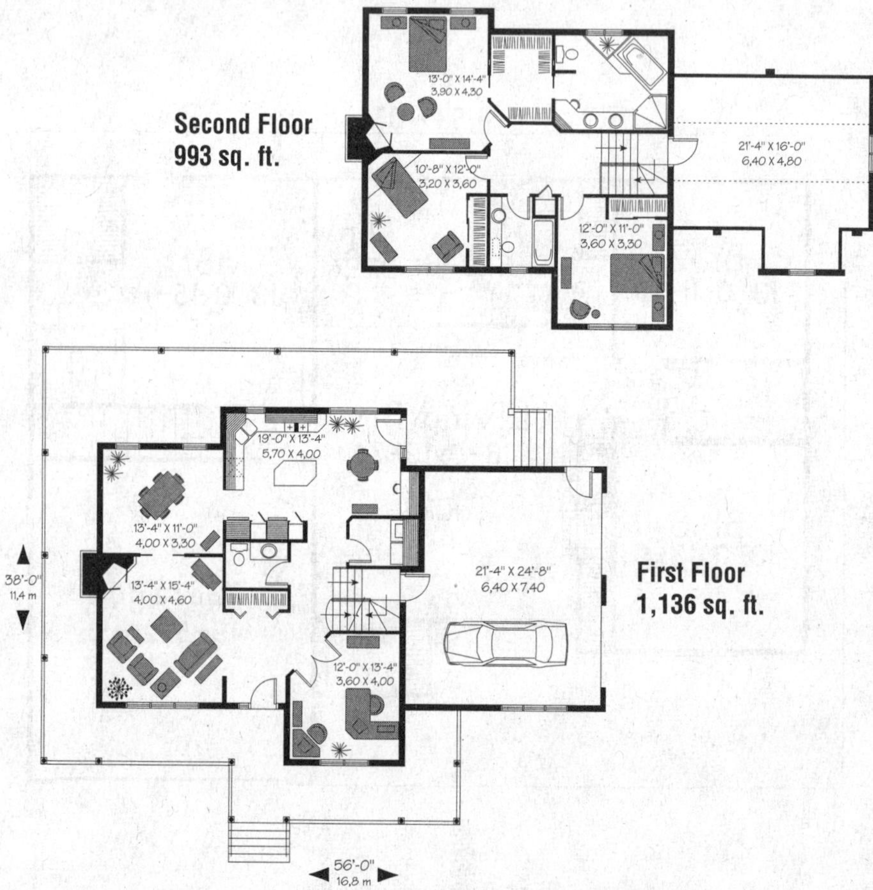
Second Floor
993 sq. ft.
13'-0" X 14'-4"
3,90 X 4,30
10'-8" X 12'-0"
3,20 X 3,60
12'-0" X 11'-0"
3,60 X 3,30
21'-4" X 16'-0"
6,40 X 4,80
19'-0" X 13'-4"
5,70 X 4,00
13'-4" X 11'-0"
4,00 X 3,30
13'-4" X 15'-4"
4,00 X 4,60
21'-4" X 24'-8"
6,40 X 7,40
12'-0" X 13'-4"
3,60 X 4,00
38'-0"
11,4 m
56'-0"
16,8 m
First Floor
1,136 sq. ft.

Special features

- Energy efficient home with 2" x 6" exterior walls
- Home office has a double-door entry and is secluded from other living areas
- Corner fireplace in living area is a nice focal point
- Bonus room above the garage has an additional 407 square feet of living area
- 3 bedrooms, 2 1/2 baths, 2-car side entry garage
- Basement foundation

TO ORDER BLUEPRINTS USE THE FORM ON PAGE 15 OR CALL TOLL-FREE 1-877-671-6036

View thousands more home plans online at www.familyhandyman.com/homeplans

The Family
Handyman

Plan #708-0729

Gracious Atrium Ranch

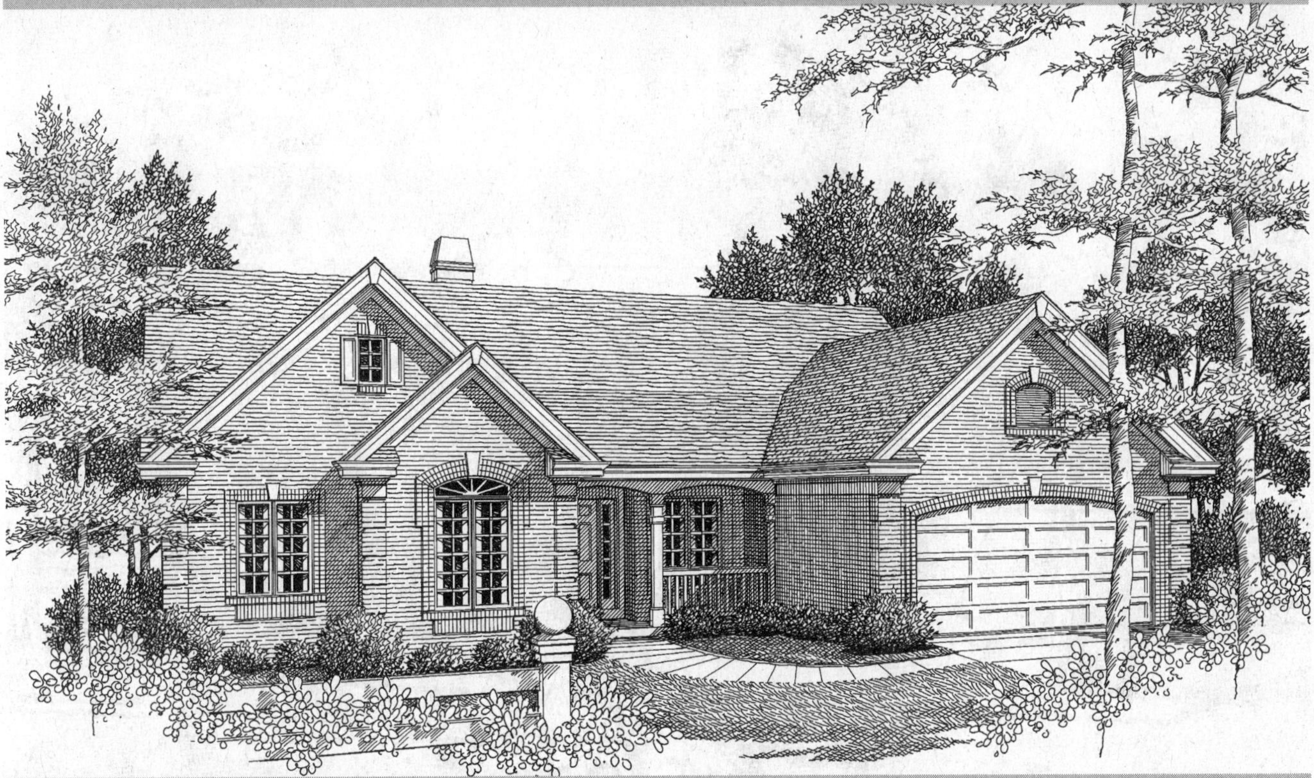

2,218 total square feet of living area | **Price Code D**

Rear View

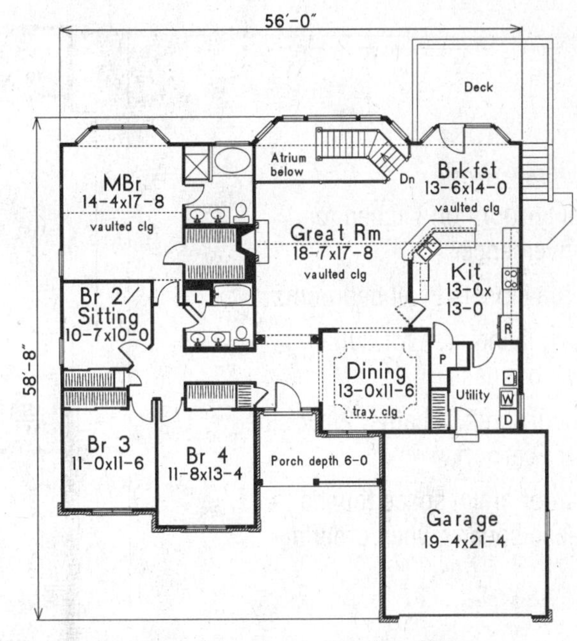
56'-0"
Deck
Atrium below
Dn
Brk fst
13-6x14-0
vaulted clg
MBr
14-4x17-8
vaulted clg
Great Rm
18-7x17-8
vaulted clg
Kit
13-0x
13-0
Br 2/
Sitting
10-7x10-0
L
R
P
Dining
13-0x11-6
tray clg
Utility
W
D
58'-8"
Br 3
11-0x11-6
Br 4
11-8x13-4
Porch depth 6-0
Garage
19-4x21-4

First Floor
2,218 sq. ft.

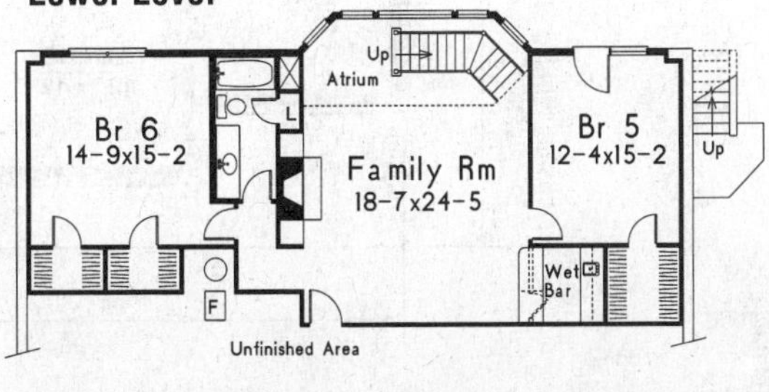

Special features

- Great room has arched entry, bay windowed atrium with staircase and a fireplace
- Breakfast room offers bay window and snack bar open to kitchen with laundry nearby
- Atrium open to 1,217 square feet of optional living area below
- 4 bedrooms, 2 baths, 2-car garage
- Walk-out basement foundation

Optional Lower Level

Up
Atrium
Br 6
14-9x15-2
L
Family Rm
18-7x24-5
Br 5
12-4x15-2
Up
Wet Bar
F
Unfinished Area

The Family
Handyman

Plan #708-BF-DR1819

Central Living Areas Away From Bedrooms

2,424 total square feet of living area **Price Code D**

Special features

- Utility room off kitchen for convenience
- Large closets in all bedrooms
- Open living area for added spaciousness
- 3 bedrooms, 2 baths, 2-car side entry carport
- Slab or crawl space foundation, please specify when ordering

STORAGE
10' x 6'
STORAGE
10' x 6'
CARPORT
22' x 20'
ATTIC STAIRS
PATIO
64'
UTILITY
11' x 6'
WASH
DRY
SHV'S
PANT
RANGE
KITCHEN
12' x 11'
SINK
D.W.
REF.
BAR
LIVING
20' x 18'
SLOPE
12' HIGH CEILING
SLOPE
CLO.
BATH
LIN
BATH
HEAT
W.H.
MASTER SUITE
16' x 14'
HALL
SHV
CLO.
CLO.
CLO.
EATING
12' x 10'
DINING
12' x 12'
ENTRY
PORCH
BED RM.
14' x 12'
BED RM.
14' x 12'
58'

TO ORDER BLUEPRINTS USE THE FORM ON PAGE 15 OR CALL TOLL-FREE 1-877-671-6036

View thousands more home plans online at www.familyhandyman.com/homeplans

Plan #708-VL-1925

Dormers And Porch Are Charming Touches

1,925 total square feet of living area

Price Code C

Second Floor
596 sq. ft.

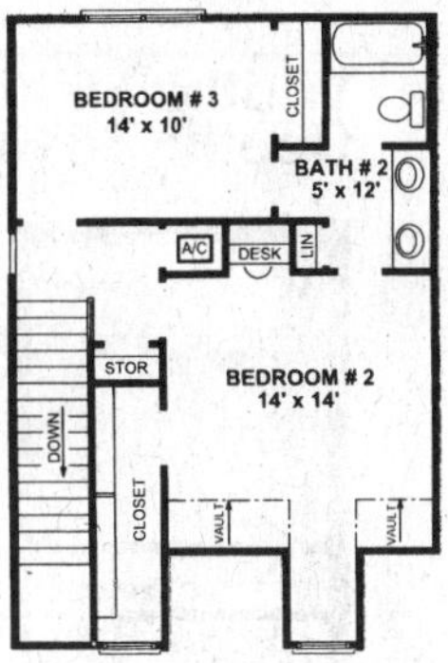

BEDROOM # 3 14' x 10'
CLOSET
BATH # 2 5' x 12'
A/C
DESK
LIN
STOR
BEDROOM # 2 14' x 14'
DOWN
CLOSET
VAULT
VAULT

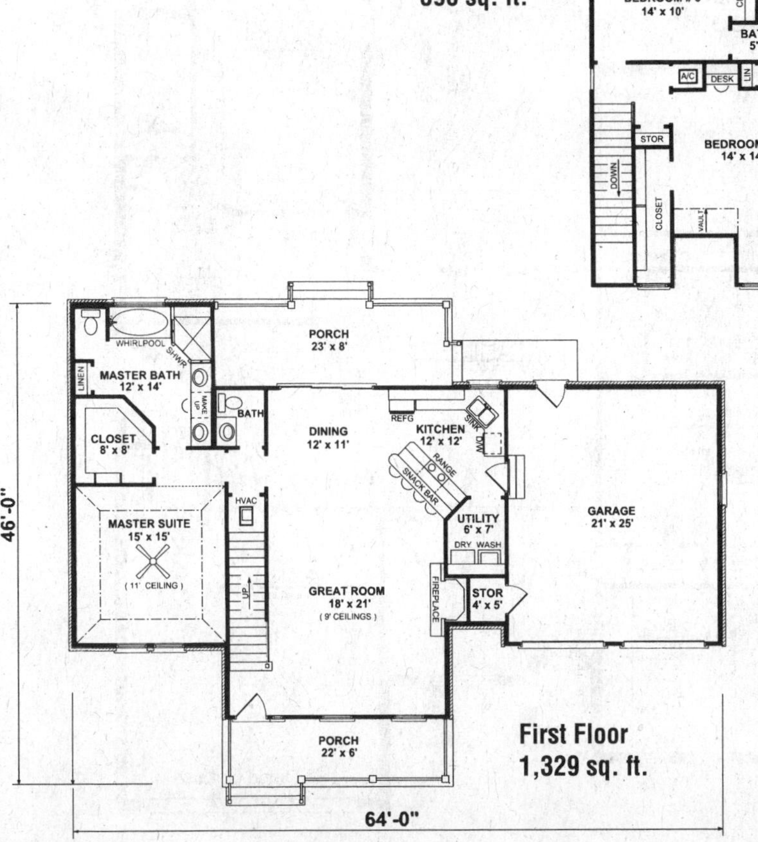

PORCH 23' x 8'
WHIRLPOOL
SHWR
LINEN
MASTER BATH 12' x 14'
MAKE UP
BATH
CLOSET 8' x 8'
DINING 12' x 11'
REFG
KITCHEN 12' x 12'
SINK
DW
RANGE
SNACK BAR
HVAC
MASTER SUITE 15' x 15'
(11' CEILING)
UTILITY 6' x 7'
DRY WASH
GARAGE 21' x 25'
UP
GREAT ROOM 18' x 21'
(9' CEILINGS)
FIREPLACE
STOR 4' x 5'
PORCH 22' x 6'
46'-0"
64'-0"

First Floor
1,329 sq. ft.

Special features

- Angled snack bar in kitchen provides extra dining space overlooking into the great room and dining area
- Wonderful master bath includes sunny whirlpool tub, corner oversized shower and a makeup counter
- Dining area has sliding glass doors leading to the outdoors
- 3 bedrooms, 2 1/2 baths, 2-car garage
- Slab or crawl space foundation, please specify when ordering

TO ORDER BLUEPRINTS USE THE FORM ON PAGE 15 OR CALL TOLL-FREE 1-877-671-6036

View thousands more home plans online at www.familyhandyman.com/homeplans

The Family
Handyman

Plan #708-DL-19603L2

Beautiful Brickwork Adds Elegance

1,960 total square feet of living area | **Price Code C**

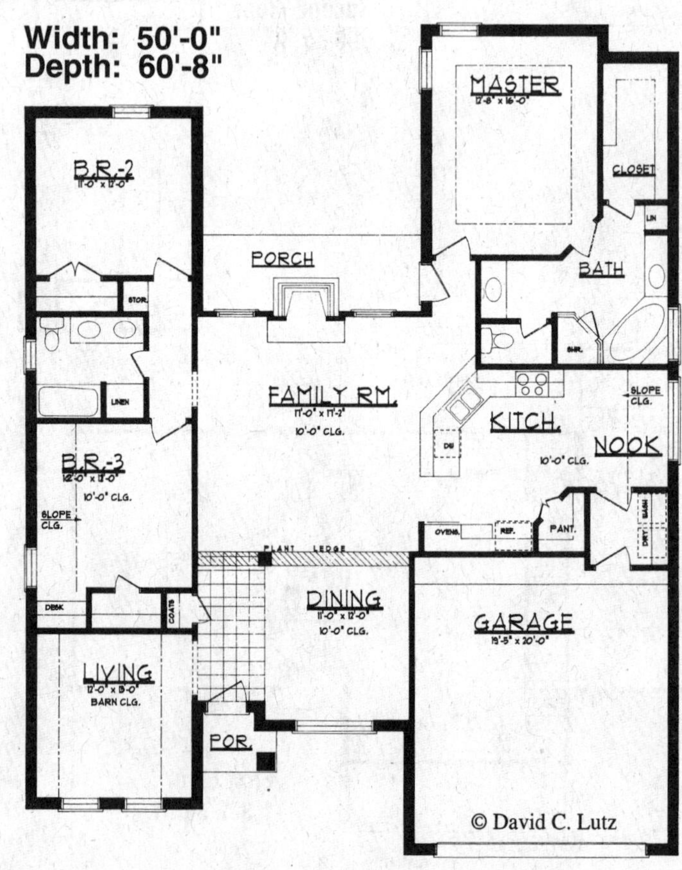
Width: 50'-0"
Depth: 60'-8"
MASTER
CLOSET
LIN.
BATH
B.R.-2
STOR.
LINEN
PORCH
FAMILY RM.
10'-0" CLG.
KITCH.
10'-0" CLG.
NOOK
SLOPE CLG.
B.R.-3
10'-0" CLG.
SLOPE CLG.
DESK
COATS
OVENS
REF.
PANT.
PLANT LEDGE
DINING
10'-0" CLG.
GARAGE
LIVING
BARN CLG.
POR.
© David C. Lutz

Special features

- Open floor plan is suitable for an active family
- Desk space in bedroom #3 is ideal for a young student
- Effective design creates enclosed courtyard in rear of home
- 3 bedrooms, 2 baths, 2-car garage
- Slab foundation

TO ORDER BLUEPRINTS USE THE FORM ON PAGE 15 OR CALL TOLL-FREE 1-877-671-6036

View thousands more home plans online at www.familyhandyman.com/homeplans

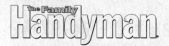

Plan #708-0775

Generous Closets In All The Bedrooms

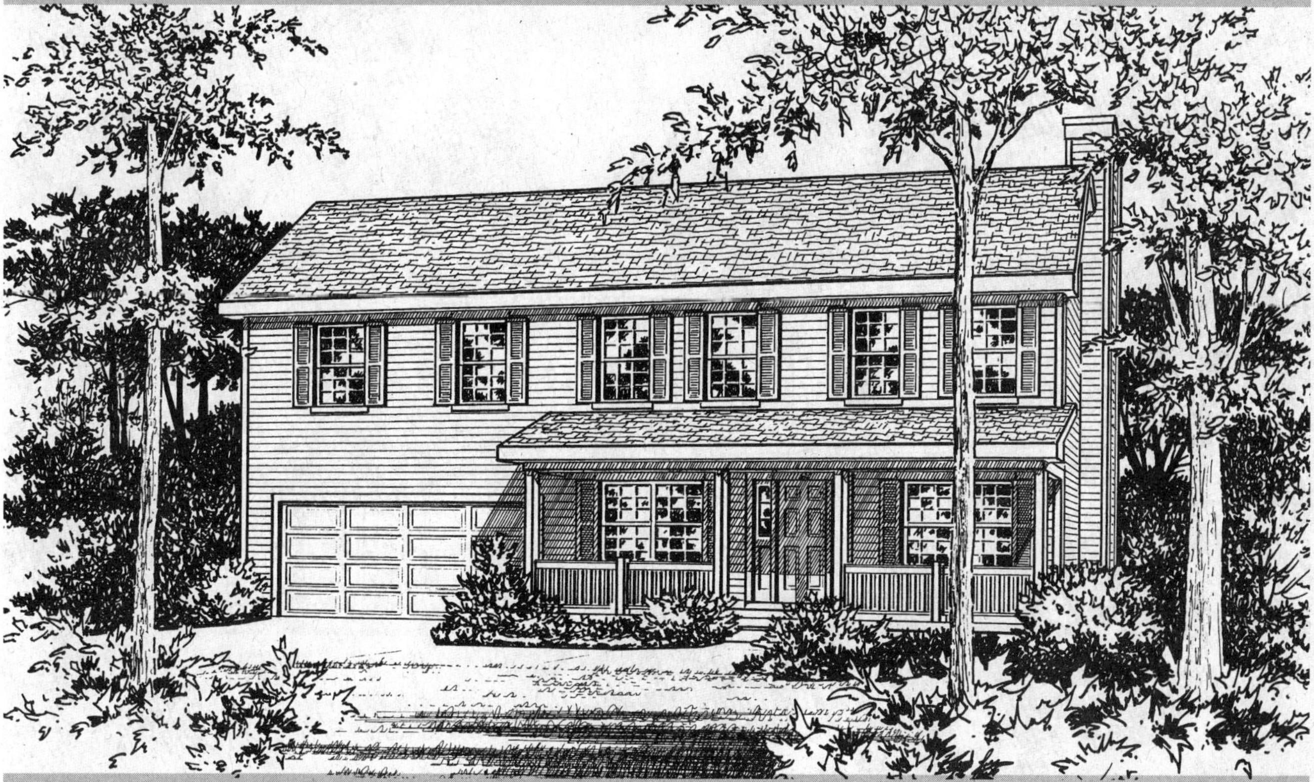

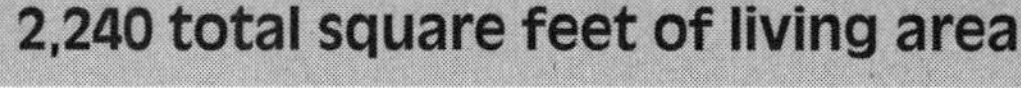

2,240 total square feet of living area **Price Code D**

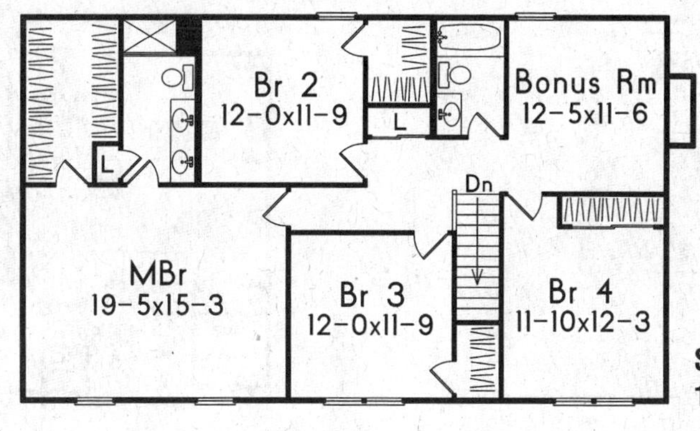
Br 2
12-0x11-9
L
Bonus Rm
12-5x11-6
L
Dn
MBr
19-5x15-3
Br 3
12-0x11-9
Br 4
11-10x12-3

Second Floor
1,344 sq. ft.

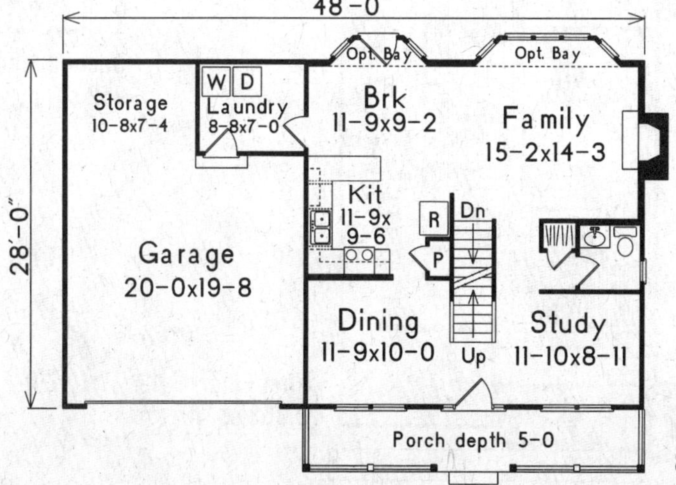
48'-0"
28'-0"
Opt. Bay
Opt. Bay
W D
Storage
10-8x7-4
Laundry
8-8x7-0
Brk
11-9x9-2
Family
15-2x14-3
Kit
11-9x
9-6
R
Dn
P
Garage
20-0x19-8
Dining
11-9x10-0
Up
Study
11-10x8-11
Porch depth 5-0

First Floor
896 sq. ft.

Special features

- Floor plan makes good use of space above garage allowing for four bedrooms and a bonus room on the second floor
- Formal dining room easily accessible to kitchen
- Cozy family room with fireplace and sunny bay window
- 4 bedrooms, 2 1/2 baths, 2-car garage
- Basement foundation

The Family
Handyman

Plan #708-MG-97162

Elegant Design With Many Extras

HO ZHAER INC.

3,304 total square feet of living area **Price Code F**

Special features

- First floor guest bedroom has access to bath and a walk-in closet
- Second floor has loft area at the top of the stairs
- Kitchen has center island and extra storage
- Luxurious master bedroom located on first floor for privacy
- 5 bedrooms, 4 baths, 2-car side entry garage
- Basement foundation

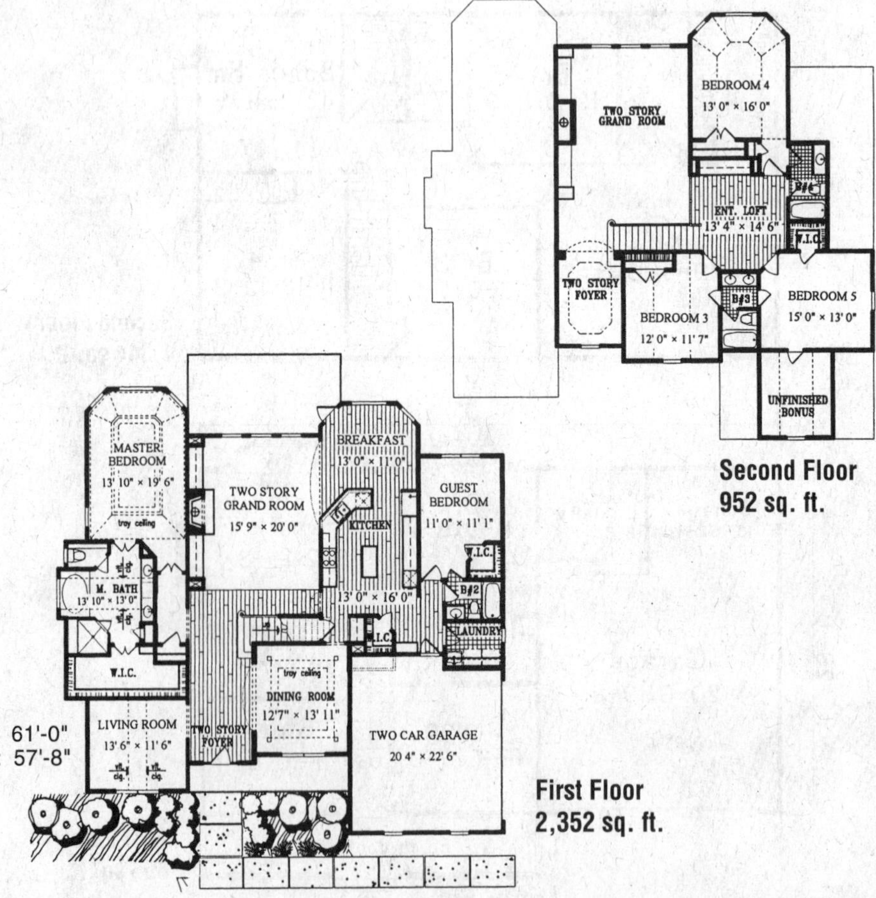
TWO STORY GRAND ROOM
BEDROOM 4
13' 0" × 16' 0"
ENT. LOFT
13' 4" × 14' 6"
B#4
W.I.C.
TWO STORY FOYER
BEDROOM 3
12' 0" × 11' 7"
B#3
BEDROOM 5
15' 0" × 13' 0"
UNFINISHED BONUS
MASTER BEDROOM
13' 10" × 19' 6"
tray ceiling
TWO STORY GRAND ROOM
15' 9" × 20' 0"
BREAKFAST
13' 0" × 11' 0"
KITCHEN
13' 0" × 16' 0"
GUEST BEDROOM
11' 0" × 11' 1"
W.I.C.
B#2
LAUNDRY
M. BATH
13' 10" × 13' 0"
W.I.C.
tray ceiling
DINING ROOM
12'7" × 13' 11"
LIVING ROOM
13' 6" × 11' 6"
TWO STORY FOYER
TWO CAR GARAGE
20 4" × 22' 6"

Second Floor
952 sq. ft.

Width: 61'-0"
Depth: 57'-8"

First Floor
2,352 sq. ft.

TO ORDER BLUEPRINTS USE THE FORM ON PAGE 15 OR CALL TOLL-FREE 1-877-671-6036

View thousands more home plans online at www.familyhandyman.com/homeplans

The Family
Handyman

Plan #708-0382

Central Living Area Keeps Bedrooms Private

1,546 total square feet of living area **Price Code C**

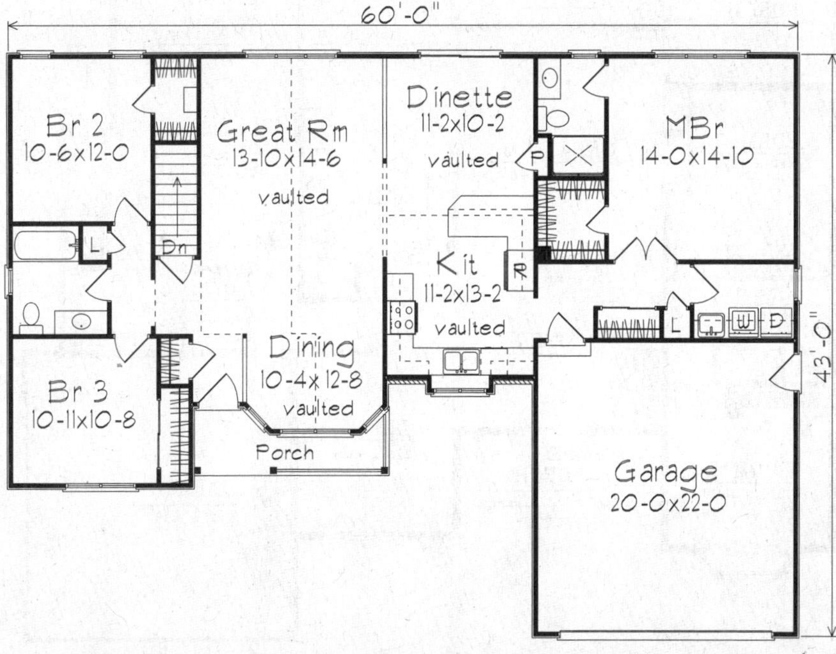
60'-0"
43'-0"
Br 2
10-6x12-0
Great Rm
13-10x14-6
vaulted
Dinette
11-2x10-2
vaulted
MBr
14-0x14-10
Kit
11-2x13-2
vaulted
Dining
10-4x12-8
vaulted
Br 3
10-11x10-8
Porch
Garage
20-0x22-0
Dn
L
P
R
W
D

Special features

- Spacious, open rooms create a casual atmosphere
- Master bedroom is secluded for privacy
- Dining room features large bay window
- Kitchen and dinette combine for added space and include access to the outdoors
- Large laundry room includes convenient sink
- 3 bedrooms, 2 baths, 2-car garage
- Basement foundation

TO ORDER BLUEPRINTS USE THE FORM ON PAGE 15 OR CALL TOLL-FREE 1-877-671-6036

View thousands more home plans online at www.familyhandyman.com/homeplans

The Family
Handyman

Plan #708-DDI-101-102

All The Comforts Of Home

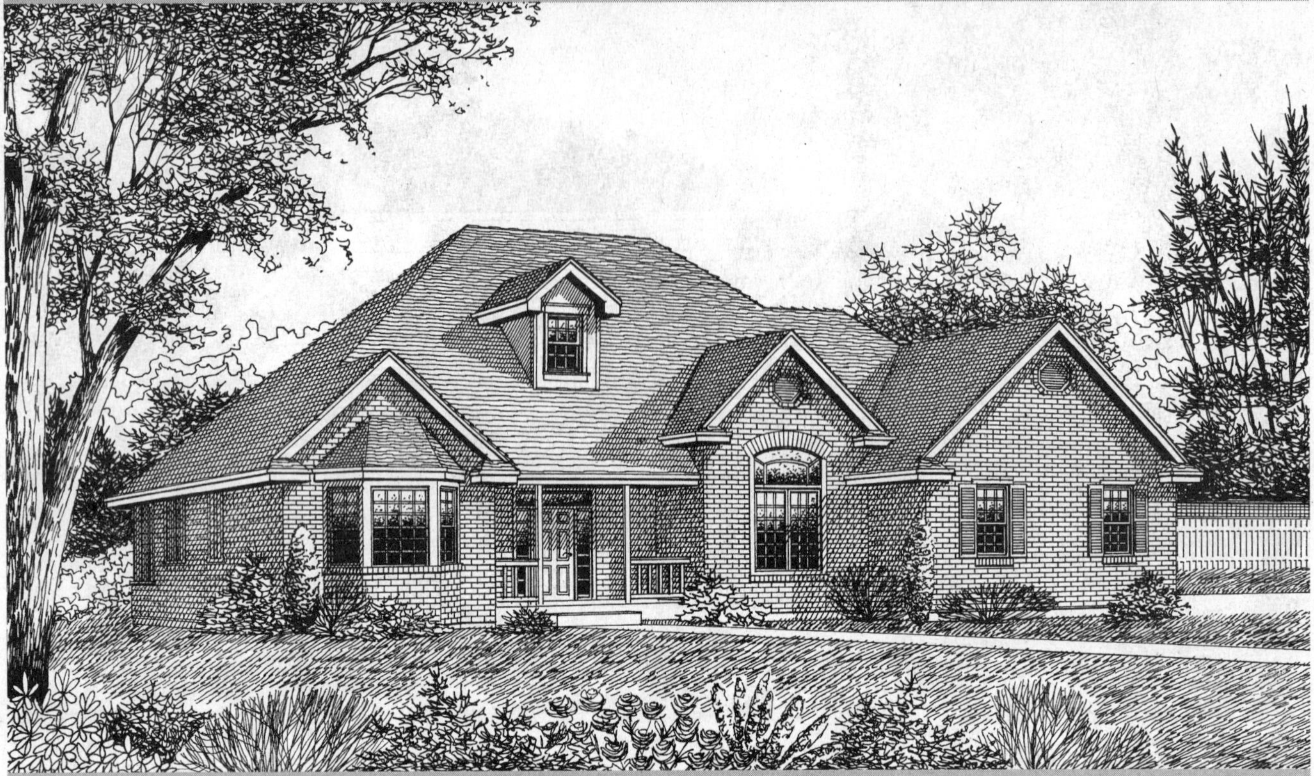

2,148 total square feet of living area **Price Code C**

Special features

- Spacious and open floor plan with covered porch and back porches
- 11' ceilings in great room, kitchen, nook and foyer
- 9' ceilings on first floor
- 3 bedrooms, 2 baths, 2-car side entry garage
- Basement foundation

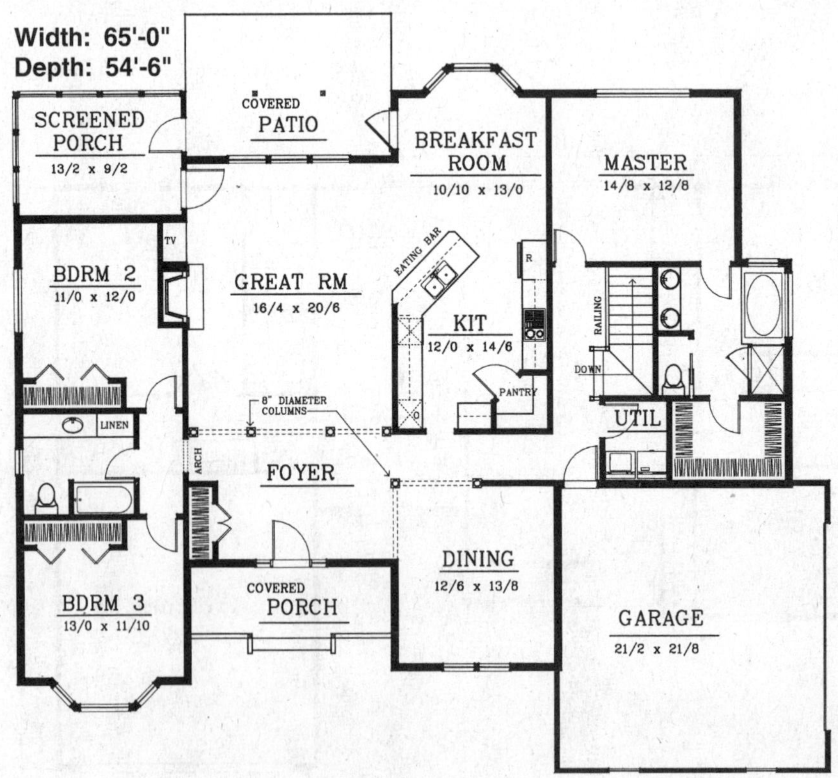
Width: 65'-0"
Depth: 54'-6"
COVERED PATIO
SCREENED PORCH
13/2 x 9/2
BREAKFAST ROOM
10/10 x 13/0
MASTER
14/8 x 12/8
TV
BDRM 2
11/0 x 12/0
GREAT RM
16/4 x 20/6
EATING BAR
R
KIT
12/0 x 14/6
RAILING
DOWN
PANTRY
8" DIAMETER COLUMNS
LINEN
UTIL
ARCH
FOYER
COVERED PORCH
DINING
12/6 x 13/8
BDRM 3
13/0 x 11/10
GARAGE
21/2 x 21/8

Three Bedroom Luxury In A Small Home

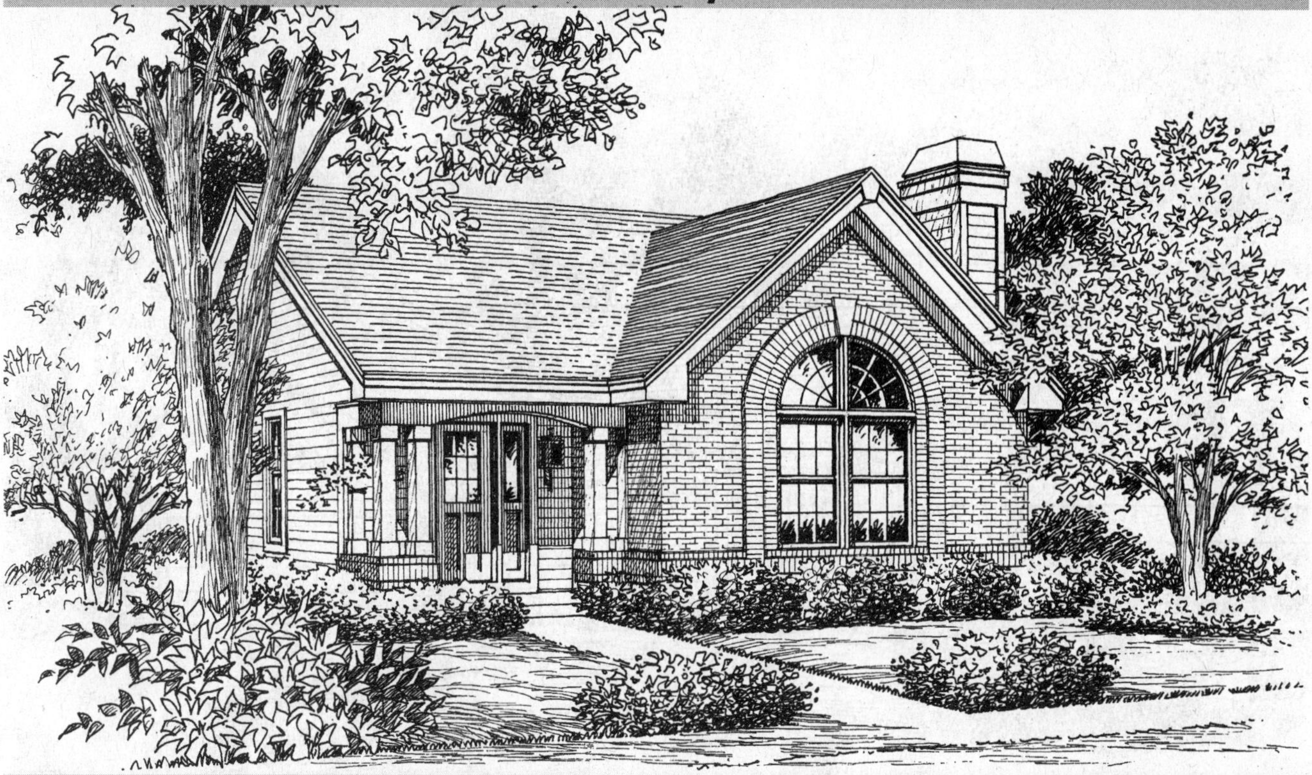

1,161 total square feet of living area

Price Code AA

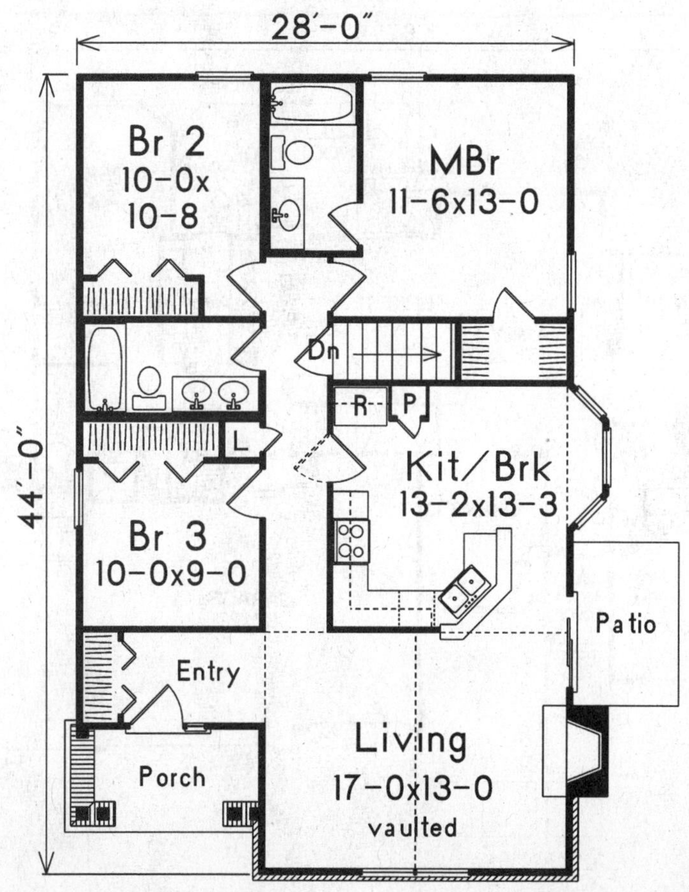

28′-0″
44′-0″
Br 2
10-0x
10-8
MBr
11-6x13-0
Dn
R
P
L
Kit/Brk
13-2x13-3
Br 3
10-0x9-0
Patio
Entry
Living
17-0x13-0
vaulted
Porch

Special features

- Brickwork and feature window add elegance to home for a narrow lot
- Living room enjoys a vaulted ceiling, fireplace and opens to kitchen area
- U-shaped kitchen offers a breakfast area with bay window, snack bar and built-in pantry
- 3 bedrooms, 2 baths
- Basement foundation

TO ORDER BLUEPRINTS USE THE FORM ON PAGE 15 OR CALL TOLL-FREE 1-877-671-6036

The Family
Handyman

Plan #708-UDG-97008

Spacious Ranch Style

© Urban Design Group, Inc.
A
B
D

2,086 total square feet of living area **Price Code C**

Special features

- Corner garden tub graces private master bath
- Kitchen and breakfast room have terrific placement connecting to family room which creates a feeling of openness
- Secluded den makes an ideal office space
- 9' ceilings throughout this home
- 3 bedrooms, 2 1/2 baths, 3-car garage
- Basement foundation

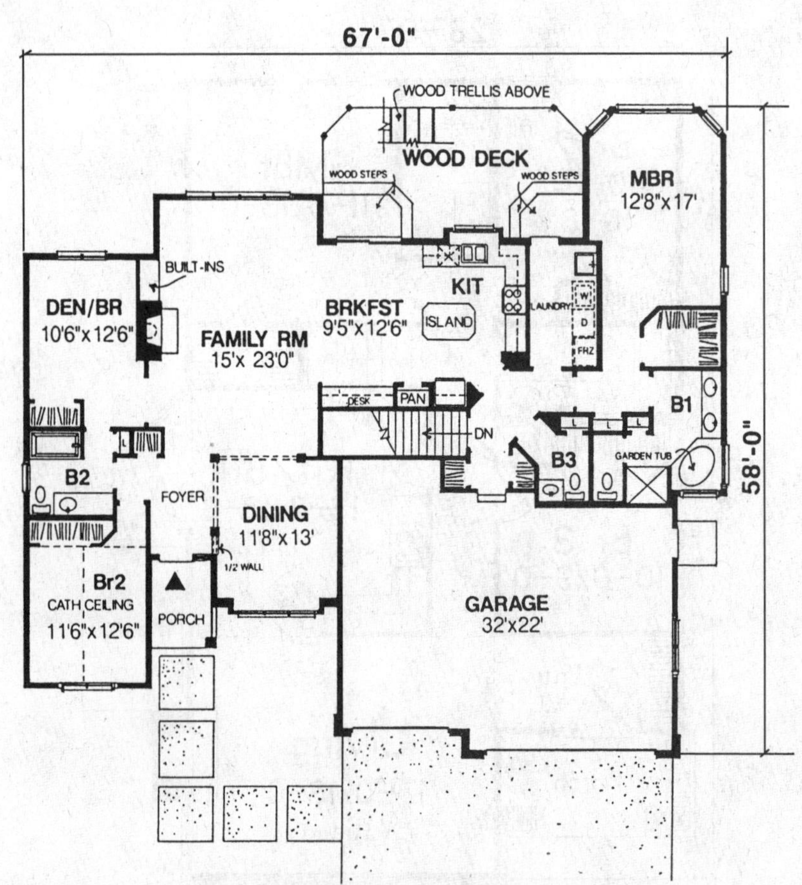
67'-0"
WOOD TRELLIS ABOVE
WOOD DECK
WOOD STEPS
WOOD STEPS
MBR
12'8"x17'
BUILT-INS
DEN/BR
10'6"x12'6"
BRKFST
9'5"x12'6"
KIT
ISLAND
LAUNDRY
FAMILY RM
15'x 23'0"
DESK
PAN
DN
B1
B2
B3
GARDEN TUB
58'-0"
FOYER
DINING
11'8"x13'
1/2 WALL
Br2
CATH CEILING
11'6"x12'6"
PORCH
GARAGE
32'x22'

Plan #708-0529

Layout Creates Large Open Living Area

1,285 total square feet of living area **Price Code B**

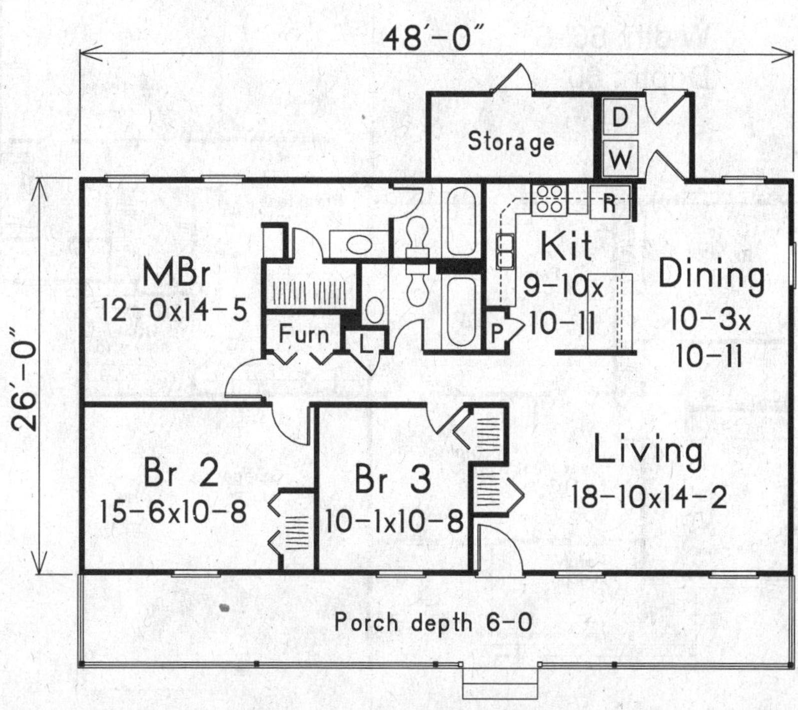
48′-0″
26′-0″
Storage
D
W
R
Kit
9-10x
10-11
Dining
10-3x
10-11
MBr
12-0x14-5
Furn
L
P
Br 2
15-6x10-8
Br 3
10-1x10-8
Living
18-10x14-2
Porch depth 6-0

Special features

- Accommodating home with ranch-style porch
- Large storage area on back of home
- Master bedroom includes dressing area, private bath and built-in bookcase
- Kitchen features pantry, breakfast bar and complete view to dining room
- 3 bedrooms, 2 baths
- Crawl space foundation, drawings also include basement and slab foundations

TO ORDER BLUEPRINTS USE THE FORM ON PAGE 15 OR CALL TOLL-FREE 1-877-671-6036

View thousands more home plans online at www.familyhandyman.com/homeplans

The Family
Handyman

Plan #708-GM-1849

Vaulted Rear Porch

1,849 total square feet of living area

Price Code C

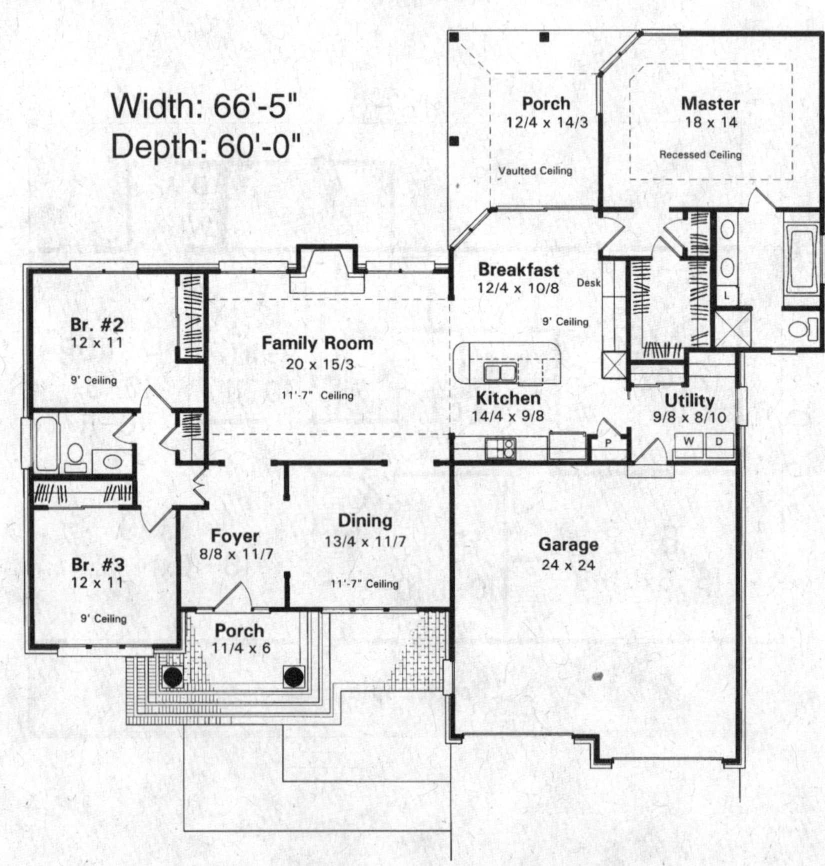
Width: 66'-5"
Depth: 60'-0"
Porch
12/4 x 14/3
Vaulted Ceiling
Master
18 x 14
Recessed Ceiling
Breakfast
12/4 x 10/8
Desk
9' Ceiling
Br. #2
12 x 11
9' Ceiling
Family Room
20 x 15/3
11'-7" Ceiling
Kitchen
14/4 x 9/8
Utility
9/8 x 8/10
W
D
P
L
Foyer
8/8 x 11/7
Dining
13/4 x 11/7
11'-7" Ceiling
Garage
24 x 24
Br. #3
12 x 11
9' Ceiling
Porch
11/4 x 6

Special features

- Open floor plan creates an airy feeling
- Kitchen and breakfast area include center island, pantry and built-in desk
- Master bedroom has private entrance off breakfast area and a view of vaulted porch
- 3 bedrooms, 2 baths, 2-car garage
- Crawl space or slab foundation, please specify when ordering

TO ORDER BLUEPRINTS USE THE FORM ON PAGE 15 OR CALL TOLL-FREE 1-877-671-6036

View thousands more home plans online at www.familyhandyman.com/homeplans

The Family
Handyman

Plan #708-0495

Compact Home Maximizes Space

987 total square feet of living area

Price Code AA

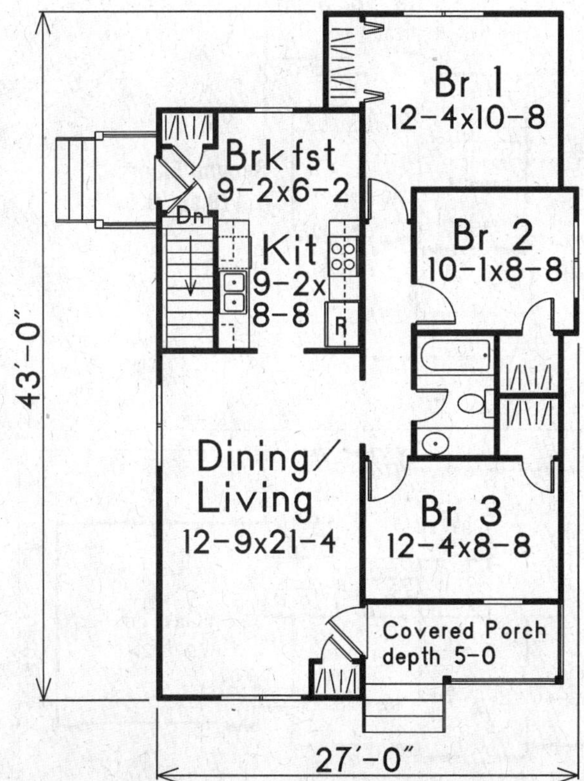
Br 1
12-4x10-8
Brkfst
9-2x6-2
Dn
Kit
9-2x
8-8
R
Br 2
10-1x8-8
Dining/
Living
12-9x21-4
Br 3
12-4x8-8
Covered Porch
depth 5-0
43'-0"
27'-0"

Special features

- Galley kitchen opens into cozy breakfast room
- Convenient coat closets located by both entrances
- Dining/living room combined for expansive open area
- Breakfast room has access to the outdoors
- Front porch great for enjoying outdoor living
- 3 bedrooms, 1 bath
- Basement foundation

Plan #708-0184

Stately Facade Features Impressive Front Balcony

2,411 total square feet of living area | **Price Code D**

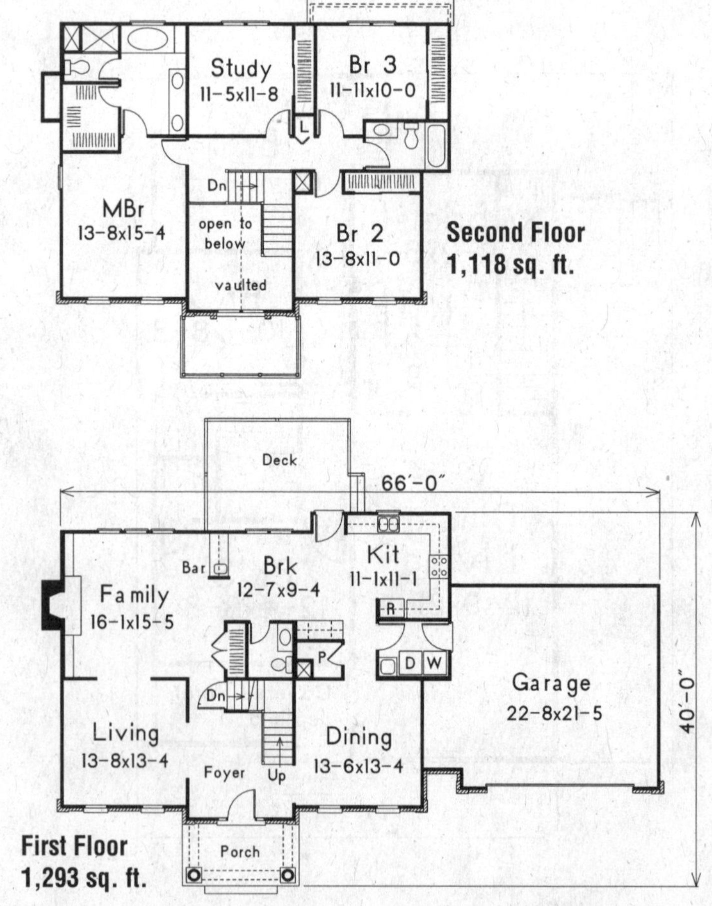

Study
11-5x11-8
Br 3
11-11x10-0
Dn
MBr
13-8x15-4
open to below
vaulted
Br 2
13-8x11-0
Second Floor
1,118 sq. ft.
Deck
66'-0"
Bar
Brk
12-7x9-4
Kit
11-1x11-1
Family
16-1x15-5
D W
Garage
22-8x21-5
40'-0"
Dn
Living
13-8x13-4
Dining
13-6x13-4
Foyer
Up
Porch
First Floor
1,293 sq. ft.

Special features

- Elegant entrance features a two-story vaulted foyer
- Large family room enhanced by masonry fireplace and wet bar
- Master bedroom suite includes walk-in closet, oversized tub and separate shower
- Second floor study could easily convert to a fourth bedroom
- 3 bedrooms, 2 1/2 baths, 2-car garage
- Basement foundation, drawings also include slab and crawl space foundations

TO ORDER BLUEPRINTS USE THE FORM ON PAGE 15 OR CALL TOLL-FREE 1-877-671-6036

View thousands more home plans online at www.familyhandyman.com/homeplans

Summer Home Or Year-Round

1,403 total square feet of living area

Price Code A

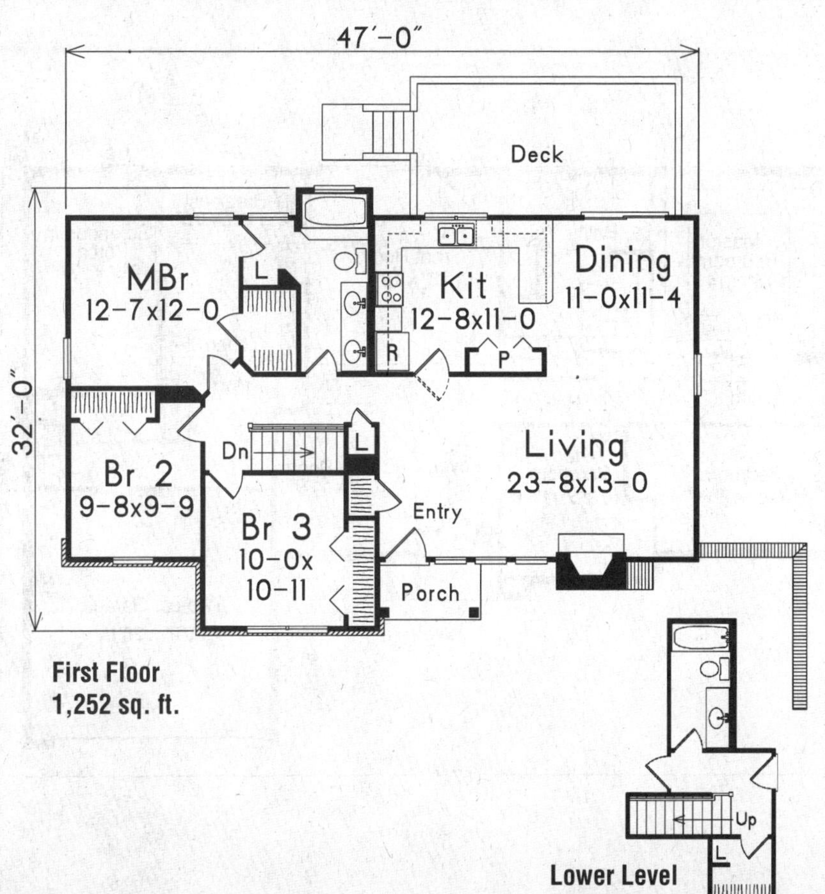
47'-0"
32'-0"
Deck
MBr
12-7x12-0
L
Kit
12-8x11-0
R
P
Dining
11-0x11-4
Br 2
9-8x9-9
Dn
L
Living
23-8x13-0
Br 3
10-0x
10-11
Entry
Porch
Up
L

First Floor
1,252 sq. ft.

Lower Level
151 sq. ft.

Special features

- Impressive living areas for a modest-sized home
- Special master/hall bath has linen storage, step-up tub and lots of window light
- Spacious closets everywhere you look
- 3 bedrooms, 2 baths, 2-car drive under garage and second bath on lower level
- Basement foundation

The Family
Handyman

Plan #708-SRD-123

Sloped Ceilings Throughout

1,782 total square feet of living area **Price Code B**

Special features

- Outstanding breakfast area accesses the outdoors through French doors
- Generous counter space and cabinets combine to create an ideal kitchen
- The master bedroom is enhanced with a beautiful bath featuring a whirlpool tub and double-bowl vanity
- 3 bedrooms, 2 baths, 2-car garage
- Basement foundation

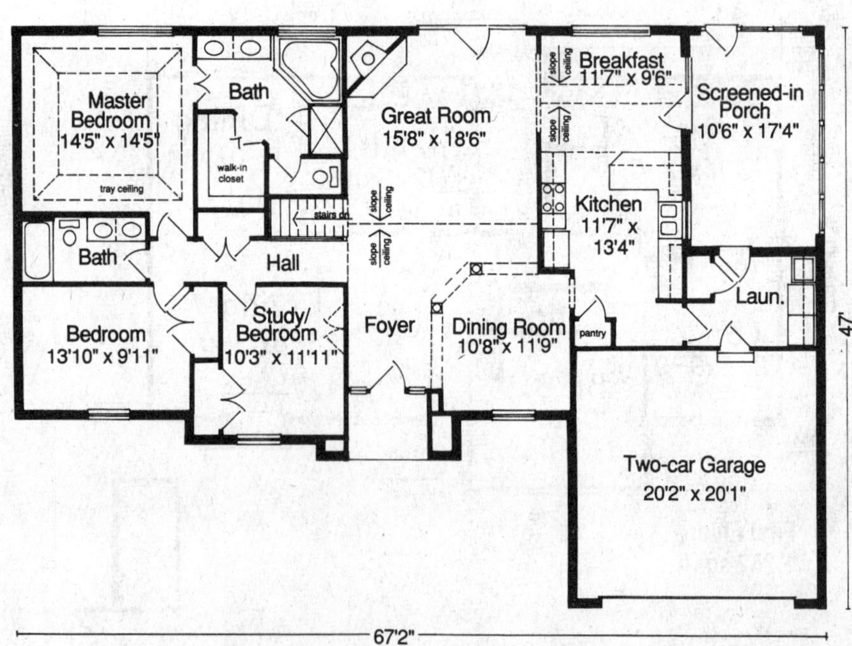
Master Bedroom
14'5" x 14'5"
tray ceiling
Bath
walk-in closet
Great Room
15'8" x 18'6"
slope ceiling
stairs dn.
Breakfast
11'7" x 9'6"
Screened-in Porch
10'6" x 17'4"
Kitchen
11'7" x 13'4"
Bath
Hall
Laun.
Bedroom
13'10" x 9'11"
Study/ Bedroom
10'3" x 11'11"
Foyer
Dining Room
10'8" x 11'9"
pantry
Two-car Garage
20'2" x 20'1"
67'2"
47'

TO ORDER BLUEPRINTS USE THE FORM ON PAGE 15 OR CALL TOLL-FREE 1-877-671-6036

View thousands more home plans online at www.familyhandyman.com/homeplans

The Family
Handyman

Plan #708-NDG-663

Amenity-Full Master Bath

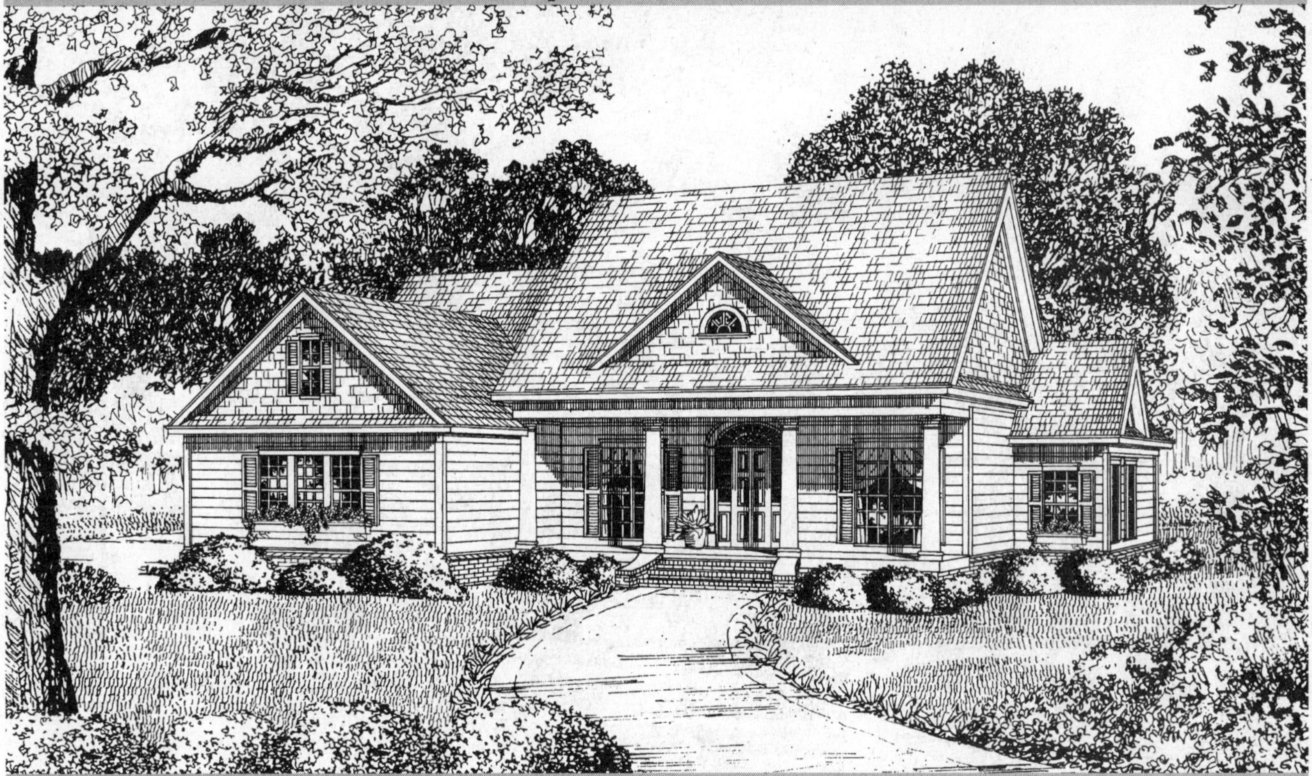

2,716 total square feet of living area **Price Code E**

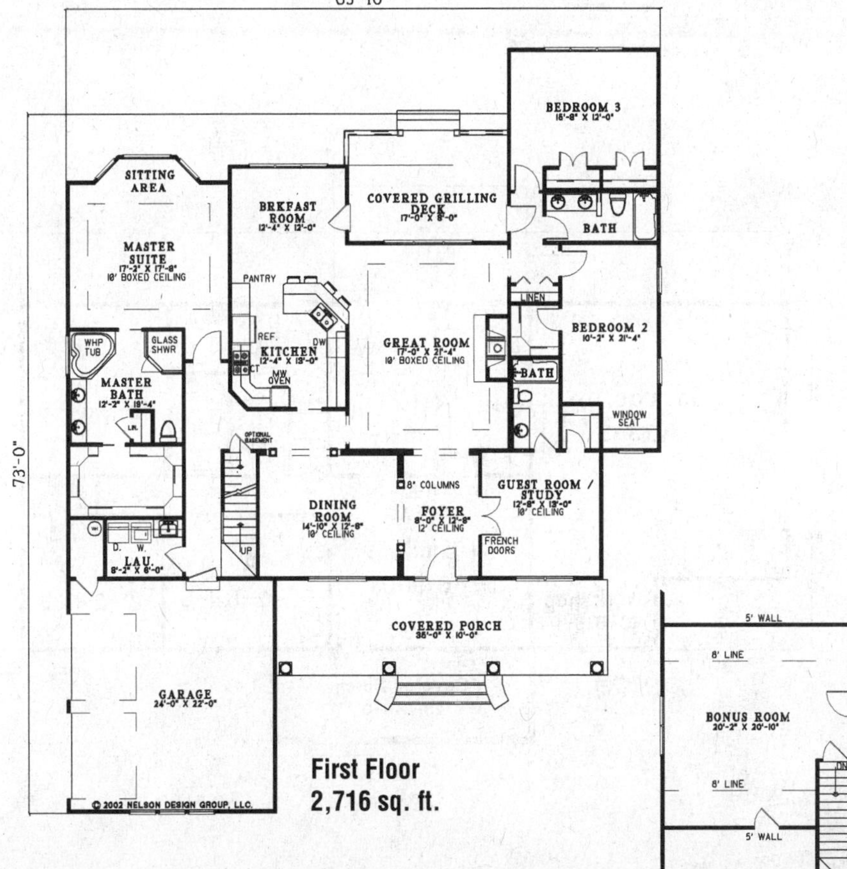
63'-10"
73'-0"
SITTING AREA
MASTER SUITE
BRKFAST ROOM
COVERED GRILLING DECK
BEDROOM 3
BATH
PANTRY
LINEN
REF.
DW
KITCHEN
GREAT ROOM
BEDROOM 2
WHP TUB
GLASS SHWR
MASTER BATH
BATH
WINDOW SEAT
8' COLUMNS
GUEST ROOM / STUDY
DINING ROOM
FOYER
FRENCH DOORS
UP
D. W.
LAU.
COVERED PORCH
GARAGE
© 2002 NELSON DESIGN GROUP, LLC.
5' WALL
8' LINE
BONUS ROOM
8' LINE
5' WALL

First Floor
2,716 sq. ft.

Optional
Second Floor

Special features

- Master suite has lots of privacy from other bedrooms
- 10' ceiling in formal dining room makes an impression
- Bonus room on second floor has an additional 438 square feet of living area
- 4 bedrooms, 4 baths, 2-car side entry garage
- Crawl space or slab foundation, please specify when ordering

TO ORDER BLUEPRINTS USE THE FORM ON PAGE 15 OR CALL TOLL-FREE 1-877-671-6036

View thousands more home plans online at www.familyhandyman.com/homeplans

The Family
Handyman

Plan #708-0217

Functional Layout For Comfortable Living

1,360 total square feet of living area **Price Code A**

Special features

- Kitchen/dining room features island work space and plenty of dining area
- Master bedroom with large walk-in closet and private bath
- Laundry room adjacent to the kitchen for easy access
- Convenient workshop in garage
- Large closets in secondary bedrooms
- 3 bedrooms, 2 baths, 2-car side entry garage
- Basement foundation, drawings also include crawl space and slab foundations

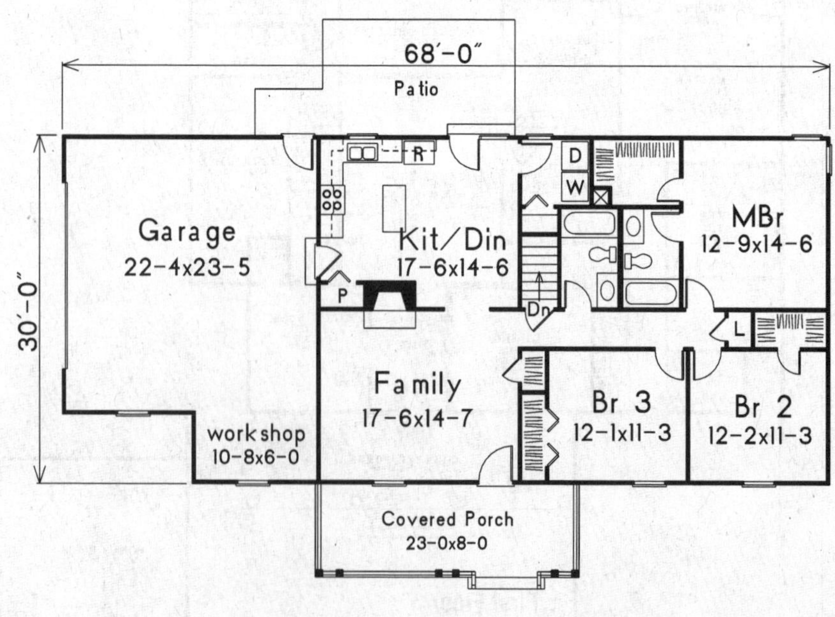
68′-0″
Patio
30′-0″
Garage
22-4x23-5
R
D
W
Kit/Din
17-6x14-6
MBr
12-9x14-6
P
Dn
L
Family
17-6x14-7
Br 3
12-1x11-3
Br 2
12-2x11-3
workshop
10-8x6-0
Covered Porch
23-0x8-0

TO ORDER BLUEPRINTS USE THE FORM ON PAGE 15 OR CALL TOLL-FREE 1-877-671-6036

View thousands more home plans online at www.familyhandyman.com/homeplans

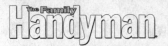

Dormer And Covered Porch Add To Country Charm

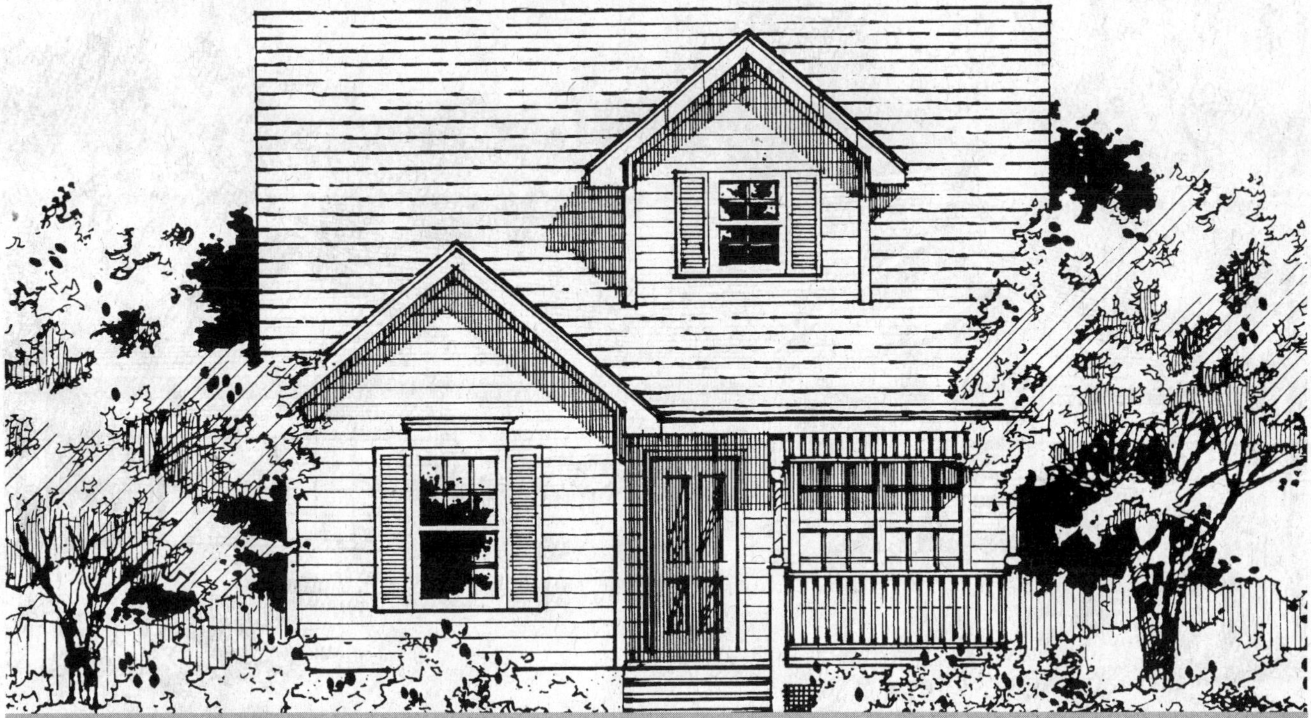

954 total square feet of living area

Price Code AA

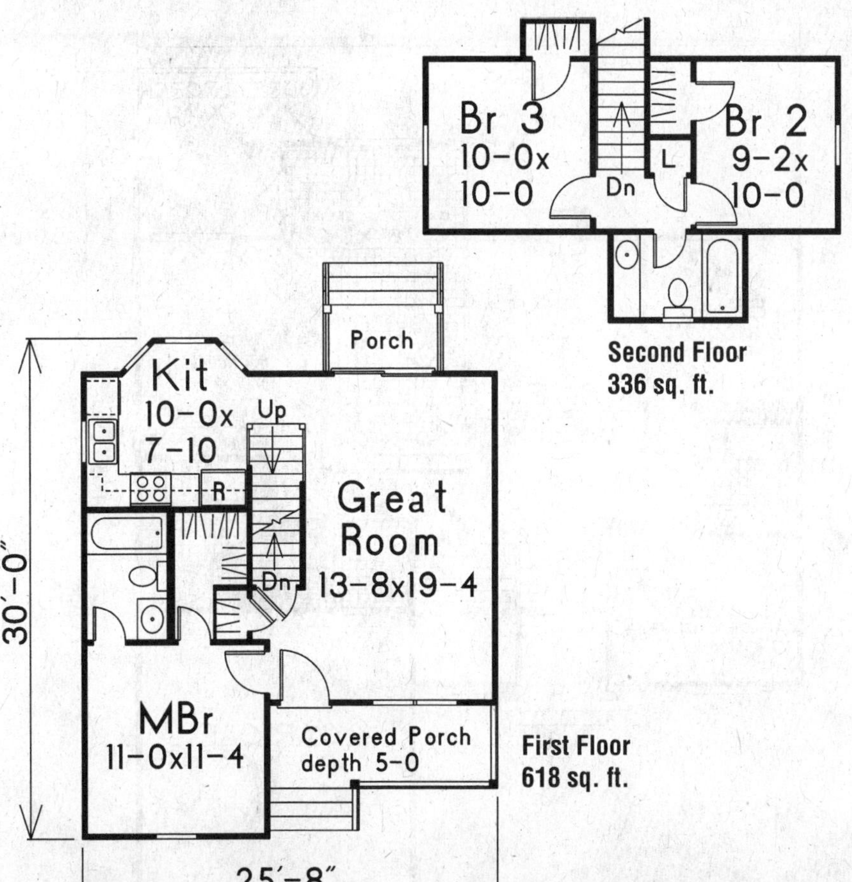
Br 3
10-0x
10-0
Dn
L
Br 2
9-2x
10-0
Porch
Kit
10-0x
7-10
Up
R
Great
Room
13-8x19-4
Dn
MBr
11-0x11-4
Covered Porch
depth 5-0
30'-0"
25'-8"

Second Floor
336 sq. ft.

First Floor
618 sq. ft.

Special features

- Kitchen has cozy bayed eating area
- Master bedroom has a walk-in closet and private bath
- Large great room has access to the back porch
- Convenient coat closet near front entry
- 3 bedrooms, 2 baths
- Basement foundation

Plan #708-JA-66096

Comfortable Ranch

1,495 total square feet of living area **Price Code A**

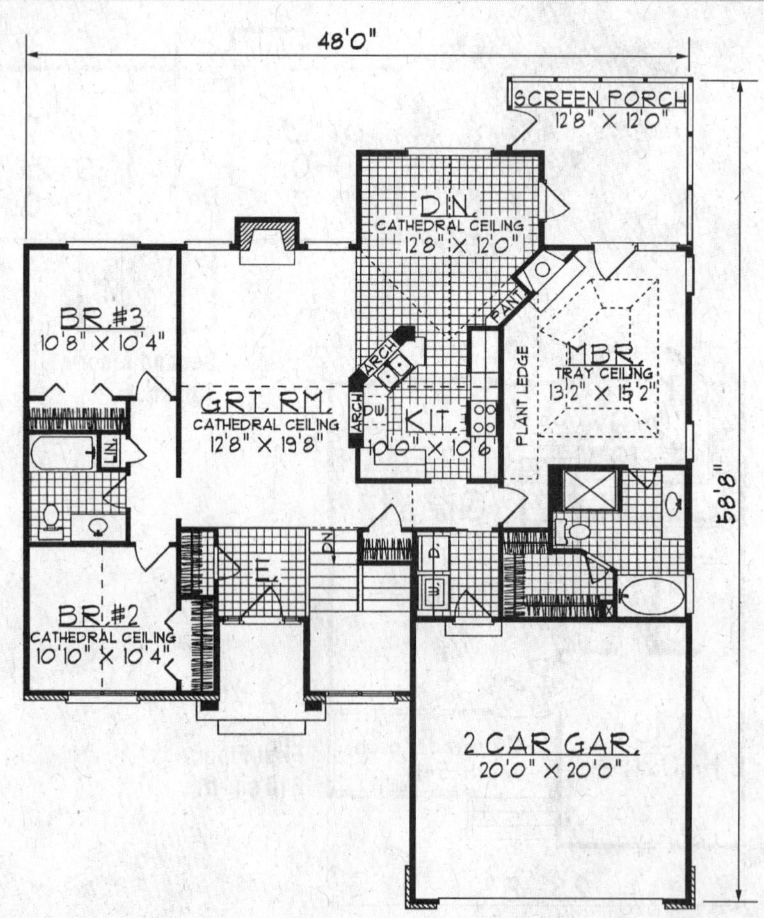

48'0"
58'8"
SCREEN PORCH
12'8" X 12'0"
DN.
CATHEDRAL CEILING
12'8" X 12'0"
PANT
MBR.
TRAY CEILING
13'2" X 15'2"
PLANT LEDGE
ARCH
ARCH
DW
KIT.
10'0" X 10'6"
BR.#3
10'8" X 10'4"
GRT. RM.
CATHEDRAL CEILING
12'8" X 19'8"
LIN.
E.
DN
BR.#2
CATHEDRAL CEILING
10'10" X 10'4"
2 CAR GAR.
20'0" X 20'0"

Special features

- Dining room has vaulted ceiling creating a large formal gathering area with access to a screened porch
- Cathedral ceiling in great room adds spaciousness
- Nice-sized entry with coat closet
- 3 bedrooms, 2 baths, 2-car garage
- Basement foundation

TO ORDER BLUEPRINTS USE THE FORM ON PAGE 15 OR CALL TOLL-FREE 1-877-671-6036

View thousands more home plans online at www.familyhandyman.com/homeplans

Innovative Ranch Has Cozy Corner Patio

1,092 total square feet of living area **Price Code AA**

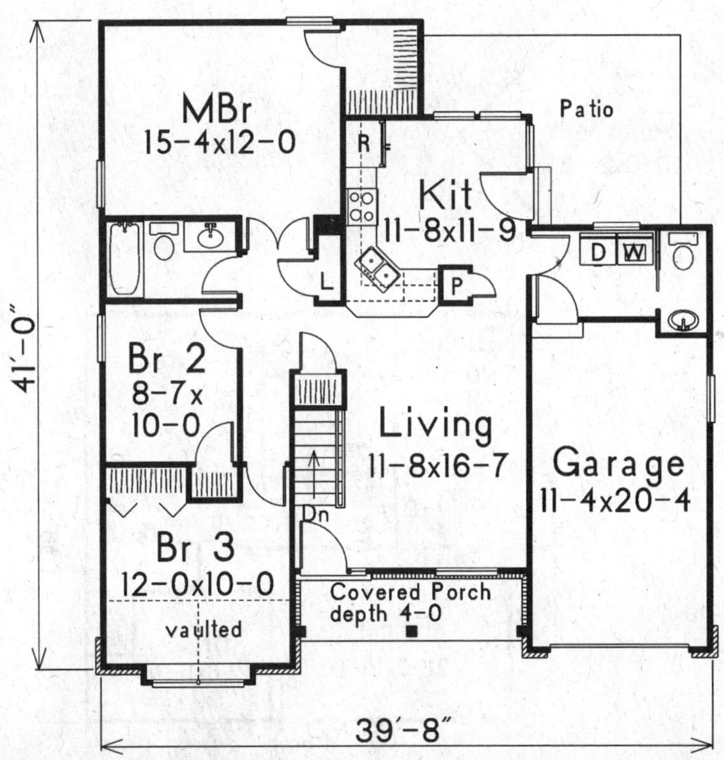
MBr
15–4x12–0
Patio
R
Kit
11–8x11–9
L
P
D
W
Br 2
8–7x
10–0
Living
11–8x16–7
Garage
11–4x20–4
Dn
Br 3
12–0x10–0
vaulted
Covered Porch
depth 4–0
41'–0"
39'–8"

Special features

- Box window and inviting porch with dormers create a charming facade
- Eat-in kitchen offers a pass-through breakfast bar, corner window wall to patio, pantry and convenient laundry with half bath
- Master bedroom features double entry doors and walk-in closet
- 3 bedrooms, 1 1/2 baths, 1-car garage
- Basement foundation

Plan #708-0203

Rambling Country Bungalow

1,475 total square feet of living area **Price Code B**

Special features

- Family room features a high ceiling and prominent corner fireplace
- Kitchen with island counter and garden window makes a convenient connection between the family and dining rooms
- Hallway leads to three bedrooms all with large walk-in closets
- Covered breezeway joins main house and garage
- Full-width covered porch entry lends a country touch
- 3 bedrooms, 2 baths, 2-car side entry garage
- Slab foundation, drawings also include crawl space foundation

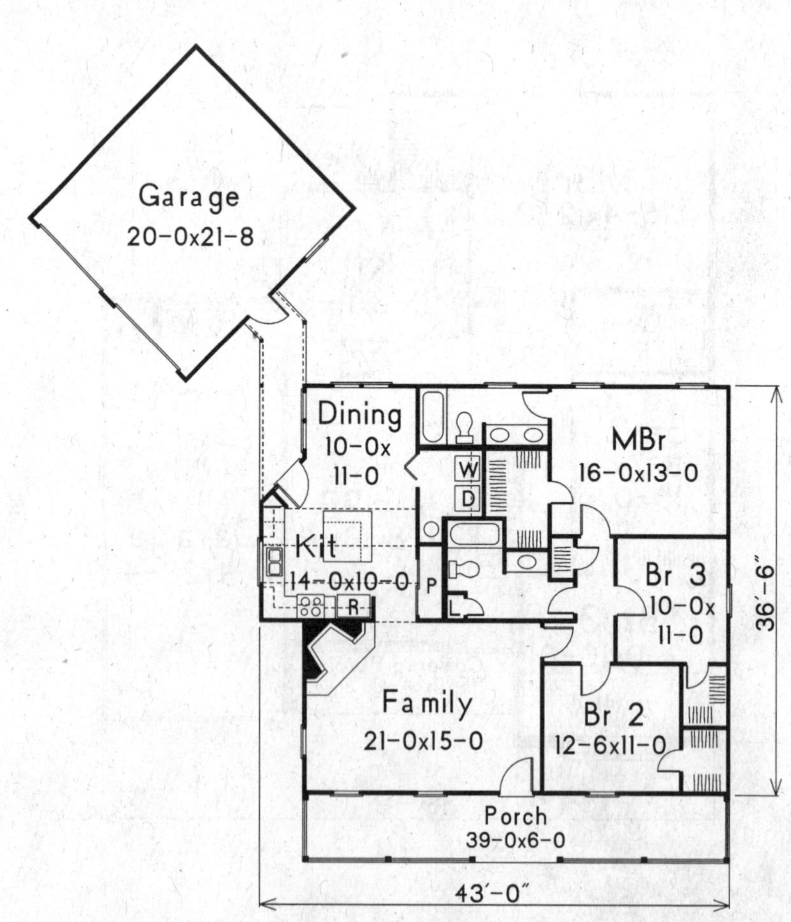

Garage
20-0x21-8
Dining
10-0x
11-0
W
D
MBr
16-0x13-0
Kit
14-0x10-0
P
R
L
Br 3
10-0x
11-0
Family
21-0x15-0
Br 2
12-6x11-0
Porch
39-0x6-0
36'-6"
43'-0"

TO ORDER BLUEPRINTS USE THE FORM ON PAGE 15 OR CALL TOLL-FREE 1-877-671-6036

View thousands more home plans online at www.familyhandyman.com/homeplans

Plan #708-0494

Compact Home, Perfect Fit For Narrow Lot

1,085 total square feet of living area

Price Code AA

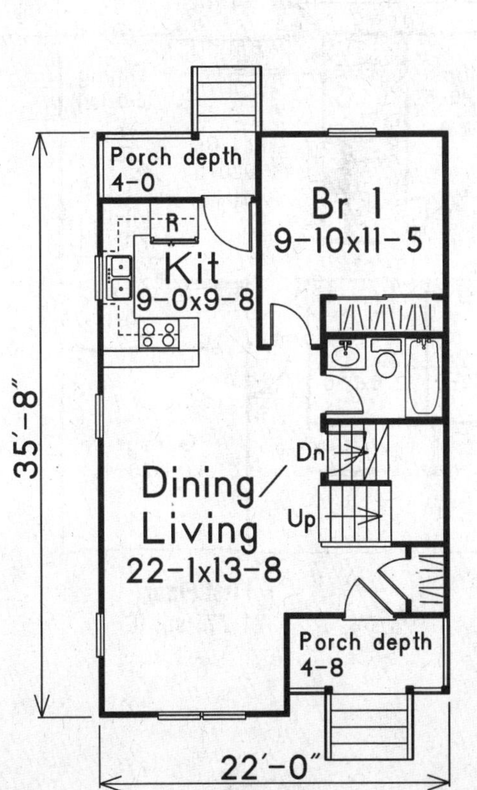

Porch depth
4-0
R
Kit
9-0x9-8
Br 1
9-10x11-5
Dn
Dining/
Living
22-1x13-8
Up
Porch depth
4-8
35'-8"
22'-0"

First Floor
685 sq. ft.

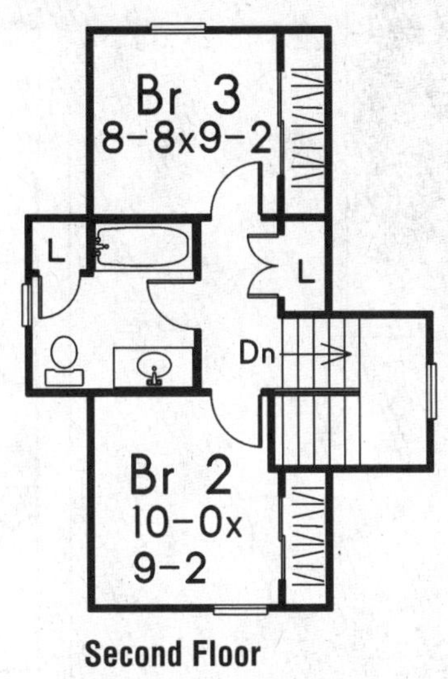

Br 3
8-8x9-2
L
L
Dn
Br 2
10-0x
9-2

Second Floor
400 sq. ft.

Special features

- Rear porch is a handy access through the kitchen
- Convenient hall linen closet located on the second floor
- Breakfast bar in kitchen offers additional counterspace
- Living and dining rooms combine for an open living atmosphere
- 3 bedrooms, 2 baths
- Basement foundation

TO ORDER BLUEPRINTS USE THE FORM ON PAGE 15 OR CALL TOLL-FREE 1-877-671-6036

View thousands more home plans online at www.familyhandyman.com/homeplans

Plan #708-0710

Affordable Atrium Ranch

2,334 total square feet of living area | **Price Code D**

Rear View

Special features

- Roomy front porch gives home a country flavor
- Vaulted great room boasts a fireplace, TV alcove, pass-through snack bar to kitchen and atrium featuring bayed window wall and ascending stair to family room
- Oversized master bedroom and bath features a vaulted ceiling, double entry doors and large walk-in closet
- 3 bedrooms, 2 baths, 2-car garage
- Walk-out basement foundation

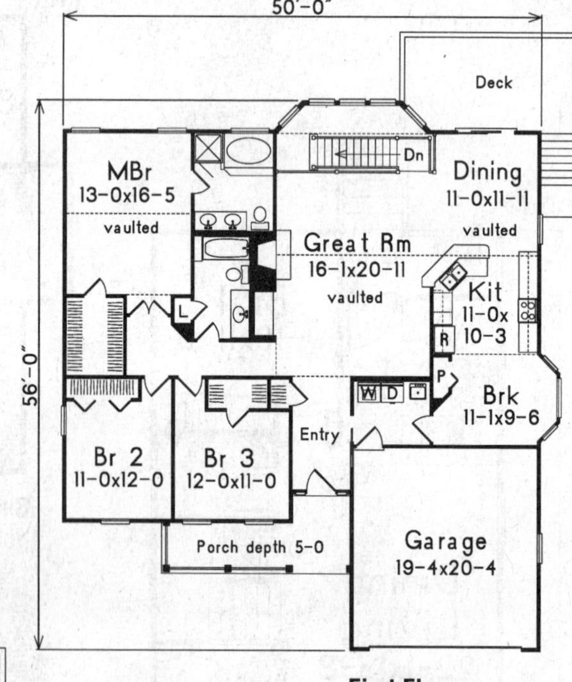
50'-0"
56'-0"
Deck
Dn
MBr
13-0x16-5
vaulted
Dining
11-0x11-11
vaulted
Great Rm
16-1x20-11
vaulted
Kit
11-0x
10-3
R
P
W D
Brk
11-1x9-6
Entry
Br 2
11-0x12-0
Br 3
12-0x11-0
Porch depth 5-0
Garage
19-4x20-4

First Floor
1,777 sq. ft.

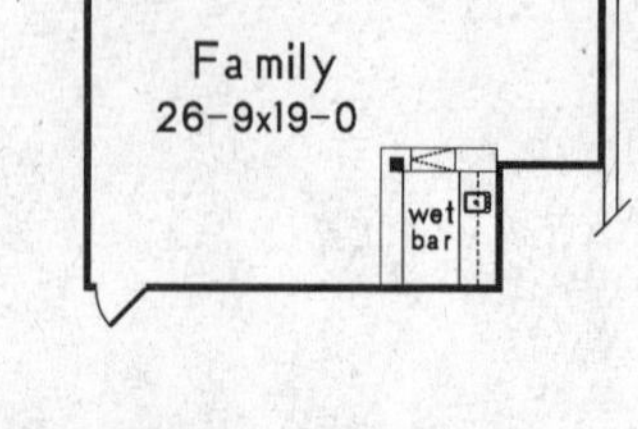

Lower Level
557 sq. ft.

Up
Family
26-9x19-0
wet bar

TO ORDER BLUEPRINTS USE THE FORM ON PAGE 15 OR CALL TOLL-FREE 1-877-671-6036

View thousands more home plans online at www.familyhandyman.com/homeplans

Plan #708-JA-79298

Amenity Full Ranch

2,229 total square feet of living area

Price Code D

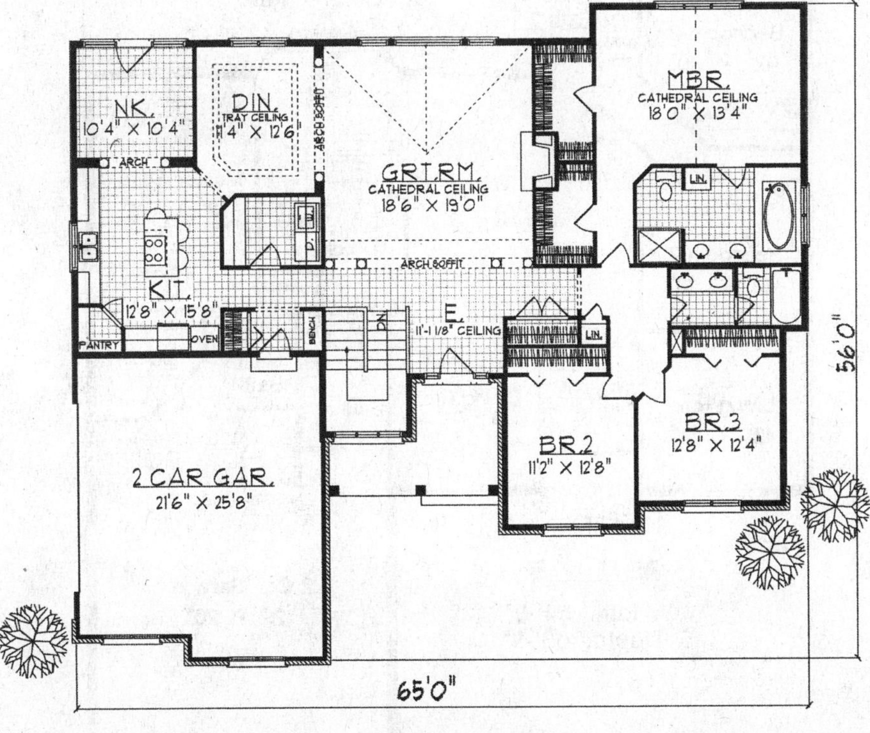

NK.
10'4" X 10'4"
DIN.
TRAY CEILING
11'4" X 12'6"
ARCH
GRT.RM.
CATHEDRAL CEILING
18'6" X 19'0"
MBR.
CATHEDRAL CEILING
18'0" X 13'4"
LIN.
ARCH SOFFIT
KIT.
12'8" X 15'8"
E.
11'-1 1/8" CEILING
DN
BENCH
PANTRY
OVEN
LIN.
BR.2
11'2" X 12'8"
BR.3
12'8" X 12'4"
2 CAR GAR.
21'6" X 25'8"
56'0"
65'0"

Special features

- Welcoming and expansive front porch
- Dining room has tray ceiling
- Sunny nook with arched soffit creates an inviting entry
- 3 bedrooms, 2 baths, 2-car garage
- Basement foundation

TO ORDER BLUEPRINTS USE THE FORM ON PAGE 15 OR CALL TOLL-FREE 1-877-671-6036

View thousands more home plans online at www.familyhandyman.com/homeplans

The Family
Handyman

Plan #708-HDS-1806

Trio Of Dormers Adds Curb Appeal

1,806 total square feet of living area **Price Code C**

Special features

- Covered porch in the rear of the home adds an outdoor living area
- Private and formal living room
- Kitchen has snack counter that extends into family room
- 3 bedrooms, 2 baths, 2-car garage
- Slab foundation

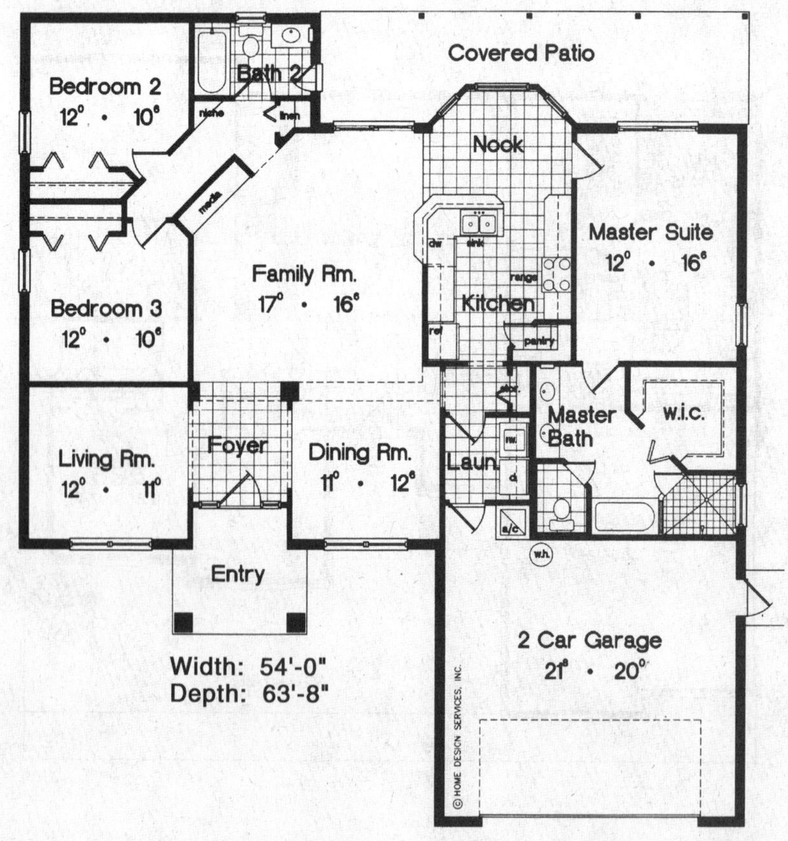
Covered Patio
Bedroom 2
12⁰ · 10⁶
Bath 2
niche
linen
Nook
media
Master Suite
12⁰ · 16⁶
Family Rm.
17⁰ · 16⁶
dw
sink
range
Kitchen
ref
pantry
Bedroom 3
12⁰ · 10⁶
Master Bath
W.i.c.
Living Rm.
12⁰ · 11⁰
Foyer
Dining Rm.
11⁰ · 12⁶
Laun.
a/c
w.h.
Entry
2 Car Garage
21⁸ · 20⁰
Width: 54'-0"
Depth: 63'-8"
© HOME DESIGN SERVICES, INC.

TO ORDER BLUEPRINTS USE THE FORM ON PAGE 15 OR CALL TOLL-FREE 1-877-671-6036

View thousands more home plans online at www.familyhandyman.com/homeplans

Elegance In A Starter Or Retirement Home

888 total square feet of living area **Price Code AAA**

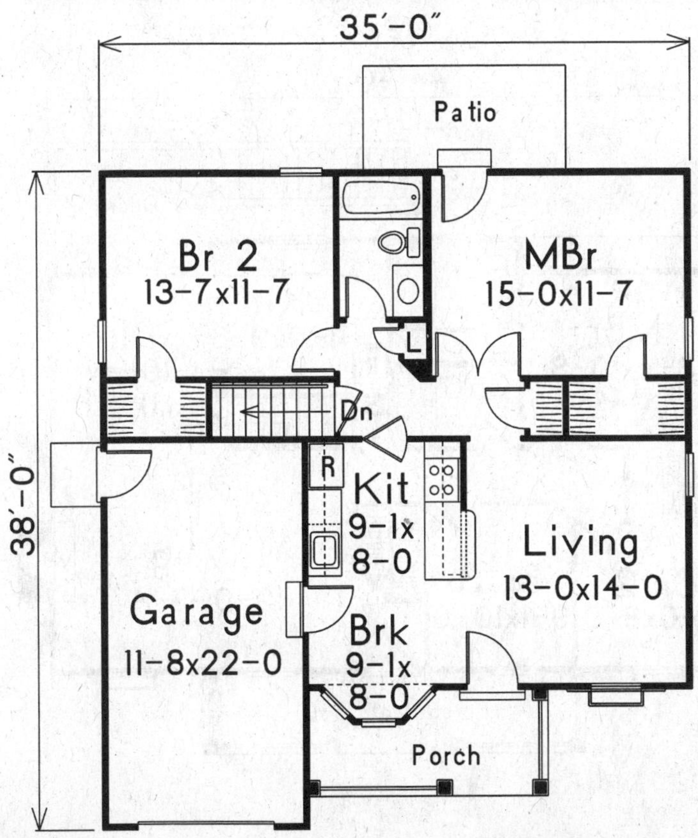
35′-0″
38′-0″
Patio
Br 2
13-7x11-7
MBr
15-0x11-7
L
Dn
R
Kit
9-1x
8-0
Living
13-0x14-0
Garage
11-8x22-0
Brk
9-1x
8-0
Porch

Special features

- Home features an eye-catching exterior and includes a spacious porch
- The breakfast room with bay window is open to living room and adjoins kitchen with pass-through snack bar
- The bedrooms are quite roomy and feature walk-in closets
- The master bedroom has double entry doors and access to rear patio
- 2 bedrooms, 1 bath, 1-car garage
- Basement foundation

TO ORDER BLUEPRINTS USE THE FORM ON PAGE 15 OR CALL TOLL-FREE 1-877-671-6036

View thousands more home plans online at www.familyhandyman.com/homeplans

The Family
Handyman

Plan #708-0477

Enchanting Country Cottage

1,140 total square feet of living area | **Price Code AA**

Special features

- Open and spacious living and dining areas for family gatherings
- Well-organized kitchen with an abundance of cabinetry and a built-in pantry
- Roomy master bath features double-bowl vanity
- 3 bedrooms, 2 baths, 2-car drive under garage
- Basement foundation

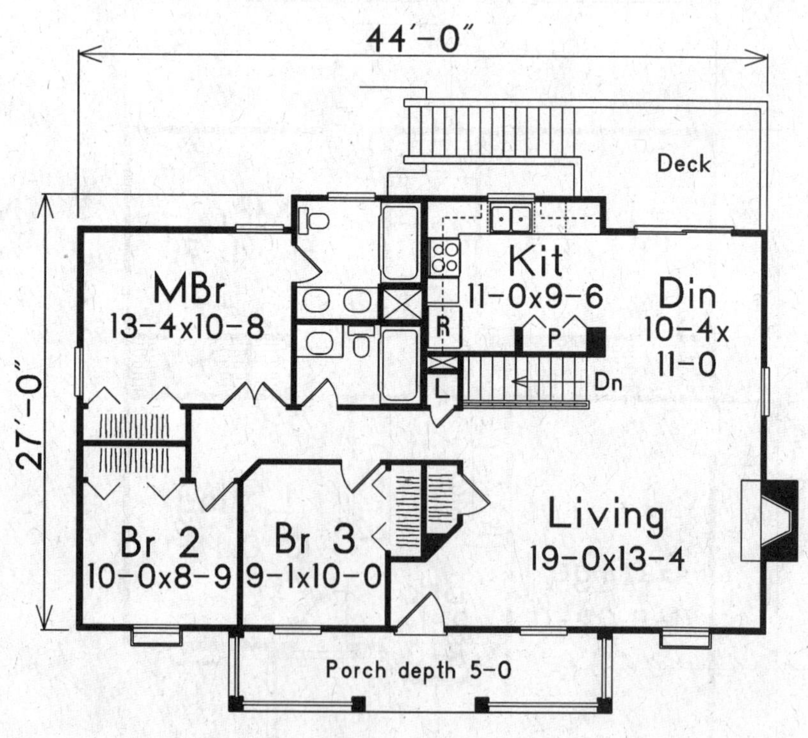
44'-0"
27'-0"
Deck
MBr
13-4x10-8
Kit
11-0x9-6
Din
10-4x
11-0
R
P
L
Dn
Br 2
10-0x8-9
Br 3
9-1x10-0
Living
19-0x13-4
Porch depth 5-0

TO ORDER BLUEPRINTS USE THE FORM ON PAGE 15 OR CALL TOLL-FREE 1-877-671-6036
View thousands more home plans online at www.familyhandyman.com/homeplans

The Family Handyman

Plan #708-VL2162

This Ranch Has A Tudor Influence

2,162 total square feet of living area **Price Code C**

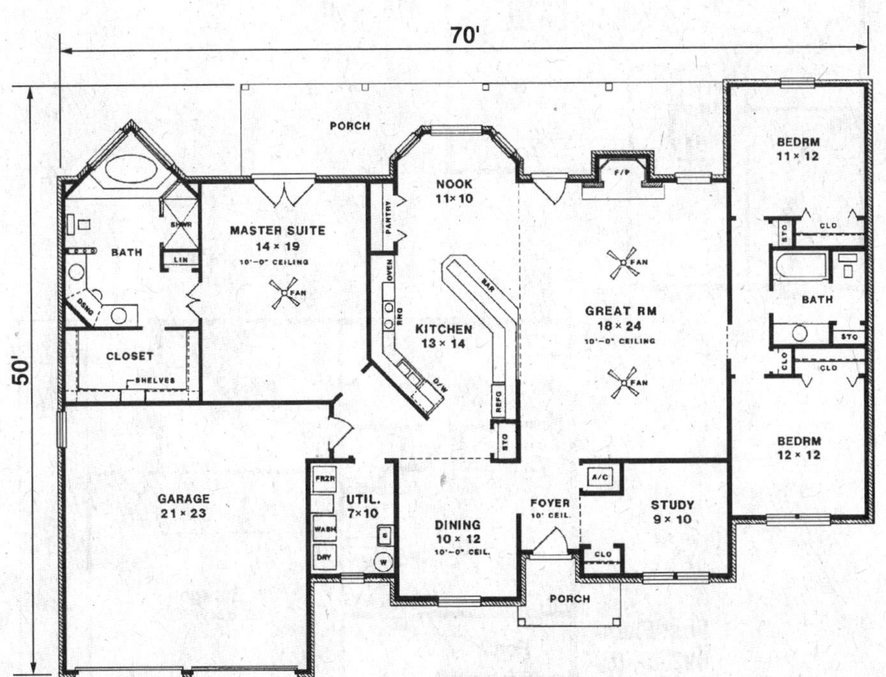
70'
50'
PORCH
NOOK
11×10
BEDRM
11 × 12
F/P
MASTER SUITE
14 × 19
10'-0" CEILING
BATH
PANTRY
FAN
GREAT RM
18 × 24
10'-0" CEILING
KITCHEN
13 × 14
BAR
BATH
CLOSET
SHELVES
BEDRM
12 × 12
GARAGE
21 × 23
UTIL.
7×10
DINING
10 × 12
10'-0" CEIL.
FOYER
10' CEIL.
STUDY
9 × 10
A/C
CLO
PORCH

Special features

- 10' ceilings in great room, dining room, master suite and foyer
- Enormous great room overlooks kitchen with oversized snack bar
- Luxurious master bath boasts a triangular whirlpool tub drenched in light from large windows
- 3 bedrooms, 2 baths, 2-car garage
- Crawl space or slab foundation, please specify when ordering

The Family
Handyman

Plan #708-GH-24326

Family Room Has Cozy Fireplace

1,505 total square feet of living area

Price Code B

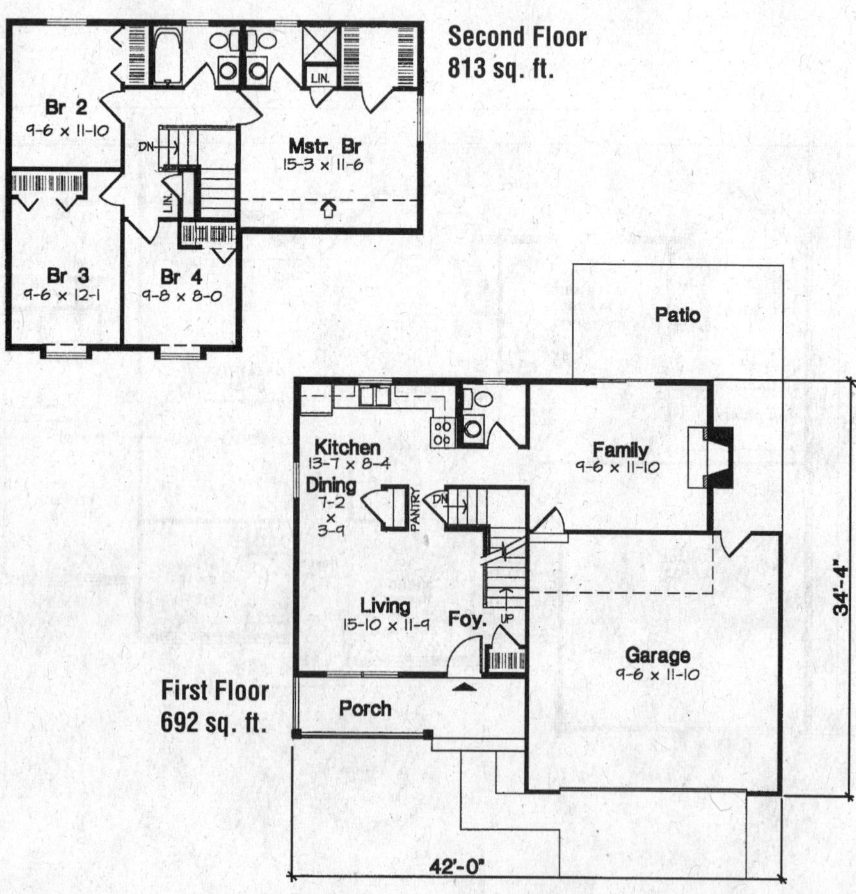

Second Floor
813 sq. ft.
Br 2
9-6 x 11-10
DN
Mstr. Br
15-3 x 11-6
LIN.
LIN.
Br 3
9-6 x 12-1
Br 4
9-8 x 8-0
Patio
Kitchen
13-7 x 8-4
Dining
7-2
x
3-9
PANTRY
DN
Family
9-6 x 11-10
Living
15-10 x 11-9
Foy.
UP
Garage
9-6 x 11-10
34'-4"
First Floor
692 sq. ft.
Porch
42'-0"

Special features

- Spacious living room opens into the dining area which flows into an efficient kitchen
- All bedrooms located on the second floor for privacy
- Master bedroom has a large walk-in closet and a private bath with step-in shower
- 4 bedrooms, 2 1/2 baths, 2-car garage
- Basement, crawl space or slab foundation, please specify when ordering

TO ORDER BLUEPRINTS USE THE FORM ON PAGE 15 OR CALL TOLL-FREE 1-877-671-6036

View thousands more home plans online at www.familyhandyman.com/homeplans

The Family
Handyman

Plan #708-0799

Bedrooms Separate From Rest Of Home

1,849 total square feet of living area **Price Code C**

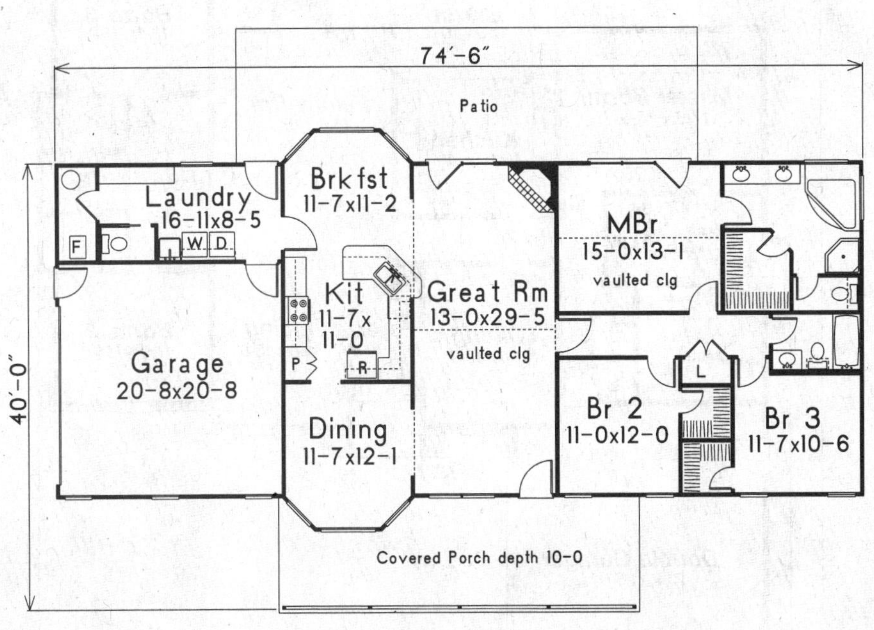
74'-6"
Patio
Brkfst
11-7x11-2
Laundry
16-11x8-5
F
W
D
MBr
15-0x13-1
vaulted clg
Kit
11-7x
11-0
P
R
Great Rm
13-0x29-5
vaulted clg
Garage
20-8x20-8
L
Br 2
11-0x12-0
Br 3
11-7x10-6
Dining
11-7x12-1
Covered Porch depth 10-0
40'-0"

Special features

- Enormous laundry/mud room has many extras including storage area and half bath
- Lavish master bath has corner jacuzzi tub, double sinks, separate shower and walk-in closet
- Secondary bedrooms include walk-in closets
- Kitchen has wrap-around eating counter and is positioned between formal dining area and breakfast room for convenience
- 3 bedrooms, 2 1/2 baths, 2-car side entry garage
- Slab foundation, drawings also include crawl space foundation

Plan #708-JV-2221-A

Impressive Ranch With Many Amenities

2,221 total square feet of living area **Price Code D**

Special features

- Kitchen and breakfast room combine for convenience
- A jack and jill bath is shared by bedrooms #2 and #3
- Decorative columns enhance the entrance of the formal living room
- 3 bedrooms, 2 1/2 baths, 2-car side entry garage
- Basement foundation

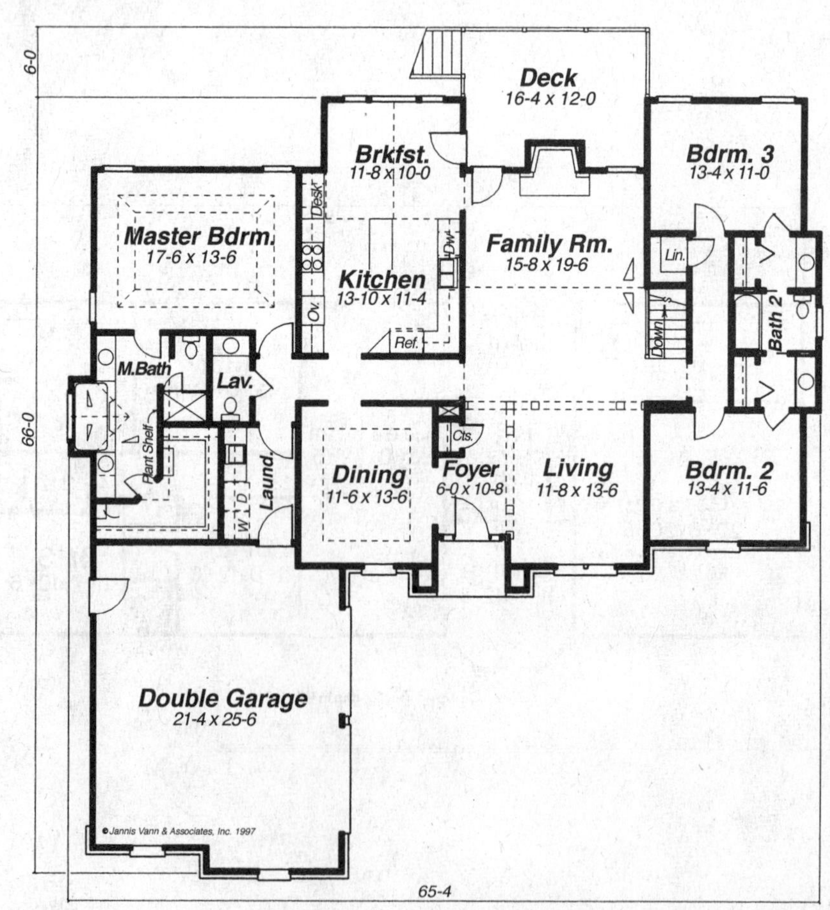
6-0
Deck
16-4 x 12-0
Brkfst.
11-8 x 10-0
Bdrm. 3
13-4 x 11-0
Master Bdrm.
17-6 x 13-6
Desk
Dw
Kitchen
13-10 x 11-4
Family Rm.
15-8 x 19-6
Lin.
Ov.
Ref.
Down
Bath 2
M.Bath
Lav.
66-0
Plant Shelf
Laund.
W D
Dining
11-6 x 13-6
Foyer
6-0 x 10-8
Cls.
Living
11-8 x 13-6
Bdrm. 2
13-4 x 11-6
Double Garage
21-4 x 25-6
©Jannis Vann & Associates, Inc. 1997
65-4

TO ORDER BLUEPRINTS USE THE FORM ON PAGE 15 OR CALL TOLL-FREE 1-877-671-6036

View thousands more home plans online at www.familyhandyman.com/homeplans

The Family
Handyman

Plan #708-0228

Blends Open And Private Living Areas

1,996 total square feet of living area | **Price Code C**

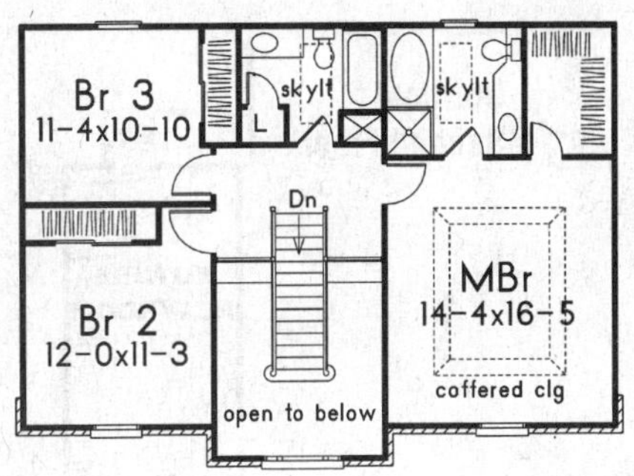
Br 3
11-4x10-10
skylt
L
skylt
Dn
MBr
14-4x16-5
Br 2
12-0x11-3
coffered clg
open to below

Second Floor
859 sq. ft.

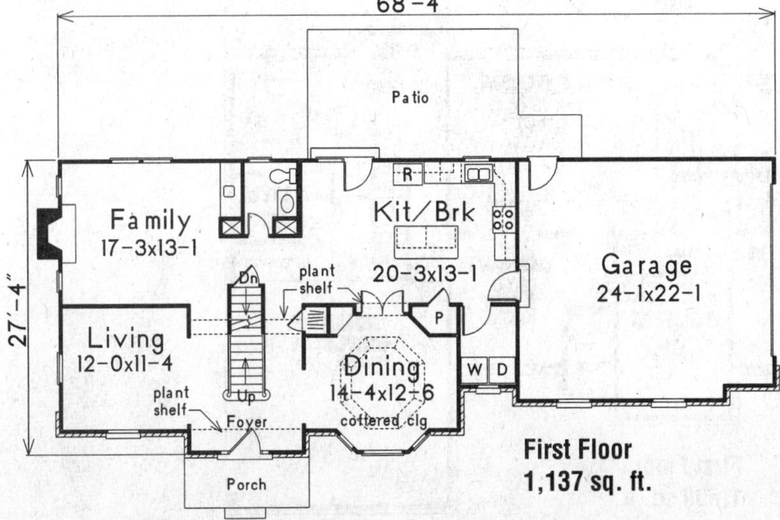
68'-4"
27'-4"
Patio
R
Family
17-3x13-1
Kit/Brk
20-3x13-1
Dn
plant shelf
Garage
24-1x22-1
P
Living
12-0x11-4
Dining
14-4x12-6
W
D
plant shelf
Up
Foyer
coffered clg
Porch

First Floor
1,137 sq. ft.

Special features

- Dining area features octagon-shaped coffered ceiling and built-in china cabinet
- Both the master bath and second floor bath have cheerful skylights
- Family room includes wet bar and fireplace flanked by attractive quarter round windows
- 9' ceilings throughout first floor with plant shelving in foyer and dining area
- 3 bedrooms, 2 1/2 baths, 2-car side entry garage
- Basement foundation, drawings also include crawl space and slab foundations

TO ORDER BLUEPRINTS USE THE FORM ON PAGE 15 OR CALL TOLL-FREE 1-877-671-6036

View thousands more home plans online at www.familyhandyman.com/homeplans

The Family
Handyman

Plan #708-CHD-16-33

Stunning All Brick Ranch

1,699 total square feet of living area

Price Code B

<u>*Special features*</u>

- Master suite is filled with luxury including a private bath with glass shower, oversized tub, large walk-in closet and double vanity
- Wonderful kitchen and breakfast room arrangement makes great use of space
- Bonus room on second floor has an additional 260 square feet of living area
- 3 bedrooms, 2 baths, 2-car side entry garage
- Slab foundation

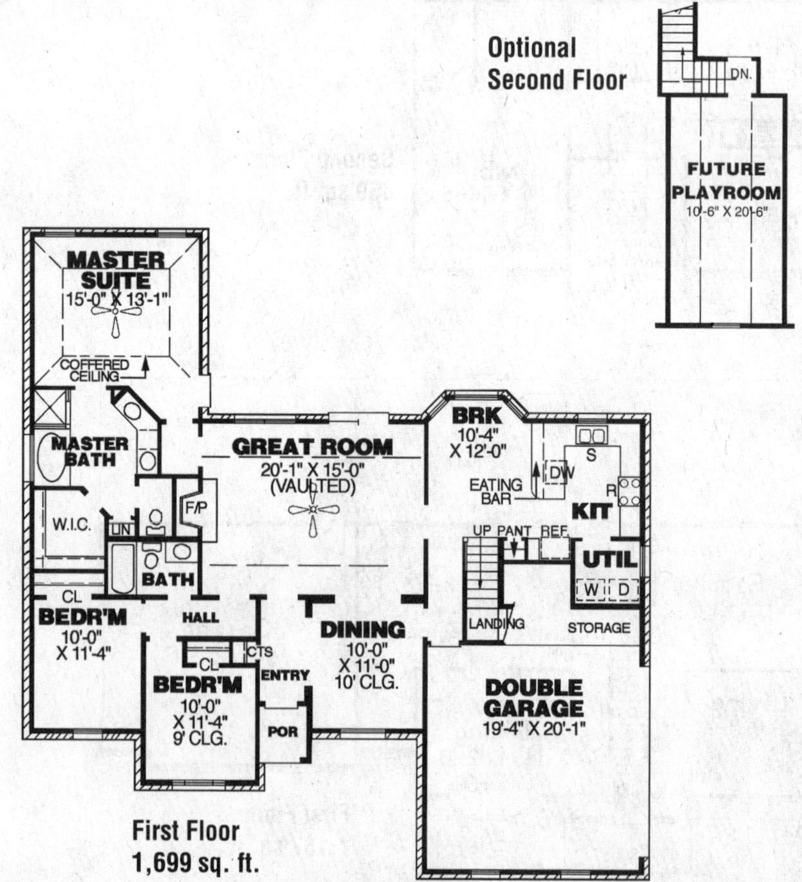

Optional Second Floor
DN.
FUTURE PLAYROOM
10'-6" X 20'-6"
MASTER SUITE
15'-0" X 13'-1"
COFFERED CEILING
MASTER BATH
W.I.C.
LIN
F/P
GREAT ROOM
20'-1" X 15'-0"
(VAULTED)
BRK
10'-4"
X 12'-0"
DW
S
R
EATING BAR
KIT
UP
PANT
REF.
UTIL
W D
LANDING
STORAGE
BATH
CL
BEDR'M
10'-0"
X 11'-4"
HALL
DINING
10'-0"
X 11'-0"
10' CLG.
CL
CTS
ENTRY
BEDR'M
10'-0"
X 11'-4"
9' CLG.
POR
DOUBLE GARAGE
19'-4" X 20'-1"
First Floor
1,699 sq. ft.

TO ORDER BLUEPRINTS USE THE FORM ON PAGE 15 OR CALL TOLL-FREE 1-877-671-6036

View thousands more home plans online at www.familyhandyman.com/homeplans

Open Ranch Design Gives Expansive Look

1,630 total square feet of living area | **Price Code B**

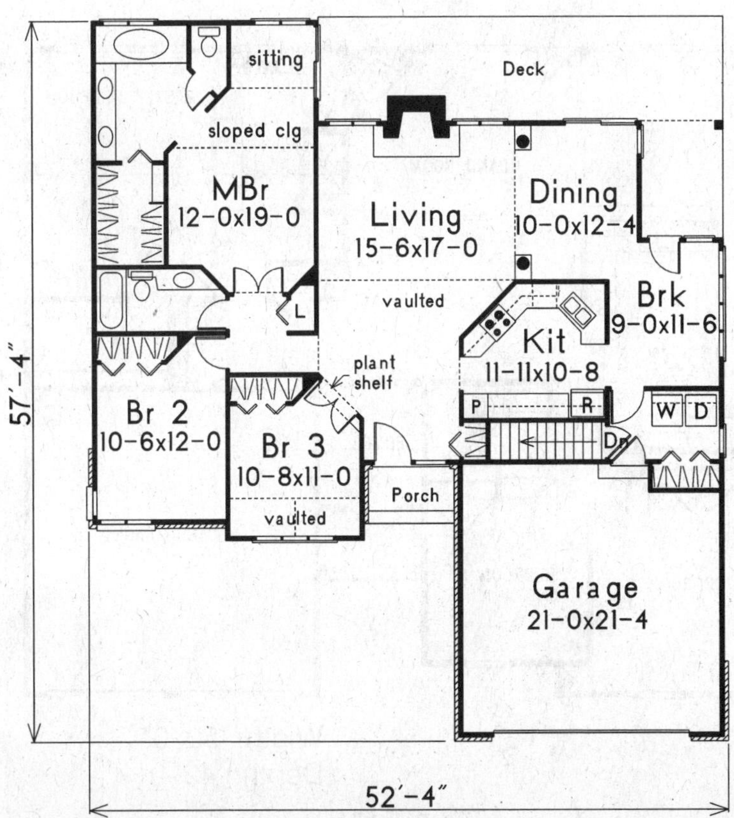
sitting
Deck
sloped clg
MBr
12-0x19-0
Living
15-6x17-0
Dining
10-0x12-4
vaulted
L
Brk
9-0x11-6
Kit
11-11x10-8
plant shelf
P
R
W
D
D
Br 2
10-6x12-0
Br 3
10-8x11-0
Porch
vaulted
Garage
21-0x21-4
57'-4"
52'-4"

Special features

- Crisp facade and full windows front and back offer open viewing
- Wrap-around rear deck is accessible from breakfast room, dining room and master bedroom
- Vaulted ceiling in living room and master bedroom
- Sitting area and large walk-in closet complement master bedroom
- 3 bedrooms, 2 baths, 2-car garage
- Basement foundation

Plan #708-MG-9305

Corner Fireplace In Grand Room

1,606 total square feet of living area **Price Code B**

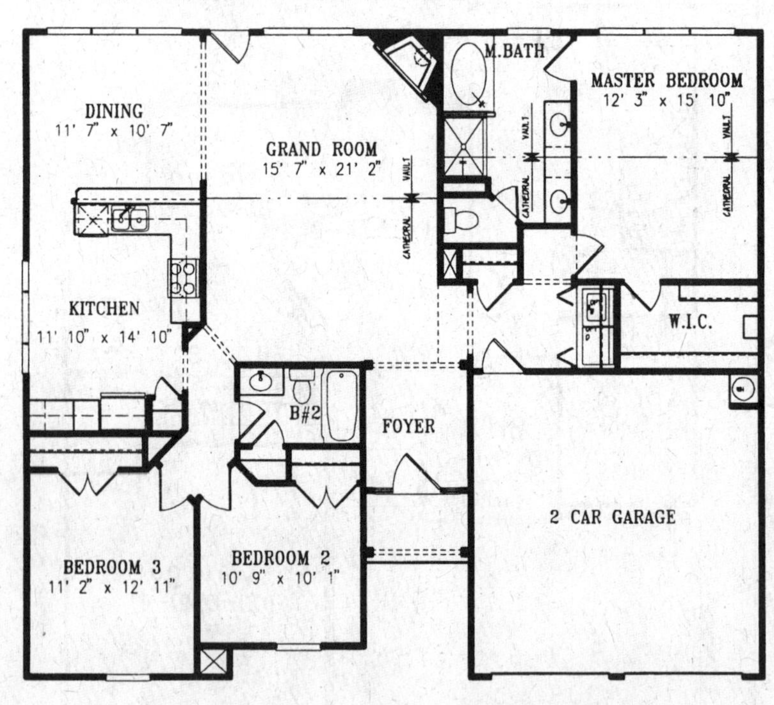
M.BATH
MASTER BEDROOM
12' 3" x 15' 10"
DINING
11' 7" x 10' 7"
GRAND ROOM
15' 7" x 21' 2"
CATHEDRAL VAULT
KITCHEN
11' 10" x 14' 10"
W.I.C.
B#2
FOYER
2 CAR GARAGE
BEDROOM 3
11' 2" x 12' 11"
BEDROOM 2
10' 9" x 10' 1"

Width: 50'-0"
Depth: 42'-0"

Special features

- Kitchen has snack bar which overlooks dining area for convenience
- Master bedroom has lots of windows with a private bath and large walk-in closet
- Cathedral vault in great room adds spaciousness
- 3 bedrooms, 2 baths, 2-car garage
- Slab foundation

TO ORDER BLUEPRINTS USE THE FORM ON PAGE 15 OR CALL TOLL-FREE 1-877-671-6036

View thousands more home plans online at www.familyhandyman.com/homeplans

The Family Handyman

Plan #708-0265

Economical Ranch For Easy Living

1,314 total square feet of living area **Price Code A**

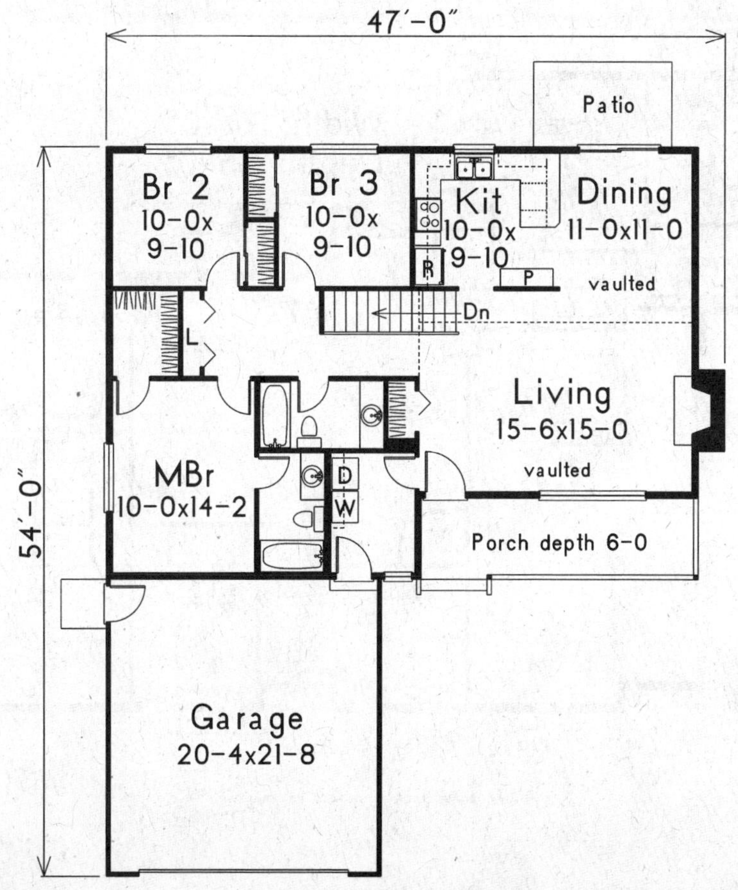
47'-0"
Patio
Br 2
10-0x
9-10
Br 3
10-0x
9-10
Kit
10-0x
9-10
Dining
11-0x11-0
vaulted
R
P
Dn
L
Living
15-6x15-0
vaulted
MBr
10-0x14-2
D
W
Porch depth 6-0
54'-0"
Garage
20-4x21-8

Special features

- Energy efficient home with 2" x 6" exterior walls
- Covered porch adds immediate appeal and welcoming charm
- Open floor plan combined with vaulted ceiling offers spacious living
- Functional kitchen complete with pantry and eating bar
- Cozy fireplace in the living room
- Private master bedroom features a large walk-in closet and bath
- 3 bedrooms, 2 baths, 2-car garage
- Basement foundation

The Family
Handyman

Plan #708-DL-25454L1

Sunny Sitting Area In Master Suite

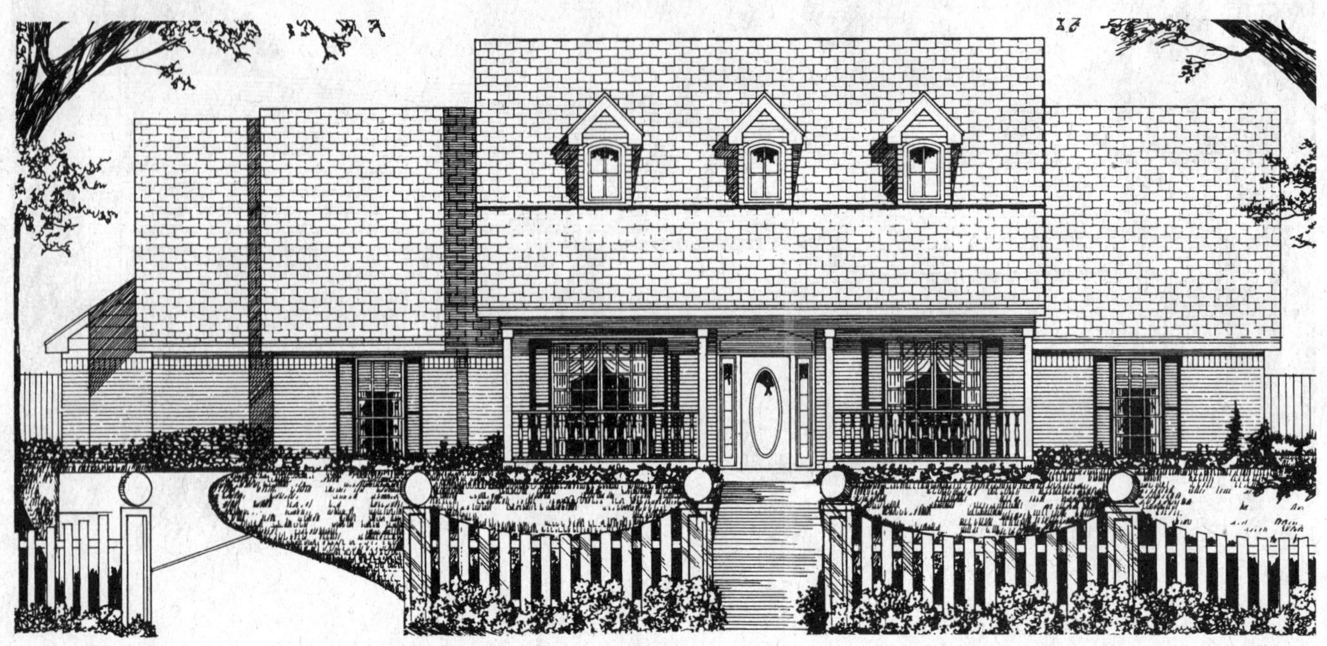

2,545 total square feet of living area **Price Code D**

Special features

- Beautiful covered front porch gives country appeal
- Open family room has 10' ceiling
- Kitchen has abundant counterspace
- 4 bedrooms, 2 1/2 baths, 3-car side entry garage
- Slab foundation

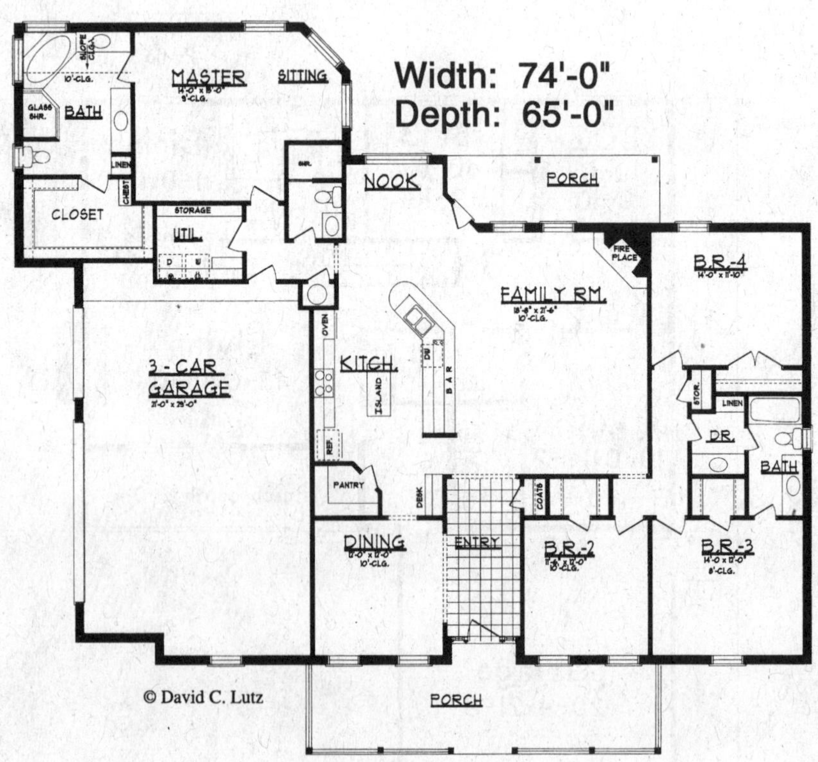
Width: 74'-0"
Depth: 65'-0"
MASTER
SITTING
BATH
GLASS SHR.
LINEN
CLOSET
STORAGE
UTIL.
NOOK
PORCH
FIRE PLACE
FAMILY RM.
B.R.-4
3 - CAR GARAGE
KITCH.
ISLAND
BAR
OVEN
REF.
PANTRY
DESK
COATS
STOR.
LINEN
DR.
BATH
DINING
ENTRY
B.R.-2
B.R.-3
PORCH
© David C. Lutz

TO ORDER BLUEPRINTS USE THE FORM ON PAGE 15 OR CALL TOLL-FREE 1-877-671-6036

View thousands more home plans online at www.familyhandyman.com/homeplans

The Family
Handyman

Plan #708-0335

Wonderful Great Room

1,865 total square feet of living area **Price Code D**

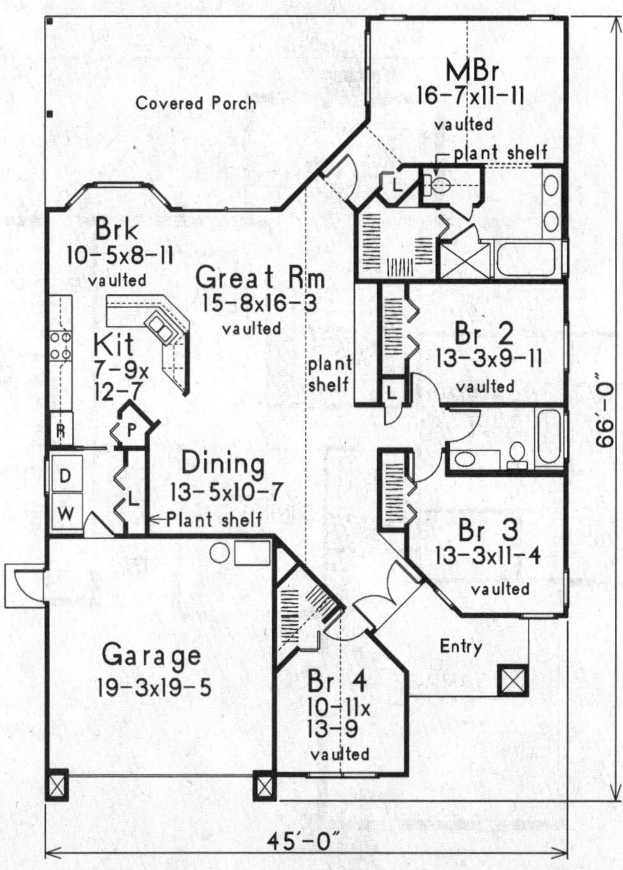
Covered Porch
MBr
16-7x11-11
vaulted
plant shelf
Brk
10-5x8-11
vaulted
Great Rm
15-8x16-3
vaulted
Kit
7-9x
12-7
plant
shelf
Br 2
13-3x9-11
vaulted
Dining
13-5x10-7
Plant shelf
Br 3
13-3x11-4
vaulted
Entry
Garage
19-3x19-5
Br 4
10-11x
13-9
vaulted
66'-0"
45'-0"

Special features

- Large foyer opens into expansive dining area and great room
- Home features vaulted ceilings throughout
- Master suite features bath with double-bowl vanity, shower, tub and toilet in separate room for privacy
- 4 bedrooms, 2 baths, 2-car garage
- Slab foundation, drawings also include crawl space foundation

TO ORDER BLUEPRINTS USE THE FORM ON PAGE 15 OR CALL TOLL-FREE 1-877-671-6036

View thousands more home plans online at www.familyhandyman.com/homeplans

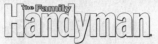

Plan #708-RDD-2050-7A

Traditional Styling

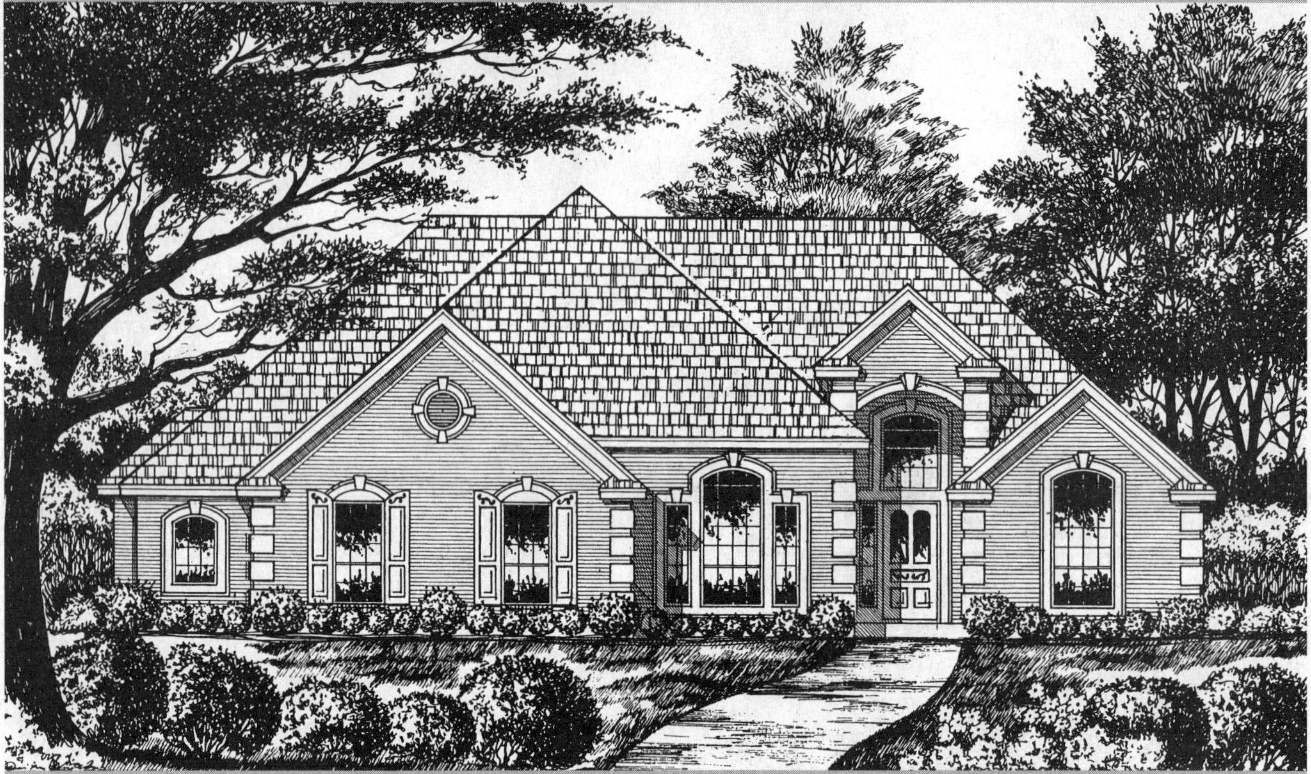

2,050 total square feet of living area

Price Code C

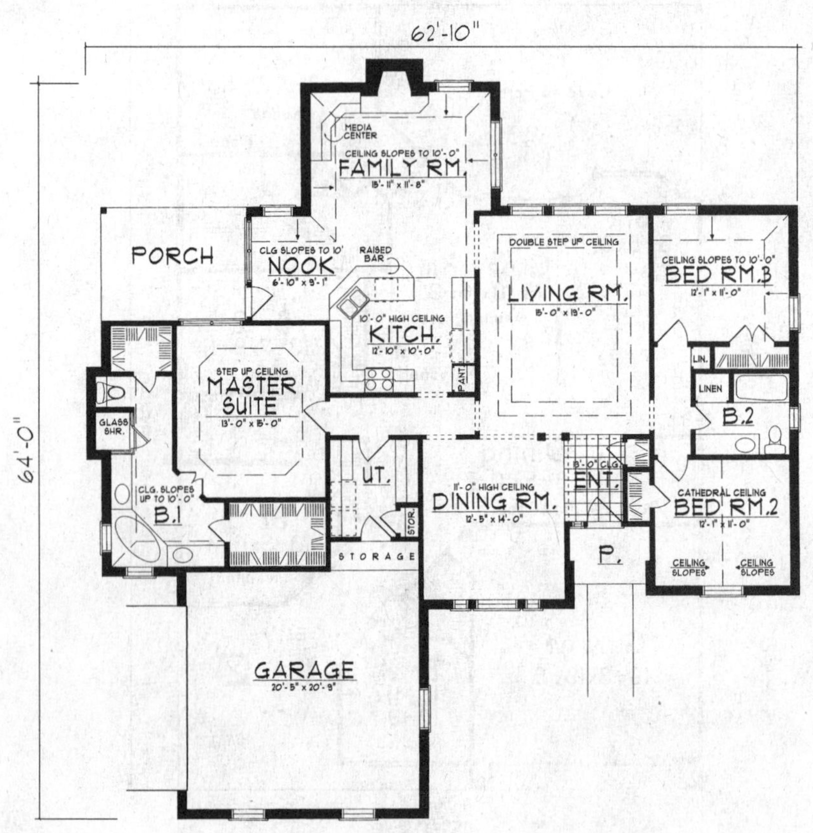
62'-10"
64'-0"
MEDIA CENTER
CEILING SLOPES TO 10'-0"
FAMILY RM.
PORCH
CLG SLOPES TO 10'
NOOK
RAISED BAR
DOUBLE STEP UP CEILING
LIVING RM.
CEILING SLOPES TO 10'-0"
BED RM.3
10'-0" HIGH CEILING
KITCH.
STEP UP CEILING
MASTER SUITE
PANT
LIN.
LINEN
B.2
GLASS SHR.
UT.
ENT.
CLG. SLOPES UP TO 10'-0"
B.1
11'-0" HIGH CEILING
DINING RM.
CATHEDRAL CEILING
BED RM.2
STOR
STORAGE
P.
CEILING SLOPES
CEILING SLOPES
GARAGE

Special features

- Living room immersed in sunlight from wall of windows
- Master suite with amenities like double walk-in closets, private bath and view onto covered porch
- Cozy family room with built-in shelves and fireplace
- 3 bedrooms, 2 baths, 2-car side entry garage
- Slab or crawl space foundation, please specify when ordering

The Family
Handyman

Plan #708-0809

Stylish Retreat For A Narrow Lot

1,084 total square feet of living area **Price Code AA**

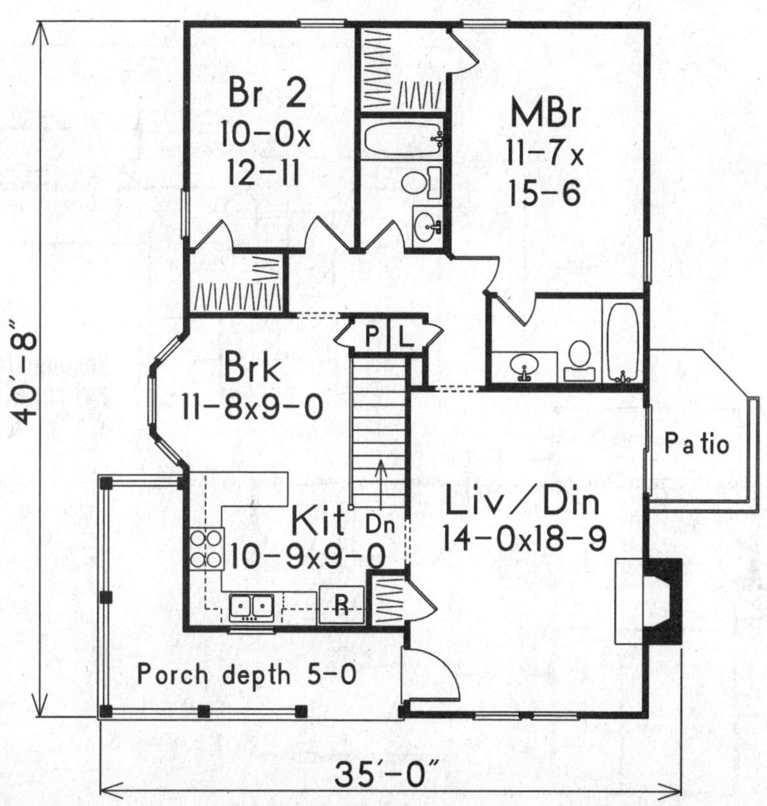
Br 2
10-0x
12-11
MBr
11-7x
15-6
P
L
Brk
11-8x9-0
Patio
Kit
Dn
10-9x9-0
R
Liv/Din
14-0x18-9
Porch depth 5-0
40'-8"
35'-0"

Special features

- Delightful country porch for quiet evenings
- Living room has a front feature window which invites the sun and includes a fireplace and dining area with private patio
- The U-shaped kitchen features lots of cabinets and bayed breakfast room with built-in pantry
- Both bedrooms have walk-in closets and access to their own bath
- 2 bedrooms, 2 baths
- Basement foundation

Second Floor Is A Child's Dream

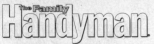

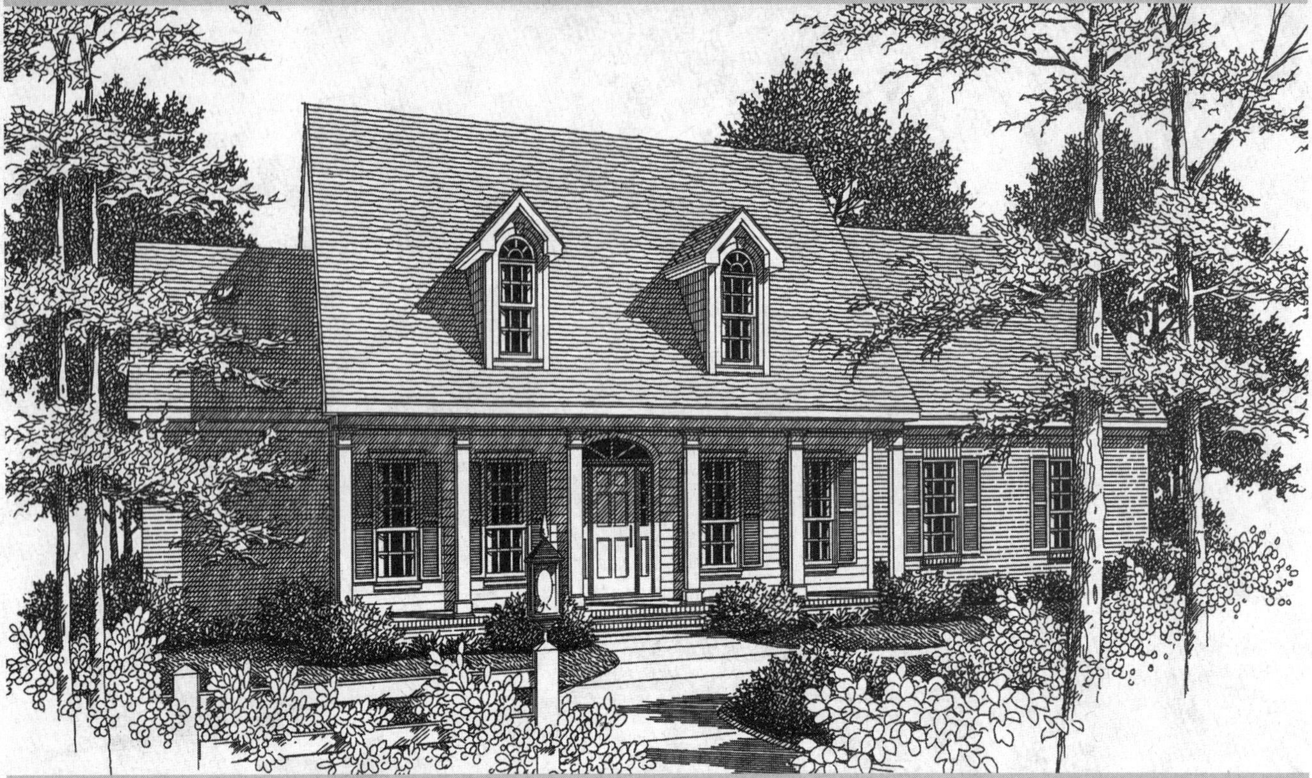

2,279 total square feet of living area | Price Code D

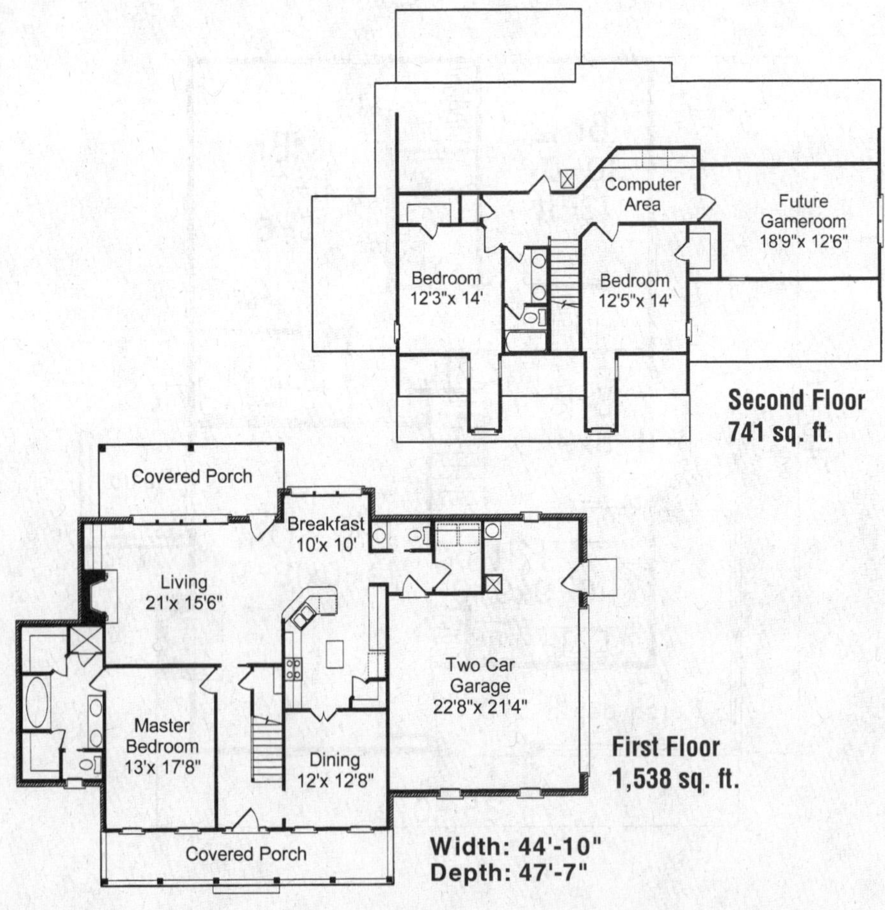
Computer Area
Future Gameroom 18'9"x 12'6"
Bedroom 12'3"x 14'
Bedroom 12'5"x 14'
Second Floor 741 sq. ft.
Covered Porch
Breakfast 10'x 10'
Living 21'x 15'6"
Two Car Garage 22'8"x 21'4"
Master Bedroom 13'x 17'8"
Dining 12'x 12'8"
Covered Porch
First Floor 1,538 sq. ft.
Width: 44'-10"
Depth: 47'-7"

<u>*Special features*</u>

- Kitchen overlooks living area with fireplace and lots of windows
- Conveniently located first floor master bedroom
- Second floor features computer area with future game room space
- 3 bedrooms, 2 1/2 baths, 2-car side entry garage
- Slab foundation

The Family
Handyman

Plan #708-0503

Open Living Spaces

1,000 total square feet of living area **Price Code AA**

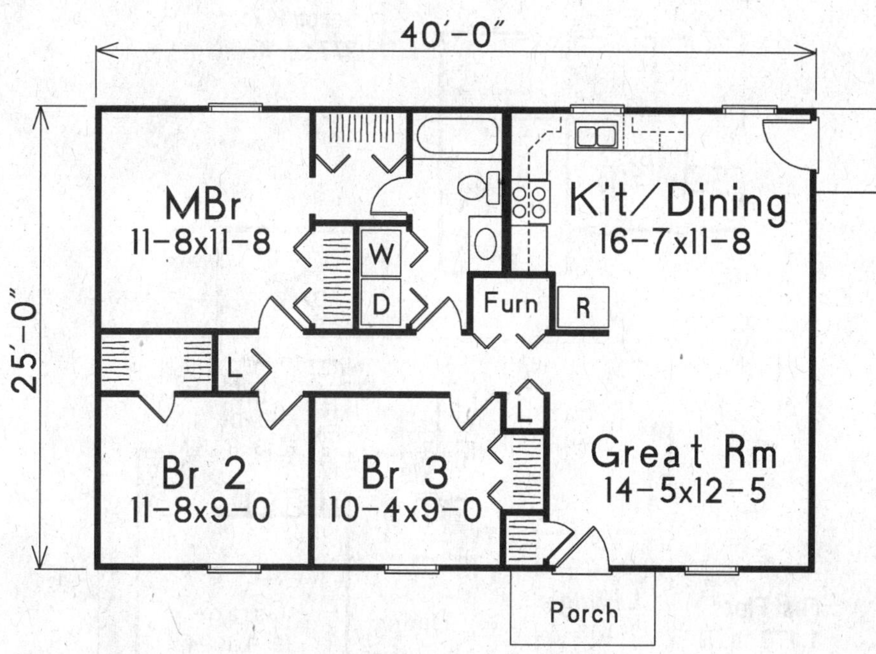
40′–0″
25′–0″
MBr
11–8x11–8
W
D
Furn
R
Kit/Dining
16–7x11–8
L
L
Br 2
11–8x9–0
Br 3
10–4x9–0
Great Rm
14–5x12–5
Porch

Special features

- Bath includes convenient closeted laundry area
- Master bedroom includes double closets and private access to bath
- Foyer features handy coat closet
- L-shaped kitchen provides easy access outdoors
- 3 bedrooms, 1 bath
- Crawl space foundation, drawings also include basement and slab foundations

The Family Handyman

Plan #708-0318

Spacious Family Room For Growing Families

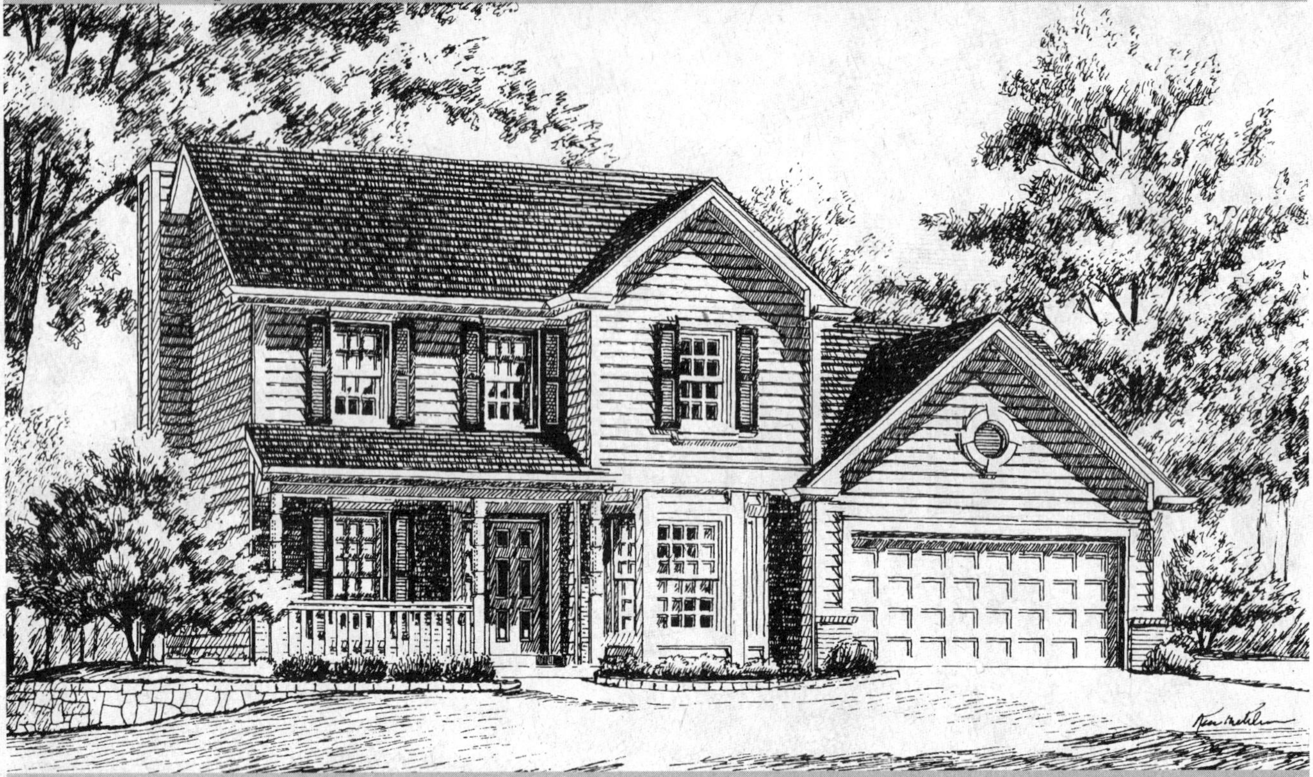

2,147 total square feet of living area

Price Code C

Special features

- Living and dining rooms adjacent to entry foyer for easy access
- Kitchen conveniently located next to sunny breakfast nook
- Master bedroom includes large walk-in closet and luxurious bath
- Breakfast area offers easy access to deck
- 4 bedrooms, 2 1/2 baths, 2-car garage
- Basement foundation

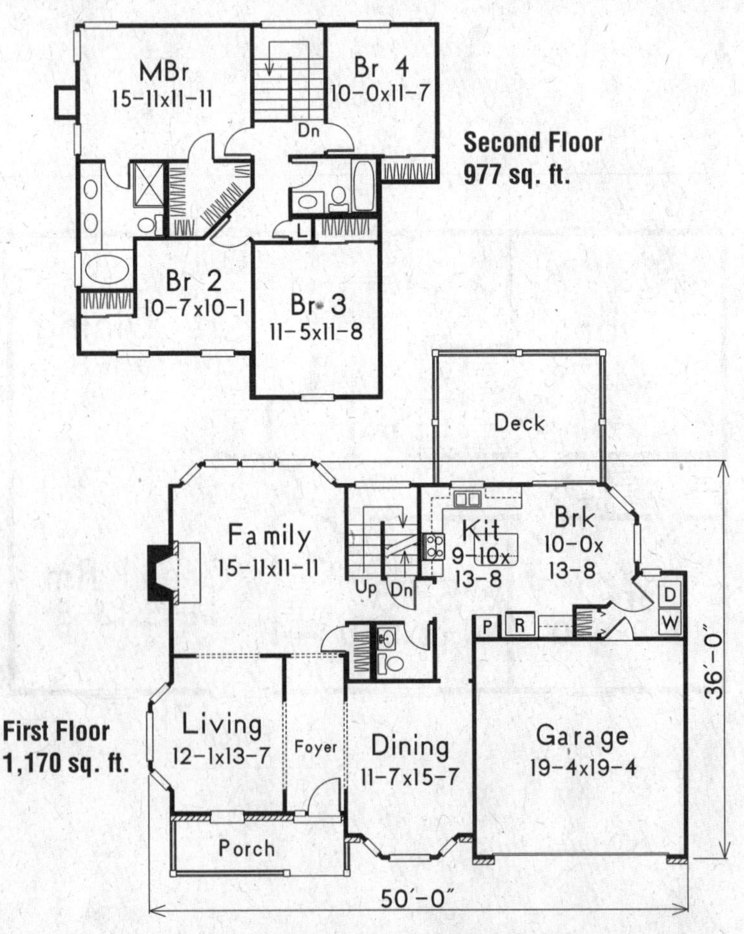
MBr
15-11x11-11
Br 4
10-0x11-7
Dn
L
Br 2
10-7x10-1
Br 3
11-5x11-8
Second Floor
977 sq. ft.
Deck
Family
15-11x11-11
Up
Dn
Kit
9-10x
13-8
Brk
10-0x
13-8
D
W
P
R
Living
12-1x13-7
Foyer
Dining
11-7x15-7
Garage
19-4x19-4
Porch
First Floor
1,170 sq. ft.
36'-0"
50'-0"

Plan #708-0823

Sensational Home Designed For Views

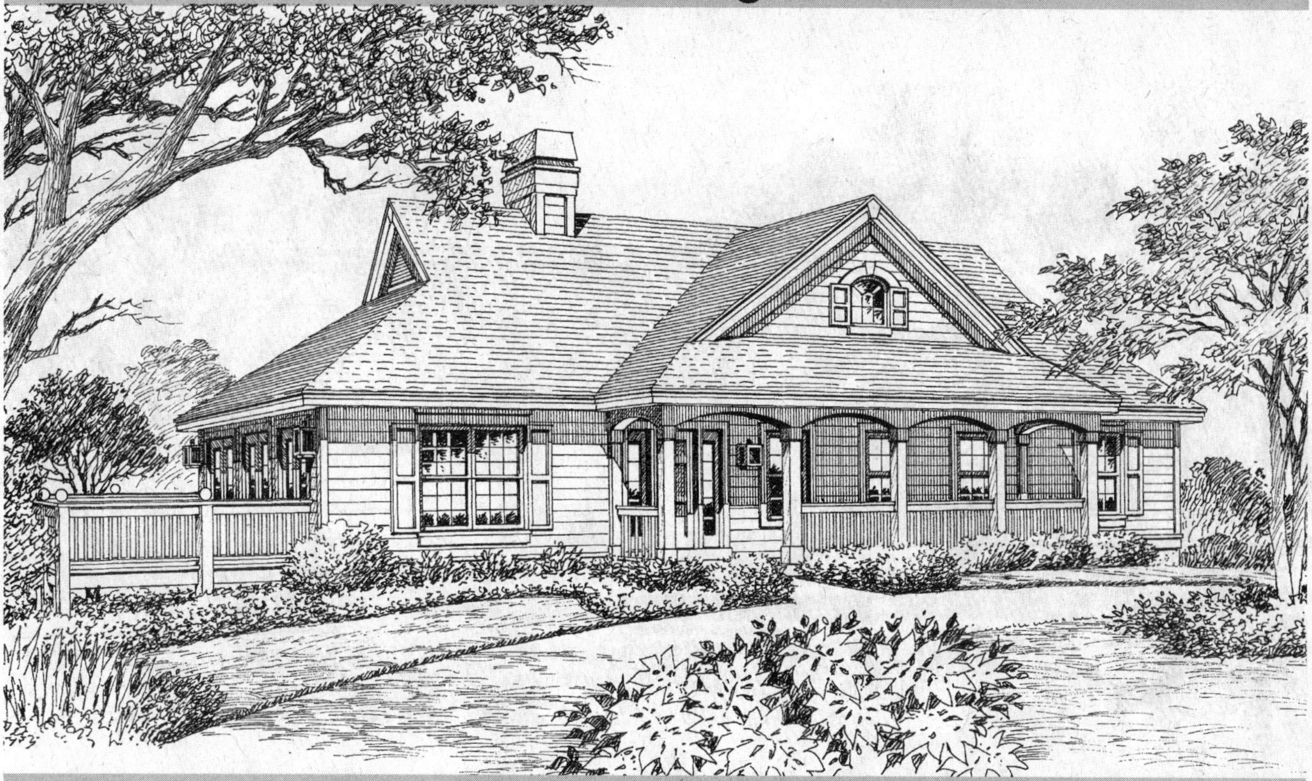

1,621 total square feet of living area **Price Code B**

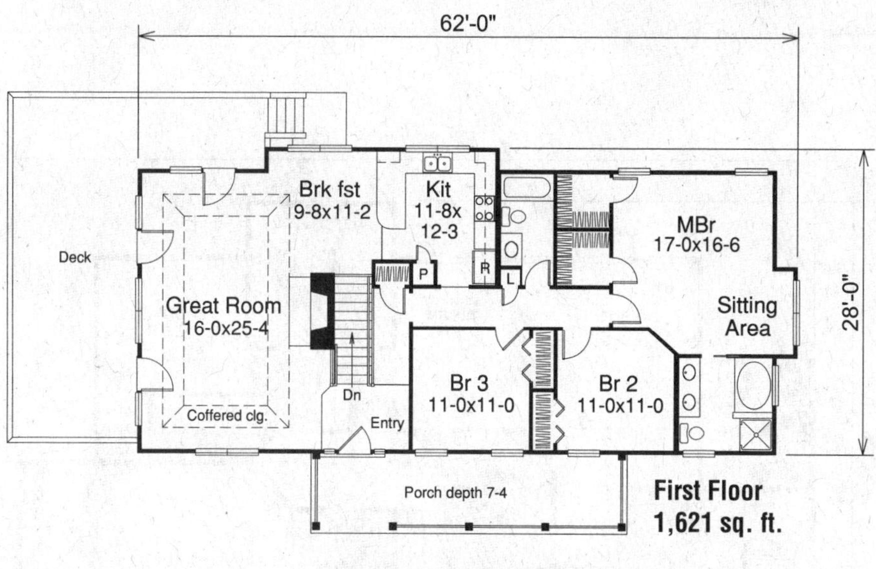

62'-0"
28'-0"
Deck
Brk fst
9-8x11-2
Kit
11-8x
12-3
P
R
L
MBr
17-0x16-6
Great Room
16-0x25-4
Sitting
Area
Br 3
11-0x11-0
Br 2
11-0x11-0
Dn
Entry
Coffered clg.
Porch depth 7-4

First Floor
1,621 sq. ft.

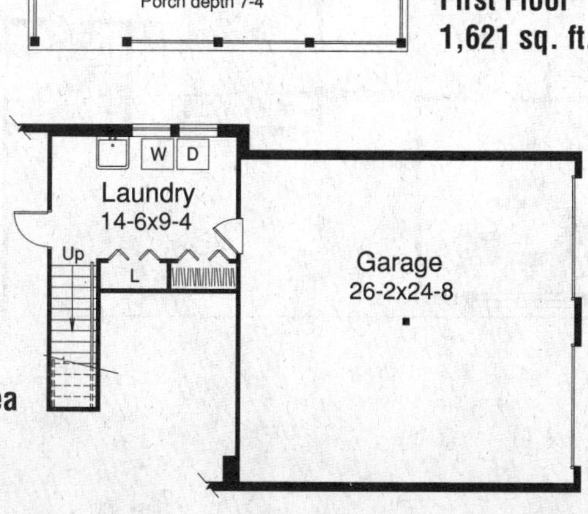

W D
Laundry
14-6x9-4
Up
L
Garage
26-2x24-8

Lower Level With Optional Laundry Area

Special features

- The front exterior includes an attractive gable-end arched window and extra deep porch
- A grand-scale great room enjoys a coffered ceiling, fireplace, access to the wrap-around deck and is brightly lit with numerous French doors and windows
- The master bedroom suite has a sitting area, his and hers walk-in closets and a luxury bath
- 223 square feet of optional laundry area on the lower level
- 3 bedrooms, 2 baths, 2-car drive under side entry garage
- Basement foundation

TO ORDER BLUEPRINTS USE THE FORM ON PAGE 15 OR CALL TOLL-FREE 1-877-671-6036

The Family
Handyman

Plan #708-JFD-10-1436-1

Dramatic Cathedral Ceilings

M. MAXON

1,436 total square feet of living area **Price Code A**

Special features

- Covered entry is inviting
- Kitchen has handy breakfast bar which overlooks great room and dining room
- Private master suite with bath and walk-in closet is separate from other bedrooms
- 3 bedrooms, 2 baths, 2-car garage
- Basement foundation

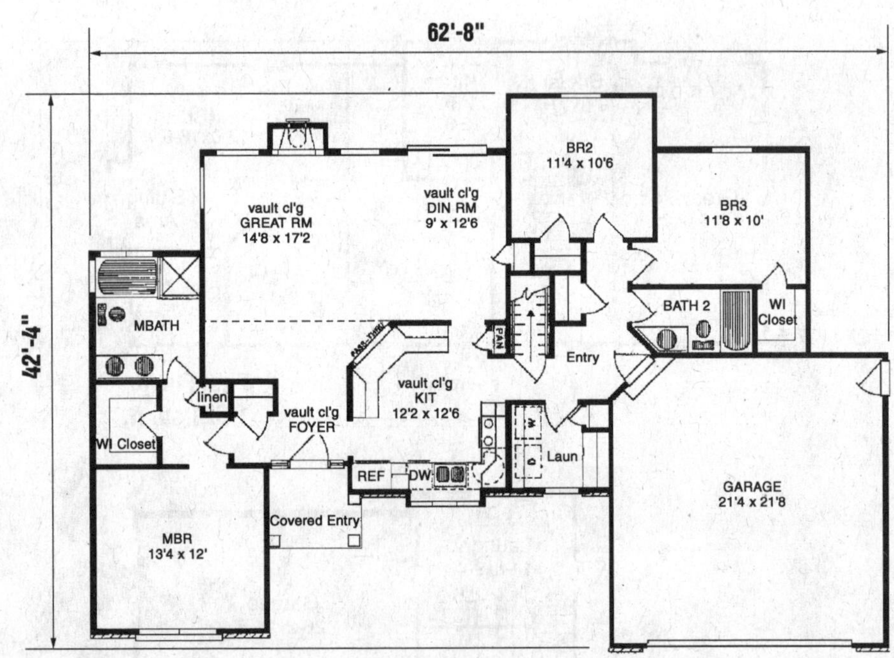
62'-8"
42'-4"
BR2
11'4 x 10'6
BR3
11'8 x 10'
vault cl'g
GREAT RM
14'8 x 17'2
vault cl'g
DIN RM
9' x 12'6
MBATH
BATH 2
WI Closet
PAN
Entry
vault cl'g
KIT
12'2 x 12'6
linen
vault cl'g
FOYER
WI Closet
REF
DW
Laun
GARAGE
21'4 x 21'8
MBR
13'4 x 12'
Covered Entry

TO ORDER BLUEPRINTS USE THE FORM ON PAGE 15 OR CALL TOLL-FREE 1-877-671-6036

View thousands more home plans online at www.familyhandyman.com/homeplans

Plan #708-0370

Atrium's Dramatic Ambiance, Compliments Of Windows

1,721 total square feet of living area **Price Code C**

Rear View

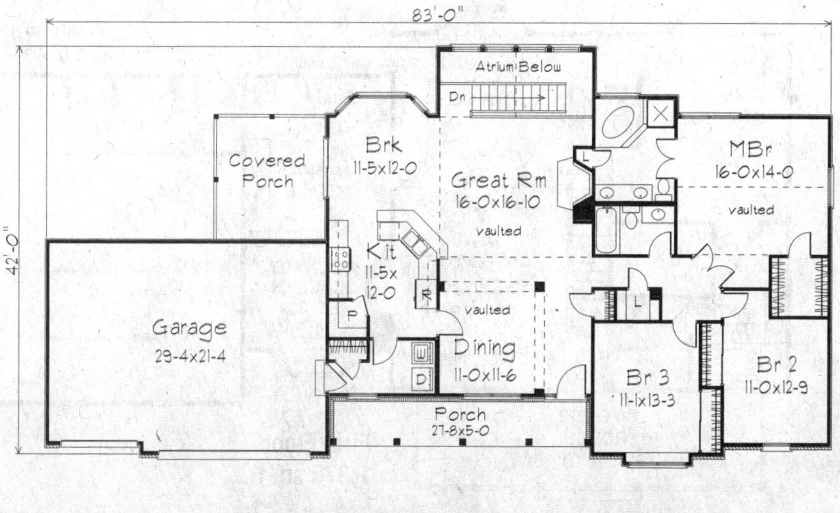

83'-0"
42'-0"
Atrium Below
Dn
Brk 11-5x12-0
Covered Porch
Great Rm 16-0x16-10 vaulted
MBr 16-0x14-0 vaulted
Kit 11-5x12-0
vaulted
Garage 29-4x21-4
Dining 11-0x11-6
Br 3 11-1x13-3
Br 2 11-0x12-9
Porch 27-8x5-0

Special features

- Roof dormers add great curb appeal
- Vaulted dining and great rooms immersed in light from atrium window wall
- Breakfast room opens onto covered porch
- Functionally designed kitchen
- 3 bedrooms, 2 baths, 3-car garage
- Walk-out basement foundation, drawings also include crawl space and slab foundations

TO ORDER BLUEPRINTS USE THE FORM ON PAGE 15 OR CALL TOLL-FREE 1-877-671-6036

View thousands more home plans online at www.familyhandyman.com/homeplans

Plan #708-AX-93311

Affordable Country-Style Living

1,945 total square feet of living area **Price Code D**

Special features

- Great room has a stepped ceiling and a fireplace
- Bayed dining area with stepped ceiling and French door leading to a covered porch
- Master bedroom has a tray ceiling, a bay window and a large walk-in closet
- 3 bedrooms, 2 1/2 baths, 2-car side entry garage
- Basement, crawl space or slab foundation, please specify when ordering

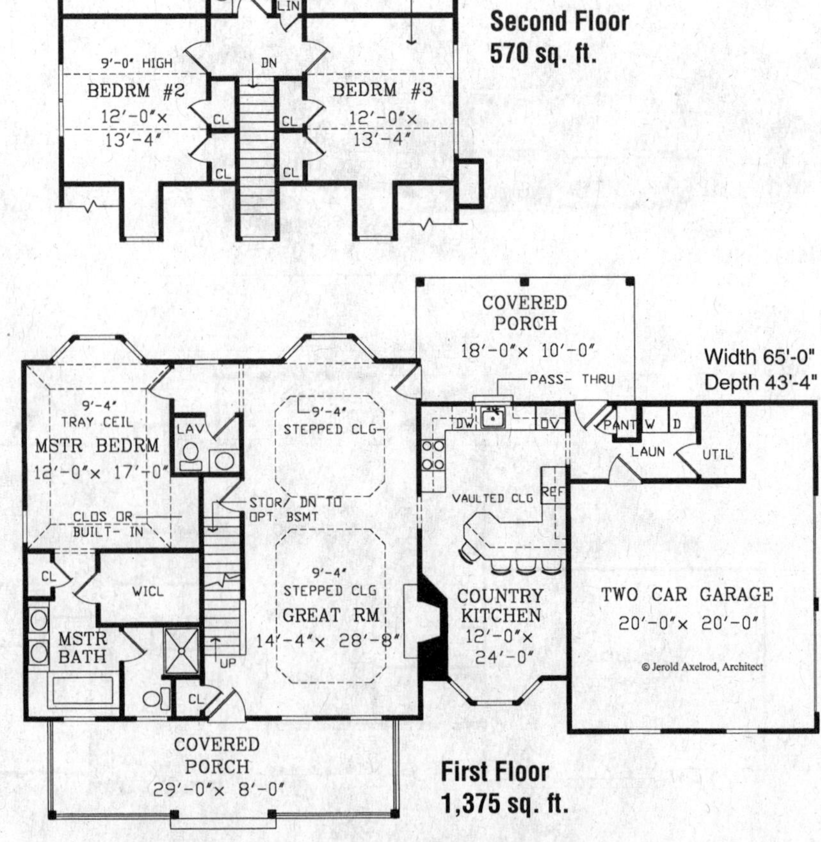
BATH
VAULTED CLG
LIN
9'-0" HIGH
DN
BEDRM #2
12'-0"× 13'-4"
CL
CL
BEDRM #3
12'-0"× 13'-4"
CL
CL
Second Floor
570 sq. ft.
COVERED PORCH
18'-0"× 10'-0"
PASS- THRU
Width 65'-0"
Depth 43'-4"
9'-4" TRAY CEIL
MSTR BEDRM
12'-0"× 17'-0"
LAV
9'-4" STEPPED CLG
DW
DW
PANT
W
D
LAUN
UTIL
STOR/ DN TO OPT. BSMT
VAULTED CLG
REF
CLOS OR BUILT- IN
CL
WICL
9'-4" STEPPED CLG
GREAT RM
14'-4"× 28'-8"
COUNTRY KITCHEN
12'-0"× 24'-0"
TWO CAR GARAGE
20'-0"× 20'-0"
MSTR BATH
UP
CL
© Jerold Axelrod, Architect
COVERED PORCH
29'-0"× 8'-0"
First Floor
1,375 sq. ft.

TO ORDER BLUEPRINTS USE THE FORM ON PAGE 15 OR CALL TOLL-FREE 1-877-671-6036

View thousands more home plans online at www.familyhandyman.com/homeplans

The Family
Handyman

Plan #708-FDG-7773

One-Level Living At Its Best

1,653 total square feet of living area **Price Code B**

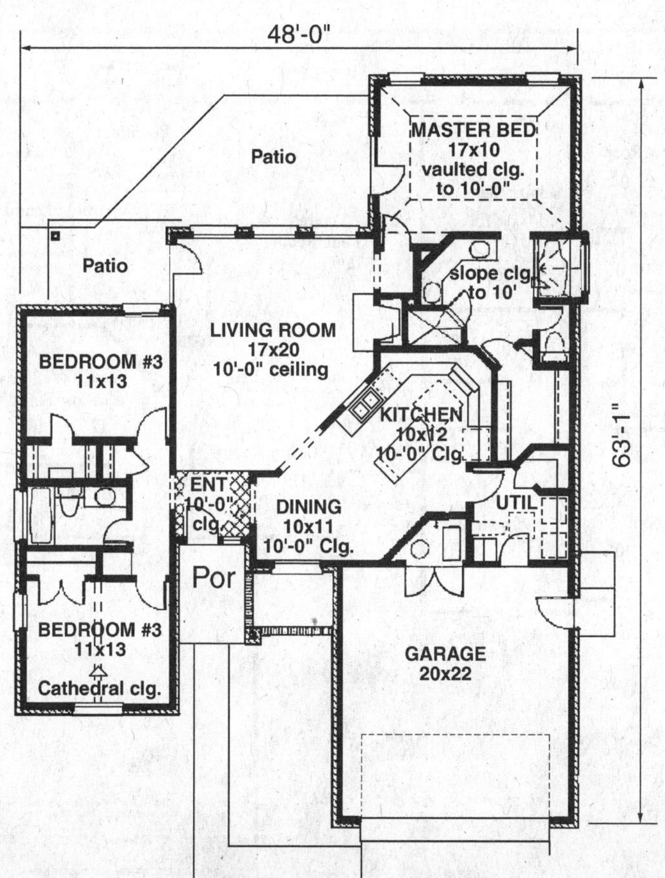
48'-0"
63'-1"
Patio
MASTER BED
17x10
vaulted clg.
to 10'-0"
Patio
slope clg
to 10'
LIVING ROOM
17x20
10'-0" ceiling
BEDROOM #3
11x13
KITCHEN
10x12
10'-0" Clg.
ENT
10'-0"
clg.
DINING
10x11
10'-0" Clg.
UTIL
Por
BEDROOM #3
11x13
Cathedral clg.
GARAGE
20x22

Special features

- Open kitchen accesses living room and backyard through sliding glass doors
- Master bedroom is separated from rest of the bedrooms for privacy
- Handy work island in kitchen
- 3 bedrooms, 2 baths, 2-car garage
- Slab foundation

Plan #708-FB1119

Bayed Breakfast Room

1,915 total square feet of living area **Price Code C**

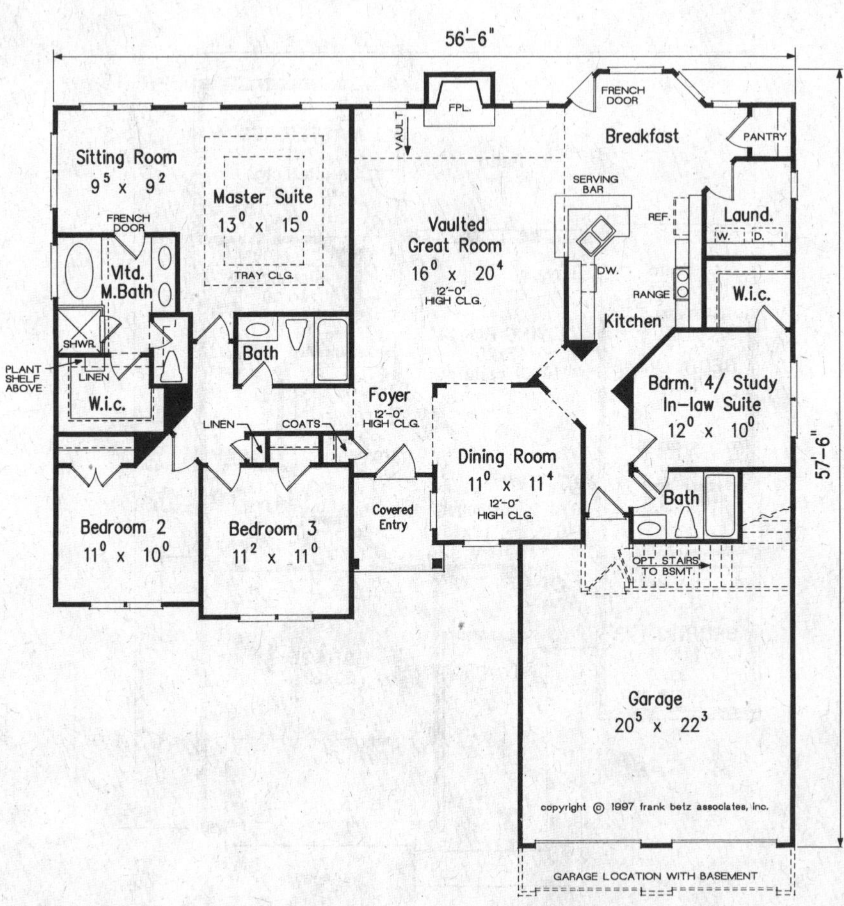
56'-6"
FPL.
VAULT
FRENCH DOOR
Breakfast
PANTRY
Sitting Room
9^5 x 9^2
Master Suite
13^0 x 15^0
TRAY CLG.
FRENCH DOOR
Vtd. M.Bath
SHWR.
LINEN
W.i.c.
PLANT SHELF ABOVE
Bath
SERVING BAR
Vaulted Great Room
16^0 x 20^4
12'-0" HIGH CLG.
REF.
DW.
RANGE
Laund.
W. D.
W.i.c.
Kitchen
Bdrm. 4/ Study In-law Suite
12^0 x 10^0
Foyer
12'-0" HIGH CLG.
LINEN
COATS
Dining Room
11^0 x 11^4
12'-0" HIGH CLG.
Covered Entry
Bath
OPT. STAIRS TO BSMT.
Bedroom 2
11^0 x 10^0
Bedroom 3
11^2 x 11^0
57'-6"
Garage
20^5 x 22^3
copyright © 1997 frank betz associates, inc.
GARAGE LOCATION WITH BASEMENT

Special features

- Large breakfast area overlooks vaulted great room
- Master suite has cheerful sitting room and a private bath
- Plan features unique in-law suite with private bath and walk-in closet
- 4 bedrooms, 3 baths, 2-car garage
- Walk-out basement, slab or crawl space foundation, please specify when ordering

TO ORDER BLUEPRINTS USE THE FORM ON PAGE 15 OR CALL TOLL-FREE 1-877-671-6036

View thousands more home plans online at www.familyhandyman.com/homeplans

The Family
Handyman

Plan #708-0747

Classic Atrium Ranch With Rooms To Spare

1,977 total square feet of living area | **Price Code C**

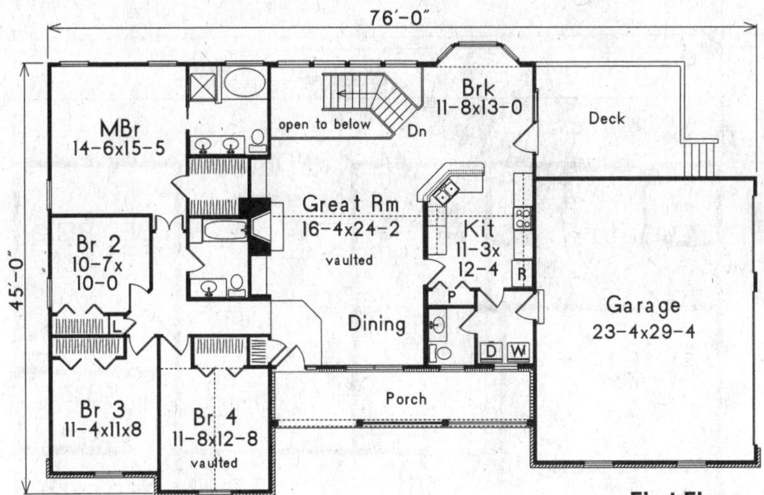
76'-0"
45'-0"
MBr
14-6x15-5
open to below
Dn
Brk
11-8x13-0
Deck
Great Rm
16-4x24-2
vaulted
Kit
11-3x
12-4
Br 2
10-7x
10-0
Dining
Garage
23-4x29-4
Br 3
11-4x11x8
Br 4
11-8x12-8
vaulted
Porch

First Floor
1,977 sq. ft.

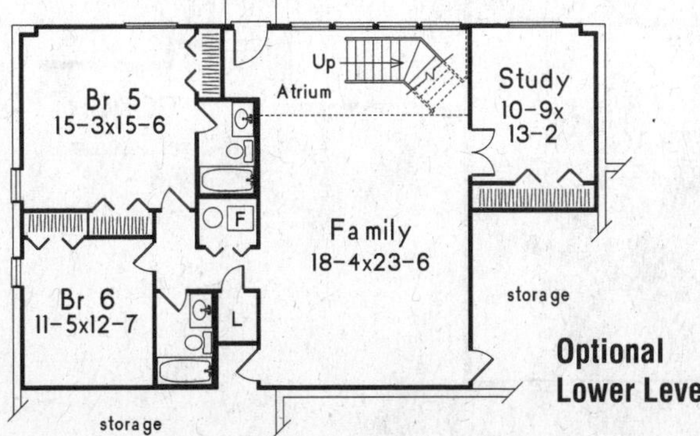
Up
Atrium
Br 5
15-3x15-6
Study
10-9x
13-2
Family
18-4x23-6
Br 6
11-5x12-7
storage
storage

Optional
Lower Level

Special features

- Classic traditional exterior always in style
- Spacious great room boasts a vaulted ceiling, dining area, atrium with elegant staircase and feature windows
- Atrium open to 1,416 square feet of optional living area below which consists of an optional family room, two bedrooms, two baths and a study
- 4 bedrooms, 2 1/2 baths, 3-car side entry garage
- Walk-out basement foundation

TO ORDER BLUEPRINTS USE THE FORM ON PAGE 15 OR CALL TOLL-FREE 1-877-671-6036

The Family
Handyman

Plan #708-RDD-1374-9

Scalloped Front Porch

1,374 total square feet of living area

Price Code A

Special features

- Garage has extra storage space
- Spacious living room has fireplace
- Well-designed kitchen with adjacent breakfast nook
- Separated master suite maintains privacy
- 3 bedrooms, 2 baths, 2-car garage
- Slab or crawl space foundation, please specify when ordering

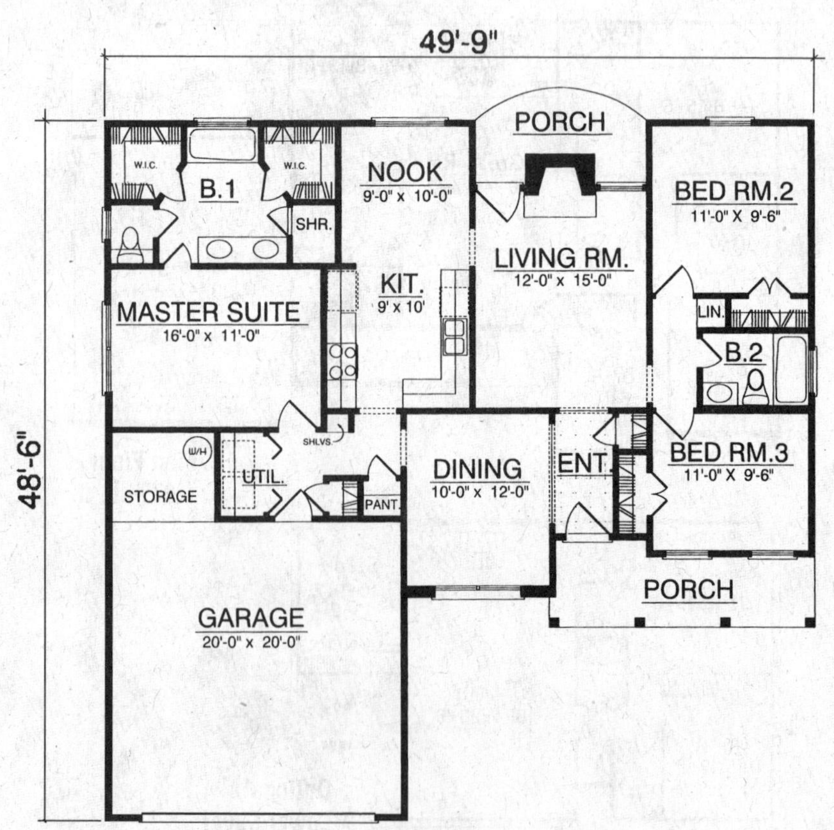

49'-9"
48'-6"
PORCH
W.I.C.
B.1
W.I.C.
SHR.
NOOK
9'-0" x 10'-0"
LIVING RM.
12'-0" x 15'-0"
BED RM.2
11'-0" X 9'-6"
KIT.
9' x 10'
MASTER SUITE
16'-0" x 11'-0"
LIN.
B.2
W/H
SHLVS.
UTIL.
STORAGE
PANT.
DINING
10'-0" x 12'-0"
ENT.
BED RM.3
11'-0" X 9'-6"
PORCH
GARAGE
20'-0" x 20'-0"

TO ORDER BLUEPRINTS USE THE FORM ON PAGE 15 OR CALL TOLL-FREE 1-877-671-6036

View thousands more home plans online at www.familyhandyman.com/homeplans

Uncommon Style With This Ranch

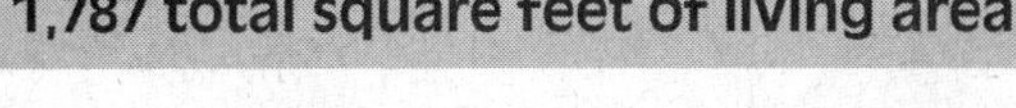

1,787 total square feet of living area **Price Code B**

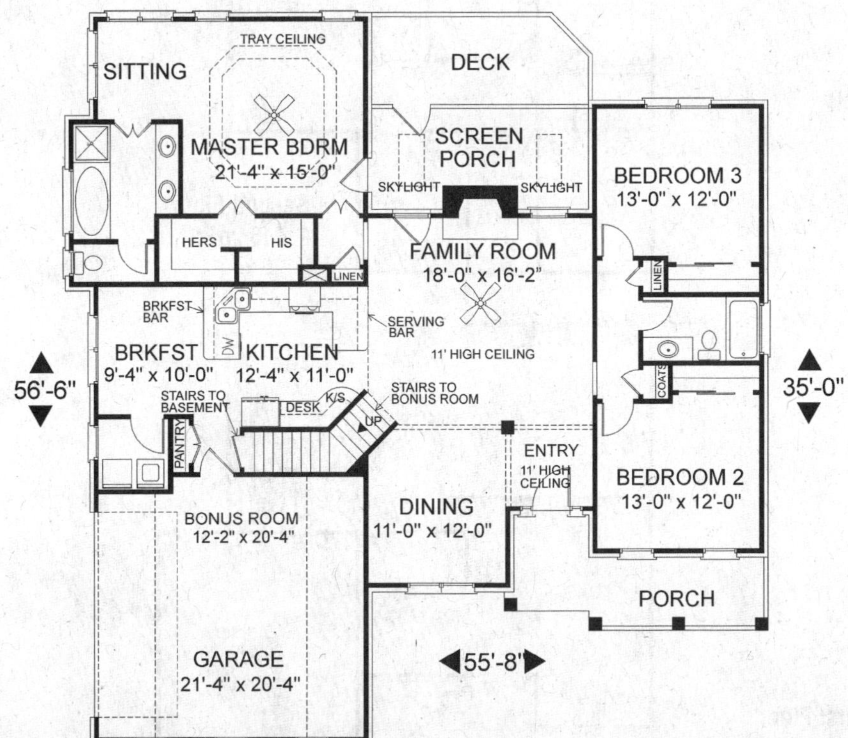
TRAY CEILING
SITTING
DECK
MASTER BDRM
21'-4" x 15'-0"
SCREEN PORCH
SKYLIGHT
SKYLIGHT
BEDROOM 3
13'-0" x 12'-0"
HERS
HIS
LINEN
FAMILY ROOM
18'-0" x 16'-2"
BRKFST BAR
SERVING BAR
DW
BRKFST
9'-4" x 10'-0"
KITCHEN
12'-4" x 11'-0"
11' HIGH CEILING
COATS
56'-6"
35'-0"
STAIRS TO BASEMENT
DESK
K/S
STAIRS TO BONUS ROOM
UP
PANTRY
ENTRY
11' HIGH CEILING
BEDROOM 2
13'-0" x 12'-0"
BONUS ROOM
12'-2" x 20'-4"
DINING
11'-0" x 12'-0"
PORCH
GARAGE
21'-4" x 20'-4"
55'-8"

Special features

- Skylights brighten screened porch which connects to family room and deck outdoors
- Master bedroom features a comfortable sitting area, large private bath and direct access to screened porch
- Kitchen has serving bar which extends dining into family room
- 3 bedrooms, 2 baths, 2-car side entry garage
- Basement, crawl space or slab foundation, please specify when ordering

TO ORDER BLUEPRINTS USE THE FORM ON PAGE 15 OR CALL TOLL-FREE 1-877-671-6036

View thousands more home plans online at www.familyhandyman.com/homeplans

The Family
Handyman

Plan #708-0365

Impressive Two-Story Entry Boasts Popular T-Stair

2,336 total square feet of living area **Price Code D**

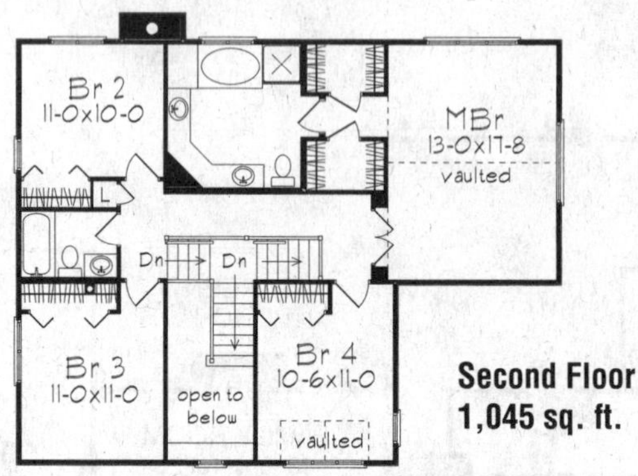

Br 2
11-0x10-0
MBr
13-0x17-8
vaulted
Dn
Dn
Br 3
11-0x11-0
open to below
Br 4
10-6x11-0
vaulted

Second Floor
1,045 sq. ft.

Special features

- Stately sunken living room with partially vaulted ceiling and classic arched transom windows
- Family room features plenty of windows and a fireplace with flanking bookshelves
- 4 bedrooms, 2 1/2 baths, 2-car garage
- Basement foundation

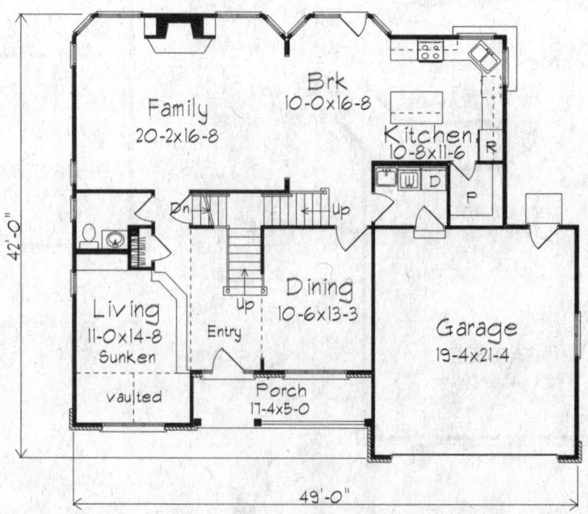

Family
20-2x16-8
Brk
10-0x16-8
Kitchen
10-8x11-6
R
W
D
P
Dn
Up
Up
Living
11-0x14-8
Sunken
vaulted
Entry
Dining
10-6x13-3
Porch
17-4x5-0
Garage
19-4x21-4
42'-0"
49'-0"

First Floor
1,291 sq. ft.

TO ORDER BLUEPRINTS USE THE FORM ON PAGE 15 OR CALL TOLL-FREE 1-877-671-6036

View thousands more home plans online at www.familyhandyman.com/homeplans

The Family
Handyman

Plan #708-DBI-2461

Convenient Wet Bar

1,850 total square feet of living area

Price Code C

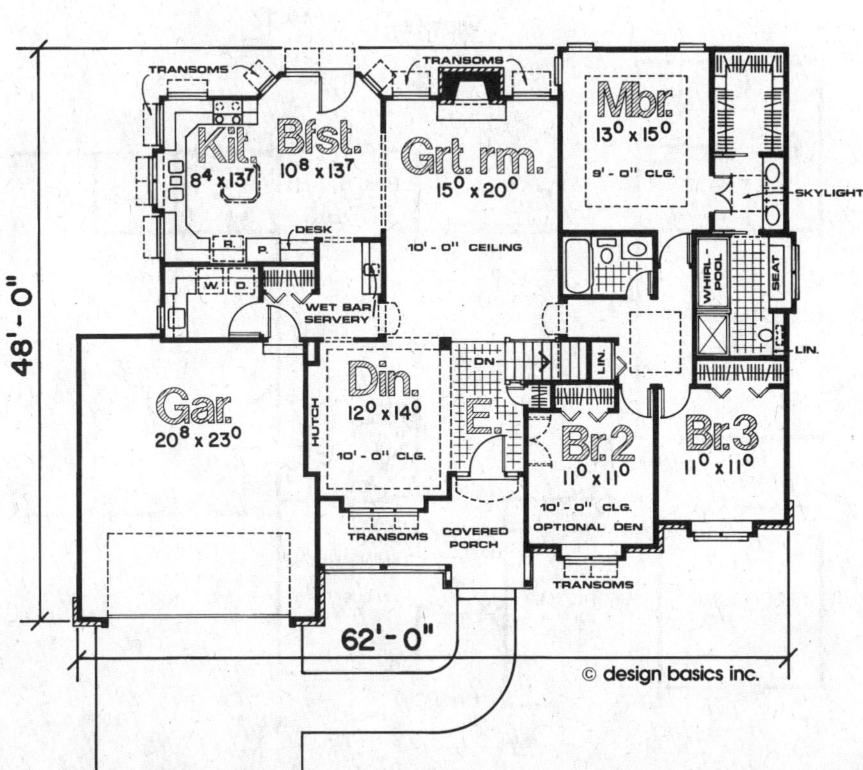
TRANSOMS
TRANSOMS
Kit.
8^4 x 13^7
Bfst.
10^8 x 13^7
Grt. rm.
15^0 x 20^0
10'-0" CEILING
Mbr.
13^0 x 15^0
9'-0" CLG.
SKYLIGHT
DESK
R.
P.
W.
D.
WET BAR
SERVERY
WHIRL-POOL
SEAT
LIN.
LIN.
DN
Gar.
20^8 x 23^0
HUTCH
Din.
12^0 x 14^0
10'-0" CLG.
E.
Br. 2
11^0 x 11^0
10'-0" CLG.
OPTIONAL DEN
Br. 3
11^0 x 11^0
TRANSOMS
COVERED PORCH
TRANSOMS
48'-0"
62'-0"
© design basics inc.

Special features

- Oversized rooms throughout
- Great room spotlights fireplace with sunny windows on both sides
- Master bedroom has private skylighted bath
- Interesting wet bar between kitchen and dining area is an added bonus when entertaining
- 3 bedrooms, 2 baths, 2-car garage
- Basement foundation

TO ORDER BLUEPRINTS USE THE FORM ON PAGE 15 OR CALL TOLL-FREE 1-877-671-6036

Plan #708-LBD-18-11A

Formal Facade

1,890 total square feet of living area

Price Code C

Special features

- 10' ceilings give this home a spacious feel
- Efficient kitchen has breakfast bar which overlooks living room
- Master bedroom has private bath with walk-in closet
- 3 bedrooms, 2 baths, 2-car side entry garage
- Crawl space or slab foundation, please specify when ordering

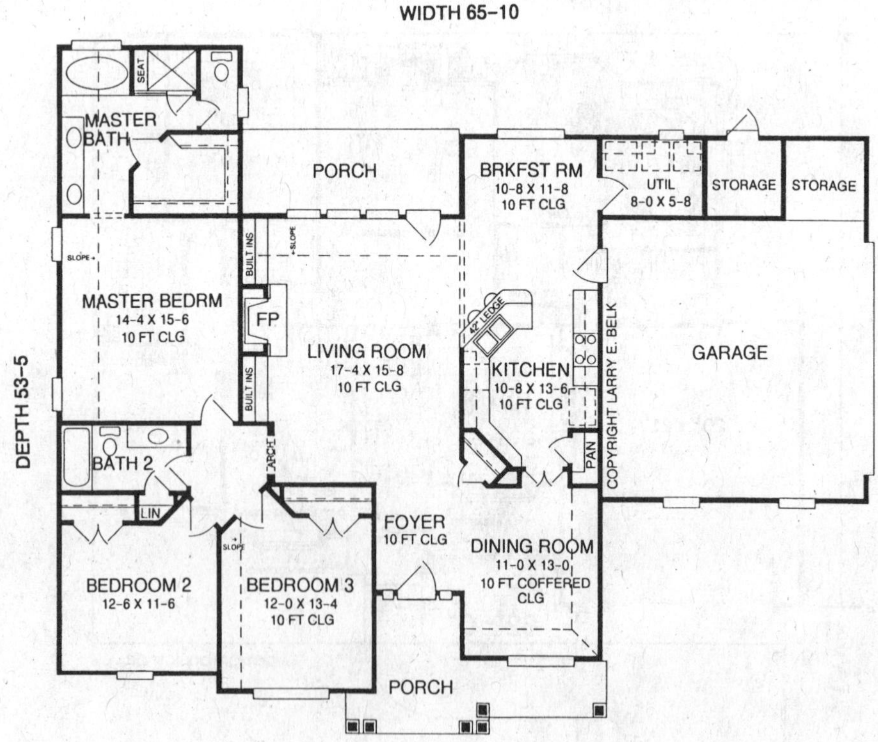
WIDTH 65–10
DEPTH 53–5
SEAT
MASTER BATH
PORCH
BRKFST RM
10-8 X 11-8
10 FT CLG
UTIL
8-0 X 5-8
STORAGE
STORAGE
SLOPE
BUILT INS
SLOPE
MASTER BEDRM
14-4 X 15-6
10 FT CLG
FP
LIVING ROOM
17-4 X 15-8
10 FT CLG
42" LEDGE
KITCHEN
10-8 X 13-6
10 FT CLG
COPYRIGHT LARRY E. BELK
GARAGE
BUILT INS
ARCH
BATH 2
PAN
LIN
FOYER
10 FT CLG
SLOPE
DINING ROOM
11-0 X 13-0
10 FT COFFERED CLG
BEDROOM 2
12-6 X 11-6
BEDROOM 3
12-0 X 13-4
10 FT CLG
PORCH

TO ORDER BLUEPRINTS USE THE FORM ON PAGE 15 OR CALL TOLL-FREE 1-877-671-6036

View thousands more home plans online at www.familyhandyman.com/homeplans

The Family
Handyman

Plan #708-0449

Charming House, Spacious And Functional

2,505 total square feet of living area — **Price Code D**

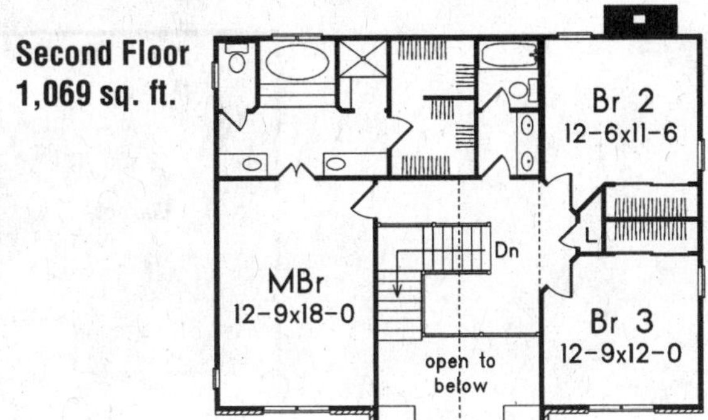

Br 2
12-6x11-6
L
Dn
MBr
12-9x18-0
Br 3
12-9x12-0
open to below

Second Floor
1,069 sq. ft.

Special features

- The garage features extra storage area and ample work space
- Laundry room accessible from the garage and the outdoors
- Deluxe raised tub and immense walk-in closet grace master bath
- 3 bedrooms, 2 1/2 baths, 2-car side entry garage
- Basement foundation, drawings also include crawl space foundation

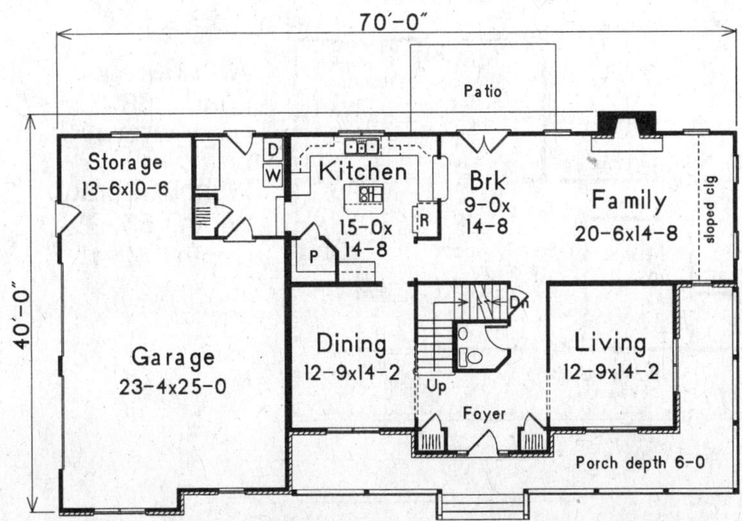

70'-0"
40'-0"
Patio
Storage
13-6x10-6
D
W
Kitchen
15-0x
14-8
R
P
Brk
9-0x
14-8
Family
20-6x14-8
sloped clg
Dn
Garage
23-4x25-0
Dining
12-9x14-2
Up
Foyer
Living
12-9x14-2
Porch depth 6-0

First Floor
1,436 sq. ft.

TO ORDER BLUEPRINTS USE THE FORM ON PAGE 15 OR CALL TOLL-FREE 1-877-671-6036

View thousands more home plans online at www.familyhandyman.com/homeplans

The Family
Handyman

Plan #708-GM-1550

Private Bedroom Area

1,550 total square feet of living area | **Price Code B**

Special features

- Wrap-around front porch is an ideal gathering place
- Handy snack bar is positioned so kitchen flows into family room
- Master bedroom has many amenities
- 3 bedrooms, 2 baths, 2-car detached garage
- Slab or crawl space foundation, please specify when ordering

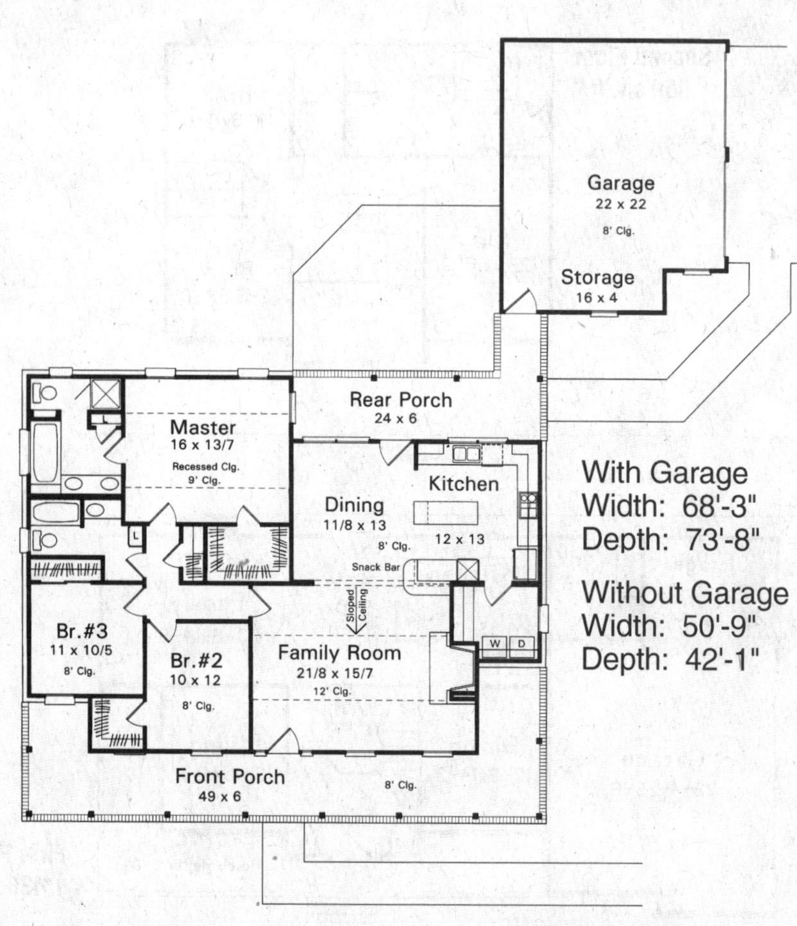
Garage
22 x 22
8' Clg.
Storage
16 x 4
Rear Porch
24 x 6
Master
16 x 13/7
Recessed Clg.
9' Clg.
Dining
11/8 x 13
8' Clg.
Kitchen
12 x 13
Snack Bar
Sloped Ceiling
W D
Br.#3
11 x 10/5
8' Clg.
Br.#2
10 x 12
8' Clg.
Family Room
21/8 x 15/7
12' Clg.
Front Porch
49 x 6
8' Clg.
With Garage
Width: 68'-3"
Depth: 73'-8"
Without Garage
Width: 50'-9"
Depth: 42'-1"

TO ORDER BLUEPRINTS USE THE FORM ON PAGE 15 OR CALL TOLL-FREE 1-877-671-6036

View thousands more home plans online at www.familyhandyman.com/homeplans

Plan #708-BF-3007

Plenty Of Built-Ins

3,012 total square feet of living area

Price Code E

Second Floor
810 sq. ft.

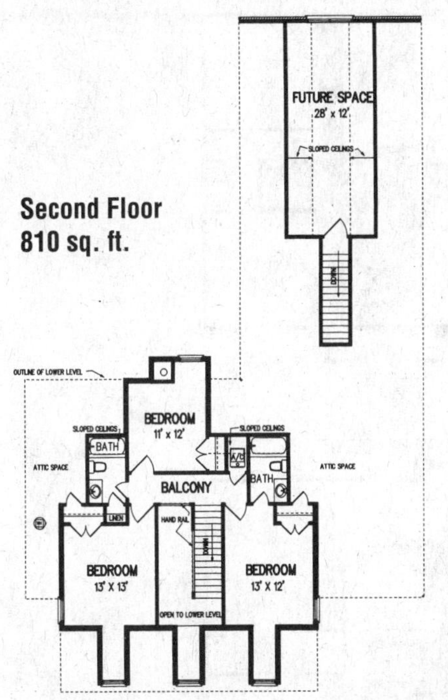
FUTURE SPACE
28' x 12'
SLOPED CEILINGS
OUTLINE OF LOWER LEVEL
BEDROOM
11' x 12'
SLOPED CEILINGS
BATH
ATTIC SPACE
BALCONY
BATH
LINEN
HAND RAIL
BEDROOM
13' X 13'
BEDROOM
13' X 12'
OPEN TO LOWER LEVEL

First Floor
2,202 sq. ft.

Width: 62'-0"
Depth: 86'-0"

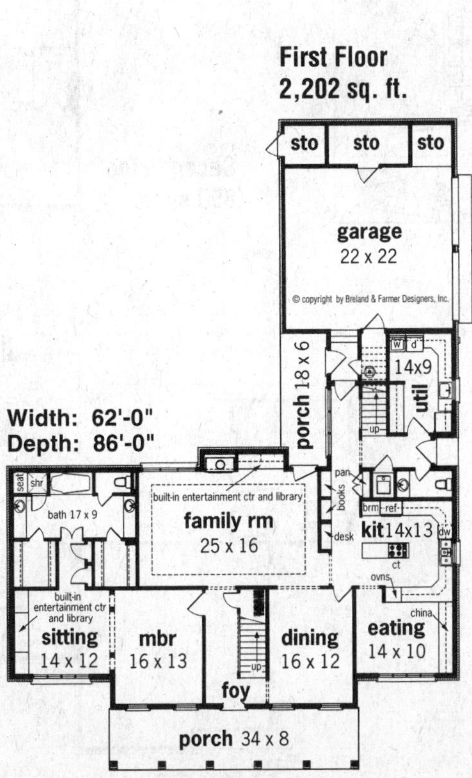
sto
sto
sto
garage
22 x 22
© copyright by Breland & Farmer Designers, Inc.
porch 18 x 6
14x9
util
up
pan
books
desk
brm
ref
kit 14x13
dw
ct
ovns
china
eating
14 x 10
seat
shr
bath 17 x 9
built-in entertainment ctr and library
family rm
25 x 16
built-in entertainment ctr and library
sitting
14 x 12
mbr
16 x 13
dining
16 x 12
up
foy
porch 34 x 8

Special features

- Master suite has sitting area with entertainment center/ library
- Utility room has a sink and includes lots of storage and counterspace
- Future space above the garage has an additional 336 square feet of living area
- 4 bedrooms, 3 1/2 baths, 2-car side entry garage
- Crawl space, slab or basement foundation, please specify when ordering

TO ORDER BLUEPRINTS USE THE FORM ON PAGE 15 OR CALL TOLL-FREE 1-877-671-6036

View thousands more home plans online at www.familyhandyman.com/homeplans

The Family
Handyman

Plan #708-0366

Irresistible Grandeur

2,624 total square feet of living area — **Price Code E**

Interior View - Master Bath

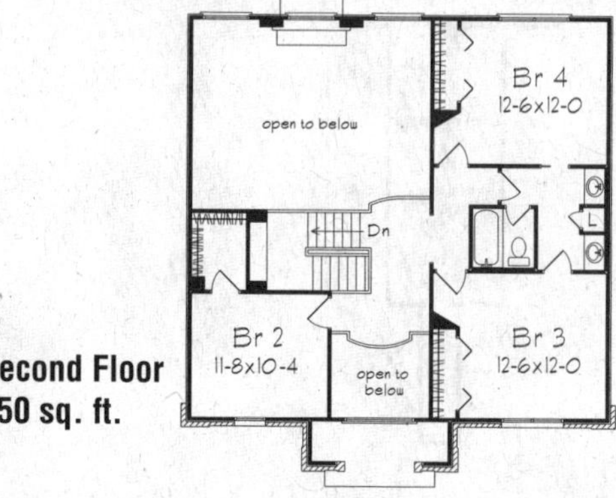
open to below
Br 4
12-6x12-0
Dn
Br 2
11-8x10-4
open to below
Br 3
12-6x12-0

Second Floor
850 sq. ft.

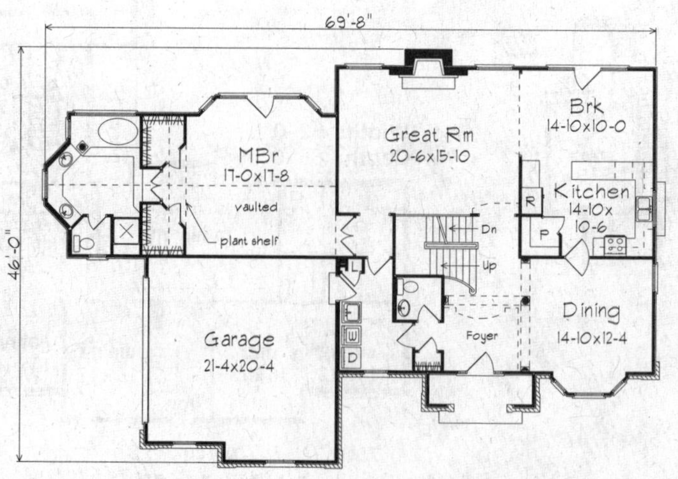
69'-8"
46'-0"
MBr
17-0x17-8
vaulted
plant shelf
Great Rm
20-6x15-10
Brk
14-10x10-0
R
Kitchen
14-10x
10-6
P
Dn
Up
Foyer
Dining
14-10x12-4
Garage
21-4x20-4
W
D

First Floor
1,774 sq. ft.

Special features

- Dramatic two-story entry opens to bayed dining room through classic colonnade
- Magnificent great room with 18' ceiling brightly lit with three palladian windows
- Master suite includes bay window, walk-in closets, plant shelves and sunken bath
- 4 bedrooms, 2 1/2 baths, 2-car side entry garage
- Basement foundation

TO ORDER BLUEPRINTS USE THE FORM ON PAGE 15 OR CALL TOLL-FREE 1-877-671-6036
View thousands more home plans online at www.familyhandyman.com/homeplans

The Family
Handyman

Plan #708-0306

Circular Stairway Adds To Front Entry

2,360 total square feet of living area | **Price Code D**

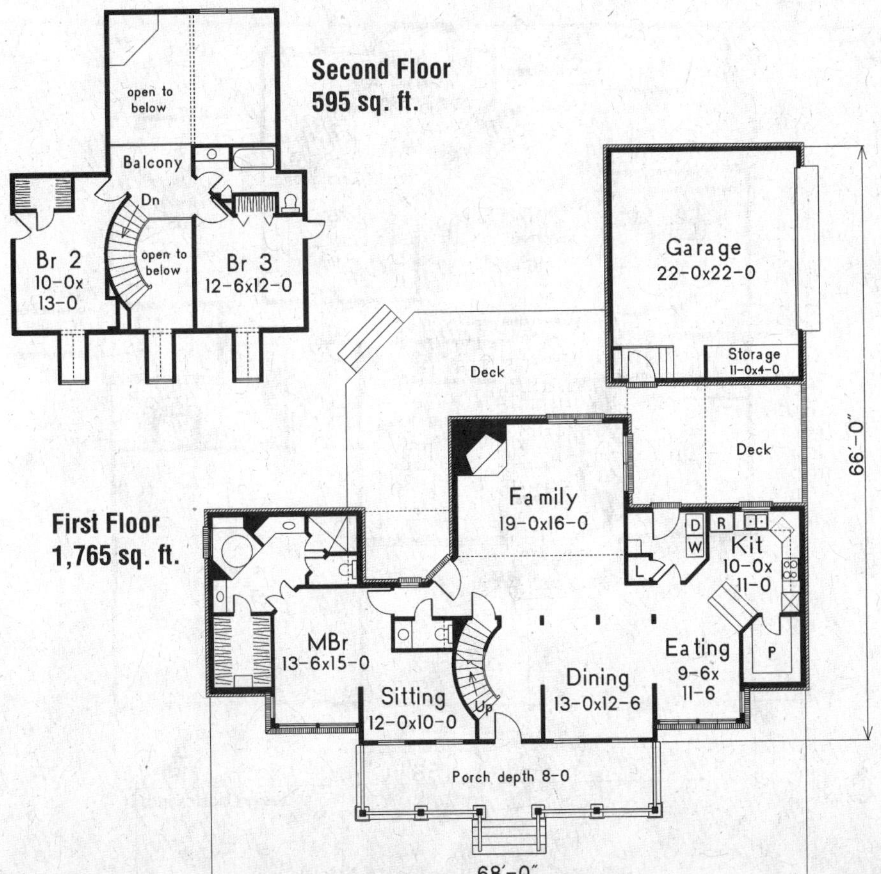
open to below
Balcony
Dn
Br 2
10-0x
13-0
open to below
Br 3
12-6x12-0
Garage
22-0x22-0
Storage
11-0x4-0
Deck
Deck
Family
19-0x16-0
Kit
10-0x
11-0
MBr
13-6x15-0
Eating
9-6x
11-6
Dining
13-0x12-6
Sitting
12-0x10-0
Up
Porch depth 8-0
68'-0"
66'-0"

Second Floor
595 sq. ft.

First Floor
1,765 sq. ft.

Special features

- Master bedroom includes sitting area and large bath
- Sloped family room ceiling provides view from second floor balcony
- Kitchen features island bar and walk-in butler's pantry
- 3 bedrooms, 2 1/2 baths, 2-car side entry garage
- Crawl space foundation, drawings also include slab and basement foundations

TO ORDER BLUEPRINTS USE THE FORM ON PAGE 15 OR CALL TOLL-FREE 1-877-671-6036

View thousands more home plans online at www.familyhandyman.com/homeplans

Plan #708-DBI-1748-19

Whirlpool With Skylight Above

1,911 total square feet of living area

Price Code C

Special features

- Large entry opens into beautiful great room with angled see-through fireplace
- Terrific design includes kitchen and breakfast area with adjacent sunny bayed hearth room
- Luxury master suite has privacy from other bedrooms
- 3 bedrooms, 2 baths, 2-car garage
- Basement foundation

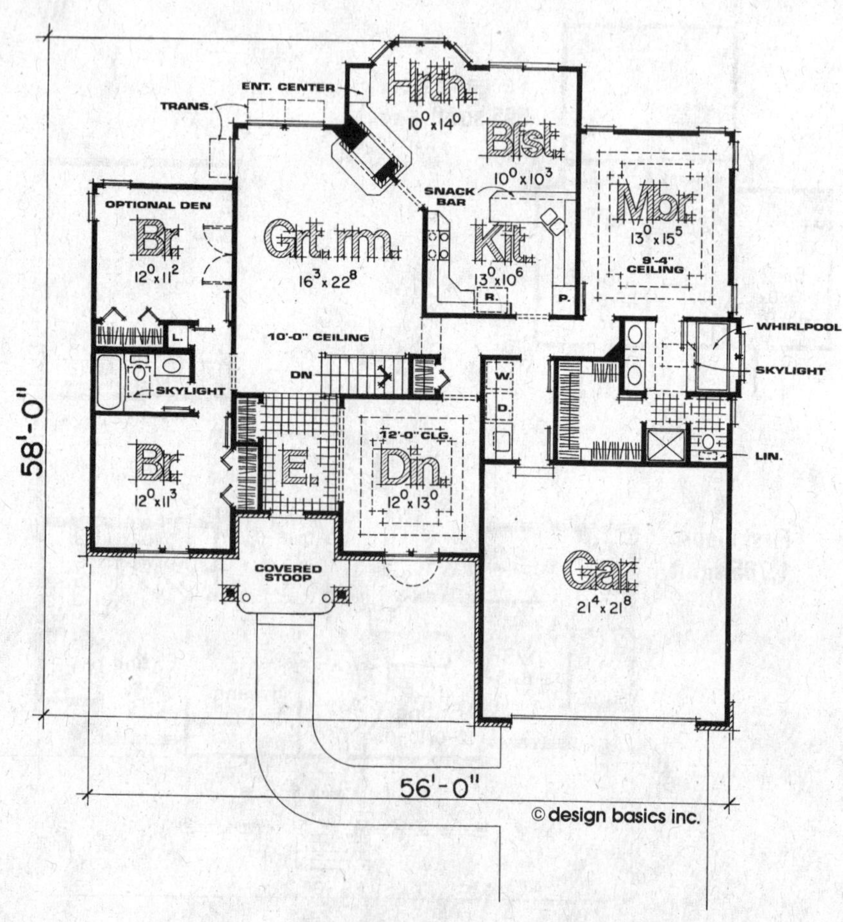
ENT. CENTER
TRANS.
Hrth.
$10^0 x 14^0$
Bfst.
$10^0 x 10^3$
SNACK BAR
OPTIONAL DEN
Br.
$12^0 x 11^2$
Grt. rm.
$16^3 x 22^8$
Kit.
$13^0 x 10^6$
R.
P.
Mbr.
$13^0 x 15^5$
9'-4" CEILING
WHIRLPOOL
SKYLIGHT
L.
10'-0" CEILING
DN
SKYLIGHT
W.
D.
LIN.
Br.
$12^0 x 11^3$
E.
12'-0" CLG.
Din.
$12^0 x 13^0$
COVERED STOOP
Gar.
$21^4 x 21^8$
58'-0"
56'-0"
© design basics inc.

TO ORDER BLUEPRINTS USE THE FORM ON PAGE 15 OR CALL TOLL-FREE 1-877-671-6036

View thousands more home plans online at www.familyhandyman.com/homeplans

The Family
Handyman

Plan #708-0702

Lovely, Spacious Floor Plan

1,558 total square feet of living area

Price Code B

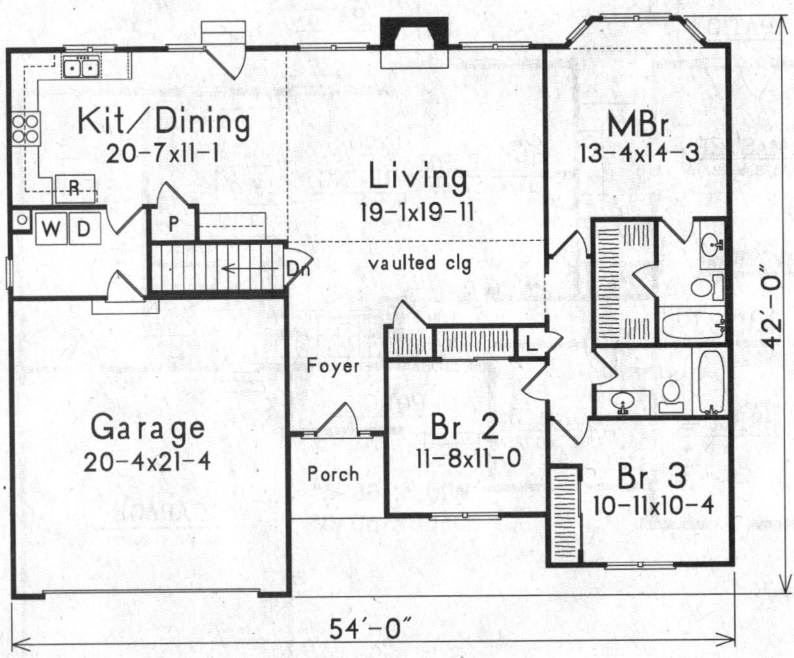
Kit/Dining
20-7x11-1
R
W D
P
Living
19-1x19-11
vaulted clg
Dn
MBr
13-4x14-3
L
Foyer
Garage
20-4x21-4
Porch
Br 2
11-8x11-0
Br 3
10-11x10-4
42'-0"
54'-0"

Special features

- Spacious utility room located conveniently between garage and kitchen/dining area
- Private bedrooms separated off main living area by hallway
- Enormous living area with fireplace and vaulted ceiling opens to kitchen and dining area
- Master bedroom enhanced with large bay window, walk-in closet and private bath
- 3 bedrooms, 2 baths, 2-car garage
- Basement foundation

Plan #708-DDI-98-106

Fabulous Curb Appeal

1,588 total square feet of living area **Price Code B**

Special features

- Workshop in garage ideal for storage and projects
- 12' vaulted master suite has his and hers closets as well as a lovely bath with bayed soaking tub and compartmentalized shower and toilet area
- Lovely arched entry to 14' vaulted great room that flows open to the dining room and sky-lit kitchen
- 3 bedrooms, 2 baths, 2-car garage
- Basement foundation

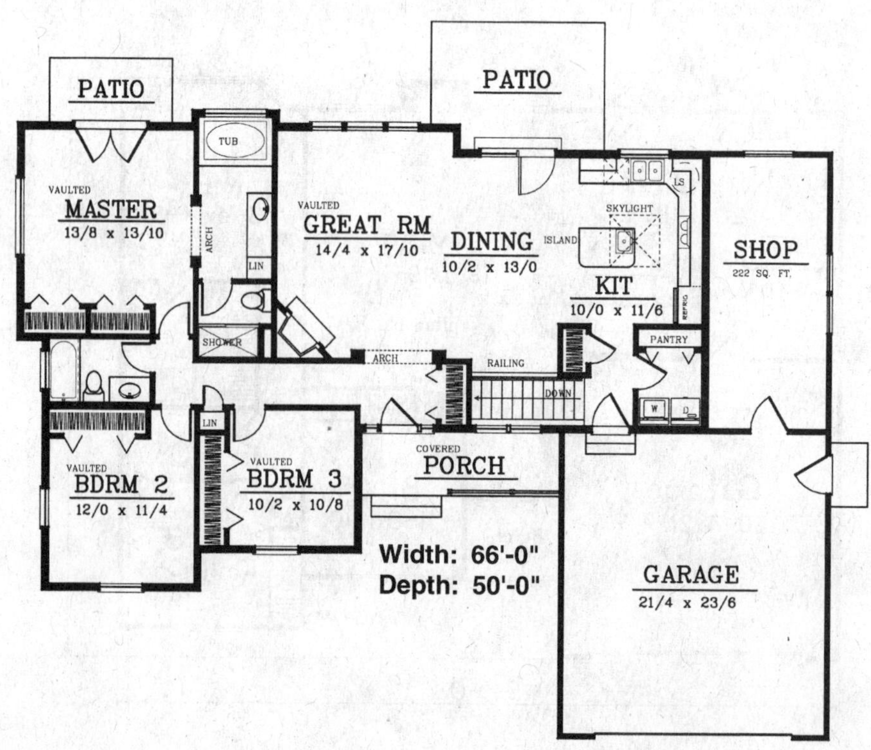
PATIO
PATIO
TUB
VAULTED
MASTER
13/8 x 13/10
ARCH
LIN
SHOWER
VAULTED
GREAT RM
14/4 x 17/10
DINING
10/2 x 13/0
SKYLIGHT
ISLAND
KIT
10/0 x 11/6
SHOP
222 SQ. FT.
PANTRY
ARCH
RAILING
DOWN
LIN
VAULTED
BDRM 2
12/0 x 11/4
VAULTED
BDRM 3
10/2 x 10/8
COVERED
PORCH
Width: 66'-0"
Depth: 50'-0"
GARAGE
21/4 x 23/6

TO ORDER BLUEPRINTS USE THE FORM ON PAGE 15 OR CALL TOLL-FREE 1-877-671-6036

View thousands more home plans online at www.familyhandyman.com/homeplans

The Family
Handyman

Plan #708-0493

Open Layout Ensures Easy Living

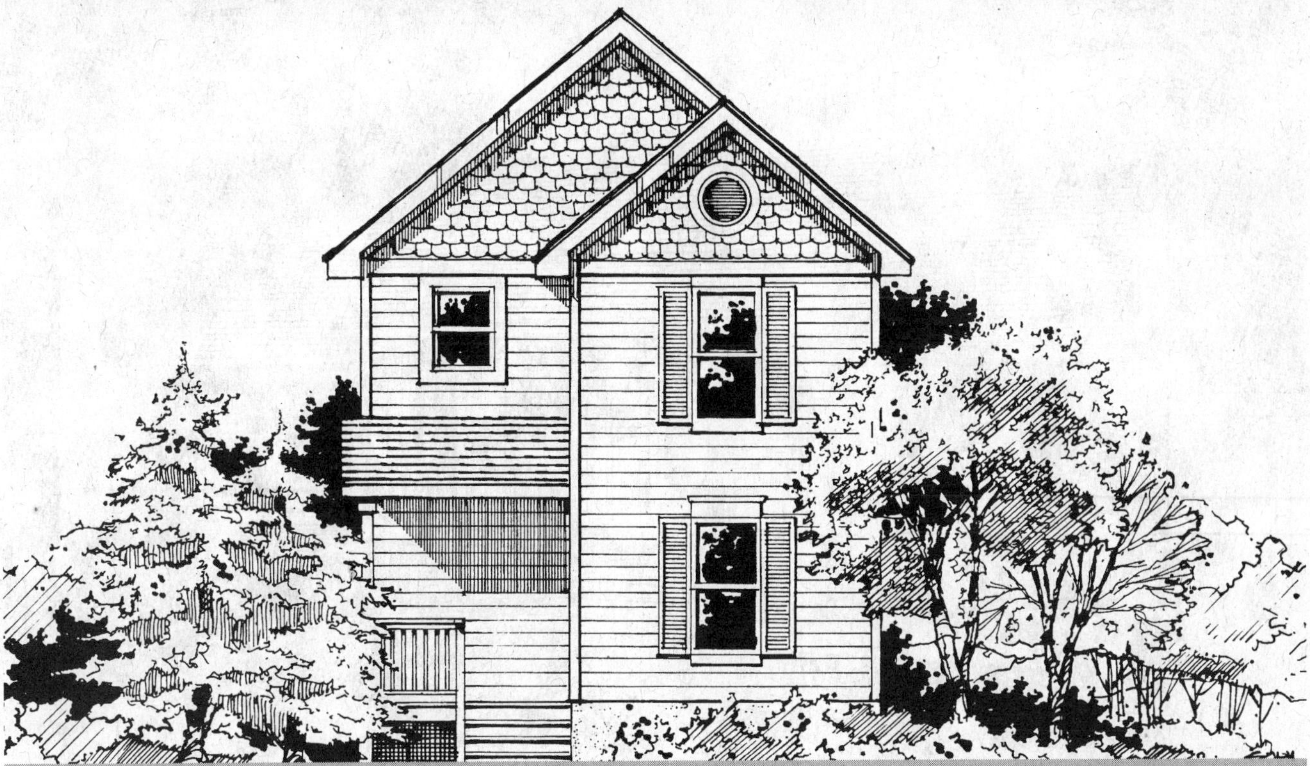

976 total square feet of living area | **Price Code AA**

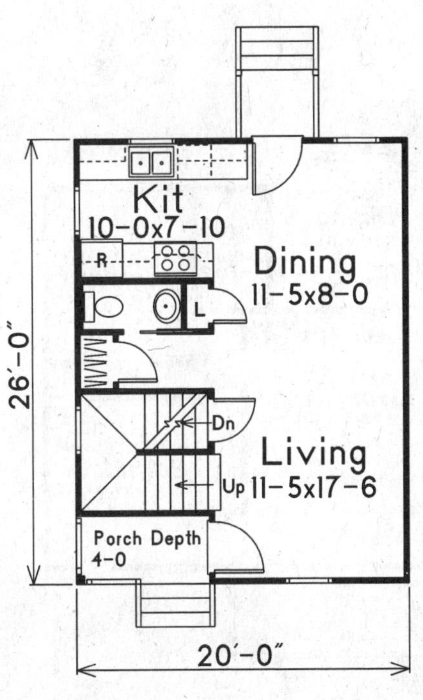
Kit
10-0x7-10
R
Dining
11-5x8-0
L
Dn
Living
Up 11-5x17-6
Porch Depth
4-0
26'-0"
20'-0"

First Floor
488 sq. ft.

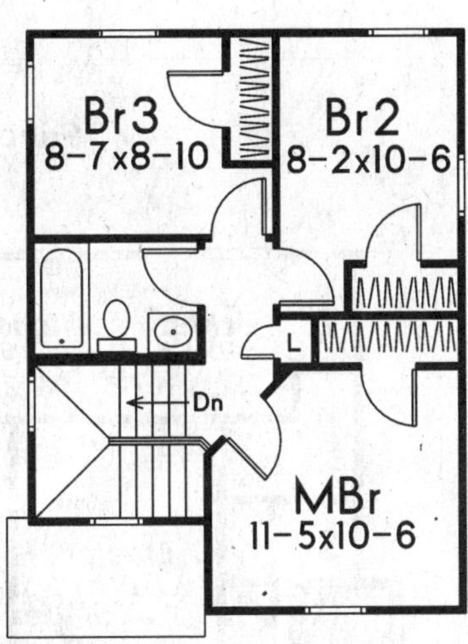
Br3
8-7x8-10
Br2
8-2x10-6
L
Dn
MBr
11-5x10-6

Second Floor
488 sq. ft.

Special features

- Cozy front porch opens into large living room
- Convenient half bath is located on first floor
- All bedrooms are located on second floor for privacy
- Dining room has access to the outdoors
- 3 bedrooms, 1 1/2 baths
- Basement foundation

Formal Country Charm

1,325 total square feet of living area

Price Code A

Special features

- Sloped ceiling and a fireplace in living area creates a cozy feeling
- Formal dining and breakfast areas have an efficiently designed kitchen between them
- Master bedroom has a walk-in closet with luxurious private bath
- 3 bedrooms, 2 baths, 2-car drive under garage
- Basement foundation

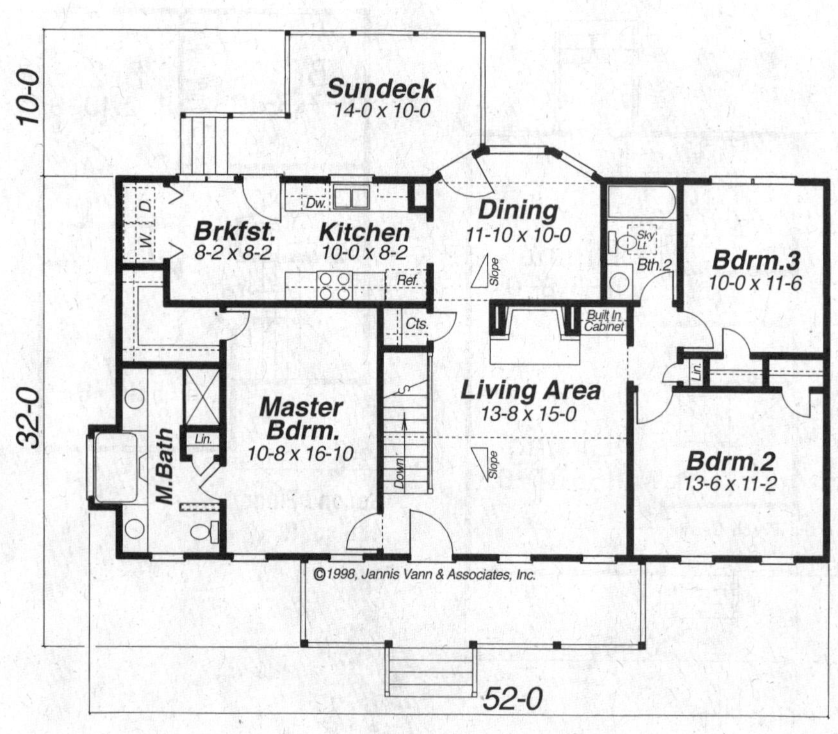
Sundeck
14-0 x 10-0
10-0
Brkfst.
8-2 x 8-2
Kitchen
10-0 x 8-2
Dining
11-10 x 10-0
Dw.
Ref.
W
D
Slope
Sky Lt.
Bth.2
Bdrm.3
10-0 x 11-6
Cts.
Built In Cabinet
Lin.
32-0
Master
Bdrm.
10-8 x 16-10
Living Area
13-8 x 15-0
M.Bath
Lin.
Down
Bdrm.2
13-6 x 11-2
©1998, Jannis Vann & Associates, Inc.
52-0

TO ORDER BLUEPRINTS USE THE FORM ON PAGE 15 OR CALL TOLL-FREE 1-877-671-6036

View thousands more home plans online at www.familyhandyman.com/homeplans

The Family
Handyman

Plan #708-0774

Open Floor Plan With Extra Amenities

1,680 total square feet of living area

Price Code B

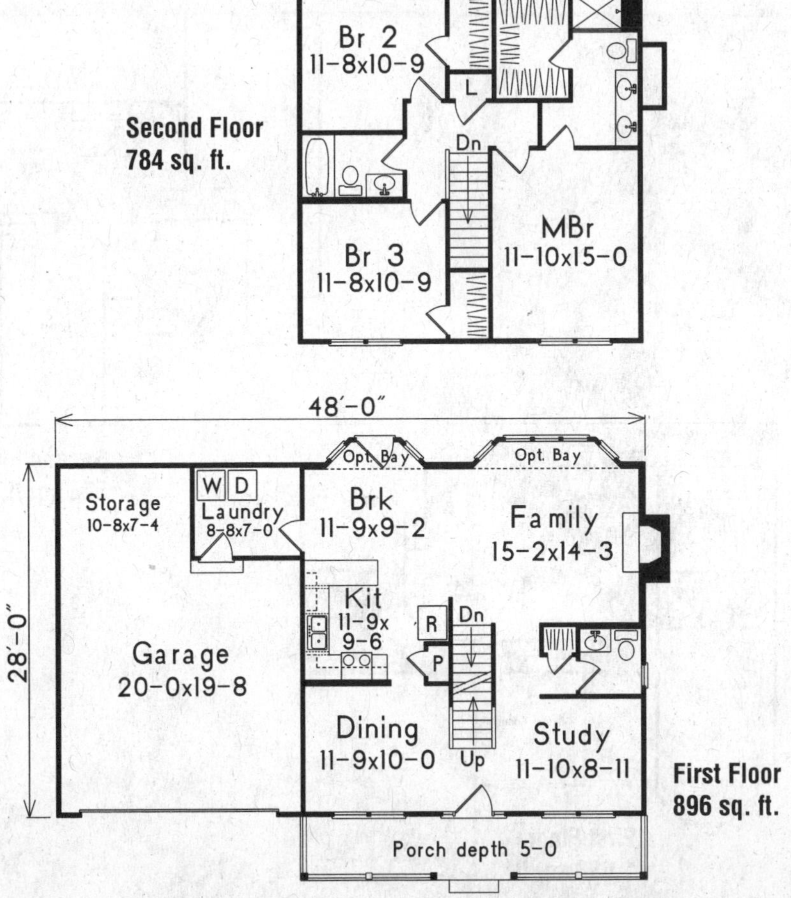
Second Floor
784 sq. ft.
Br 2
11-8x10-9
L
Dn
MBr
11-10x15-0
Br 3
11-8x10-9
48'-0"
28'-0"
Opt. Bay
Opt. Bay
W D
Storage
10-8x7-4
Laundry
8-8x7-0
Brk
11-9x9-2
Family
15-2x14-3
Kit
11-9x
9-6
R
Dn
P
Garage
20-0x19-8
Dining
11-9x10-0
Up
Study
11-10x8-11
First Floor
896 sq. ft.
Porch depth 5-0

Special features

- Compact and efficient layout in an affordable package
- Second floor has three bedrooms all with oversized closets
- All bedrooms on second floor for privacy
- 3 bedrooms, 2 1/2 baths, 2-car garage
- Basement foundation

TO ORDER BLUEPRINTS USE THE FORM ON PAGE 15 OR CALL TOLL-FREE 1-877-671-6036

View thousands more home plans online at www.familyhandyman.com/homeplans

The Family
Handyman

Plan #708-FB-1224

Striking Turret Created By Sitting Area

2,246 total square feet of living area **Price Code D**

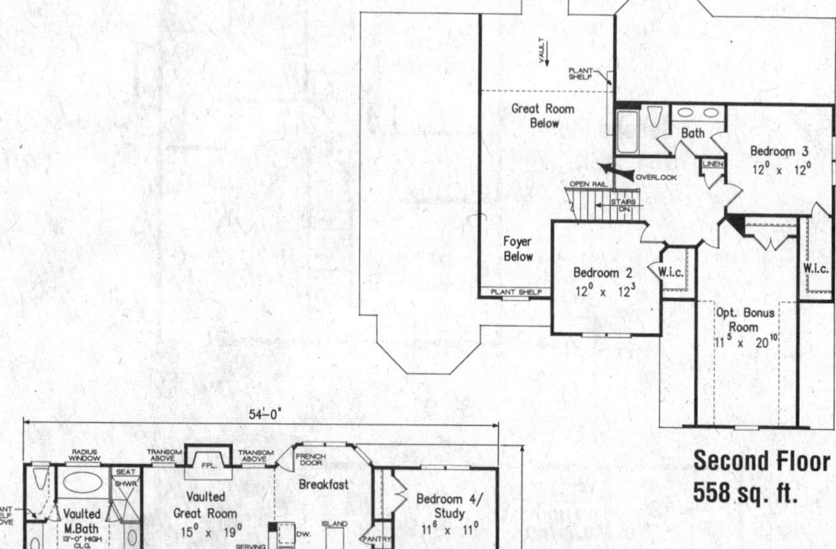
VAULT
PLANT SHELF
Great Room Below
Bath
Bedroom 3
12^0 x 12^0
LINEN
OVERLOOK
OPEN RAIL
STAIRS DN.
Foyer Below
Bedroom 2
12^0 x 12^3
W.i.c.
W.i.c.
PLANT SHELF
Opt. Bonus Room
11^5 x 20^{10}

Second Floor
558 sq. ft.

Special features

- Elegant two-story foyer
- Master suite has sitting area with bay window
- Breakfast area near kitchen
- Bedroom #4 easily converts to an office
- Optional bonus room has an additional 269 square feet of living area
- 4 bedrooms, 3 baths, 2-car side entry garage
- Walk-out basement, slab or crawl space foundation, please specify when ordering

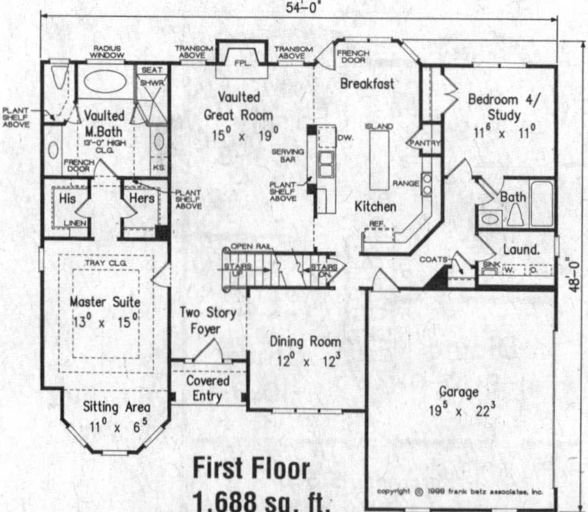
54'-0"
48'-0"
RADIUS WINDOW
TRANSOM ABOVE
TRANSOM ABOVE
FRENCH DOOR
SEAT
SHWR
FPL.
PLANT SHELF ABOVE
Vaulted M.Bath
Vaulted Great Room
15^0 x 19^0
Breakfast
Bedroom 4/ Study
11^6 x 11^0
ISLAND
DW.
PANTRY
SERVING BAR
FRENCH DOOR
His
Hers
LINEN
PLANT SHELF ABOVE
Kitchen
RANGE
REF.
Bath
Laund.
COATS
OPEN RAIL
STAIRS
TRAY CLG.
Master Suite
13^0 x 15^0
Two Story Foyer
Dining Room
12^0 x 12^3
Covered Entry
Sitting Area
11^0 x 6^5
Garage
19^5 x 22^3
copyright © 1998 frank betz associates, inc.

First Floor
1,688 sq. ft.

TO ORDER BLUEPRINTS USE THE FORM ON PAGE 15 OR CALL TOLL-FREE 1-877-671-6036

View thousands more home plans online at www.familyhandyman.com/homeplans

Plan #708-0227

Sculptured Roof Line And Facade Add Charm

1,674 total square feet of living area **Price Code B**

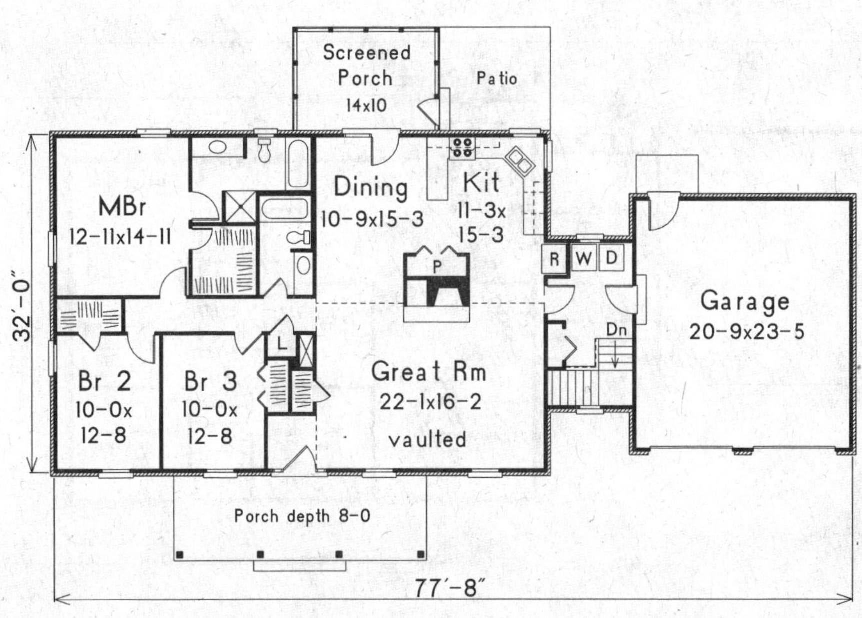

Screened Porch 14x10
Patio
MBr 12-11x14-11
Dining 10-9x15-3
Kit 11-3x 15-3
P
R
W
D
Garage 20-9x23-5
Dn
L
Br 2 10-0x 12-8
Br 3 10-0x 12-8
Great Rm 22-1x16-2 vaulted
32'-0"
Porch depth 8-0
77'-8"

Special features

- Great room, dining area and kitchen, surrounded with vaulted ceiling, central fireplace and log bin
- Convenient laundry/mud room located between garage and family area with handy stairs to basement
- Easily expandable screened porch and adjacent patio with access from dining area
- Master bedroom features full bath with tub, separate shower and walk-in closet
- 3 bedrooms, 2 baths, 2-car garage
- Basement foundation, drawings also include crawl space and slab foundations

The Family
Handyman

Lovely Arched Touches On The Covered Porch

1,594 total square feet of living area **Price Code B**

Special features

- Corner fireplace in the great room creates a cozy feel
- Spacious kitchen combines with the dining room creating a terrific gathering place
- A handy family and guest entrance is a casual and convenient way to enter the home
- 3 bedrooms, 2 baths, 2-car garage
- Slab or crawl space foundation, please specify when ordering

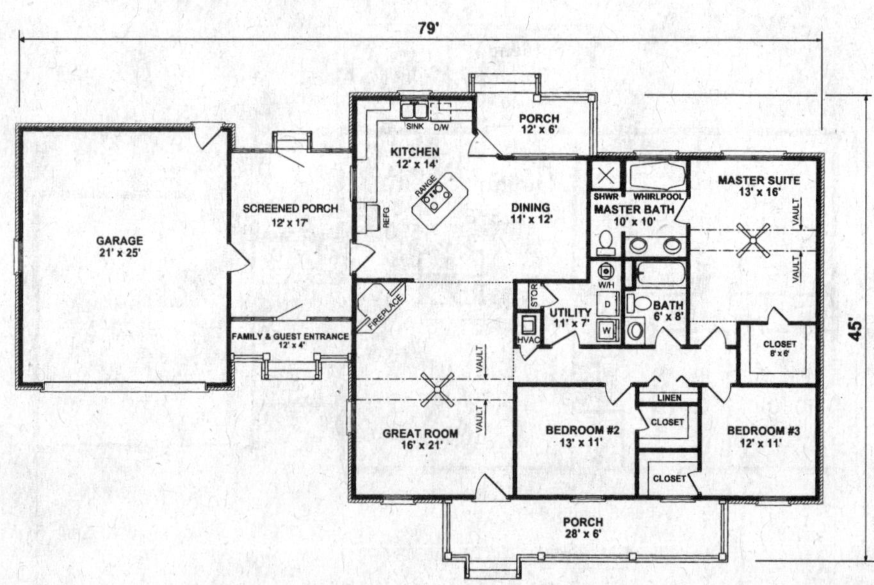
79'
PORCH 12' x 6'
SINK
D/W
KITCHEN 12' x 14'
RANGE
REFG
SCREENED PORCH 12' x 17'
GARAGE 21' x 25'
DINING 11' x 12'
SHWR
WHIRLPOOL
MASTER BATH 10' x 10'
MASTER SUITE 13' x 16'
VAULT
VAULT
W/H
STOR
FIREPLACE
UTILITY 11' x 7'
HVAC
BATH 6' x 8'
CLOSET 8' x 6'
45'
FAMILY & GUEST ENTRANCE 12' x 4'
VAULT
VAULT
LINEN
CLOSET
GREAT ROOM 16' x 21'
BEDROOM #2 13' x 11'
BEDROOM #3 12' x 11'
CLOSET
PORCH 28' x 6'

TO ORDER BLUEPRINTS USE THE FORM ON PAGE 15 OR CALL TOLL-FREE 1-877-671-6036

View thousands more home plans online at www.familyhandyman.com/homeplans

Plan #708-HP-C659

Modern Rustic Design

1,118 total square feet of living area **Price Code AA**

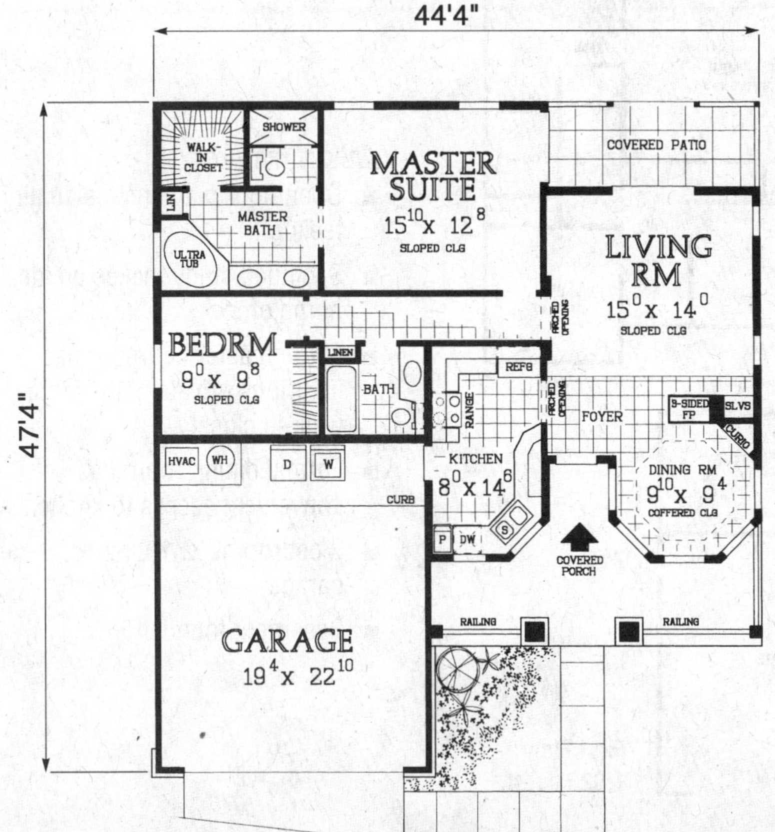
44'4"
47'4"
SHOWER
WALK-IN CLOSET
LIN
MASTER BATH
ULTRA TUB
MASTER SUITE
15^10 x 12^8
SLOPED CLG
COVERED PATIO
LIVING RM
15^0 x 14^0
SLOPED CLG
ARCHED OPENING
BEDRM
9^0 x 9^8
SLOPED CLG
LINEN
BATH
REFG
RANGE
FOYER
3-SIDED FP
SLVS
CURIO
HVAC
WH
D
W
KITCHEN
8^0 x 14^6
DINING RM
9^10 x 9^4
COFFERED CLG
CURB
P
DW
S
COVERED PORCH
RAILING
RAILING
GARAGE
19^4 x 22^10

Special features

- Convenient kitchen has direct access into garage and looks out onto front covered porch
- The covered patio is enjoyed by both the living room and master suite
- Octagon-shaped dining room adds interest to the front exterior while the interior is sunny and bright
- 2 bedrooms, 2 baths, 2-car garage
- Slab foundation

TO ORDER BLUEPRINTS USE THE FORM ON PAGE 15 OR CALL TOLL-FREE 1-877-671-6036

View thousands more home plans online at www.familyhandyman.com/homeplans

The Family
Handyman

Plan #708-JFD-20-1868-1

Plenty Of Closet Space

1,868 total square feet of living area

Price Code C

Second Floor
848 sq. ft.

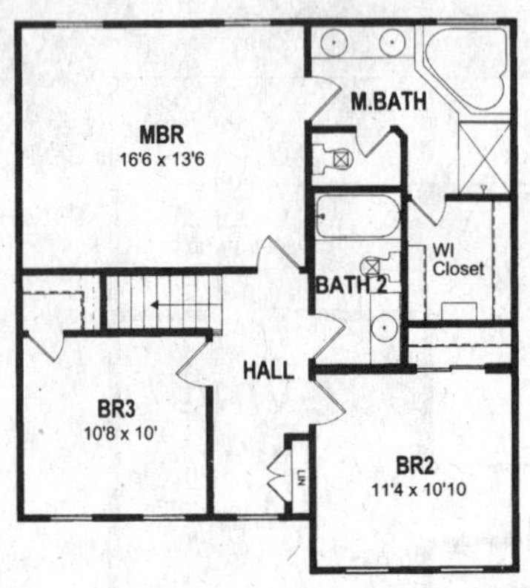
MBR
16'6 x 13'6
M.BATH
WI
Closet
BATH 2
HALL
BR3
10'8 x 10'
BR2
11'4 x 10'10

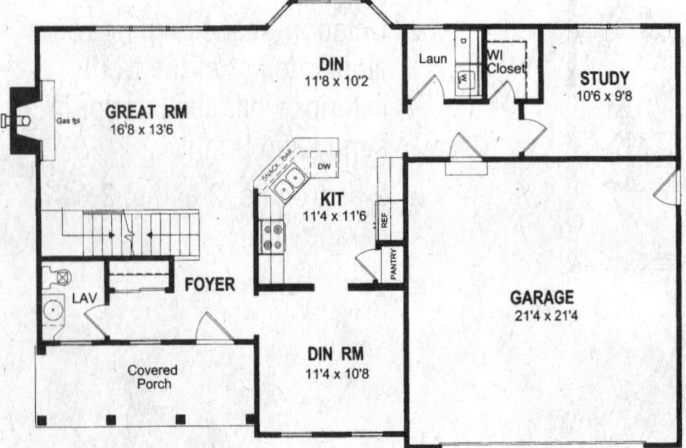
DIN
11'8 x 10'2
Laun
WI
Closet
STUDY
10'6 x 9'8
GREAT RM
16'8 x 13'6
KIT
11'4 x 11'6
DW
REF
PANTRY
FOYER
LAV
GARAGE
21'4 x 21'4
Covered
Porch
DIN RM
11'4 x 10'8

First Floor
1,020 sq. ft.

Width: 52'-8"
Depth: 34'-0"

Special features

- Open floor plan creates an airy feeling
- Secluded study makes an ideal home office
- Large master bedroom has luxurious private bath with a walk-in closet
- Formal dining room has convenient access to kitchen
- 3 bedrooms, 2 1/2 baths, 2-car garage
- Basement foundation

TO ORDER BLUEPRINTS USE THE FORM ON PAGE 15 OR CALL TOLL-FREE 1-877-671-6036

View thousands more home plans online at www.familyhandyman.com/homeplans

Unique Split Foyer Design

1,720 total square feet of living area

Price Code B

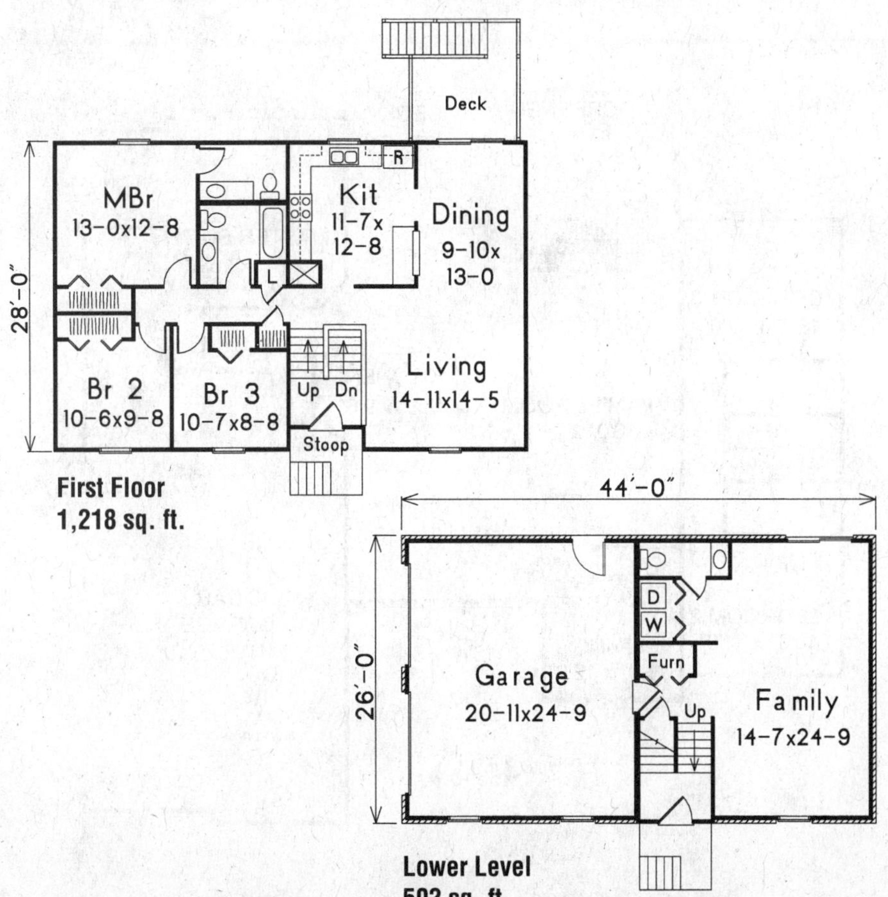
Deck
MBr
13-0x12-8
Kit
11-7x
12-8
Dining
9-10x
13-0
28'-0"
Living
14-11x14-5
Br 2
10-6x9-8
Br 3
10-7x8-8
Up
Dn
Stoop
R
L
44'-0"
26'-0"
Garage
20-11x24-9
D
W
Furn
Up
Family
14-7x24-9

First Floor
1,218 sq. ft.

Lower Level
502 sq. ft.

Special features

- Lower level includes large family room with laundry area and half bath
- L-shaped kitchen has a convenient serving bar and pass-through to dining area
- Private half bath in master bedroom
- 3 bedrooms, 1 full bath, 2 half baths, 2-car drive under garage
- Basement foundation

The Family
Handyman

Plan #708-AP-1911

Elegant Arched Front Porch Attracts Attention

1,992 total square feet of living area **Price Code C**

Special features

- Bayed breakfast room overlooks outdoor deck and connects to screened porch
- Private formal living room in the front of the home could easily be converted to a home office or study
- Compact, yet efficient kitchen is conveniently situated between the breakfast and dining rooms
- 3 bedrooms, 2 1/2 baths, 3-car side entry garage
- Basement, crawl space or slab foundation, please specify when ordering

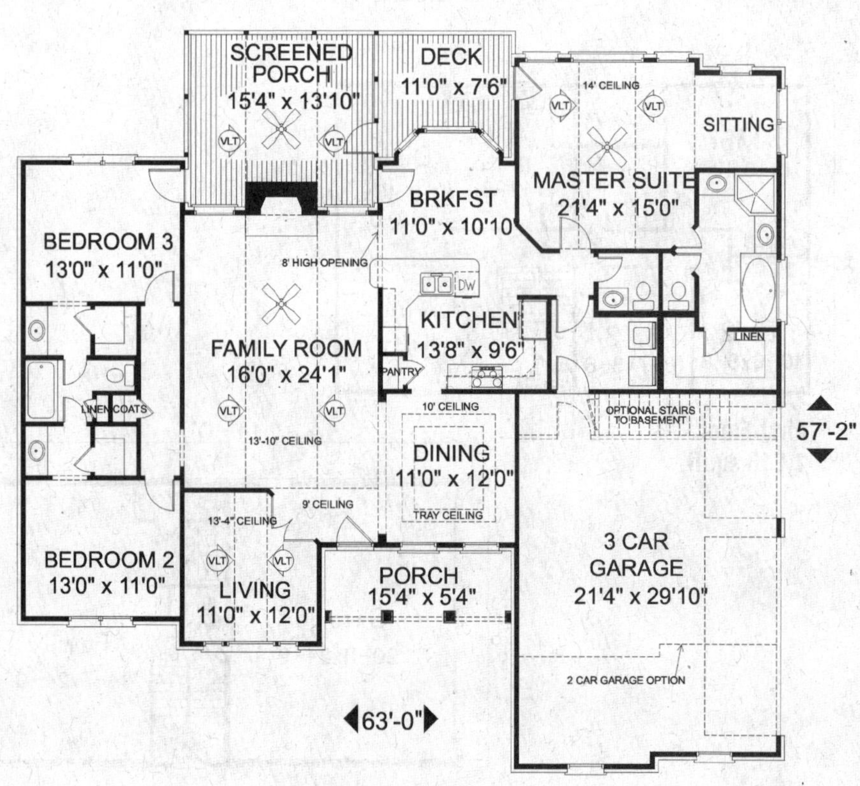
SCREENED PORCH
15'4" x 13'10"
DECK
11'0" x 7'6"
14' CEILING
SITTING
MASTER SUITE
21'4" x 15'0"
BRKFST
11'0" x 10'10"
BEDROOM 3
13'0" x 11'0"
8' HIGH OPENING
DW
KITCHEN
13'8" x 9'6"
FAMILY ROOM
16'0" x 24'1"
PANTRY
LINEN
COATS
LINEN
10' CEILING
OPTIONAL STAIRS TO BASEMENT
57'-2"
13'-10" CEILING
DINING
11'0" x 12'0"
9' CEILING
TRAY CEILING
13'-4" CEILING
BEDROOM 2
13'0" x 11'0"
LIVING
11'0" x 12'0"
PORCH
15'4" x 5'4"
3 CAR GARAGE
21'4" x 29'10"
2 CAR GARAGE OPTION
63'-0"

TO ORDER BLUEPRINTS USE THE FORM ON PAGE 15 OR CALL TOLL-FREE 1-877-671-6036

View thousands more home plans online at www.familyhandyman.com/homeplans

Plan #708-0393

See-Through Fireplace Joins Gathering Rooms

1,684 total square feet of living area **Price Code B**

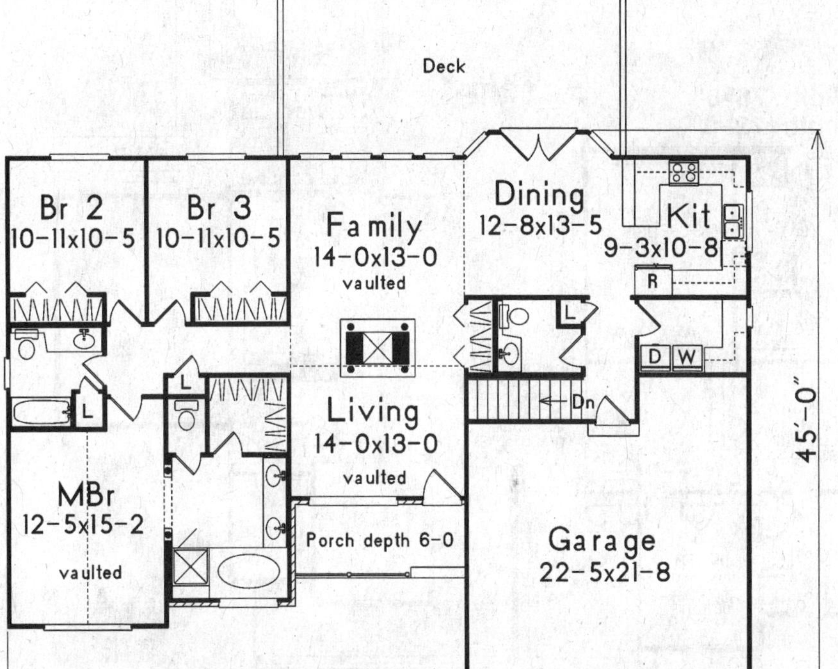
Deck
Br 2
10-11x10-5
Br 3
10-11x10-5
Family
14-0x13-0
vaulted
Dining
12-8x13-5
Kit
9-3x10-8
R
D W
Dn
Living
14-0x13-0
vaulted
MBr
12-5x15-2
vaulted
Porch depth 6-0
Garage
22-5x21-8
45'-0"
60'-0"

Special features

- Convenient double-doors in dining area provide access to large deck
- Family room features several large windows for brightness
- Bedrooms separate from living areas for privacy
- Master bedroom suite offers bath with walk-in closet, double-bowl vanity and both a shower and whirlpool tub
- 3 bedrooms, 2 1/2 baths, 2-car garage
- Basement foundation

TO ORDER BLUEPRINTS USE THE FORM ON PAGE 15 OR CALL TOLL-FREE 1-877-671-6036

View thousands more home plans online at www.familyhandyman.com/homeplans

The Family
Handyman

Plan #708-GSD-1260

Many Decorative Touches Throughout

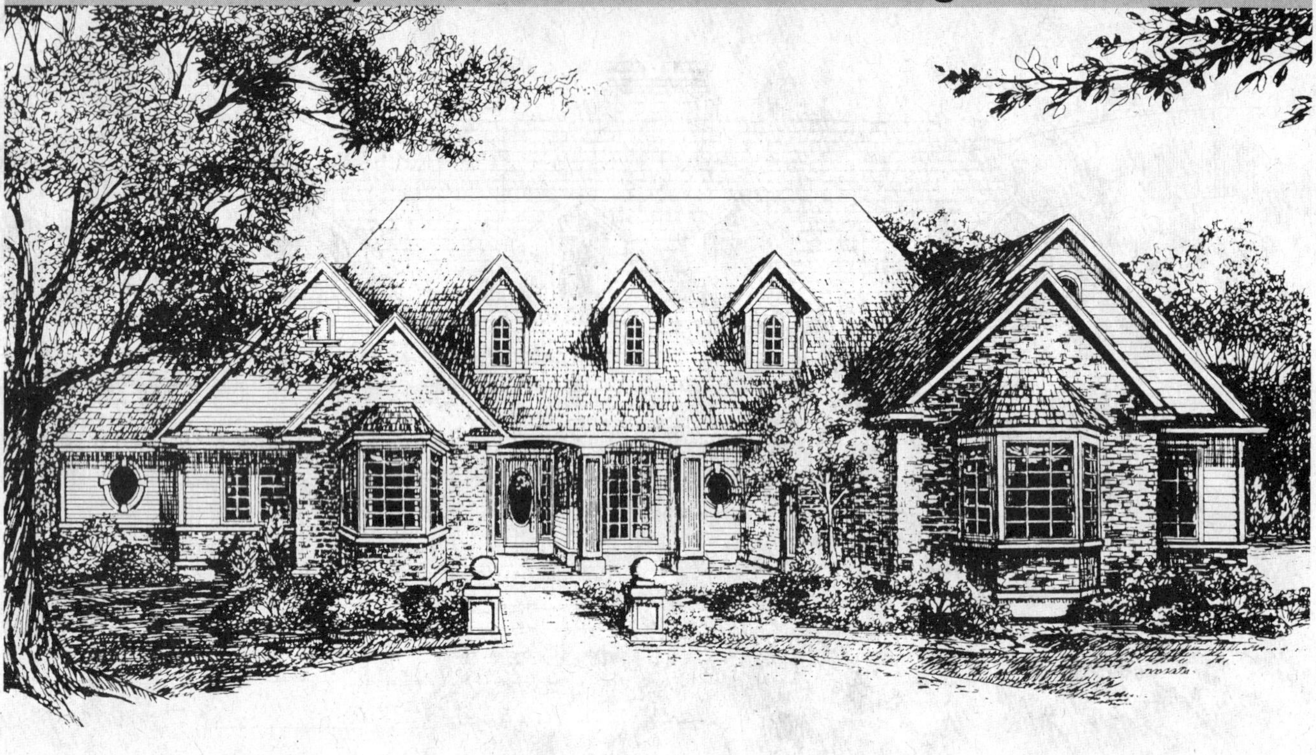

2,788 total square feet of living area **Price Code E**

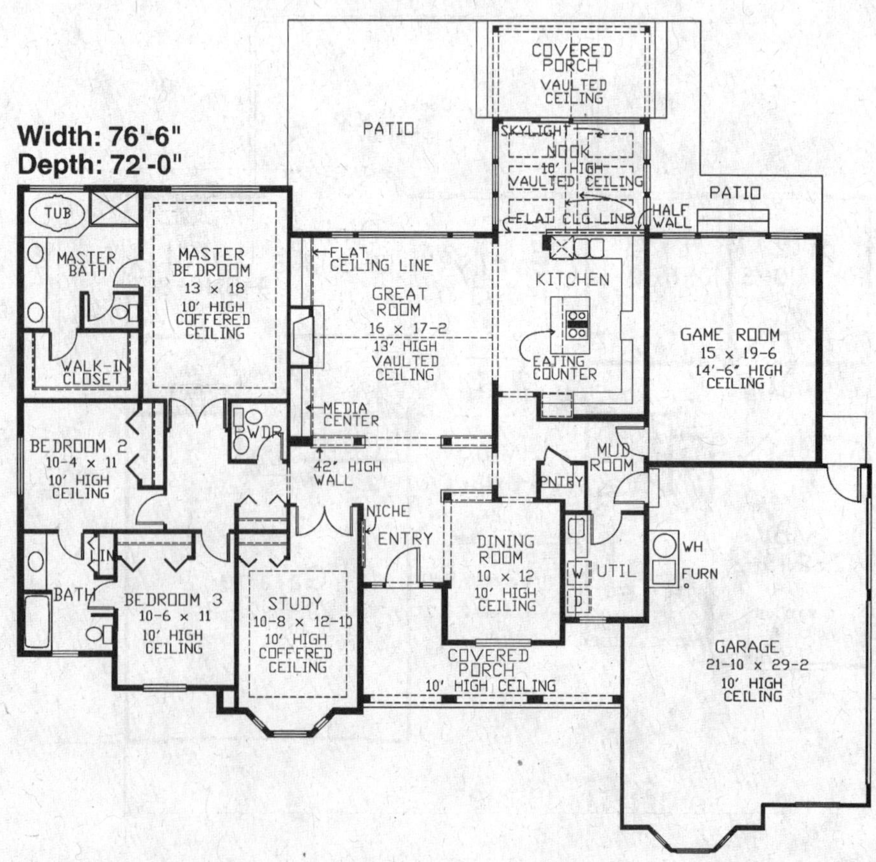
Width: 76'-6"
Depth: 72'-0"
COVERED PORCH
VAULTED CEILING
PATIO
SKYLIGHT
NOOK
10' HIGH VAULTED CEILING
FLAT CLG LINE
HALF WALL
PATIO
TUB
MASTER BATH
MASTER BEDROOM
13 x 18
10' HIGH COFFERED CEILING
WALK-IN CLOSET
FLAT CEILING LINE
GREAT ROOM
16 x 17-2
13' HIGH VAULTED CEILING
KITCHEN
EATING COUNTER
GAME ROOM
15 x 19-6
14'-6" HIGH CEILING
MEDIA CENTER
PWDR
BEDROOM 2
10-4 x 11
10' HIGH CEILING
42" HIGH WALL
MUD ROOM
PNTRY
NICHE
ENTRY
DINING ROOM
10 x 12
10' HIGH CEILING
LIN
BATH
BEDROOM 3
10-6 x 11
10' HIGH CEILING
STUDY
10-8 x 12-10
10' HIGH COFFERED CEILING
UTIL
WH
FURN
COVERED PORCH
10' HIGH CEILING
GARAGE
21-10 x 29-2
10' HIGH CEILING

Special features

- Breakfast nook flooded with sunlight from skylights
- Fireplace in great room framed by media center and shelving
- Large game room is secluded for active children
- 3 bedrooms, 2 1/2 baths, 3-car side entry garage
- Crawl space foundation

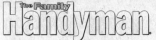

Gabled, Covered Front Porch

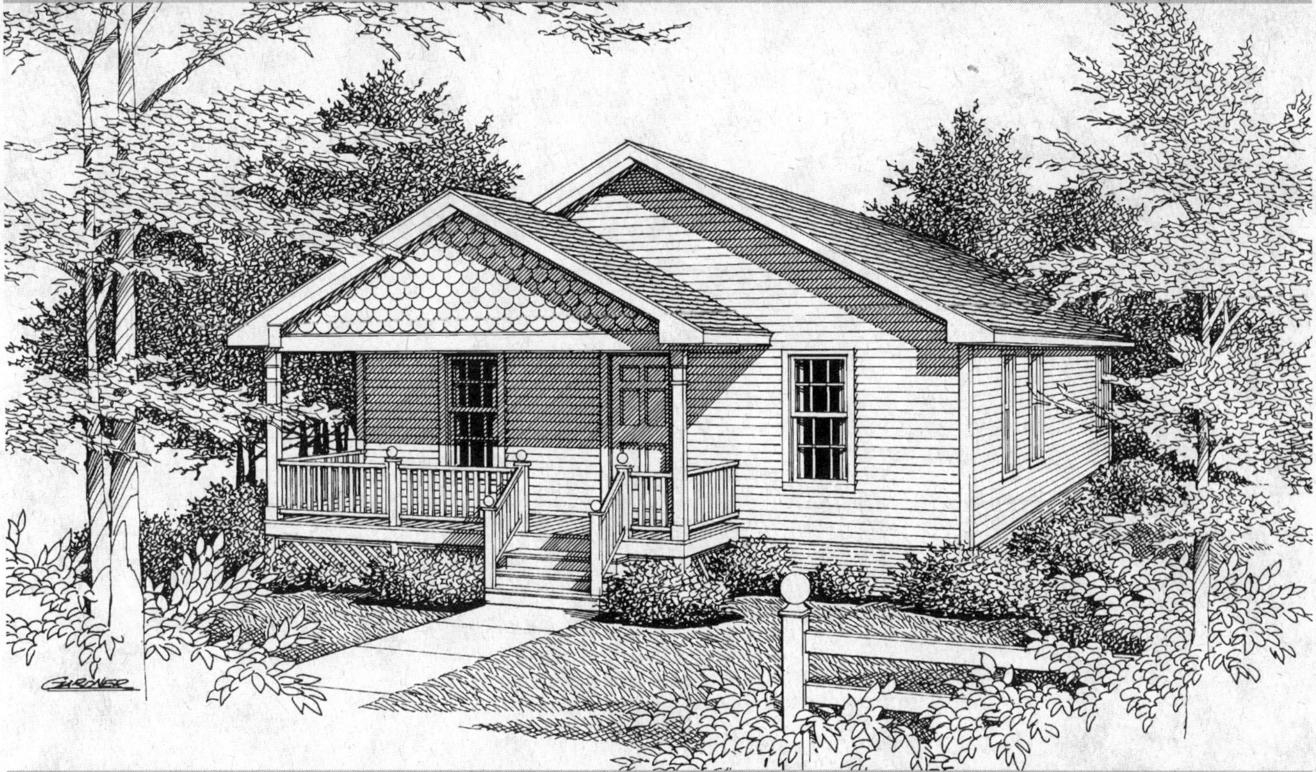

1,320 total square feet of living area

Price Code A

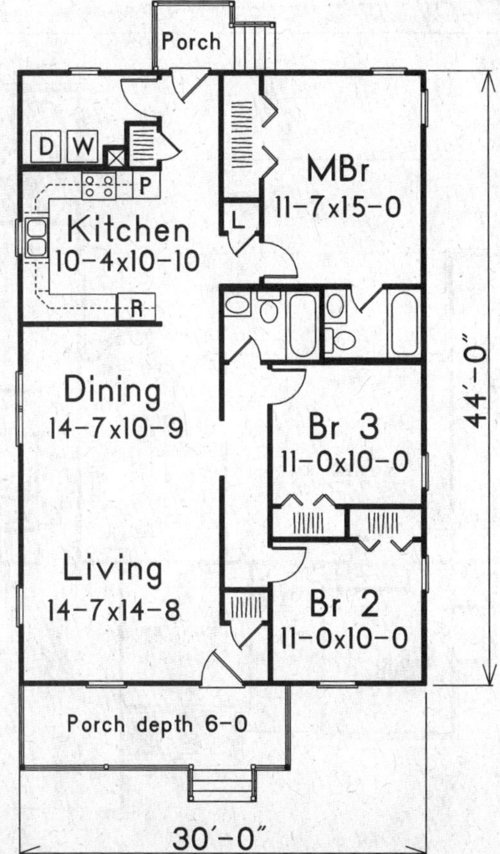
Porch
D
W
P
MBr
11-7x15-0
L
Kitchen
10-4x10-10
R
Dining
14-7x10-9
Br 3
11-0x10-0
44'-0"
Living
14-7x14-8
Br 2
11-0x10-0
Porch depth 6-0
30'-0"

Special features

- Functional U-shaped kitchen features pantry
- Large living and dining areas join to create an open atmosphere
- Secluded master bedroom includes private full bath
- Covered front porch opens into large living area with convenient coat closet
- Utility/laundry room located near the kitchen
- 3 bedrooms, 2 baths
- Crawl space foundation

The Family
Handyman

Plan #708-NDG-190

Attractive Exterior

2,107 total square feet of living area **Price Code C**

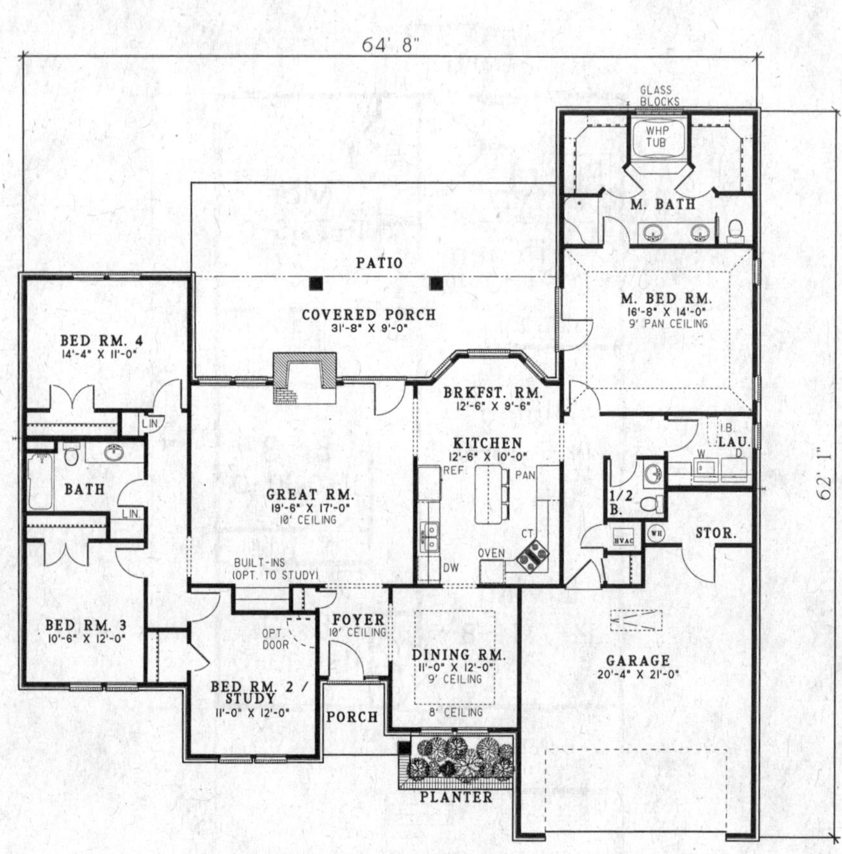
64' 8"
62' 1"
GLASS BLOCKS
WHP TUB
M. BATH
PATIO
M. BED RM.
16'-8" X 14'-0"
9' PAN CEILING
COVERED PORCH
31'-8" X 9'-0"
BED RM. 4
14'-4" X 11'-0"
BRKFST. RM.
12'-6" X 9'-6"
LIN
I.B.
LAU.
KITCHEN
12'-6" X 10'-0"
REF
PAN
BATH
GREAT RM.
19'-6" X 17'-0"
10' CEILING
1/2 B.
LIN
HVAC
WH
STOR.
CT
OVEN
DW
BUILT-INS
(OPT. TO STUDY)
BED RM. 3
10'-6" X 12'-0"
OPT DOOR
FOYER
10' CEILING
DINING RM.
11'-0" X 12'-0"
9' CEILING
GARAGE
20'-4" X 21'-0"
BED RM. 2 / STUDY
11'-0" X 12'-0"
PORCH
8' CEILING
PLANTER

Special features

- Master bedroom is separate from other bedrooms for privacy
- Spacious breakfast room and kitchen include center island with eating space
- Centralized great room has fireplace and easy access to any area in the home
- 4 bedrooms, 2 1/2 baths, 2-car garage
- Crawl space, basement, walk-out basement or slab foundation, please specify when ordering

TO ORDER BLUEPRINTS USE THE FORM ON PAGE 15 OR CALL TOLL-FREE 1-877-671-6036

View thousands more home plans online at www.familyhandyman.com/homeplans

The Family
Handyman

Plan #708-0505

Spacious Dining And Living Areas

1,104 total square feet of living area **Price Code AA**

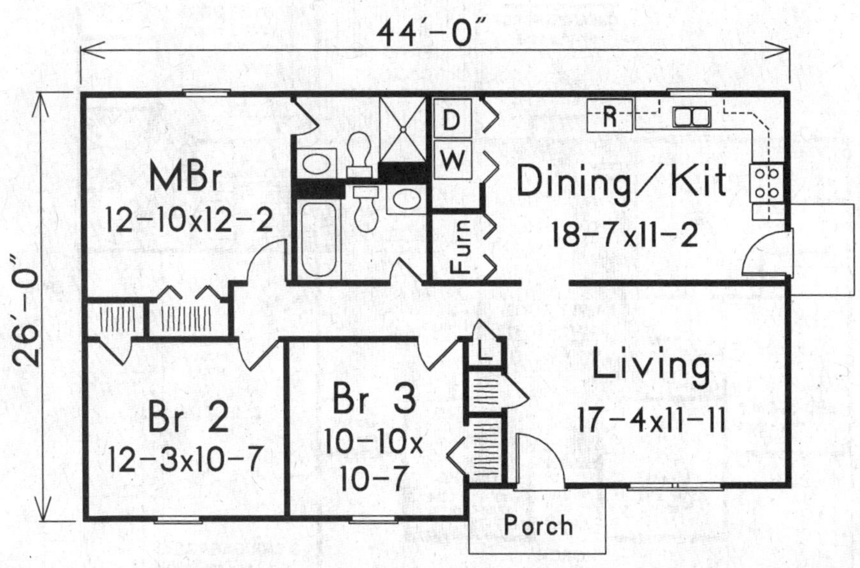
44′–0″
26′–0″
MBr
12–10x12–2
D
W
R
Dining/Kit
18–7x11–2
Furn
L
Living
17–4x11–11
Br 2
12–3x10–7
Br 3
10–10x
10–7
Porch

Special features

- Master bedroom includes private bath
- Convenient side entrance to dining area/kitchen
- Laundry area located near kitchen
- Large living area creates a comfortable atmosphere
- 3 bedrooms, 2 baths
- Crawl space foundation, drawings also include basement and slab foundations

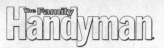

Inviting Vaulted Entry

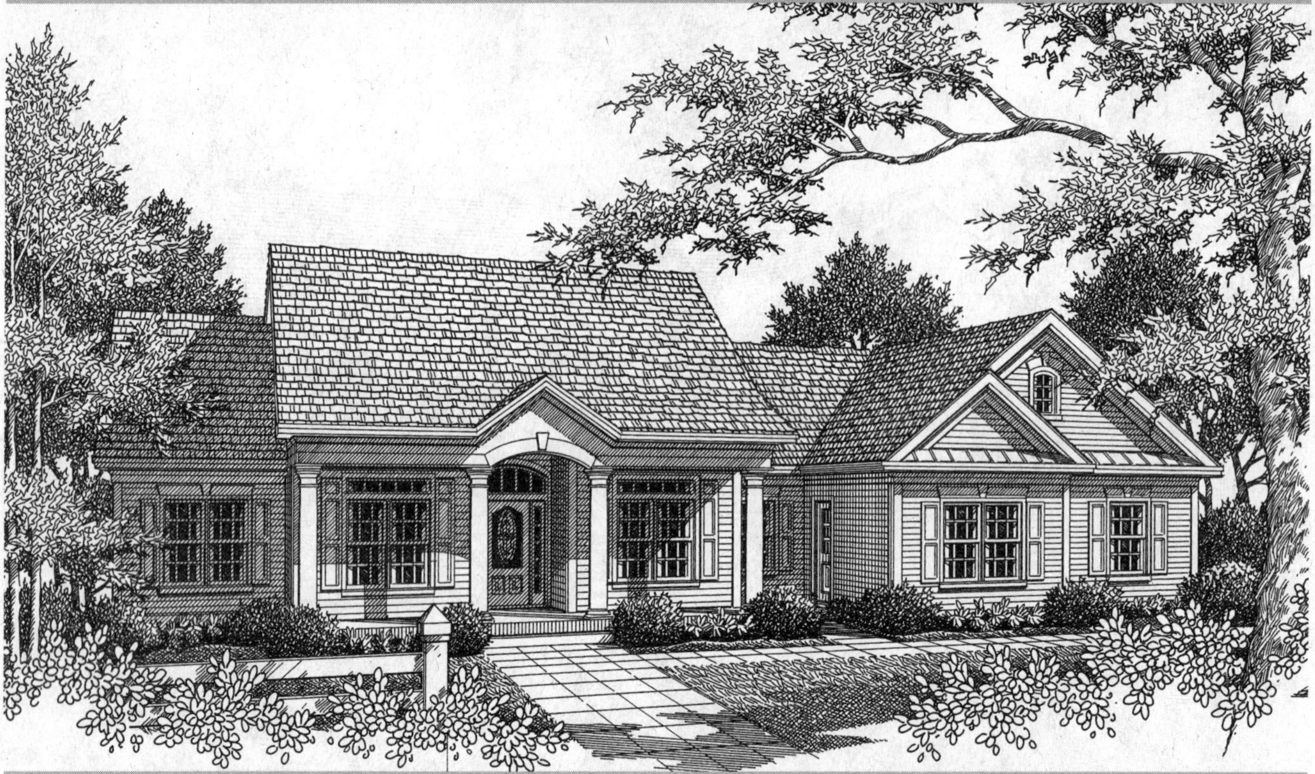

2,097 total square feet of living area | **Price Code C**

Special features

- Angled kitchen, family room and eating area adds interest to this home
- Family room includes a T.V. niche making this a cozy place to relax
- Sumptuous master bedroom includes sitting area, double walk-in closets and a full bath
- 3 bedrooms, 3 baths, 3-car side entry garage
- Crawl space or slab foundation, please specify when ordering

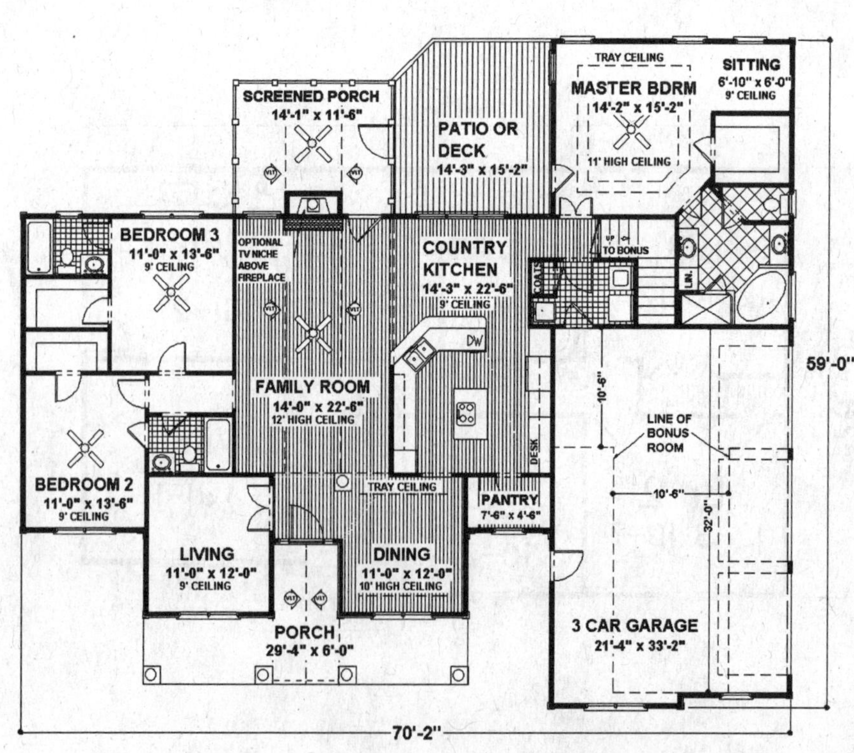
SCREENED PORCH
14'-1" x 11'-6"
PATIO OR DECK
14'-3" x 15'-2"
TRAY CEILING
MASTER BDRM
14'-2" x 15'-2"
11' HIGH CEILING
SITTING
6'-10" x 6'-0"
9' CEILING
BEDROOM 3
11'-0" x 13'-6"
9' CEILING
OPTIONAL TV NICHE ABOVE FIREPLACE
COUNTRY KITCHEN
14'-3" x 22'-6"
9' CEILING
UP TO BONUS
DW
FAMILY ROOM
14'-0" x 22'-6"
12' HIGH CEILING
DESK
59'-0"
10'-6"
LINE OF BONUS ROOM
10'-6"
32'-0"
BEDROOM 2
11'-0" x 13'-6"
9' CEILING
TRAY CEILING
PANTRY
7'-6" x 4'-6"
LIVING
11'-0" x 12'-0"
9' CEILING
DINING
11'-0" x 12'-0"
10' HIGH CEILING
PORCH
29'-4" x 6'-0"
3 CAR GARAGE
21'-4" x 33'-2"
70'-2"

The Family Handyman

Plan #708-SRD-150

Enchanting One-Level Home

1,508 total square feet of living area **Price Code B**

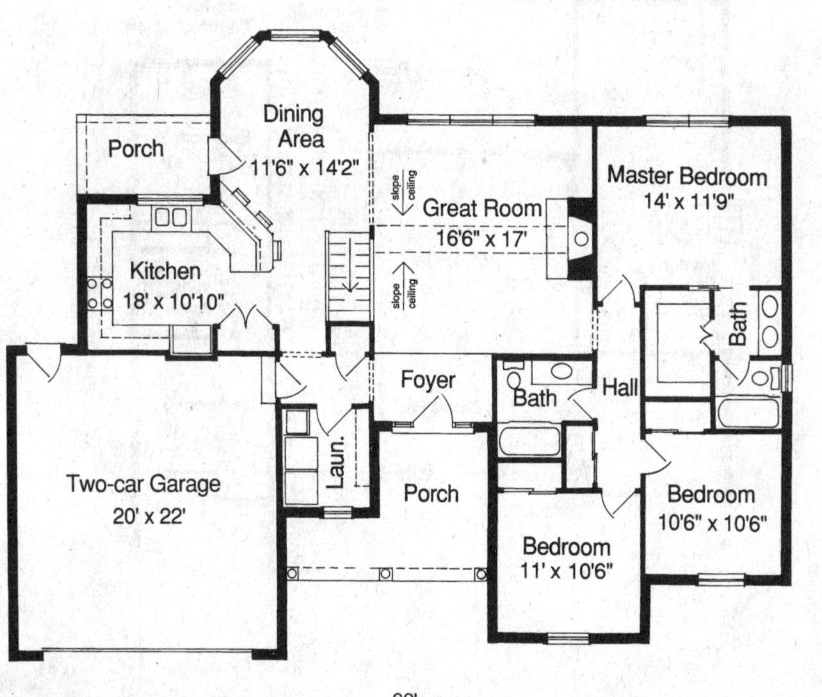
Dining Area 11'6" x 14'2"
Porch
Great Room 16'6" x 17'
slope ceiling
slope ceiling
Master Bedroom 14' x 11'9"
Kitchen 18' x 10'10"
Bath
Foyer
Bath
Hall
Two-car Garage 20' x 22'
Laun.
Porch
Bedroom 10'6" x 10'6"
Bedroom 11' x 10'6"
47'
60'

Special features

- Grand opening between rooms creates a spacious effect
- Additional room for quick meals or serving a larger crowd is provided at the breakfast bar
- Sunny dining area accesses the outdoors as well
- 3 bedrooms, 2 baths, 2-car garage
- Basement or crawl space foundation, please specify when ordering

The Family
Handyman

Plan #708-HDS-1993

Country Living At Its Finest

© HOME DESIGN SERVICES, INC.

J.N. HANSEN S.D.G.

1,993 total square feet of living area **Price Code C**

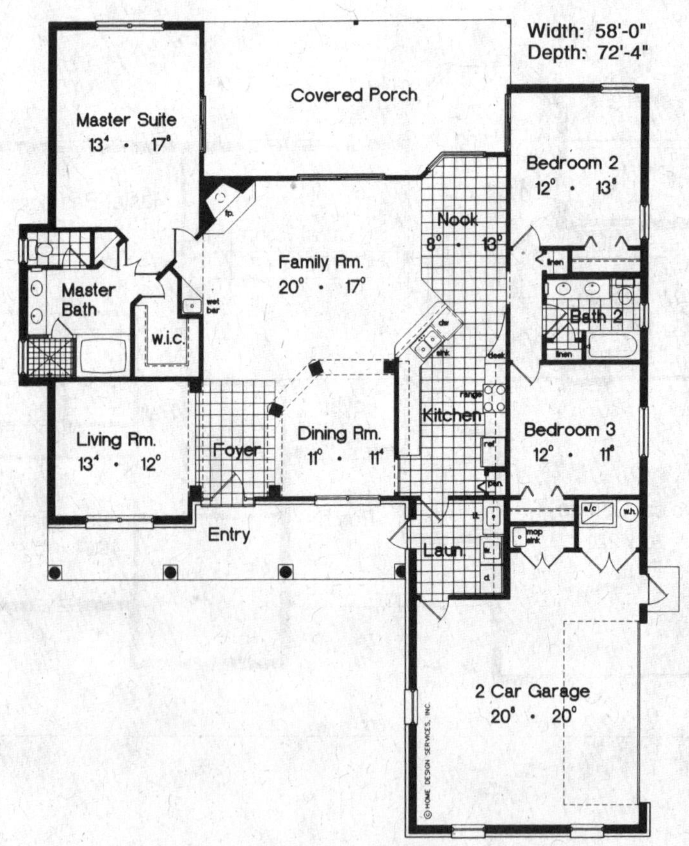
Width: 58'-0"
Depth: 72'-4"
Covered Porch
Master Suite
13⁴ · 17⁸
Bedroom 2
12⁰ · 13⁸
Nook
8⁰ · 13⁰
Family Rm.
20⁰ · 17⁰
Master
Bath
w.i.c.
wet bar
Bath 2
linen
Kitchen
range
Living Rm.
13⁴ · 12⁰
Foyer
Dining Rm.
11⁰ · 11⁶
Bedroom 3
12⁰ · 11⁸
Entry
Laun
mop sink
2 Car Garage
20⁸ · 20⁰
© HOME DESIGN SERVICES, INC.

Special features

- Kitchen and nook share open view onto the covered porch
- Ample-sized secondary bedrooms
- Well-designed master bath
- 3 bedrooms, 2 baths, 2-car side entry garage
- Slab foundation

TO ORDER BLUEPRINTS USE THE FORM ON PAGE 15 OR CALL TOLL-FREE 1-877-671-6036

View thousands more home plans online at www.familyhandyman.com/homeplans

The Family Handyman

Plan #708-0759

Duo Atrium For Fantastic Views

2,125 total square feet of living area **Price Code C**

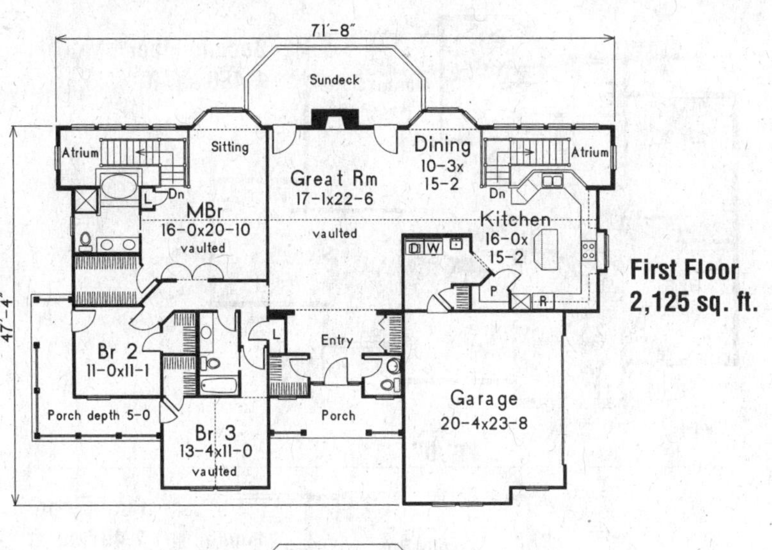
71'-8"
Sundeck
Atrium
Sitting
Great Rm
17-1x22-6
Dining
10-3x
15-2
Atrium
Dn
MBr
16-0x20-10
vaulted
vaulted
Dn
Kitchen
16-0x
15-2
DW
P
R
47'-4"
Br 2
11-0x11-1
L
Entry
Garage
20-4x23-8
Porch depth 5-0
Porch
Br 3
13-4x11-0
vaulted

First Floor
2,125 sq. ft.

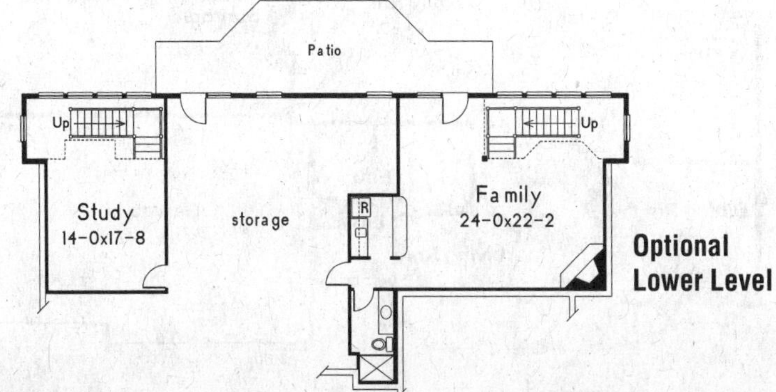
Patio
Up
Up
Study
14-0x17-8
storage
R
Family
24-0x22-2

Optional
Lower Level

Special features

- A cozy porch leads to the vaulted great room with fireplace through the entry which has a walk-in closet and bath
- Large and well-arranged kitchen offers spectacular views from its cantilevered sink cabinetry through a two-story atrium window wall
- Master bedroom boasts a sitting room, large walk-in closet and bath with garden tub overhanging a brightly lit atrium
- 1,047 square feet of optional living area on the lower level featuring a study and family room with walk-in bar and full bath below the kitchen
- 3 bedrooms, 2 1/2 baths, 2-car side entry garage
- Walk-out basement foundation

The Family
Handyman

Plan #708-GH-24594

Impressive Family Home

2,957 total square feet of living area **Price Code E**

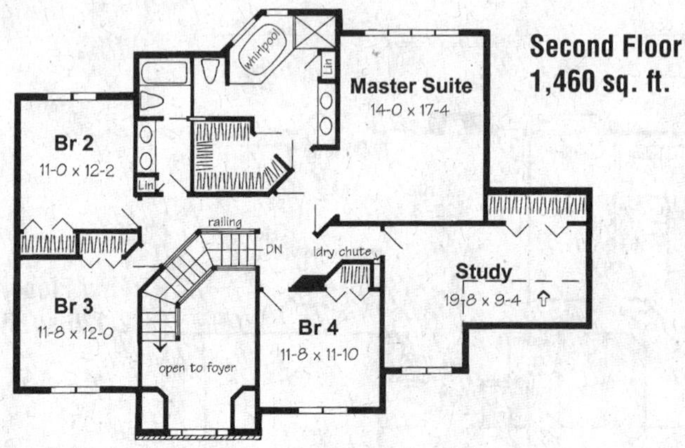

Second Floor
1,460 sq. ft.
whirlpool
Lin
Master Suite
14-0 x 17-4
Br 2
11-0 x 12-2
Lin
railing
DN
ldry chute
Study
19-8 x 9-4
Br 3
11-8 x 12-0
Br 4
11-8 x 11-10
open to foyer

Special features

- Angled staircase to second floor demands attention
- 9' ceilings throughout first floor
- Step-down into cozy sunken family room to find bookshelves and a large fireplace
- Second floor study would make an ideal home office away from the main living areas
- 4 bedrooms, 2 1/2 baths, 3-car garage
- Basement, crawl space or slab foundation, please specify when ordering

76'-0"

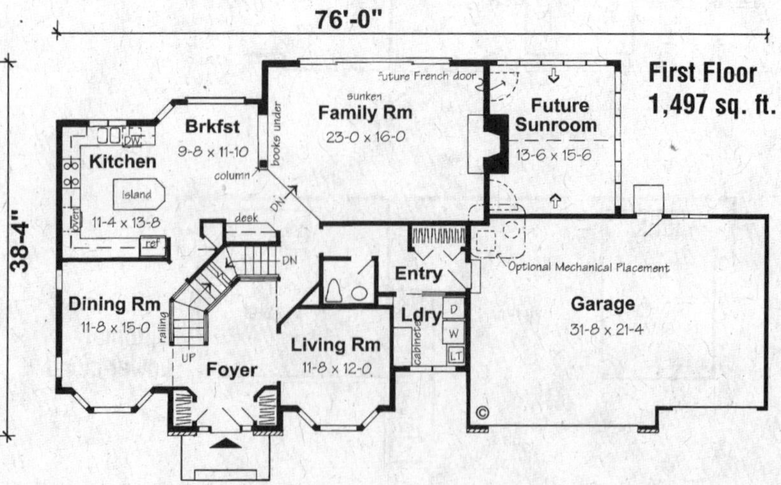

First Floor
1,497 sq. ft.
38'-4"
Future French door
sunken
Family Rm
23-0 x 16-0
Future
Sunroom
13-6 x 15-6
Brkfst
9-8 x 11-10
books under
column
DW
Kitchen
Island
11-4 x 13-8
oven
ref
deck
DN
Optional Mechanical Placement
Entry
Dining Rm
11-8 x 15-0
railing
UP
Foyer
Living Rm
11-8 x 12-0
Ldry
cabinets
D
W
LT
Garage
31-8 x 21-4

TO ORDER BLUEPRINTS USE THE FORM ON PAGE 15 OR CALL TOLL-FREE 1-877-671-6036

View thousands more home plans online at www.familyhandyman.com/homeplans

The Family
Handyman

Plan #708-0178

Elegant Two-Story Exterior And Entry

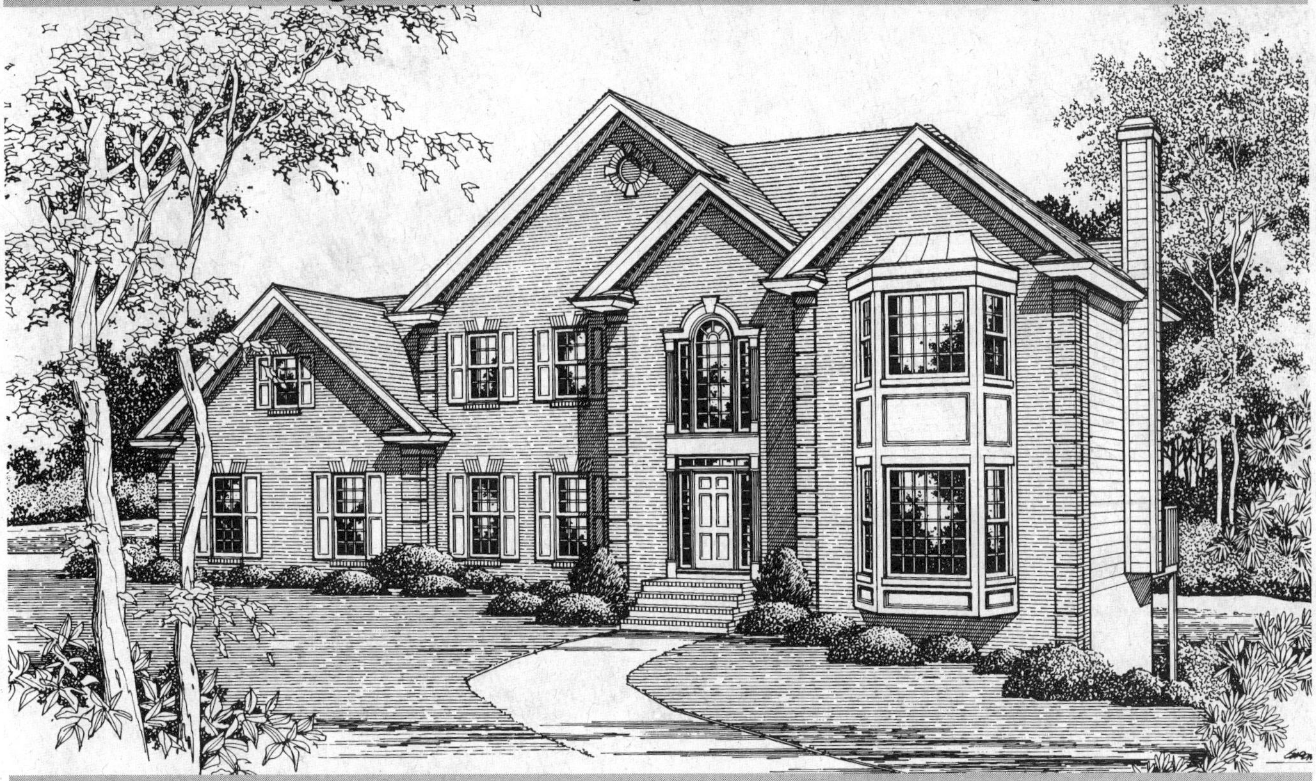

2,846 total square feet of living area — **Price Code E**

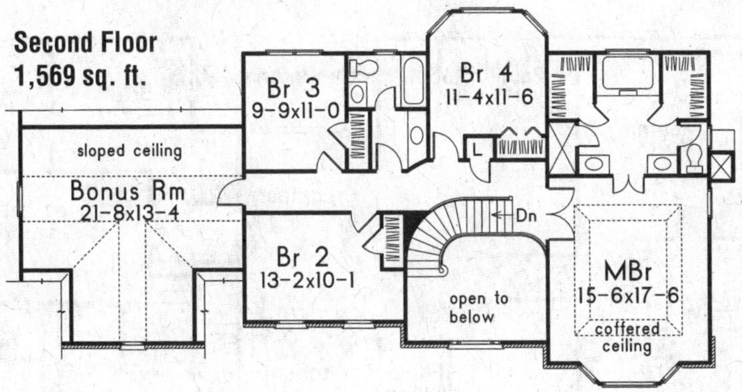
Second Floor
1,569 sq. ft.
Br 3
9-9x11-0
Br 4
11-4x11-6
L
sloped ceiling
Bonus Rm
21-8x13-4
Dn
Br 2
13-2x10-1
open to
below
MBr
15-6x17-6
coffered
ceiling

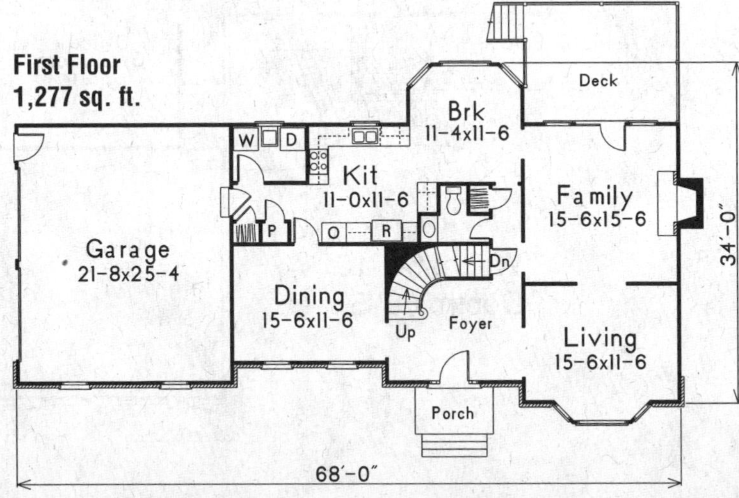
First Floor
1,277 sq. ft.
Deck
Brk
11-4x11-6
W
D
Kit
11-0x11-6
P
O
R
Family
15-6x15-6
Garage
21-8x25-4
Dn
Dining
15-6x11-6
Up
Foyer
Living
15-6x11-6
34'-0"
Porch
68'-0"

Special features

- 9' ceilings on first floor and 8' ceilings on second floor
- Bonus room over garage is included in the square footage
- Prominent double-bay windows and two-story foyer add brightness and space to both floors
- Master suite with double-door entry and coffered ceiling includes an elaborate bath with large tub, separate shower and individual walk-in closets
- 4 bedrooms, 2 1/2 baths, 2-car side entry garage
- Basement foundation, drawings also include slab and crawl space foundations

TO ORDER BLUEPRINTS USE THE FORM ON PAGE 15 OR CALL TOLL-FREE 1-877-671-6036

Plan #708-GM-2361

Office/Game Room With Separate Entrance

2,361 total square feet of living area **Price Code D**

Special features

- Enormous breakfast area and kitchen area create a perfect gathering place
- Family room enhanced with wall of windows and a large fireplace
- Office/gameroom easily accessible through separate side entrance
- 4 bedrooms, 3 baths, 2-car side entry garage
- Basement foundation

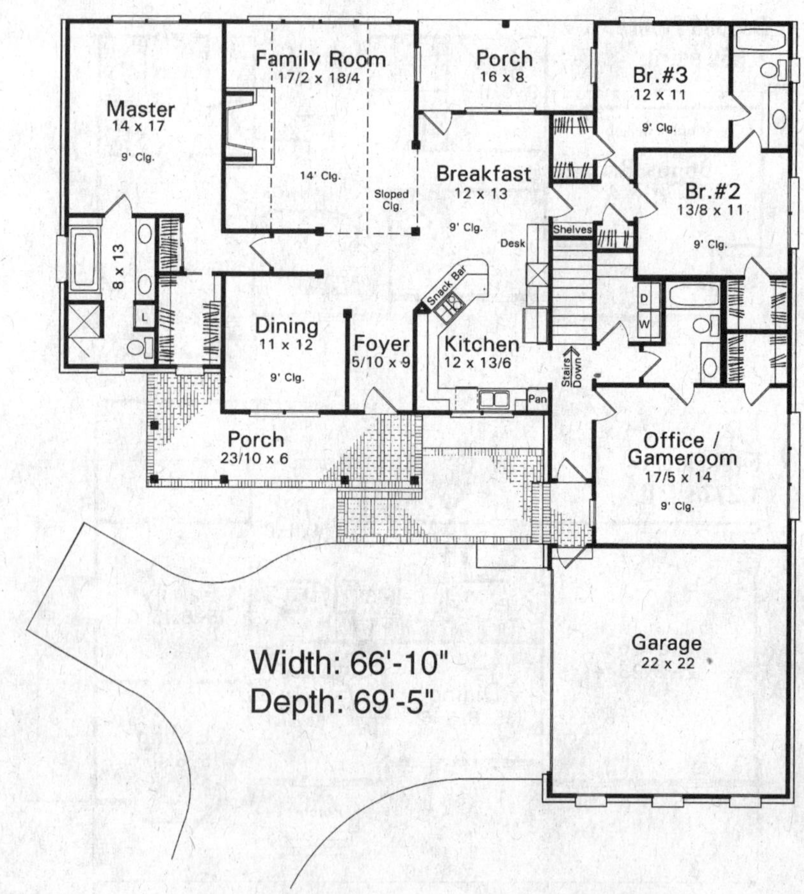
Family Room
17/2 x 18/4
14' Clg.
Sloped Clg.
Porch
16 x 8
Br.#3
12 x 11
9' Clg.
Master
14 x 17
9' Clg.
Breakfast
12 x 13
9' Clg.
Desk
Shelves
Br.#2
13/8 x 11
9' Clg.
8 x 13
L
Snack Bar
D
W
Dining
11 x 12
9' Clg.
Foyer
5/10 x 9
Kitchen
12 x 13/6
Pan
Stairs Down
Porch
23/10 x 6
Office / Gameroom
17/5 x 14
9' Clg.
Garage
22 x 22
Width: 66'-10"
Depth: 69'-5"

TO ORDER BLUEPRINTS USE THE FORM ON PAGE 15 OR CALL TOLL-FREE 1-877-671-6036

View thousands more home plans online at www.familyhandyman.com/homeplans

The Family
Handyman

Plan #708-0678

Pillared Front Porch Generates Charm And Warmth

1,567 total square feet of living area **Price Code C**

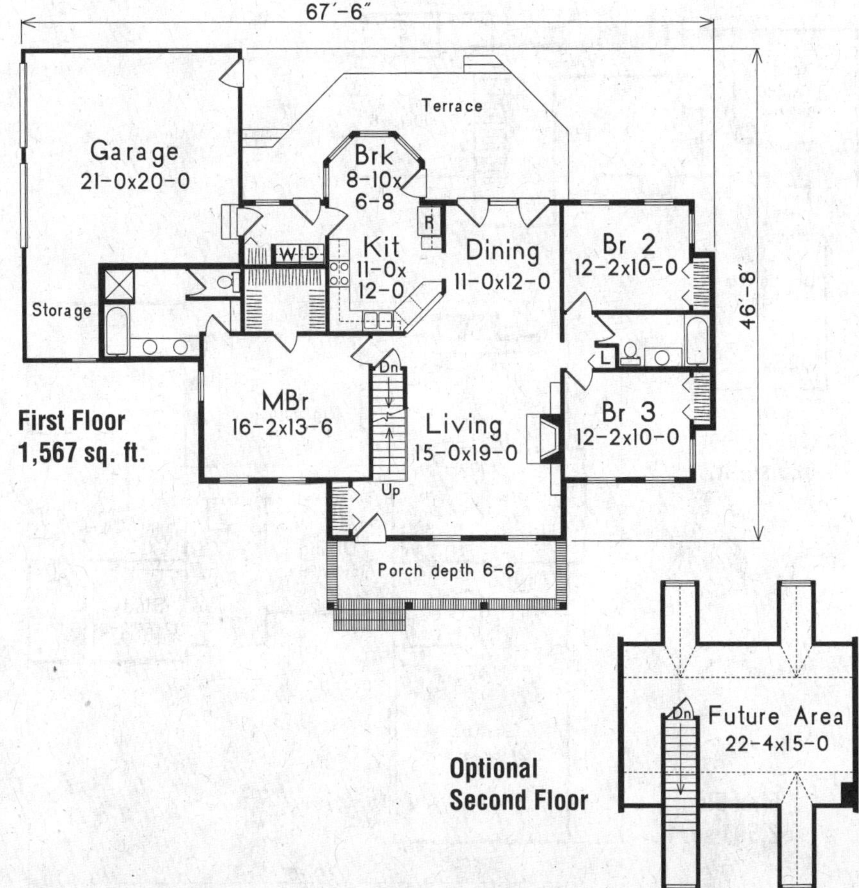
67'-6"
46'-8"
Terrace
Garage
21-0x20-0
Brk
8-10x
6-8
R
Kit
11-0x
12-0
W D
Dining
11-0x12-0
Br 2
12-2x10-0
Storage
L
MBr
16-2x13-6
Dn
Living
15-0x19-0
Br 3
12-2x10-0
Up
Porch depth 6-6
First Floor
1,567 sq. ft.
Dn
Future Area
22-4x15-0
Optional
Second Floor

Special features

- Living room flows into dining room shaped by an angled pass-through into the kitchen
- Cheerful, windowed dining area
- Master bedroom separated from other bedrooms for privacy
- Future area available on the second floor has an additional 338 square feet of living area
- 3 bedrooms, 2 baths, 2-car side entry garage
- Basement foundation, drawings also include slab foundation

Plan #708-0160

Luxury Home Abounds With Amenities

4,120 total square feet of living area **Price Code G**

Special features

- Spacious rooms on both floors include two bedroom suites
- Elaborate master bedroom with a fireplace, double walk-in closets, deluxe tub and two private entrances
- Family room and kitchen form a large living area which includes a fireplace, corner window and vaulted ceiling
- 4 bedrooms, 3 baths, 2 half baths, 2-car side entry garage
- Partial basement/crawl space foundation

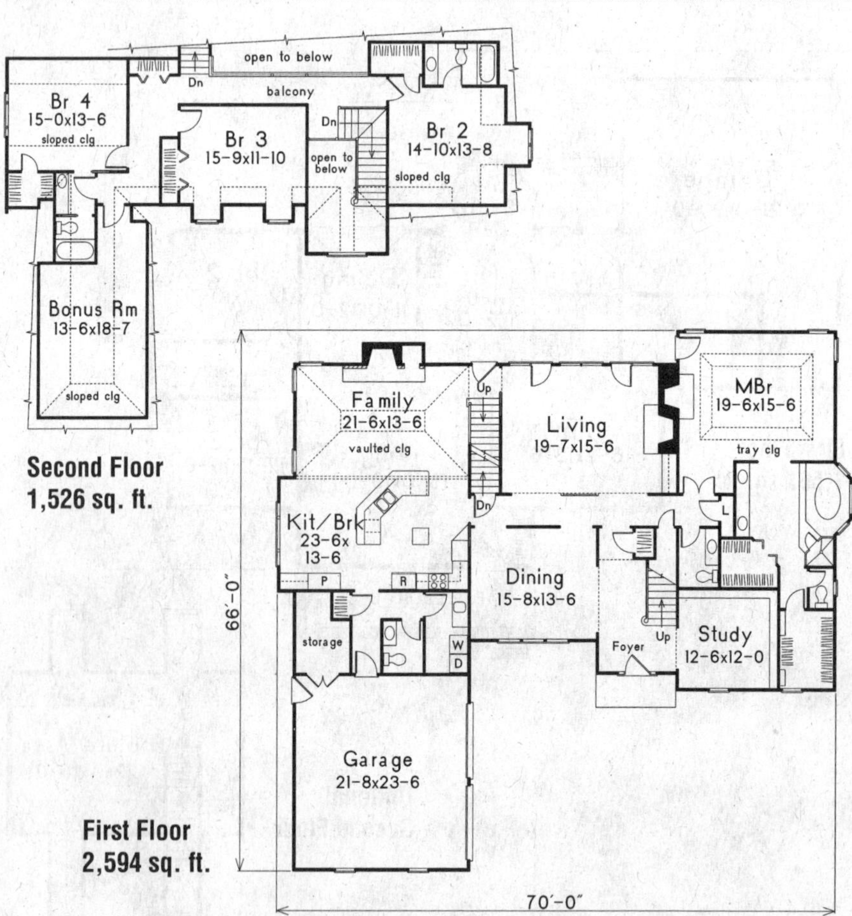

open to below
balcony
Dn
Br 4
15-0x13-6
sloped clg
Br 3
15-9x11-10
open to below
Br 2
14-10x13-8
sloped clg
Bonus Rm
13-6x18-7
sloped clg
Family
21-6x13-6
vaulted clg
Up
Living
19-7x15-6
MBr
19-6x15-6
tray clg
Kit/Brk
23-6x
13-6
P
R
Dn
Dining
15-8x13-6
storage
W
D
Foyer
Up
Study
12-6x12-0
Garage
21-8x23-6
66'-0"
70'-0"

Second Floor
1,526 sq. ft.

First Floor
2,594 sq. ft.

TO ORDER BLUEPRINTS USE THE FORM ON PAGE 15 OR CALL TOLL-FREE 1-877-671-6036

View thousands more home plans online at www.familyhandyman.com/homeplans

Efficient Ranch With Country Charm

1,364 total square feet of living area

Price Code A

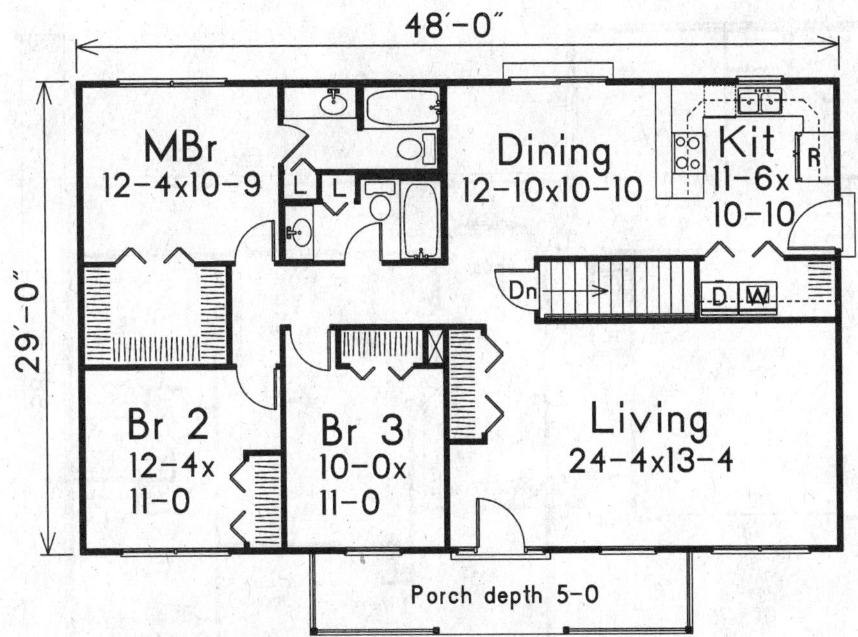
48'-0"
29'-0"
MBr
12-4x10-9
L
L
Dining
12-10x10-10
Kit
11-6x
10-10
R
Dn
D
W
Br 2
12-4x
11-0
Br 3
10-0x
11-0
Living
24-4x13-4
Porch depth 5-0

Special features

- Master suite features spacious walk-in closet and private bath
- Great room highlighted with several windows
- Kitchen with snack bar adjacent to dining area
- Plenty of storage space throughout
- 3 bedrooms, 2 baths, optional 2-car garage
- Basement foundation, drawings also include crawl space foundation

Plan #708-VL2069

Covered Porch Adds Charm

2,069 total square feet of living area **Price Code C**

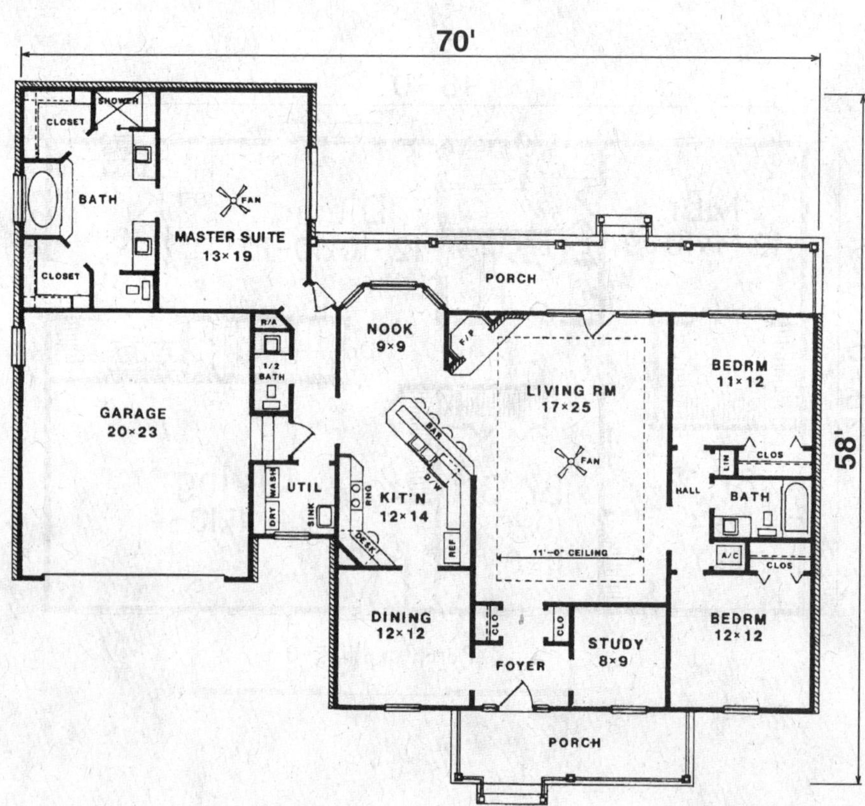
70'
58'
CLOSET
SHOWER
BATH
FAN
MASTER SUITE
13×19
CLOSET
PORCH
NOOK
9×9
F/P
R/A
1/2 BATH
GARAGE
20×23
BAR
D/W
LIVING RM
17×25
FAN
BEDRM
11×12
LIN
CLOS
HALL
BATH
WASH
DRY
UTIL
RNG
SINK
KIT'N
12×14
DESK
REF
11'-0" CEILING
A/C
CLOS
DINING
12×12
CLO
CLO
STUDY
8×9
FOYER
BEDRM
12×12
PORCH

Special features

- 9' ceilings throughout this home
- Kitchen has many amenities including a snack bar
- Large front and rear porches
- 3 bedrooms, 2 1/2 baths, 2-car garage
- Slab or crawl space foundation, please specify when ordering

Comfortable Home Has Character

1,482 total square feet of living area

Price Code A

Second Floor
587 sq. ft.
14'-8" X 11'-0"
4,40 X 3,30
14'-8" X 12'-4"
4,40 X 3,70
12'-0" X 9'-0"
3,60 X 2,70
24'-8" X 12'-4"
7,40 X 3,70
11'-4" X 13'-8"
3,40 X 4,10
36'-0"
10,8 m
38'-0"
11,4 m
First Floor
895 sq. ft.

Special features

- Energy efficient home with 2" x 6" exterior walls
- Corner fireplace warms living area
- Screened porch is spacious and connects to other living areas in the home
- Two bedrooms on second floor share a spacious bath
- 2 bedrooms, 1 1/2 baths
- Basement foundation

Plan #708-BF-2107

Expansive Counter Space

2,123 total square feet of living area

Price Code E

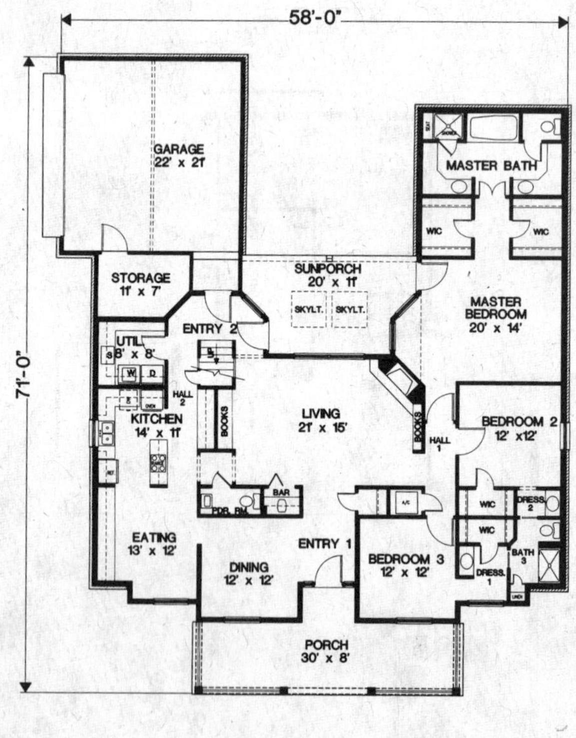
58'-0"
71'-0"
GARAGE
22' x 21'
STORAGE
11' x 7'
SUNPORCH
20' x 11'
SKYLT.
SKYLT.
MASTER BATH
WIC
WIC
MASTER BEDROOM
20' x 14'
ENTRY 2
UTIL
8' x 8'
HALL 2
KITCHEN
14' x 11'
BOOKS
LIVING
21' x 15'
BOOKS
HALL 1
BEDROOM 2
12' x12'
BAR
PDR. RM.
WIC
DRESS. 2
WIC
EATING
13' x 12'
DINING
12' x 12'
ENTRY 1
BEDROOM 3
12' x 12'
DRESS. 1
BATH 3
PORCH
30' x 8'

First Floor
2,123 sq. ft.

Special features

- Energy efficient home with 2" x 6" exterior walls
- Living room has wood burning fireplace, built-in bookshelves and a wet bar
- Skylights make sun porch bright and comfortable
- Unfinished attic has an additional 450 square feet of living area
- 3 bedrooms, 2 1/2 baths, 2-car side entry garage
- Crawl space, slab or basement foundation, please specify when ordering

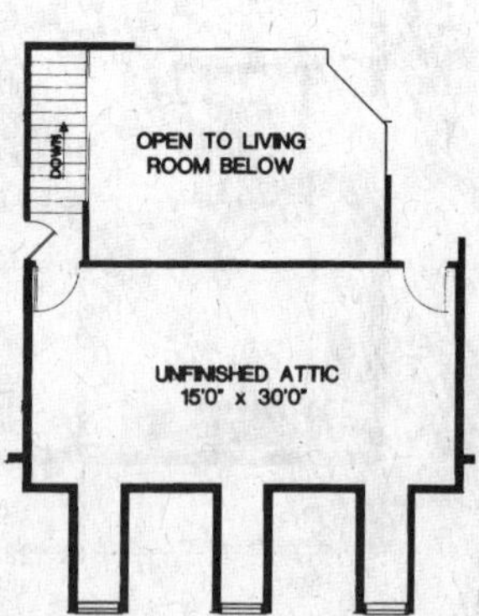
DOWN
OPEN TO LIVING ROOM BELOW
UNFINISHED ATTIC
15'0" x 30'0"

Optional
Second Floor

TO ORDER BLUEPRINTS USE THE FORM ON PAGE 15 OR CALL TOLL-FREE 1-877-671-6036

The Family
Handyman

Plan #708-0295

Dormers And Stone Veneer Add Exterior Appeal

1,609 total square feet of living area

Price Code B

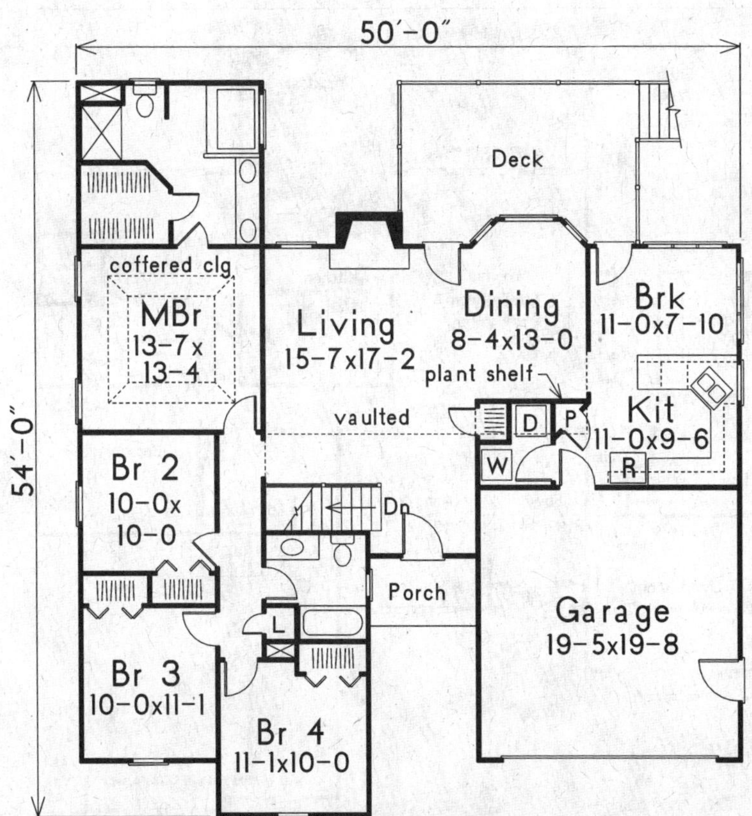

50′–0″
54′–0″
Deck
coffered clg
MBr
13–7x
13–4
Living
15–7x17–2
Dining
8–4x13–0
Brk
11–0x7–10
plant shelf
Kit
11–0x9–6
vaulted
D
P
W
R
Br 2
10–0x
10–0
Dn
Porch
Garage
19–5x19–8
L
Br 3
10–0x11–1
Br 4
11–1x10–0

Special features

- Efficient kitchen with corner pantry and adjacent laundry room
- Breakfast room boasts plenty of windows and opens onto rear deck
- Master bedroom features tray ceiling and private deluxe bath
- Entry opens into large living area with fireplace
- 4 bedrooms, 2 baths, 2-car garage
- Basement foundation

TO ORDER BLUEPRINTS USE THE FORM ON PAGE 15 OR CALL TOLL-FREE 1-877-671-6036

View thousands more home plans online at www.familyhandyman.com/homeplans

Plan #708-FB-930

Bounty Of Bay Windows

2,322 total square feet of living area — **Price Code D**

Special features

- Vaulted family room has fireplace and access to kitchen
- Decorative columns and arched openings surround dining area
- Master suite has a sitting room and grand scale bath
- Kitchen includes island with serving bar
- 3 bedrooms, 2 1/2 baths, 2-car side entry garage
- Walk-out basement, crawl space or slab foundation, please specify when ordering

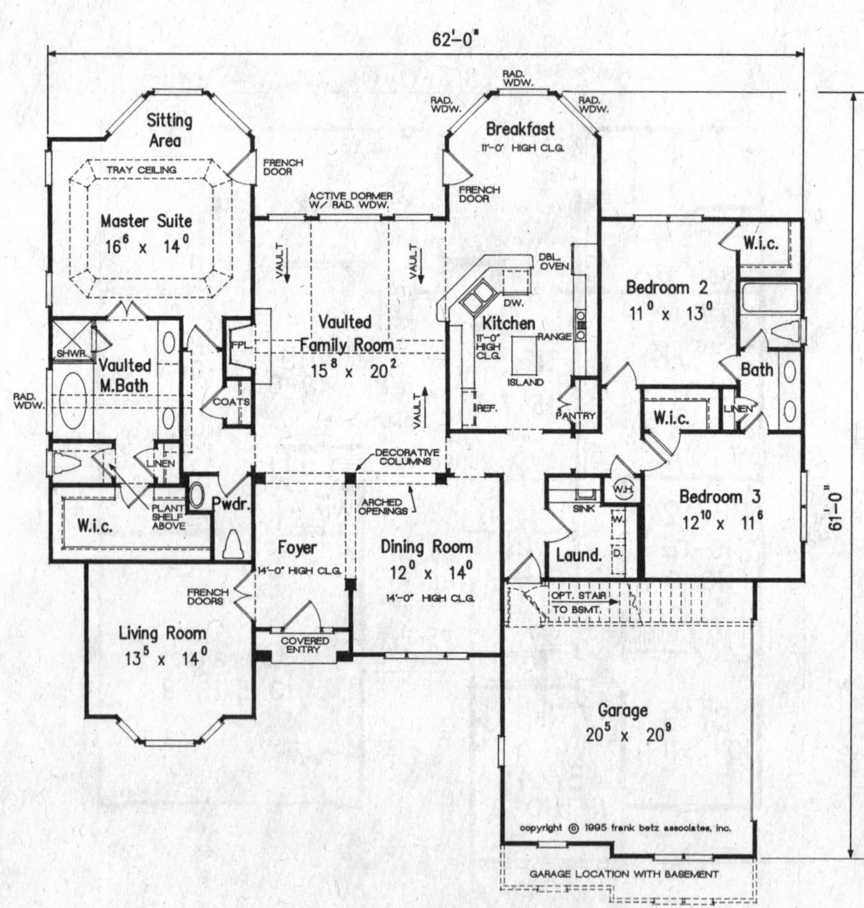
62'-0"
RAD. WDW.
RAD. WDW.
RAD. WDW.
RAD. WDW.
Sitting Area
Breakfast
11'-0' HIGH CLG.
FRENCH DOOR
FRENCH DOOR
TRAY CEILING
Master Suite
16^{6} x 14^{0}
ACTIVE DORMER W/ RAD. WDW.
VAULT
VAULT
VAULT
DBL. OVEN
DW.
Kitchen
11'-0" HIGH CLG.
RANGE
ISLAND
REF.
PANTRY
W.i.c.
Bedroom 2
11^{0} x 13^{0}
Bath
LINEN
W.i.c.
SHWR.
Vaulted M.Bath
FPL.
Vaulted Family Room
15^{8} x 20^{2}
COATS
LINEN
DECORATIVE COLUMNS
PLANT SHELF ABOVE
Pwdr.
W.i.c.
ARCHED OPENINGS
W.H.
SINK
W.
D.
Laund.
Bedroom 3
12^{10} x 11^{6}
61'-0"
Foyer
14'-0" HIGH CLG.
Dining Room
12^{0} x 14^{0}
14'-0" HIGH CLG.
OPT. STAIR TO BSMT.
FRENCH DOORS
Living Room
13^{5} x 14^{0}
COVERED ENTRY
Garage
20^{5} x 20^{9}
copyright © 1995 frank betz associates, inc.
GARAGE LOCATION WITH BASEMENT

The Family
Handyman

Plan #708-0437

Double French Doors Grace Living Room

2,333 total square feet of living area **Price Code D**

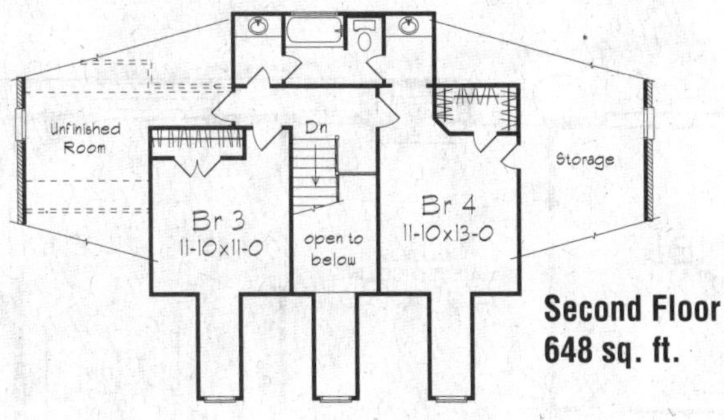
Unfinished Room
Dn
Storage
Br 3
11-10x11-0
open to below
Br 4
11-10x13-0

Second Floor
648 sq. ft.

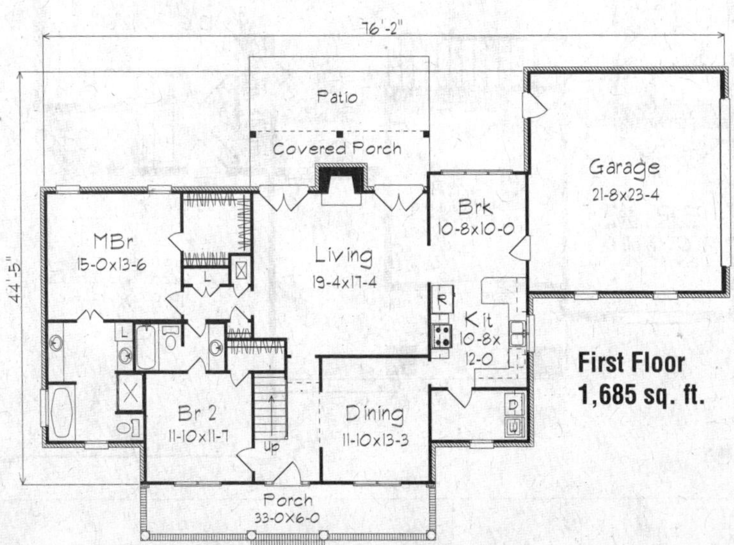
76'-2"
44'-5"
Patio
Covered Porch
Garage
21-8x23-4
MBr
15-0x13-6
Living
19-4x17-4
Brk
10-8x10-0
Kit
10-8x
12-0
Br 2
11-10x11-7
Up
Dining
11-10x13-3
Porch
33-0X6-0

First Floor
1,685 sq. ft.

Special features

- 9' ceilings on first floor
- Master bedroom features a large walk-in closet and an inviting double-door entry into a spacious bath
- Convenient laundry room located near kitchen
- 4 bedrooms, 3 baths, 2-car side entry garage
- Slab foundation, drawings also include crawl space and partial crawl space/basement foundations

TO ORDER BLUEPRINTS USE THE FORM ON PAGE 15 OR CALL TOLL-FREE 1-877-671-6036

View thousands more home plans online at www.familyhandyman.com/homeplans

The Family Handyman

Plan #708-JA-81098

Dramatic Open Layout

1,537 total square feet of living area **Price Code B**

Special features

- Vaulted ceilings in foyer and living room welcome guests
- Kitchen offers eating bar and pantry
- Living room features a fireplace flanked by large windows
- 3 bedrooms, 2 baths, 2-car garage
- Basement foundation

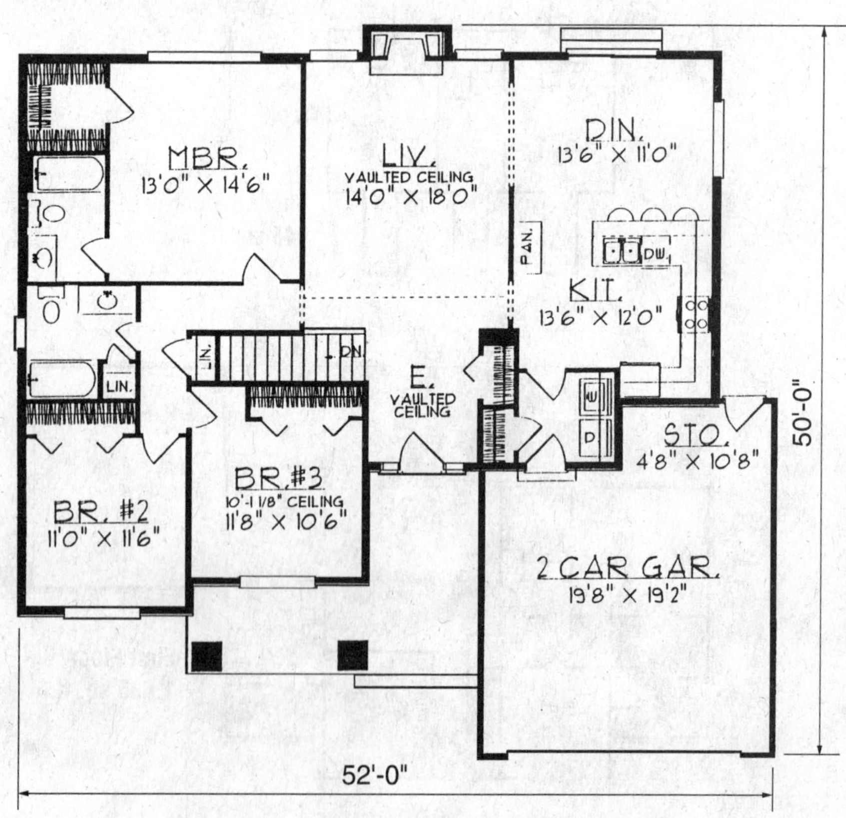
MBR.
13'0" X 14'6"
LIV.
VAULTED CEILING
14'0" X 18'0"
DIN.
13'6" X 11'0"
PAN.
DW
KIT.
13'6" X 12'0"
LIN.
DN.
E.
VAULTED CEILING
LIN.
W
D
STO.
4'8" X 10'8"
BR. #2
11'0" X 11'6"
BR. #3
10'-1 1/8" CEILING
11'8" X 10'6"
2 CAR GAR.
19'8" X 19'2"
50'-0"
52'-0"

TO ORDER BLUEPRINTS USE THE FORM ON PAGE 15 OR CALL TOLL-FREE 1-877-671-6036

View thousands more home plans online at www.familyhandyman.com/homeplans

Plan #708-0744

Home Features Generous Room Sizes

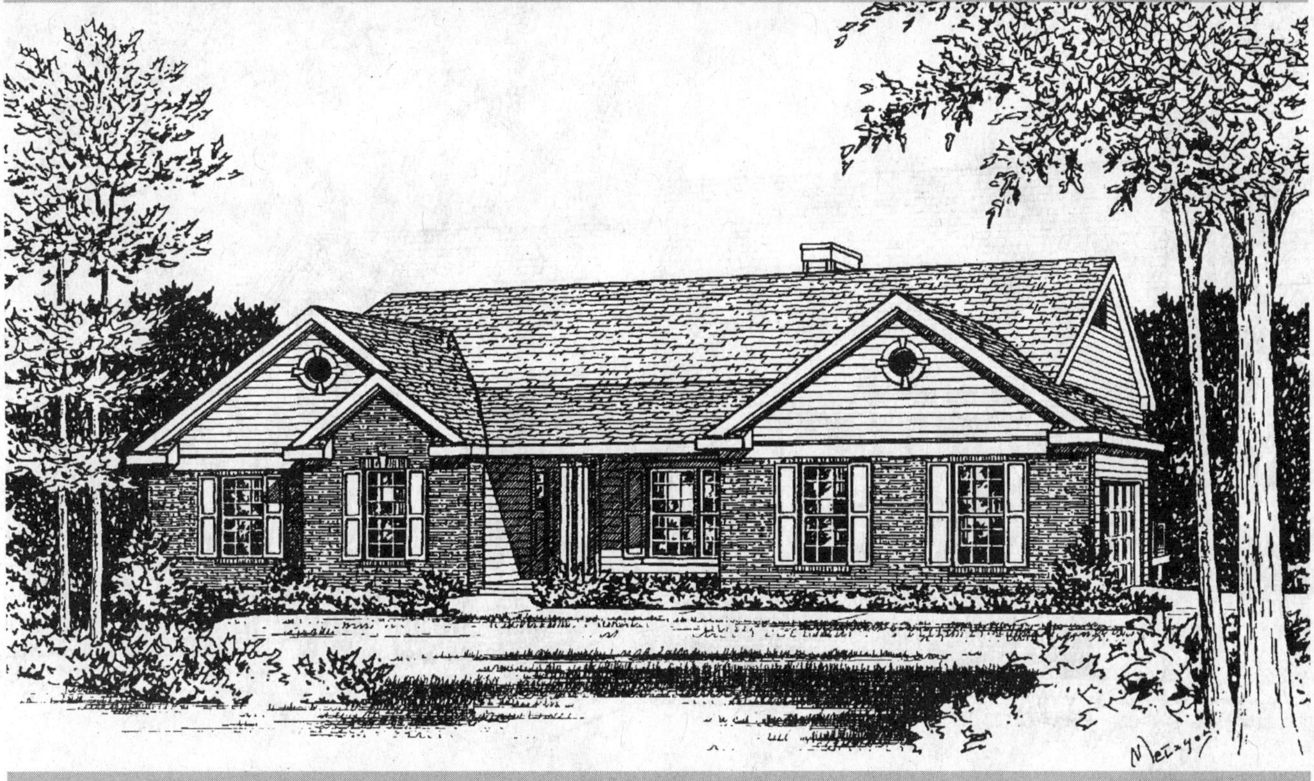

2,164 total square feet of living area **Price Code C**

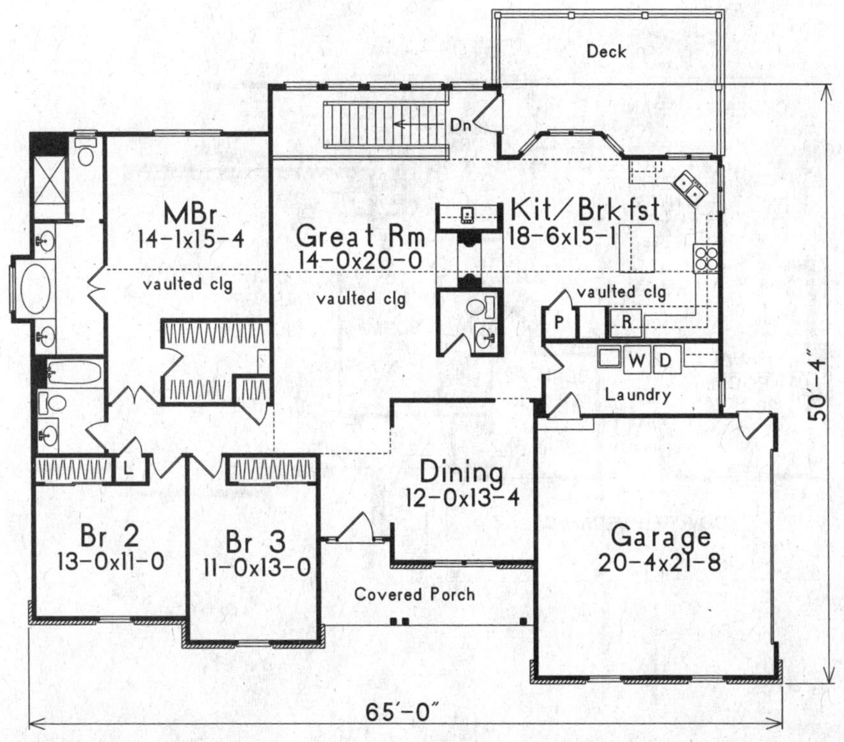

Deck
Dn
MBr
14-1x15-4
vaulted clg
Great Rm
14-0x20-0
vaulted clg
Kit/Brkfst
18-6x15-1
vaulted clg
P
R
W
D
Laundry
L
Dining
12-0x13-4
Br 2
13-0x11-0
Br 3
11-0x13-0
Garage
20-4x21-8
Covered Porch
50'-4"
65'-0"

Special features

- Great design for entertaining with wet bar and see-through fireplace in great room
- Plenty of closet space
- Vaulted ceiling enlarges the master bedroom, great room and kitchen/breakfast area
- Great room features great view to the rear of the home
- 3 bedrooms, 2 1/2 baths, 2-car side entry garage
- Basement foundation

The Family
Handyman

Plan #708-FDG-7963-L

Inviting Covered Verandas

1,830 total square feet of living area **Price Code C**

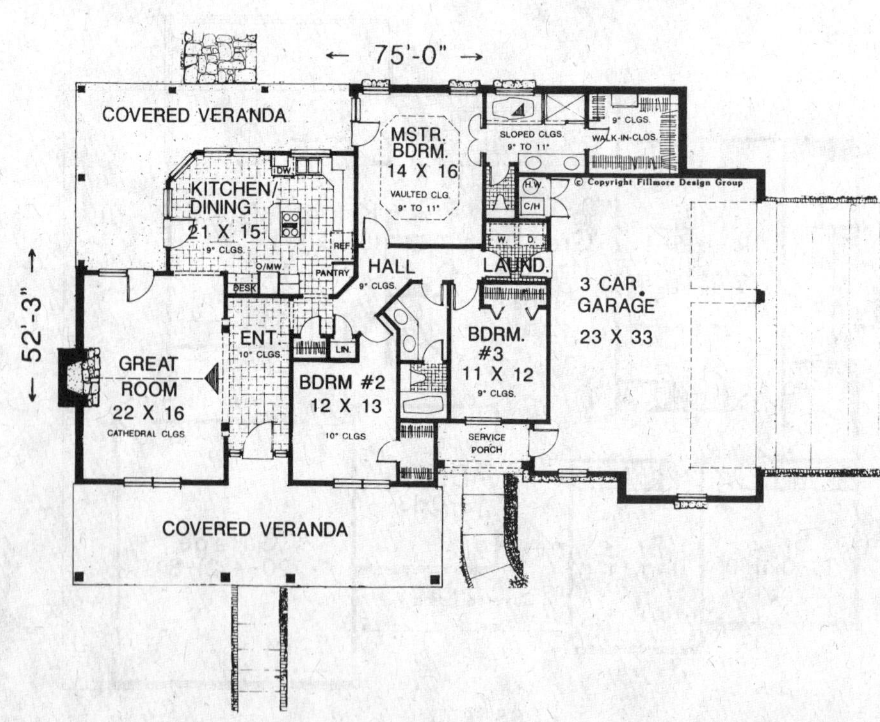

75'-0"
52'-3"
COVERED VERANDA
KITCHEN/ DINING
21 X 15
9" CLGS.
DW
REF
PANTRY
D/MW
DESK
MSTR. BDRM.
14 X 16
VAULTED CLG.
9" TO 11"
SLOPED CLGS.
9" TO 11"
9" CLGS.
WALK-IN-CLOS.
H.W.
C/H
© Copyright Fillmore Design Group
W. D.
LAUND.
HALL
9" CLGS.
3 CAR GARAGE
23 X 33
ENT.
10" CLGS.
LIN.
GREAT ROOM
22 X 16
CATHEDRAL CLGS.
BDRM #2
12 X 13
10" CLGS.
BDRM. #3
11 X 12
9" CLGS.
SERVICE PORCH
COVERED VERANDA

Special features

- Inviting covered verandas in the front and rear of the home
- Great room has fireplace and cathedral ceiling
- Handy service porch allows easy access
- Master suite has vaulted ceiling and private bath
- 3 bedrooms, 2 baths, 3-car side entry garage
- Basement, crawl space or slab foundation, please specify when ordering

The Family
Handyman

Plan #708-SH-SEA-245

Quaint Home Made For Country Living

1,578 total square feet of living area **Price Code B**

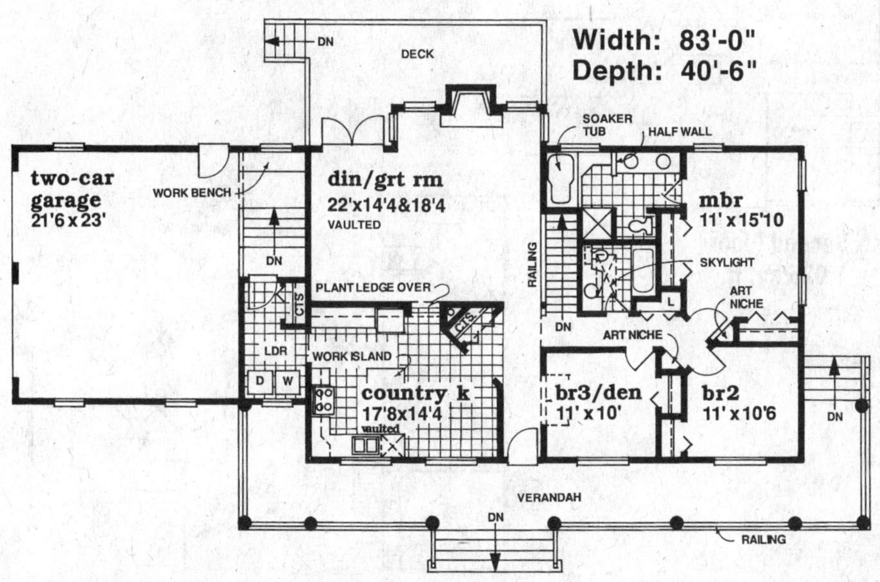
Width: 83'-0"
Depth: 40'-6"
DN
DECK
SOAKER TUB
HALF WALL
two-car garage 21'6 x 23'
WORK BENCH
din/grt rm 22'x14'4&18'4 VAULTED
mbr 11' x 15'10
SKYLIGHT
DN
PLANT LEDGE OVER
RAILING
ART NICHE
DN
ART NICHE
LDR
WORK ISLAND
D
W
country k 17'8x14'4 vaulted
br3/den 11' x 10'
br2 11' x 10'6
DN
VERANDAH
DN
RAILING

Special features

- A fireplace warms the great room and is flanked by windows overlooking the rear deck
- Bedrooms are clustered on one side of the home for privacy from living areas
- Master bedroom has unique art niche at its entry and a private bath with separate tub and shower
- 3 bedrooms, 2 baths, 2-car side entry garage
- Basement or crawl space foundation, please specify when ordering

Plan #708-0405

Striking Double Arched Entry

3,494 total square feet of living area — **Price Code F**

Special features

- Majestic two-story foyer opens into living and dining rooms, both framed by arched columns
- Balcony overlooks large living area featuring French doors to covered porch
- Luxurious master suite
- Convenient game room supports lots of activities
- 4 bedrooms, 3 1/2 baths, 3-car side entry garage
- Slab foundation, drawings also include crawl space foundation

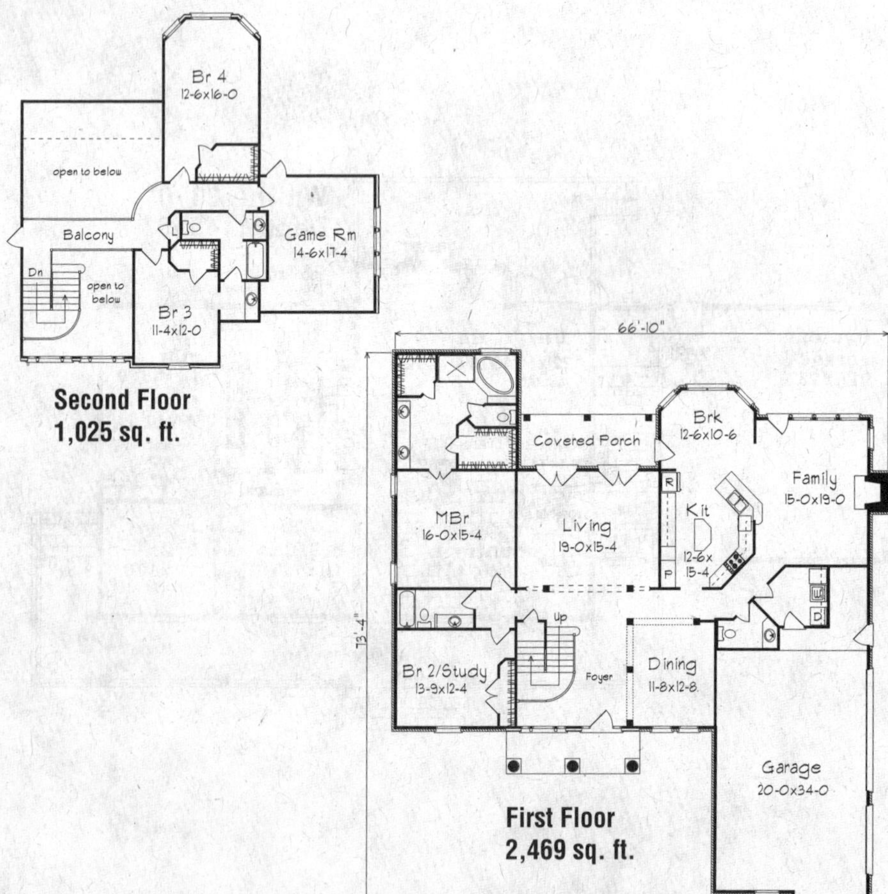
Br 4
12-6x16-0
open to below
Balcony
Dn
open to below
Br 3
11-4x12-0
Game Rm
14-6x17-4
Second Floor
1,025 sq. ft.
66'-10"
73'-4"
Covered Porch
Brk
12-6x10-6
Family
15-0x19-0
MBr
16-0x15-4
Living
19-0x15-4
Kit
12-6x
15-4
Up
Br 2/Study
13-9x12-4
Foyer
Dining
11-8x12-8
Garage
20-0x34-0
First Floor
2,469 sq. ft.

TO ORDER BLUEPRINTS USE THE FORM ON PAGE 15 OR CALL TOLL-FREE 1-877-671-6036

View thousands more home plans online at www.familyhandyman.com/homeplans

The Family
Handyman

Plan #708-LBD-19-23A

Circle-Top Details

1,932 total square feet of living area

Price Code C

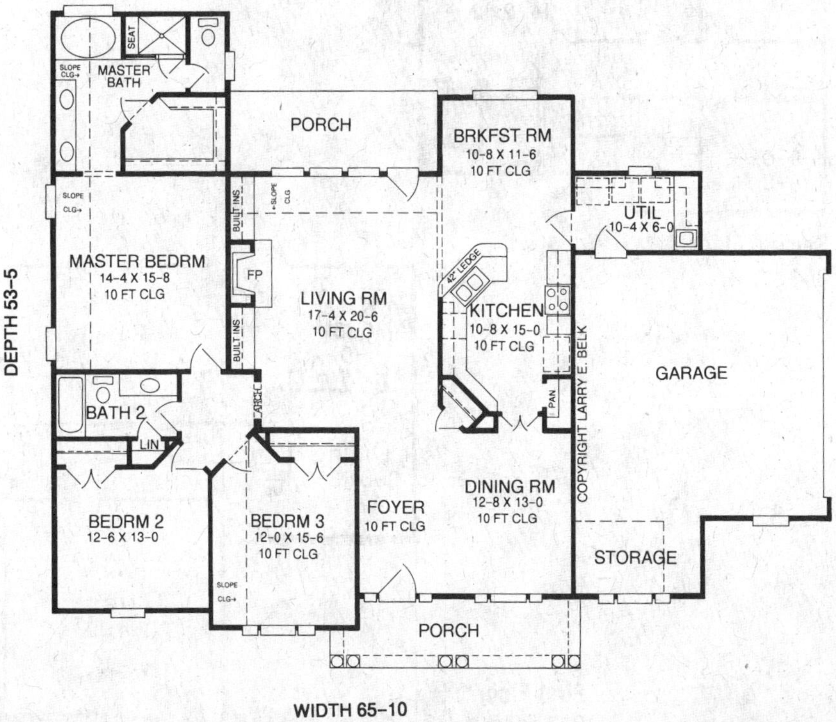

MASTER BATH
SEAT
SLOPE CLG+
PORCH
BRKFST RM
10-8 X 11-6
10 FT CLG
SLOPE CLG+
BUILT INS
MASTER BEDRM
14-4 X 15-8
10 FT CLG
FP
LIVING RM
17-4 X 20-6
10 FT CLG
42" LEDGE
KITCHEN
10-8 X 15-0
10 FT CLG
UTIL
10-4 X 6-0
GARAGE
PAN
COPYRIGHT LARRY E. BELK
DEPTH 53-5
BATH 2
LIN
BEDRM 2
12-6 X 13-0
BEDRM 3
12-0 X 15-6
10 FT CLG
FOYER
10 FT CLG
DINING RM
12-8 X 13-0
10 FT CLG
STORAGE
PORCH
WIDTH 65-10

Special features

- Double arches form entrance to this elegantly styled home
- Two palladian windows add distinction to facade
- Kitchen has angled eating bar opening to the breakfast and living rooms
- 3 bedrooms, 2 baths, 2-car side entry garage
- Crawl space or slab foundation, please specify when ordering

Plan #708-0656

Smaller Home Offers Stylish Exterior

1,700 total square feet of living area

Price Code B

Special features

- Two-story entry with T-stair is illuminated with decorative oval window
- Skillfully designed U-shaped kitchen has a built-in pantry
- All bedrooms have generous closet storage and are common to spacious hall with walk-in cedar closet
- 4 bedrooms, 2 1/2 baths, 2-car side entry garage
- Basement foundation

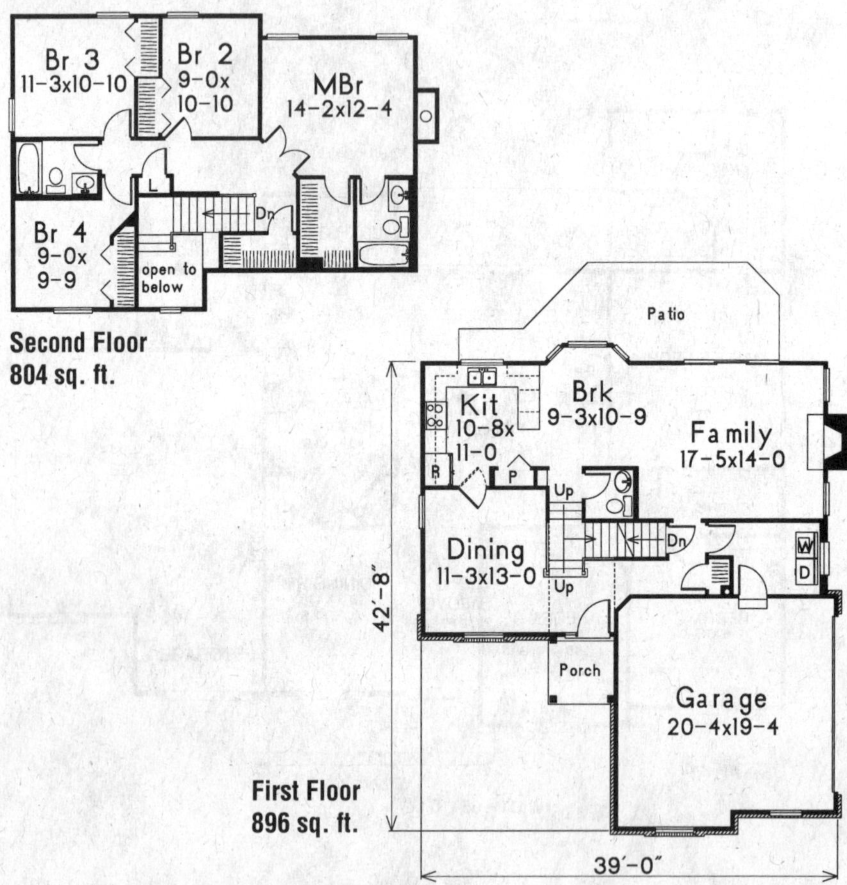

Br 3
11-3x10-10
Br 2
9-0x
10-10
MBr
14-2x12-4
L
Dn
Br 4
9-0x
9-9
open to
below
Patio
Kit
10-8x
11-0
Brk
9-3x10-9
Family
17-5x14-0
R
P
Up
Dining
11-3x13-0
Dn
Up
W
D
42'-8"
Porch
Garage
20-4x19-4
39'-0"

Second Floor
804 sq. ft.

First Floor
896 sq. ft.

TO ORDER BLUEPRINTS USE THE FORM ON PAGE 15 OR CALL TOLL-FREE 1-877-671-6036

View thousands more home plans online at www.familyhandyman.com/homeplans

The Family
Handyman

Open Dining And Living Areas

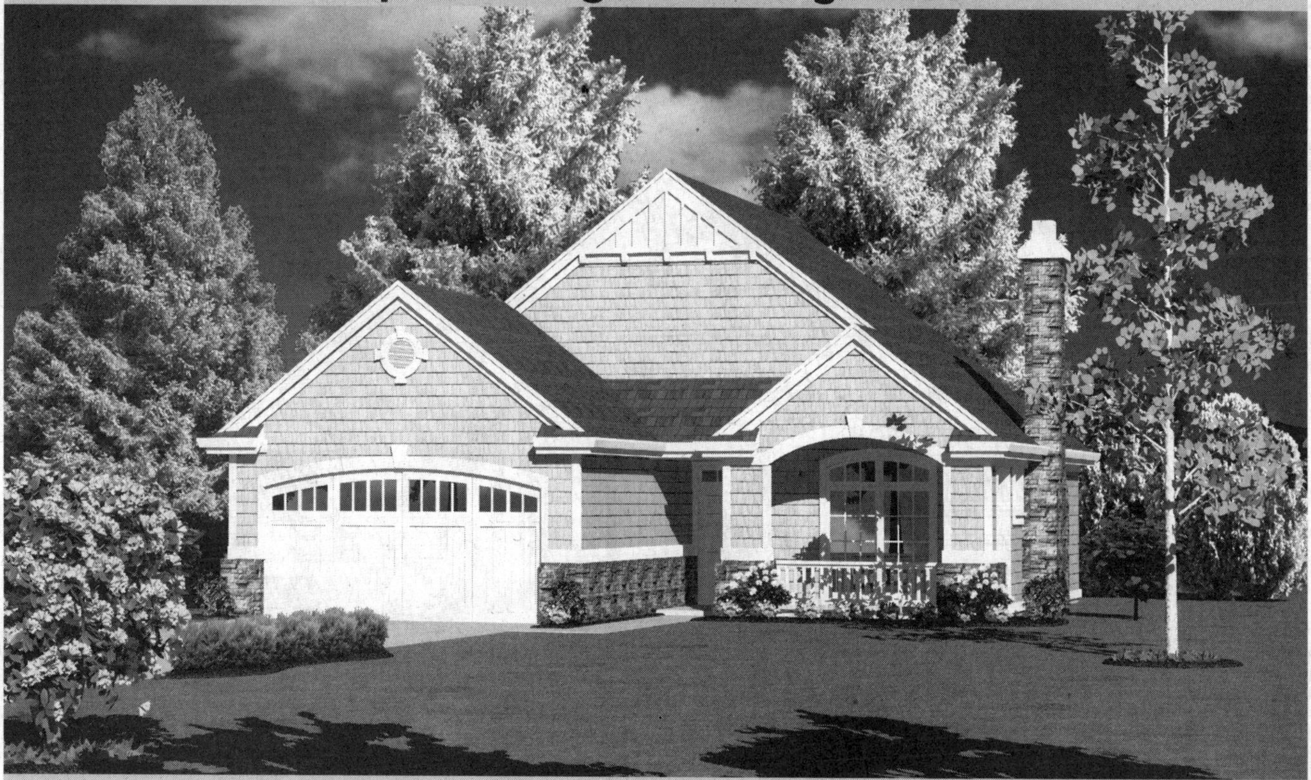

1,275 total square feet of living area **Price Code C**

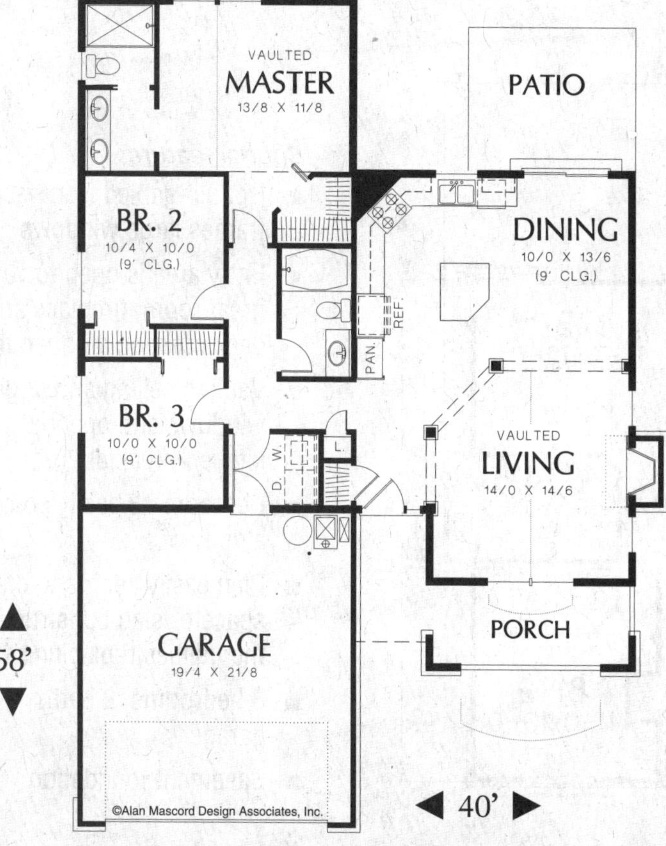
VAULTED
MASTER
13/8 X 11/8
PATIO
BR. 2
10/4 X 10/0
(9' CLG.)
DINING
10/0 X 13/6
(9' CLG.)
REF.
PAN.
BR. 3
10/0 X 10/0
(9' CLG.)
D.
W.
L.
VAULTED
LIVING
14/0 X 14/6
PORCH
GARAGE
19/4 X 21/8
58'
40'
©Alan Mascord Design Associates, Inc.

Special features

- Center island in the kitchen expands the kitchen into the dining area
- Decorative columns keep the living area open to other areas
- Covered front porch adds charm to the entry
- 3 bedrooms, 2 baths, 2-car garage
- Crawl space foundation

TO ORDER BLUEPRINTS USE THE FORM ON PAGE 15 OR CALL TOLL-FREE 1-877-671-6036

Plan #708-0105

Distinctive Ranch Has A Larger Look

1,360 total square feet of living area **Price Code A**

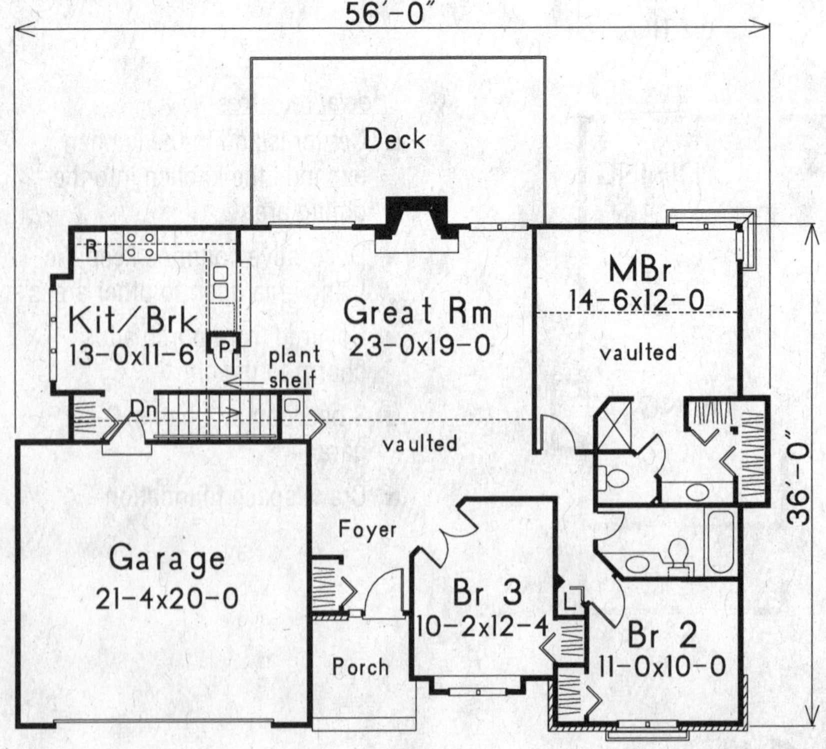
56'-0"
Deck
R
Kit/Brk
13-0x11-6
P
plant shelf
Great Rm
23-0x19-0
MBr
14-6x12-0
vaulted
Dn
vaulted
36'-0"
Garage
21-4x20-0
Foyer
Br 3
10-2x12-4
L
Br 2
11-0x10-0
Porch

Special features

- Double-gabled front facade frames large windows
- Entry area is open to vaulted great room, fireplace and rear deck creating an open feel
- Vaulted ceiling and large windows add openness to kitchen/breakfast room
- Bedroom #3 easily converts to a den
- Plan easily adapts to crawl space or slab construction, with the utilities replacing the stairs
- 3 bedrooms, 2 baths, 2-car garage
- Basement foundation

The Family
Handyman

Plan #708-0253

Impressive Corner Fireplace Highlights The Living Area

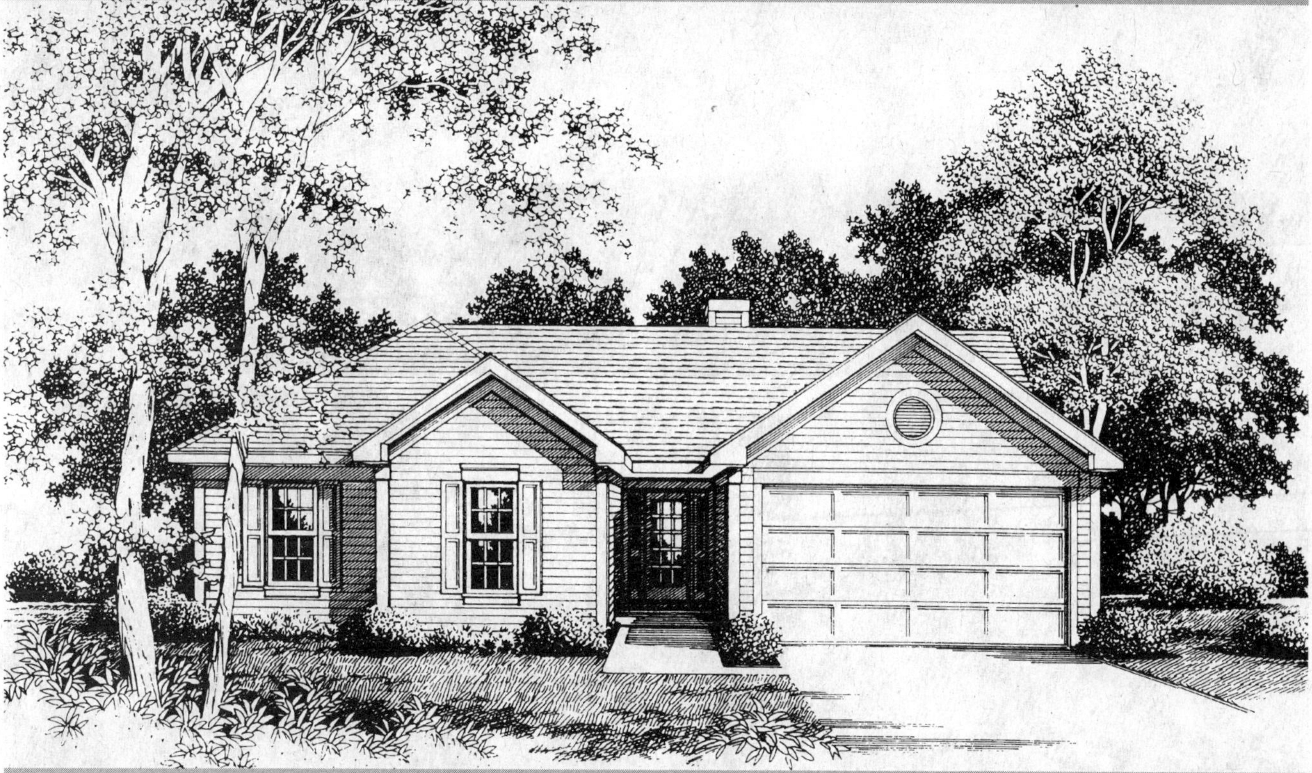

1,458 total square feet of living area

Price Code A

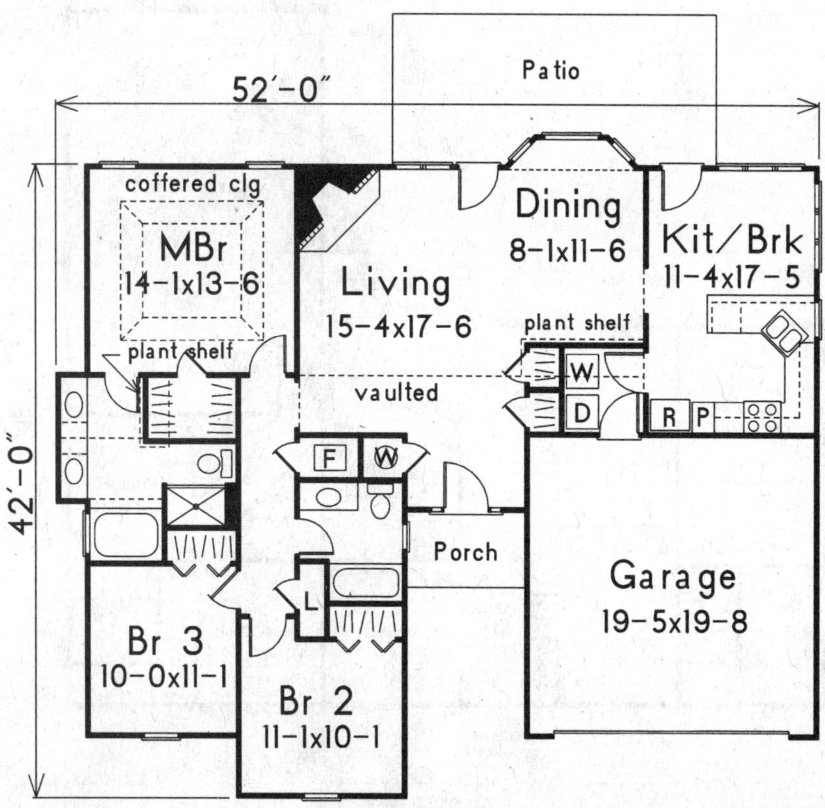
Patio
52′-0″
42′-0″
coffered clg
MBr
14-1x13-6
plant shelf
Living
15-4x17-6
Dining
8-1x11-6
Kit/Brk
11-4x17-5
plant shelf
vaulted
W
D
R
P
F
W
Porch
Garage
19-5x19-8
L
Br 3
10-0x11-1
Br 2
11-1x10-1

Special features

- Convenient snack bar joins kitchen with breakfast room
- Large living room has fireplace, plenty of windows, vaulted ceiling and nearby plant shelf
- Master bedroom offers a private bath with vaulted ceiling, walk-in closet, plant shelf and coffered ceiling
- Corner windows provide abundant light in breakfast room
- 3 bedrooms, 2 baths, 2-car garage
- Crawl space foundation, drawings also include slab foundation

The Family
Handyman

Plan #708-DH-2323

Private Master Bedroom

2,293 total square feet of living area **Price Code D**

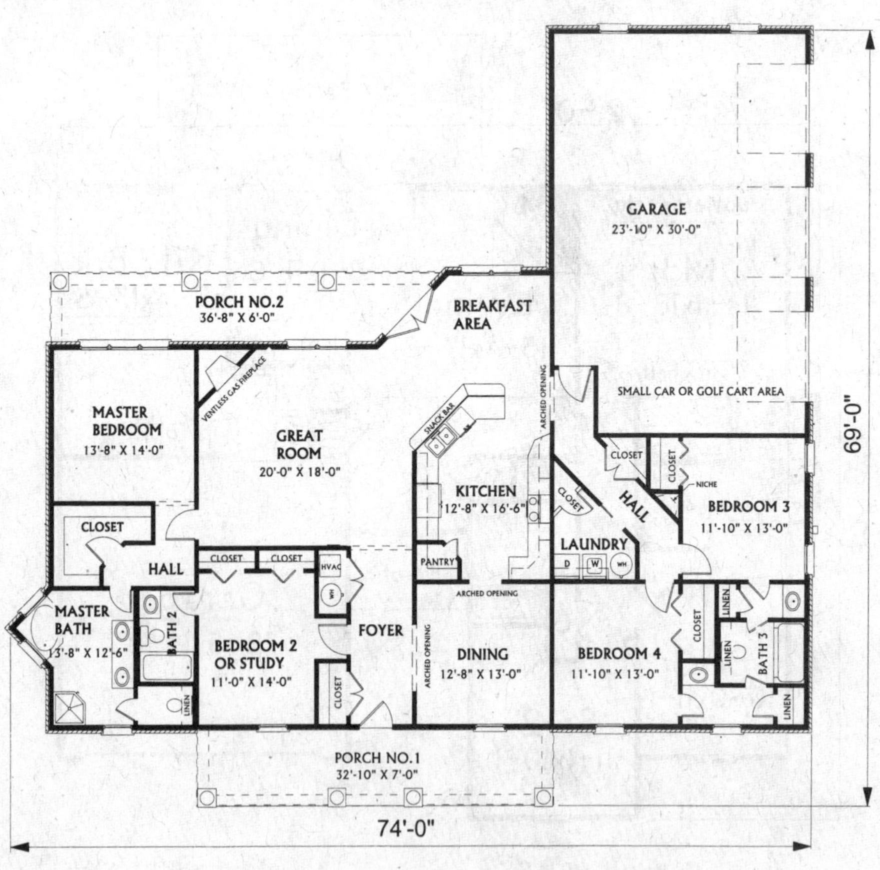
PORCH NO.2
36'-8" X 6'-0"
BREAKFAST AREA
GARAGE
23'-10" X 30'-0"
SMALL CAR OR GOLF CART AREA
MASTER BEDROOM
13'-8" X 14'-0"
VENTLESS GAS FIREPLACE
GREAT ROOM
20'-0" X 18'-0"
SNACK BAR
KITCHEN
12'-8" X 16'-6"
ARCHED OPENING
CLOSET
HALL
NICHE
BEDROOM 3
11'-10" X 13'-0"
LAUNDRY
PANTRY
CLOSET
HALL
CLOSET
CLOSET
HVAC
ARCHED OPENING
MASTER BATH
13'-8" X 12'-6"
BATH 2
LINEN
BEDROOM 2
OR STUDY
11'-0" X 14'-0"
CLOSET
FOYER
ARCHED OPENING
DINING
12'-8" X 13'-0"
BEDROOM 4
11'-10" X 13'-0"
CLOSET
LINEN
LINEN
BATH 3
LINEN
PORCH NO.1
32'-10" X 7'-0"
74'-0"
69'-0"

Special features

- The arched opening near the kitchen leads to all the two of the secondary bedrooms
- Bedroom #2/study could easily convert to an office area
- Corner fireplace in great room demands attention
- 4 bedrooms, 3 baths, 3-car side entry garage
- Crawl space or slab foundation, please specify when ordering

TO ORDER BLUEPRINTS USE THE FORM ON PAGE 15 OR CALL TOLL-FREE 1-877-671-6036

View thousands more home plans online at www.familyhandyman.com/homeplans

The Family
Handyman

Plan #708-0320

Classic Three Bedroom

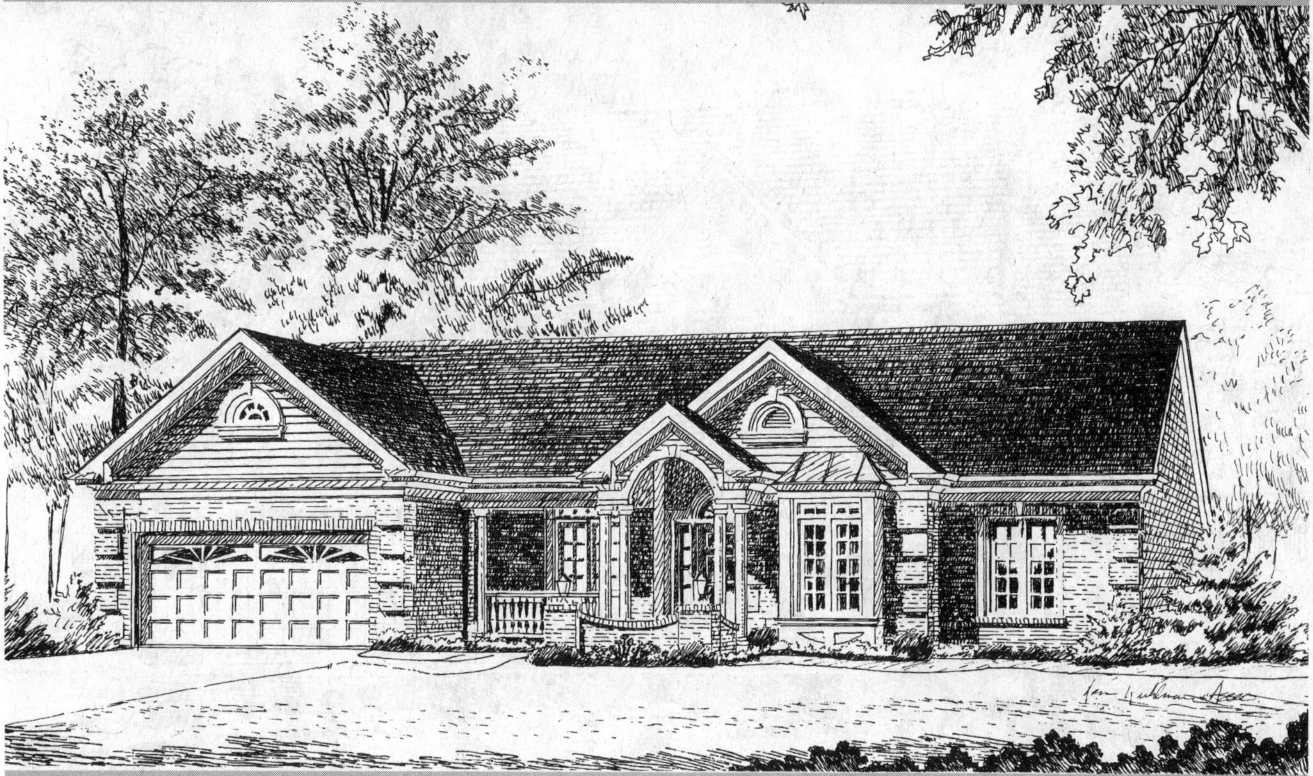

2,061 total square feet of living area **Price Code D**

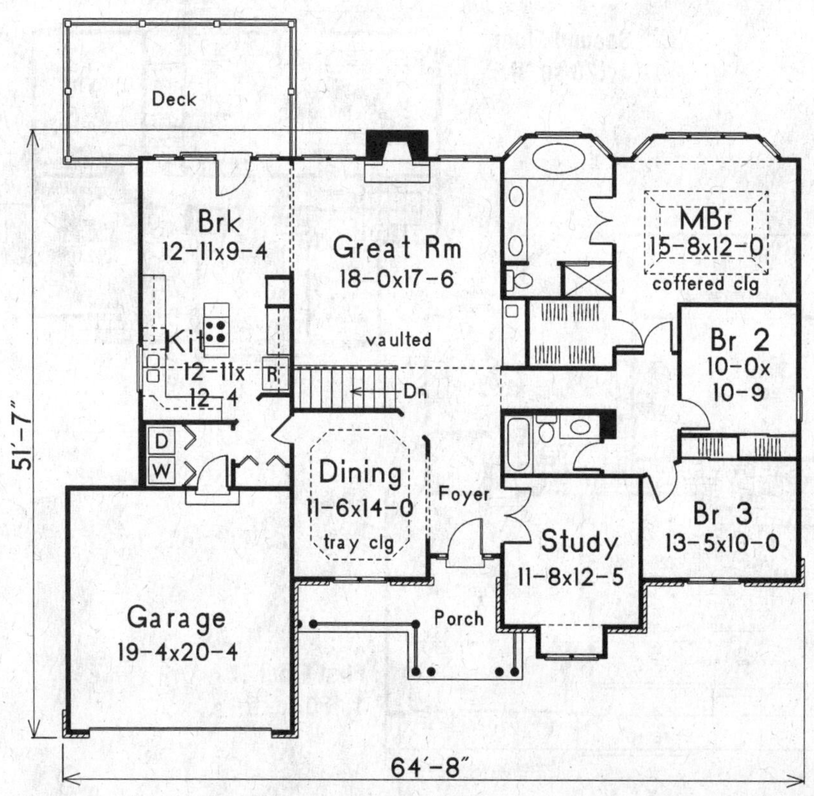
Deck
Brk
12-11x9-4
Great Rm
18-0x17-6
vaulted
MBr
15-8x12-0
coffered clg
Br 2
10-0x
10-9
Kit
12-11x
12-4
R
Dn
D
W
Dining
11-6x14-0
tray clg
Foyer
Study
11-8x12-5
Br 3
13-5x10-0
Porch
Garage
19-4x20-4
51'-7"
64'-8"

Special features

- Convenient entrance from garage into home through laundry room
- Master bedroom features walk-in closet and double-door entrance into master bath with oversized tub
- Formal dining room with tray ceiling
- Kitchen features island cooktop and adjacent breakfast room
- 3 bedrooms, 2 baths, 2-car garage
- Basement foundation

Plan #708-DBI-2408

Cozy Family Home

2,270 total square feet of living area

Price Code D

Special features

- Great room and hearth room share see-through fireplace
- Oversized rooms throughout
- First floor has terrific floor plan for entertaining with large kitchen, breakfast area and adjacent great room
- 4 bedrooms, 2 1/2 baths, 2-car garage
- Basement foundation

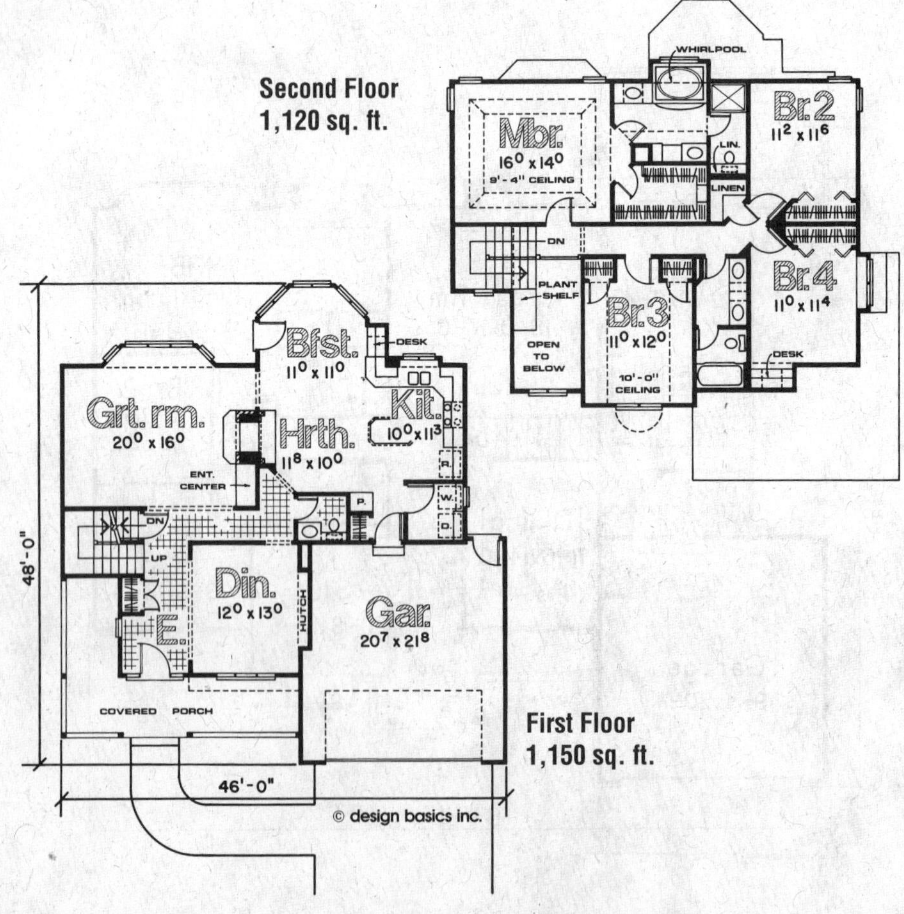
Second Floor
1,120 sq. ft.
WHIRLPOOL
Mbr.
16⁰ x 14⁰
9'-4" CEILING
Br. 2
11² x 11⁶
LIN.
LINEN
DN
PLANT SHELF
OPEN TO BELOW
Br. 3
11⁰ x 12⁰
10'-0" CEILING
Br. 4
11⁰ x 11⁴
DESK
Bfst.
11⁰ x 11⁰
DESK
Grt. rm.
20⁰ x 16⁰
Hrth.
11⁸ x 10⁰
Kit.
10⁰ x 11³
ENT. CENTER
P.
R.
W.
D.
DN
UP
Din.
12⁰ x 13⁰
HUTCH
Gar.
20⁷ x 21⁸
E.
COVERED PORCH
48'-0"
46'-0"
© design basics inc.
First Floor
1,150 sq. ft.

TO ORDER BLUEPRINTS USE THE FORM ON PAGE 15 OR CALL TOLL-FREE 1-877-671-6036

View thousands more home plans online at www.familyhandyman.com/homeplans

The Family
Handyman

Plan #708-0374

Combined Family And Breakfast Areas

2,213 total square feet of living area **Price Code E**

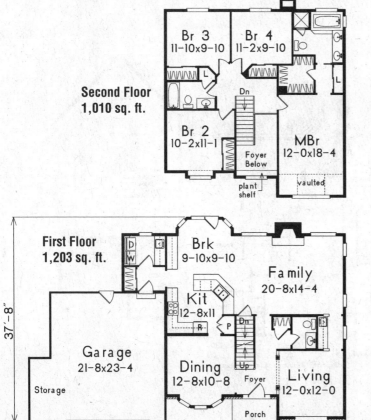

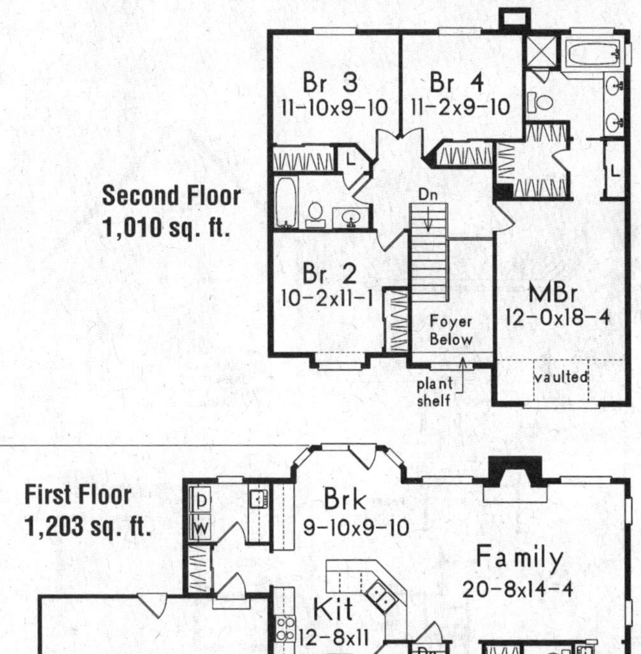
Second Floor
1,010 sq. ft.
Br 3
11-10x9-10
Br 4
11-2x9-10
L
L
Dn
Br 2
10-2x11-1
MBr
12-0x18-4
Foyer
Below
plant
shelf
vaulted
First Floor
1,203 sq. ft.
D
W
Brk
9-10x9-10
Family
20-8x14-4
Kit
12-8x11
R
P
Dn
Up
Garage
21-8x23-4
Storage
Dining
12-8x10-8
Foyer
Living
12-0x12-0
Porch
37'-8"
59'-8"

Special features

- Angled kitchen counter overlooks living room with large fireplace
- Hallway between family and living areas provides extra storage and convenient sink for entertaining
- Large master bedroom features vaulted ceiling and elegant master bath with walk-in closet
- Second floor open to foyer below and features distinctive plant shelf
- 4 bedrooms, 2 1/2 baths, 2-car garage
- Basement foundation

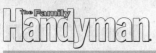

Plan #708-FDG-8729-L

Double Bays Accent Front

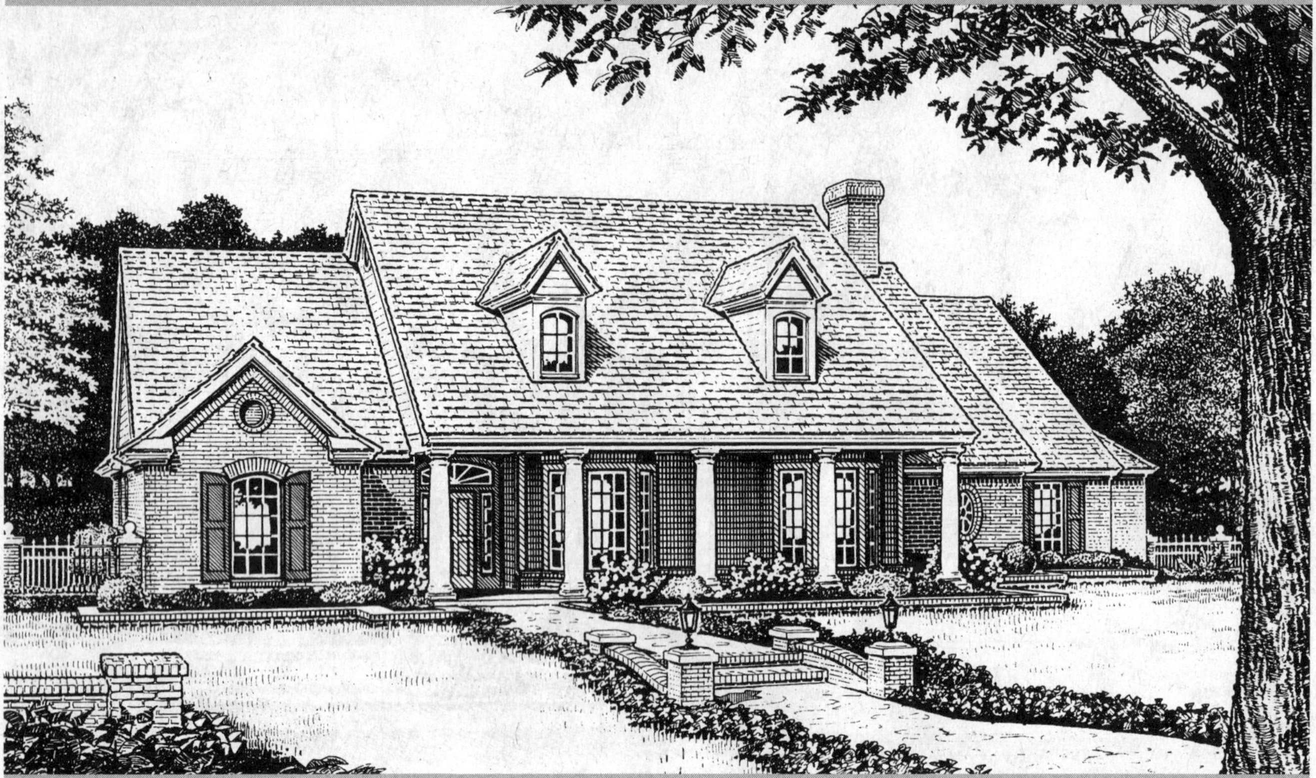

2,529 total square feet of living area

Price Code D

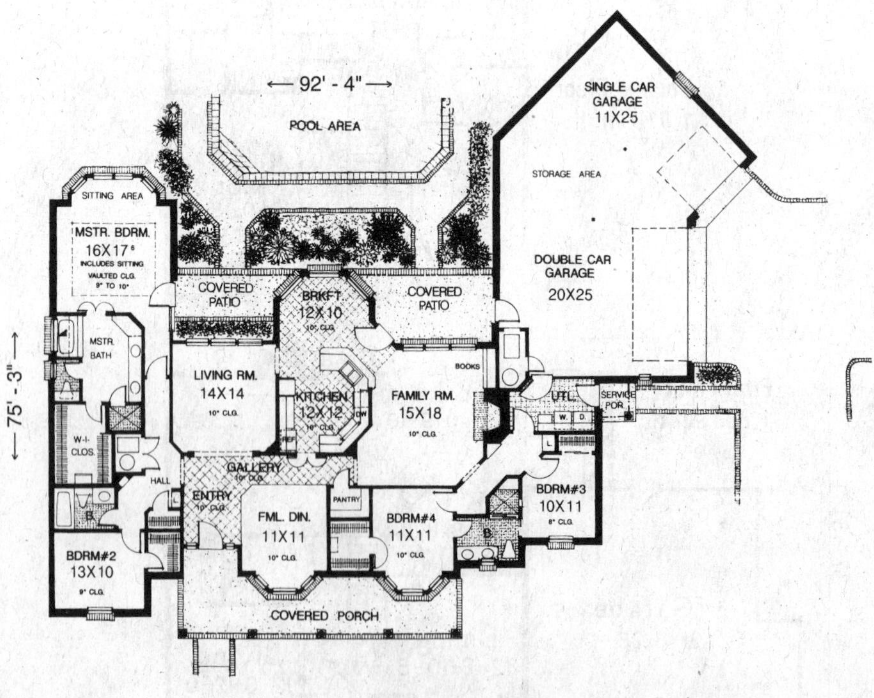
92' - 4"
POOL AREA
SINGLE CAR GARAGE 11X25
STORAGE AREA
SITTING AREA
MSTR. BDRM. 16X17[6]
INCLUDES SITTING VAULTED CLG. 9" TO 10"
COVERED PATIO
BRKFT. 12X10
COVERED PATIO
DOUBLE CAR GARAGE 20X25
MSTR. BATH
LIVING RM. 14X14
10" CLG.
KITCHEN 12X12
FAMILY RM. 15X18
10" CLG.
BOOKS
UTL.
SERVICE POR.
75' - 3"
W-I-CLOS.
GALLERY
HALL
ENTRY
PANTRY
FML. DIN. 11X11
BDRM#4 11X11
BDRM#3 10X11
BDRM#2 13X10
9" CLG.
COVERED PORCH

Special features

- Kitchen and breakfast area are located between the family and living rooms for easy access
- Master bedroom includes sitting area, private bath and access to covered patio
- 4 bedrooms, 3 baths, 3-car side entry garage
- Slab foundation

Plan #708-SRD-147

A Touch Of Old World Charm

2,320 total square feet of living area **Price Code D**

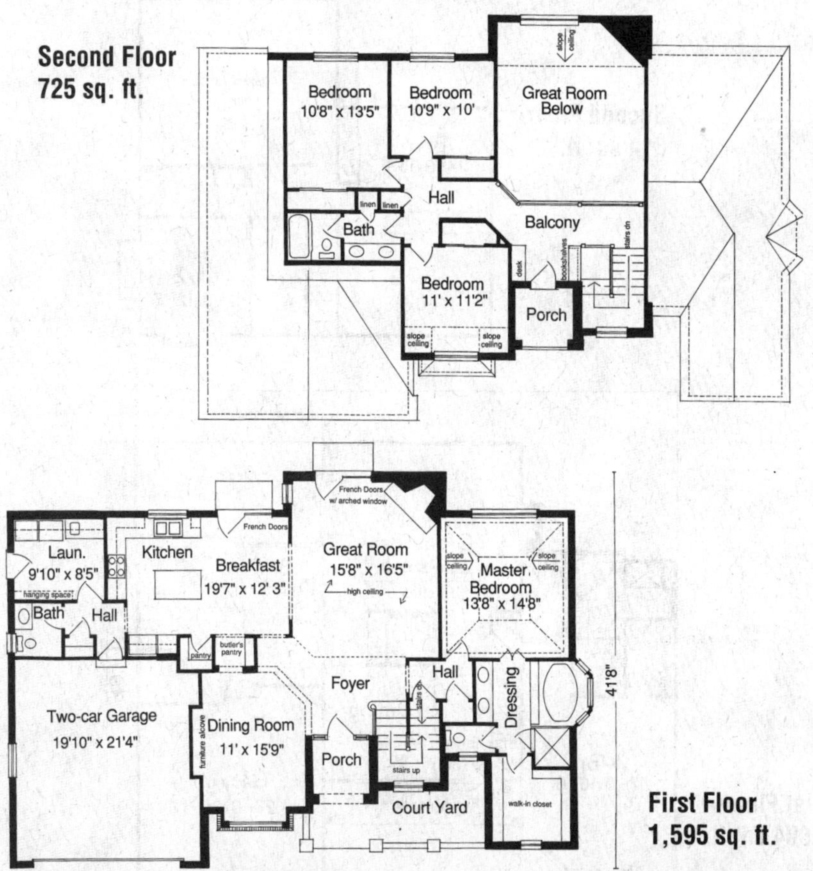
Second Floor
725 sq. ft.
Bedroom
10'8" x 13'5"
Bedroom
10'9" x 10'
Great Room
Below
slope ceiling
Hall
linen
linen
Bath
Balcony
stairs dn
bookshelves
desk
Bedroom
11' x 11'2"
Porch
slope ceiling
slope ceiling
French Doors w/ arched window
French Doors
Laun.
9'10" x 8'5"
hanging space
Kitchen
Breakfast
19'7" x 12' 3"
Great Room
15'8" x 16'5"
high ceiling
slope ceiling
slope ceiling
Master
Bedroom
13'8" x 14'8"
Bath
Hall
butler's pantry
pantry
Two-car Garage
19'10" x 21'4"
furniture alcove
Dining Room
11' x 15'9"
Foyer
Hall
Dressing
stairs dn
stairs up
Porch
Court Yard
walk-in closet
41'8"
61'
First Floor
1,595 sq. ft.

Special features

- From the foyer, there is a panoramic view of the dramatic great room and formal dining room
- A butler's pantry is strategically placed between formal dining room and kitchen/breakfast room
- French doors add light and style to the breakfast room
- 4 bedrooms, 2 1/2 baths, 2-car garage
- Basement foundation

TO ORDER BLUEPRINTS USE THE FORM ON PAGE 15 OR CALL TOLL-FREE 1-877-671-6036

View thousands more home plans online at www.familyhandyman.com/homeplans

Plan #708-0170

Handsome Home With Spacious Living Areas

2,618 total square feet of living area **Price Code E**

Special features

- Stylish front facade with covered porch and distinctive window treatment
- Great room features vaulted ceiling, skylights and large fireplace
- Master bedroom and bath has two large walk-in closets, separate oversized tub and shower, first floor convenience and privacy
- Kitchen overlooks the deck and features circle-top windows and corner window view from the sink
- 4 bedrooms, 2 1/2 baths, 2-car garage
- Basement foundation

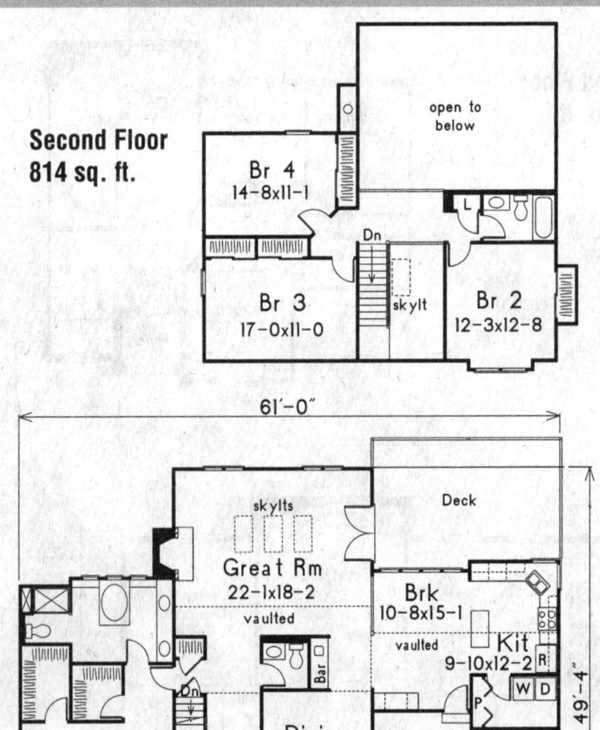

open to below
Br 4
14-8x11-1
L
Dn
Br 3
17-0x11-0
skylt
Br 2
12-3x12-8
61'-0"
skylts
Deck
Great Rm
22-1x18-2
vaulted
Brk
10-8x15-1
vaulted
Kit
9-10x12-2
R
Bar
Dn
P
W D
Dining
12-3x12-5
Entry
Up
MBr
17-0x16-0
Porch depth 4-0
Garage
20-8x20-1
49'-4"

Second Floor
814 sq. ft.

First Floor
1,804 sq. ft.

TO ORDER BLUEPRINTS USE THE FORM ON PAGE 15 OR CALL TOLL-FREE 1-877-671-6036

View thousands more home plans online at www.familyhandyman.com/homeplans

Plan #708-AX-93308

Wrap-Around Porch Adds To Farmhouse Style

1,793 total square feet of living area

Price Code B

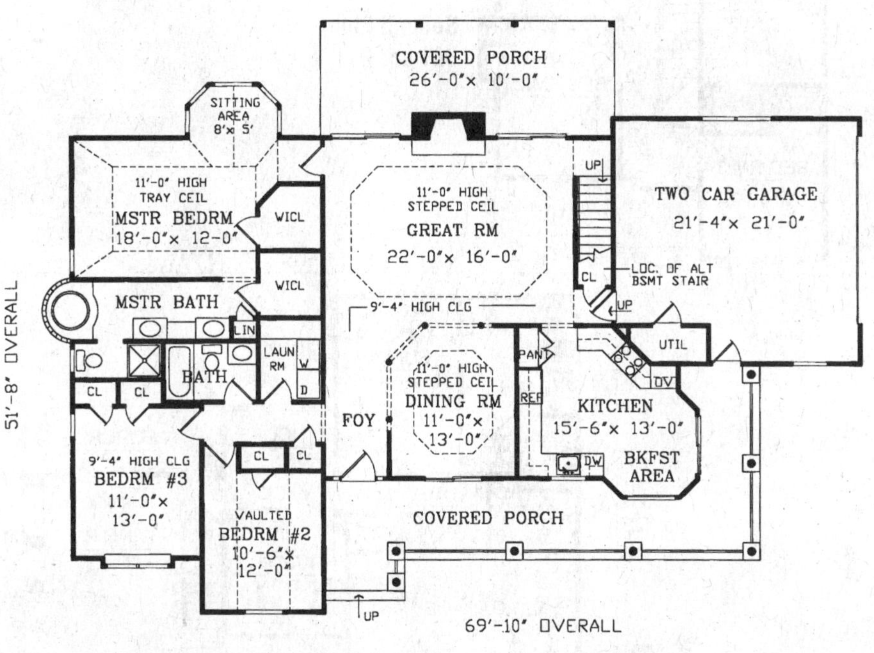

COVERED PORCH
26'-0"x 10'-0"
SITTING AREA
8'x 5'
11'-0" HIGH TRAY CEIL
MSTR BEDRM
18'-0"x 12-0"
WICL
WICL
11'-0" HIGH STEPPED CEIL
GREAT RM
22'-0"x 16'-0"
UP
TWO CAR GARAGE
21'-4"x 21'-0"
CL
LOC. OF ALT BSMT STAIR
UP
9'-4" HIGH CLG
MSTR BATH
LIN
LAUN RM
W
D
BATH
CL
CL
PANT
UTIL
DW
11'-0" HIGH STEPPED CEIL
DINING RM
11'-0"x 13'-0"
REF
KITCHEN
15'-6"x 13'-0"
BKFST AREA
DW
FOY
9'-4" HIGH CLG
BEDRM #3
11'-0"x 13'-0"
CL
CL
VAULTED
BEDRM #2
10'-6"x 12'-0"
COVERED PORCH
UP
51'-8" OVERALL
69'-10" OVERALL

Special features

- A beautiful foyer leads into the great room which has a fireplace flanked by two sets of beautifully transomed doors both leading to a large covered porch
- Dramatic eat-in kitchen includes an abundance of cabinets and workspace in an exciting angled shape
- Delightful master bedroom has many amenities
- Optional bonus room has an additional 779 square feet of living area
- 3 bedrooms, 2 baths, 2-car side entry garage
- Basement, crawl space or slab foundation, please specify when ordering

Plan #708-RDD-1896-9

Appealing Master Suite

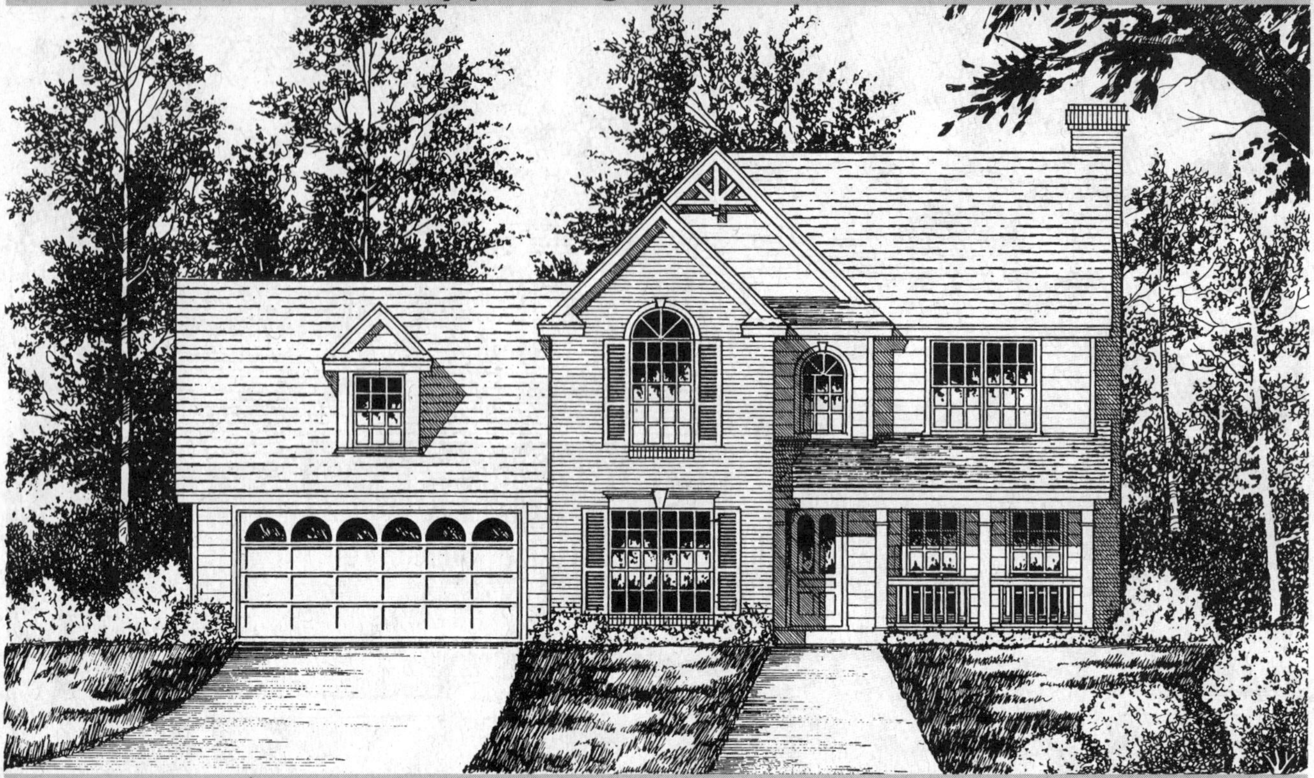

1,896 total square feet of living area

Price Code C

Special features

- Living room has lots of windows, a media center and a fireplace
- Centrally located kitchen with breakfast nook
- Extra storage in garage
- Covered porch in front and rear of home
- Optional balcony on second floor
- 4 bedrooms, 2 1/2 baths, 2-car garage
- Basement, crawl space or slab foundation, please specify when ordering

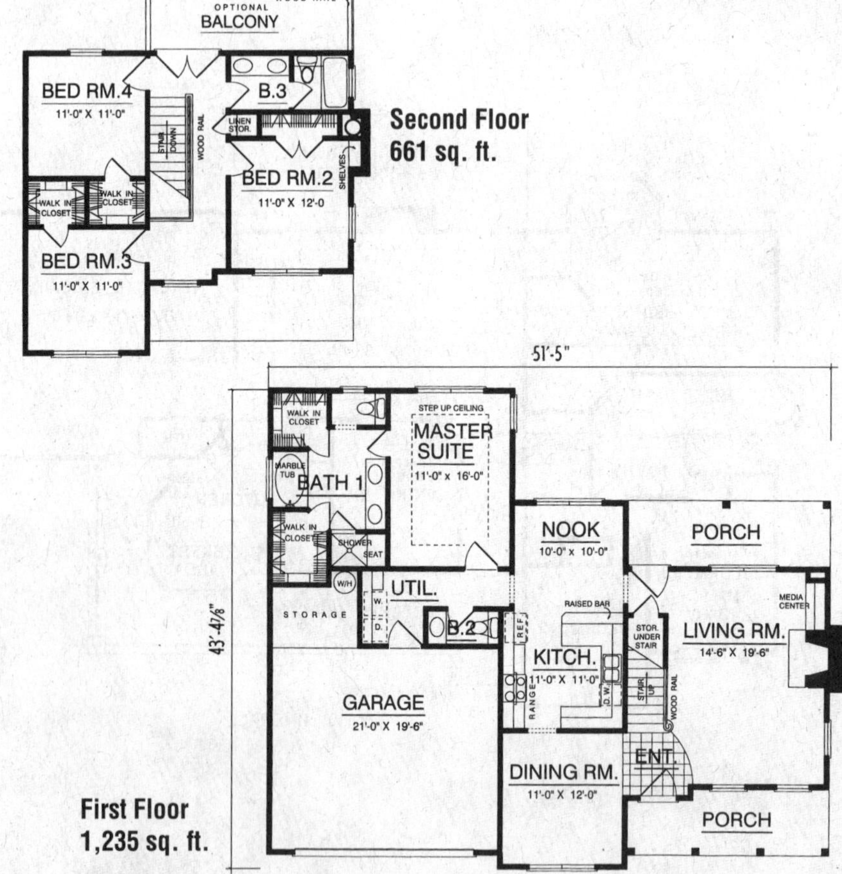

WOOD RAIL
OPTIONAL BALCONY
BED RM.4
11'-0" X 11'-0"
B.3
LINEN STOR.
BED RM.2
11'-0" X 12'-0
SHELVES
WALK IN CLOSET
WALK IN CLOSET
BED RM.3
11'-0" X 11'-0"
Second Floor
661 sq. ft.
51'-5"
43'-4 1/8"
WALK IN CLOSET
STEP UP CEILING
MASTER SUITE
11'-0" x 16'-0"
MARBLE TUB
BATH 1
WALK IN CLOSET
SHOWER SEAT
NOOK
10'-0" x 10'-0"
PORCH
W/H
UTIL.
STORAGE
B.2
RAISED BAR
KITCH.
11'-0" X 11'-0"
STOR. UNDER STAIR
MEDIA CENTER
LIVING RM.
14'-6" X 19'-6"
GARAGE
21'-0" X 19'-6"
ENT.
DINING RM.
11'-0" X 12'-0"
PORCH
First Floor
1,235 sq. ft.

TO ORDER BLUEPRINTS USE THE FORM ON PAGE 15 OR CALL TOLL-FREE 1-877-671-6036

View thousands more home plans online at www.familyhandyman.com/homeplans

The Family
Handyman

Plan #708-UDG-97010

Terrific Traditional Brick Two-Story

© Urban Design Group, Inc.

2,900 total square feet of living area — **Price Code E**

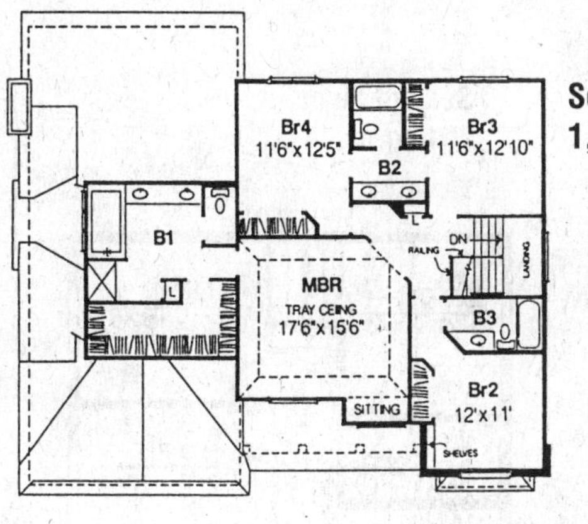
Br4
11'6"x12'5"
Br3
11'6"x12'10"
B2
B1
DN
RAILING
LANDING
MBR
TRAY CEING
17'6"x15'6"
B3
Br2
12'x11'
SITTING
SHELVES

Second Floor
1,386 sq. ft.

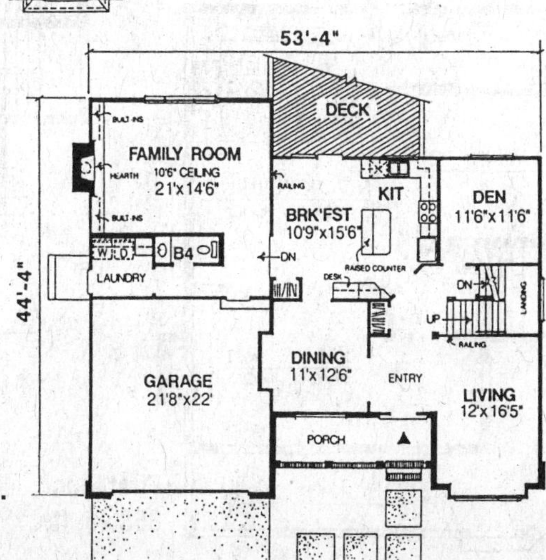
53'-4"
44'-4"
DECK
FAMILY ROOM
10'6" CEILING
21'x14'6"
BUILT-INS
HEARTH
RAILING
KIT
DEN
11'6"x11'6"
BRK'FST
10'9"x15'6"
W D
B4
DN
LAUNDRY
RAISED COUNTER
DESK
DN
UP
RAILING
DINING
11'x12'6"
ENTRY
GARAGE
21'8"x22'
LIVING
12'x16'5"
PORCH

First Floor
1,514 sq. ft.

Special features

- Master bedroom includes small sitting nook and spacious walk-in closet
- Formal living and dining rooms in the front of the home
- 9' ceilings on first floor
- 4 bedrooms, 3 1/2 baths, 2-car garage
- Basement foundation

TO ORDER BLUEPRINTS USE THE FORM ON PAGE 15 OR CALL TOLL-FREE 1-877-671-6036

View thousands more home plans online at www.familyhandyman.com/homeplans

The Family
Handyman

Plan #708-DDI-95-234

Craftsman Cottage

1,649 total square feet of living area — **Price Code B**

Special features

- Energy efficient home with 2" x 6" exterior walls
- Ideal design for a narrow lot
- Country kitchen includes an island and eating bar
- Master bedroom has 12' vaulted ceiling and a charming arched window
- 4 bedrooms, 2 1/2 baths, 2-car side entry garage
- Basement or crawl space foundation, please specify when ordering

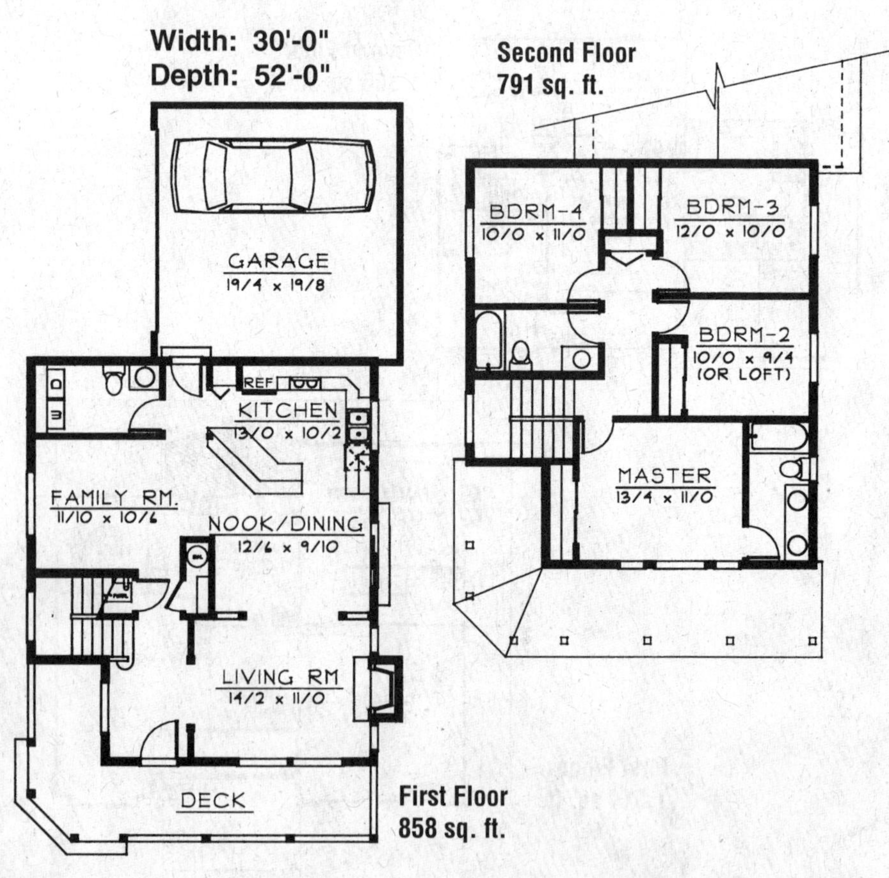
Width: 30'-0"
Depth: 52'-0"
Second Floor
791 sq. ft.
GARAGE
19/4 x 19/8
BDRM-4
10/0 x 11/0
BDRM-3
12/0 x 10/0
BDRM-2
10/0 x 9/4
(OR LOFT)
MASTER
13/4 x 11/0
REF
KITCHEN
13/0 x 10/2
FAMILY RM.
11/10 x 10/6
NOOK/DINING
12/6 x 9/10
LIVING RM
14/2 x 11/0
DECK
First Floor
858 sq. ft.

TO ORDER BLUEPRINTS USE THE FORM ON PAGE 15 OR CALL TOLL-FREE 1-877-671-6036

View thousands more home plans online at www.familyhandyman.com/homeplans

Traditional Classic, Modern Features Abound

3,035 total square feet of living area

Price Code E

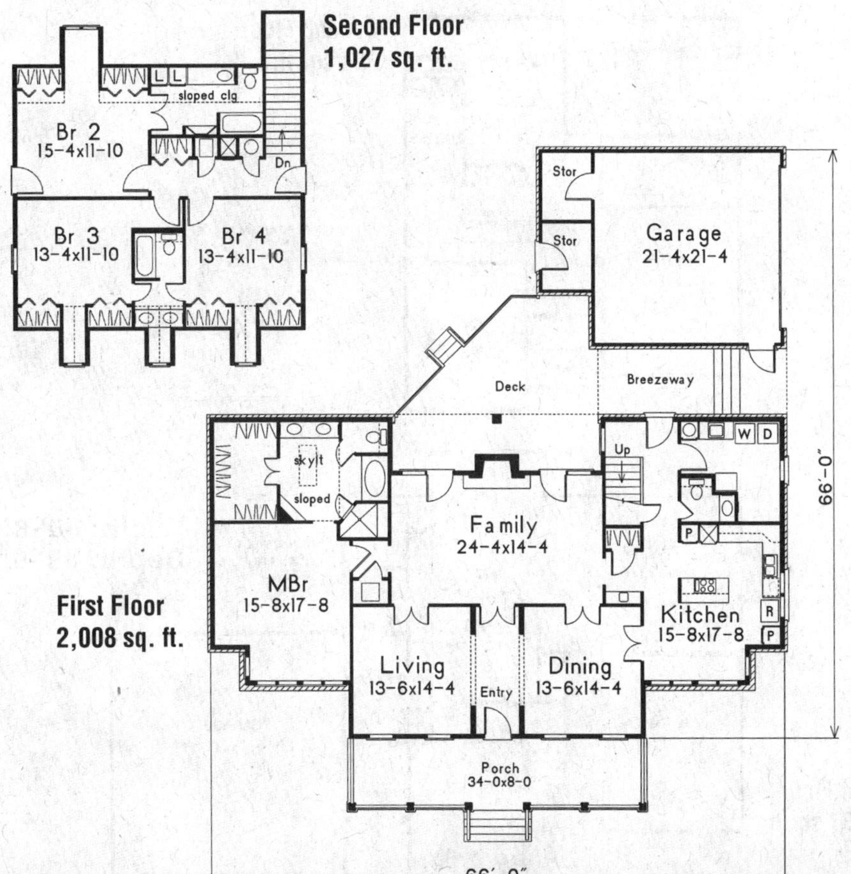
Second Floor
1,027 sq. ft.
sloped clg
Br 2
15-4x11-10
Dn
Br 3
13-4x11-10
Br 4
13-4x11-10
Stor
Stor
Garage
21-4x21-4
Deck
Breezeway
skylt
sloped
Up
W
D
P
Family
24-4x14-4
MBr
15-8x17-8
Kitchen
15-8x17-8
R
P
First Floor
2,008 sq. ft.
Living
13-6x14-4
Entry
Dining
13-6x14-4
Porch
34-0x8-0
66'-0"
66'-0"

Special features

- Front facade includes large porch
- Private master bedroom with windowed sitting area, walk-in closet, sloped ceiling and skylight
- Formal living and dining rooms adjoin the family room through attractive French doors
- Energy efficient home with 2" x 6" exterior walls
- 4 bedrooms, 3 1/2 baths, 2-car side entry garage
- Crawl space foundation, drawings also include slab and basement foundations

TO ORDER BLUEPRINTS USE THE FORM ON PAGE 15 OR CALL TOLL-FREE 1-877-671-6036

View thousands more home plans online at www.familyhandyman.com/homeplans

Plan #708-JFD-20-2121-1

Optional Study

2,121 total square feet of living area **Price Code C**

Special features

- Delightful kitchen space overlooks dining and family rooms
- Optional study has an additional 148 square feet of living area
- Garage is a useful secondary entrance
- Optional bonus room has an additional 334 square feet of living area
- 4 bedrooms, 3 1/2 baths, 2-car garage
- Basement foundation

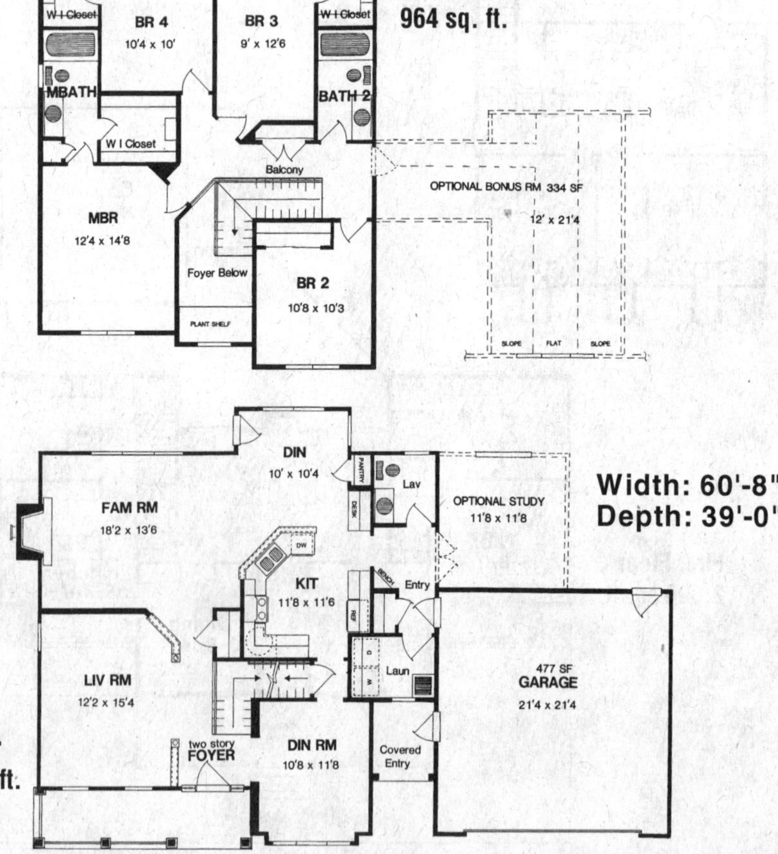
Second Floor
964 sq. ft.
W I Closet
BR 4
10'4 x 10'
BR 3
9' x 12'6
W I Closet
MBATH
BATH 2
W I Closet
Balcony
OPTIONAL BONUS RM 334 SF
12' x 21'4
MBR
12'4 x 14'8
Foyer Below
BR 2
10'8 x 10'3
PLANT SHELF
SLOPE
FLAT
SLOPE
DIN
10' x 10'4
PANTRY
DESK
Lav
OPTIONAL STUDY
11'8 x 11'8
Width: 60'-8"
Depth: 39'-0"
FAM RM
18'2 x 13'6
DW
KIT
11'8 x 11'6
BENCH
Entry
REF
Laun
477 SF
GARAGE
21'4 x 21'4
LIV RM
12'2 x 15'4
two story
FOYER
DIN RM
10'8 x 11'8
Covered
Entry

First Floor
1,157 sq. ft.

TO ORDER BLUEPRINTS USE THE FORM ON PAGE 15 OR CALL TOLL-FREE 1-877-671-6036

View thousands more home plans online at www.familyhandyman.com/homeplans

The Family
Handyman

Plan #708-0712

Country Home With Front Orientation

2,029 total square feet of living area **Price Code D**

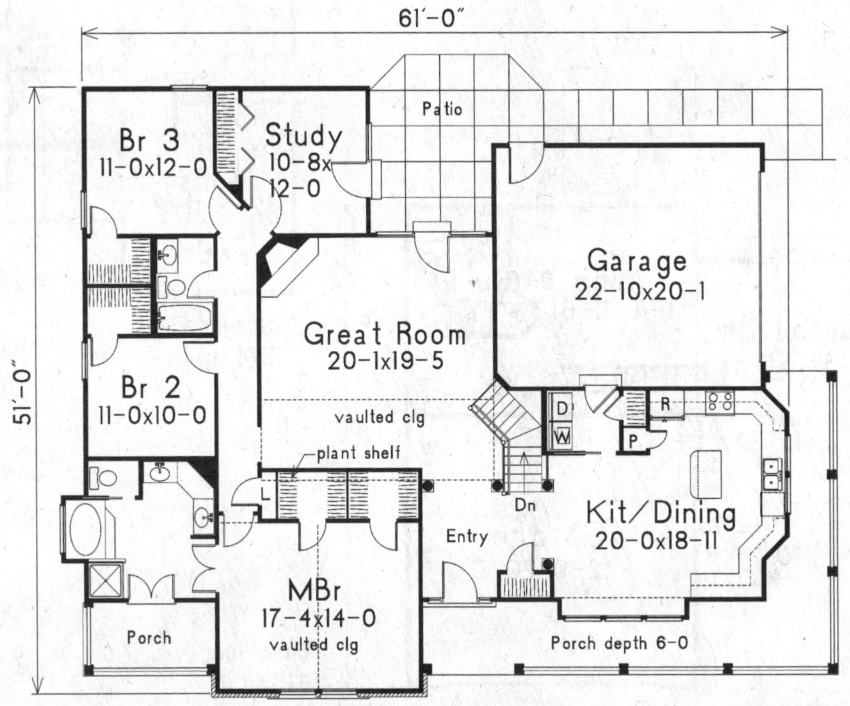

61'-0"
51'-0"
Patio
Br 3
11-0x12-0
Study
10-8x
12-0
Garage
22-10x20-1
Great Room
20-1x19-5
vaulted clg
plant shelf
Br 2
11-0x10-0
L
D
W
R
P
Dn
Kit/Dining
20-0x18-11
Entry
MBr
17-4x14-0
vaulted clg
Porch
Porch depth 6-0

Special features

- Stonework, gables, roof dormer and double porches create a country flavor
- Kitchen enjoys extravagant cabinetry and counterspace in a bay, island snack bar, built-in pantry and cheery dining area with multiple tall windows
- Angled stair descends from large entry with wood columns and is open to vaulted great room with corner fireplace
- Master bedroom boasts his and hers walk-in closets, double-doors leading to an opulent master bath and private porch
- 4 bedrooms, 2 baths, 2-car side entry garage
- Basement foundation

The Family
Handyman

Plan #708-0487

Spacious Vaulted Great Room

1,189 total square feet of living area **Price Code AA**

Special features

- All bedrooms are located on the second floor
- Dining room and kitchen both have views of the patio
- Convenient half bath located near the kitchen
- Master bedroom has private bath
- 3 bedrooms, 2 1/2 baths, 2-car garage
- Basement foundation

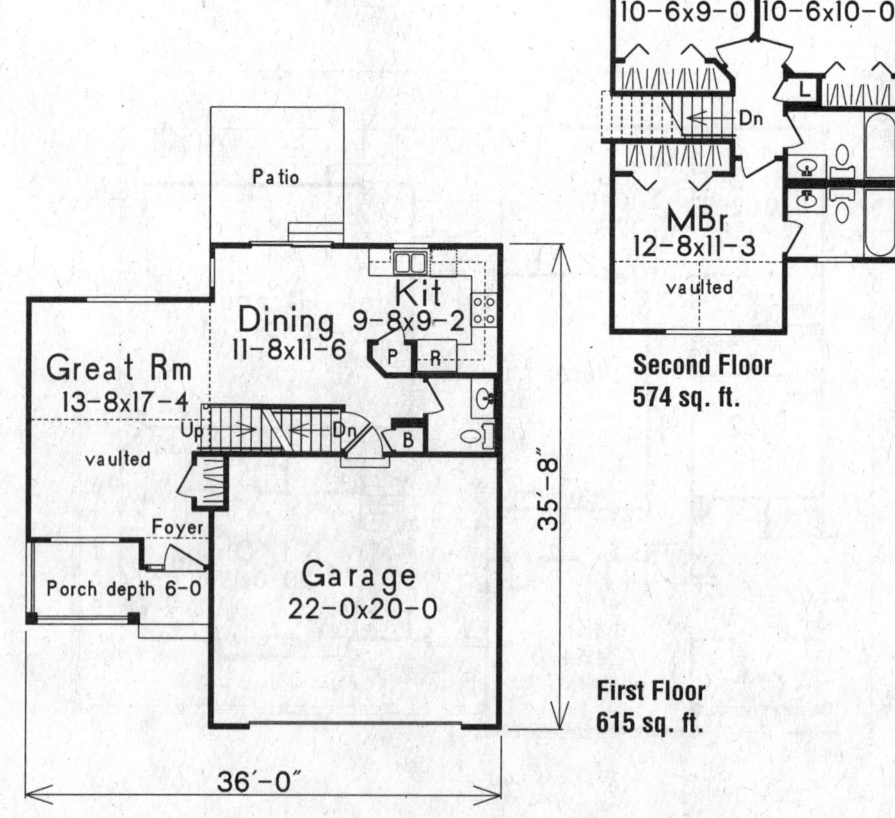
Br 2
10-6x9-0
Br 3
10-6x10-0
L
Dn
MBr
12-8x11-3
vaulted
Patio
Kit
9-8x9-2
Dining
11-8x11-6
P
R
Great Rm
13-8x17-4
Up
Dn
B
vaulted
Foyer
Porch depth 6-0
Garage
22-0x20-0
35′-8″
36′-0″

Second Floor
574 sq. ft.

First Floor
615 sq. ft.

TO ORDER BLUEPRINTS USE THE FORM ON PAGE 15 OR CALL TOLL-FREE 1-877-671-6036

View thousands more home plans online at www.familyhandyman.com/homeplans

The Family
Handyman

Plan #708-CHD-29-58

Grand Covered Entry

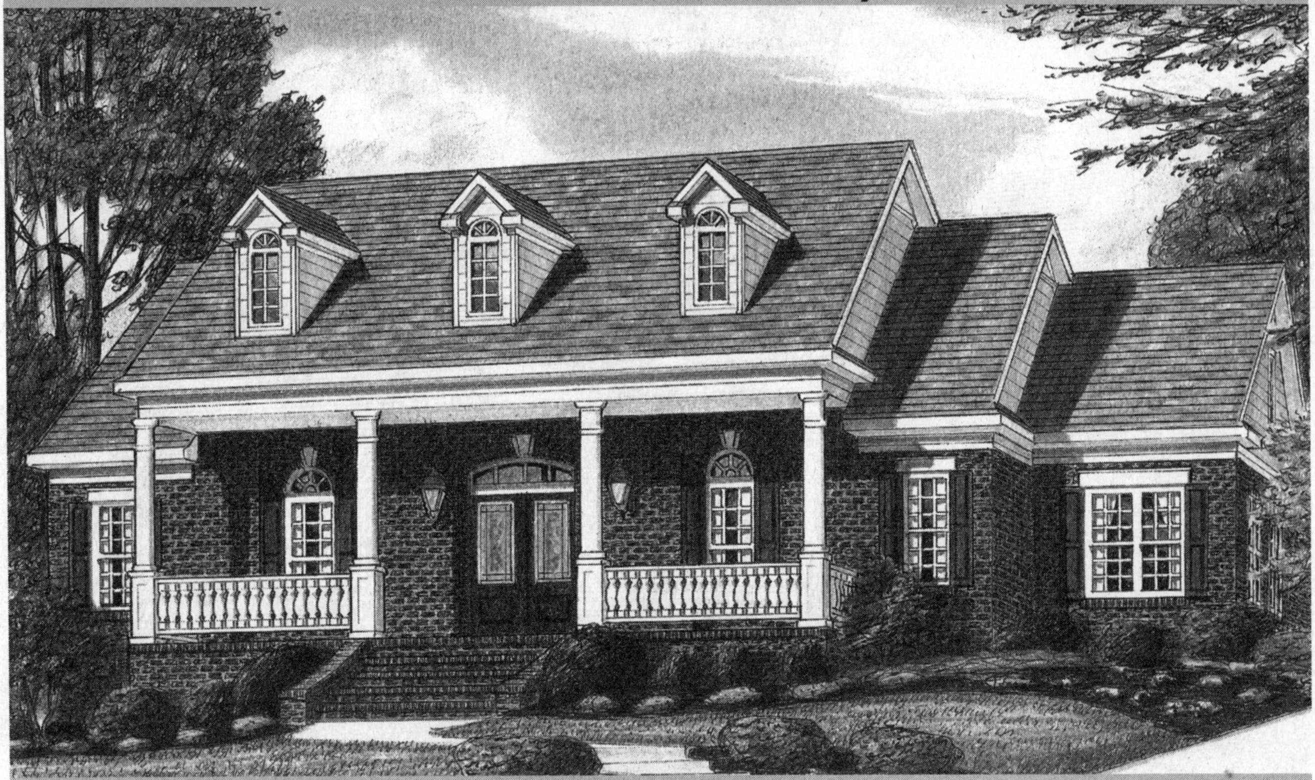

3,369 total square feet of living area

Price Code F

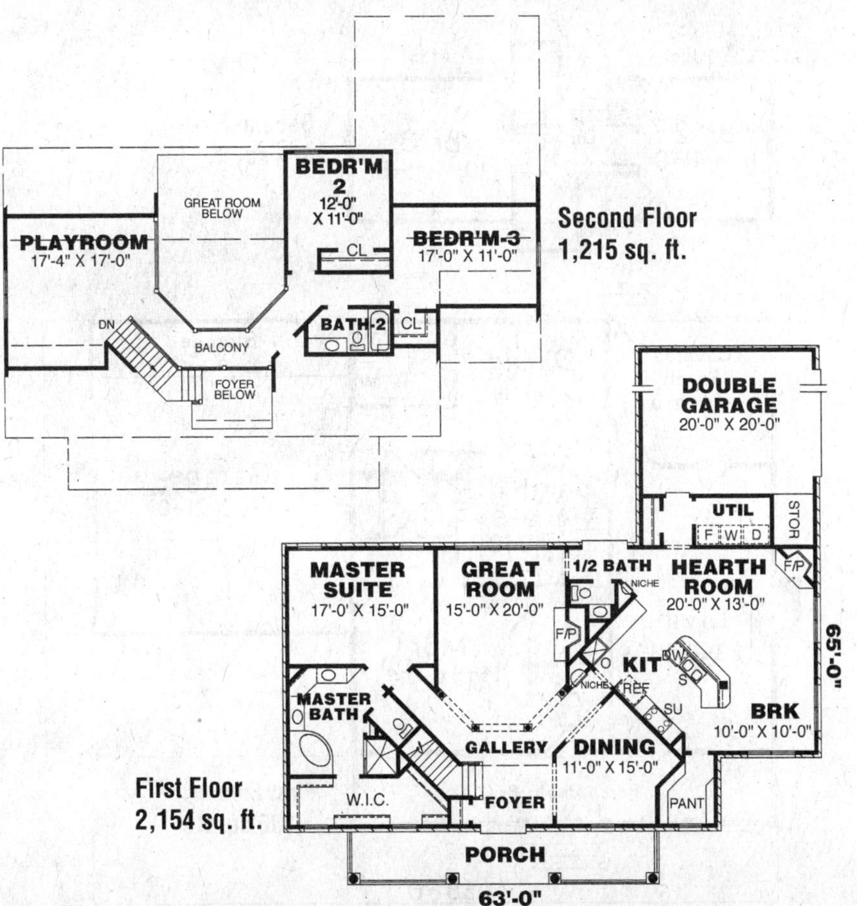
BEDR'M 2
12'-0" X 11'-0"
GREAT ROOM BELOW
PLAYROOM
17'-4" X 17'-0"
BEDR'M-3
17'-0" X 11'-0"
CL
BATH-2
CL
DN
BALCONY
FOYER BELOW
Second Floor
1,215 sq. ft.
DOUBLE GARAGE
20'-0" X 20'-0"
UTIL
STOR
F W D
MASTER SUITE
17'-0' X 15'-0"
GREAT ROOM
15'-0" X 20'-0"
1/2 BATH
NICHE
HEARTH ROOM
20'-0" X 13'-0"
F/P
F/P
KIT
NICHE
REF
DW
S
SU
65'-0"
MASTER BATH
BRK
10'-0" X 10'-0"
GALLERY
DINING
11'-0" X 15'-0"
W.I.C.
FOYER
PANT
PORCH
63'-0"
First Floor
2,154 sq. ft.

Special features

- Large playroom overlooks to great room below and makes a great casual family area
- Extra storage is located in garage
- Well-planned hearth room and kitchen are open and airy
- Foyer flows into unique diagonal gallery area creating a dramatic entrance into the great room
- 3 bedrooms, 2 1/2 baths, 2-car side entry garage
- Walk-out basement foundation

Plan #708-0291

Roomy Two-Story Has Screened-In Rear Porch

1,600 total square feet of living area

Price Code B

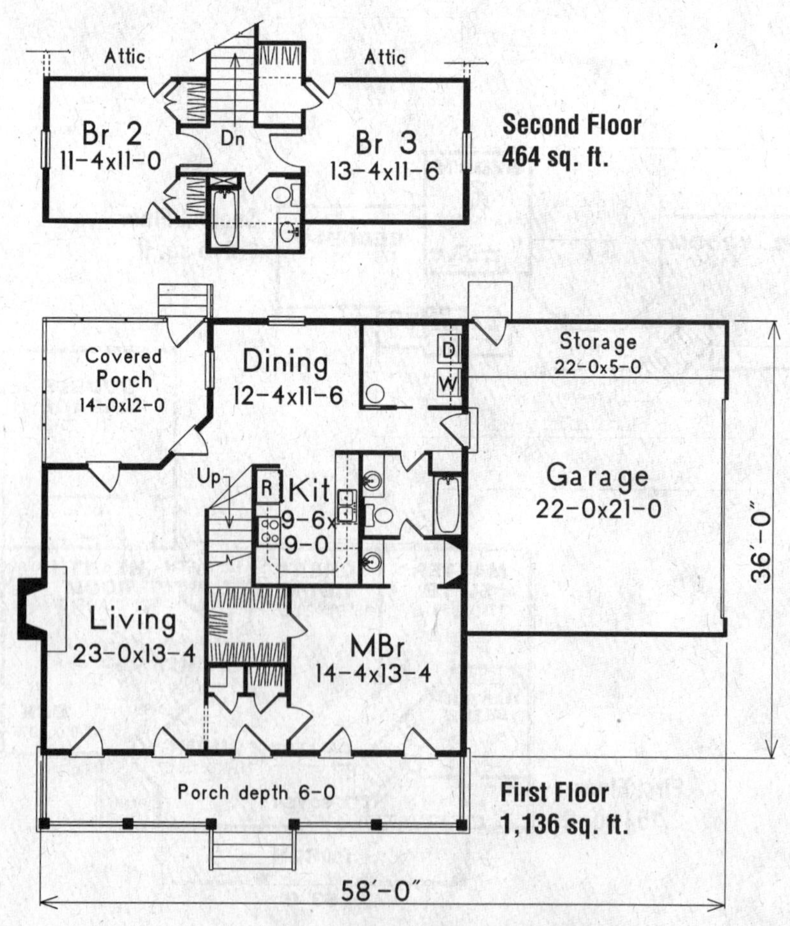
Attic
Attic
Br 2
11-4x11-0
Dn
Br 3
13-4x11-6
Second Floor
464 sq. ft.
Covered Porch
14-0x12-0
Dining
12-4x11-6
D
W
Storage
22-0x5-0
Up
R
Kit
9-6x
9-0
Garage
22-0x21-0
36'-0"
Living
23-0x13-4
MBr
14-4x13-4
Porch depth 6-0
First Floor
1,136 sq. ft.
58'-0"

Special features

- Energy efficient home with 2" x 6" exterior walls
- First floor master bedroom accessible from two points of entry
- Master bedroom dressing area includes separate vanities and a mirrored make-up counter
- Second floor bedrooms with generous storage, share a full bath
- 3 bedrooms, 2 baths, 2-car side entry garage
- Crawl space foundation, drawings also include slab foundation

TO ORDER BLUEPRINTS USE THE FORM ON PAGE 15 OR CALL TOLL-FREE 1-877-671-6036

View thousands more home plans online at www.familyhandyman.com/homeplans

The Family
Handyman

Plan #708-0280

Half-Round Highlights And Gables Unify The Facade

1,847 total square feet of living area **Price Code C**

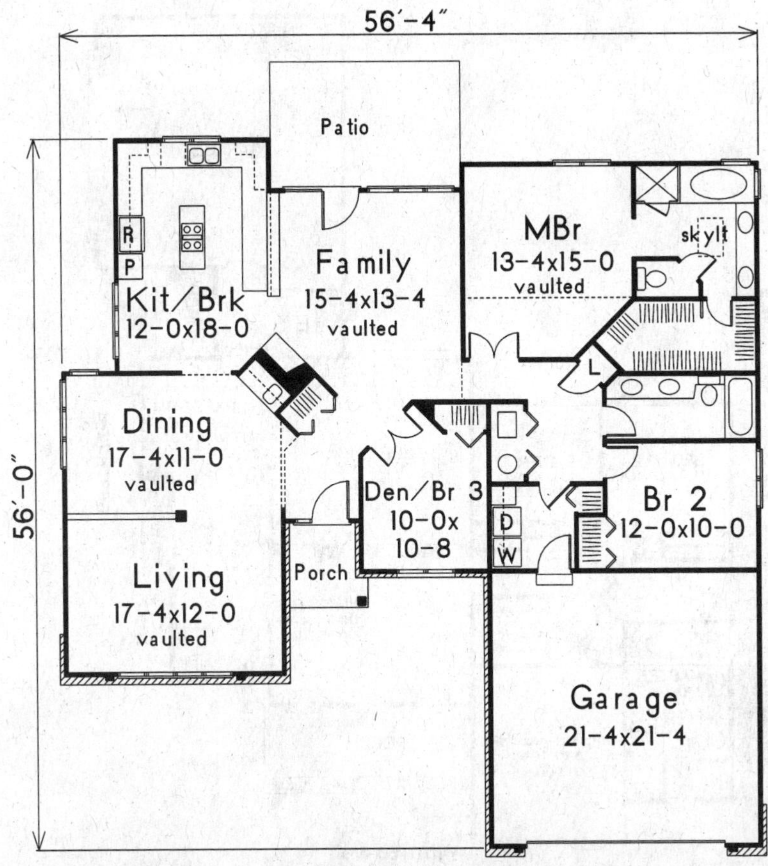
56′-4″
Patio
MBr
13-4x15-0
vaulted
skylt
R
P
Kit/Brk
12-0x18-0
Family
15-4x13-4
vaulted
L
Dining
17-4x11-0
vaulted
Den/Br 3
10-0x
10-8
D
W
Br 2
12-0x10-0
56′-0″
Porch
Living
17-4x12-0
vaulted
Garage
21-4x21-4

Special features

- Kitchen includes island cooktop and sunny breakfast area
- Master bedroom features vaulted ceilings and skylighted bath with large tub, separate shower and walk-in closet
- Service bar eases entertaining in vaulted dining and living rooms
- Family room, complete with corner fireplace, accesses outdoor patio
- 3 bedrooms, 2 baths, 2-car garage
- Slab foundation

TO ORDER BLUEPRINTS USE THE FORM ON PAGE 15 OR CALL TOLL-FREE 1-877-671-6036
View thousands more home plans online at www.familyhandyman.com/homeplans

The Family
Handyman

Plan #708-LBD-17-14A

Covered Porches All Around

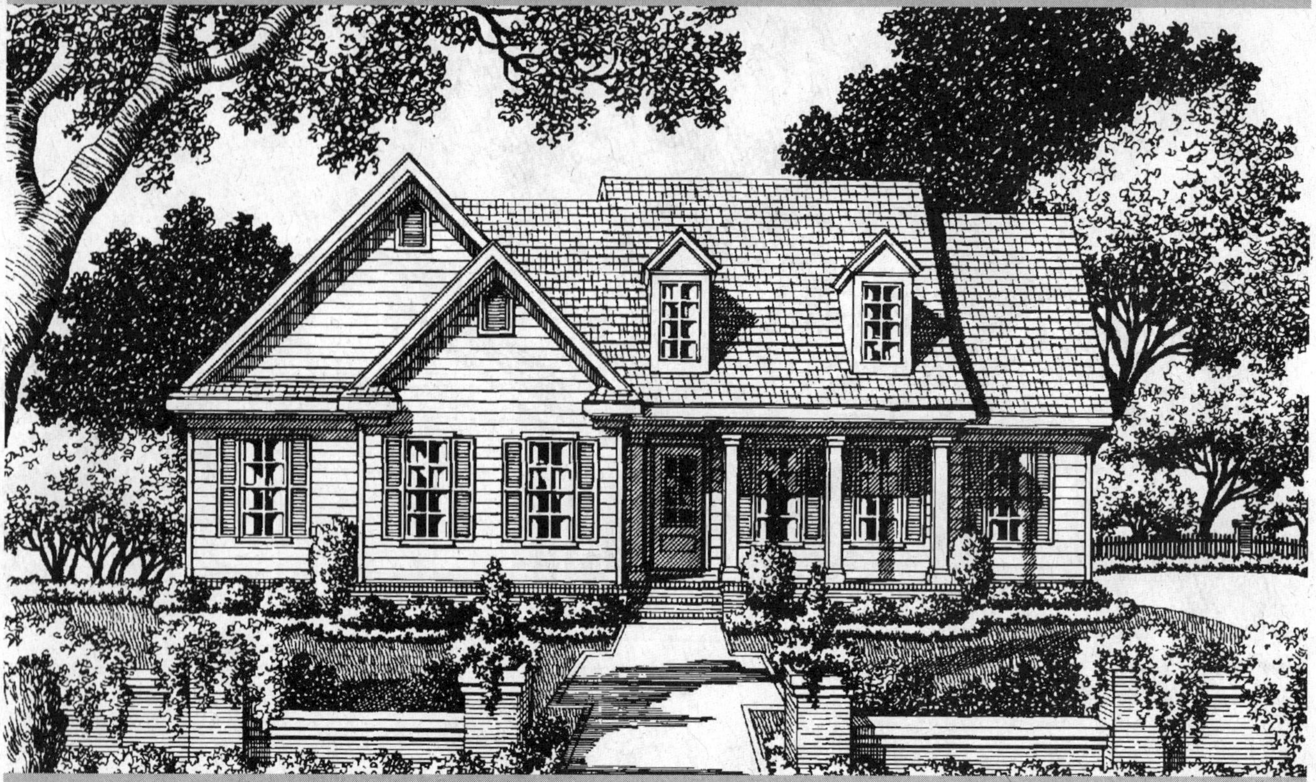

1,725 total square feet of living area — **Price Code B**

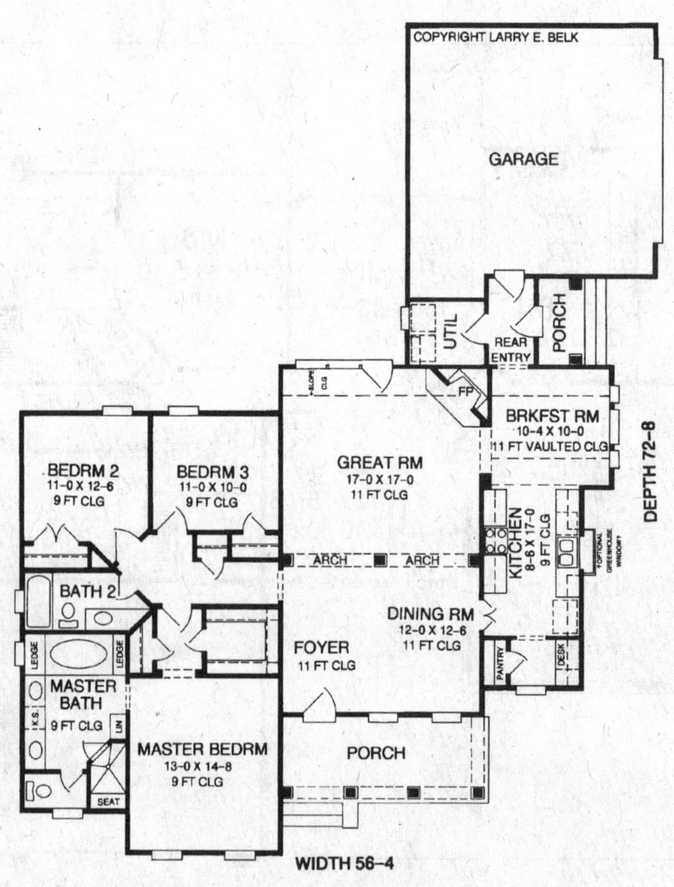
COPYRIGHT LARRY E. BELK
GARAGE
UTIL
REAR ENTRY
PORCH
FP
BRKFST RM
10-4 X 10-0
11 FT VAULTED CLG
GREAT RM
17-0 X 17-0
11 FT CLG
BEDRM 2
11-0 X 12-6
9 FT CLG
BEDRM 3
11-0 X 10-0
9 FT CLG
KITCHEN
8-6 X 17-0
9 FT CLG
ARCH
ARCH
BATH 2
DINING RM
12-0 X 12-6
11 FT CLG
FOYER
11 FT CLG
PANTRY
DESK
LEDGE
LEDGE
MASTER BATH
9 FT CLG
LIN
MASTER BEDRM
13-0 X 14-8
9 FT CLG
PORCH
SEAT
WIDTH 56–4
DEPTH 72–8

Special features

- Spectacular arches when entering the foyer
- Dining room has double-doors leading to the kitchen
- Unique desk area off kitchen is ideal for computer work station
- 3 bedrooms, 2 baths, 2-car side entry garage
- Slab or crawl space foundation, please specify when ordering

Plan #708-0349

Striking Curb Appeal

2,204 total square feet of living area **Price Code D**

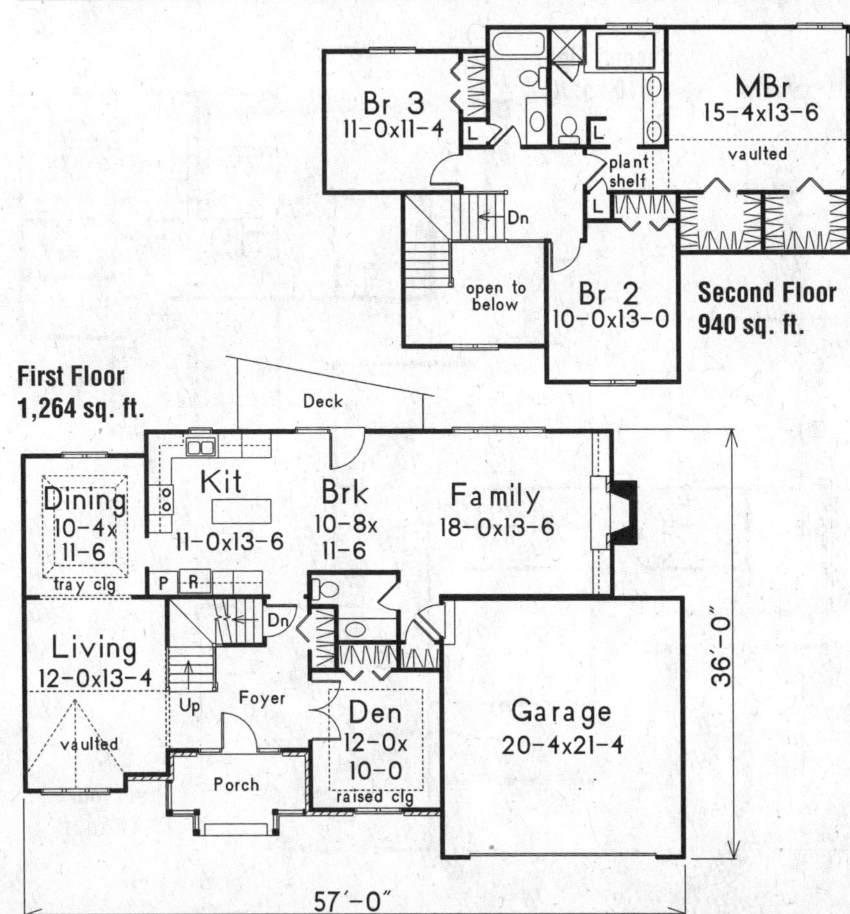

Br 3
11-0x11-4
MBr
15-4x13-6
vaulted
plant shelf
Dn
open to below
Br 2
10-0x13-0
Second Floor
940 sq. ft.
First Floor
1,264 sq. ft.
Deck
Dining
10-4x
11-6
tray clg
Kit
11-0x13-6
Brk
10-8x
11-6
Family
18-0x13-6
Living
12-0x13-4
vaulted
Up
Foyer
Dn
Den
12-0x
10-0
raised clg
Porch
Garage
20-4x21-4
36'-0"
57'-0"

Special features

- First floor den offers the flexibility of an office, study or fourth bedroom
- Large island kitchen with breakfast bar next to family room provides open living space
- Second floor balcony overlooks entry below
- Master bedroom features double walk-in closets, private bath with step-up tub and double-bowl vanity
- 3 bedrooms, 2 1/2 baths, 2-car garage
- Basement foundation

The Family
Handyman

Plan #708-0413

Distinctive Country Porch

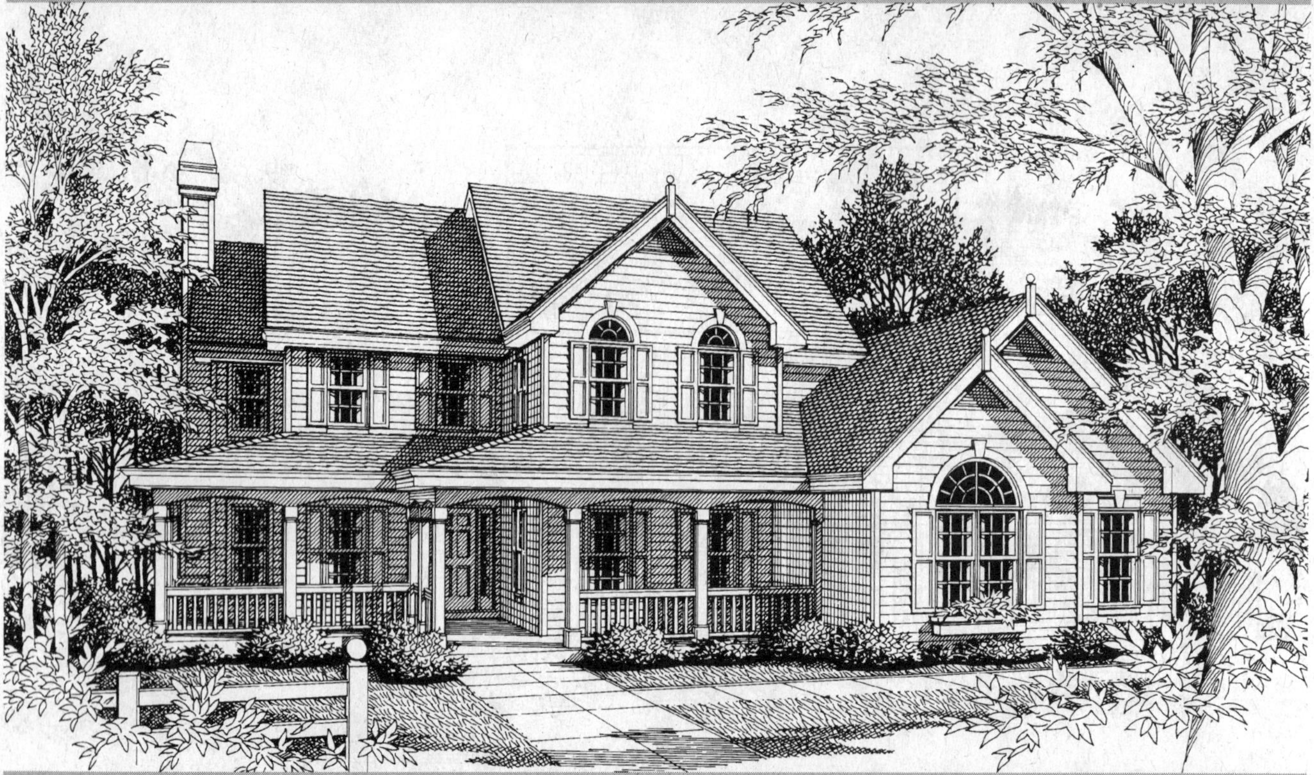

2,182 total square feet of living area **Price Code D**

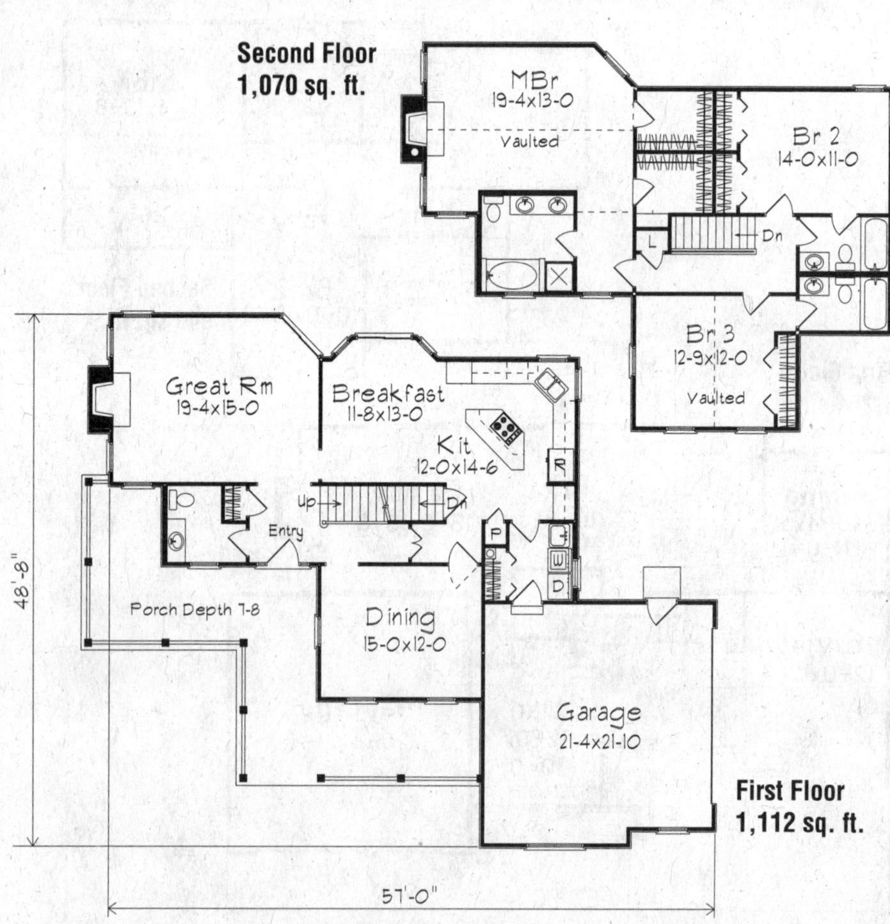
Second Floor
1,070 sq. ft.
MBr
19-4x13-0
Vaulted
Br 2
14-0x11-0
Dn
L
Br 3
12-9x12-0
Vaulted
Great Rm
19-4x15-0
Breakfast
11-8x13-0
Kit
12-0x14-6
R
Up
Dn
Entry
P
W
D
Porch Depth 7-8
Dining
15-0x12-0
Garage
21-4x21-10
48'-8"
57'-0"
First Floor
1,112 sq. ft.

Special features

- Meandering porch creates an inviting look
- Generous great room has four double-hung windows and gliding doors to exterior
- Highly functional kitchen features island/breakfast bar, menu desk and convenient pantry
- Each secondary bedroom includes generous closet and private bath
- 3 bedrooms, 3 1/2 baths, 2-car side entry garage
- Basement foundation

The Family
Handyman

Plan #708-HP-C662

Secluded Master Suite

1,937 total square feet of living area **Price Code C**

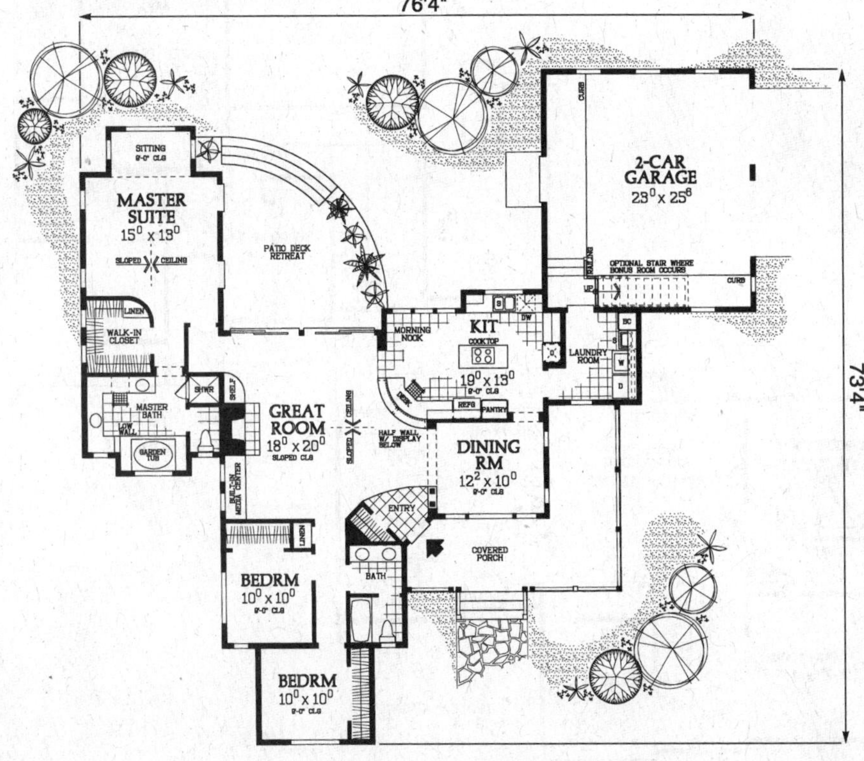
76'4"
73'4"
SITTING
MASTER SUITE
$15^0 \times 13^0$
SLOPED CEILING
PATIO DECK RETREAT
2-CAR GARAGE
$23^0 \times 25^6$
OPTIONAL STAIR WHERE BONUS ROOM OCCURS
CURB
KIT
COOKTOP
$19^0 \times 13^0$
MORNING NOOK
DW
LAUNDRY ROOM
LINEN
WALK-IN CLOSET
MASTER BATH
LOW WALL
GARDEN TUB
SHWR
GREAT ROOM
$18^0 \times 20^0$
SLOPED CLG
REFG
PANTRY
HALF WALL W/ DISPLAY BELOW
DINING RM
$12^2 \times 10^0$
ENTRY
COVERED PORCH
BEDRM
$10^0 \times 10^0$
BATH
BEDRM
$10^0 \times 10^0$

Special features

- Upscale great room offers a sloped ceiling, fireplace with extended hearth and built-in shelves for an entertainment center
- Gourmet kitchen includes a cooktop island counter and a quaint morning room
- Master suite features a sloped ceiling, cozy sitting room, walk-in closet and a private bath with whirlpool tub
- 3 bedrooms, 2 baths, 2-car side entry garage
- Crawl space foundation

Plan #708-MG-96183

Brick Traditional

2,737 total square feet of living area

Price Code E

Special features

- T-stairs make any room easily accessible
- Two-story foyer and grand room create spacious feeling
- Master bedroom has gorgeous bay window and a sitting area
- Bedroom #4 has its own private bath
- 5 bedrooms, 4 baths, 2-car side entry garage
- Basement foundation

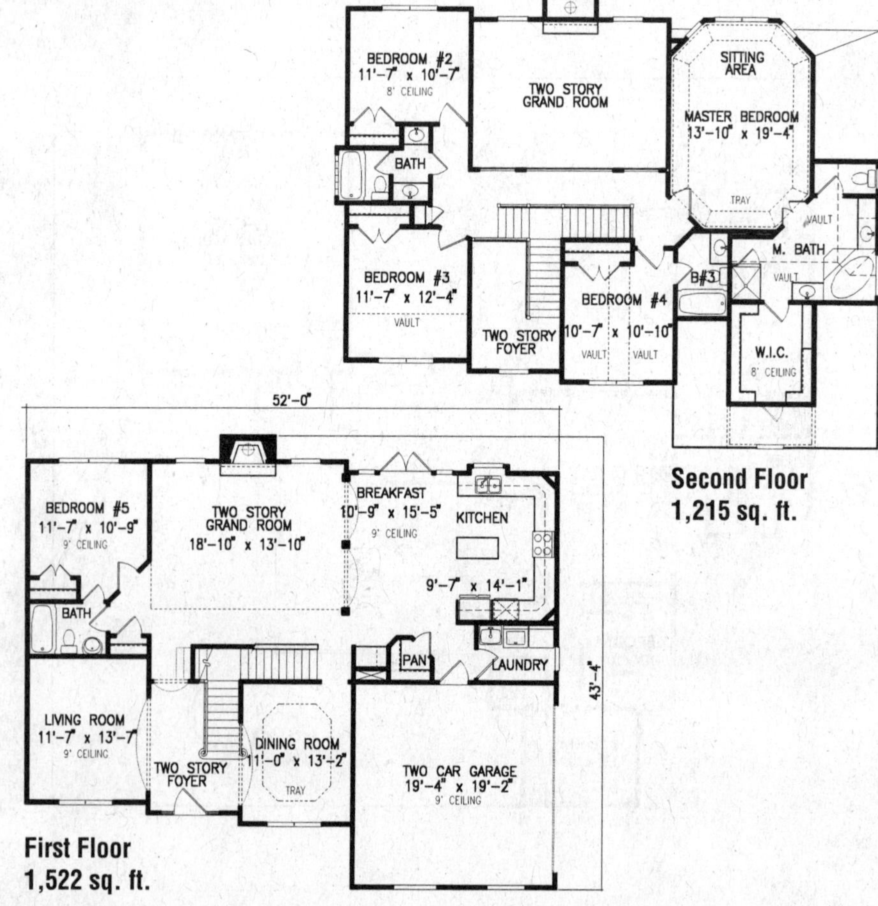
BEDROOM #2
11'-7" x 10'-7"
8' CEILING
TWO STORY
GRAND ROOM
SITTING
AREA
MASTER BEDROOM
13'-10" x 19'-4"
TRAY
BATH
VAULT
M. BATH
VAULT
BEDROOM #3
11'-7" x 12'-4"
VAULT
B#3
BEDROOM #4
10'-7" x 10'-10"
VAULT
VAULT
TWO STORY
FOYER
W.I.C.
8' CEILING
52'-0"
BEDROOM #5
11'-7" x 10'-9"
9' CEILING
TWO STORY
GRAND ROOM
18'-10" x 13'-10"
BREAKFAST
10'-9" x 15'-5"
9' CEILING
KITCHEN
9'-7" x 14'-1"
BATH
PAN
LAUNDRY
43'-4"
LIVING ROOM
11'-7" x 13'-7"
9' CEILING
TWO STORY
FOYER
DINING ROOM
11'-0" x 13'-2"
TRAY
TWO CAR GARAGE
19'-4" x 19'-2"
9' CEILING

Second Floor
1,215 sq. ft.

First Floor
1,522 sq. ft.

TO ORDER BLUEPRINTS USE THE FORM ON PAGE 15 OR CALL TOLL-FREE 1-877-671-6036

View thousands more home plans online at www.familyhandyman.com/homeplans

The Family
Handyman

Plan #708-UD-E141

Central Gathering Room

3,272 total square feet of living area

Price Code F

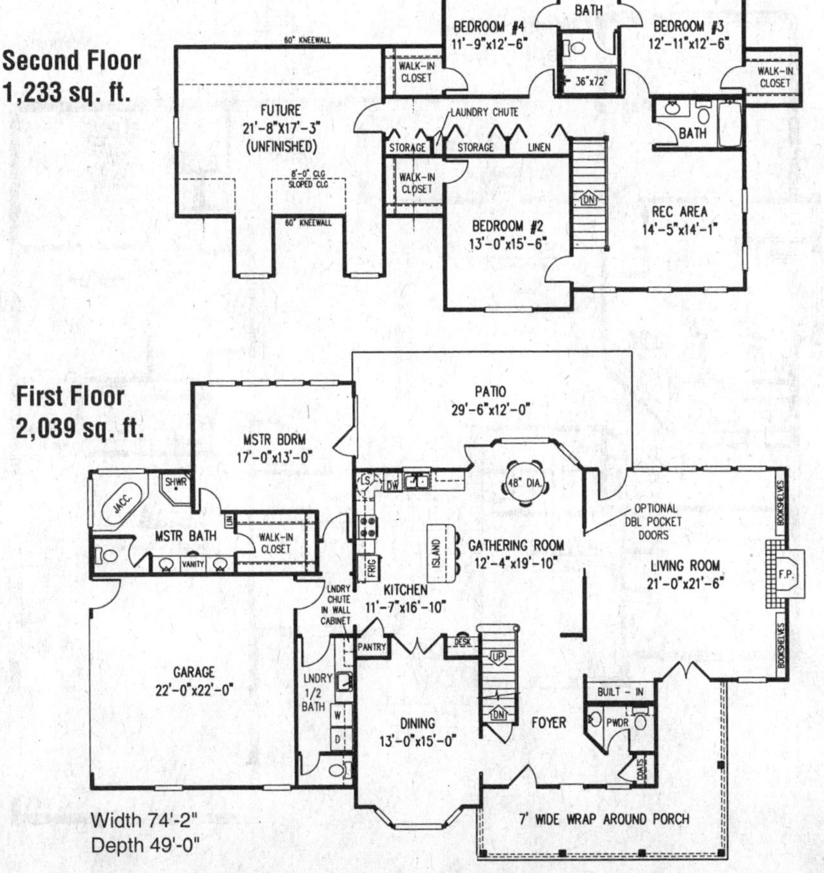
Second Floor
1,233 sq. ft.
60" KNEEWALL
FUTURE
21'-8"x17'-3"
(UNFINISHED)
8'-0" CLG
SLOPED CLG
WALK-IN CLOSET
BEDROOM #4
11'-9"x12'-6"
BATH
BEDROOM #3
12'-11"x12'-6"
36"x72"
WALK-IN CLOSET
LAUNDRY CHUTE
STORAGE
STORAGE
LINEN
BATH
BEDROOM #2
13'-0"x15'-6"
DN
REC AREA
14'-5"x14'-1"
First Floor
2,039 sq. ft.
PATIO
29'-6"x12'-0"
MSTR BDRM
17'-0"x13'-0"
SHWR
JACC.
MSTR BATH
VANITY
WALK-IN CLOSET
DW
48" DIA.
FRIG
ISLAND
GATHERING ROOM
12'-4"x19'-10"
OPTIONAL
DBL POCKET
DOORS
LIVING ROOM
21'-0"x21'-6"
BOOKSHELVES
F.P.
LNDRY CHUTE IN WALL CABINET
KITCHEN
11'-7"x16'-10"
PANTRY
UP
GARAGE
22'-0"x22'-0"
LNDRY
1/2 BATH
W
D
DINING
13'-0"x15'-0"
DN
FOYER
BUILT - IN
PWDR
COATS
7' WIDE WRAP AROUND PORCH
Width 74'-2"
Depth 49'-0"

Special features

- Living room with fireplace accesses rear patio and wrap-around front porch
- Large formal dining room
- Master bedroom has walk-in closet and deluxe bath
- 4 bedrooms, 3 full baths, 2 half baths, 2-car side entry garage
- Basement, crawl space or slab foundation, please specify when ordering

TO ORDER BLUEPRINTS USE THE FORM ON PAGE 15 OR CALL TOLL-FREE 1-877-671-6036

View thousands more home plans online at www.familyhandyman.com/homeplans

Plan #708-DL-35355LS2

Amenity Full Master Suite

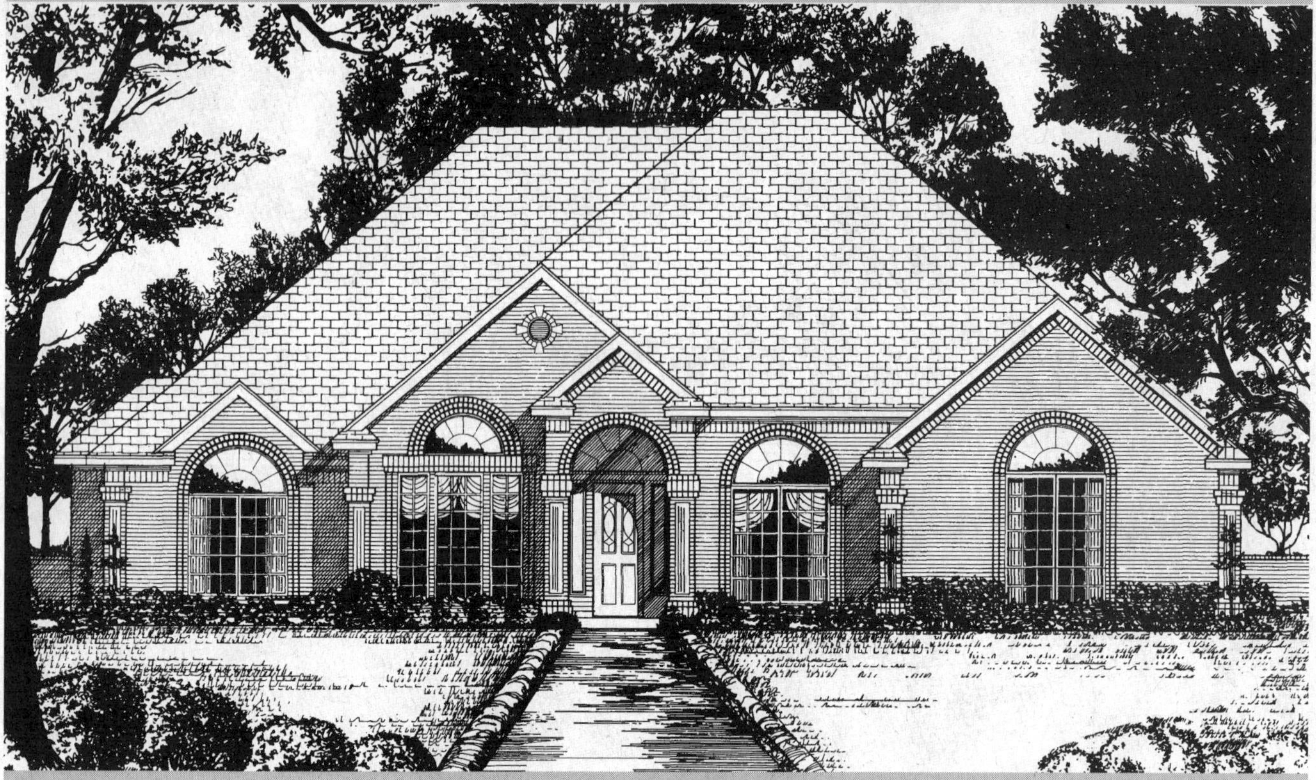

3,535 total square feet of living area **Price Code F**

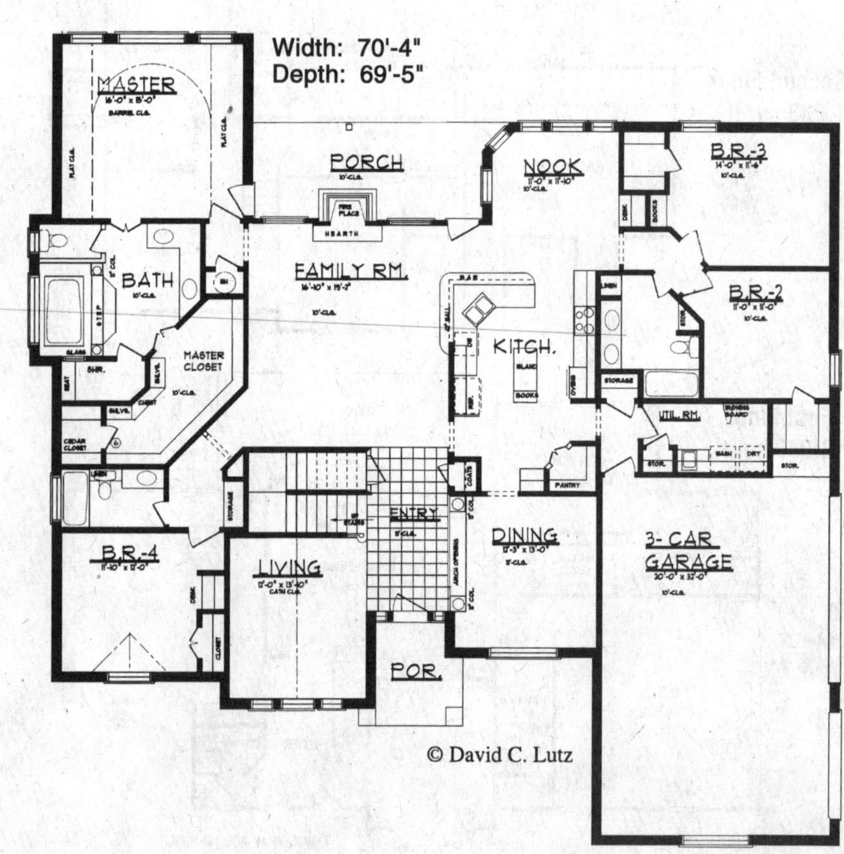
Width: 70'-4"
Depth: 69'-5"
MASTER
PORCH
NOOK
B.R.-3
BATH
FAMILY RM.
KITCH.
B.R.-2
MASTER CLOSET
UTIL. RM.
ENTRY
DINING
3- CAR GARAGE
B.R.-4
LIVING
POR.
© David C. Lutz

Special features

- Arched windows and entrance give luxurious look to exterior
- Optional bonus area on second floor has an additional 685 square feet of living area
- Arched opening and decorative columns give elegance to dining area
- 5 bedrooms, 4 baths, 3-car side entry garage
- Slab foundation

Country Accents Make This Home

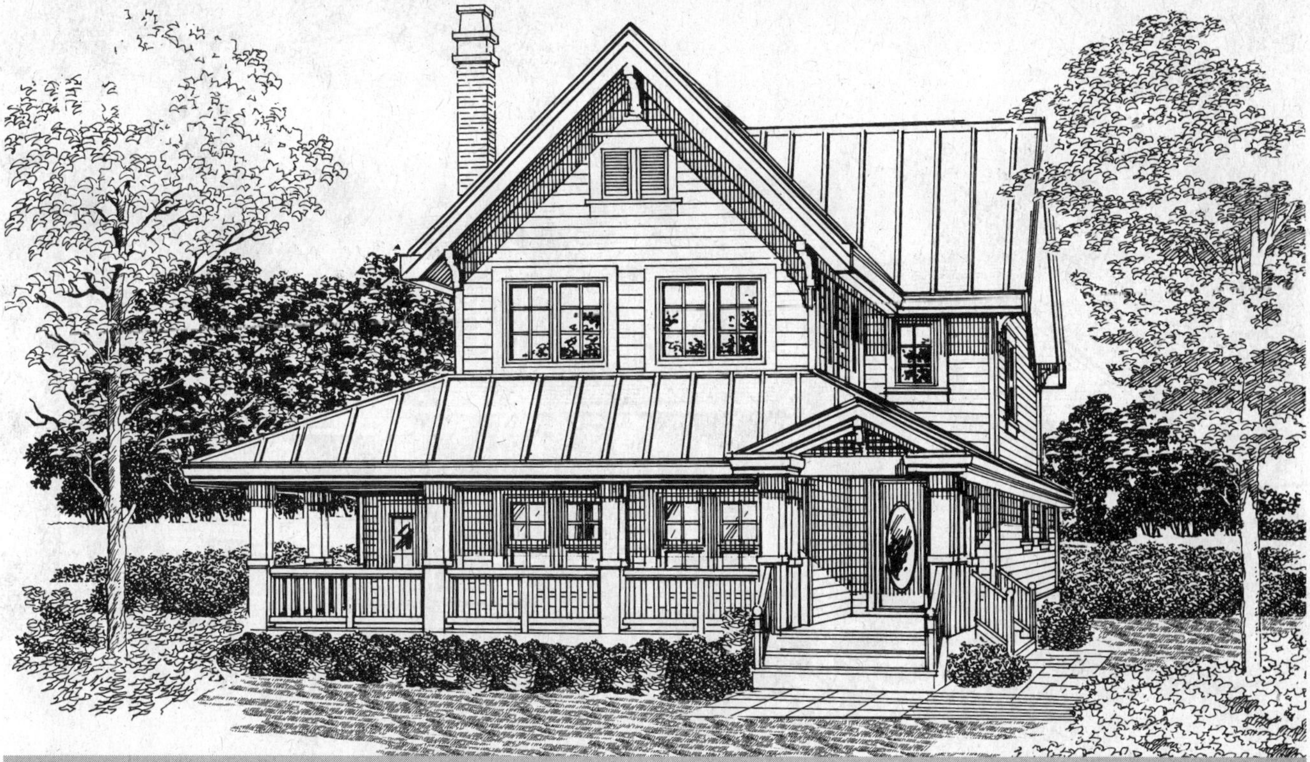

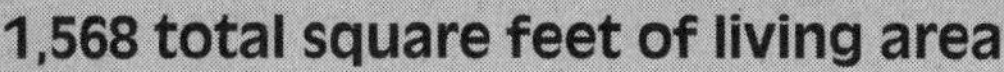

1,568 total square feet of living area

Price Code B

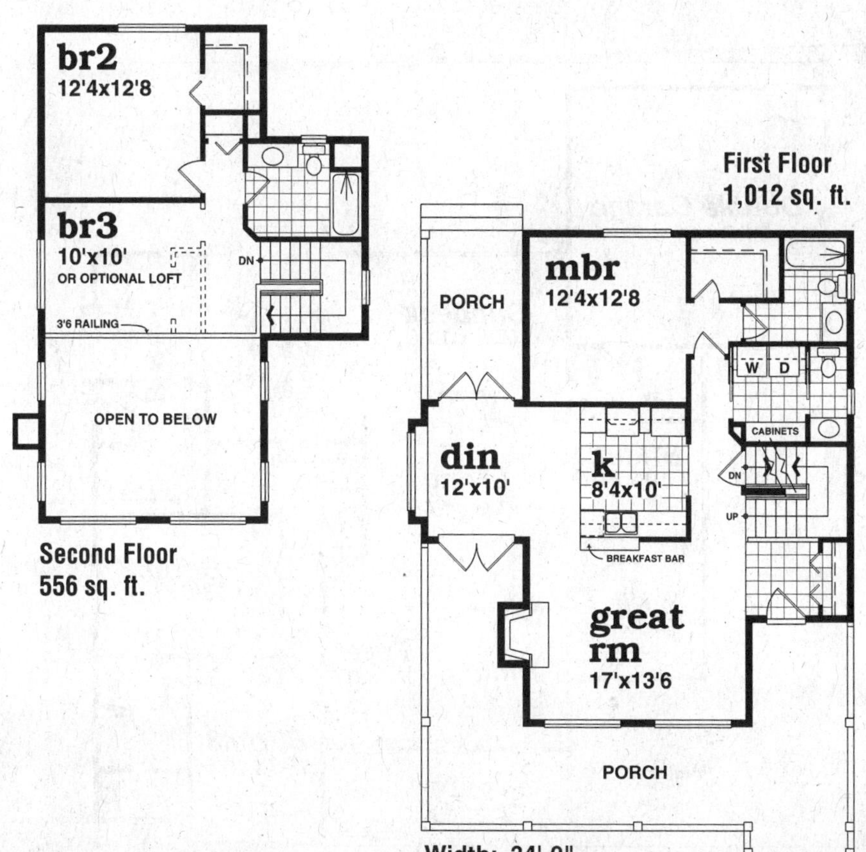
br2
12'4x12'8
br3
10'x10'
OR OPTIONAL LOFT
DN
3'6 RAILING
OPEN TO BELOW
Second Floor
556 sq. ft.
First Floor
1,012 sq. ft.
mbr
12'4x12'8
PORCH
W
D
CABINETS
DN
UP
din
12'x10'
k
8'4x10'
BREAKFAST BAR
great rm
17'x13'6
PORCH
Width: 34'-0"
Depth: 38'-0"

Special features

- Master bedroom is located on first floor for convenience
- Cozy great room has fireplace
- Dining room has access to both the front and rear porches
- Two secondary bedrooms and a bath complete the second floor
- 3 bedrooms, 2 1/2 baths
- Basement or crawl space foundation, please specify when ordering

TO ORDER BLUEPRINTS USE THE FORM ON PAGE 15 OR CALL TOLL-FREE 1-877-671-6036

Plan #708-JV-2012-A-SJ

Classy Master Bedroom

2,012 total square feet of living area **Price Code C**

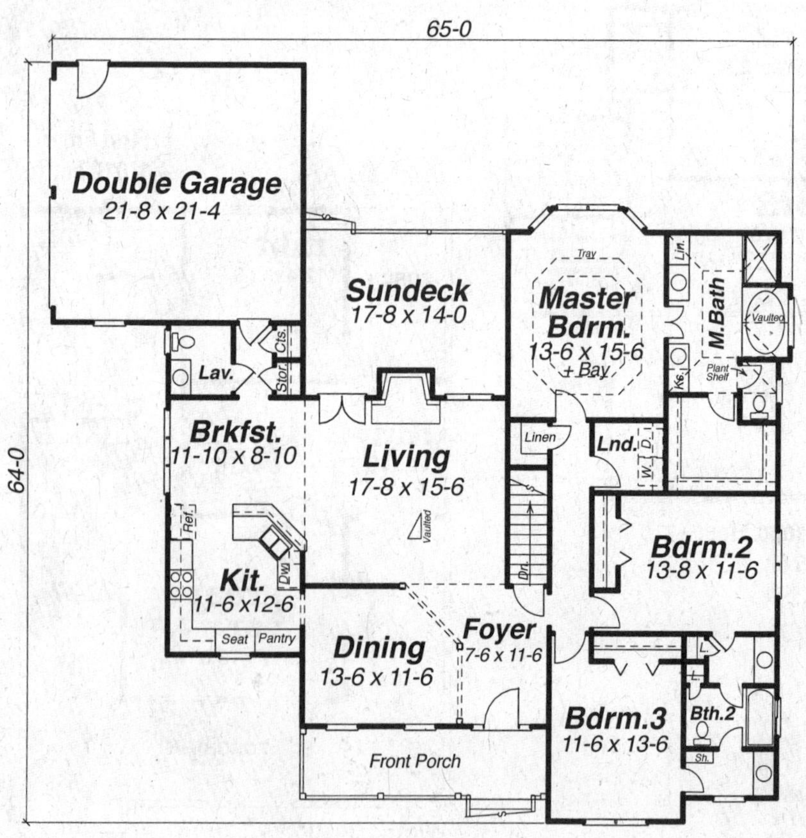
65-0
64-0
Double Garage
21-8 x 21-4
Sundeck
17-8 x 14-0
Master
Bdrm.
13-6 x 15-6
+ Bay
Tray
Lin.
M.Bath
Vaulted
Plant Shelf
Lav.
Cts.
Stor.
Brkfst.
11-10 x 8-10
Living
17-8 x 15-6
Vaulted
Linen
Lnd.
W
D
Ref.
Dw
Kit.
11-6 x 12-6
Seat
Pantry
Dn.
Bdrm.2
13-8 x 11-6
Foyer
7-6 x 11-6
Dining
13-6 x 11-6
Bdrm.3
11-6 x 13-6
Bth.2
Sh.
Front Porch

Special features

- Kitchen with eat-in breakfast bar overlooks breakfast room
- Sunny living room is open and airy with vaulted ceiling
- Secondary bedrooms with convenient vanities skillfully share bath
- 3 bedrooms, 2 1/2 baths, 2-car side entry garage
- Basement foundation

TO ORDER BLUEPRINTS USE THE FORM ON PAGE 15 OR CALL TOLL-FREE 1-877-671-6036

View thousands more home plans online at www.familyhandyman.com/homeplans

The Family
Handyman

Plan #708-0223

Clean, Practical Colonial

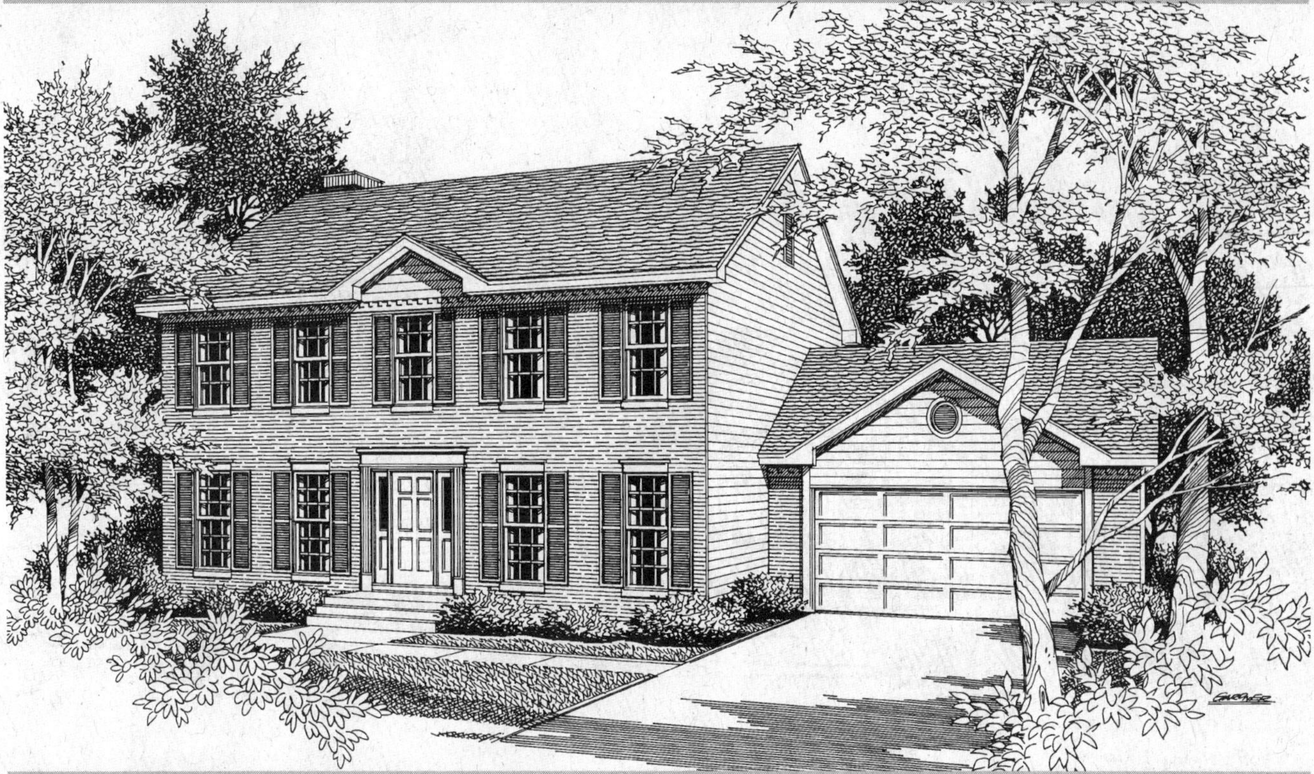

2,328 total square feet of living area **Price Code D**

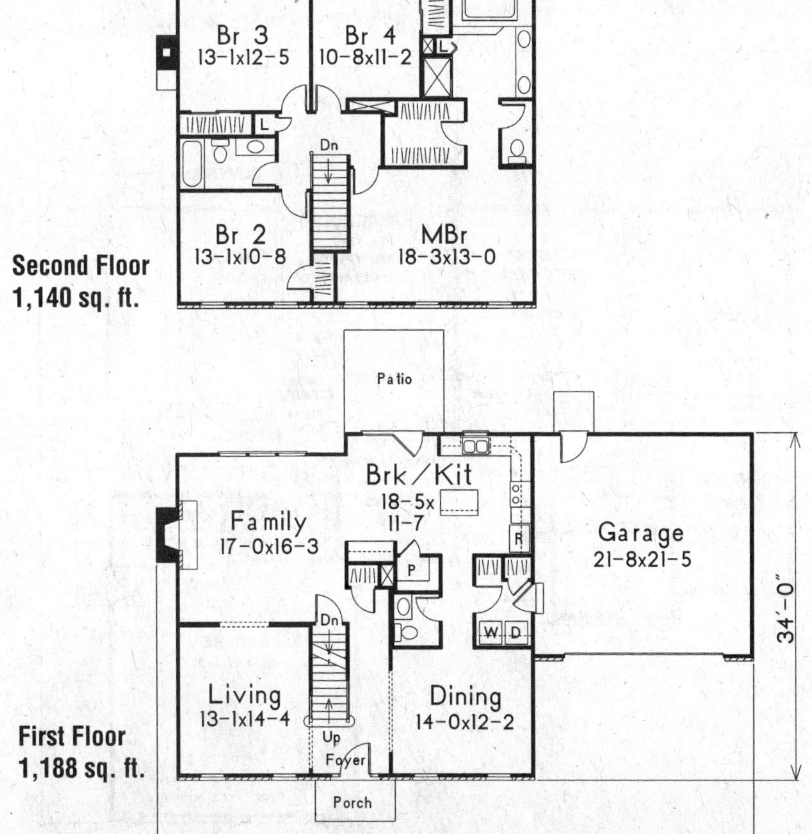

Br 3
13-1x12-5
Br 4
10-8x11-2
Dn
Br 2
13-1x10-8
MBr
18-3x13-0
Second Floor
1,140 sq. ft.
Patio
Brk / Kit
18-5x
11-7
Family
17-0x16-3
Garage
21-8x21-5
P
R
W D
Dn
Living
13-1x14-4
Up
Foyer
Dining
14-0x12-2
First Floor
1,188 sq. ft.
Porch
34'-0"
60'-0"

Special features

- Formal living and dining rooms feature floor-to-ceiling windows
- Kitchen with island counter and pantry makes cooking a delight
- Expansive master bedroom has luxury bath with double vanity and walk-in closet
- 4 bedrooms, 2 1/2 baths, 2-car garage
- Basement foundation, drawings also include slab and crawl space foundations

Plan #708-GSD-1123

Bedrooms Separated From Living Areas

1,734 total square feet of living area **Price Code B**

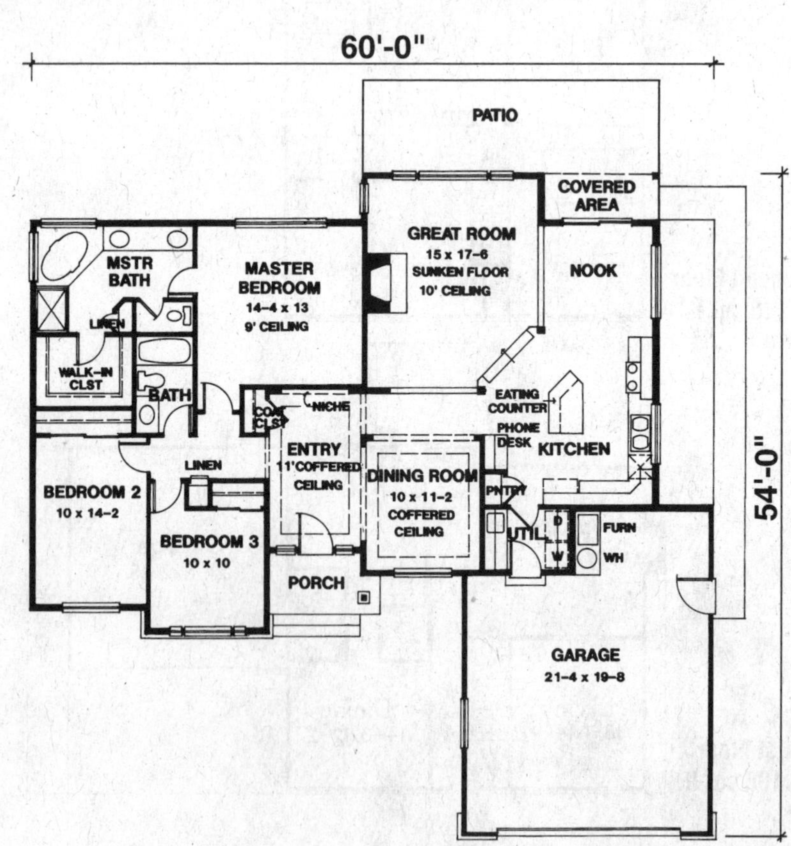

60'-0"
54'-0"
PATIO
COVERED AREA
GREAT ROOM
15 x 17-6
SUNKEN FLOOR
10' CEILING
NOOK
MSTR BATH
MASTER BEDROOM
14-4 x 13
9' CEILING
LINEN
WALK-IN CLST
BATH
NICHE
EATING COUNTER
PHONE DESK
KITCHEN
ENTRY
11' COFFERED CEILING
DINING ROOM
10 x 11-2
COFFERED CEILING
PNTRY
UTIL
FURN
WH
BEDROOM 2
10 x 14-2
LINEN
BEDROOM 3
10 x 10
PORCH
GARAGE
21-4 x 19-8

Special features

- Large entry with coffered ceiling and display niches
- Sunken great room has 10' ceiling
- Kitchen island includes eating counter
- 9' ceiling in master bedroom
- Master bath features corner tub and double sinks
- 3 bedrooms, 2 baths, 2-car garage
- Crawl space foundation

TO ORDER BLUEPRINTS USE THE FORM ON PAGE 15 OR CALL TOLL-FREE 1-877-671-6036

View thousands more home plans online at www.familyhandyman.com/homeplans

The Family
Handyman

Plan #708-0357

Vaulted Ceilings Add Dimension

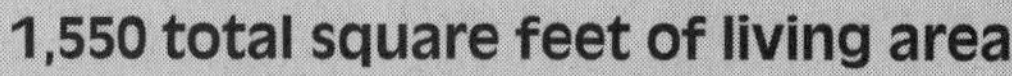

1,550 total square feet of living area **Price Code B**

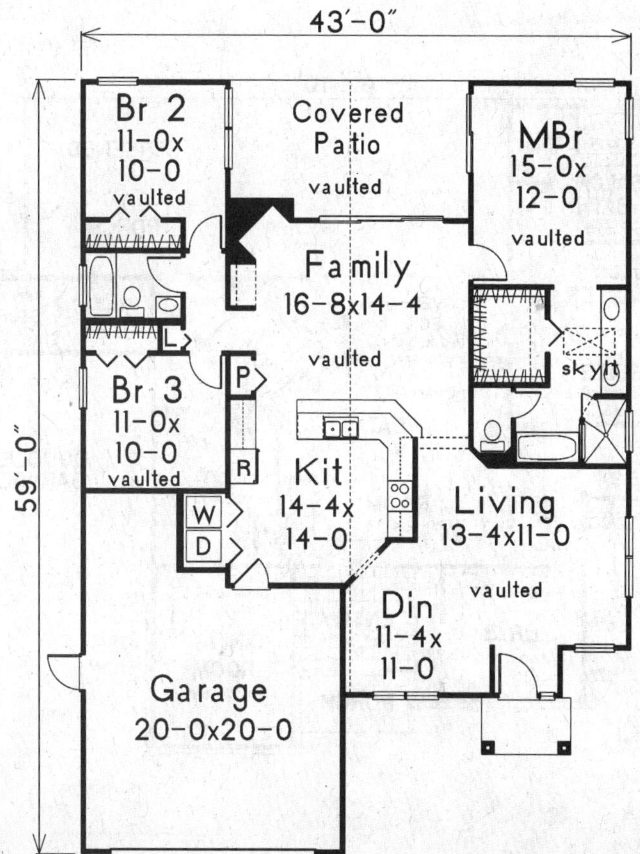
43′-0″
59′-0″
Br 2
11-0x
10-0
vaulted
Covered
Patio
vaulted
MBr
15-0x
12-0
vaulted
Family
16-8x14-4
vaulted
L
P
skylt
Br 3
11-0x
10-0
vaulted
R
Kit
14-4x
14-0
Living
13-4x11-0
vaulted
W
D
Din
11-4x
11-0
Garage
20-0x20-0

Special features

- Cozy corner fireplace provides focal point in family room
- Master bedroom features large walk-in closet, skylight and separate tub and shower
- Convenient laundry closet
- Kitchen with pantry and break-fast bar connects to family room
- Family room and master bedroom access covered patio
- 3 bedrooms, 2 baths, 2-car garage
- Slab foundation

TO ORDER BLUEPRINTS USE THE FORM ON PAGE 15 OR CALL TOLL-FREE 1-877-671-6036

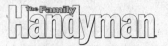

Great Room Atrium Door Accesses Covered Deck

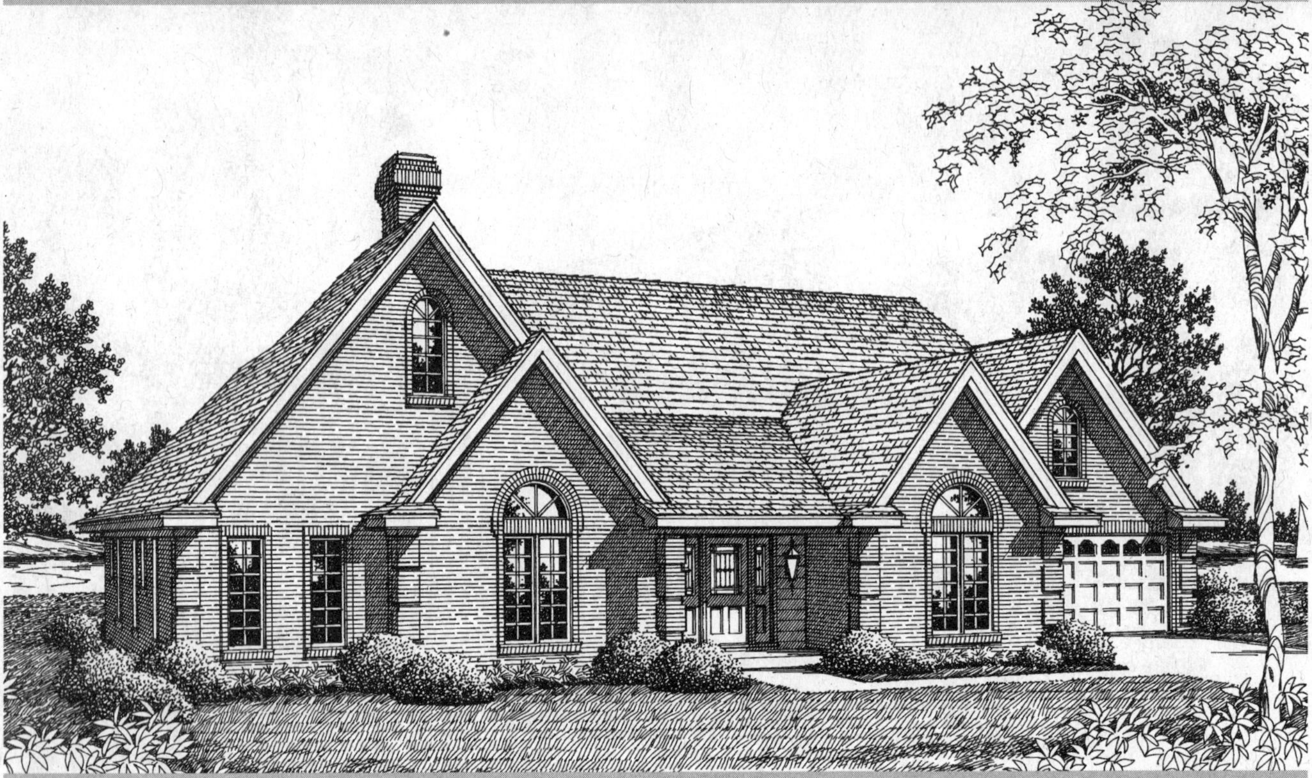

2,079 total square feet of living area

Price Code C

Special features

- Large formal entry foyer with openings to formal dining area and great room
- Great room has built-in bookshelves, a fireplace, and a coffered ceiling
- Unique angled morning room with bay windows overlooks covered deck
- Master bath with double walk-in closets, step-up tub, separate shower and a coffered ceiling
- 3 bedrooms, 2 baths, 2-car garage
- Slab or crawl space foundation, please specify when ordering

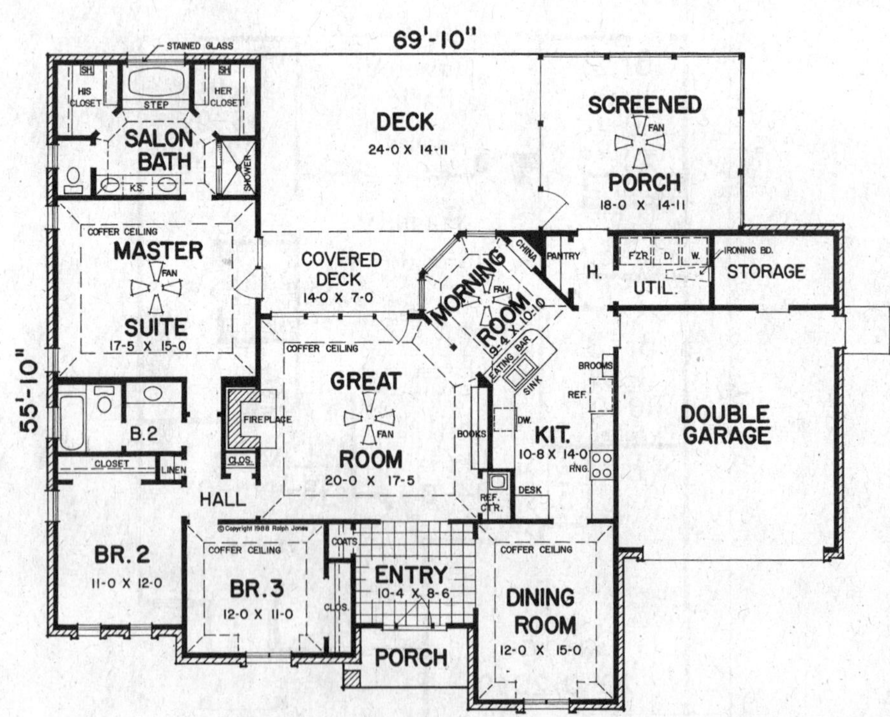
69'-10"
55'-10"
STAINED GLASS
HIS CLOSET
STEP
HER CLOSET
SALON BATH
SHOWER
DECK
24-0 X 14-11
SCREENED PORCH
18-0 X 14-11
FAN
COFFER CEILING
MASTER SUITE
17-5 X 15-0
COVERED DECK
14-0 X 7-0
MORNING ROOM
9-4 X 10-10
CHINA
PANTRY
H.
UTIL.
IRONING BD.
STORAGE
EATING BAR
SINK
BROOMS
REF.
GREAT ROOM
20-0 X 17-5
FIREPLACE
BOOKS
KIT.
10-8 X 14-0
DW.
RNG.
DESK
REF. CTR.
DOUBLE GARAGE
B.2
CLOSET
LINEN
CLOS.
HALL
BR. 2
11-0 X 12-0
BR. 3
12-0 X 11-0
COATS
ENTRY
10-4 X 8-6
CLOS.
PORCH
DINING ROOM
12-0 X 15-0

TO ORDER BLUEPRINTS USE THE FORM ON PAGE 15 OR CALL TOLL-FREE 1-877-671-6036

View thousands more home plans online at www.familyhandyman.com/homeplans

The Family
Handyman

Plan #708-0173

Compact Home For Functional Living

1,220 total square feet of living area

Price Code A

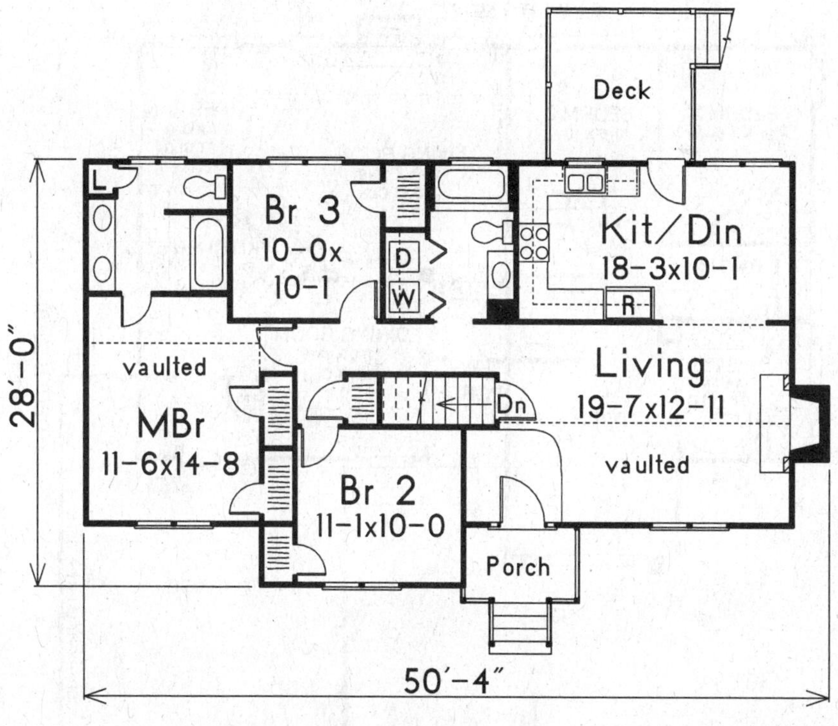
Deck
Br 3
10-0x
10-1
D
W
Kit/Din
18-3x10-1
R
vaulted
Living
19-7x12-11
Dn
MBr
11-6x14-8
vaulted
Br 2
11-1x10-0
Porch
28'-0"
50'-4"

Special features

- Vaulted ceilings add luxury to living room and master bedroom
- Spacious living room accented with a large fireplace and hearth
- Gracious dining area is adjacent to the convenient wrap-around kitchen
- Washer and dryer handy to the bedrooms
- Covered porch entry adds appeal
- Rear sun deck adjoins dining area
- 3 bedrooms, 2 baths, 2-car drive under garage
- Basement foundation

The Family
Handyman

Plan #708-LBD-15-4A

Open Living In This Ranch

COPYRIGHT 1991 LARRY E. BELK

1,575 total square feet of living area — **Price Code B**

Special features

- Decorative columns separate dining room from living room and foyer
- Kitchen has plenty of workspace
- Spacious walk-in closet in master bedroom
- 3 bedrooms, 2 baths, 2-car garage
- Slab or crawl space foundation, please specify when ordering

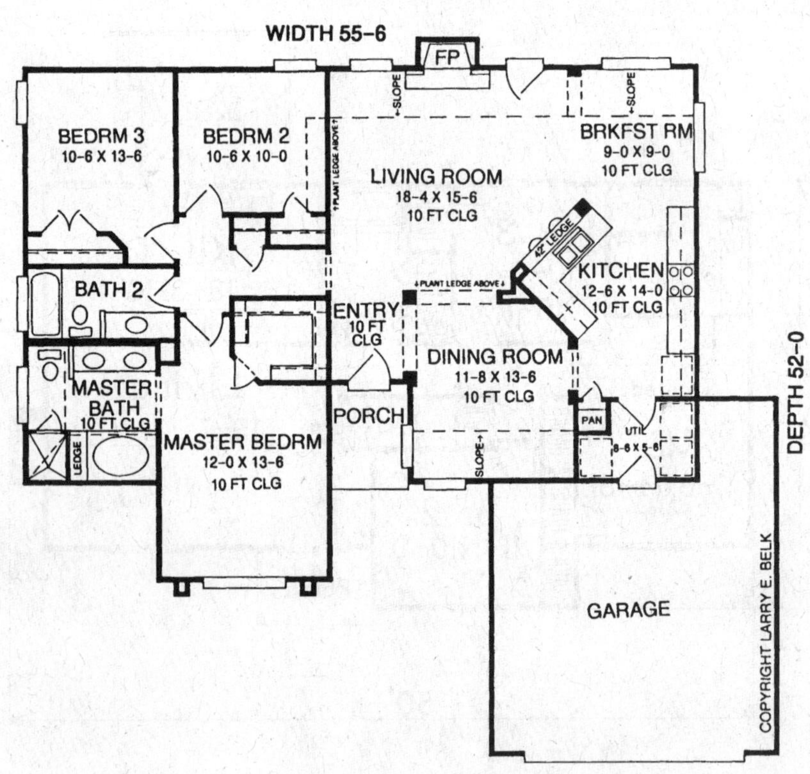
WIDTH 55-6
FP
SLOPE
SLOPE
BEDRM 3
10-6 X 13-6
BEDRM 2
10-6 X 10-0
PLANT LEDGE ABOVE
LIVING ROOM
18-4 X 15-6
10 FT CLG
BRKFST RM
9-0 X 9-0
10 FT CLG
42" LEDGE
KITCHEN
12-6 X 14-0
10 FT CLG
PLANT LEDGE ABOVE
BATH 2
ENTRY
10 FT
CLG
DINING ROOM
11-8 X 13-6
10 FT CLG
MASTER
BATH
10 FT CLG
PORCH
PAN
UTIL
8-6 X 5-8
LEDGE
MASTER BEDRM
12-0 X 13-6
10 FT CLG
SLOPE
DEPTH 52-0
GARAGE
COPYRIGHT LARRY E. BELK

The Family
Handyman

Plan #708-0425

Great Room Forms Core Of This Home

2,076 total square feet of living area — **Price Code C**

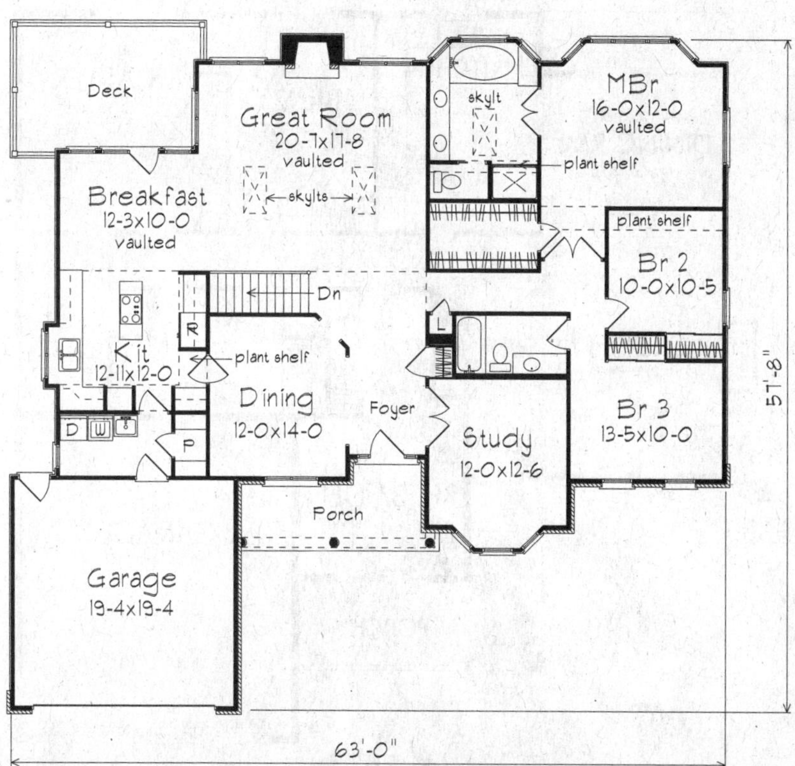
Deck
Great Room
20-7x17-8
vaulted
skylts
skylt
MBr
16-0x12-0
vaulted
plant shelf
Breakfast
12-3x10-0
vaulted
plant shelf
Br 2
10-0x10-5
Dn
R
L
Kit
12-11x12-0
plant shelf
Dining
12-0x14-0
Foyer
Study
12-0x12-6
Br 3
13-5x10-0
D
W
P
Porch
Garage
19-4x19-4
57'-8"
63'-0"

Special features

- Vaulted great room has fireplace flanked by windows and skylights that welcome the sun
- Kitchen leads to vaulted breakfast room and rear deck
- Study located off foyer provides great location for home office
- Large bay windows grace master bedroom and bath
- 3 bedrooms, 2 baths, 2-car garage
- Basement foundation

TO ORDER BLUEPRINTS USE THE FORM ON PAGE 15 OR CALL TOLL-FREE 1-877-671-6036

The Family
Handyman

Plan #708-AMD-1112

Modest Ranch Is A Great Layout For Family Living

1,557 total square feet of living area

Price Code C

Special features

- Vaulted dining room extends off the great room and features a eye-catching plant shelf above
- Double closets adorn the vaulted master bedroom which also features a private bath with tub and shower
- Bedroom #3/den has the option to add double-doors creating the feeling of a home office if needed
- 3 bedrooms, 2 baths, 2-car garage
- Crawl space foundation

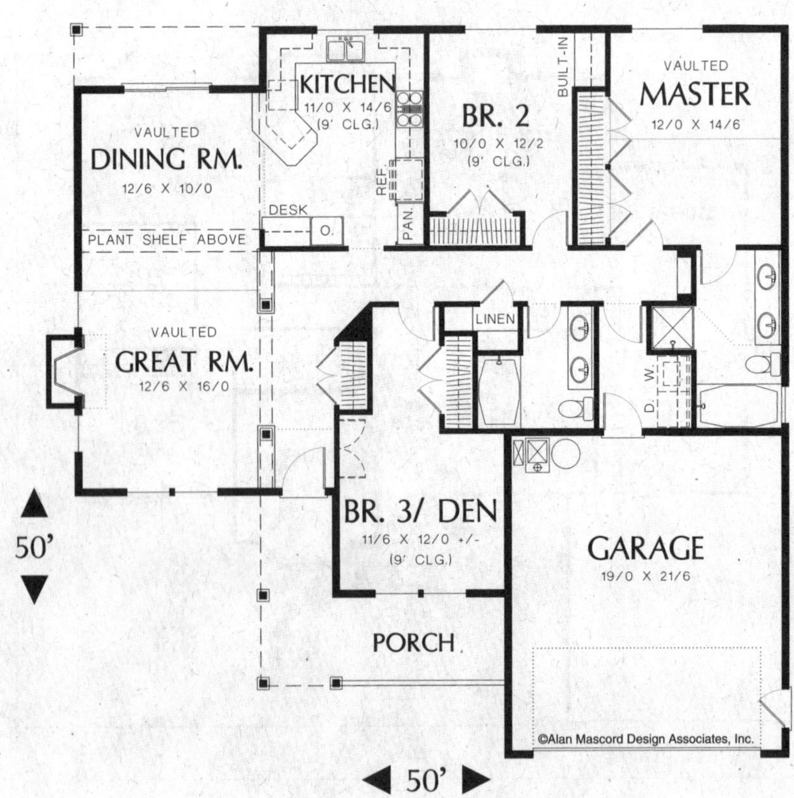
KITCHEN
11/0 X 14/6
(9' CLG.)
VAULTED
DINING RM.
12/6 X 10/0
DESK
O.
PLANT SHELF ABOVE
REF.
PAN.
BR. 2
10/0 X 12/2
(9' CLG.)
BUILT-IN
VAULTED
MASTER
12/0 X 14/6
LINEN
W.
D.
VAULTED
GREAT RM.
12/6 X 16/0
BR. 3/ DEN
11/6 X 12/0 +/-
(9' CLG.)
GARAGE
19/0 X 21/6
PORCH
50'
50'
©Alan Mascord Design Associates, Inc.

TO ORDER BLUEPRINTS USE THE FORM ON PAGE 15 OR CALL TOLL-FREE 1-877-671-6036

View thousands more home plans online at www.familyhandyman.com/homeplans

The Family
Handyman

Plan #708-0322

Open Breakfast/Family Room Combination

2,135 total square feet of living area

Price Code D

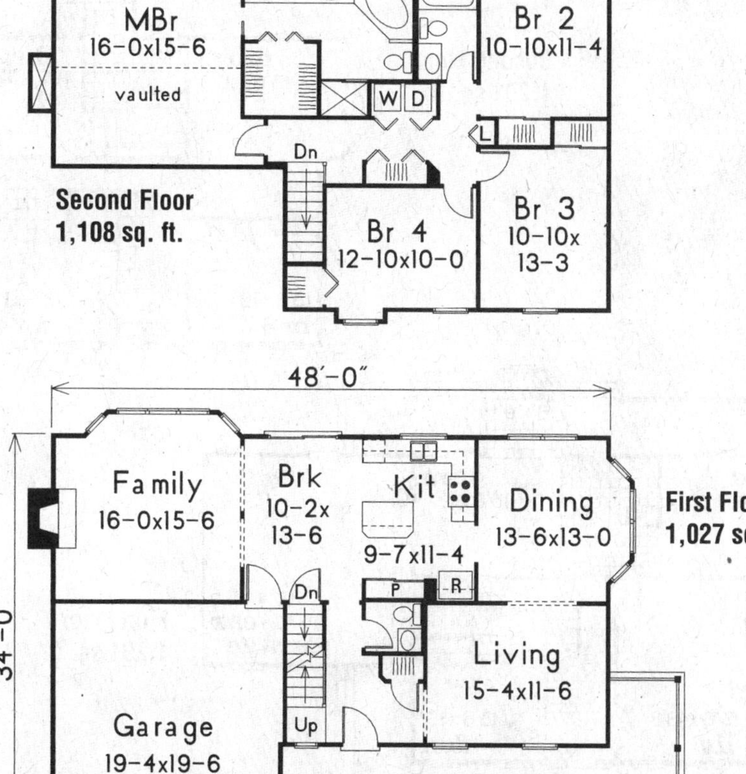
MBr
16-0x15-6
vaulted
W
D
Br 2
10-10x11-4
L
Dn
Br 3
10-10x
13-3
Br 4
12-10x10-0
Second Floor
1,108 sq. ft.
48'-0"
34'-0"
Family
16-0x15-6
Brk
10-2x
13-6
Kit
9-7x11-4
Dining
13-6x13-0
First Floor
1,027 sq. ft.
Dn
P
R
Living
15-4x11-6
Garage
19-4x19-6
Up
Porch depth 6-0

Special features

- Family room features extra space, impressive fireplace and full wall of windows that joins breakfast room creating a spacious entertainment area
- Washer and dryer conveniently located on the second floor
- Kitchen features island counter and pantry
- 4 bedrooms, 2 1/2 baths, 2-car garage
- Basement foundation

The Family
Handyman

Plan #708-SH-SEA-100

Traditional Farmhouse Feeling With This Home

2,582 total square feet of living area **Price Code D**

Special features

- Both the family and living rooms are warmed by hearths
- The master suite on the second floor has a bayed sitting room and a private bath with whirlpool tub
- Old-fashioned window seat in second floor landing is a charming touch
- 4 bedrooms, 3 baths, 2-car side entry garage
- Basement or crawl space foundation, please specify when ordering

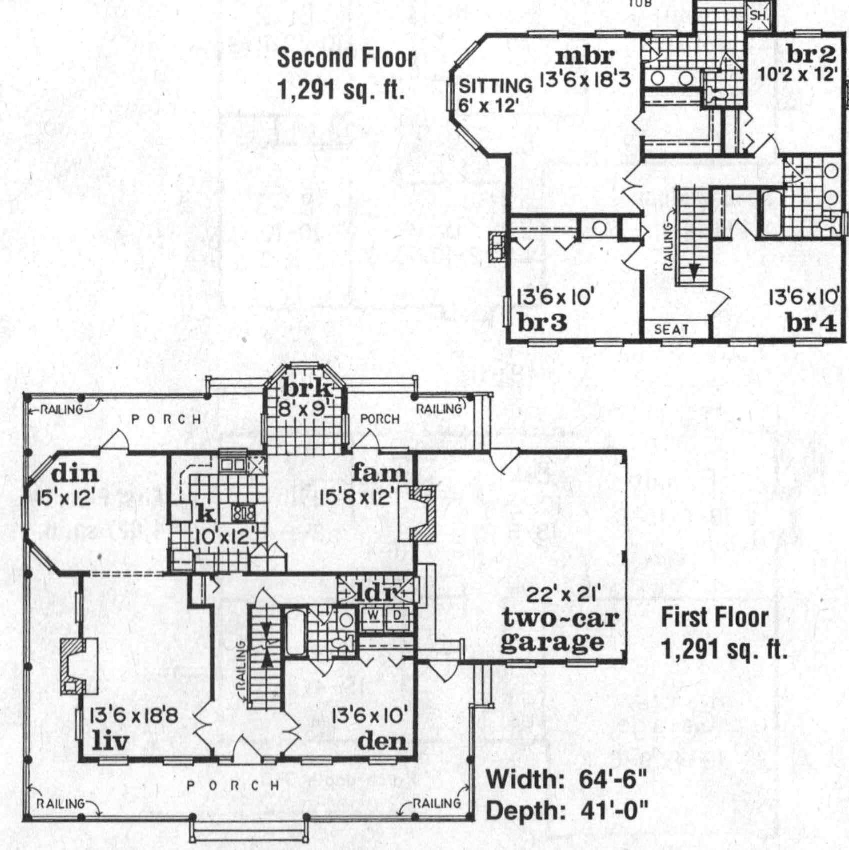
Second Floor
1,291 sq. ft.
WHIRLPOOL TUB
SH
mbr
13'6 x 18'3
SITTING
6' x 12'
br2
10'2 x 12'
RAILING
13'6 x 10'
br3
SEAT
13'6 x 10'
br4
brk
8' x 9'
RAILING
PORCH
PORCH
RAILING
din
15' x 12'
k
10' x 12'
fam
15'8 x 12'
ldr
W D
22' x 21'
two-car garage
RAILING
13'6 x 18'8
liv
13'6 x 10'
den
PORCH
RAILING
RAILING
First Floor
1,291 sq. ft.
Width: 64'-6"
Depth: 41'-0"

TO ORDER BLUEPRINTS USE THE FORM ON PAGE 15 OR CALL TOLL-FREE 1-877-671-6036

View thousands more home plans online at www.familyhandyman.com/homeplans

Plan #708-0670

Brick And Siding Enhance This Traditional Home

1,170 total square feet of living area **Price Code AA**

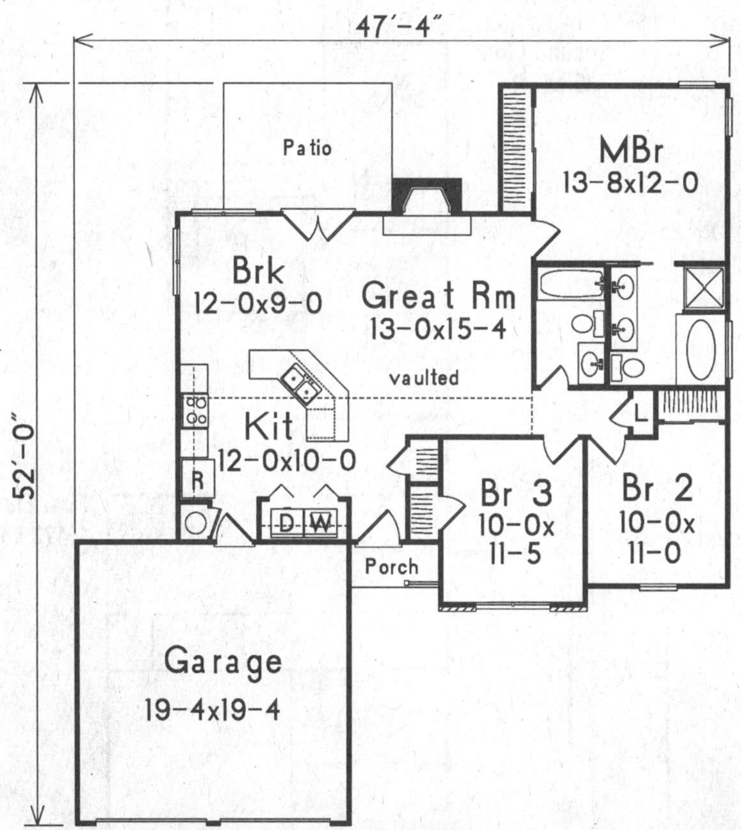
47'-4"
52'-0"
Patio
MBr
13-8x12-0
Brk
12-0x9-0
Great Rm
13-0x15-4
vaulted
Kit
12-0x10-0
R
DW
L
Br 3
10-0x
11-5
Br 2
10-0x
11-0
Porch
Garage
19-4x19-4

Special features

- Master bedroom enjoys privacy at the rear of this home
- Kitchen has angled bar that overlooks great room and breakfast area
- Living areas combine to create a greater sense of spaciousness
- Great room has a cozy fireplace
- 3 bedrooms, 2 baths, 2-car garage
- Slab foundation

TO ORDER BLUEPRINTS USE THE FORM ON PAGE 15 OR CALL TOLL-FREE 1-877-671-6036

View thousands more home plans online at www.familyhandyman.com/homeplans

The Family
Handyman

Plan #708-0356

Balcony Enjoys Spectacular Views In Atrium Home

2,806 total square feet of living area **Price Code E**

Rear View

Second Floor
785 sq. ft.

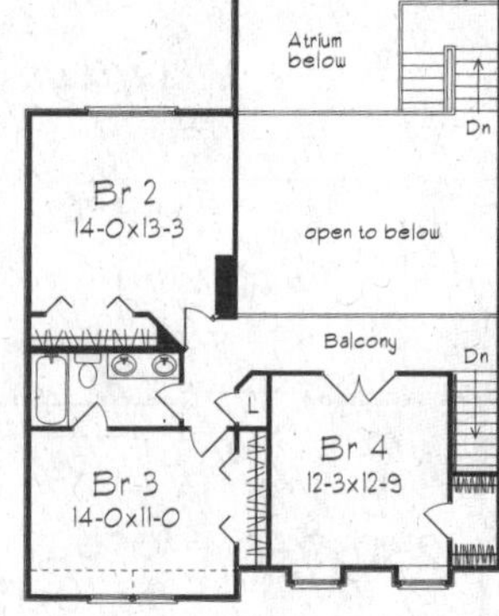
Atrium
below
Dn
Br 2
14-0x13-3
open to below
Balcony
Dn
L
Br 4
12-3x12-9
Br 3
14-0x11-0

Special features

- Harmonious charm throughout
- Sweeping balcony and vaulted ceiling soar above spacious great room and walk-in bar
- 4 bedrooms, 2 1/2 baths, 2-car garage
- Walk-out basement foundation

Lower Level
548 sq. ft.

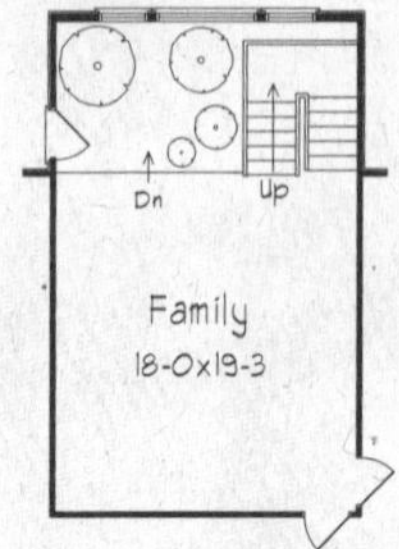
Dn
Up
Family
18-0x19-3

54'-8"
Atrium
below
Deck
Dn
Dining
10-2x13-3
Kit
11-0x
13-3
R
Great Rm
18-0x19-10
vaulted
vaulted
Bar
W
D
P
51'-0"
MBr
14-0x16-9
Foyer
Up
Porch
Garage
21-4x21-4

First Floor
1,473 sq. ft.

TO ORDER BLUEPRINTS USE THE FORM ON PAGE 15 OR CALL TOLL-FREE 1-877-671-6036

View thousands more home plans online at www.familyhandyman.com/homeplans

Plan #708-CHP-2233-B-21

Traditional Brick Ranch

2,697 total square feet of living area **Price Code E**

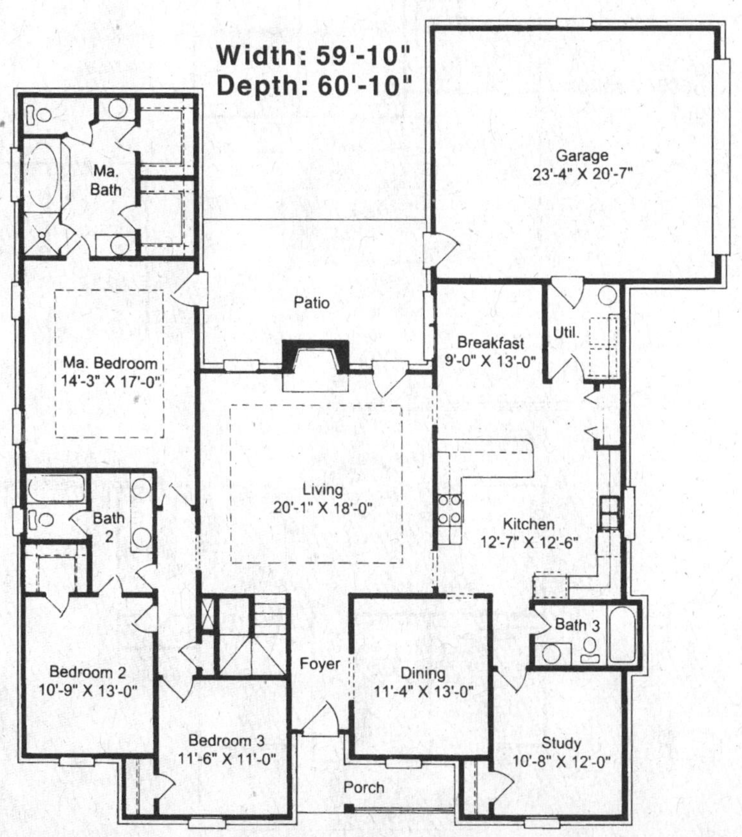
Width: 59'-10"
Depth: 60'-10"
Ma. Bath
Garage
23'-4" X 20'-7"
Patio
Ma. Bedroom
14'-3" X 17'-0"
Breakfast
9'-0" X 13'-0"
Util.
Living
20'-1" X 18'-0"
Kitchen
12'-7" X 12'-6"
Bath 2
Bath 3
Foyer
Bedroom 2
10'-9" X 13'-0"
Dining
11'-4" X 13'-0"
Bedroom 3
11'-6" X 11'-0"
Study
10'-8" X 12'-0"
Porch

Special features

- Secluded study with full bath nearby is an ideal guest room or office
- Master bedroom has access to outdoor patio
- 351 square feet of additional unfinished living space available in the attic
- 3 bedrooms, 3 baths, 2-car side entry garage
- Slab foundation

TO ORDER BLUEPRINTS USE THE FORM ON PAGE 15 OR CALL TOLL-FREE 1-877-671-6036

View thousands more home plans online at www.familyhandyman.com/homeplans

The Family Handyman

Plan #708-UD-D162

Wrap-Around Porch Adds Outdoor Style

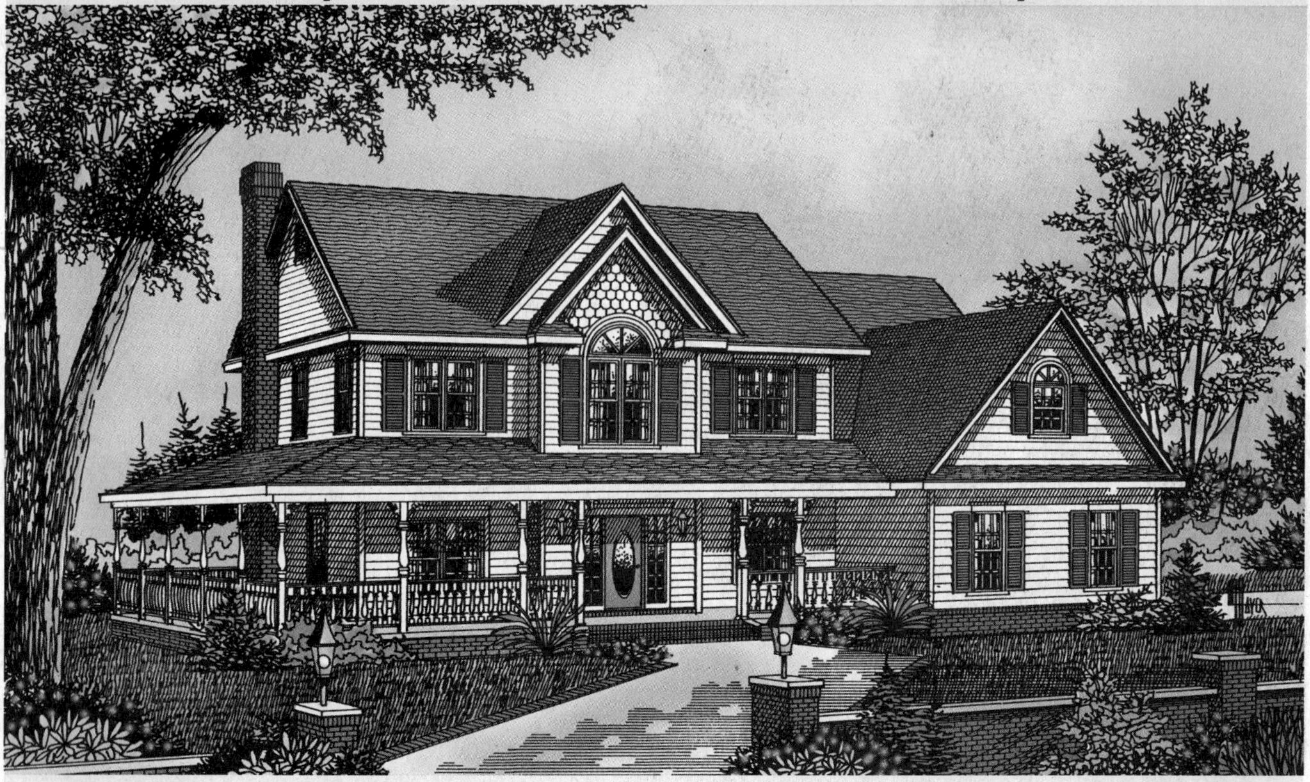

2,198 total square feet of living area

Price Code C

Special features

- Great room features a warm fireplace flanked by bookshelves for storage
- Double French doors connect the formal dining room to the kitchen
- An oversized laundry room has extra counterspace
- 4 bedrooms, 2 1/2 baths, 2-car side entry garage with shop/storage
- Basement, crawl space or slab foundation, please specify when ordering

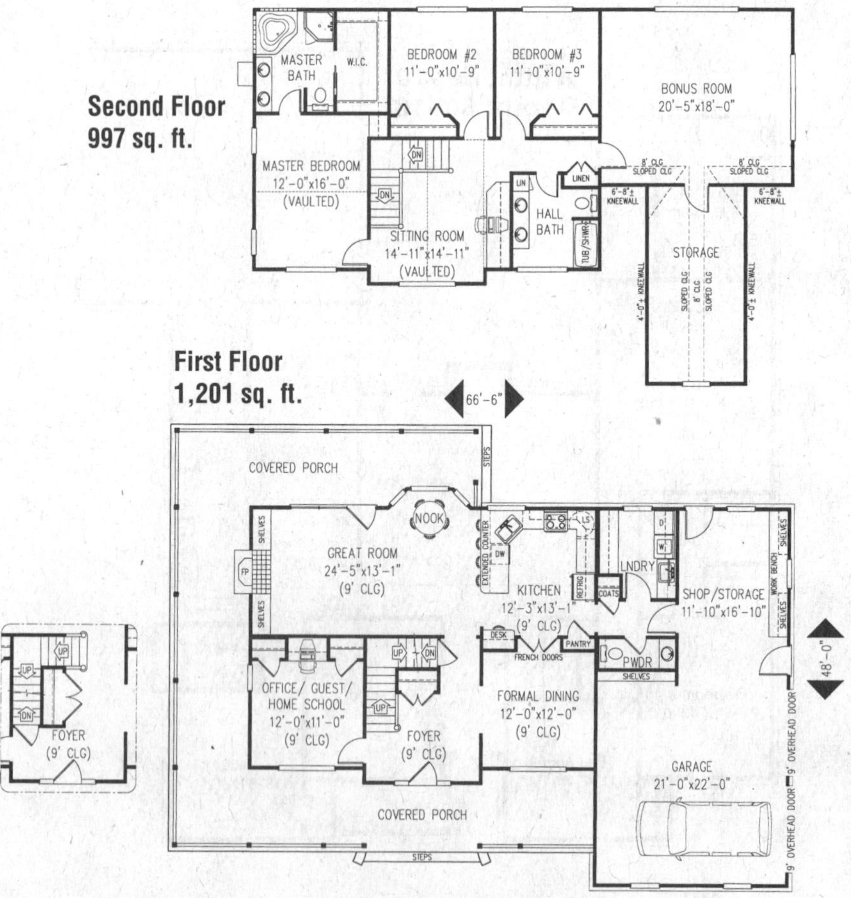

Second Floor
997 sq. ft.
MASTER BATH
W.I.C.
BEDROOM #2
11'-0"x10'-9"
BEDROOM #3
11'-0"x10'-9"
BONUS ROOM
20'-5"x18'-0"
MASTER BEDROOM
12'-0"x16'-0"
(VAULTED)
SITTING ROOM
14'-11"x14'-11"
(VAULTED)
HALL BATH
LINEN
STORAGE
First Floor
1,201 sq. ft.
66'-6"
COVERED PORCH
NOOK
GREAT ROOM
24'-5"x13'-1"
(9' CLG)
KITCHEN
12'-3"x13'-1"
(9' CLG)
LNDRY
SHOP/STORAGE
11'-10"x16'-10"
48'-0"
PANTRY
PWDR
FRENCH DOORS
OFFICE/ GUEST/ HOME SCHOOL
12'-0"x11'-0"
(9' CLG)
FOYER
(9' CLG)
FORMAL DINING
12'-0"x12'-0"
(9' CLG)
GARAGE
21'-0"x22'-0"
COVERED PORCH
STEPS

TO ORDER BLUEPRINTS USE THE FORM ON PAGE 15 OR CALL TOLL-FREE 1-877-671-6036

View thousands more home plans online at www.familyhandyman.com/homeplans

Plan #708-0418

Two-Story Solarium Welcomes The Sun

3,850 total square feet of living area

Price Code F

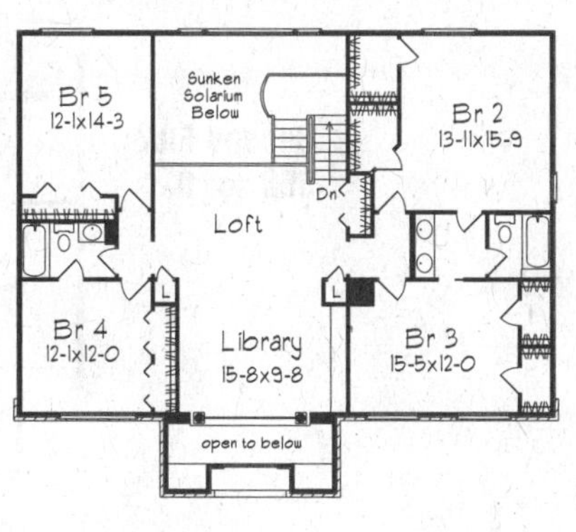
Br 5
12-1x14-3
Sunken
Solarium
Below
Br 2
13-11x15-9
Dn
Loft
Br 4
12-1x12-0
Library
15-8x9-8
Br 3
15-5x12-0
open to below

Second Floor
1,544 sq. ft.

Interior View

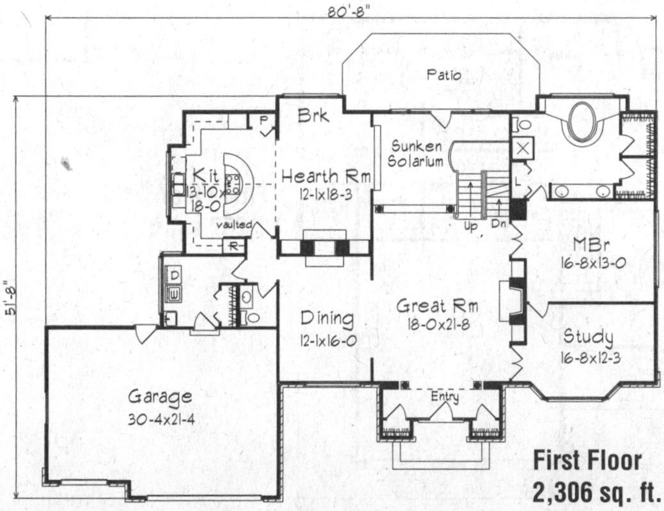

80'-8"
Patio
Brk
Sunken
Solarium
Kit
13-10x
18-0
Hearth Rm
12-1x18-3
vaulted
Up
Dn
MBr
16-8x13-0
51'-8"
Dining
12-1x16-0
Great Rm
18-0x21-8
Study
16-8x12-3
Garage
30-4x21-4
Entry

First Floor
2,306 sq. ft.

Special features

- Entry, with balcony above, leads into a splendid great room with sunken solarium
- Kitchen layout boasts a half-circle bar and cooktop island with banquet-sized dining nearby
- Solarium features U-shaped stairs with balcony and arched window
- Master suite includes luxurious bath and large study with bay window
- 5 bedrooms, 3 1/2 baths, 3-car garage
- Basement foundation

TO ORDER BLUEPRINTS USE THE FORM ON PAGE 15 OR CALL TOLL-FREE 1-877-671-6036

View thousands more home plans online at www.familyhandyman.com/homeplans

Plan #708-VL-1815

Terrific Screened Porch Off Dining Room

1,815 total square feet of living area **Price Code C**

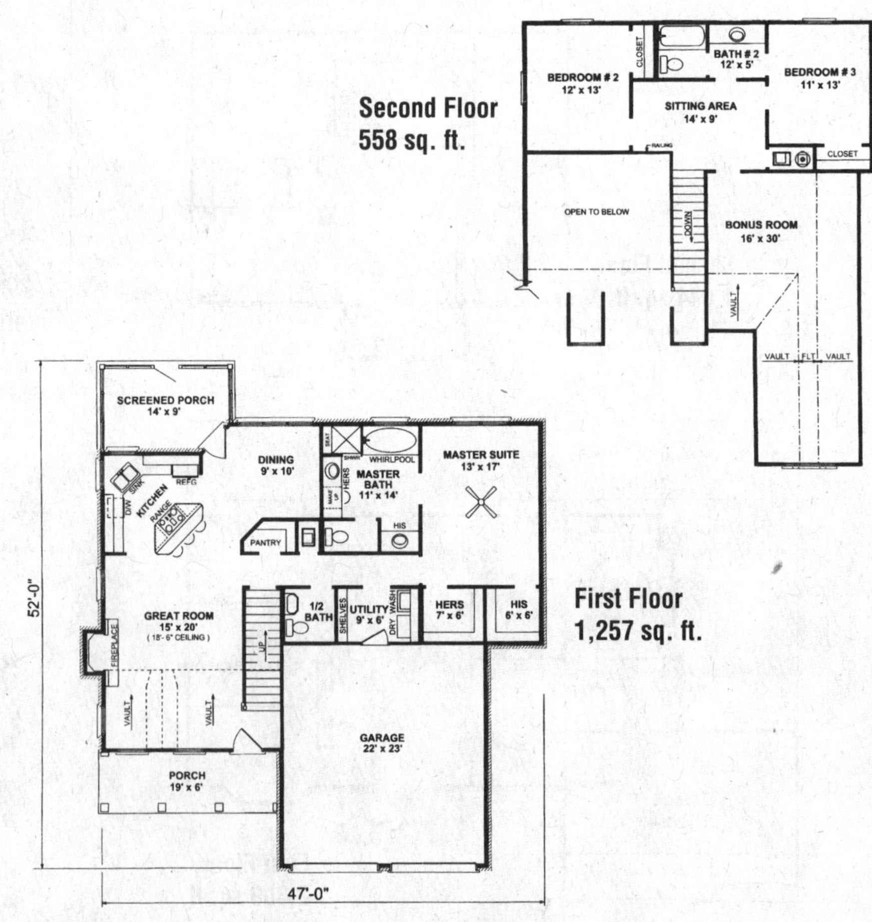

Second Floor
558 sq. ft.
CLOSET
BATH # 2
12' x 5'
BEDROOM # 2
12' x 13'
BEDROOM # 3
11' x 13'
SITTING AREA
14' x 9'
RAILING
CLOSET
OPEN TO BELOW
DOWN
BONUS ROOM
16' x 30'
VAULT
VAULT
FLT
VAULT
SCREENED PORCH
14' x 9'
DINING
9' x 10'
WHIRLPOOL
MASTER SUITE
13' x 17'
MASTER BATH
11' x 14'
HERS
HIS
KITCHEN
REFG
RANGE
PANTRY
GREAT ROOM
15' x 20'
(18'-6" CEILING)
FIREPLACE
UP
1/2 BATH
UTILITY
9' x 6'
SHELVES
WASH
DRY
HERS
7' x 6'
HIS
6' x 6'
VAULT
VAULT
GARAGE
22' x 23'
PORCH
19' x 6'
52'-0"
47'-0"
First Floor
1,257 sq. ft.

Special features

- Center island in kitchen creates an extra dining space as well as a cooking area
- Large vaulted great room has a fireplace centered on one wall for coziness
- The second floor features a centralized sitting area ideal for casual living space
- Bonus room on the second floor has an additional 426 square feet of living area
- 3 bedrooms, 2 1/2 baths, 2-car garage
- Slab or crawl space foundation, please specify when ordering

TO ORDER BLUEPRINTS USE THE FORM ON PAGE 15 OR CALL TOLL-FREE 1-877-671-6036

View thousands more home plans online at www.familyhandyman.com/homeplans

Bay Window Graces Luxury Master Bedroom

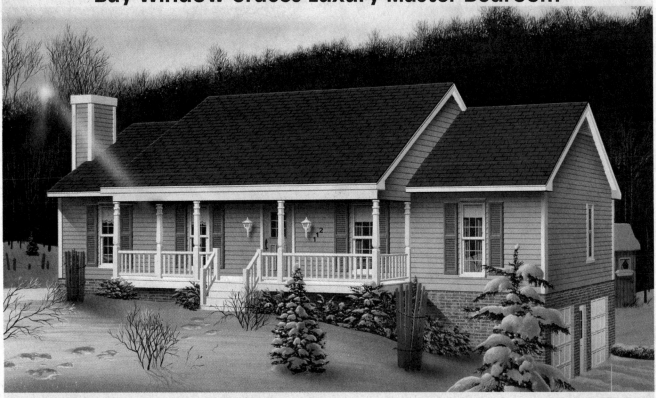

1,668 total square feet of living area **Price Code C**

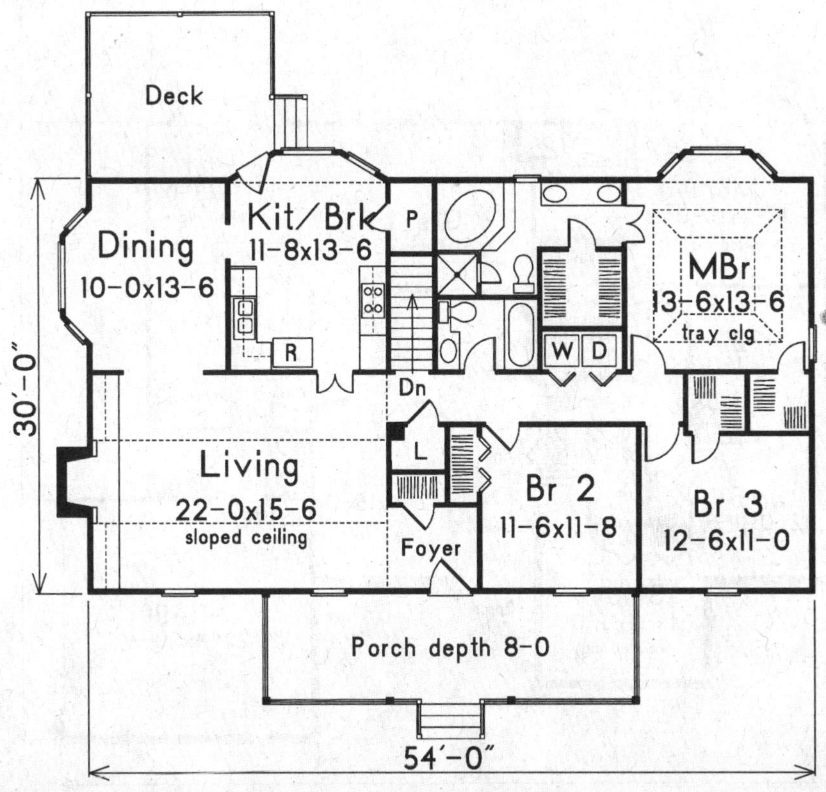
Deck
Dining
10-0x13-6
Kit/Brk
11-8x13-6
P
R
Dn
MBr
13-6x13-6
tray clg
W D
Living
22-0x15-6
sloped ceiling
L
Foyer
Br 2
11-6x11-8
Br 3
12-6x11-0
Porch depth 8-0
30'-0"
54'-0"

Special features

- Large bay windows in breakfast area, master bedroom and dining room
- Extensive walk-in closets and storage spaces throughout the home
- Handy covered entry porch
- Large living room has fireplace, built-in bookshelves and sloped ceiling
- 3 bedrooms, 2 baths, 2-car drive under garage
- Basement foundation

Classic Elegance

2,483 total square feet of living area

Price Code D

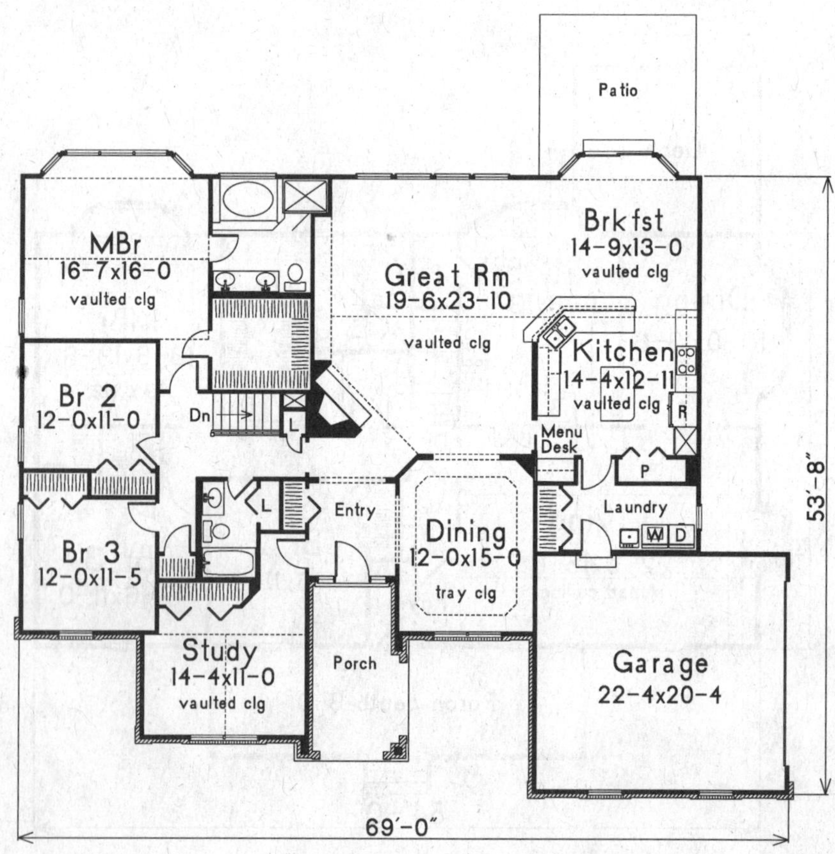
Patio
MBr
16-7x16-0
vaulted clg
Great Rm
19-6x23-10
vaulted clg
Brkfst
14-9x13-0
vaulted clg
Kitchen
14-4x12-11
vaulted clg
R
Menu
Desk
P
Laundry
W
D
Br 2
12-0x11-0
Dn
L
Br 3
12-0x11-5
L
Entry
Dining
12-0x15-0
tray clg
Study
14-4x11-0
vaulted clg
Porch
Garage
22-4x20-4
53'-8"
69'-0"

Special features

- A large entry porch with open brick arches and palladian door welcomes guests
- The vaulted great room features an entertainment center alcove and ideal layout for furniture placement
- Dining room is extra large with a stylish tray ceiling
- Study can easily be converted to a fourth bedroom
- 3 bedrooms, 2 baths, 2-car side entry garage
- Basement foundation

TO ORDER BLUEPRINTS USE THE FORM ON PAGE 15 OR CALL TOLL-FREE 1-877-671-6036

View thousands more home plans online at www.familyhandyman.com/homeplans

The Family
Handyman

Plan #708-AP-1516

Covered Rear Porch Is A Nice Dining Place

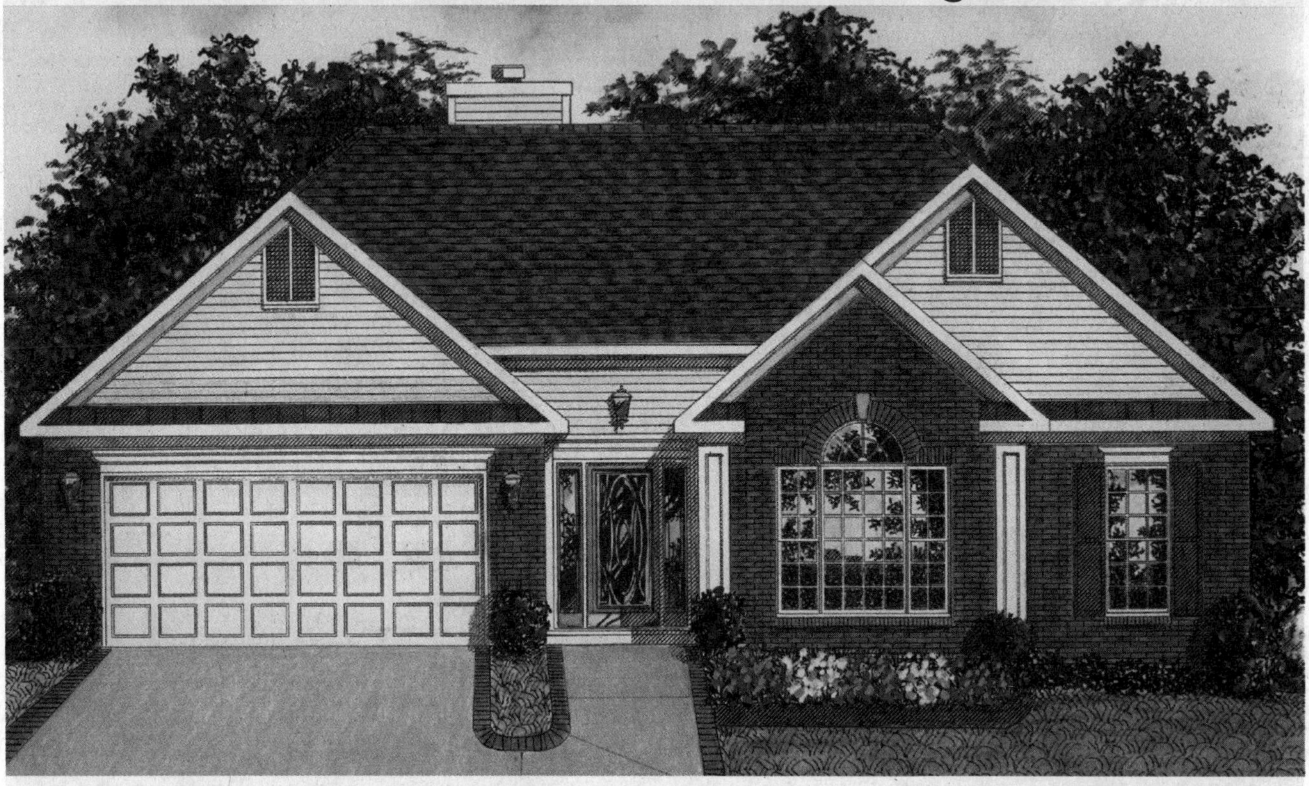

1,593 total square feet of living area

Price Code C

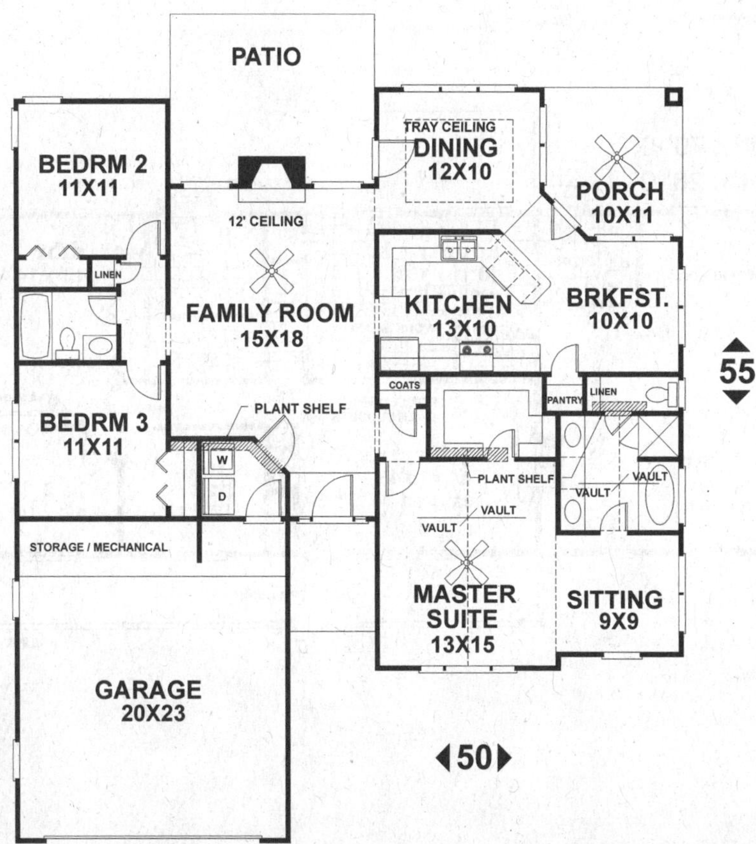
PATIO
BEDRM 2
11X11
TRAY CEILING
DINING
12X10
PORCH
10X11
12' CEILING
LINEN
FAMILY ROOM
15X18
KITCHEN
13X10
BRKFST.
10X10
55
COATS
PANTRY
LINEN
PLANT SHELF
BEDRM 3
11X11
W
D
PLANT SHELF
VAULT
VAULT
VAULT
VAULT
STORAGE / MECHANICAL
MASTER
SUITE
13X15
SITTING
9X9
GARAGE
20X23
50

Special features

- Large sitting area is enjoyed by the master bedroom which also features a walk-in closet and bath
- Centrally located kitchen accesses the family, dining and breakfast rooms with ease
- Storage/mechanical area is ideal for seasonal storage or hobby supplies
- 3 bedrooms, 2 baths, 2-car garage
- Basement, crawl space or slab foundation, please specify when ordering

The Family
Handyman

Plan #708-SH-SEA-242

Vaulted Ceilings Add A Sense Of Spaciousness

1,408 total square feet of living area **Price Code A**

<u>*Special features*</u>

- A bright country kitchen boasts an abundance of counterspace and cupboards
- The front entry is sheltered by a broad verandah
- A spa tub is brightened by a box bay window in the master bath
- 3 bedrooms, 2 baths, 2-car side entry garage
- Basement or crawl space foundation, please specify when ordering

Width: 70'-0"
Depth: 28'-0"

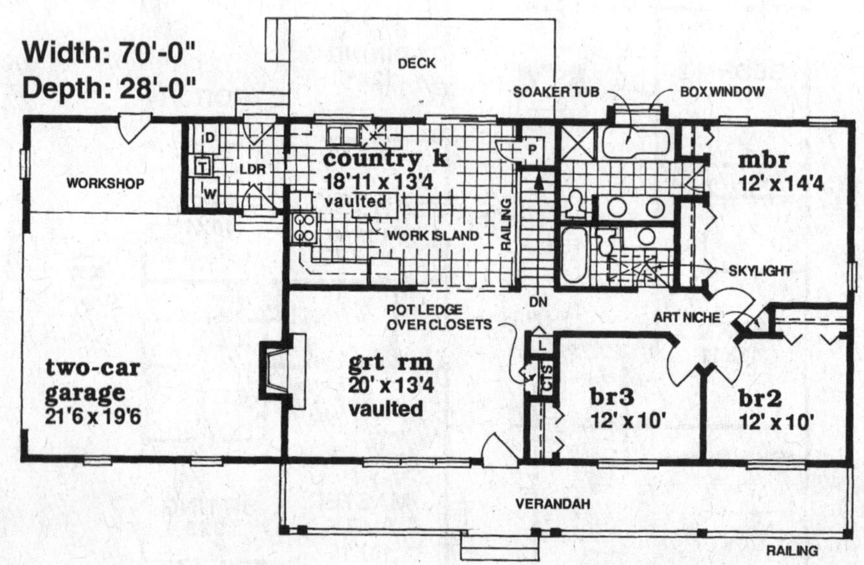
DECK
SOAKER TUB
BOX WINDOW
D
T
W
LDR
WORKSHOP
country k
18'11 x 13'4
vaulted
P
WORK ISLAND
RAILING
mbr
12' x 14'4
SKYLIGHT
DN
ART NICHE
POT LEDGE
OVER CLOSETS
L
CLS
two-car
garage
21'6 x 19'6
grt rm
20' x 13'4
vaulted
br3
12' x 10'
br2
12' x 10'
VERANDAH
RAILING

TO ORDER BLUEPRINTS USE THE FORM ON PAGE 15 OR CALL TOLL-FREE 1-877-671-6036
View thousands more home plans online at www.familyhandyman.com/homeplans

The Family
Handyman

Plan #708-0709

Great Looks Accentuated By Elliptical Brick Arches

2,521 total square feet of living area **Price Code D**

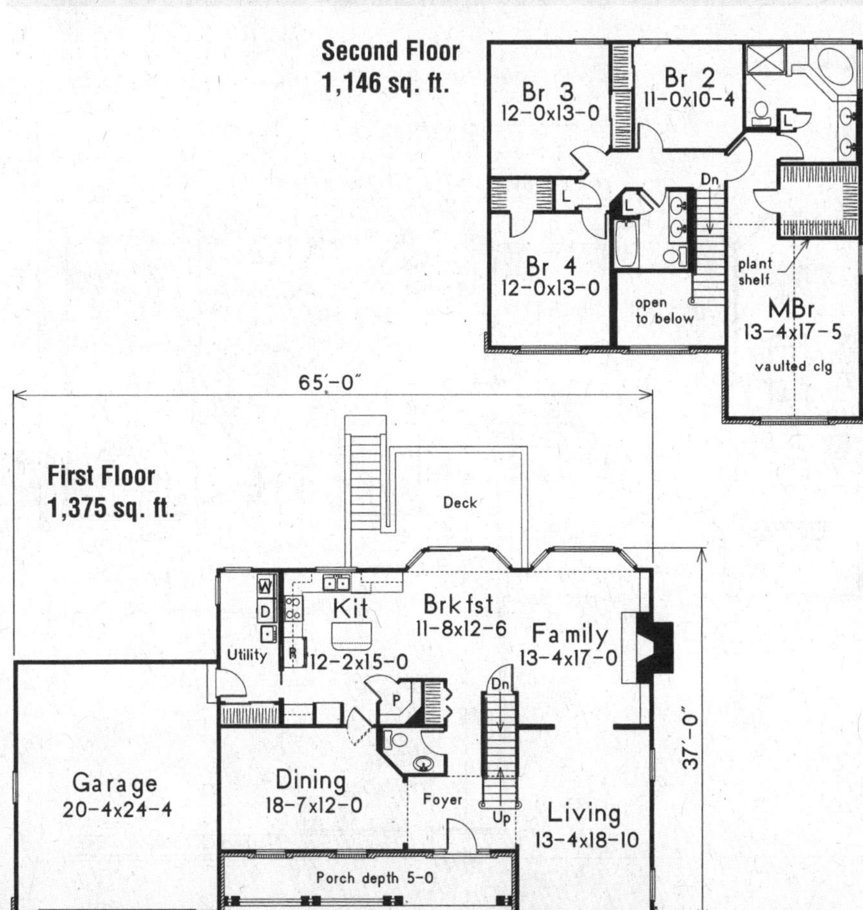
Second Floor
1,146 sq. ft.
Br 3
12-0x13-0
Br 2
11-0x10-4
Br 4
12-0x13-0
Dn
plant shelf
open to below
MBr
13-4x17-5
vaulted clg
65'-0"
First Floor
1,375 sq. ft.
Deck
Kit
12-2x15-0
Brkfst
11-8x12-6
Family
13-4x17-0
Utility
Dn
Garage
20-4x24-4
Dining
18-7x12-0
Foyer
Up
Living
13-4x18-10
Porch depth 5-0
37'-0"

Special features

- Large living and dining rooms are a plus for formal entertaining or large family gatherings
- Informal kitchen, breakfast and family rooms feature a 37' vista and double bay windows
- Generous-sized master bedroom and three secondary bedrooms grace the second floor
- 4 bedrooms, 2 1/2 baths, 2-car garage
- Basement foundation

TO ORDER BLUEPRINTS USE THE FORM ON PAGE 15 OR CALL TOLL-FREE 1-877-671-6036

The Family
Handyman

Plan #708-DBI-9120

Luxurious Ranch Has It All

3,312 total square feet of living area **Price Code F**

Special features

- Impressive front entry commands attention with an enormous living room straight ahead
- A casual family room and breakfast area combine to create a terrific gathering place just off the kitchen
- A second entry near the master bedroom is a convenient way into the home directly from the garage
- 3 bedrooms, 2 1/2 baths, 3-car side entry garage
- Slab foundation

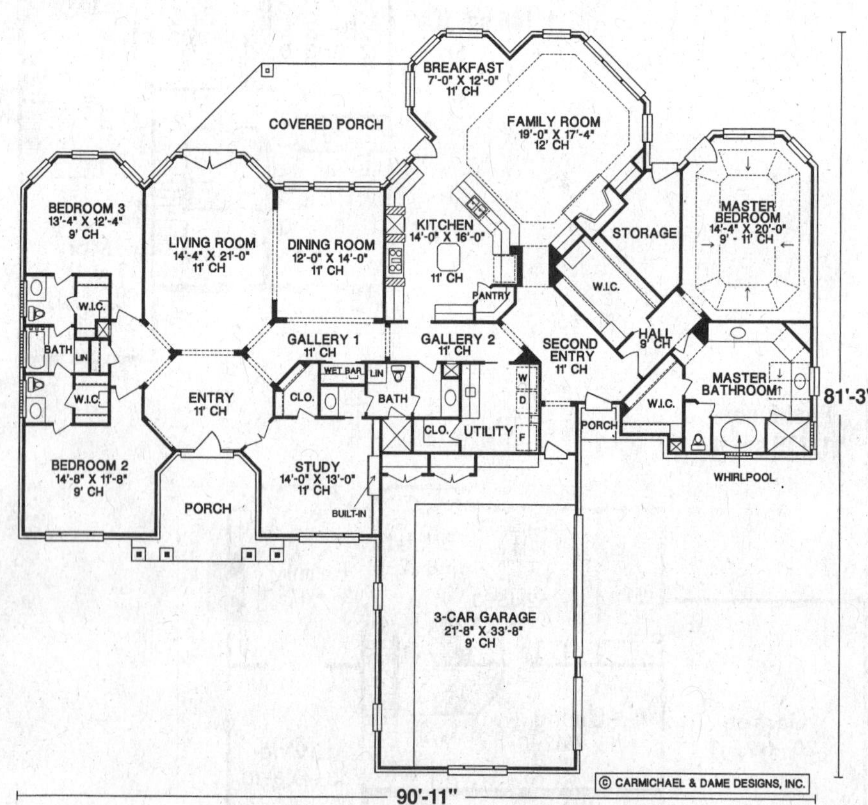
BREAKFAST
7'-0" X 12'-0"
11' CH
COVERED PORCH
FAMILY ROOM
19'-0" X 17'-4"
12' CH
BEDROOM 3
13'-4" X 12'-4"
9' CH
LIVING ROOM
14'-4" X 21'-0"
11' CH
DINING ROOM
12'-0" X 14'-0"
11' CH
KITCHEN
14'-0" X 16'-0"
11' CH
PANTRY
STORAGE
MASTER
BEDROOM
14'-4" X 20'-0"
9' - 11' CH
W.I.C.
BATH
LIN
W.I.C.
GALLERY 1
11' CH
GALLERY 2
11' CH
SECOND
ENTRY
11' CH
HALL
9' CH
WET BAR
LIN
CLO.
BATH
W
D
F
ENTRY
11' CH
CLO.
UTILITY
PORCH
W.I.C.
MASTER
BATHROOM
WHIRLPOOL
BEDROOM 2
14'-8" X 11'-8"
9' CH
STUDY
14'-0" X 13'-0"
11' CH
BUILT-IN
PORCH
3-CAR GARAGE
21'-8" X 33'-8"
9' CH
81'-3"
90'-11"
© CARMICHAEL & DAME DESIGNS, INC.

TO ORDER BLUEPRINTS USE THE FORM ON PAGE 15 OR CALL TOLL-FREE 1-877-671-6036

View thousands more home plans online at www.familyhandyman.com/homeplans

Plan #708-0219

Arched Elegance

3,222 total square feet of living area

Price Code F

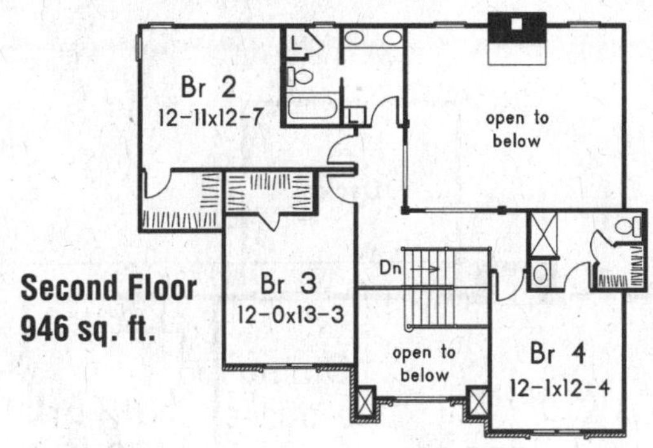
Br 2
12-11x12-7
L
open to
below
Dn
Br 3
12-0x13-3
open to
below
Br 4
12-1x12-4

Second Floor
946 sq. ft.

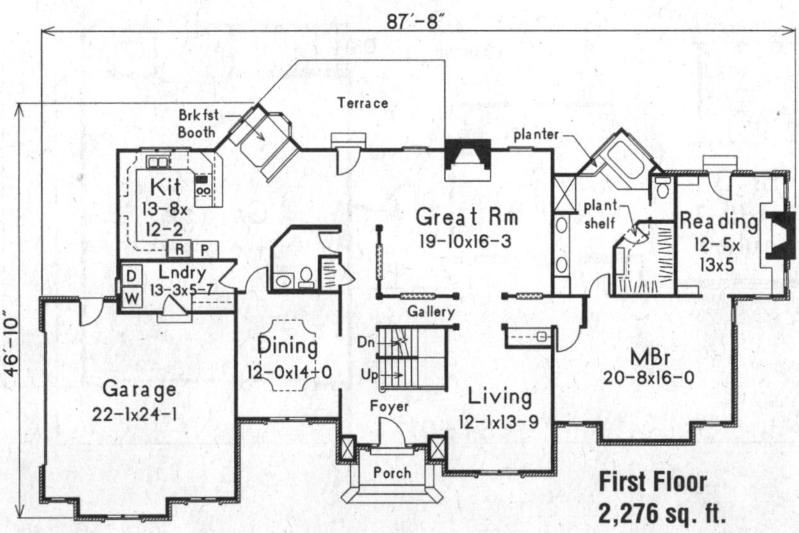
87'-8"
46'-10"
Terrace
Brkfst
Booth
planter
Kit
13-8x
12-2
R
P
Great Rm
19-10x16-3
plant
shelf
Reading
12-5x
13x5
D
W
Lndry
13-3x5-7
Gallery
Dining
12-0x14-0
Dn
Up
MBr
20-8x16-0
Garage
22-1x24-1
Foyer
Living
12-1x13-9
Porch

First Floor
2,276 sq. ft.

Special features

- Two-story foyer features central staircase and views to second floor, dining and living rooms
- Built-in breakfast booth surrounded by windows
- Gourmet kitchen with view to the great room
- Two-story great room features large fireplace and arched openings to the second floor
- Elegant master suite has separate reading room with bookshelves and fireplace
- 4 bedrooms, 3 1/2 baths, 2-car side entry garage
- Basement foundation, drawings also include crawl space and slab foundations

The Family
Handyman

Plan #708-0229

Vaulted Ceilings And Light Add Dimension

1,676 total square feet of living area **Price Code B**

Special features

- The living area skylights and large breakfast room with bay window provide plenty of sunlight
- The master bedroom has a walk-in closet and both the secondary bedrooms have large closets
- Vaulted ceilings, plant shelving and a fireplace provide a quality living area
- 3 bedrooms, 2 baths, 2-car garage
- Basement foundation, drawings also include crawl space and slab foundations

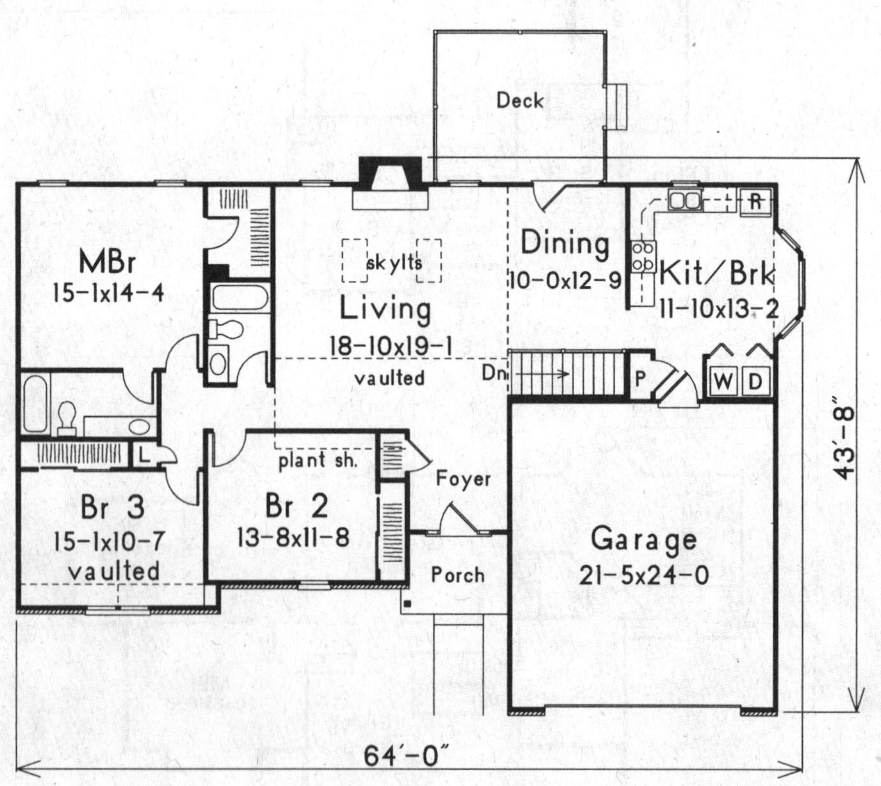
Deck
MBr
15-1x14-4
skylts
Living
18-10x19-1
vaulted
Dining
10-0x12-9
Kit/Brk
11-10x13-2
R
Dn
P
W
D
L
plant sh.
Foyer
Br 3
15-1x10-7
vaulted
Br 2
13-8x11-8
Porch
Garage
21-5x24-0
43'-8"
64'-0"

TO ORDER BLUEPRINTS USE THE FORM ON PAGE 15 OR CALL TOLL-FREE 1-877-671-6036

View thousands more home plans online at www.familyhandyman.com/homeplans

Country Comfort

3,025 total square feet of living area **Price Code E**

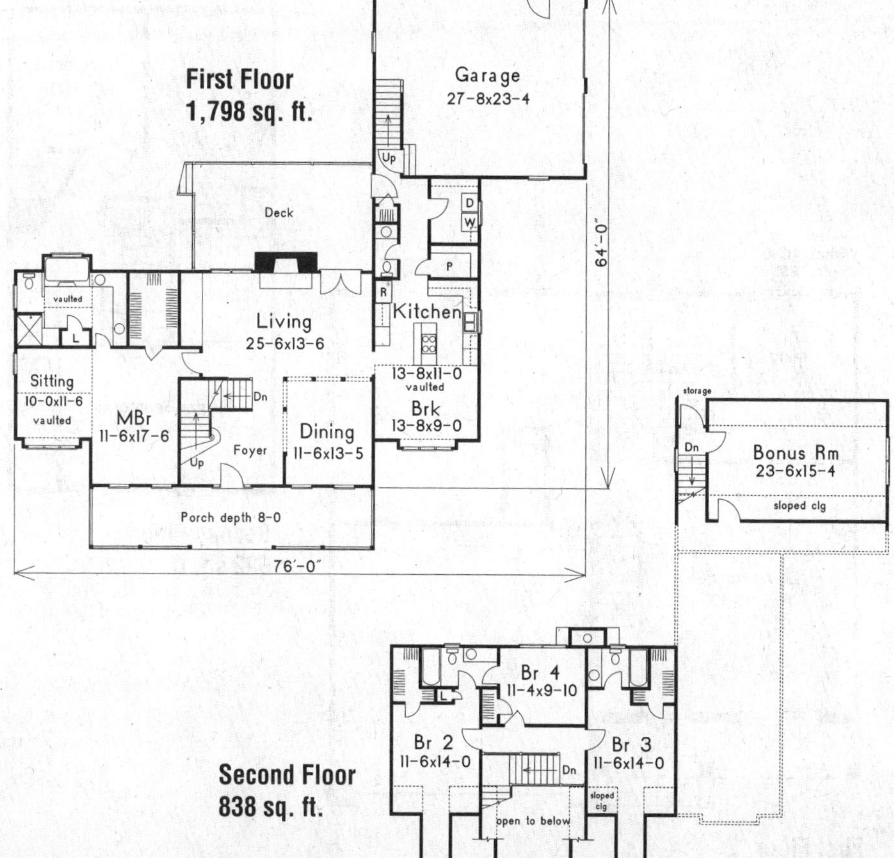
First Floor
1,798 sq. ft.
Garage
27-8x23-4
Up
Deck
D
W
P
R
Kitchen
vaulted
L
Living
25-6x13-6
13-8x11-0
vaulted
Brk
13-8x9-0
Sitting
10-0x11-6
vaulted
MBr
11-6x17-6
Dn
Foyer
Up
Dining
11-6x13-5
Porch depth 8-0
76'-0"
64'-0"
storage
Dn
Bonus Rm
23-6x15-4
sloped clg
Br 4
11-4x9-10
L
Br 2
11-6x14-0
Dn
Br 3
11-6x14-0
sloped clg
open to below
Second Floor
838 sq. ft.

Special features

- Bonus room above garage has its own private entrance - great for home office, hobby or exercise room
- Master suite has generous walk-in closet, luxurious bath and a vaulted sitting area
- Spacious kitchen has an island cooktop and vaulted breakfast nook
- Bonus room above garage has an additional 389 square feet of living area
- 4 bedrooms, 3 1/2 baths, 2-car side entry garage, 1-car drive under garage
- Basement foundation

The Family
Handyman

Plan #708-HDS-1670

Charming Two-Story With Porch

1,670 total square feet of living area **Price Code B**

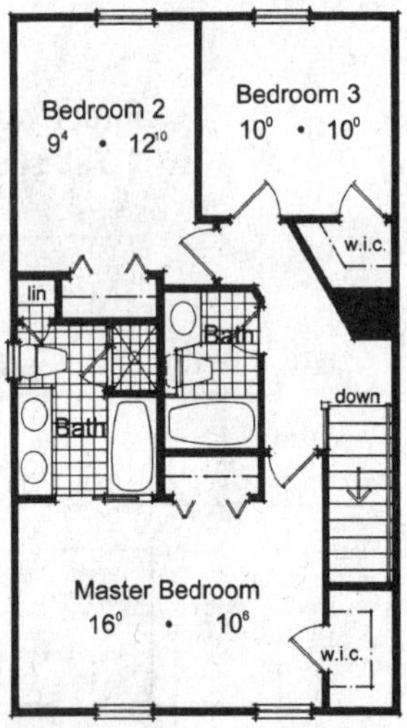

Special features

- Lots of closet space throughout
- Family room is flooded with sunlight from many windows
- Open living areas make this home appear larger
- 4 bedrooms, 2 1/2 baths, 2-car garage
- Basement foundation

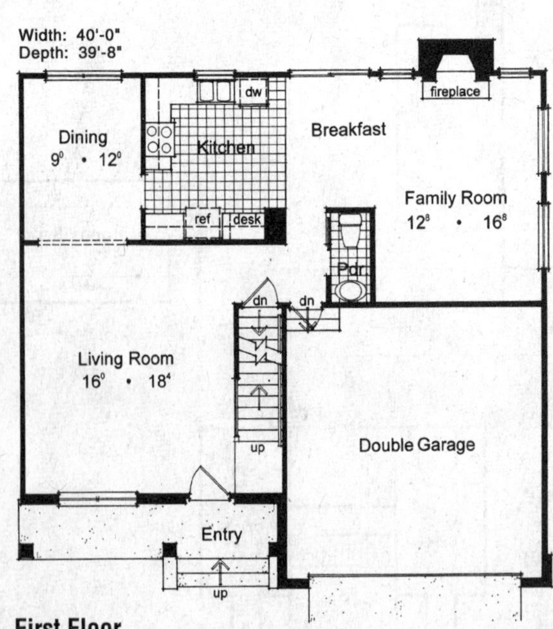
Width: 40'-0"
Depth: 39'-8"
dw
fireplace
Dining
9° • 12°
Kitchen
Breakfast
Family Room
12⁸ • 16⁸
ref
desk
Pdr
dn
dn
Living Room
16° • 18⁴
up
Double Garage
Entry
up

First Floor
978 sq. ft.

Bedroom 2
9⁴ • 12¹⁰

Bedroom 3
10° • 10°

w.i.c.

lin

Bath

Bath

down

Master Bedroom
16° • 10⁶

w.i.c.

Second Floor
692 sq. ft.

TO ORDER BLUEPRINTS USE THE FORM ON PAGE 15 OR CALL TOLL-FREE 1-877-671-6036

View thousands more home plans online at www.familyhandyman.com/homeplans

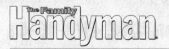

Designed For Handicap Access

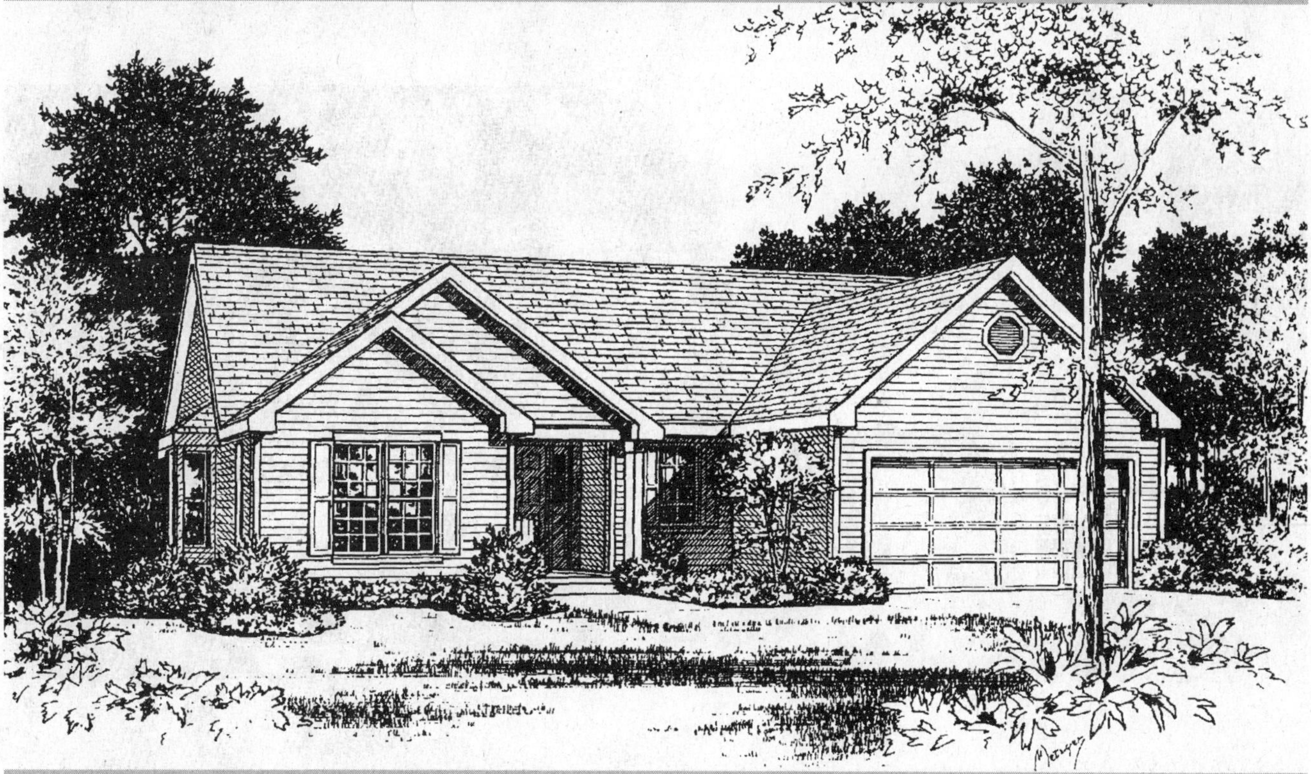

1,578 total square feet of living area **Price Code B**

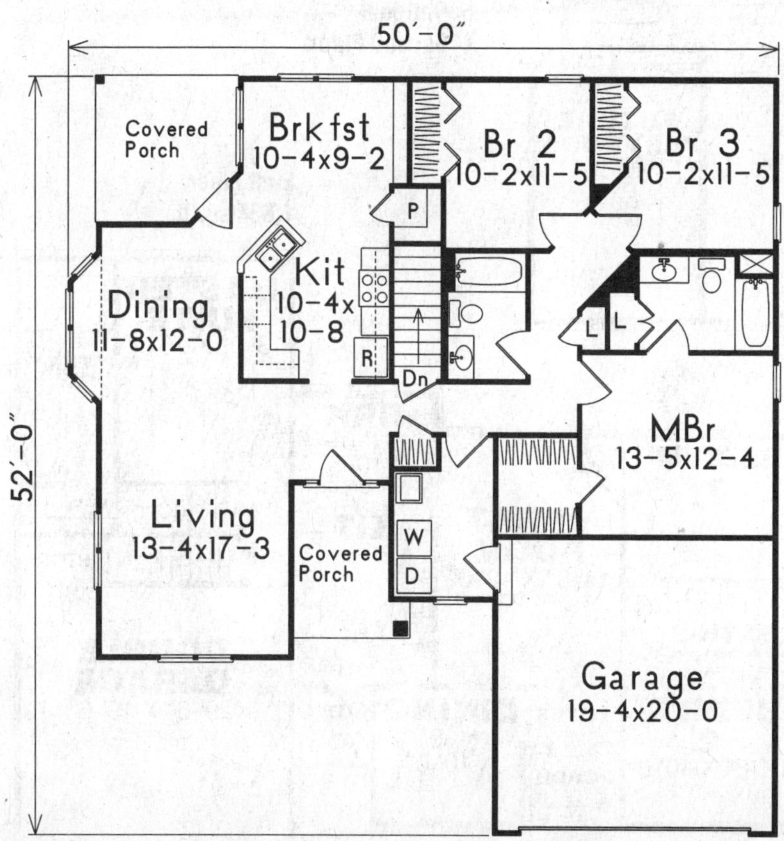
50′-0″
52′-0″
Covered
Porch
Brk fst
10-4x9-2
Br 2
10-2x11-5
Br 3
10-2x11-5
P
Kit
10-4x
10-8
Dining
11-8x12-0
R
Dn
L
L
MBr
13-5x12-4
Living
13-4x17-3
W
D
Covered
Porch
Garage
19-4x20-0

Special features

- Plenty of closet, linen and storage space
- Covered porches in the front and rear of the home add charm to this design
- Open floor plan has unique angled layout
- 3 bedrooms, 2 baths, 2-car garage
- Basement foundation

Plan #708-CHD-16-41

Vaulted Ceilings Throughout Home

1,634 total square feet of living area — **Price Code B**

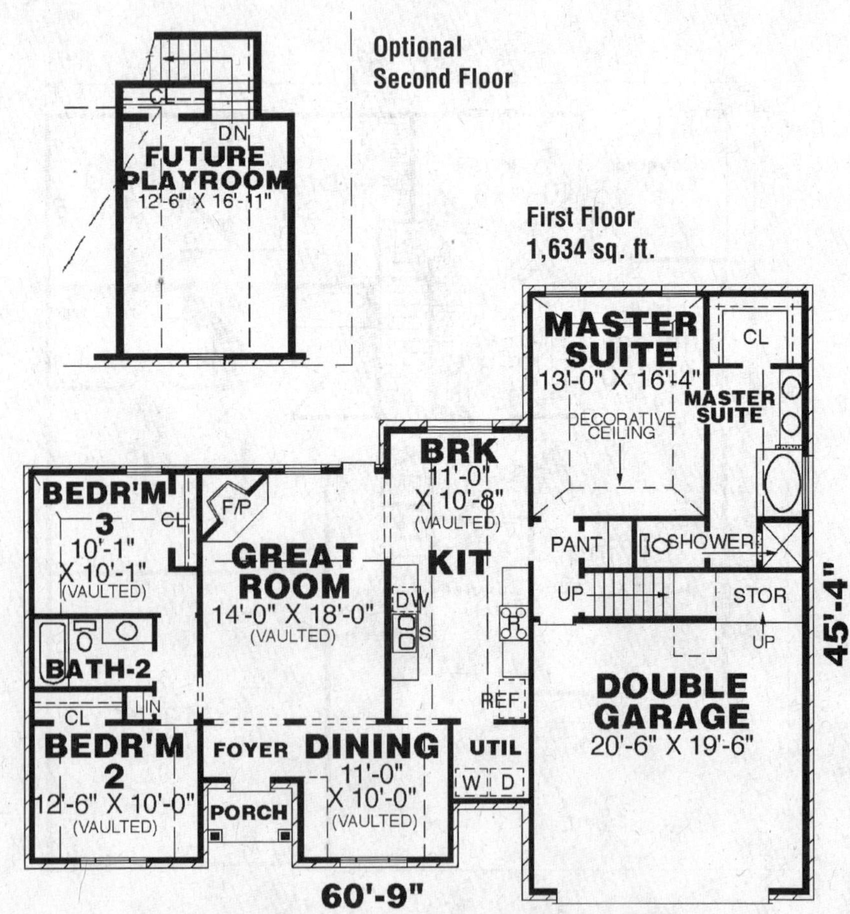
Optional
Second Floor
CL
DN
FUTURE
PLAYROOM
12'-6" X 16'-11"
First Floor
1,634 sq. ft.
MASTER
SUITE
13'-0" X 16'-4"
CL
MASTER
SUITE
DECORATIVE
CEILING
BRK
11'-0"
X 10'-8"
(VAULTED)
BEDR'M
3
10'-1"
X 10'-1"
(VAULTED)
CL
F/P
GREAT
ROOM
14'-0" X 18'-0"
(VAULTED)
KIT
DW
S
PANT
SHOWER
UP
STOR
UP
45'-4"
BATH-2
LIN
CL
REF
DOUBLE
GARAGE
20'-6" X 19'-6"
BEDR'M
2
12'-6" X 10'-0"
(VAULTED)
FOYER
DINING
11'-0"
X 10'-0"
(VAULTED)
UTIL
W D
PORCH
60'-9"

Special features

- Enter foyer to find a nice-sized dining room to the right and a cozy great room with fireplace straight ahead
- Secluded master suite offers privacy from other bedrooms and living areas
- Plenty of storage throughout this home
- Future playroom on the second floor has an additional 256 square feet of living area
- 3 bedrooms, 2 baths, 2-car garage
- Slab foundation

Dormers Add Southern Accents

2,651 total square feet of living area **Price Code E**

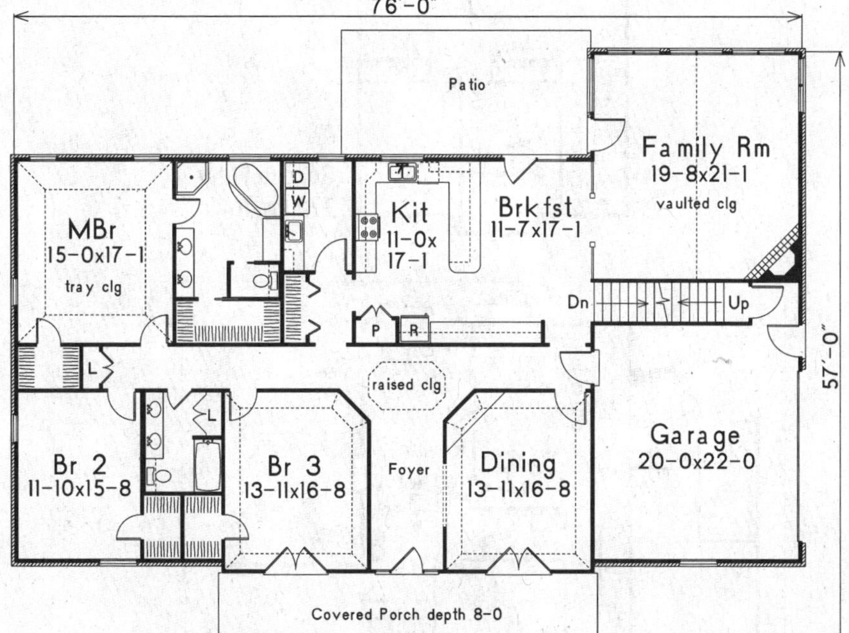
76'-0"
57'-0"
Patio
Family Rm
19-8x21-1
vaulted clg
MBr
15-0x17-1
tray clg
D
W
Kit
11-0x
17-1
Brk fst
11-7x17-1
Dn
Up
P
R
L
raised clg
L
Br 2
11-10x15-8
Br 3
13-11x16-8
Foyer
Dining
13-11x16-8
Garage
20-0x22-0
Covered Porch depth 8-0

Special features

- Vaulted family room has corner fireplace and access to breakfast room and outdoor patio
- Dining room has double-door entry from covered front porch and a beautiful built-in corner display area
- Master bedroom has 10' tray ceiling, private bath and two walk-in closets
- Kitchen has enormous counterspace with plenty of eating area and overlooks a cheerful breakfast room
- 3 bedrooms, 2 baths, 2-car side entry garage
- Basement foundation, drawings also include crawl space and slab foundations

The Family
Handyman

Plan #708-0426

Balcony Offers Sweeping Views

2,444 total square feet of living area | **Price Code D**

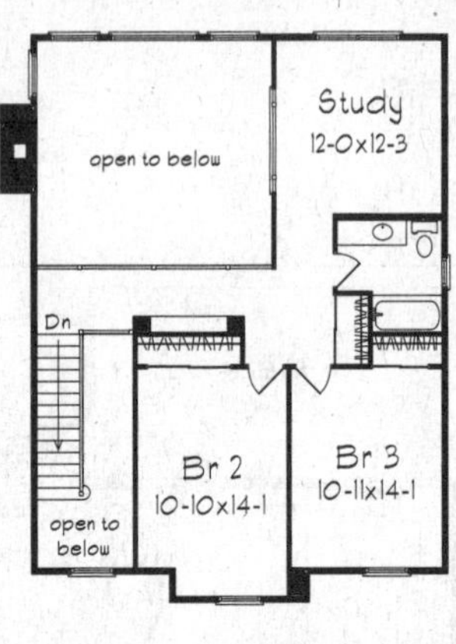
Study
12-0x12-3
open to below
Dn
Br 2
10-10x14-1
Br 3
10-11x14-1
open to below

Second Floor
772 sq. ft.

Special features

- Laundry room with work space, pantry and coat closet adjacent to kitchen
- Two bedrooms, study, full bath and plenty of closets on second floor
- Large walk-in closet and private bath make this master suite one you're sure to enjoy
- Kitchen with cooktop island and easy access to living area
- 3 bedrooms, 2 1/2 baths, 2-car side entry garage
- Basement foundation

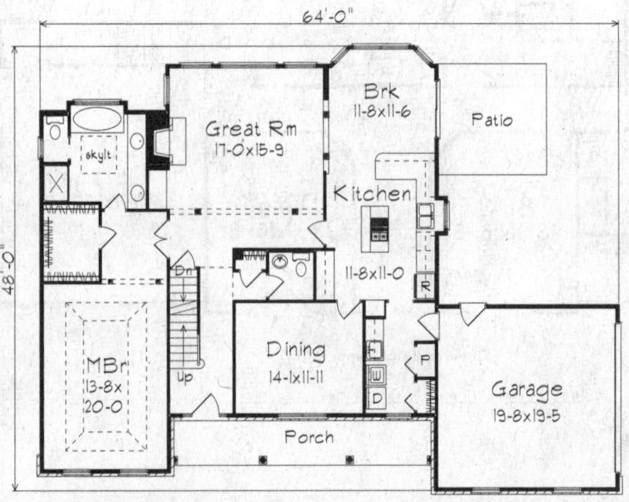
64'-0"
48'-0"
Brk
11-8x11-6
Patio
Great Rm
17-0x15-9
skylt
Kitchen
11-8x11-0
Dn
Up
MBr
13-8x
20-0
Dining
14-1x11-11
Garage
19-8x19-5
Porch

First Floor
1,672 sq. ft.

TO ORDER BLUEPRINTS USE THE FORM ON PAGE 15 OR CALL TOLL-FREE 1-877-671-6036

View thousands more home plans online at www.familyhandyman.com/homeplans

Plan #708-BF-2108

Two-Story Living Room

2,194 total square feet of living area | **Price Code C**

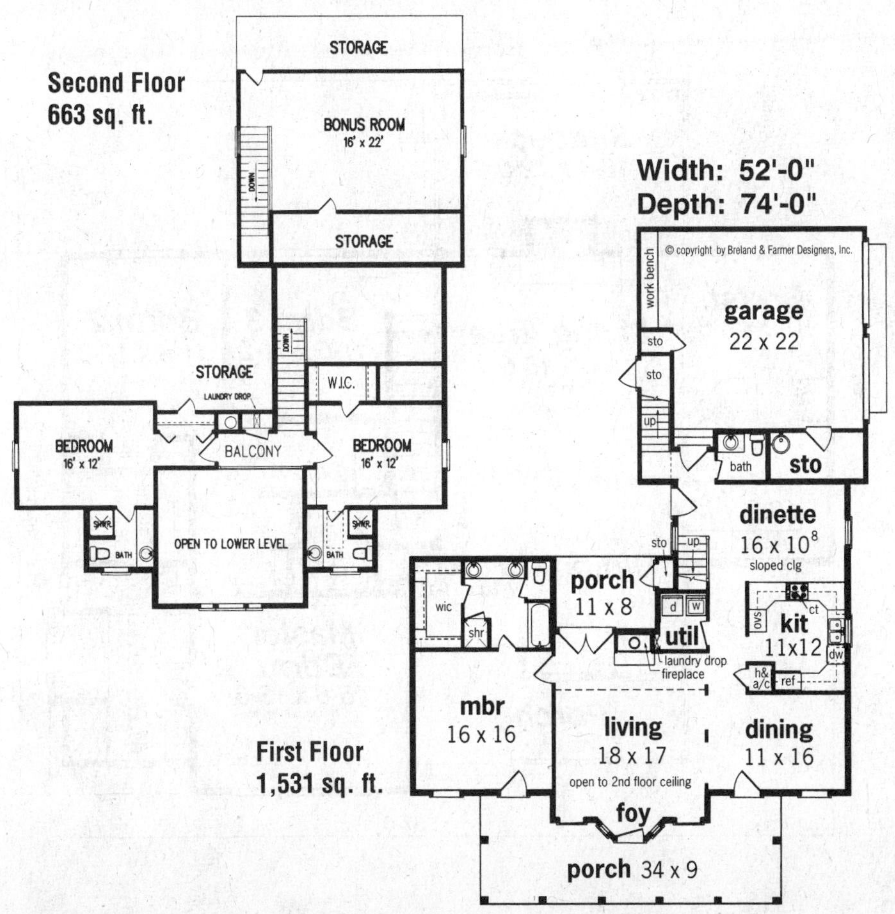

Second Floor
663 sq. ft.
STORAGE
BONUS ROOM
16' x 22'
DOWN
STORAGE
STORAGE
LAUNDRY DROP
W.I.C.
BEDROOM
16' x 12'
BALCONY
BEDROOM
16' x 12'
SHWR.
BATH
OPEN TO LOWER LEVEL
SHWR.
BATH
Width: 52'-0"
Depth: 74'-0"
© copyright by Breland & Farmer Designers, Inc.
work bench
garage
22 x 22
sto
sto
up
bath
sto
dinette
16 x 10⁸
sloped clg
sto
up
porch
11 x 8
wic
shr
d
w
util
laundry drop
fireplace
kit
11x12
ovs
ct
dw
h&a/c
ref
mbr
16 x 16
living
18 x 17
open to 2nd floor ceiling
dining
11 x 16
First Floor
1,531 sq. ft.
foy
porch 34 x 9

Special features

- Energy efficient home with 2" x 6" exterior walls
- Utility room has laundry drop conveniently located next to kitchen
- Both second floor bedrooms have large closets and their own bath
- 3 bedrooms, 3 1/2 baths, 2-car side entry garage
- Crawl space, slab or basement foundation, please specify when ordering

TO ORDER BLUEPRINTS USE THE FORM ON PAGE 15 OR CALL TOLL-FREE 1-877-671-6036

Plan #708-JV-1772-A-SJ

Scalloped Porch Cornice Adds Flair

1,772 total square feet of living area | Price Code B

Special features

- Dramatic palladian window and scalloped porch are attention grabbers
- Island kitchen sink allows for easy access and views into the living/breakfast areas
- Washer and dryer closet easily accessible from all bedrooms
- 3 bedrooms, 2 baths, 3-car drive under garage
- Basement foundation

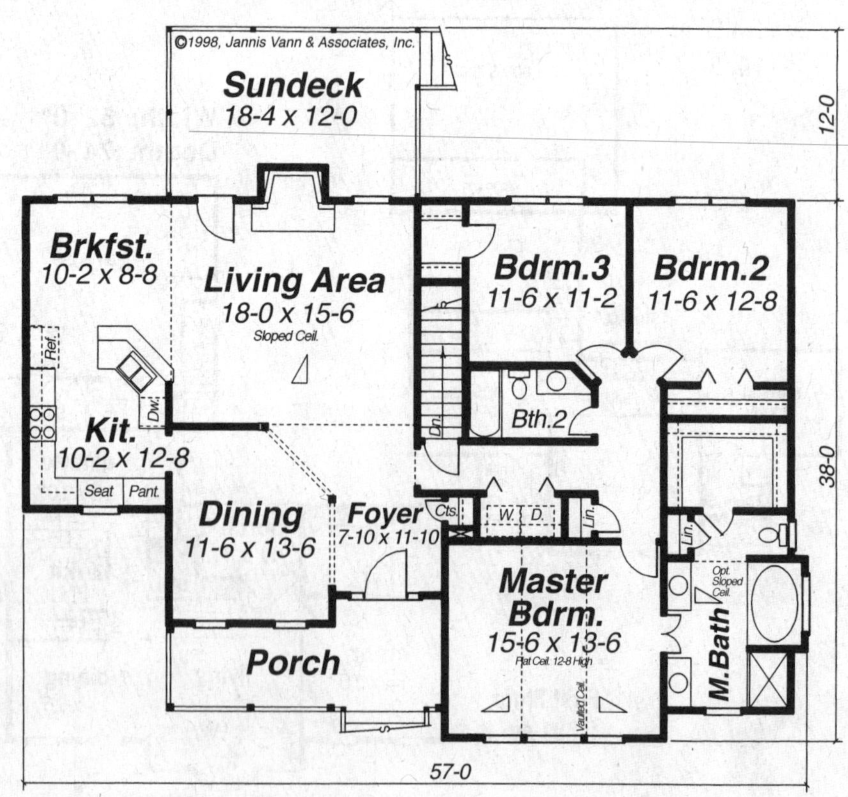

©1998, Jannis Vann & Associates, Inc.
Sundeck
18-4 x 12-0
12-0
Brkfst.
10-2 x 8-8
Living Area
18-0 x 15-6
Sloped Ceil.
Bdrm.3
11-6 x 11-2
Bdrm.2
11-6 x 12-8
Ref.
DW
Kit.
10-2 x 12-8
Seat
Pant.
Bth.2
Dn
38-0
Dining
11-6 x 13-6
Foyer
7-10 x 11-10
Cts.
W.
D.
Lin.
Master
Bdrm.
15-6 x 13-6
Flat Ceil. 12-8 High
Vaulted Ceil.
Opt. Sloped Ceil.
M.Bath
Porch
57-0

TO ORDER BLUEPRINTS USE THE FORM ON PAGE 15 OR CALL TOLL-FREE 1-877-671-6036

View thousands more home plans online at www.familyhandyman.com/homeplans

Plan #708-1117

An Enhancement To Any Neighborhood

1,440 total square feet of living area **Price Code A**

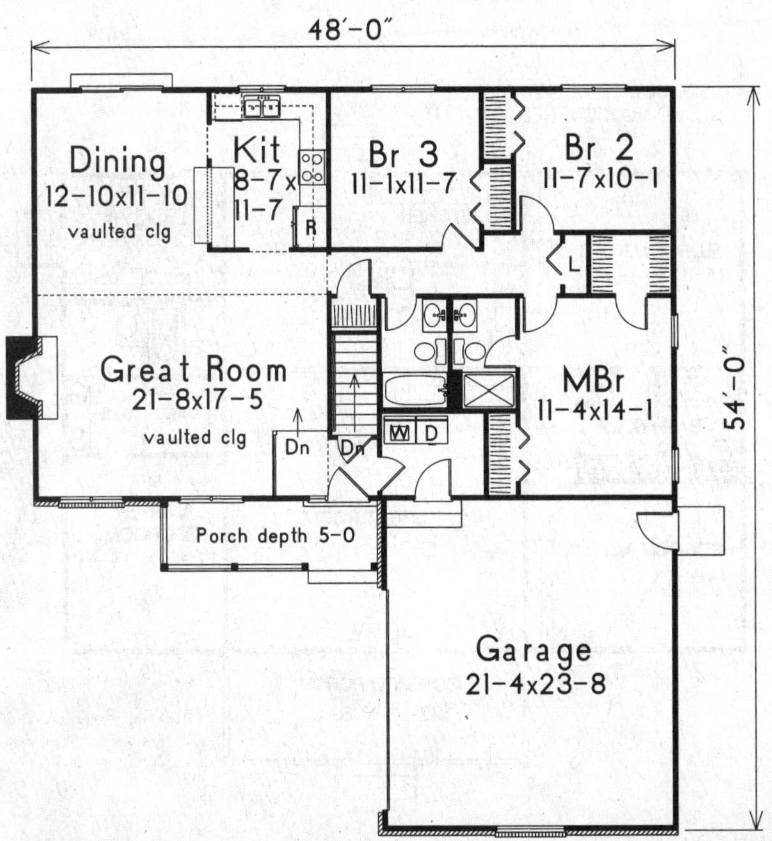

48'-0"
54'-0"
Dining
12-10x11-10
vaulted clg
Kit
8-7x
11-7
R
Br 3
11-1x11-7
Br 2
11-7x10-1
L
Great Room
21-8x17-5
vaulted clg
Dn
Dn
W
D
MBr
11-4x14-1
Porch depth 5-0
Garage
21-4x23-8

Special features

- Foyer adjoins massive-sized great room with sloping ceiling and tall masonry fireplace
- Kitchen adjoins spacious dining room and features pass-through breakfast bar
- Master suite enjoys private bath and two closets
- An oversized two-car side entry garage offers plenty of storage for bicycles, lawn equipment, etc.
- 3 bedrooms, 2 baths, 2-car side entry garage
- Basement foundation, drawings also include crawl space and slab foundations

TO ORDER BLUEPRINTS USE THE FORM ON PAGE 15 OR CALL TOLL-FREE 1-877-671-6036

Plan #708-DH-2005

Perfect Home For Family Living

1,700 total square feet of living area **Price Code B**

Special features

- Oversized laundry room has large pantry and storage area as well as access to the outdoors
- Master bedroom is separated from other bedrooms for privacy
- Raised snack bar in kitchen allows extra seating for dining
- 3 bedrooms, 2 baths
- Crawl space foundation

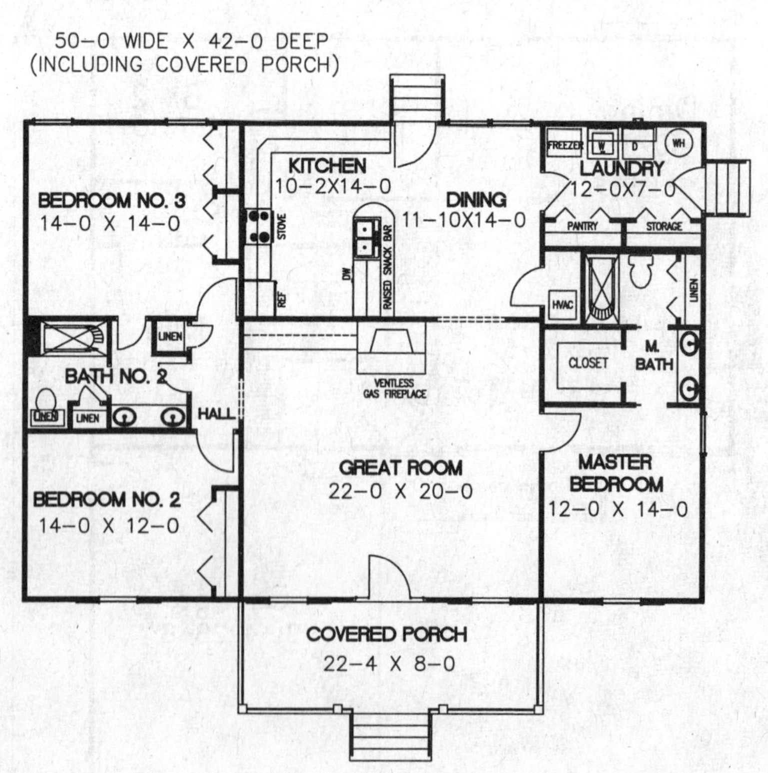
50-0 WIDE X 42-0 DEEP
(INCLUDING COVERED PORCH)
KITCHEN
10-2X14-0
DINING
11-10X14-0
FREEZER
W
D
WH
LAUNDRY
12-0X7-0
PANTRY
STORAGE
BEDROOM NO. 3
14-0 X 14-0
STOVE
REF
DW
RAISED SNACK BAR
HVAC
LINEN
LINEN
BATH NO. 2
LINEN
LINEN
HALL
CLOSET
M.
BATH
VENTLESS
GAS FIREPLACE
GREAT ROOM
22-0 X 20-0
MASTER
BEDROOM
12-0 X 14-0
BEDROOM NO. 2
14-0 X 12-0
COVERED PORCH
22-4 X 8-0

TO ORDER BLUEPRINTS USE THE FORM ON PAGE 15 OR CALL TOLL-FREE 1-877-671-6036

View thousands more home plans online at www.familyhandyman.com/homeplans

Openness In A Split-Bedroom Ranch

1,574 total square feet of living area **Price Code B**

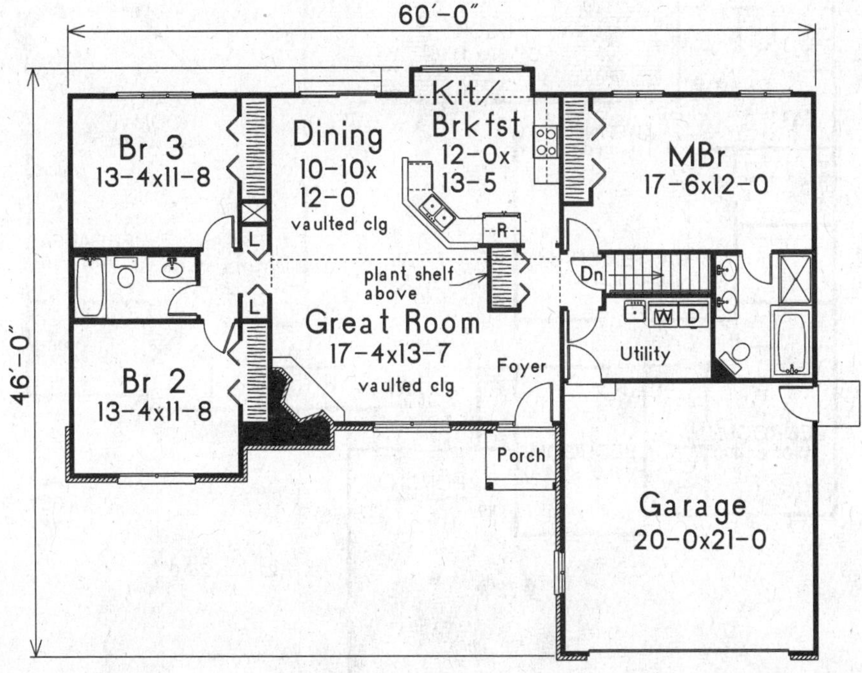
60'-0"
46'-0"
Kit/
Brkfst
12-0x
13-5
Dining
10-10x
12-0
vaulted clg
Br 3
13-4x11-8
MBr
17-6x12-0
plant shelf
above
Great Room
17-4x13-7
vaulted clg
Foyer
Dn
Utility
Br 2
13-4x11-8
Porch
Garage
20-0x21-0

Special features

- Foyer enters into open great room with corner fireplace and rear dining room with adjoining kitchen
- Two secondary bedrooms share a full bath
- Master bedroom has spacious private bath
- Garage accesses home through mud room/laundry
- 3 bedrooms, 2 baths, 2-car garage
- Basement foundation, drawings also include crawl space foundation

Plan #708-AP-2520

Grand Arched Entry

2,564 total square feet of living area **Price Code D**

Special features

- Hearth room is surrounded by kitchen, dining and breakfast rooms making it the focal point of the living areas
- Escape to the master bedroom which has a luxurious private bath and a sitting area leading to the deck outdoors
- The secondary bedrooms share a jack and jill bath and both have walk-in closets
- 3 bedrooms, 2 1/2 baths, 2-car side entry garage
- Basement, crawl space or slab foundation, please specify when ordering

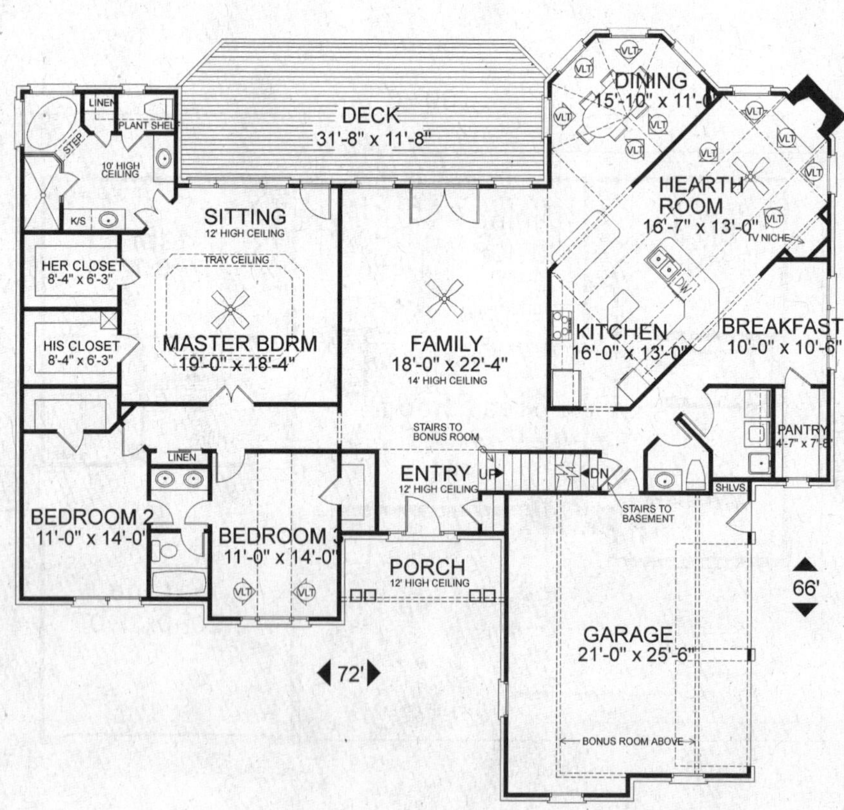
DECK
31'-8" x 11'-8"
DINING
15'-10" x 11'-0"
HEARTH ROOM
16'-7" x 13'-0"
TV NICHE
KITCHEN
16'-0" x 13'-0"
BREAKFAST
10'-0" x 10'-6"
PANTRY
4'-7" x 7'-8"
SHLVS
LINEN
PLANT SHELF
STEP
10' HIGH CEILING
K/S
SITTING
12' HIGH CEILING
TRAY CEILING
HER CLOSET
8'-4" x 6'-3"
HIS CLOSET
8'-4" x 6'-3"
MASTER BDRM
19'-0" x 18'-4"
FAMILY
18'-0" x 22'-4"
14' HIGH CEILING
STAIRS TO BONUS ROOM
ENTRY
12' HIGH CEILING
UP
DN
STAIRS TO BASEMENT
LINEN
BEDROOM 2
11'-0" x 14'-0"
BEDROOM 3
11'-0" x 14'-0"
PORCH
12' HIGH CEILING
GARAGE
21'-0" x 25'-6"
BONUS ROOM ABOVE
66'
72'

TO ORDER BLUEPRINTS USE THE FORM ON PAGE 15 OR CALL TOLL-FREE 1-877-671-6036

View thousands more home plans online at www.familyhandyman.com/homeplans

Plan #708-0748

Rambling Ranch With Country Charm

2,514 total square feet of living area **Price Code D**

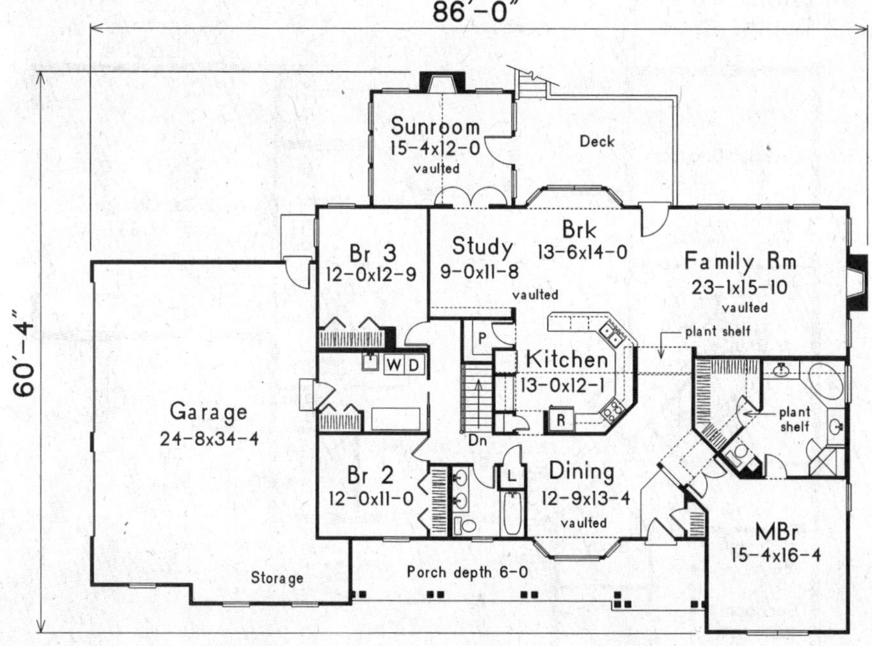

86'-0"
60'-4"
Sunroom
15-4x12-0
vaulted
Deck
Br 3
12-0x12-9
Study
9-0x11-8
vaulted
Brk
13-6x14-0
Family Rm
23-1x15-10
vaulted
plant shelf
Kitchen
13-0x12-1
Garage
24-8x34-4
Dn
Br 2
12-0x11-0
Dining
12-9x13-4
vaulted
plant shelf
MBr
15-4x16-4
Storage
Porch depth 6-0

Special features

- Expansive porch welcomes you to the foyer, spacious dining area with bay and a gallery-sized hall with plant shelf above
- A highly functional U-shaped kitchen is open to a bayed breakfast room, study and family room with a 46' vista
- Vaulted rear sunroom has fireplace
- 1,509 square feet of optional living area on the lower level with recreation room, bedroom #4 with bath and an office with storage closet
- 3 bedrooms, 2 baths, 3-car oversized side entry garage with workshop/storage area
- Walk-out basement foundation

TO ORDER BLUEPRINTS USE THE FORM ON PAGE 15 OR CALL TOLL-FREE 1-877-671-6036

View thousands more home plans online at www.familyhandyman.com/homeplans

The Family
Handyman

Plan #708-HDS-2077

Sprawling Ranch Has A Lot To Offer

2,077 total square feet of living area **Price Code C**

Special features

- Lots of storage space throughout
- Enormous covered patio adds a lot of space when entertaining
- Angled walls add appeal throughout this home
- 3 bedrooms, 2 baths, 2-car side entry garage
- Slab foundation

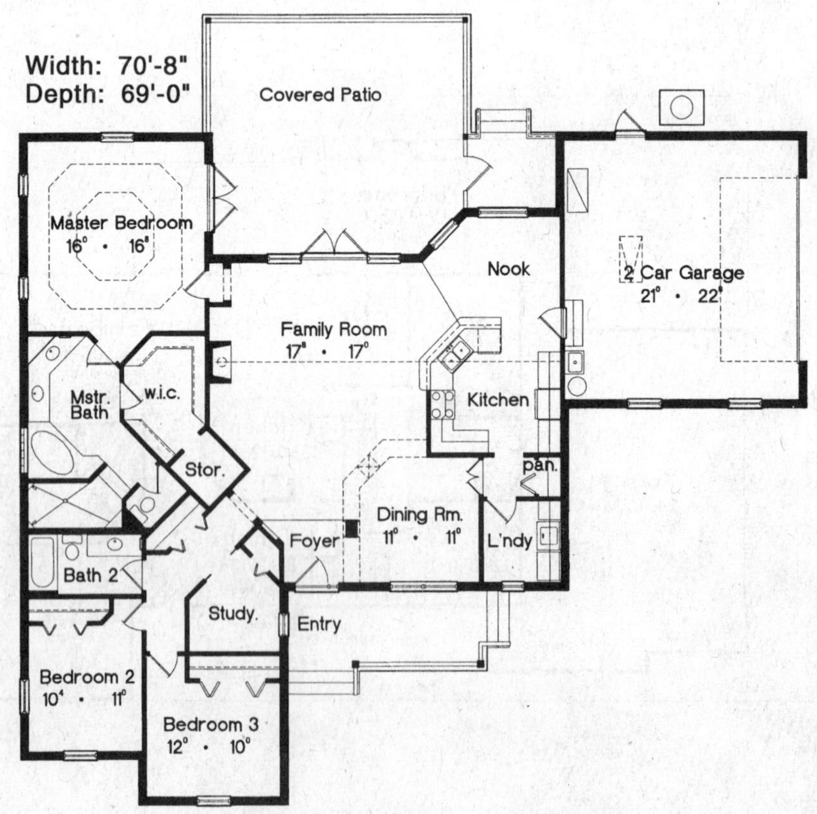

Width: 70'-8"
Depth: 69'-0"
Covered Patio
Master Bedroom
16^{0} · 16^{0}
Nook
2 Car Garage
21^{0} · 22^{0}
Family Room
17^{8} · 17^{0}
Mstr. Bath
w.i.c.
Kitchen
Stor.
pan.
Dining Rm.
11^{0} · 11^{0}
Foyer
L'ndy
Bath 2
Study.
Entry
Bedroom 2
10^{4} · 11^{0}
Bedroom 3
12^{0} · 10^{0}

TO ORDER BLUEPRINTS USE THE FORM ON PAGE 15 OR CALL TOLL-FREE 1-877-671-6036

View thousands more home plans online at www.familyhandyman.com/homeplans

The Family
Handyman

Plan #708-0389

Cozy Columned Archway Defines Foyer

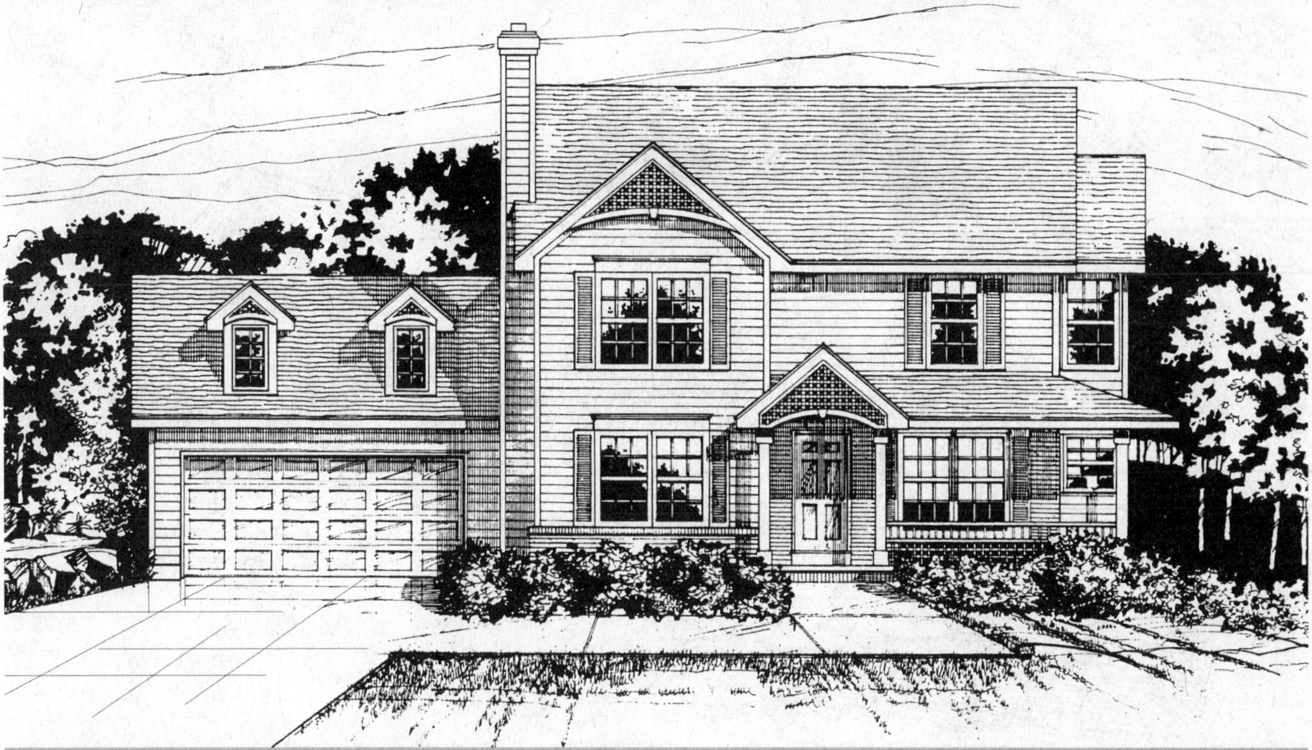

1,777 total square feet of living area — **Price Code B**

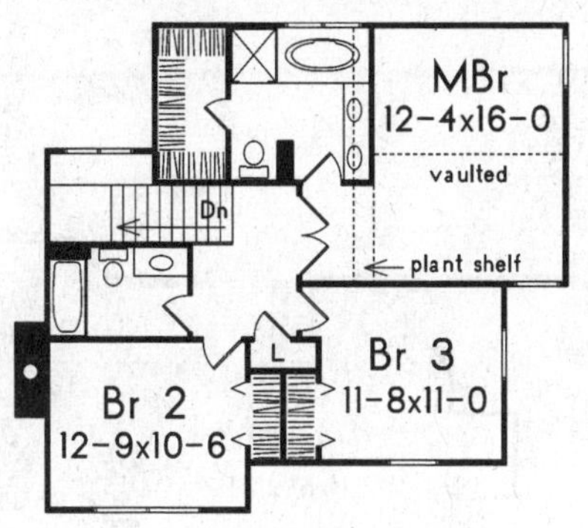
MBr
12-4x16-0
vaulted
Dn
plant shelf
Br 3
11-8x11-0
L
Br 2
12-9x10-6

Second Floor
890 sq. ft.

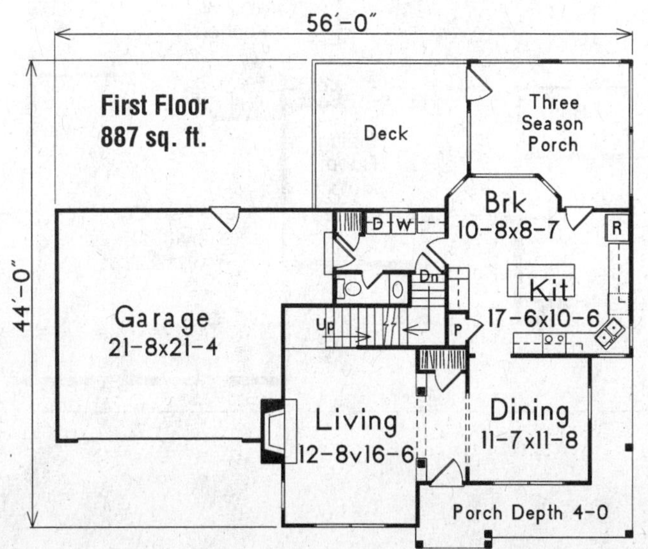
56′-0″
44′-0″
First Floor
887 sq. ft.
Deck
Three
Season
Porch
Brk
10-8x8-7
D W
R
Dn
Kit
17-6x10-6
Up
P
Garage
21-8x21-4
Living
12-8v16-6
Dining
11-7x11-8
Porch Depth 4-0

Special features

- Large master bedroom has bath with whirlpool tub, separate shower and spacious walk-in closet
- Large island kitchen with breakfast bay and access to the three-season porch
- Convenient laundry room with half bath
- 3 bedrooms, 2 1/2 baths, 2-car garage
- Basement foundation

The Family
Handyman

Plan #708-SRD-307

Perfect For A Casual Lifestyle

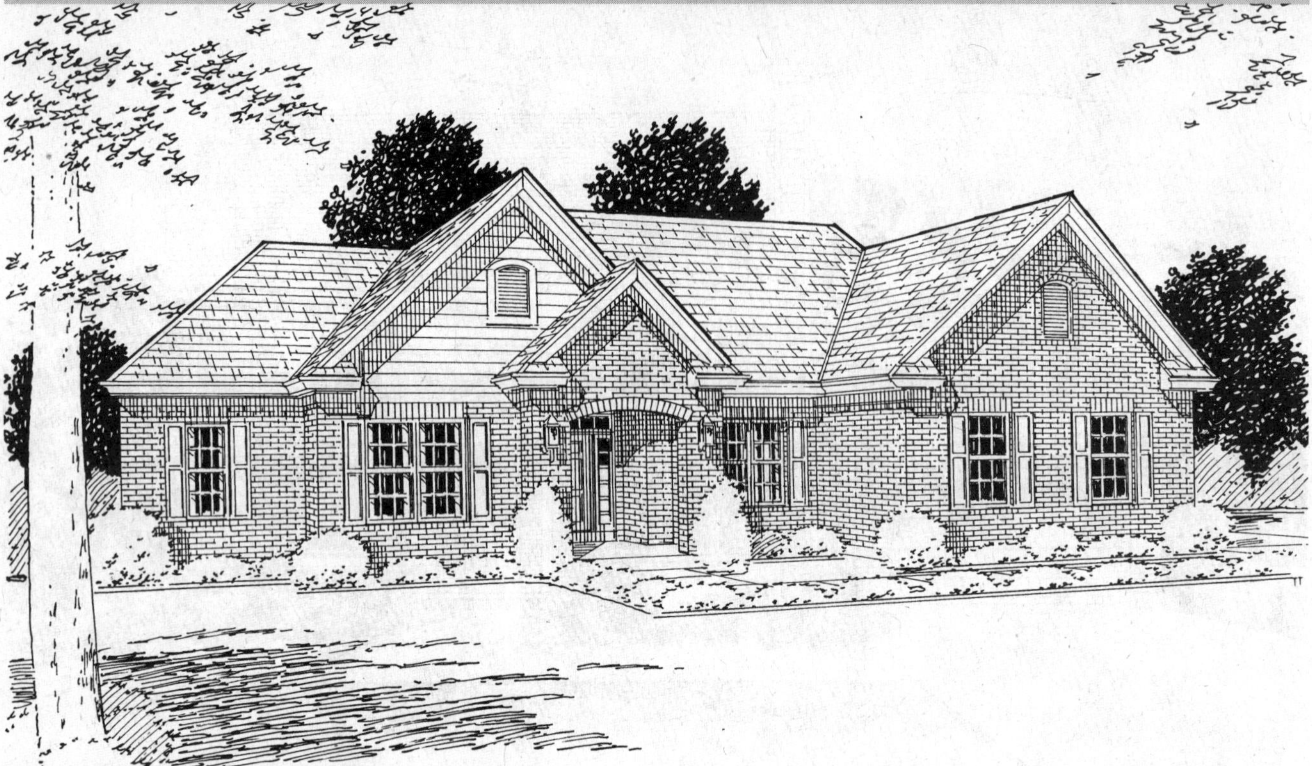

1,860 total square feet of living area **Price Code C**

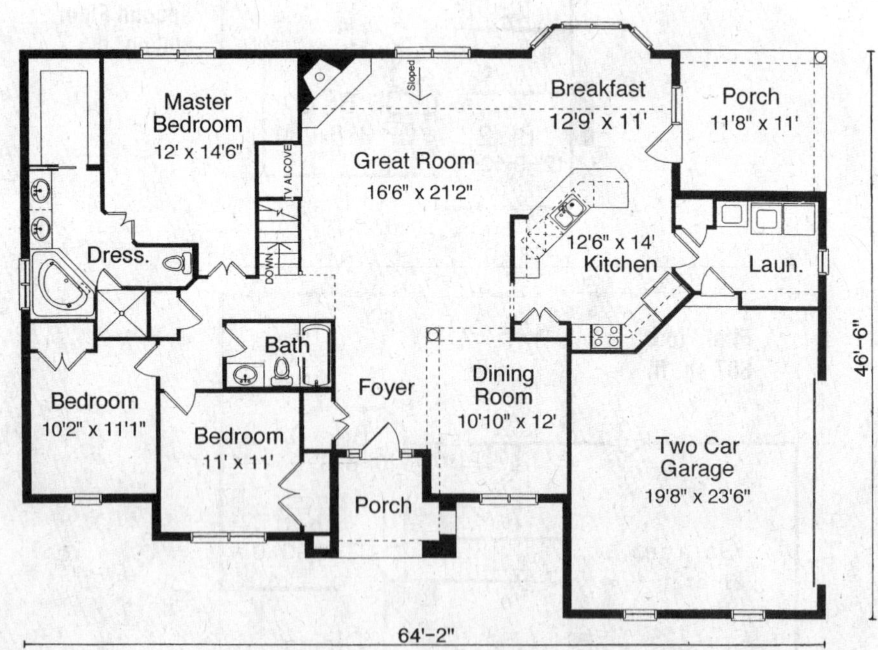
Master Bedroom
12' x 14'6"
TV ALCOVE
Sloped
Great Room
16'6" x 21'2"
Breakfast
12'9' x 11'
Porch
11'8" x 11'
12'6" x 14'
Kitchen
Laun.
Dress.
DOWN
Bath
Foyer
Dining Room
10'10" x 12'
Bedroom
10'2" x 11'1"
Bedroom
11' x 11'
Porch
Two Car Garage
19'8" x 23'6"
46'-6"
64'-2"

Special features

- French doors invite the outdoors to become part of the inside gathering places
- Comfortable master bedroom has deluxe bath, large walk-in closet and a secluded alcove
- A convenient snack bar is arranged to offer views to both the breakfast area with angled walls and the great room fireplace
- 3 bedrooms, 2 baths, 2-car side entry garage
- Basement or walk-out basement foundation, please specify when ordering

Plan #708-0348

Open Living Centers On Windowed Dining Room

2,003 total square feet of living area **Price Code D**

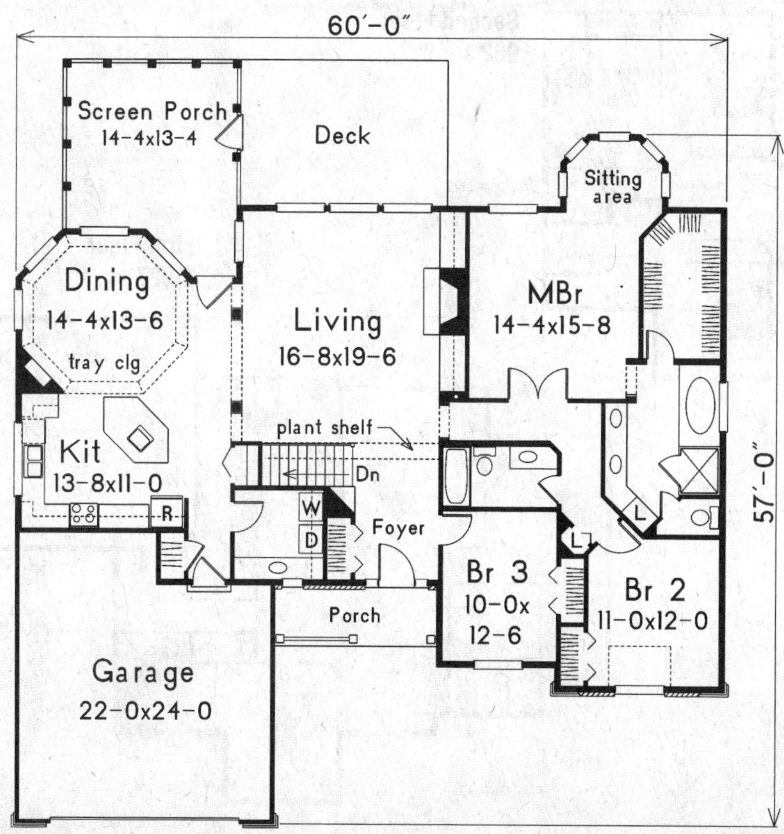

60'-0"
Screen Porch
14-4x13-4
Deck
Sitting area
Dining
14-4x13-6
tray clg
Living
16-8x19-6
MBr
14-4x15-8
plant shelf
Kit
13-8x11-0
Dn
W
D
R
Foyer
L
Br 3
10-0x
12-6
Br 2
11-0x12-0
Porch
Garage
22-0x24-0
57'-0"

Special features

- Octagon-shaped dining room with tray ceiling and deck overlook
- L-shaped island kitchen serves living and dining rooms
- Master bedroom boasts luxury bath and walk-in closet
- Living room features columns, elegant fireplace and 10' ceiling
- 3 bedrooms, 2 baths, 2-car garage
- Basement foundation

TO ORDER BLUEPRINTS USE THE FORM ON PAGE 15 OR CALL TOLL-FREE 1-877-671-6036

View thousands more home plans online at www.familyhandyman.com/homeplans

The Family
Handyman

Plan #708-DR-2615

Grand Curved Staircase Makes A Beautiful Entrance

2,889 total square feet of living area

Price Code E

Special features

- Energy efficient home with 2" x 6" exterior walls
- Cathedral ceiling in family room is impressive
- 9' ceilings throughout first floor
- Private home office located away from traffic flow
- 4 bedrooms, 3 1/2 baths, 2-car side entry garage
- Basement foundation

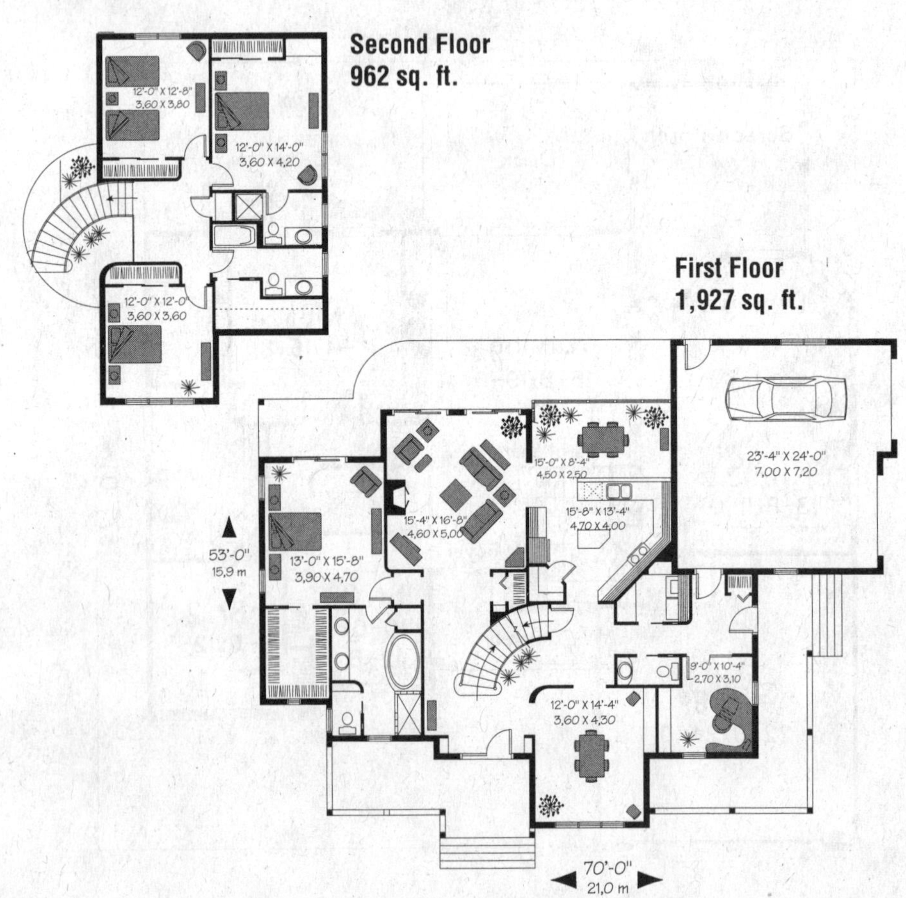
Second Floor
962 sq. ft.
12'-0" X 12'-8"
3,60 X 3,80
12'-0" X 14'-0"
3,60 X 4,20
12'-0" X 12'-0"
3,60 X 3,60
First Floor
1,927 sq. ft.
23'-4" X 24'-0"
7,00 X 7,20
15'-0" X 8'-4"
4,50 X 2,50
15'-4" X 16'-8"
4,60 X 5,00
15'-8" X 13'-4"
4,70 X 4,00
13'-0" X 15'-8"
3,90 X 4,70
53'-0"
15,9 m
9'-0" X 10'-4"
2,70 X 3,10
12'-0" X 14'-4"
3,60 X 4,30
70'-0"
21,0 m

TO ORDER BLUEPRINTS USE THE FORM ON PAGE 15 OR CALL TOLL-FREE 1-877-671-6036

View thousands more home plans online at www.familyhandyman.com/homeplans

Plan #708-0796

Colossal Great Room

1,599 total square feet of living area

Price Code B

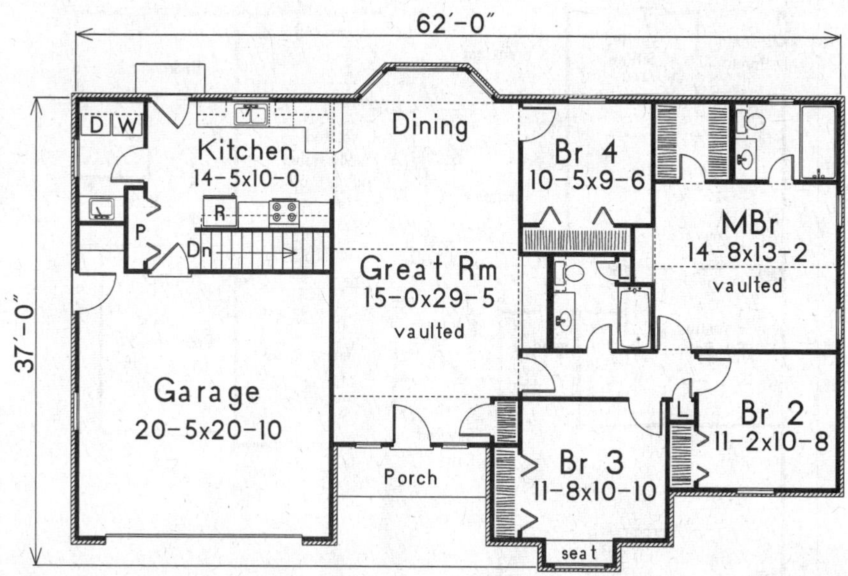

62'-0"
37'-0"
Dining
Kitchen
14-5x10-0
Br 4
10-5x9-6
MBr
14-8x13-2
vaulted
Great Rm
15-0x29-5
vaulted
Garage
20-5x20-10
Porch
Br 3
11-8x10-10
Br 2
11-2x10-8
seat

Special features

- Efficiently designed kitchen with large pantry and easy access to laundry room
- Bedroom #3 has a charming window seat
- Master bedroom has a full bath and large walk-in closet
- 4 bedrooms, 2 baths, 2-car garage
- Basement foundation, drawings also include crawl space and slab foundations

TO ORDER BLUEPRINTS USE THE FORM ON PAGE 15 OR CALL TOLL-FREE 1-877-671-6036

View thousands more home plans online at www.familyhandyman.com/homeplans

The Family
Handyman

Plan #708-FB-845

Elaborate Dining Room

1,779 total square feet of living area **Price Code B**

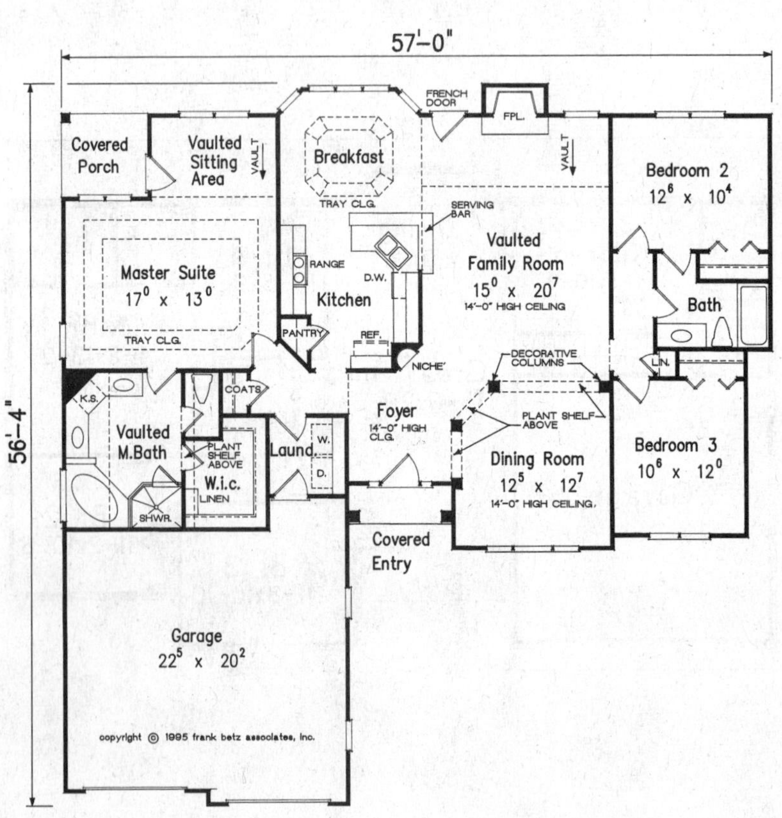
57'-0"
56'-4"
Covered Porch
Vaulted Sitting Area
VAULT
Breakfast
TRAY CLG.
FRENCH DOOR
FPL.
VAULT
Bedroom 2
12⁶ x 10⁴
SERVING BAR
Master Suite
17⁰ x 13⁰
TRAY CLG.
RANGE
D.W.
Kitchen
PANTRY
REF.
NICHE
Vaulted Family Room
15⁰ x 20⁷
14'-0" HIGH CEILING
Bath
LIN.
DECORATIVE COLUMNS
K.S.
COATS
Vaulted M.Bath
PLANT SHELF ABOVE
W.i.c.
LINEN
SHWR.
Laund.
W.
D.
Foyer
14'-0" HIGH CLG.
PLANT SHELF ABOVE
Dining Room
12⁵ x 12⁷
14'-0" HIGH CEILING
Bedroom 3
10⁶ x 12⁰
Covered Entry
Garage
22⁵ x 20²
copyright © 1995 frank betz associates, inc.

Special features

- Well-designed floor plan has vaulted family room with fireplace and access to the outdoors
- Decorative columns separate dining area from foyer
- Vaulted ceiling adds spaciousness in master bath with walk-in closet
- 3 bedrooms, 2 baths, 2-car garage
- Walk-out basement, slab or crawl space foundation, please specify when ordering

TO ORDER BLUEPRINTS USE THE FORM ON PAGE 15 OR CALL TOLL-FREE 1-877-671-6036

View thousands more home plans online at www.familyhandyman.com/homeplans

Plan #708-0739

A Special Home For Views

1,684 total square feet of living area **Price Code B**

Rear View

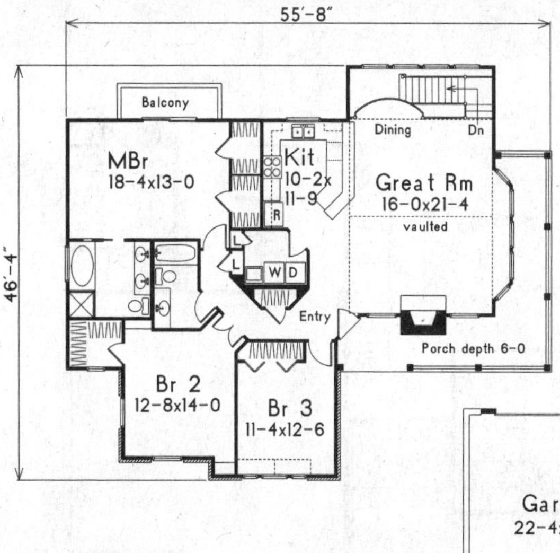

55′-8″

46′-4″

Balcony

MBr
18-4x13-0

Kit
10-2x
11-9

Dining

Dn

Great Rm
16-0x21-4
vaulted

W D

Entry

Porch depth 6-0

Br 2
12-8x14-0

Br 3
11-4x12-6

First Floor
1,684 sq. ft.

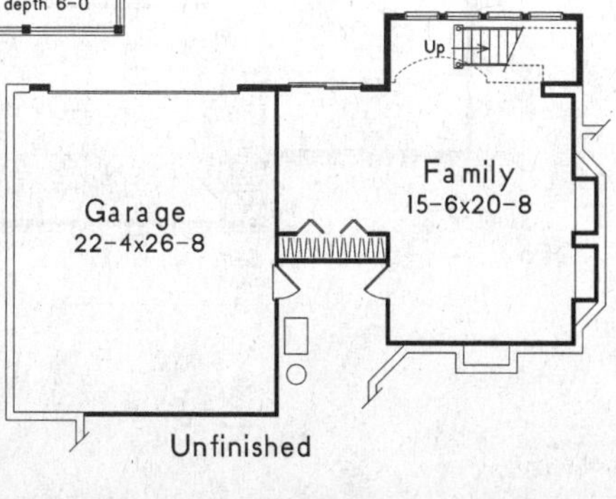

Up

Family
15-6x20-8

Garage
22-4x26-8

Unfinished

Optional
Lower Level

Special features

- Delightful wrap-around porch anchored by full masonry fireplace
- The vaulted great room includes a large bay window, fireplace, dining balcony and atrium window wall
- Double walk-in closets, large luxury bath and sliding doors to exterior balcony are a few fantastic features of the master bedroom
- Atrium open to 611 square feet of optional living area on the lower level
- 3 bedrooms, 2 baths, 2-car drive under garage
- Walk-out basement foundation

The Family
Handyman

Plan #708-0419

Organized Kitchen, Center Of Activity

1,882 total square feet of living area **Price Code C**

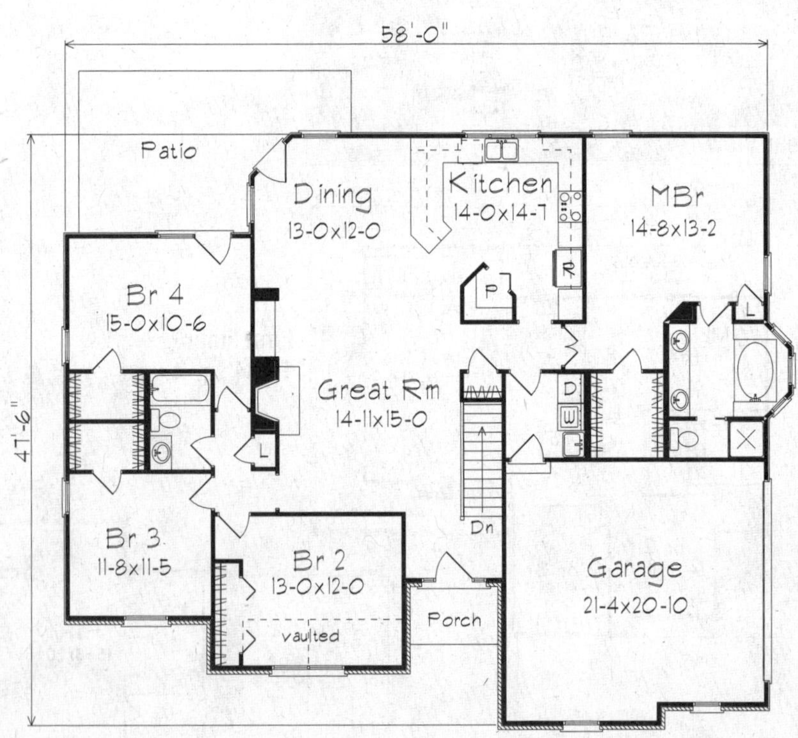
58'-0"
47'-6"
Patio
Dining
13-0x12-0
Kitchen
14-0x14-7
MBr
14-8x13-2
Br 4
15-0x10-6
Great Rm
14-11x15-0
Br 3
11-8x11-5
Br 2
13-0x12-0
vaulted
Dn
Porch
Garage
21-4x20-10

Special features

- Handsome brick facade
- Spacious great room and dining room combination brightened by unique corner windows and patio access
- Well-designed kitchen incorporates breakfast bar peninsula, sweeping casement window above sink and walk-in pantry island
- Master suite features large walk-in closet and private bath with bay window
- 4 bedrooms, 2 baths, 2-car side entry garage
- Basement foundation

TO ORDER BLUEPRINTS USE THE FORM ON PAGE 15 OR CALL TOLL-FREE 1-877-671-6036

View thousands more home plans online at www.familyhandyman.com/homeplans

Plan #708-GSD-1748

Cottage-Style Adds Charm

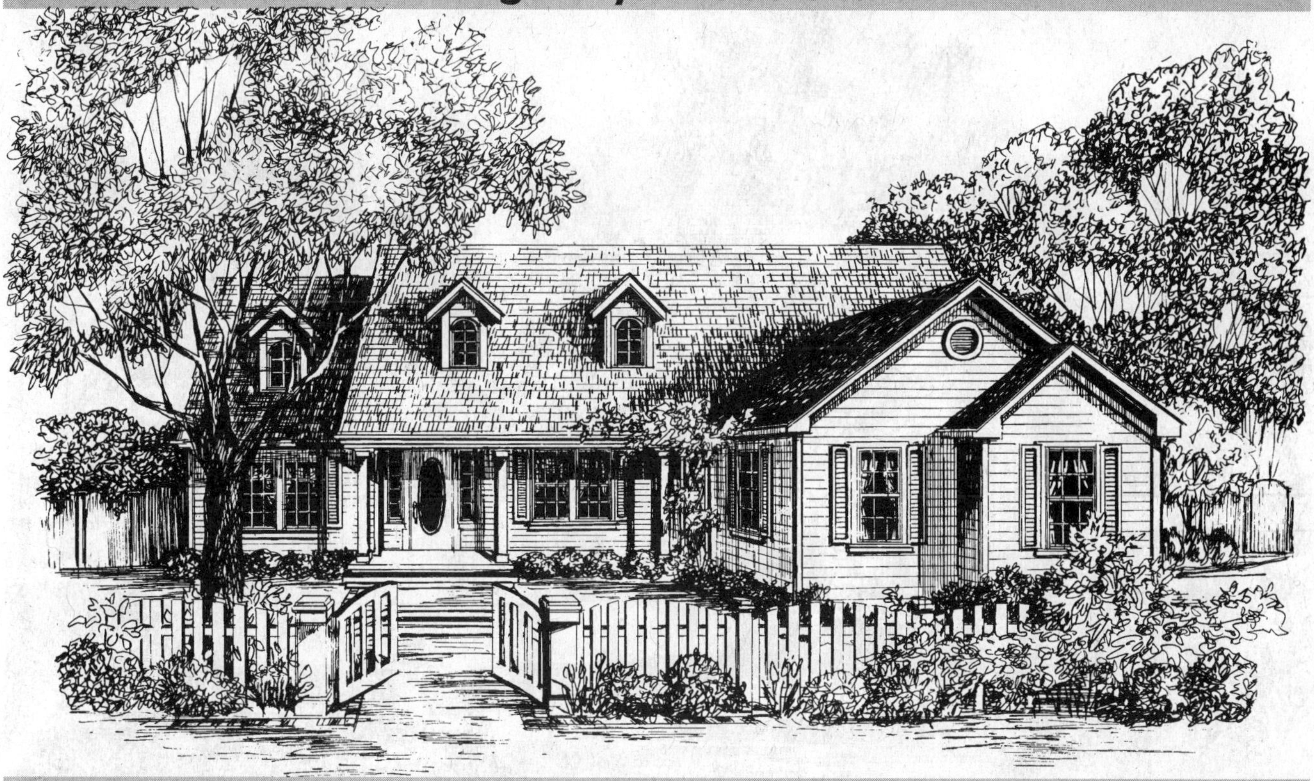

1,496 total square feet of living area **Price Code A**

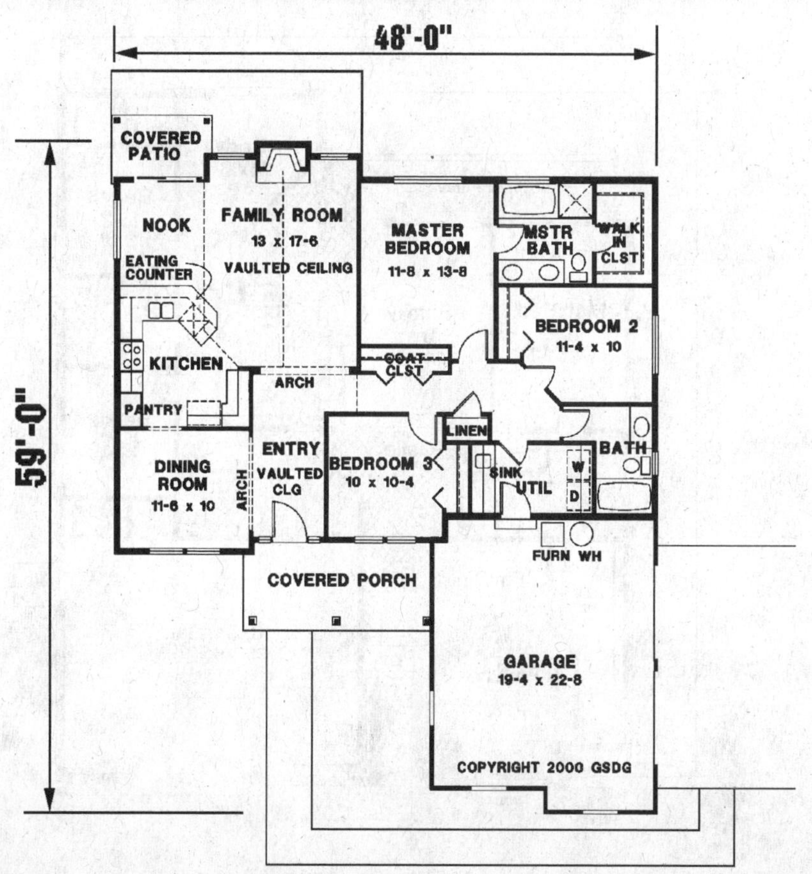
48'-0"
59'-0"
COVERED PATIO
NOOK
EATING COUNTER
FAMILY ROOM
13 x 17-6
VAULTED CEILING
MASTER BEDROOM
11-8 x 13-8
MSTR BATH
WALK IN CLST
BEDROOM 2
11-4 x 10
KITCHEN
PANTRY
ARCH
COAT CLST
LINEN
DINING ROOM
11-6 x 10
ARCH
ENTRY
VAULTED CLG
BEDROOM 3
10 x 10-4
SINK
UTIL
W
D
BATH
FURN WH
COVERED PORCH
GARAGE
19-4 x 22-8
COPYRIGHT 2000 GSDG

Special features

- Large utility room with sink and extra counterspace
- Covered patio off breakfast nook extends dining to the outdoors
- Eating counter in kitchen overlooks vaulted family room
- 3 bedrooms, 2 baths, 2-car side entry garage
- Crawl space foundation

The Family
Handyman

Plan #708-FDG-8526

Central Family Area

2,370 total square feet of living area

Price Code D

Special features

- Dramatic gallery located in front of family area
- Formal dining and living areas in the front of home are ideal for entertaining
- All bedrooms throughout this home have spacious walk-in closets
- 4 bedrooms, 2 1/2 baths, 3-car garage
- Slab foundation

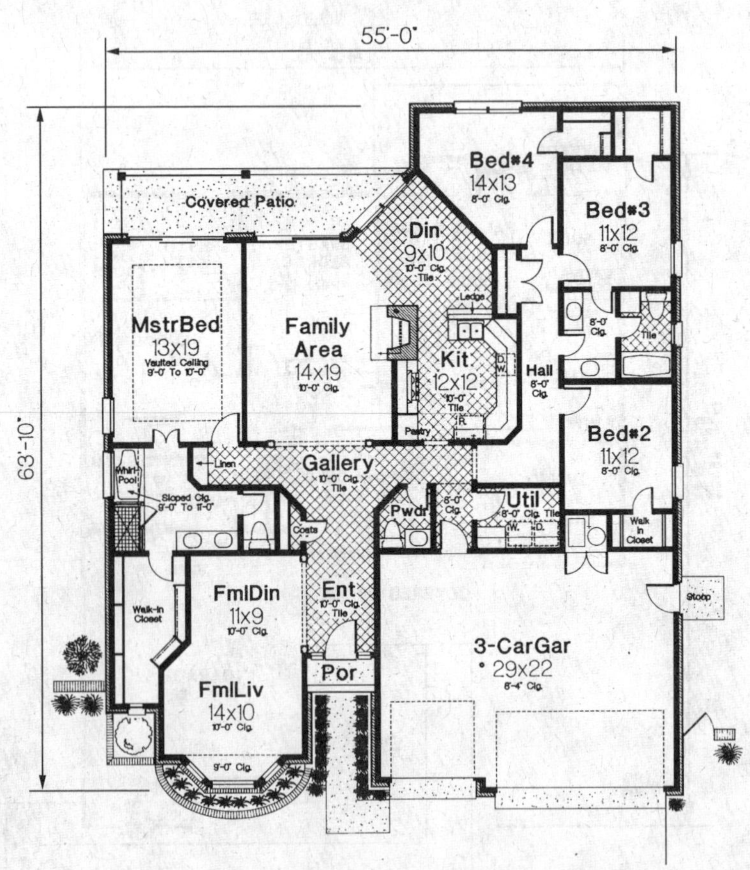

55'-0"
63'-10"
Covered Patio
Bed#4
14x13
8'-0" Clg.
Din
9x10
10'-0" Clg.
Tile
Bed#3
11x12
8'-0" Clg.
MstrBed
13x19
Vaulted Ceiling
9'-0" To 10'-0"
Family
Area
14x19
10'-0" Clg.
Ledge
Kit
12x12
10'-0"
Tile
Pantry
Hall
8'-0"
Clg.
Bed#2
11x12
8'-0" Clg.
Linen
Gallery
10'-0" Clg.
Tile
Whirl-Pool
Sloped Clg.
9'-0" To 11'-0"
Pwdr
Util
8'-0" Clg. Tile
Walk in Closet
Coats
Stoop
Walk-in Closet
FmlDin
11x9
10'-0" Clg.
Ent
10'-0" Clg.
Tile
3-CarGar
29x22
8'-4" Clg.
Por
FmlLiv
14x10
10'-0" Clg.
9'-0" Clg.

TO ORDER BLUEPRINTS USE THE FORM ON PAGE 15 OR CALL TOLL-FREE 1-877-671-6036

View thousands more home plans online at www.familyhandyman.com/homeplans

Plan #708-0312

Country Classic With Modern Floor Plan

1,921 total square feet of living area — **Price Code D**

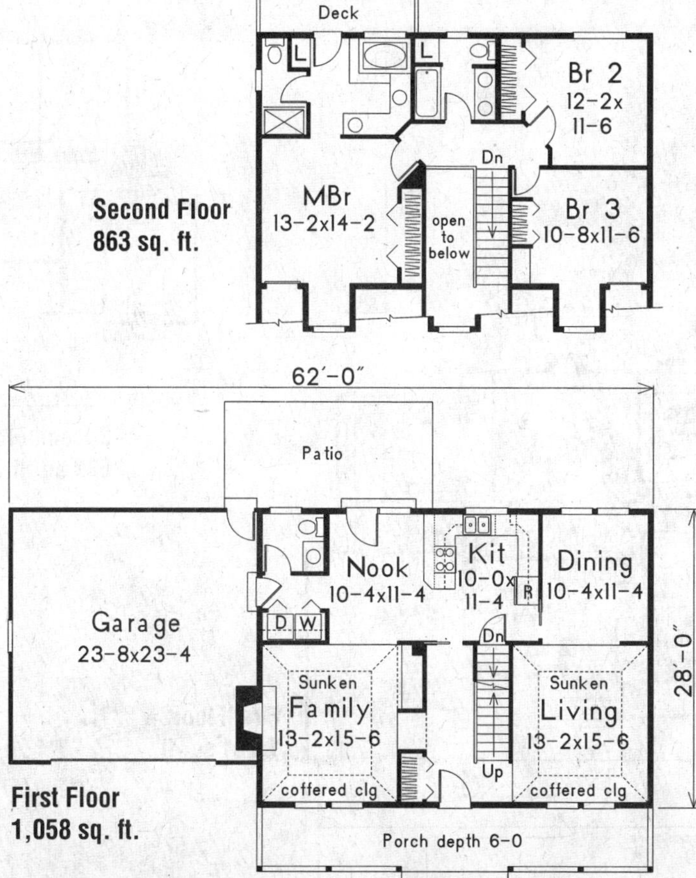
Deck
Br 2
12-2x
11-6
Dn
MBr
13-2x14-2
open
to
below
Br 3
10-8x11-6
Second Floor
863 sq. ft.
62'-0"
Patio
Nook
10-4x11-4
Kit
10-0x
11-4
R
Dining
10-4x11-4
Garage
23-8x23-4
D W
Dn
28'-0"
Sunken
Family
13-2x15-6
Sunken
Living
13-2x15-6
Up
coffered clg
coffered clg
First Floor
1,058 sq. ft.
Porch depth 6-0

Special features

- Energy efficient home with 2" x 6" exterior walls
- Sunken family room includes a built-in entertainment center and coffered ceiling
- Sunken formal living room features a coffered ceiling
- Dressing area has double sinks, spa tub, shower and French door to private deck
- Large front porch adds to home's appeal
- 3 bedrooms, 2 1/2 baths, 2-car garage
- Basement foundation

TO ORDER BLUEPRINTS USE THE FORM ON PAGE 15 OR CALL TOLL-FREE 1-877-671-6036

View thousands more home plans online at www.familyhandyman.com/homeplans

The Family
Handyman

Plan #708-DBI-2701

Den With Double-Door Entry

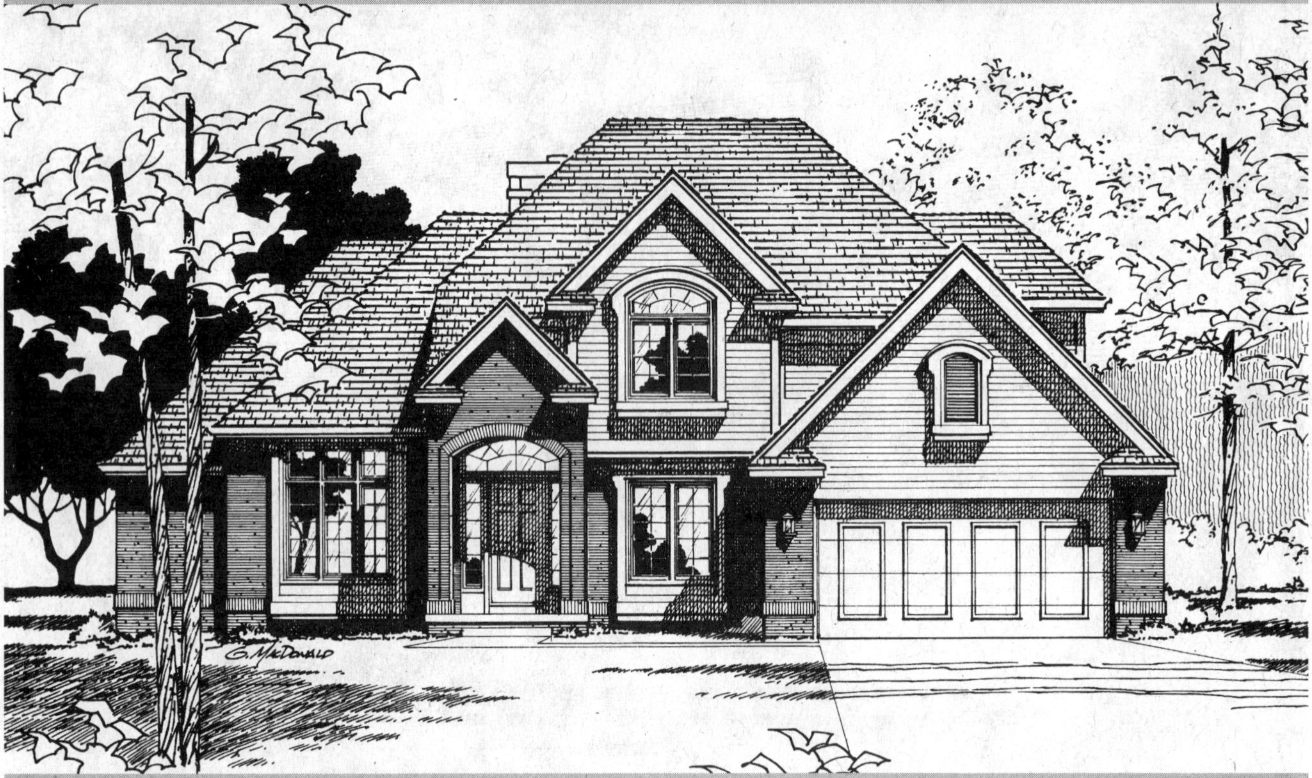

G. MacDonald

2,340 total square feet of living area

Price Code D

Special features

- Box bay windows in front of home add interest in dining room and den
- Master bedroom features one-of-a-kind design whirlpool tub
- Kitchen has lots of counter space and cabinetry stretching into breakfast area
- Centrally located wet bar for entertaining
- 4 bedrooms, 2 1/2 baths, 2-car garage
- Basement foundation

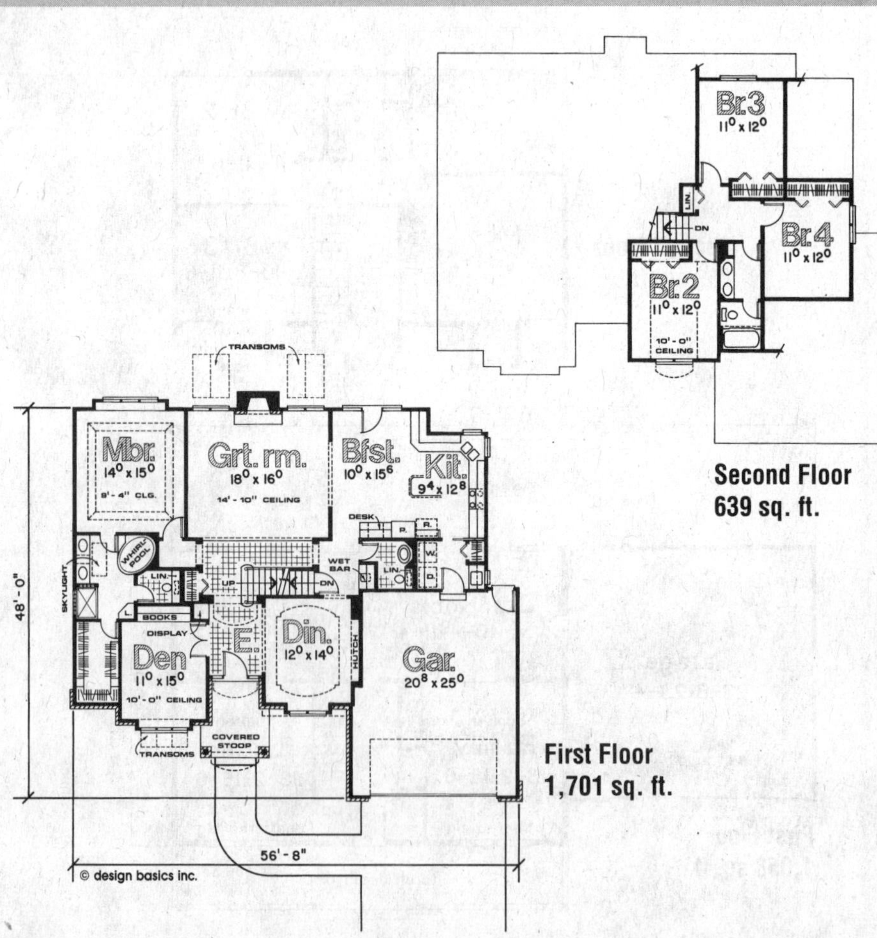

Br.3
11^{0} x 12^{0}
Br.4
11^{0} x 12^{0}
Br.2
11^{0} x 12^{0}
10'-0" CEILING
LIN.
DN
TRANSOMS
Mbr.
14^{0} x 15^{0}
9'-4" CLG.
Grt. rm.
18^{0} x 16^{0}
14'-10" CEILING
Bfst.
10^{0} x 15^{6}
Kit.
9^{4} x 12^{8}
DESK
WHIRLPOOL
WET BAR
LIN.
UP
DN
SKYLIGHT
BOOKS
DISPLAY
Den
11^{0} x 15^{0}
10'-0" CEILING
E.
Din.
12^{0} x 14^{0}
HUTCH
Gar.
20^{8} x 25^{0}
COVERED STOOP
TRANSOMS
48'-0"
56'-8"
© design basics inc.

Second Floor
639 sq. ft.

First Floor
1,701 sq. ft.

TO ORDER BLUEPRINTS USE THE FORM ON PAGE 15 OR CALL TOLL-FREE 1-877-671-6036

The Family
Handyman

Plan #708-0783

Spacious Rooms Throughout

3,035 total square feet of living area

Price Code E

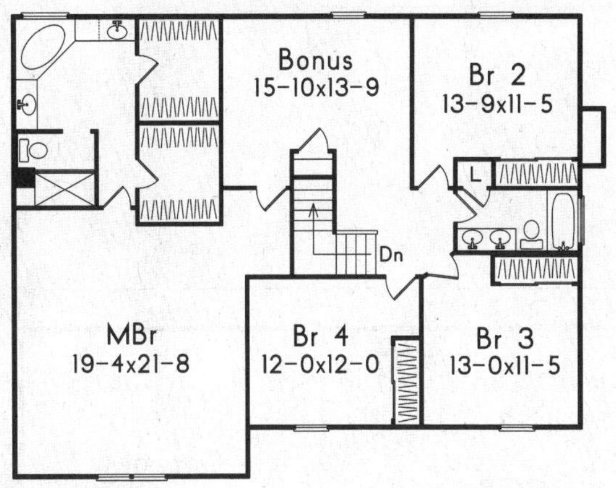
Bonus
15-10x13-9
Br 2
13-9x11-5
L
Dn
MBr
19-4x21-8
Br 4
12-0x12-0
Br 3
13-0x11-5

Second Floor
1,712 sq. ft.

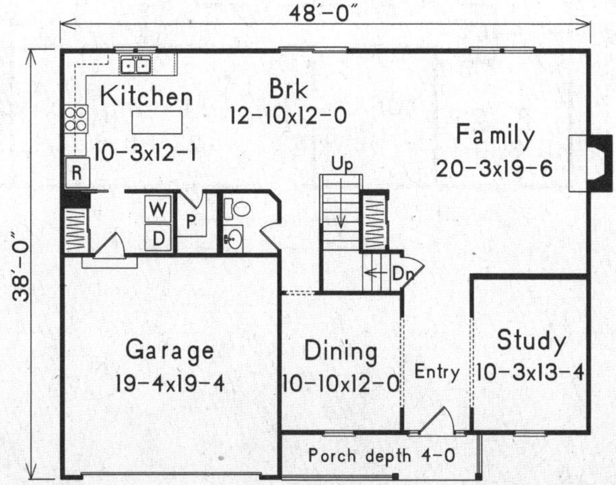
48'-0"
38'-0"
Kitchen
10-3x12-1
Brk
12-10x12-0
Family
20-3x19-6
R
W
D
P
Up
Dn
Garage
19-4x19-4
Dining
10-10x12-0
Entry
Study
10-3x13-4
Porch depth 4-0

First Floor
1,323 sq. ft.

Special features

- Master bedroom features two walk-in closets and a luxury bath
- Second floor has four bedrooms plus a bonus area ideal as an additional family area
- Unique version of traditional two-story with rooms located around central staircase
- 4 bedrooms, 2 1/2 baths, 2-car garage
- Basement foundation

The Family
Handyman

Plan #708-0515

Stylish Ranch With Rustic Charm

1,344 total square feet of living area **Price Code A**

Special features

- Family/dining room has sliding door
- Master bedroom includes private bath with shower
- Hall bath includes double vanity for added convenience
- Kitchen features U-shaped design, large pantry and laundry area
- 3 bedrooms, 2 baths, 2-car garage
- Crawl space foundation, drawings also include basement and slab foundations

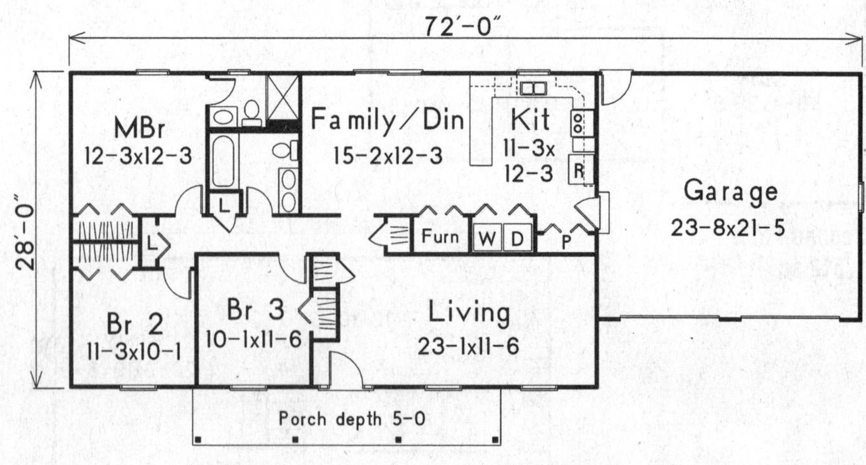
72'-0"
28'-0"
MBr
12-3x12-3
Family/Din
15-2x12-3
Kit
11-3x
12-3
R
L
L
Furn
W
D
P
Garage
23-8x21-5
Br 2
11-3x10-1
Br 3
10-1x11-6
Living
23-1x11-6
Porch depth 5-0

TO ORDER BLUEPRINTS USE THE FORM ON PAGE 15 OR CALL TOLL-FREE 1-877-671-6036

View thousands more home plans online at www.familyhandyman.com/homeplans

The Family
Handyman

Plan #708-NDG-700

Modest-Sized Home With Much To Offer

2,217 total square feet of living area — **Price Code C**

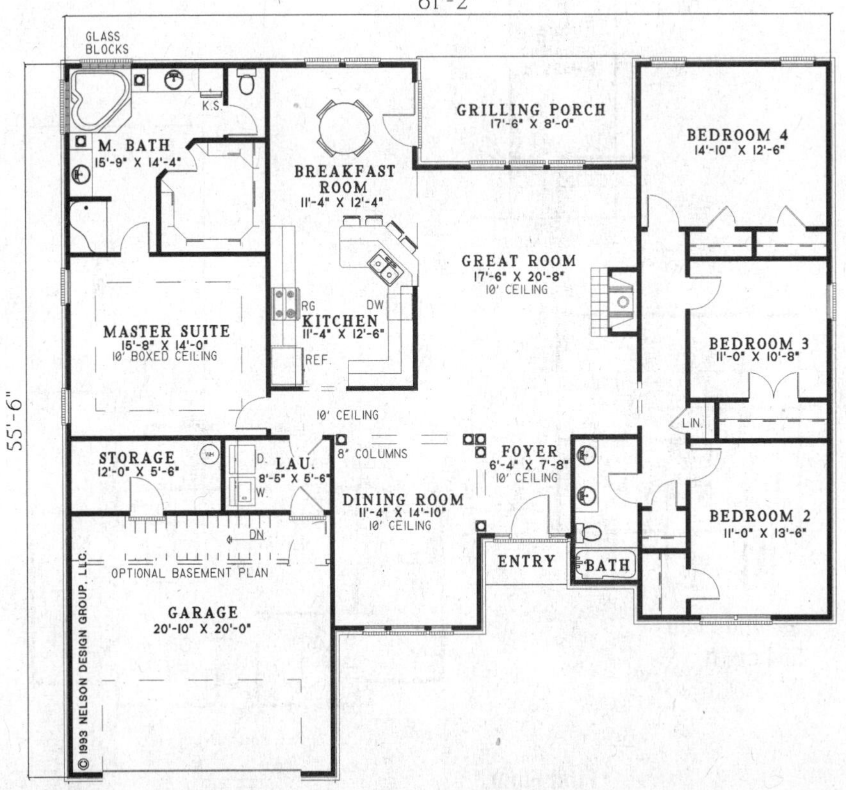
61'-2"
55'-6"
GLASS BLOCKS
K.S.
M. BATH
15'-9" X 14'-4"
BREAKFAST ROOM
11'-4" X 12'-4"
GRILLING PORCH
17'-6" X 8'-0"
BEDROOM 4
14'-10" X 12'-6"
GREAT ROOM
17'-6" X 20'-8"
10' CEILING
RG
DW
KITCHEN
11'-4" X 12'-6"
REF.
MASTER SUITE
15'-8" X 14'-0"
10' BOXED CEILING
BEDROOM 3
11'-0" X 10'-8"
10' CEILING
LIN.
STORAGE
12'-0" X 5'-6"
LAU.
8'-5" X 5'-6"
D.
W.
8" COLUMNS
FOYER
6'-4" X 7'-8"
10' CEILING
DINING ROOM
11'-4" X 14'-10"
10' CEILING
BEDROOM 2
11'-0" X 13'-6"
DN.
OPTIONAL BASEMENT PLAN
ENTRY
BATH
GARAGE
20'-10" X 20'-0"
© 1993 NELSON DESIGN GROUP, LLC.

Special features

- Great room features a fireplace and is open to the foyer, breakfast and dining rooms
- Laundry room and storage closet are located off of garage
- Secluded master suite includes a bath with a corner whirlpool tub, split vanities, corner shower and a large walk-in closet
- 4 bedrooms, 2 baths, 2-car garage
- Crawl space or slab foundation, please specify when ordering

Plan #708-0303

Distinctive Front Facade With Generous Porch

2,024 total square feet of living area

Price Code C

Special features

- King-size master bedroom with sitting area
- Living room features corner fireplace, access to covered rear porch, 18' ceiling and a balcony
- Closet for handling recyclables
- Future bonus room has an additional 475 square feet of living area
- 3 bedrooms, 2 1/2 baths, 2-car side entry garage
- Crawl space foundation, drawings also include slab and basement foundations

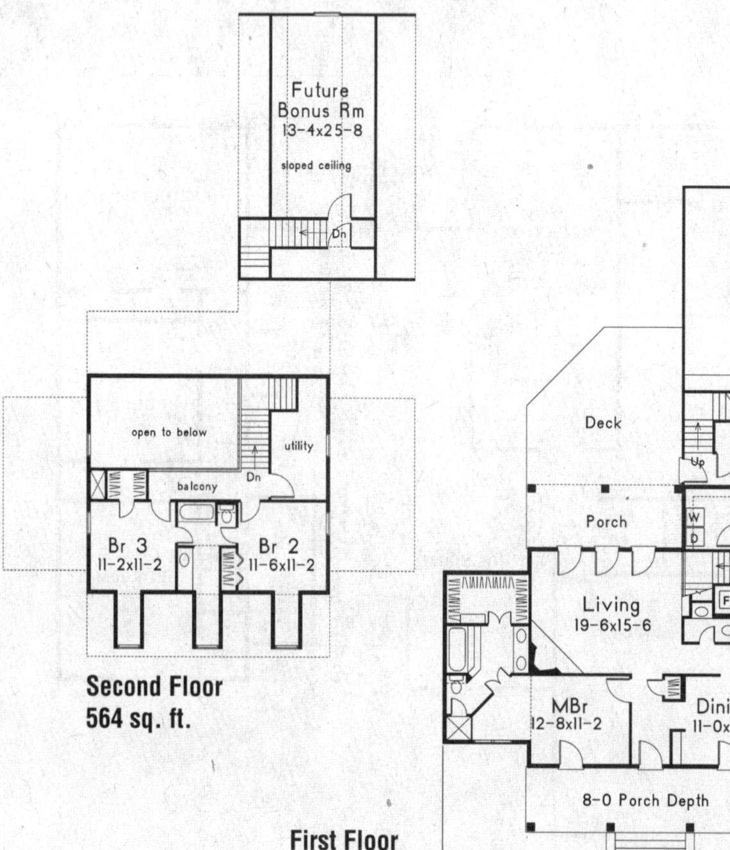
Future
Bonus Rm
13-4x25-8
sloped ceiling
Dn
open to below
utility
Dn
balcony
Br 3
11-2x11-2
Br 2
11-6x11-2
Garage
25-8x22-4
Deck
Storage
Up
Dn
Porch
W
D
Up
82'-0"
Living
19-6x15-6
Kit
10-8x
11-6
MBr
12-8x11-2
Dining
11-0x11-0
Eating
10-6x9-6
8-0 Porch Depth
54'-0"

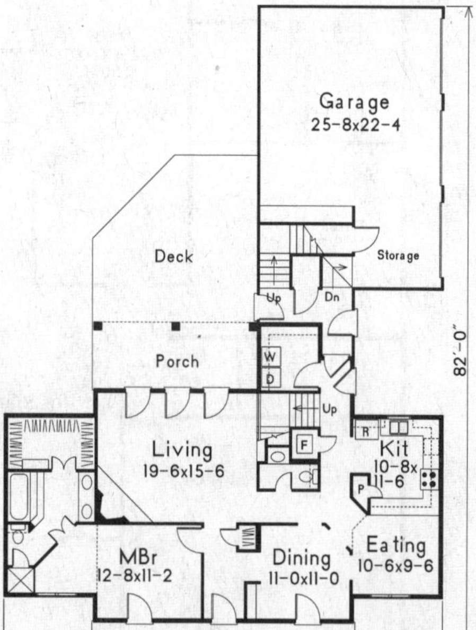

Second Floor
564 sq. ft.

First Floor
1,460 sq. ft.

TO ORDER BLUEPRINTS USE THE FORM ON PAGE 15 OR CALL TOLL-FREE 1-877-671-6036

View thousands more home plans online at www.familyhandyman.com/homeplans

The Family
Handyman

Plan #708-0721

Well-Designed Floor Plan Has Many Extras

2,437 total square feet of living area

Price Code D

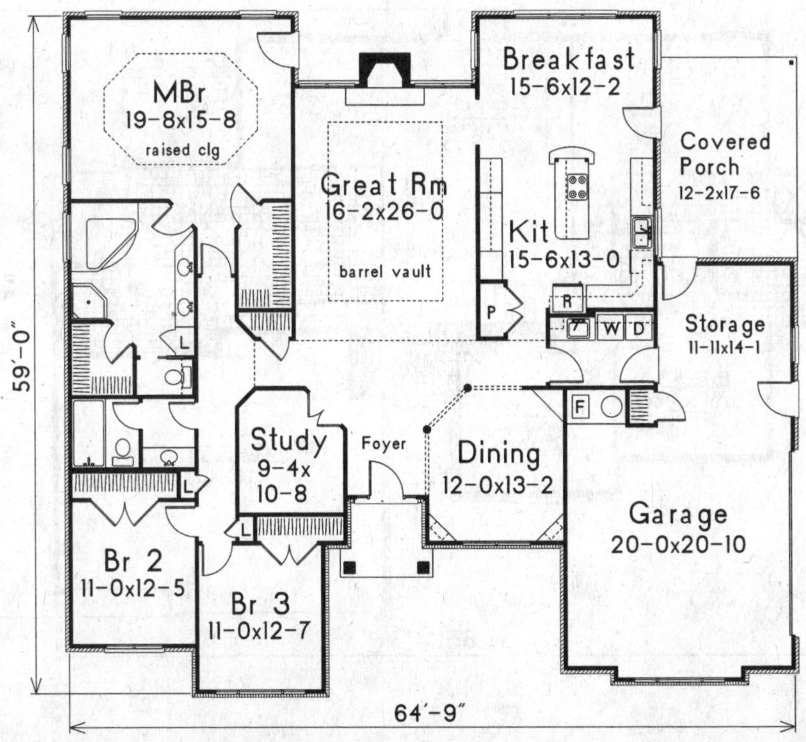
MBr
19-8x15-8
raised clg
Great Rm
16-2x26-0
barrel vault
Breakfast
15-6x12-2
Kit
15-6x13-0
Covered
Porch
12-2x17-6
Storage
11-11x14-1
Study
9-4x
10-8
Foyer
Dining
12-0x13-2
Garage
20-0x20-10
Br 2
11-0x12-5
Br 3
11-0x12-7
59'-0"
64'-9"

Special features

- Spacious breakfast area with access to the covered porch is adjacent to kitchen and great room
- Elegant dining area has columned entrance and built-in corner cabinets
- Cozy study has handsome double-door entrance off a large foyer
- Raised ceiling and lots of windows in master bedroom create a spacious, open feel
- 3 bedrooms, 2 baths, 2-car side entry garage
- Slab foundation, drawings also include crawl space foundation

TO ORDER BLUEPRINTS USE THE FORM ON PAGE 15 OR CALL TOLL-FREE 1-877-671-6036

Plan #708-JA-73897

Classic Ranch

1,794 total square feet of living area

Price Code B

Special features

- Elegant arched soffit connects the great room to the dining room
- Large kitchen has wrap-around counters, large pantry and center island
- Plenty of storage throughout
- 3 bedrooms, 2 baths, 3-car garage
- Basement foundation

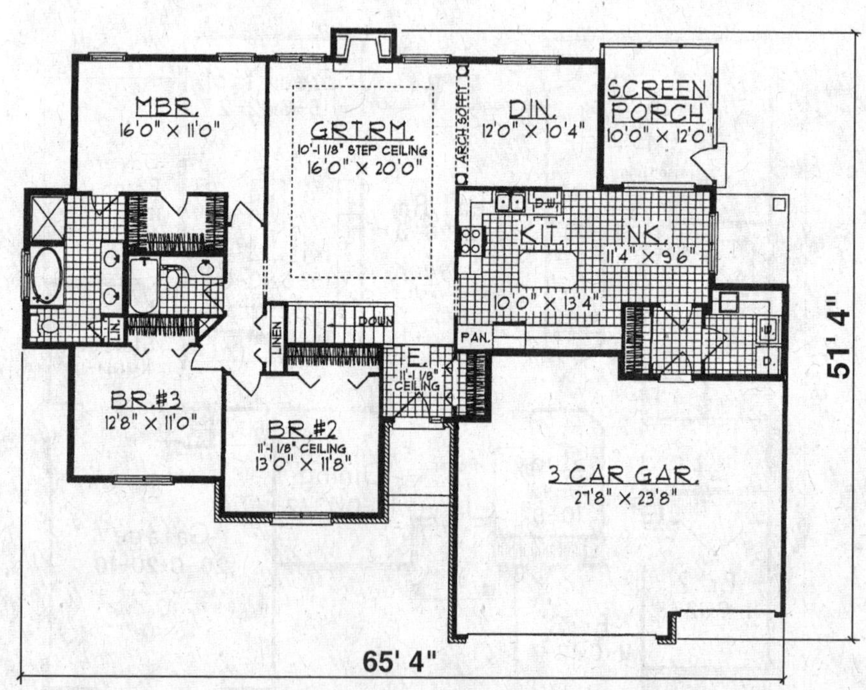
MBR.
16'0" X 11'0"
GRT.RM.
10'-1 1/8" STEP CEILING
16'0" X 20'0"
ARCH SOFFIT
DIN.
12'0" X 10'4"
SCREEN PORCH
10'0" X 12'0"
KIT.
NK.
11'4" X 9'6"
10'0" X 13'4"
PAN.
LIN.
LINEN
DOWN
E.
11'-1 1/8" CEILING
BR.#3
12'8" X 11'0"
BR.#2
11'-1 1/8" CEILING
13'0" X 11'8"
3 CAR GAR.
27'8" X 23'8"
65' 4"
51' 4"

TO ORDER BLUEPRINTS USE THE FORM ON PAGE 15 OR CALL TOLL-FREE 1-877-671-6036

View thousands more home plans online at www.familyhandyman.com/homeplans

The Family
Handyman

Plan #708-0279

Provides Family Living At Its Best

1,993 total square feet of living area **Price Code D**

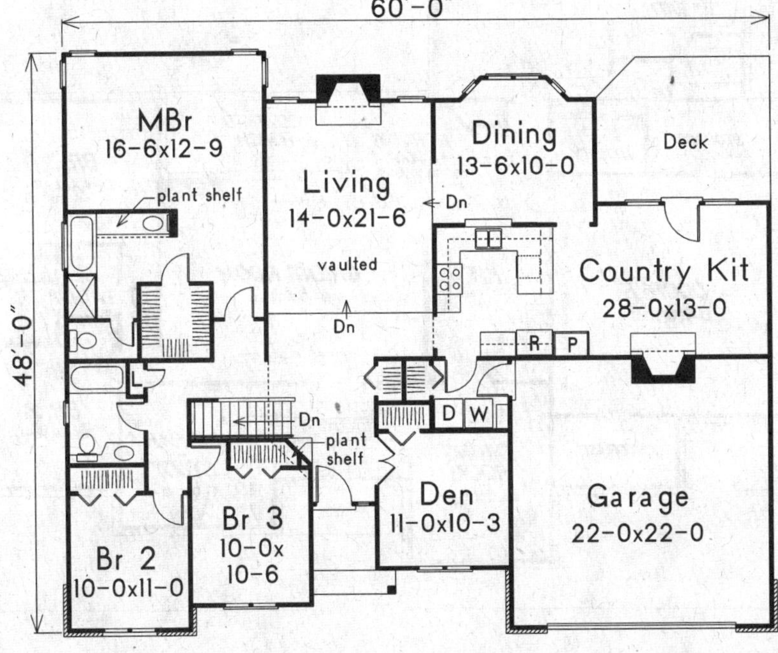

60'-0"
48'-0"
MBr
16-6x12-9
plant shelf
Living
14-0x21-6
vaulted
Dn
Dining
13-6x10-0
Dn
Deck
Country Kit
28-0x13-0
R
P
D
W
Dn
plant shelf
Br 3
10-0x
10-6
Br 2
10-0x11-0
Den
11-0x10-3
Garage
22-0x22-0

Special features

- Spacious country kitchen with fireplace and plenty of natural light from windows
- Formal dining room features large bay window and steps down to sunken living room
- Master suite features corner windows, plant shelves and deluxe private bath
- Entry opens into vaulted living room with windows flanking the fireplace
- 3 bedrooms, 2 baths, 2-car garage
- Basement foundation

The Family
Handyman

Plan #708-RJ-A22-27

Double Garage With Two Storage Areas

© Copyright MCMXCVIII – Ralph Jones

2,281 total square feet of living area — **Price Code D**

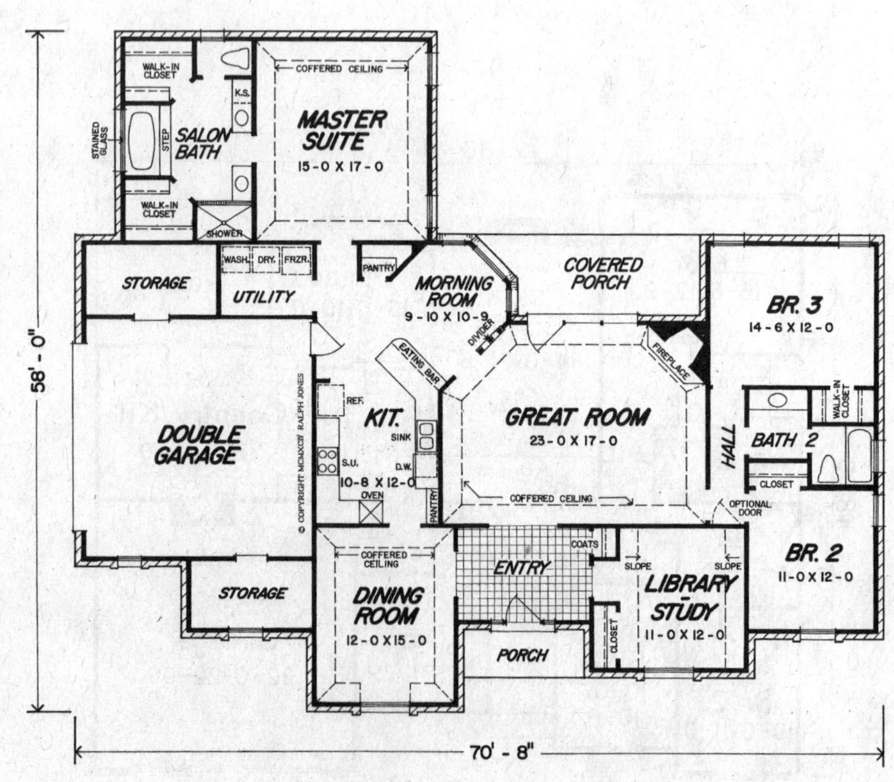
WALK-IN CLOSET
K.S.
COFFERED CEILING
STAINED GLASS
STEP
SALON BATH
MASTER SUITE
15-0 X 17-0
WALK-IN CLOSET
SHOWER
WASH
DRY.
FRZR.
PANTRY
STORAGE
UTILITY
MORNING ROOM
9-10 X 10-9
COVERED PORCH
BR. 3
14-6 X 12-0
DIVIDER
EATING BAR
FIREPLACE
58' - 0"
REF.
KIT.
SINK
S.U.
10-8 X 12-0
D.W.
OVEN
PANTRY
DOUBLE GARAGE
© COPYRIGHT MCMXCVIII RALPH JONES
GREAT ROOM
23-0 X 17-0
COFFERED CEILING
HALL
WALK-IN CLOSET
BATH 2
CLOSET
OPTIONAL DOOR
COFFERED CEILING
COATS
SLOPE
SLOPE
ENTRY
STORAGE
DINING ROOM
12-0 X 15-0
LIBRARY STUDY
11-0 X 12-0
BR. 2
11-0 X 12-0
CLOSET
PORCH
70' - 8"

Special features

- Formal dining room with coffered ceilings
- Great room with fireplace and coffered ceilings overlooks covered back porch
- Kitchen with angle eating bar adjoins angled morning room with bay window
- Salon bath has double walk-in closets, vanities, step up tub and separate shower
- 3 bedrooms, 2 baths, 2-car side entry garage
- Slab or crawl space foundation, please specify when ordering

TO ORDER BLUEPRINTS USE THE FORM ON PAGE 15 OR CALL TOLL-FREE 1-877-671-6036

View thousands more home plans online at www.familyhandyman.com/homeplans

Delightful Dormers Add Drama

3,231 total square feet of living area

Price Code G

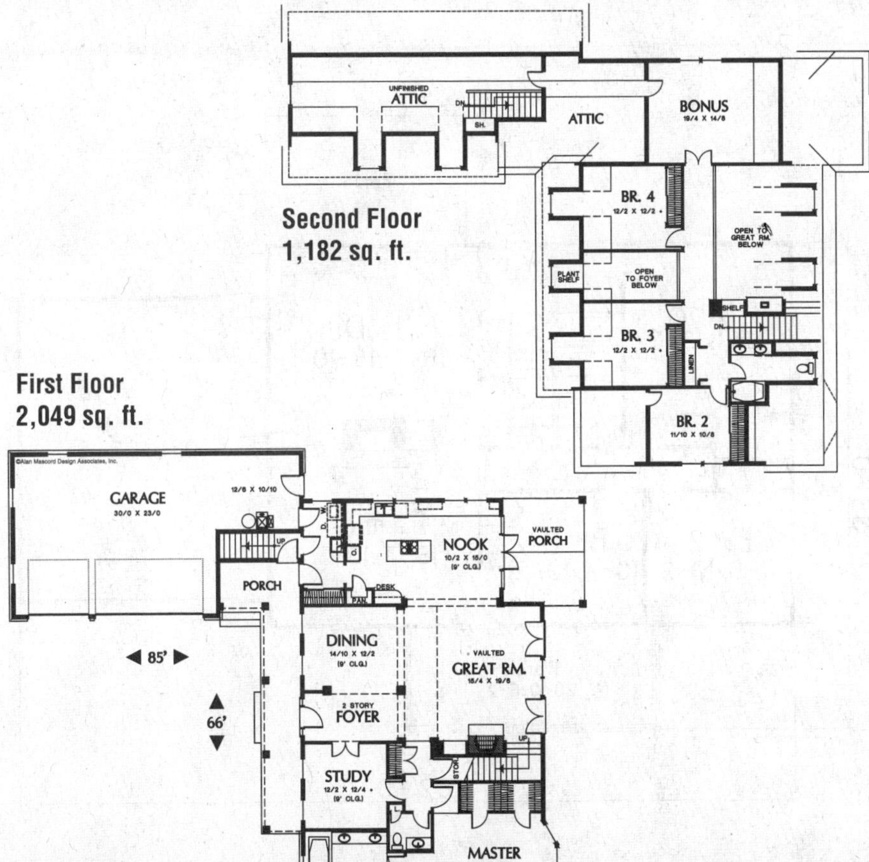

UNFINISHED ATTIC
ATTIC
BONUS
19/4 X 14/8
BR. 4
12/2 X 12/2 +
PLANT SHELF
OPEN TO FOYER BELOW
OPEN TO GREAT RM. BELOW
SHELF
BR. 3
12/2 X 12/2 +
LINEN
BR. 2
11/10 X 10/8
GARAGE
30/0 X 23/0
NOOK
10/2 X 16/0
(9' CLG.)
VAULTED PORCH
PORCH
DINING
14/10 X 12/2
(9' CLG.)
VAULTED
GREAT RM.
18/4 X 19/8
2 STORY
FOYER
STUDY
12/2 X 12/4 +
(9' CLG.)
MASTER
16/0 X 13/0 +
(9' CLG.)
85'
66'

Second Floor
1,182 sq. ft.

First Floor
2,049 sq. ft.

Special features

- Breakfast nook and kitchen combine creating a large open dining space
- A cozy and private study is convenient to the master bedroom perfect for an office
- Decorative columns enhance the formal dining room
- 1,182 square feet on the second floor includes the bonus room
- 4 bedrooms, 2 1/2 baths, 3-car garage
- Crawl space foundation

Central Fireplace Brightens Family Living

1,260 total square feet of living area **Price Code A**

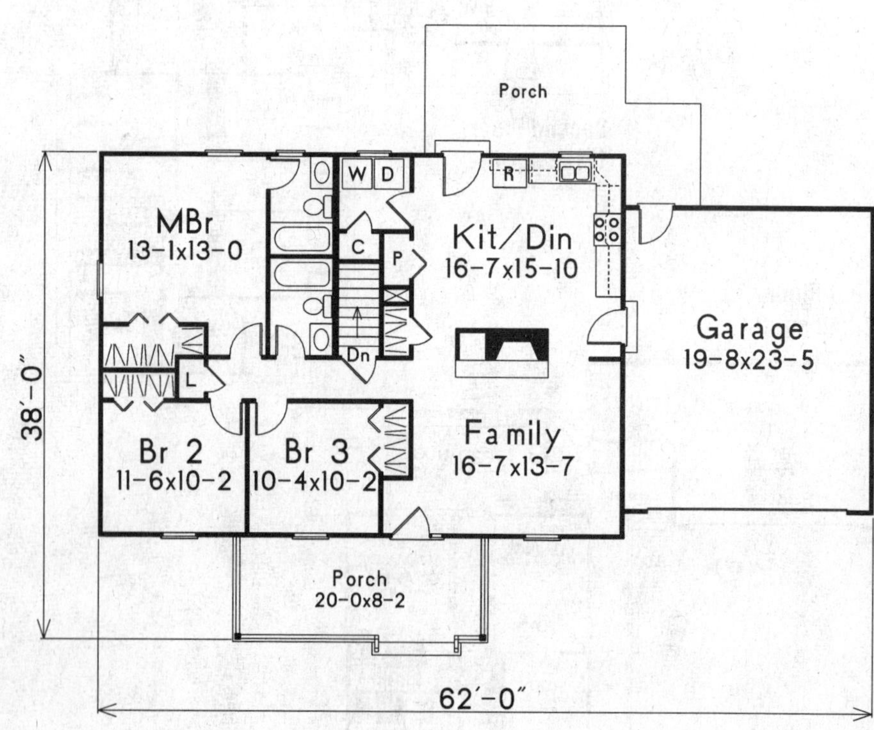
Porch
MBr
13-1x13-0
W
D
R
C
P
Kit/Din
16-7x15-10
Garage
19-8x23-5
Dn
L
Br 2
11-6x10-2
Br 3
10-4x10-2
Family
16-7x13-7
38'-0"
Porch
20-0x8-2
62'-0"

Special features

- Spacious kitchen and dining area feature large pantry, storage area, easy access to garage and laundry room
- Pleasant covered front porch adds a practical touch
- Master bedroom with a private bath adjoins two other bedrooms, all with plenty of closet space
- 3 bedrooms, 2 baths, 2-car garage
- Basement foundation, drawings also include crawl space and slab foundations

The Family
Handyman

Plan #708-GH-24701

Two-Sided Fireplace Warms This Home

1,625 total square feet of living area

Price Code B

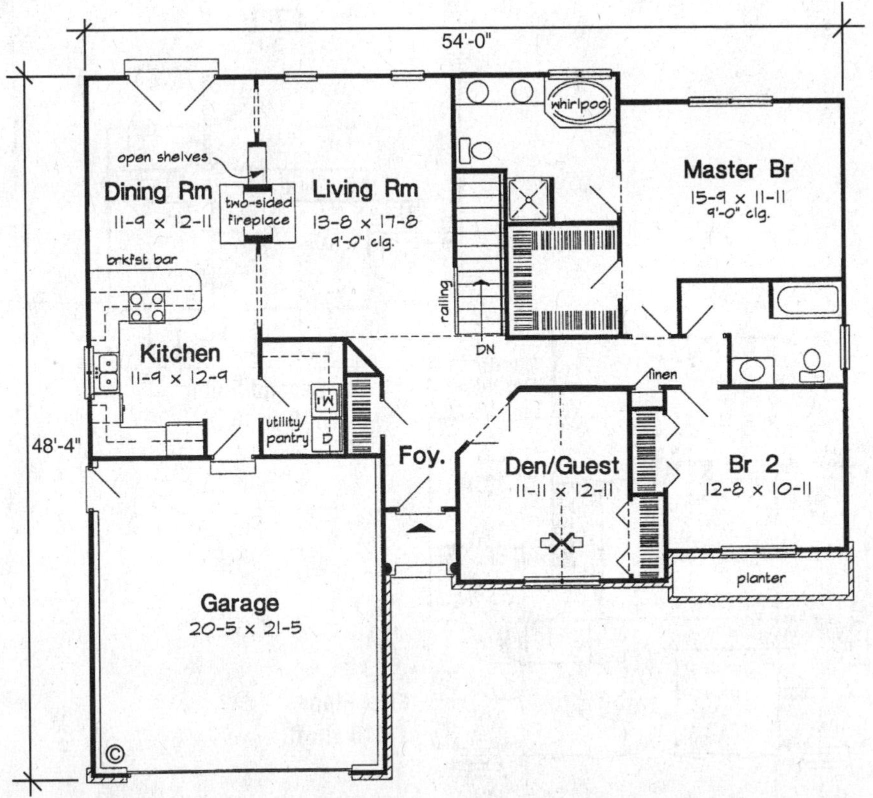
54'-0"
48'-4"
whirlpool
open shelves
Dining Rm
11-9 x 12-11
two-sided fireplace
Living Rm
13-8 x 17-8
9'-0" clg.
Master Br
15-9 x 11-11
9'-0" clg.
brkfst bar
railing
DN
Kitchen
11-9 x 12-9
linen
utility/
pantry
W
D
Foy.
Den/Guest
11-11 x 12-11
Br 2
12-8 x 10-11
planter
Garage
20-5 x 21-5
©

Special features

- Double-door in corner of den/ guest room creates an interesting entry
- Spacious master bath has both a whirlpool tub and a shower
- Welcoming planter boxes in front add curb appeal
- 3 bedrooms, 2 baths, 2-car garage
- Basement or crawl space foundation, please specify when ordering

TO ORDER BLUEPRINTS USE THE FORM ON PAGE 15 OR CALL TOLL-FREE 1-877-671-6036

View thousands more home plans online at www.familyhandyman.com/homeplans

The Family
Handyman

Plan #708-CHP-2543-A-42

Porches Bring Outdoor Living In

2,500 total square feet of living area

Price Code D

Special features

- Master bedroom has its own separate wing with front porch, double walk-in closets, private bath and access to back porch and patio
- Large unfinished gameroom on second floor has an additional 359 square feet of living area
- Living area is oversized and has a fireplace
- 3 bedrooms, 2 1/2 baths
- Basement, slab or crawl space foundation, please specify when ordering

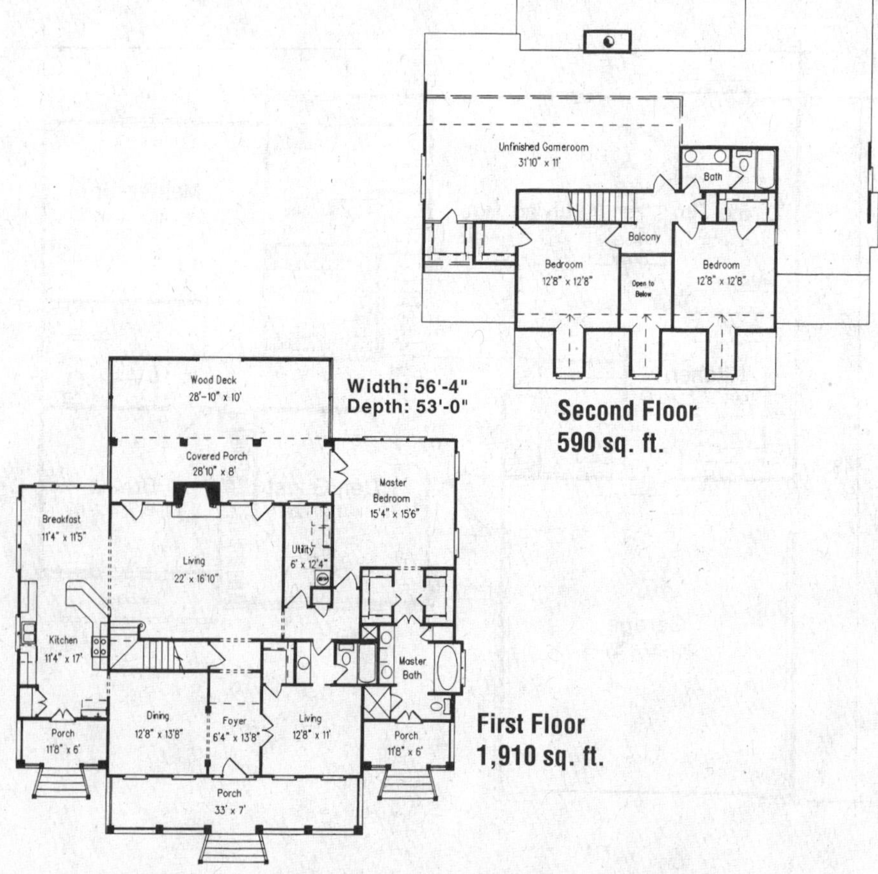
Unfinished Gameroom
31'10" x 11'
Bath
Balcony
Bedroom
12'8" x 12'8"
Open to Below
Bedroom
12'8" x 12'8"
Second Floor
590 sq. ft.
Wood Deck
28'-10" x 10'
Width: 56'-4"
Depth: 53'-0"
Covered Porch
28'10" x 8'
Master Bedroom
15'4" x 15'6"
Breakfast
11'4" x 11'5"
Living
22' x 16'10"
Utility
6' x 12'4"
Kitchen
11'4" x 17'
Master Bath
Dining
12'8" x 13'8"
Foyer
6'4" x 13'8"
Living
12'8" x 11'
Porch
11'8" x 6'
Porch
11'8" x 6'
Porch
33' x 7'
First Floor
1,910 sq. ft.

TO ORDER BLUEPRINTS USE THE FORM ON PAGE 15 OR CALL TOLL-FREE 1-877-671-6036

View thousands more home plans online at www.familyhandyman.com/homeplans

The Family
Handyman

Plan #708-0302

Stucco And Stone Add Charm To Facade

1,854 total square feet of living area **Price Code D**

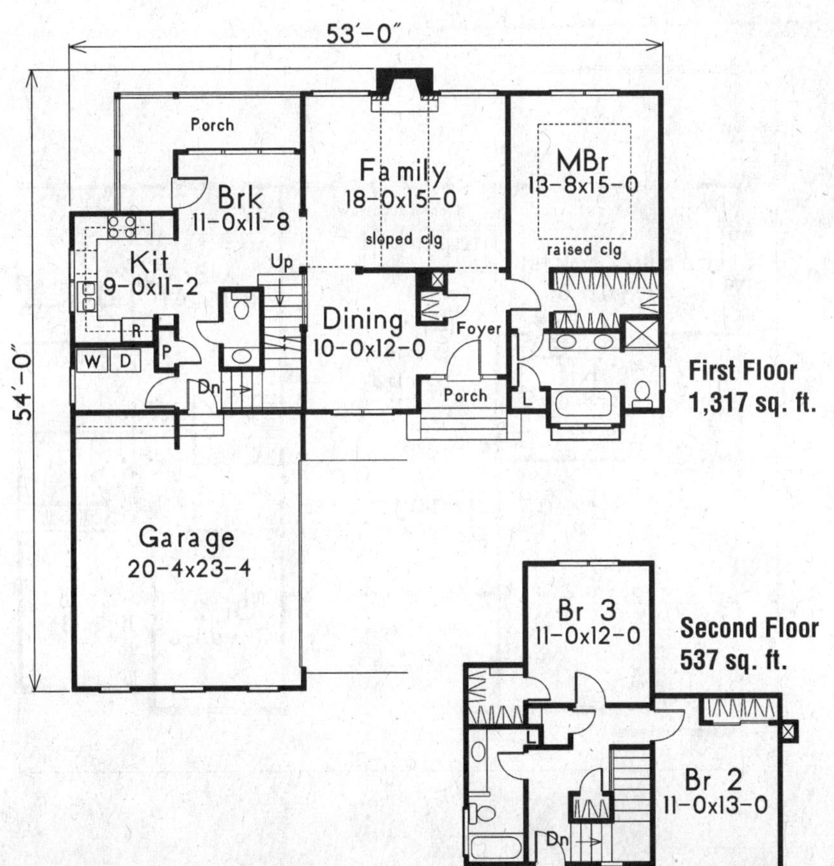

53'-0"
54'-0"
Porch
Family
18-0x15-0
sloped clg
MBr
13-8x15-0
raised clg
Brk
11-0x11-8
Kit
9-0x11-2
Up
Dining
10-0x12-0
Foyer
R
P
W
D
Dn
Porch
L
Garage
20-4x23-4
First Floor
1,317 sq. ft.
Br 3
11-0x12-0
Second Floor
537 sq. ft.
Br 2
11-0x13-0
Dn

Special features

- Front entrance enhanced by arched transom windows and rustic stone
- Isolated master bedroom with dressing area and walk-in closet
- Family room features high, sloped ceilings and large fireplace
- Breakfast area accesses covered rear porch
- 3 bedrooms, 2 1/2 baths, 2-car side entry garage
- Basement foundation

TO ORDER BLUEPRINTS USE THE FORM ON PAGE 15 OR CALL TOLL-FREE 1-877-671-6036

View thousands more home plans online at www.familyhandyman.com/homeplans

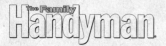

Bright, Spacious Plan With Many Features

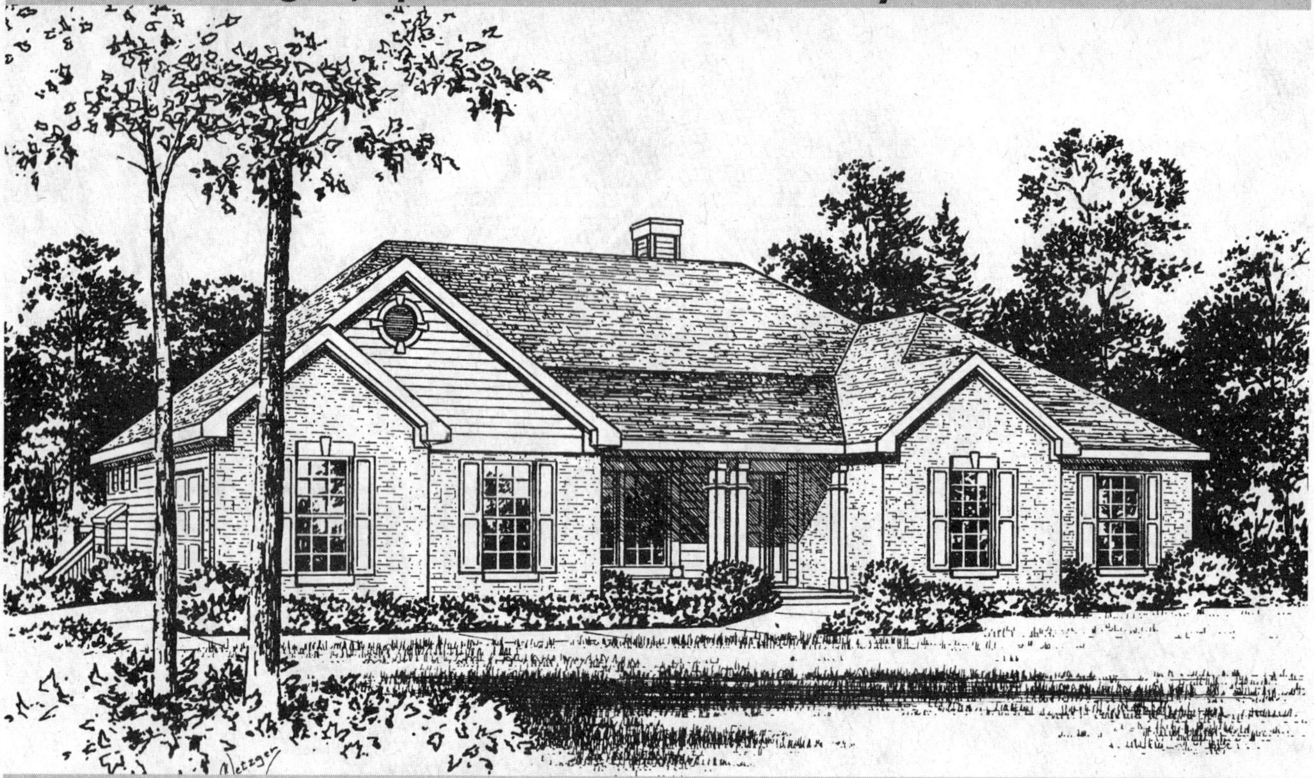

2,308 total square feet of living area **Price Code D**

Special features

- Efficient kitchen designed with many cabinets and large walk-in pantry adjoins family/breakfast area featuring a beautiful fireplace
- Dining area has architectural colonnades that separate it from living area while maintaining spaciousness
- Enter master suite through double-doors and find double walk-in closets and beautiful luxurious bath
- Living room includes vaulted ceiling, fireplace and a sunny atrium window wall creating a dramatic atmosphere
- 3 bedrooms, 2 baths, 2-car side entry garage
- Walk-out basement foundation

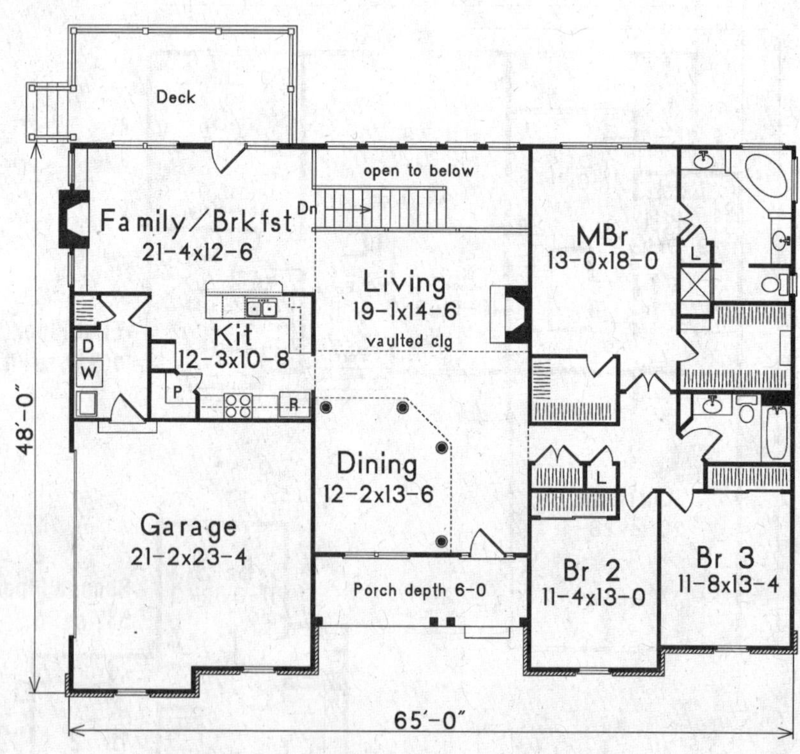
Deck
open to below
Family/Brkfst
21-4x12-6
Dn
Living
19-1x14-6
vaulted clg
MBr
13-0x18-0
Kit
12-3x10-8
D
W
P
R
L
Dining
12-2x13-6
Garage
21-2x23-4
Porch depth 6-0
Br 2
11-4x13-0
Br 3
11-8x13-4
48'-0"
65'-0"

TO ORDER BLUEPRINTS USE THE FORM ON PAGE 15 OR CALL TOLL-FREE 1-877-671-6036

Plan #708-SRD-214

A Functional Floor Plan For Family Living

1,856 total square feet of living area

Price Code C

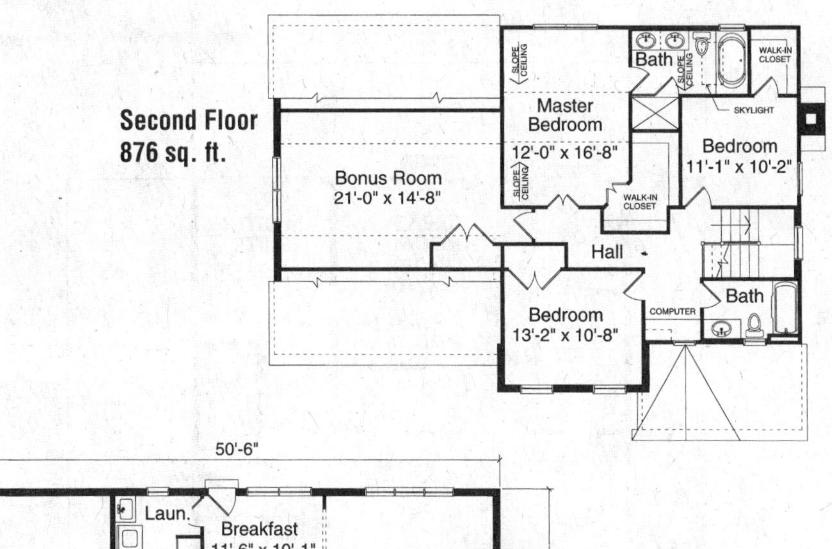
Second Floor
876 sq. ft.
Bath
WALK-IN CLOSET
SLOPE CEILING
SLOPE CEILING
SKYLIGHT
Master Bedroom
12'-0" x 16'-8"
Bedroom
11'-1" x 10'-2"
Bonus Room
21'-0" x 14'-8"
SLOPE CEILING
WALK-IN CLOSET
Hall
Bath
COMPUTER
Bedroom
13'-2" x 10'-8"

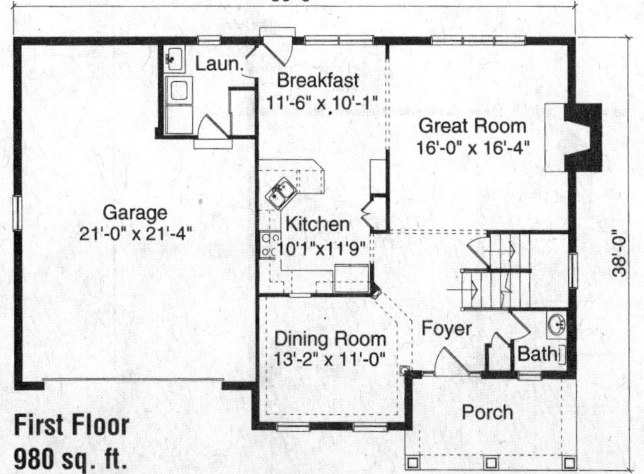
50'-6"
Laun.
Breakfast
11'-6" x 10'-1"
Great Room
16'-0" x 16'-4"
Garage
21'-0" x 21'-4"
Kitchen
10'1"x11'9"
38'-0"
Foyer
Dining Room
13'-2" x 11'-0"
Bath
Porch
First Floor
980 sq. ft.

Special features

- The roomy kitchen offers an abundance of cabinets and counter space as well as a convenient pantry
- Master bedroom includes a sloped ceiling and deluxe bath
- Bonus room on the second floor has an additional 325 square feet of living area
- 3 bedrooms, 2 1/2 baths, 2-car garage
- Walk-out basement or basement foundation, please specify when ordering

TO ORDER BLUEPRINTS USE THE FORM ON PAGE 15 OR CALL TOLL-FREE 1-877-671-6036

The Family
Handyman

Plan #708-HP-C689

Ranch-Style Home With Many Extras

1,295 total square feet of living area **Price Code A**

<u>*Special features*</u>

- Wrap-around porch is a lovely place for dining
- A fireplace gives a stunning focal point to the great room that is heightened with a sloped ceiling
- The master suite is full of luxurious touches such as a walk-in closet and a lush private bath
- 2 bedrooms, 2 baths, 2-car garage
- Basement foundation

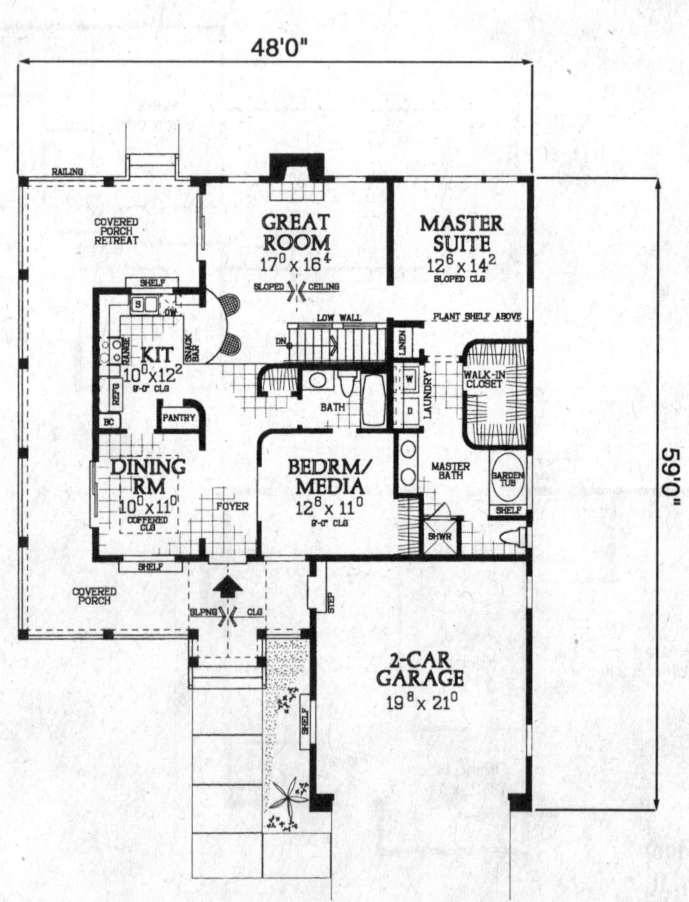
48'0"
RAILING
COVERED PORCH RETREAT
GREAT ROOM
17^0 x 16^4
SLOPED CEILING
MASTER SUITE
12^6 x 14^2
SLOPED CLG
LOW WALL
PLANT SHELF ABOVE
SHELF
KIT
10^0x12^2
9'-0" CLG
SNACK BAR
PANTRY
DN
BATH
LINEN
LAUNDRY
WALK-IN CLOSET
DINING RM
10^0x11^0
COFFERED CLG
FOYER
BEDRM/ MEDIA
12^6 x 11^0
9'-0" CLG
MASTER BATH
GARDEN TUB
SHWR
COVERED PORCH
SLPNG CLG
2-CAR GARAGE
19^8 x 21^0
59'0"

TO ORDER BLUEPRINTS USE THE FORM ON PAGE 15 OR CALL TOLL-FREE 1-877-671-6036

View thousands more home plans online at www.familyhandyman.com/homeplans

Plan #708-FB-963

Second Floor Overlook

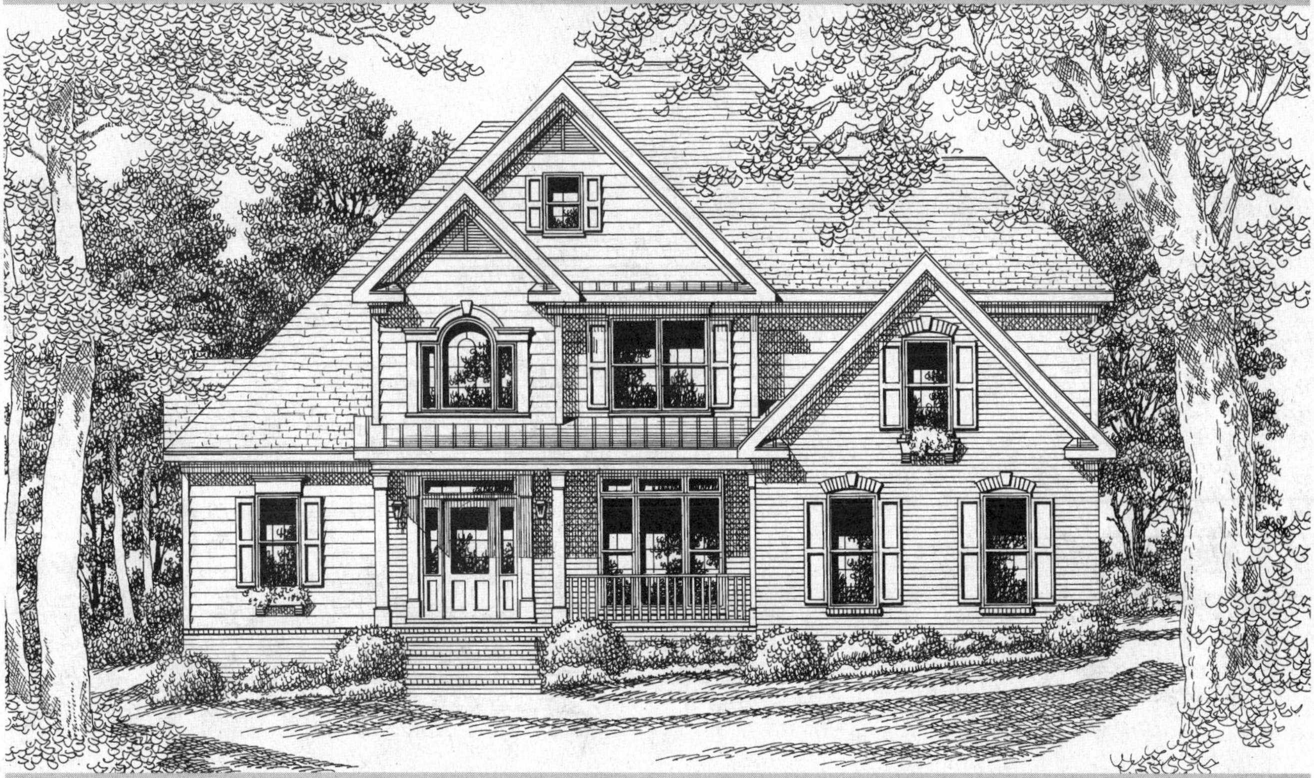

2,126 total square feet of living area **Price Code C**

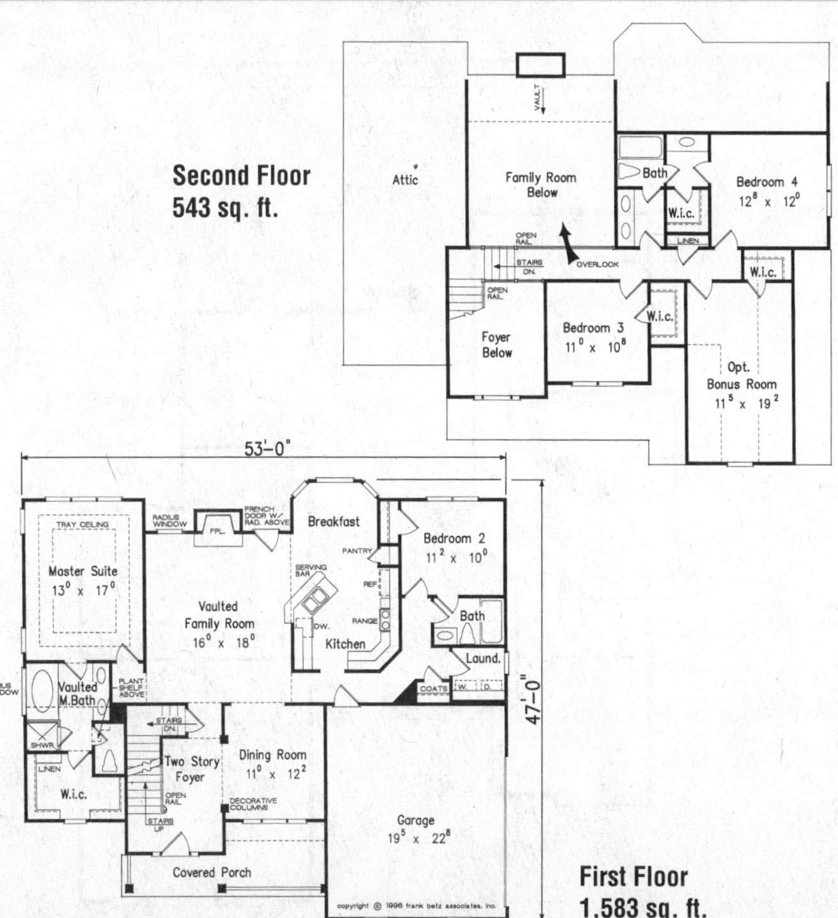
Attic
Family Room Below
VAULT
Bath
Bedroom 4
12⁸ x 12⁰
W.i.c.
LINEN
OPEN RAIL
STAIRS DN.
OVERLOOK
W.i.c.
OPEN RAIL
Foyer Below
Bedroom 3
11⁰ x 10⁸
W.i.c.
Opt. Bonus Room
11⁵ x 19²
53'-0"
47'-0"
TRAY CEILING
Master Suite
13⁰ x 17⁰
RADIUS WINDOW
FPL.
FRENCH DOOR W/ RAD. ABOVE
Breakfast
PANTRY
Bedroom 2
11² x 10⁰
SERVING BAR
REF.
Vaulted Family Room
16⁰ x 18⁰
DW.
RANGE
Kitchen
Bath
Laund.
RADIUS WINDOW
Vaulted M.Bath
PLANT SHELF ABOVE
COATS
W.
D.
STAIRS DN.
SHWR.
Two Story Foyer
Dining Room
11⁰ x 12²
LINEN
W.i.c.
OPEN RAIL
DECORATIVE COLUMNS
STAIRS UP
Garage
19⁵ x 22⁸
Covered Porch
copyright © 1996 frank betz associates, inc.

Second Floor
543 sq. ft.

First Floor
1,583 sq. ft.

Special features

- Kitchen overlooks vaulted family room with a handy serving bar
- Two-story foyer creates an airy feeling
- Second floor includes an optional bonus room with an additional 251 square feet of living area
- 4 bedrooms, 3 baths, 2-car side entry garage
- Walk-out basement, crawl space or slab foundation, please specify when ordering

TO ORDER BLUEPRINTS USE THE FORM ON PAGE 15 OR CALL TOLL-FREE 1-877-671-6036

Plan #708-0387

Casual Exterior, Filled With Great Features

1,958 total square feet of living area **Price Code C**

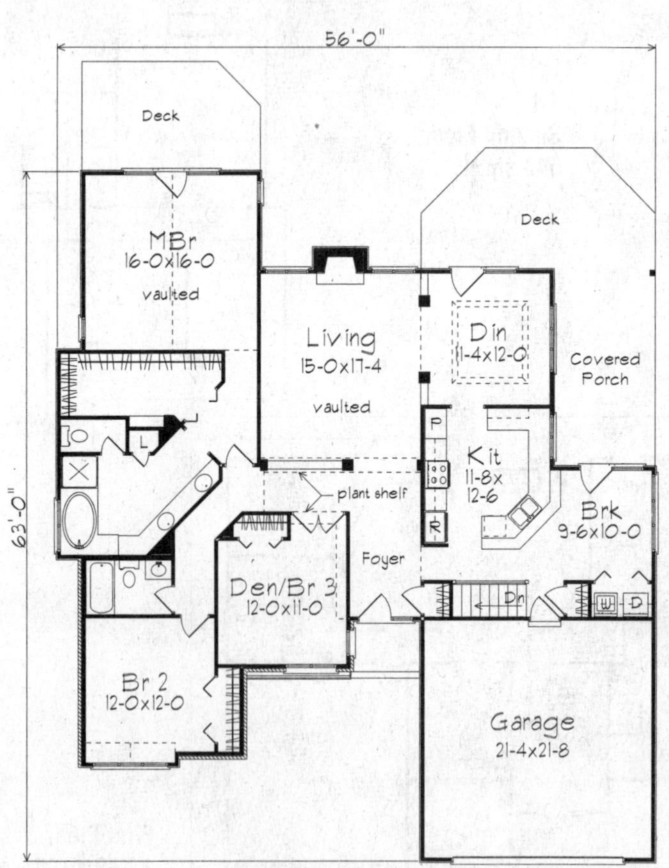

56'-0"
63'-0"
Deck
MBr
16-0x16-0
vaulted
Living
15-0x17-4
vaulted
Din
11-4x12-0
Covered
Porch
Deck
Kit
11-8x
12-6
Brk
9-6x10-0
plant shelf
Foyer
Den/Br 3
12-0x11-0
Dn
Br 2
12-0x12-0
Garage
21-4x21-8

Special features

- Large wrap-around kitchen opens to a bright cheerful breakfast area with access to large covered deck and open stairway to basement
- Kitchen nestled between the dining and breakfast rooms
- Master suite includes large walk-in closet, double-bowl vanity, garden tub and separate shower
- Foyer features attractive plant shelves and opens into living room that includes attractive central fireplace
- 3 bedrooms, 2 baths, 2-car garage
- Basement foundation

TO ORDER BLUEPRINTS USE THE FORM ON PAGE 15 OR CALL TOLL-FREE 1-877-671-6036

View thousands more home plans online at www.familyhandyman.com/homeplans

The Family
Handyman

Plan #708-FB-933

Kitchen Is A Chef's Dream

2,193 total square feet of living area **Price Code C**

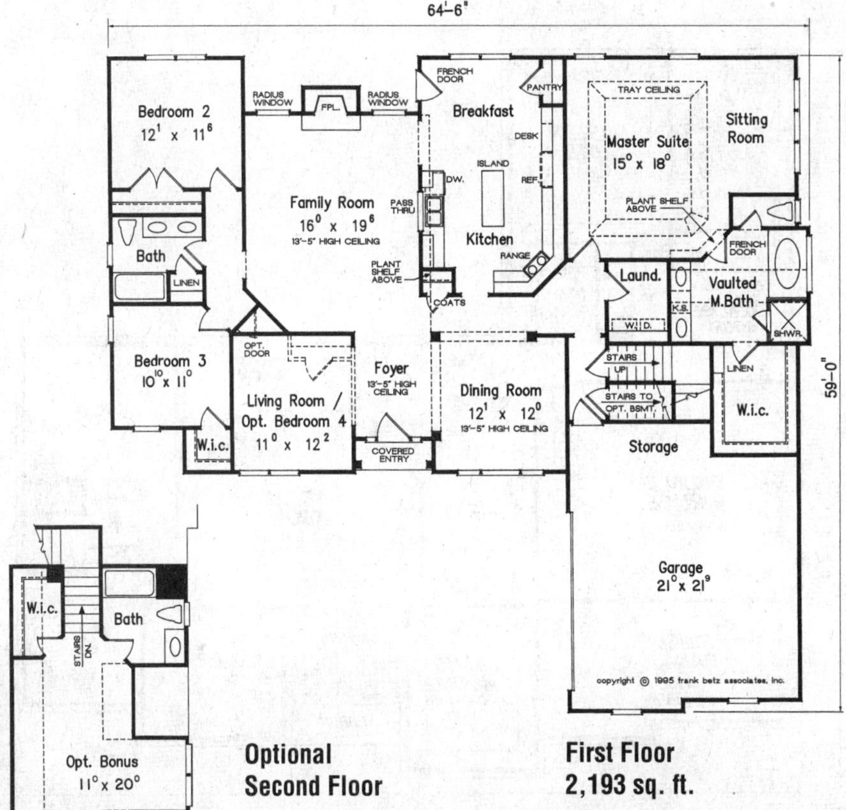
64'-6"
Bedroom 2
12^1 x 11^6
RADIUS WINDOW
FPL.
RADIUS WINDOW
FRENCH DOOR
PANTRY
Breakfast
DESK
ISLAND
REF.
DW.
TRAY CEILING
Master Suite
15^0 x 18^0
Sitting Room
Family Room
16^0 x 19^6
13'-5" HIGH CEILING
PASS THRU
Kitchen
RANGE
PLANT SHELF ABOVE
FRENCH DOOR
Bath
LINEN
PLANT SHELF ABOVE
COATS
Laund.
Vaulted M.Bath
W.D.
SHWR.
OPT. DOOR
Foyer
13'-5" HIGH CEILING
Bedroom 3
10^{10} x 11^0
Living Room / Opt. Bedroom 4
11^0 x 12^2
Dining Room
12^1 x 12^0
13'-5" HIGH CEILING
STAIRS UP
STAIRS TO OPT. BSMT.
LINEN
W.i.c.
59'-0"
W.i.c.
COVERED ENTRY
Storage
Garage
21^0 x 21^9
copyright © 1995 frank betz associates, inc.
W.i.c.
Bath
STAIRS DN.
Opt. Bonus
11^0 x 20^0

Optional Second Floor

First Floor 2,193 sq. ft.

Special features

- Master suite has sitting room
- Dining room has decorative columns and overlooks family room
- Kitchen has lots of storage
- Optional bonus room with bath on second floor has an additional 400 square feet of living area
- 3 bedrooms, 3 baths, 2-car side entry garage
- Walk-out basement, crawl space or slab foundation, please specify when ordering

TO ORDER BLUEPRINTS USE THE FORM ON PAGE 15 OR CALL TOLL-FREE 1-877-671-6036

The Family
Handyman

Plan #708-RJ-A26-15

Elegant European Styling

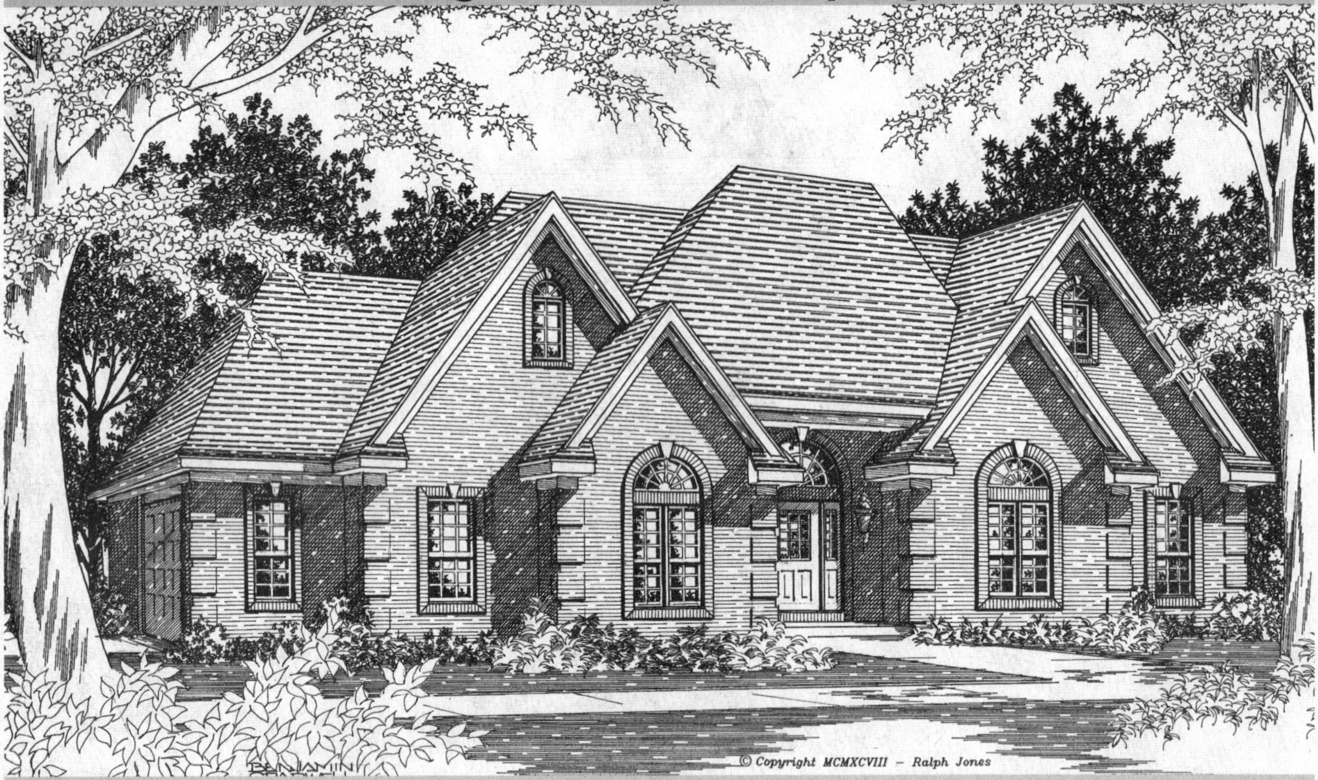

© Copyright MCMXCVIII – Ralph Jones

2,600 total square feet of living area **Price Code E**

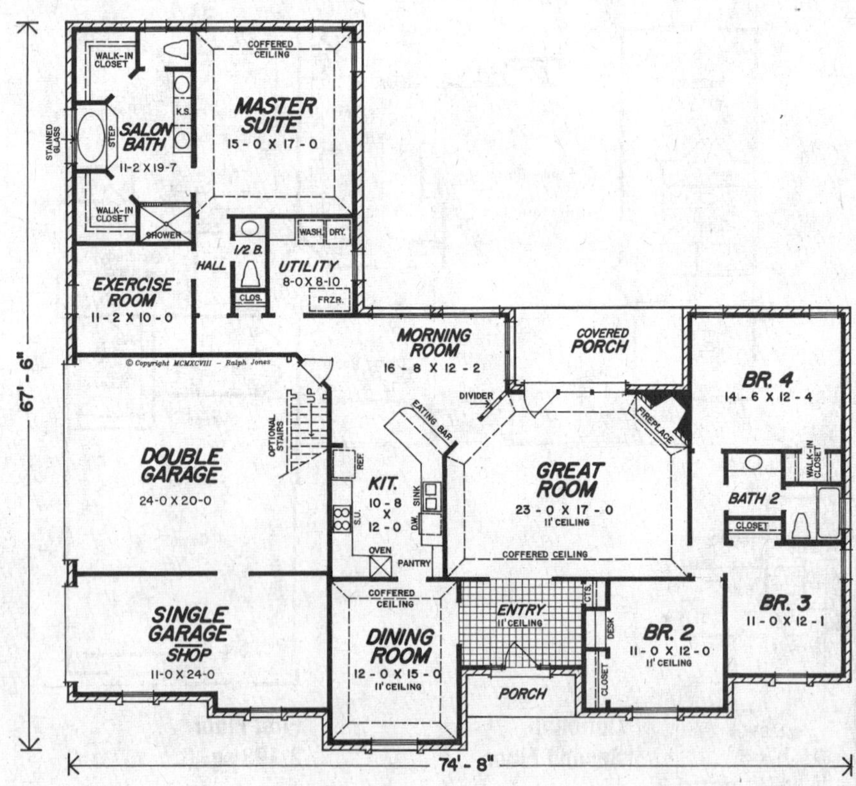
WALK-IN CLOSET
COFFERED CEILING
K.S.
MASTER SUITE
15 - 0 X 17 - 0
STAINED GLASS
STEP
SALON BATH
11-2 X 19-7
WALK-IN CLOSET
SHOWER
WASH DRY
1/2 B.
HALL
UTILITY
8-0 X 8-10
EXERCISE ROOM
11 - 2 X 10 - 0
CLOS.
FRZR.
MORNING ROOM
16 - 8 X 12 - 2
COVERED PORCH
BR. 4
14 - 6 X 12 - 4
© Copyright MCMXCVIII – Ralph Jones
UP
DIVIDER
EATING BAR
FIREPLACE
OPTIONAL STAIRS
DOUBLE GARAGE
24-0 X 20-0
REF.
KIT.
10 - 8 X 12 - 0
SINK
GREAT ROOM
23 - 0 X 17 - 0
11' CEILING
WALK-IN CLOSET
BATH 2
CLOSET
S.O.
D.W.
OVEN
PANTRY
COFFERED CEILING
COFFERED CEILING
ENTRY
11' CEILING
SINGLE GARAGE SHOP
11-0 X 24-0
DINING ROOM
12 - 0 X 15 - 0
11' CEILING
PORCH
DESK
CLOSET
BR. 2
11 - 0 X 12 - 0
11' CEILING
BR. 3
11 - 0 X 12 - 1
67' - 6"
74' - 8"

Special features

- Formal entry has large openings to dining and great rooms both with coffered ceilings
- Great room has coffered ceiling, corner fireplace and atrium doors leading to rear covered porch
- Morning room with rear view and angled eating bar
- Exercise room, or office, or computer room near master suite
- 4 bedrooms, 2 1/2 baths, 3-car side entry garage
- Slab or crawl space foundation, please specify when ordering

Plan #708-DDI-100-218

Charming Country-Style Home

2,995 total square feet of living area

Price Code E

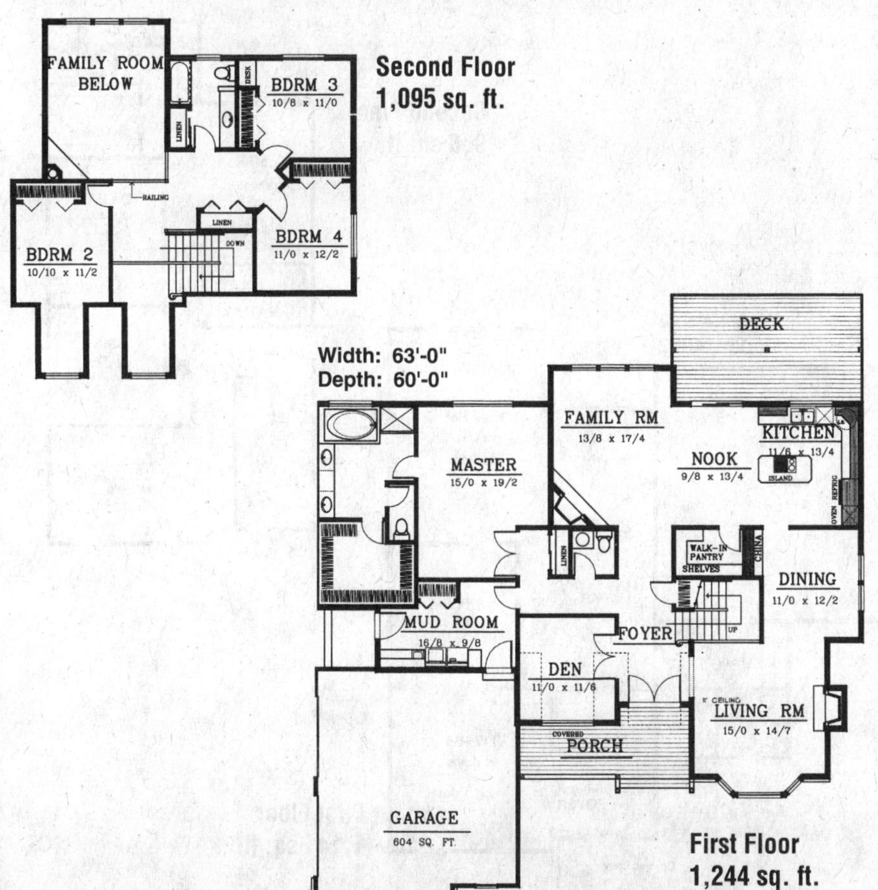
FAMILY ROOM BELOW
BDRM 3
10/8 x 11/0
LINEN
RAILING
LINEN
DOWN
BDRM 4
11/0 x 12/2
BDRM 2
10/10 x 11/2
DECK
FAMILY RM
13/8 x 17/4
KITCHEN
11/6 x 13/4
NOOK
9/8 x 13/4
ISLAND
MASTER
15/0 x 19/2
WALK-IN PANTRY SHELVES
CHINA
DINING
11/0 x 12/2
UP
MUD ROOM
16/8 x 9/8
FOYER
DEN
11/0 x 11/6
LIVING RM
15/0 x 14/7
COVERED PORCH
GARAGE
604 SQ. FT.

Second Floor
1,095 sq. ft.

Width: 63'-0"
Depth: 60'-0"

First Floor
1,244 sq. ft.

Special features

- Large island kitchen is complete with a generous walk-in pantry
- Dining room has built-in china cabinet
- First floor master bedroom offers alternate handicap accessible version
- 4 bedrooms, 2 1/2 baths, 2-car side entry garage
- Crawl space or slab foundation, please specify when ordering

TO ORDER BLUEPRINTS USE THE FORM ON PAGE 15 OR CALL TOLL-FREE 1-877-671-6036

View thousands more home plans online at www.familyhandyman.com/homeplans

Plan #708-JFD-20-2097-1

Comfortable Family Living

2,097 total square feet of living area **Price Code C**

Special features

- Formal living room connects with dining room, perfect for entertaining
- Elegant two-story foyer
- Spacious entry off garage near bath and laundry area
- Family room has cozy fireplace
- 4 bedrooms, 2 1/2 baths, 2-car side entry garage
- Basement foundation

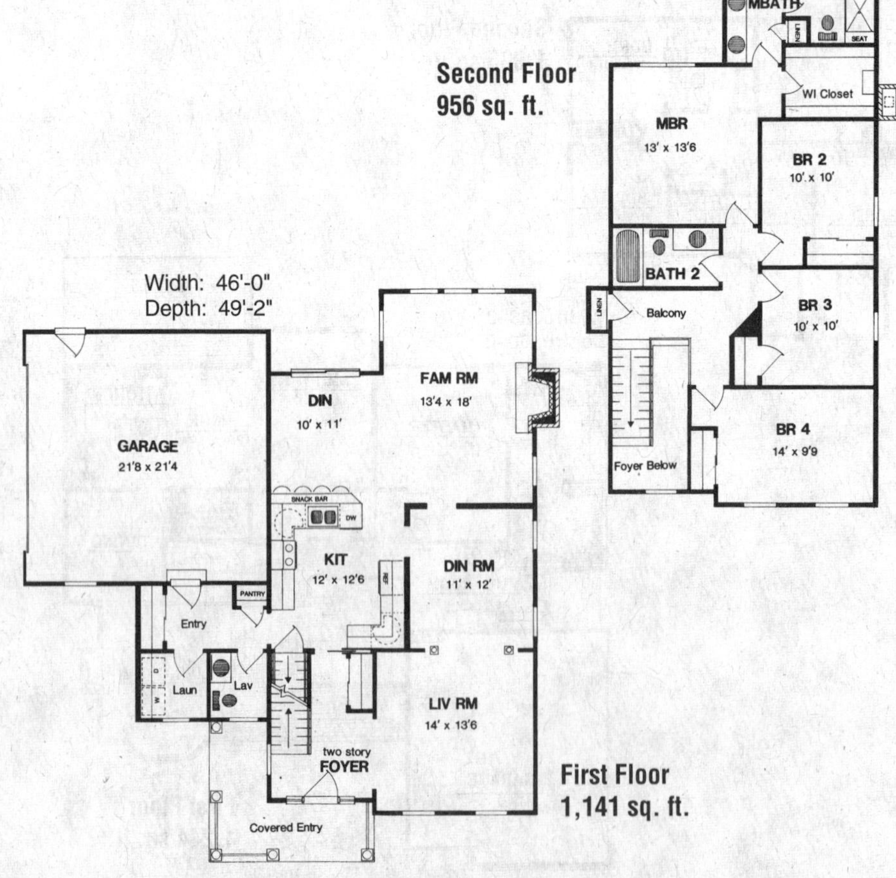

Second Floor
956 sq. ft.
MBATH
WI Closet
MBR
13' x 13'6
BR 2
10' x 10'
BATH 2
Balcony
BR 3
10' x 10'
BR 4
14' x 9'9
Foyer Below
Width: 46'-0"
Depth: 49'-2"
GARAGE
21'8 x 21'4
DIN
10' x 11'
FAM RM
13'4 x 18'
SNACK BAR
KIT
12' x 12'6
DIN RM
11' x 12'
PANTRY
Entry
Laun
Lav
LIV RM
14' x 13'6
two story
FOYER
Covered Entry
First Floor
1,141 sq. ft.

TO ORDER BLUEPRINTS USE THE FORM ON PAGE 15 OR CALL TOLL-FREE 1-877-671-6036

View thousands more home plans online at www.familyhandyman.com/homeplans

The Family
Handyman

Plan #708-0671

Large Windows Grace This Split-Level Home

1,427 total square feet of living area

Price Code A

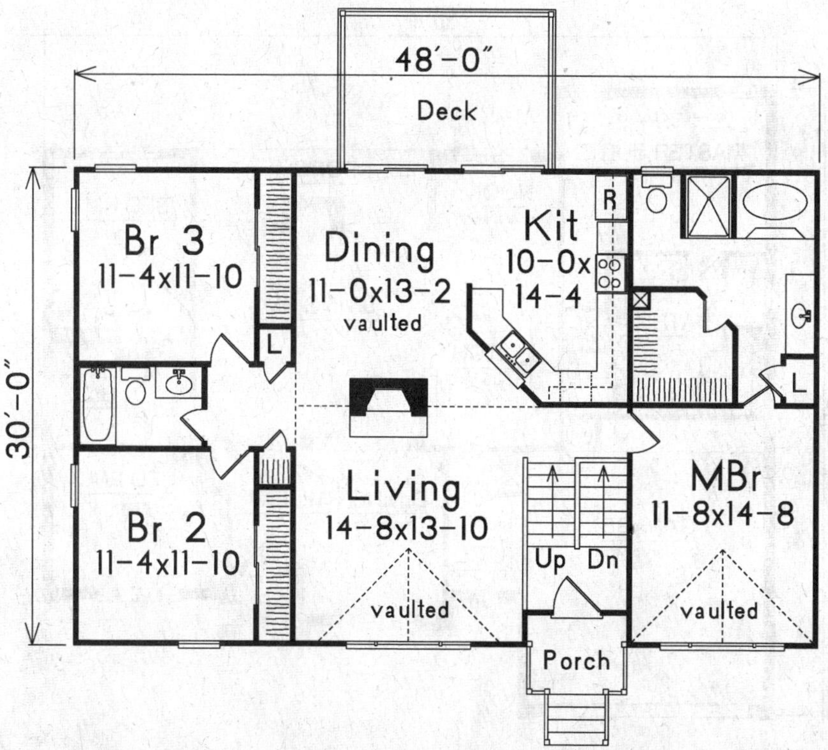
48'-0"
Deck
30'-0"
Br 3
11-4x11-10
Dining
11-0x13-2
vaulted
Kit
10-0x
14-4
R
L
Living
14-8x13-10
vaulted
MBr
11-8x14-8
vaulted
Br 2
11-4x11-10
Up
Dn
Porch

Special features

- Practical storage space situated in the garage
- Convenient laundry closet located on lower level
- Kitchen and dining area both have sliding doors that access the deck
- Large expansive space created by vaulted living and dining rooms
- 3 bedrooms, 2 baths, 2-car drive under garage
- Basement foundation

TO ORDER BLUEPRINTS USE THE FORM ON PAGE 15 OR CALL TOLL-FREE 1-877-671-6036

View thousands more home plans online at www.familyhandyman.com/homeplans

Plan #708-RDD-1791-9

Attractive Styling

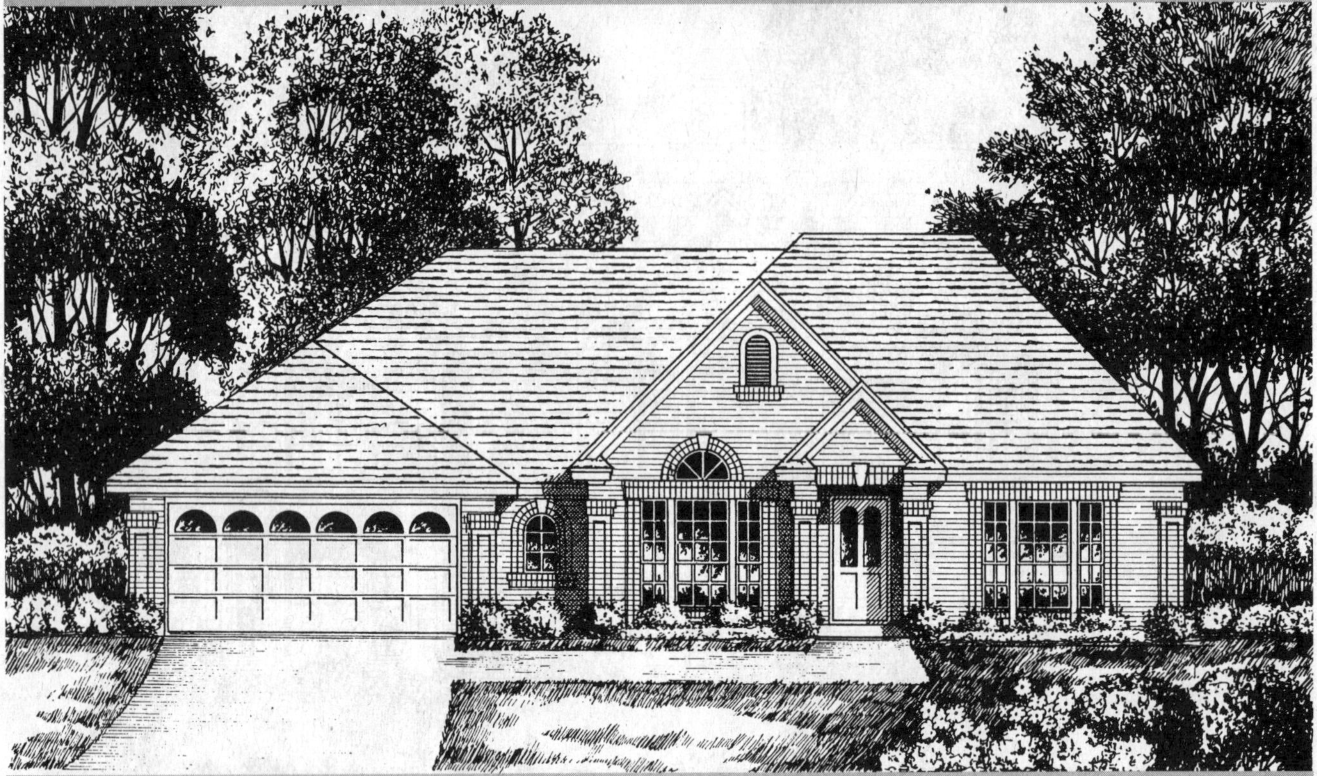

1,791 total square feet of living area **Price Code B**

Special features

- Dining area has 10' high sloped ceiling
- Kitchen opens to large living room with fireplace and access onto a covered porch
- Master suite features private bath, double walk-in closets and whirlpool tub
- 3 bedrooms, 2 baths, 2-car garage
- Slab or crawl space foundation, please specify when ordering

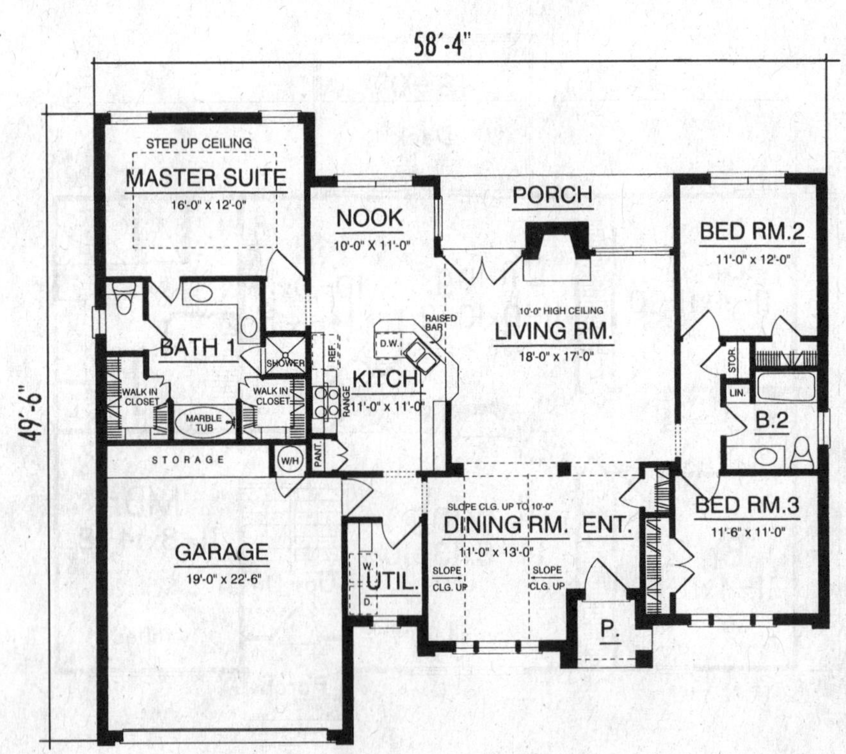

58'-4"
49'-6"
STEP UP CEILING
MASTER SUITE
16'-0" x 12'-0"
NOOK
10'-0" X 11'-0"
PORCH
BED RM.2
11'-0" x 12'-0"
RAISED BAR
D.W.
10'-0" HIGH CEILING
LIVING RM.
18'-0" x 17'-0"
BATH 1
SHOWER
REF.
KITCH
11'-0" x 11'-0"
RANGE
WALK IN CLOSET
WALK IN CLOSET
MARBLE TUB
STOR.
LIN.
B.2
STORAGE
W/H
PANT.
SLOPE CLG. UP TO 10'-0"
DINING RM.
11'-0" x 13'-0"
ENT.
BED RM.3
11'-6" x 11'-0"
GARAGE
19'-0" x 22'-6"
W.
D.
UTIL.
SLOPE CLG. UP
SLOPE CLG. UP
P.

The Family
Handyman

Plan #708-0725

Timeless Country Facade

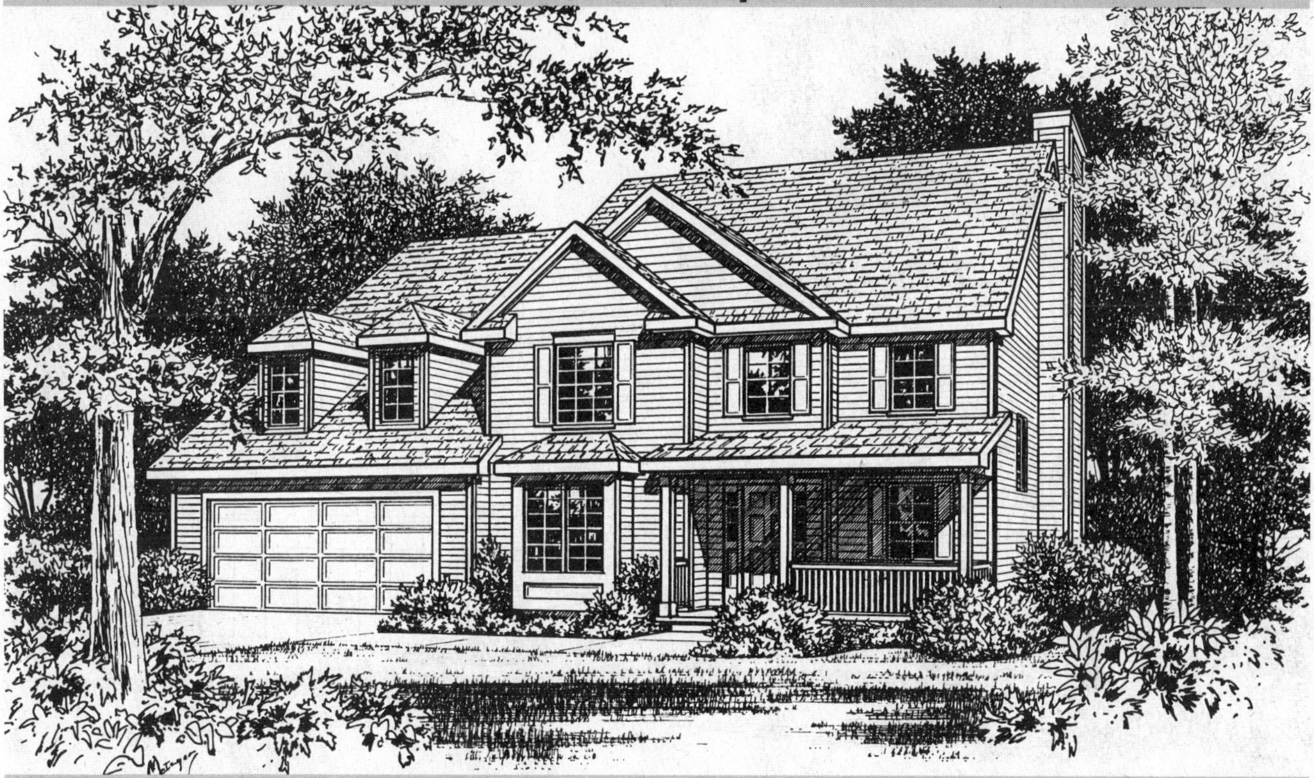

1,977 total square feet of living area | **Price Code C**

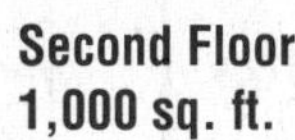

Second Floor
1,000 sq. ft.

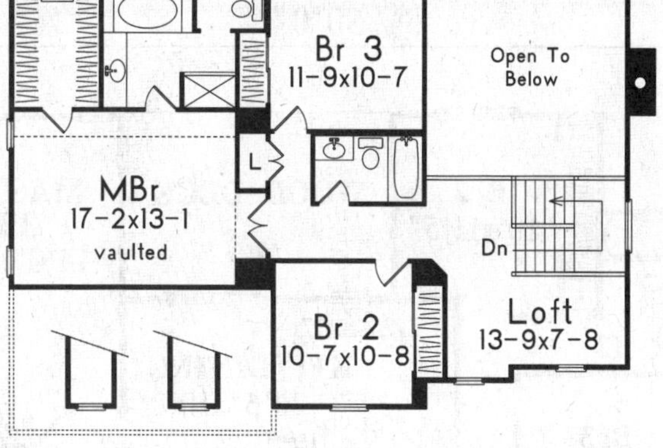
Br 3
11-9x10-7
Open To
Below
L
MBr
17-2x13-1
vaulted
Dn
Br 2
10-7x10-8
Loft
13-9x7-8

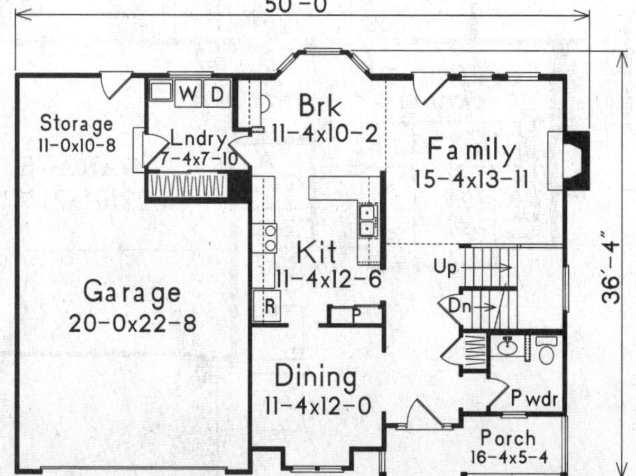
50'-0"
W D
Brk
11-4x10-2
Storage
11-0x10-8
Lndry
7-4x7-10
Family
15-4x13-11
Kit
11-4x12-6
Up
Garage
20-0x22-8
R
P
Dn
36'-4"
Dining
11-4x12-0
Pwdr
Porch
16-4x5-4

First Floor
977 sq. ft.

Special features

- An enormous entry with adjacent dining area and powder room leads to a splendid two-story family room with fireplace
- Kitchen features an abundance of cabinets, built-in pantry and breakfast room with menu desk and bay window
- A spacious vaulted master suite, two secondary bedrooms with bath and loft area adorn the second floor
- 3 bedrooms, 2 1/2 baths, 2-car garage with storage area
- Basement foundation

TO ORDER BLUEPRINTS USE THE FORM ON PAGE 15 OR CALL TOLL-FREE 1-877-671-6036

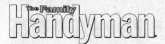

Plan #708-UDG-99003

Traditional Style With Extras

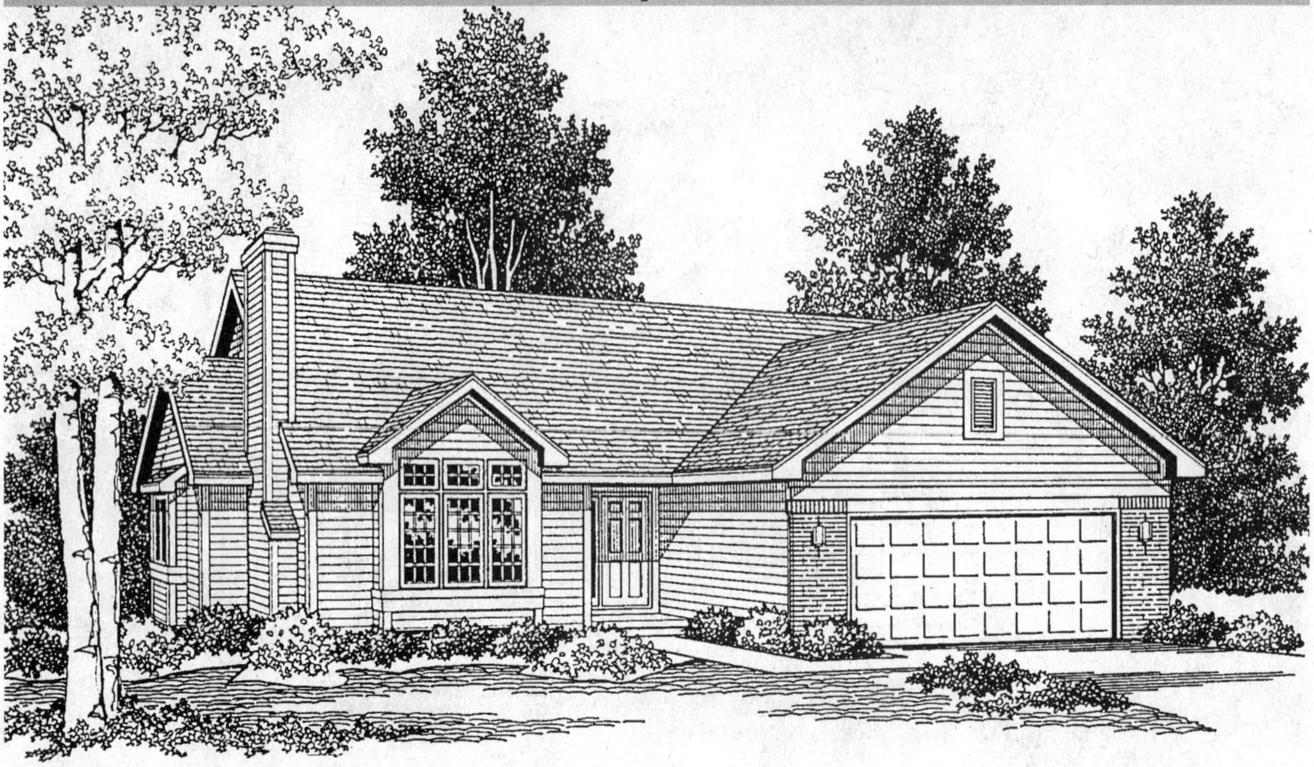

1,425 total square feet of living area | **Price Code A**

Special features

- Living room has very interesting cathedral ceiling
- Secondary bedrooms have plenty of closet space
- Raised eating counter separates kitchen and dining area
- Bedroom #3 has window seat overlooking landscape
- 3 bedrooms, 2 baths, 2-car garage
- Basement foundation

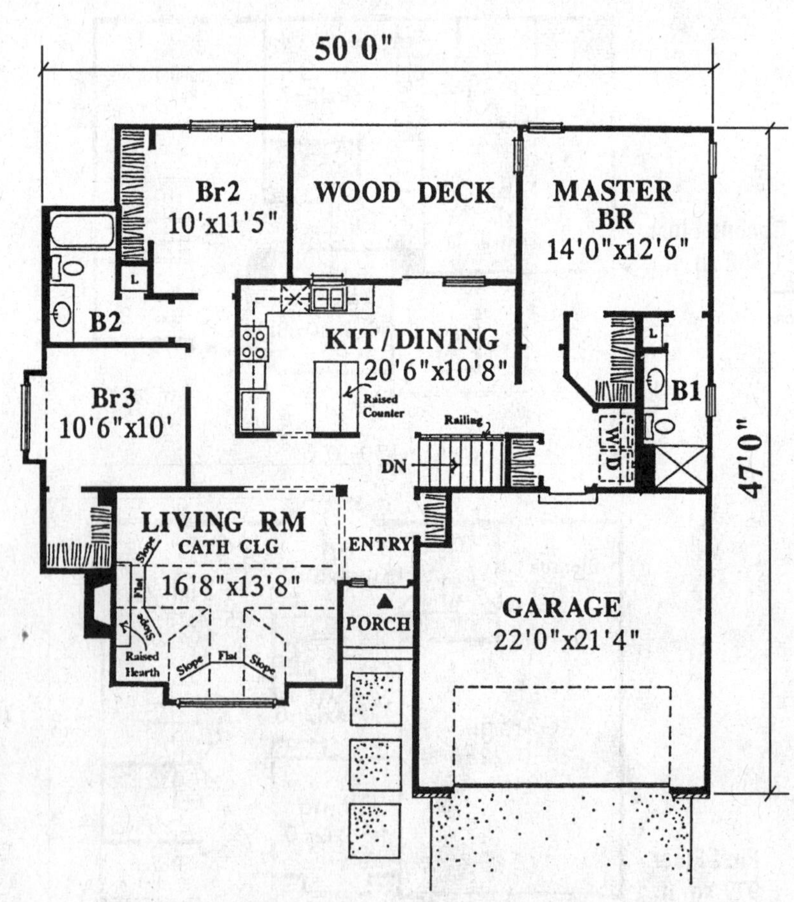
50'0"
47'0"
Br2
10'x11'5"
WOOD DECK
MASTER
BR
14'0"x12'6"
L
B2
KIT/DINING
20'6"x10'8"
Raised Counter
Br3
10'6"x10'
Railing
DN
B1
W D
LIVING RM
CATH CLG
16'8"x13'8"
ENTRY
PORCH
Slope
Flat
Raised Hearth
GARAGE
22'0"x21'4"

Plan #708-LBD-25-22A

Striking Great Room

COPYRIGHT LARRY E. BELK

2,586 total square feet of living area | **Price Code D**

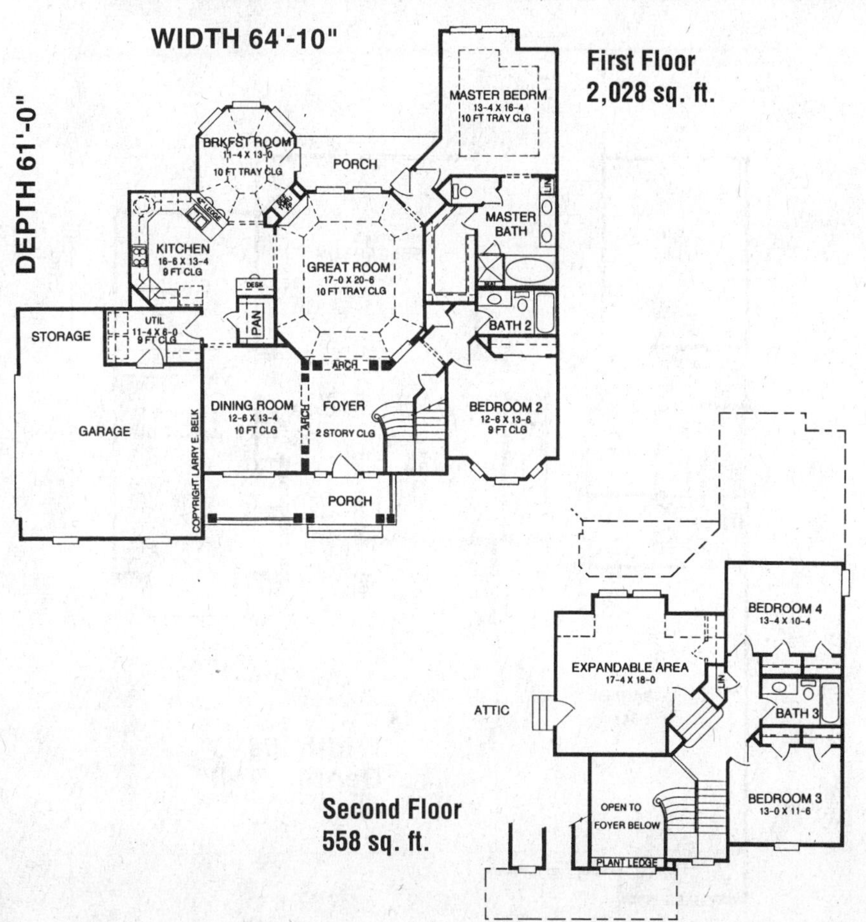
WIDTH 64'-10"
DEPTH 61'-0"
MASTER BEDRM
13-4 X 16-4
10 FT TRAY CLG
BRKFST ROOM
11-4 X 13-0
10 FT TRAY CLG
PORCH
MASTER BATH
KITCHEN
16-6 X 13-4
9 FT CLG
GREAT ROOM
17-0 X 20-6
10 FT TRAY CLG
DESK
PAN
UTIL
11-4 X 6-0
9 FT CLG
STORAGE
BATH 2
ARCH
GARAGE
DINING ROOM
12-6 X 13-4
10 FT CLG
FOYER
2 STORY CLG
BEDROOM 2
12-6 X 13-6
9 FT CLG
PORCH
COPYRIGHT LARRY E. BELK
BEDROOM 4
13-4 X 10-4
EXPANDABLE AREA
17-4 X 18-0
ATTIC
BATH 3
OPEN TO
FOYER BELOW
BEDROOM 3
13-0 X 11-6
PLANT LEDGE

First Floor
2,028 sq. ft.

Second Floor
558 sq. ft.

Special features

- Great room has impressive tray ceiling and see-through fire-place into bayed breakfast room
- Master bedroom has walk-in closet and private bath
- 4 bedrooms, 3 baths, 2-car side entry garage
- Basement, crawl space or slab foundation, please specify when ordering

TO ORDER BLUEPRINTS USE THE FORM ON PAGE 15 OR CALL TOLL-FREE 1-877-671-6036

View thousands more home plans online at www.familyhandyman.com/homeplans

Plan #708-JFD-10-2178-2

Appealing Facade

2,178 total square feet of living area **Price Code C**

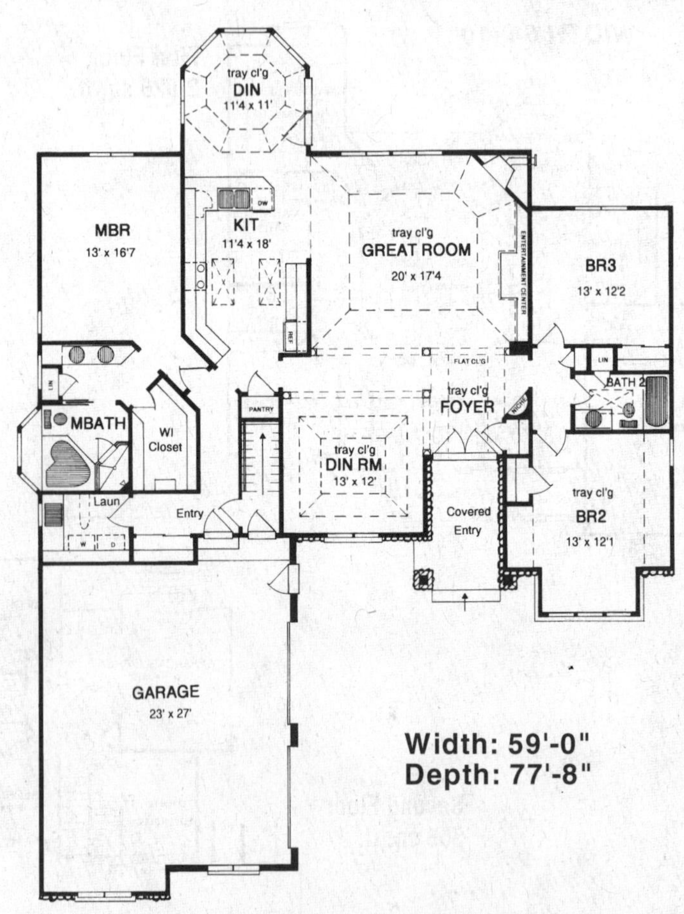

tray cl'g
DIN
11'4 x 11'
KIT
11'4 x 18'
MBR
13' x 16'7
tray cl'g
GREAT ROOM
20' x 17'4
ENTERTAINMENT CENTER
BR3
13' x 12'2
FLAT CL'G
tray cl'g
FOYER
BATH 2
MBATH
WI
Closet
PANTRY
tray cl'g
DIN RM
13' x 12'
Covered
Entry
tray cl'g
BR2
13' x 12'1
Laun
Entry
GARAGE
23' x 27'

Width: 59'-0"
Depth: 77'-8"

Special features

- Large foyer leads to a sunny great room with corner fireplace and expansive entertainment center
- Kitchen and dining area are efficiently designed
- Master bedroom has private bath with step-up tub and a bay window
- 3 bedrooms, 2 baths, 2-car side entry garage
- Basement foundation

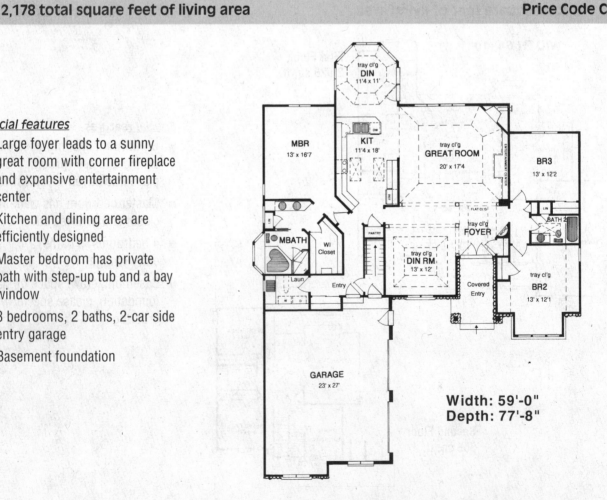

TO ORDER BLUEPRINTS USE THE FORM ON PAGE 15 OR CALL TOLL-FREE 1-877-671-6036

View thousands more home plans online at www.familyhandyman.com/homeplans

The Family
Handyman

Plan #708-0676

Comfortable One-Story Country Home

1,367 total square feet of living area

Price Code B

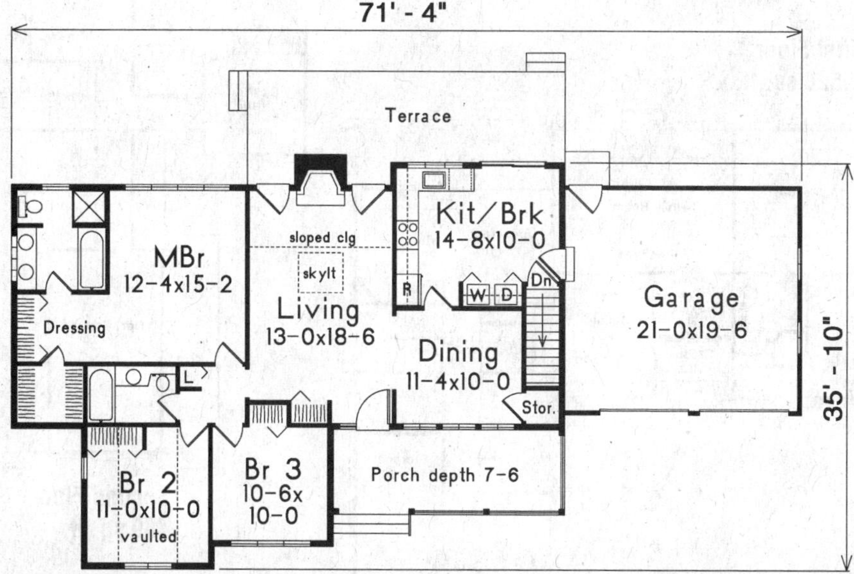
71' - 4"
Terrace
MBr
12-4x15-2
Dressing
sloped clg
skylt
Living
13-0x18-6
Kit/Brk
14-8x10-0
R
W
D
Dn
Dining
11-4x10-0
Garage
21-0x19-6
Stor.
L
Br 2
11-0x10-0
vaulted
Br 3
10-6x
10-0
Porch depth 7-6
35' - 10"

Special features

- Neat front porch shelters the entrance
- Dining room has full wall of windows and a convenient storage area
- Breakfast area leads to the rear terrace through sliding doors
- Large living room with high ceiling, skylight and fireplace
- 3 bedrooms, 2 baths, 2-car garage
- Basement foundation, drawings also include slab foundation

TO ORDER BLUEPRINTS USE THE FORM ON PAGE 15 OR CALL TOLL-FREE 1-877-671-6036

View thousands more home plans online at www.familyhandyman.com/homeplans

The Family
Handyman

Plan #708-GM-2009

Optional Bonus Room Above Garage

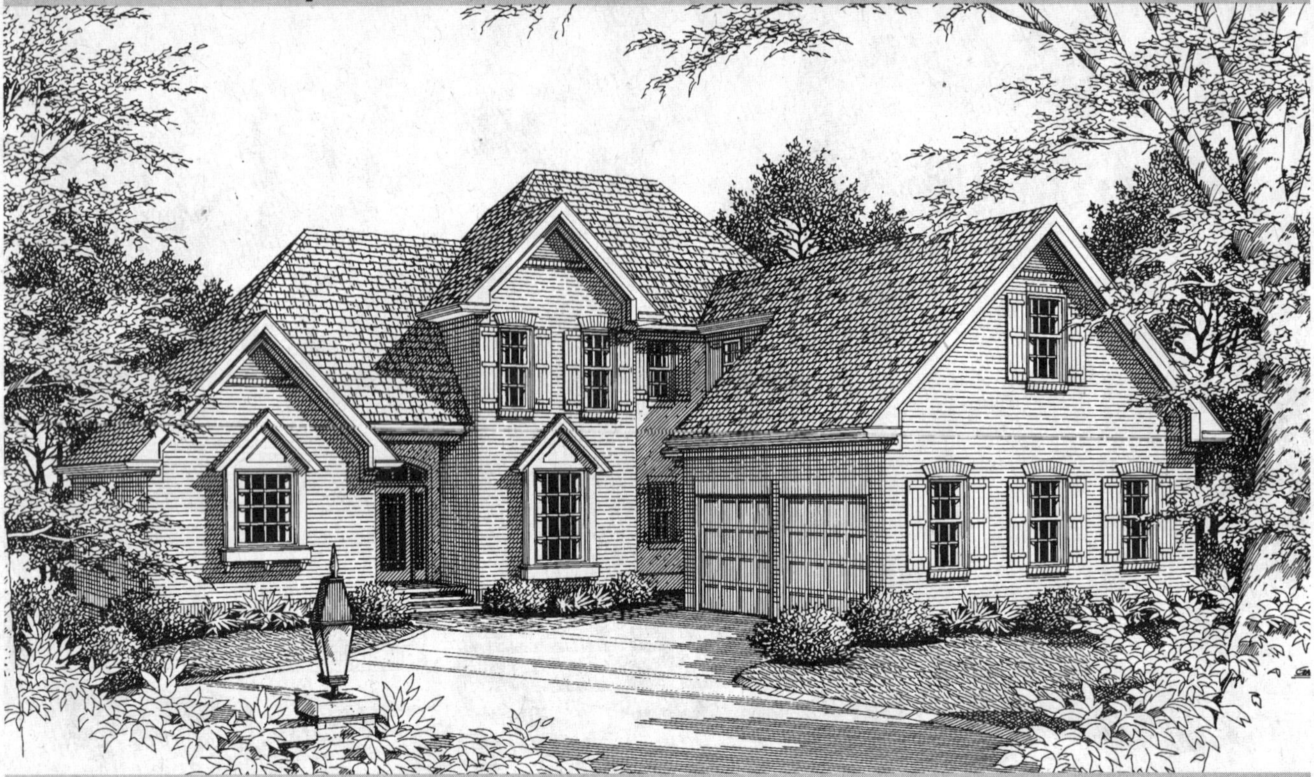

2,009 total square feet of living area

Price Code C

Special features

- Enter home and find large family room with fireplace flanked by double windows
- Cheerful breakfast area has access to skylighted porch
- Elegant dining area includes a built-in china cabinet
- 3 bedrooms, 2 baths, 2-car side entry garage
- Basement foundation

First Floor
1,520 sq. ft.

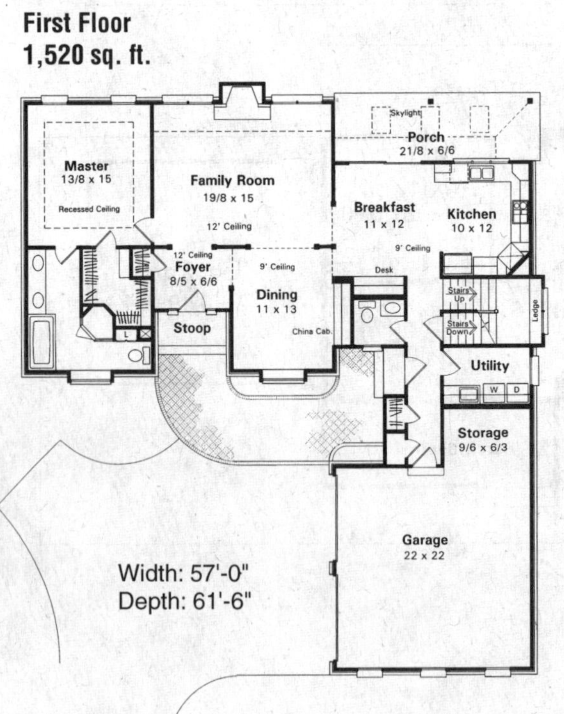
Skylight
Porch
21/8 x 6/6
Master
13/8 x 15
Recessed Ceiling
Family Room
19/8 x 15
12' Ceiling
Breakfast
11 x 12
Kitchen
10 x 12
9' Ceiling
12' Ceiling
Foyer
8/5 x 6/6
9' Ceiling
Dining
11 x 13
China Cab.
Desk
Stairs Up
Stairs Down
Ledge
Stoop
Utility
W D
Storage
9/6 x 6/3
Garage
22 x 22
Width: 57'-0"
Depth: 61'-6"

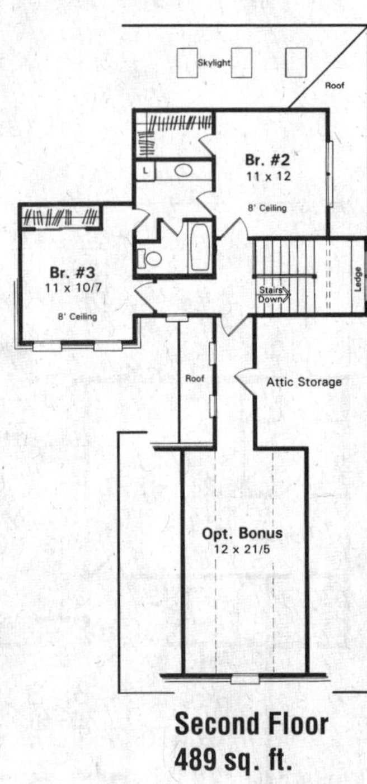
Skylight
Roof
Br. #2
11 x 12
8' Ceiling
Br. #3
11 x 10/7
8' Ceiling
Stairs Down
Ledge
Roof
Attic Storage
Opt. Bonus
12 x 21/5

Second Floor
489 sq. ft.

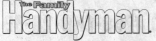

Comfortable Family Living In This Ranch

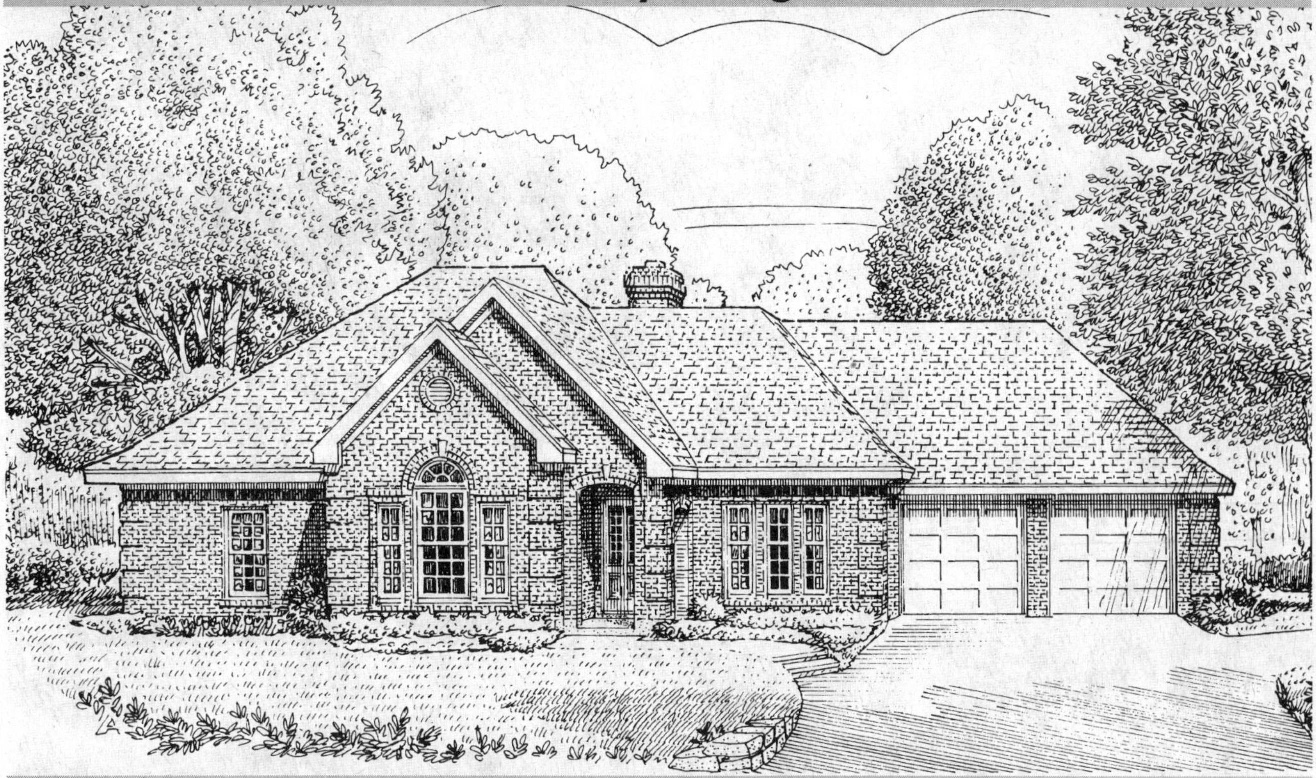

1,994 total square feet of living area **Price Code D**

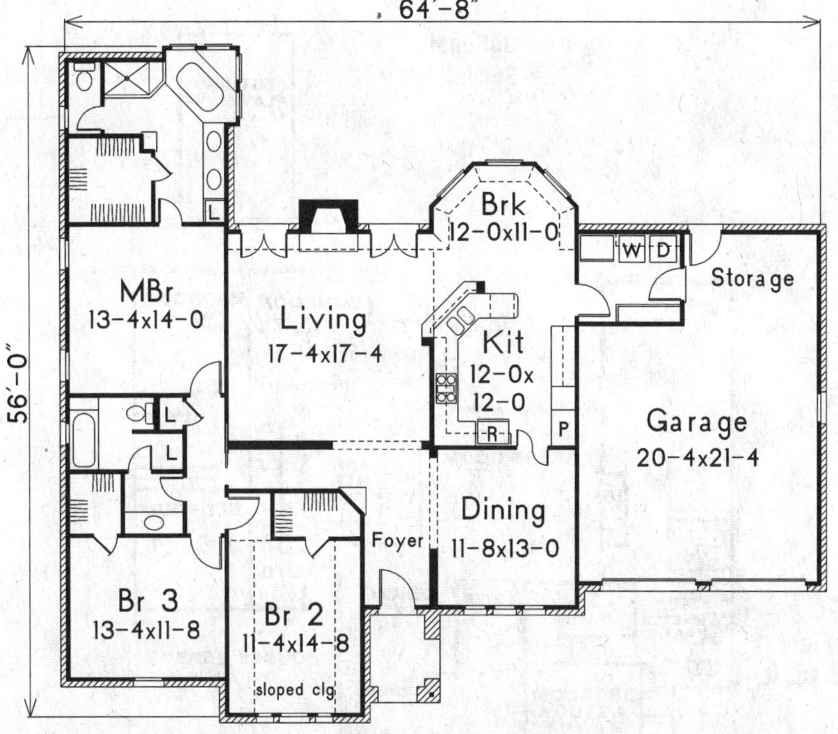
64'-8"
56'-0"
Brk
12-0x11-0
W
D
Storage
MBr
13-4x14-0
Living
17-4x17-4
Kit
12-0x
12-0
Garage
20-4x21-4
L
L
L
R
P
Dining
11-8x13-0
Foyer
Br 3
13-4x11-8
Br 2
11-4x14-8
sloped clg

Special features

- Convenient entrance from the garage into the main living area through the utility room
- Standard 9' ceilings, bedroom #2 features a 12' vaulted ceiling and a 10' ceiling in the dining room
- Master bedroom offers a full bath with oversized tub, separate shower and walk-in closet
- Entry leads to formal dining room and attractive living room with double French doors and fireplace
- 3 bedrooms, 2 baths, 2-car garage
- Slab foundation

Great Curb Appeal With Gables

2,526 total square feet of living area

Price Code D

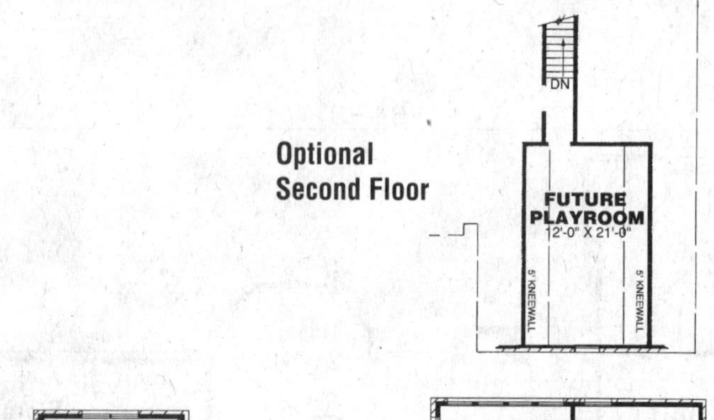
DN
FUTURE
PLAYROOM
12'-0" X 21'-0"
5' KNEEWALL
5' KNEEWALL

Optional
Second Floor

Special features

- Sunroom brightens dining areas near kitchen
- Corner whirlpool tub in master bath is a luxurious touch
- Future playroom on the second floor has an additional 341 square feet of living area
- 4 bedrooms, 3 baths, 2-car side entry garage
- Crawl space or slab foundation, please specify when ordering

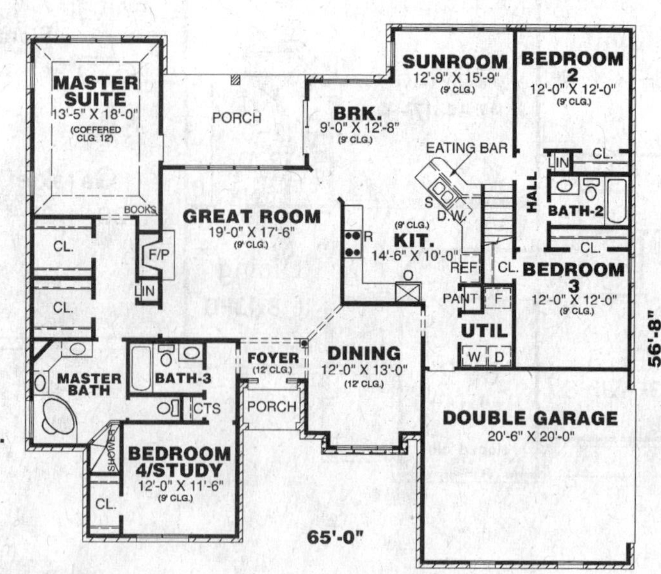
MASTER
SUITE
13'-5" X 18'-0"
(COFFERED
CLG. 12')
PORCH
BRK.
9'-0" X 12'-8"
(9' CLG.)
SUNROOM
12'-9" X 15'-9"
(9' CLG.)
BEDROOM
2
12'-0" X 12'-0"
(9' CLG.)
EATING BAR
LIN
CL.
HALL
BATH-2
BOOKS
GREAT ROOM
19'-0" X 17'-6"
(9' CLG.)
CL.
F/P
LIN
R
(9' CLG.)
KIT.
14'-6" X 10'-0"
S
D.W.
O
REF.
CL.
BEDROOM
3
12'-0" X 12'-0"
(9' CLG.)
PANT
F
UTIL
W
D
CL.
CL.
MASTER
BATH
BATH-3
CTS
FOYER
(12' CLG.)
PORCH
DINING
12'-0" X 13'-0"
(12' CLG.)
DOUBLE GARAGE
20'-6" X 20'-0"
56'-8"
SHOWER
BEDROOM
4/STUDY
12'-0" X 11'-6"
(9' CLG.)
CL.
65'-0"

First Floor
2,526 sq. ft.

TO ORDER BLUEPRINTS USE THE FORM ON PAGE 15 OR CALL TOLL-FREE 1-877-671-6036

View thousands more home plans online at www.familyhandyman.com/homeplans

The Family
Handyman

Plan #708-0691

Stylish Two-Story Provides Room For Large Family

2,730 total square feet of living area **Price Code E**

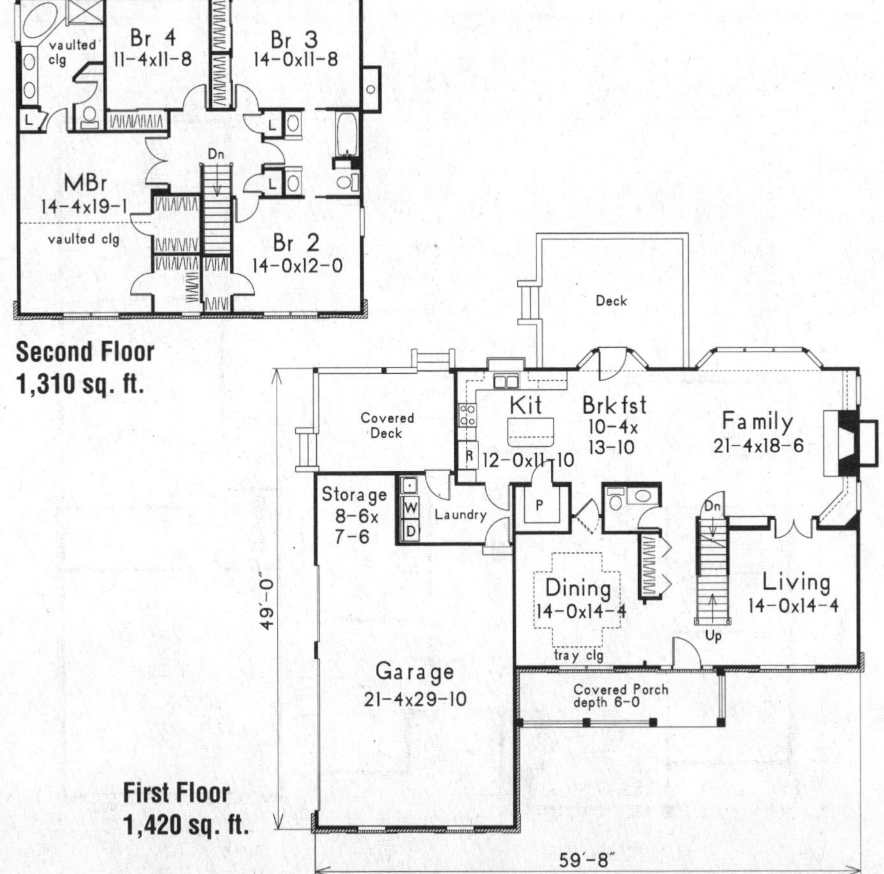

vaulted clg
Br 4
11-4x11-8
Br 3
14-0x11-8
L
Dn
MBr
14-4x19-1
vaulted clg
Br 2
14-0x12-0
Second Floor
1,310 sq. ft.
Deck
Covered Deck
Kit
12-0x11-10
R
Brkfst
10-4x
13-10
Family
21-4x18-6
Storage
8-6x
7-6
W
D
Laundry
P
Dn
Dining
14-0x14-4
tray clg
Up
Living
14-0x14-4
49'-0"
Garage
21-4x29-10
Covered Porch
depth 6-0
First Floor
1,420 sq. ft.
59'-8"

Special features

- Spacious kitchen features island and generous walk-in pantry
- Covered deck offers private retreat to the outdoors
- Large master bedroom has bath with whirlpool corner tub, separate shower and double walk-in closets
- Oversized laundry room conveniently located off kitchen
- 4 bedrooms, 2 1/2 baths, 3-car side entry garage with storage area
- Basement foundation

TO ORDER BLUEPRINTS USE THE FORM ON PAGE 15 OR CALL TOLL-FREE 1-877-671-6036

View thousands more home plans online at www.familyhandyman.com/homeplans

The Family
Handyman

Plan #708-0407

Terrific Master Suite Provides Escape

2,517 total square feet of living area **Price Code D**

Special features

- Energy efficient home with 2" x 6" exterior walls
- Central living room with large windows and attractive transoms
- Varied ceiling heights throughout home
- Secluded master suite features double-door entry, luxurious bath with separate shower, step-up whirlpool tub, double vanities and walk-in closets
- Kitchen with walk-in pantry overlooks large family room with fireplace and unique octagon-shaped breakfast room
- 4 bedrooms, 2 1/2 baths, 2-car garage
- Slab foundation, drawings also include crawl space foundation

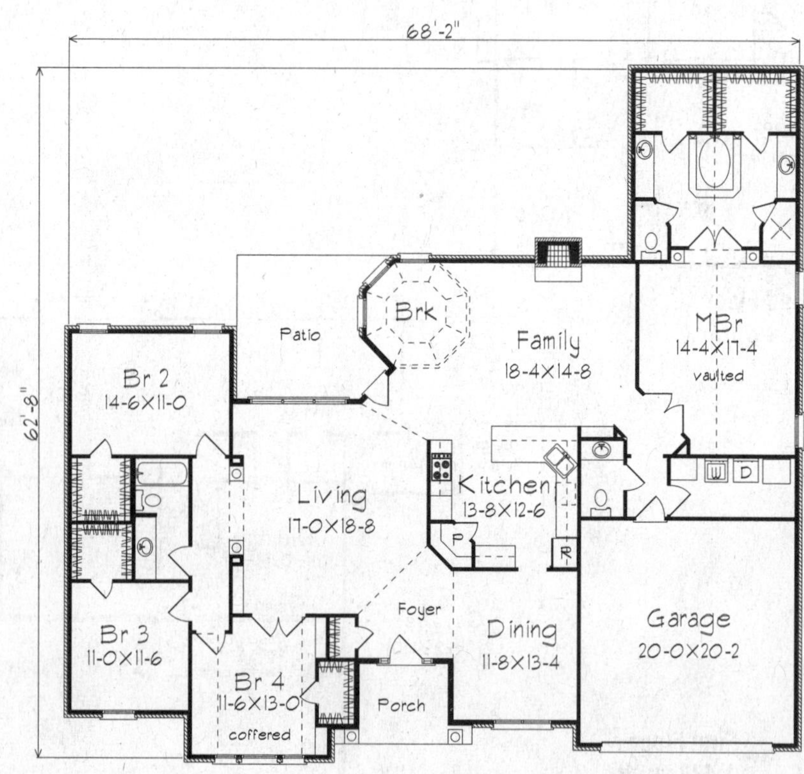
68'-2"
62'-8"
Brk
Patio
Family
18-4X14-8
MBr
14-4X17-4
vaulted
Br 2
14-6X11-0
Living
17-0X18-8
Kitchen
13-8X12-6
P
R
W
D
Foyer
Dining
11-8X13-4
Garage
20-0X20-2
Br 3
11-0X11-6
Br 4
11-6X13-0
coffered
Porch

TO ORDER BLUEPRINTS USE THE FORM ON PAGE 15 OR CALL TOLL-FREE 1-877-671-6036

View thousands more home plans online at www.familyhandyman.com/homeplans

Plan #708-0668

Efficient Layout In This Multi-Level Home

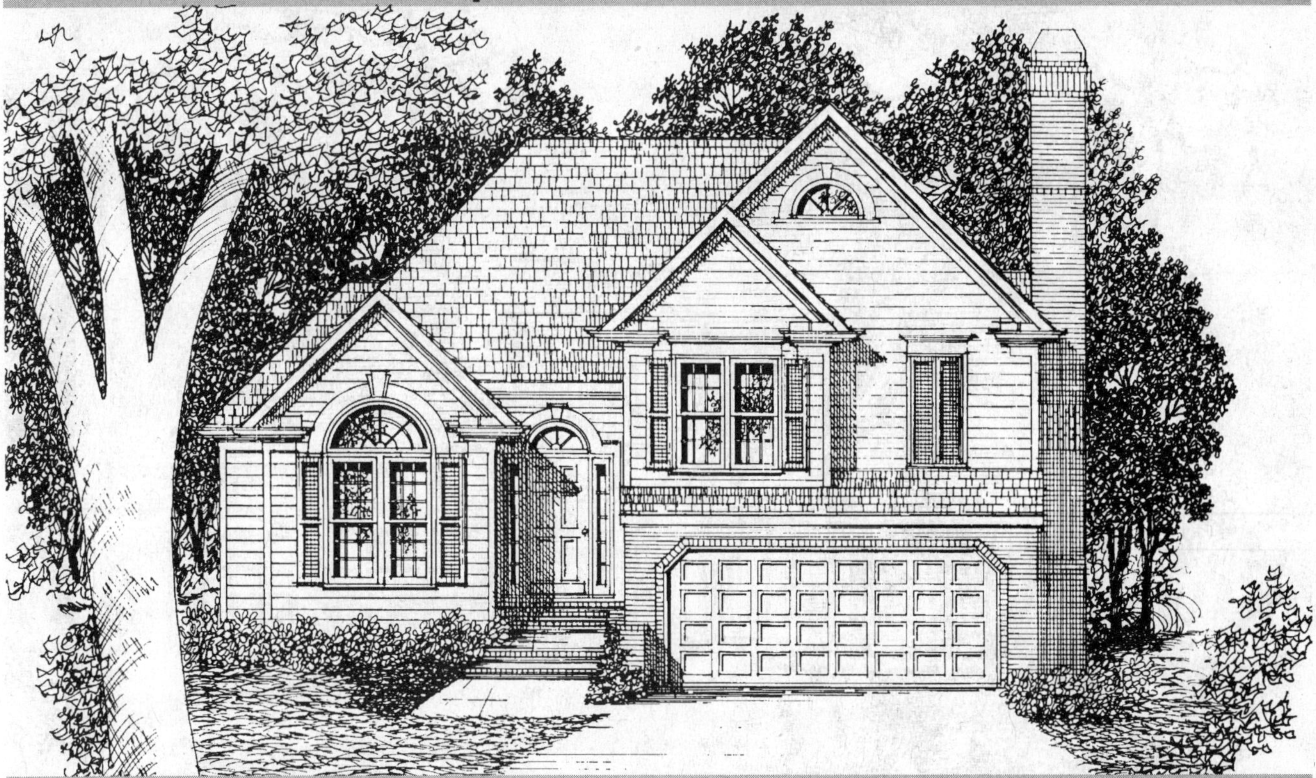

1,617 total square feet of living area

Price Code B

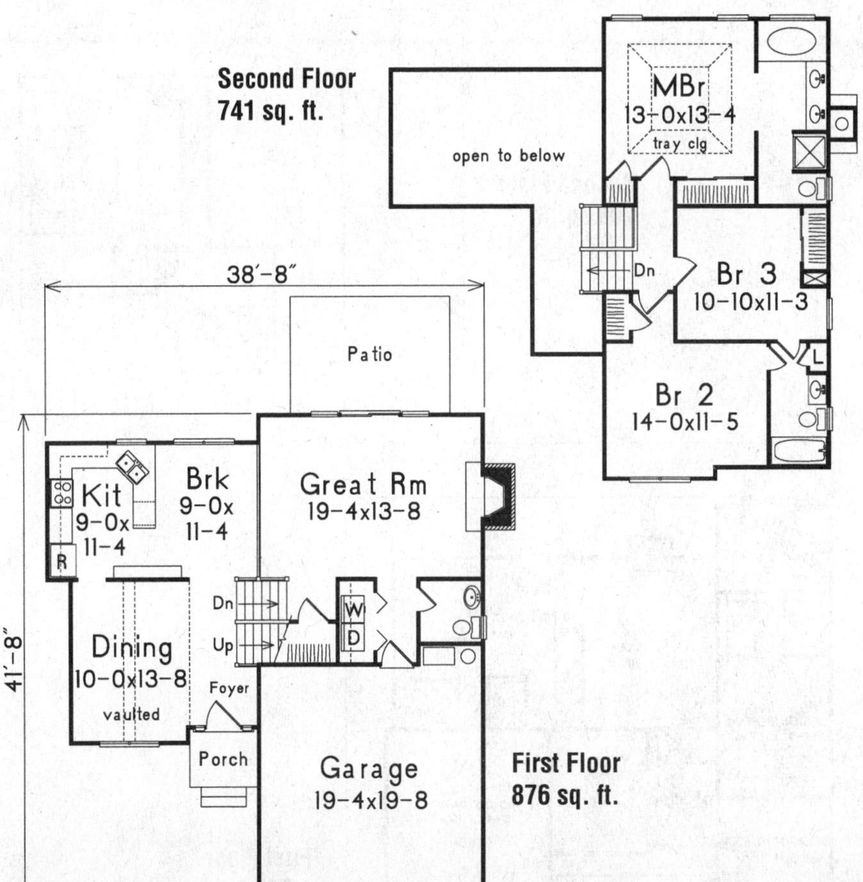

Second Floor
741 sq. ft.
open to below
MBr
13-0x13-4
tray clg
Dn
Br 3
10-10x11-3
Br 2
14-0x11-5
L
38'-8"
Patio
41'-8"
Kit
9-0x
11-4
Brk
9-0x
11-4
R
Great Rm
19-4x13-8
Dn
Up
W
D
Dining
10-0x13-8
vaulted
Foyer
Porch
Garage
19-4x19-8
First Floor
876 sq. ft.

Special features

- Kitchen and breakfast area overlook great room with fireplace
- Formal dining room features vaulted ceiling and elegant circle-top window
- All bedrooms are located on the second floor for privacy
- 3 bedrooms, 2 1/2 baths, 2-car garage
- Partial crawl space/slab foundation

The Family
Handyman

Plan #708-MG-96132

Windows Add Plenty Of Light

2,450 total square feet of living area | **Price Code D**

Special features

- Convenient first floor master bedroom has double walk-in closets and an study/living room attached
- Two-story breakfast and grand room are open and airy
- Laundry room has a sink and overhead cabinets for convenience
- 4 bedrooms, 2 1/2 baths, 2-car garage
- Basement or slab foundation, please specify when ordering

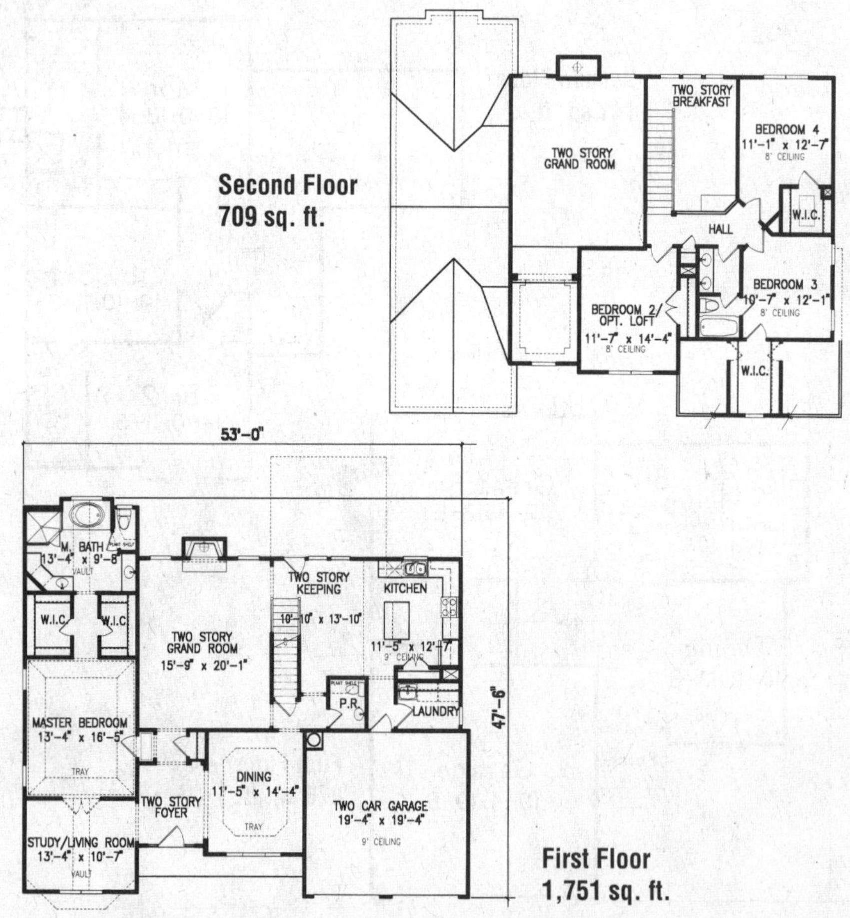
TWO STORY BREAKFAST
BEDROOM 4
11'-1" x 12'-7"
8' CEILING
TWO STORY GRAND ROOM
W.I.C.
HALL
BEDROOM 3
10'-7" x 12'-1"
8' CEILING
BEDROOM 2/ OPT. LOFT
11'-7" x 14'-4"
8' CEILING
W.I.C.
53'-0"
M. BATH
13'-4" x 9'-8"
VAULT
W.I.C.
W.I.C.
TWO STORY KEEPING
10'-10" x 13'-10"
KITCHEN
11'-5" x 12'-7"
9' CEILING
TWO STORY GRAND ROOM
15'-9" x 20'-1"
P.R.
LAUNDRY
47'-6"
MASTER BEDROOM
13'-4" x 16'-5"
TRAY
DINING
11'-5" x 14'-4"
TRAY
TWO STORY FOYER
TWO CAR GARAGE
19'-4" x 19'-4"
9' CEILING
STUDY/LIVING ROOM
13'-4" x 10'-7"
VAULT

Second Floor
709 sq. ft.

First Floor
1,751 sq. ft.

TO ORDER BLUEPRINTS USE THE FORM ON PAGE 15 OR CALL TOLL-FREE 1-877-671-6036

View thousands more home plans online at www.familyhandyman.com/homeplans

The Family
Handyman

Plan #708-JV-2726-A

Large Bay Windows Accent Traditional Look

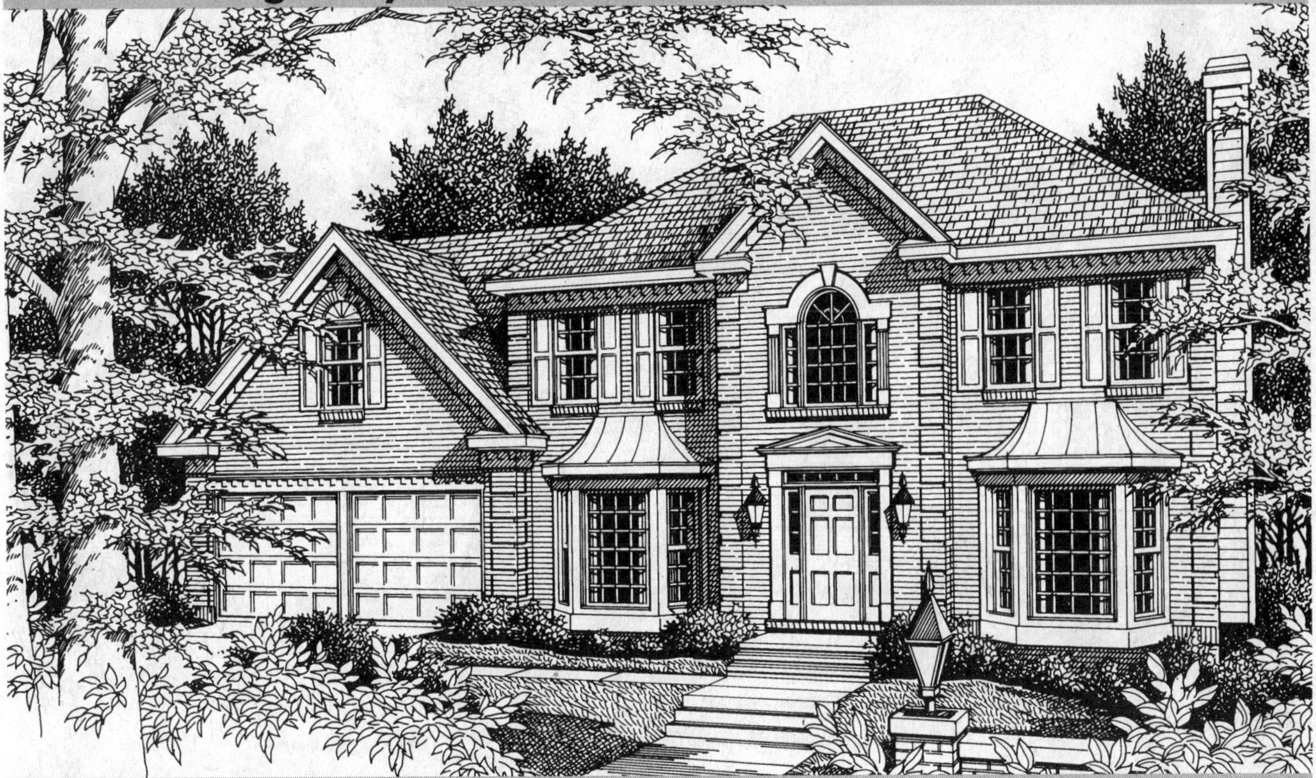

2,726 total square feet of living area

Price Code E

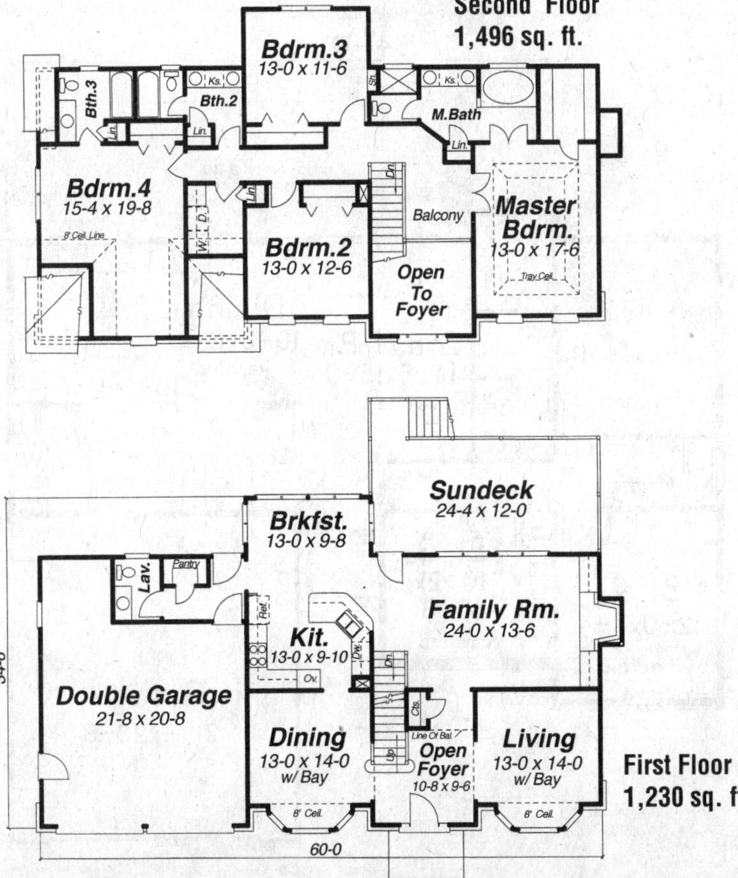
Second Floor
1,496 sq. ft.
Bdrm.3
13-0 x 11-6
Bth.3
Bth.2
M.Bath
Bdrm.4
15-4 x 19-8
Bdrm.2
13-0 x 12-6
Balcony
Open
To
Foyer
Master
Bdrm.
13-0 x 17-6
Sundeck
24-4 x 12-0
Brkfst.
13-0 x 9-8
Lav.
Pantry
Family Rm.
24-0 x 13-6
Kit.
13-0 x 9-10
Double Garage
21-8 x 20-8
34-6
Dining
13-0 x 14-0
w/ Bay
Open
Foyer
10-8 x 9-6
Living
13-0 x 14-0
w/ Bay
60-0
First Floor
1,230 sq. ft.

Special features

- French doors access master bedroom and bath
- Large family room has a fireplace, built-in bookshelves and has access to sundeck
- Large bedroom #4 has a private bath perfect for an in-law suite
- Convenient laundry room located on the second floor
- 4 bedrooms, 3 1/2 baths, 2-car garage
- Basement, crawl space or slab foundation, please specify when ordering

TO ORDER BLUEPRINTS USE THE FORM ON PAGE 15 OR CALL TOLL-FREE 1-877-671-6036

Plan #708-0267

High-Style Vaulted Ranch

1,453 total square feet of living area **Price Code A**

Special features

- Decorative vents, window trim, shutters and brick blend to create dramatic curb appeal
- Energy efficient home with 2" x 6" exterior walls
- Kitchen opens to living area and includes salad sink in the island, pantry and handy laundry room
- Exquisite master bedroom highlighted by vaulted ceiling
- Dressing area with walk-in closet, private bath and spa tub/shower
- 3 bedrooms, 2 baths, 2-car garage
- Basement foundation, drawings also include crawl space foundation

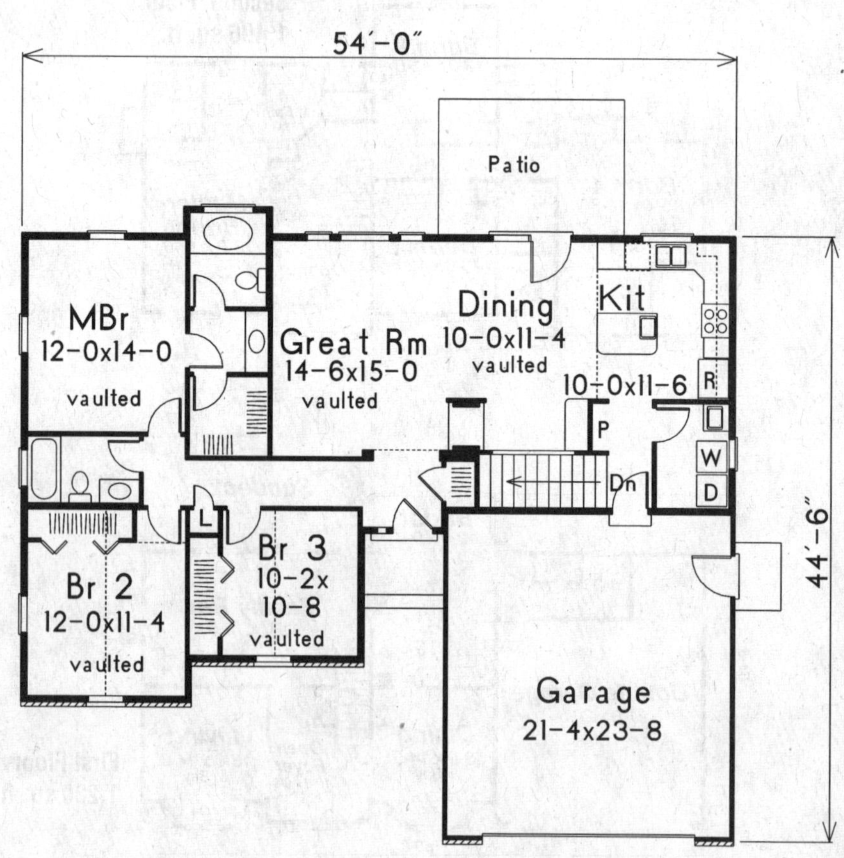
54'-0"
44'-6"
Patio
MBr
12-0x14-0
vaulted
Great Rm
14-6x15-0
vaulted
Dining
10-0x11-4
vaulted
Kit
10-0x11-6
R
P
W
D
Dn
L
Br 2
12-0x11-4
vaulted
Br 3
10-2x
10-8
vaulted
Garage
21-4x23-8

TO ORDER BLUEPRINTS USE THE FORM ON PAGE 15 OR CALL TOLL-FREE 1-877-671-6036
View thousands more home plans online at www.familyhandyman.com/homeplans

The Family
Handyman

Plan #708-0364

Traditional Exterior Boasts Exciting Interior

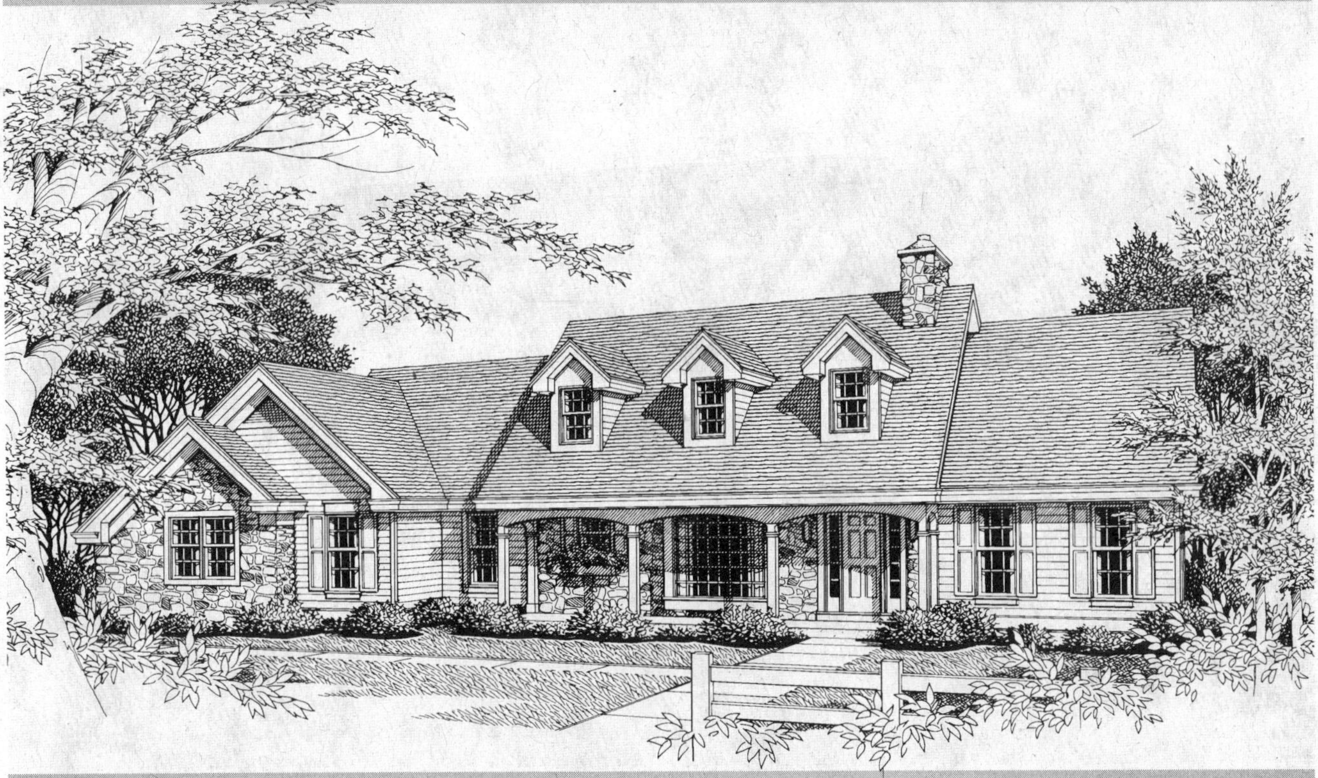

2,531 total square feet of living area **Price Code D**

Rear View

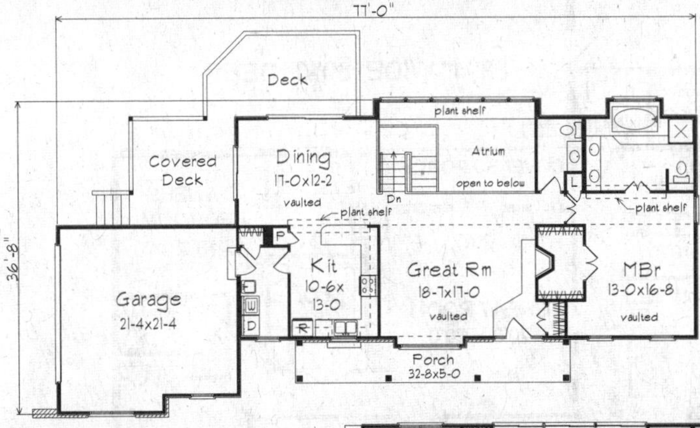
77'-0"
36'-8"
Deck
Covered Deck
Dining
17-0x12-2
vaulted
plant shelf
Atrium
open to below
Dn
plant shelf
Kit
10-6x
13-0
Great Rm
18-7x17-0
vaulted
MBr
13-0x16-8
vaulted
Garage
21-4x21-4
Porch
32-8x5-0

First Floor
1,297 sq. ft.

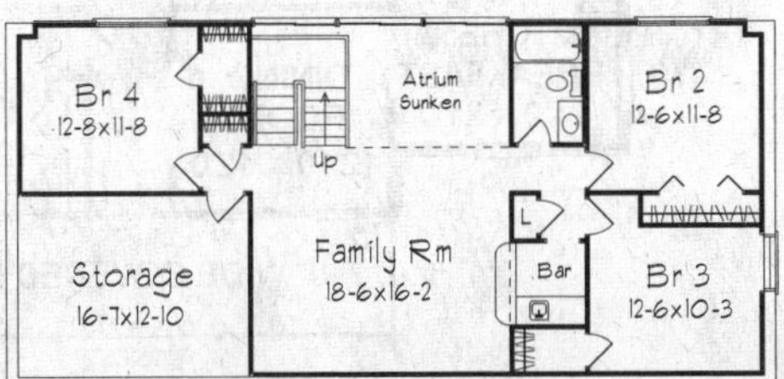
Br 4
12-8x11-8
Atrium
Sunken
Br 2
12-6x11-8
Up
Storage
16-7x12-10
Family Rm
18-6x16-2
Bar
Br 3
12-6x10-3

Lower Level
1,234 sq. ft.

Special features

- Charming porch with dormers leads into vaulted great room with atrium
- Well-designed kitchen and breakfast bar adjoin extra large laundry/mud room
- Double sinks, tub with window above and plant shelf complete vaulted master suite bath
- 4 bedrooms, 2 1/2 baths, 2-car side entry garage
- Walk-out basement foundation

TO ORDER BLUEPRINTS USE THE FORM ON PAGE 15 OR CALL TOLL-FREE 1-877-671-6036

The Family
Handyman

Plan #708-DH-2214

Traditional Southern Design With Modern Floor Plan

2,214 total square feet of living area

Price Code D

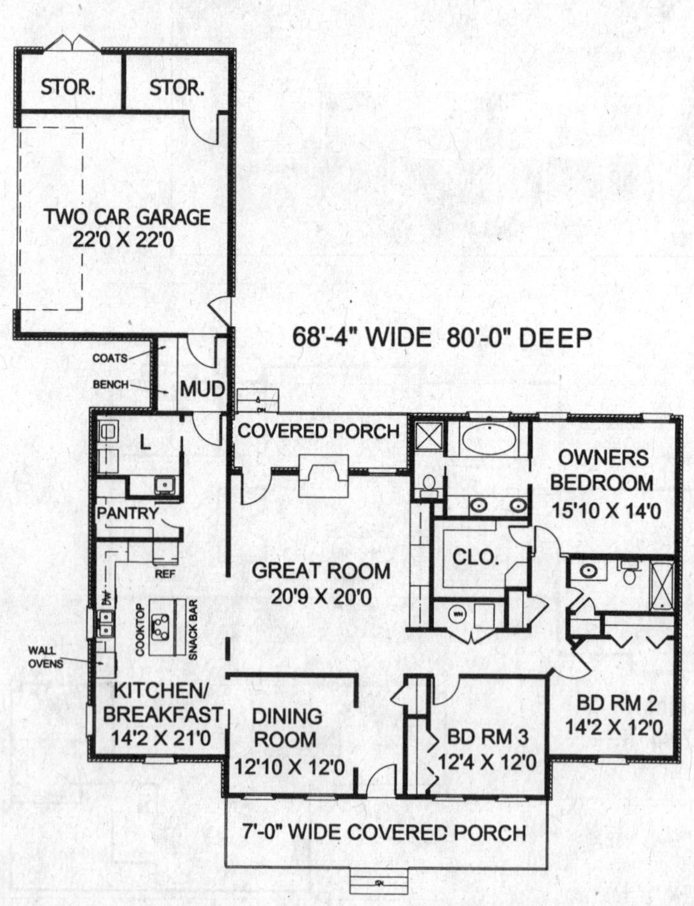
STOR.
STOR.
TWO CAR GARAGE
22'0 X 22'0
68'-4" WIDE 80'-0" DEEP
COATS
BENCH
MUD
L
COVERED PORCH
OWNERS
BEDROOM
15'10 X 14'0
PANTRY
CLO.
REF
GREAT ROOM
20'9 X 20'0
COOKTOP
SNACK BAR
WALL
OVENS
KITCHEN/
BREAKFAST
14'2 X 21'0
DINING
ROOM
12'10 X 12'0
BD RM 3
12'4 X 12'0
BD RM 2
14'2 X 12'0
7'-0" WIDE COVERED PORCH

Special features

- Great room has built-in cabinets for entertainment system, fireplace and French doors leading to private rear covered porch
- Dining room has an arched opening from foyer
- Breakfast room has lots of windows for a sunny open feel
- 3 bedrooms, 2 baths, 2-car side entry garage
- Crawl space or slab foundation, please specify when ordering

TO ORDER BLUEPRINTS USE THE FORM ON PAGE 15 OR CALL TOLL-FREE 1-877-671-6036

View thousands more home plans online at www.familyhandyman.com/homeplans

Plan #708-0510

Spacious Interior For Open Living

1,400 total square feet of living area **Price Code A**

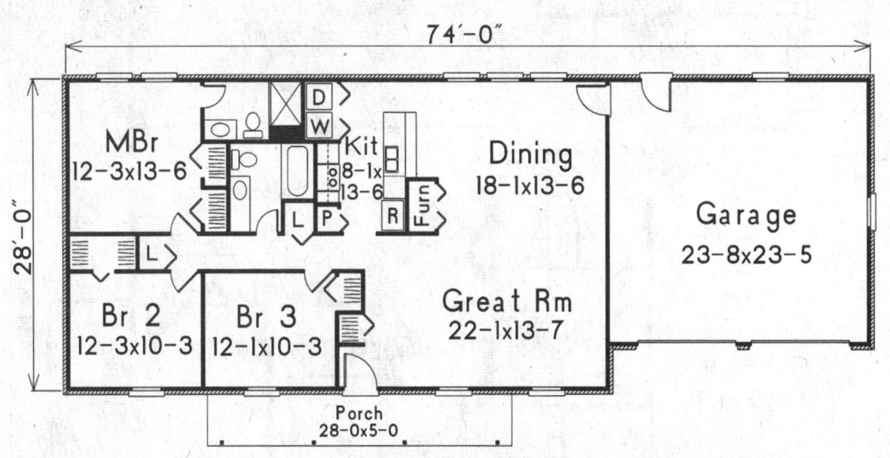
74'-0"
28'-0"
MBr
12-3x13-6
D
W
Kit
8-1x
13-6
L
P
R
Furn
Dining
18-1x13-6
Garage
23-8x23-5
L
Br 2
12-3x10-3
Br 3
12-1x10-3
Great Rm
22-1x13-7
Porch
28-0x5-0

Special features

- Front porch offers warmth and welcome
- Large great room opens into dining room creating an open living atmosphere
- Kitchen features convenient laundry area, pantry and breakfast bar
- 3 bedrooms, 2 baths, 2-car garage
- Crawl space foundation, drawings also include basement and slab foundations

Plan #708-JA-91099

Handsome Two-Story With A Tudor Feel

3,246 total square feet of living area **Price Code F**

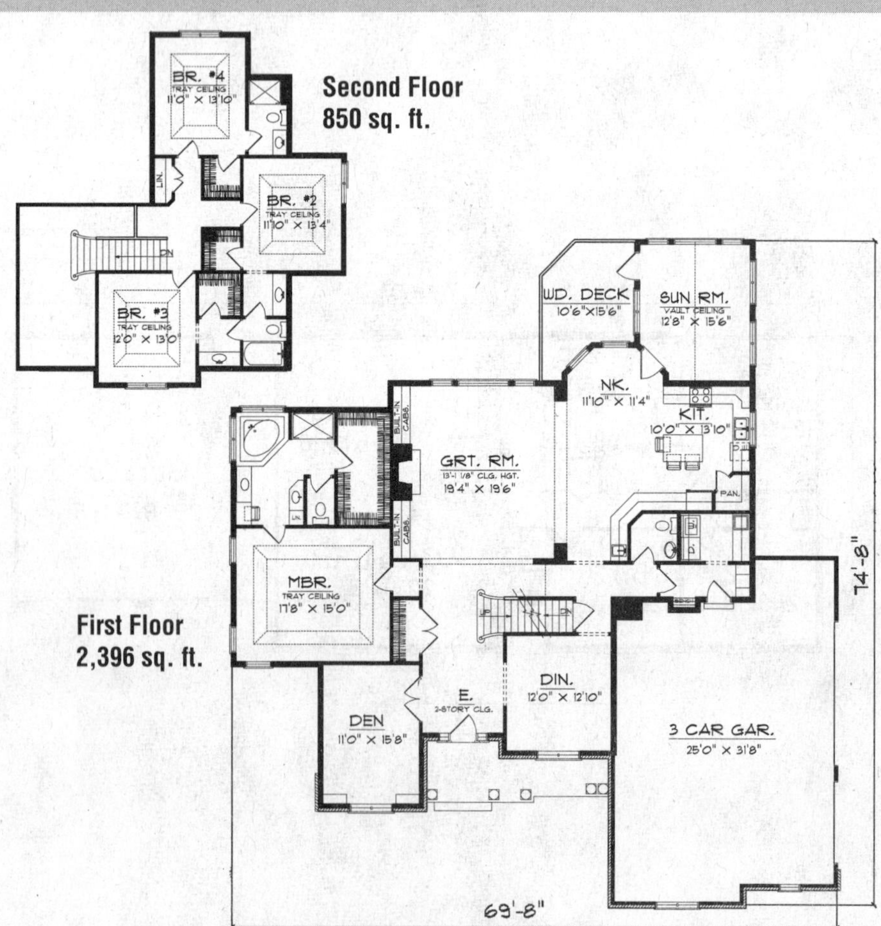

Second Floor
850 sq. ft.
BR. #4
TRAY CEILING
11'0" X 13'10"
BR. #2
TRAY CEILING
11'10" X 13'4"
BR. #3
TRAY CEILING
12'0" X 13'0"
LIN.
DN
First Floor
2,396 sq. ft.
WD. DECK
10'6"X15'6"
SUN RM.
VAULT CEILING
12'8" X 15'6"
NK.
11'10" X 11'4"
KIT.
10'0" X 13'10"
PAN.
GRT. RM.
13'-1 1/8" CLG. HGT.
19'4" X 19'6"
BUILT-IN CABS.
MBR.
TRAY CEILING
17'8" X 15'0"
DIN.
12'0" X 12'10"
E.
2-STORY CLG.
DEN
11'0" X 15'8"
3 CAR GAR.
25'0" X 31'8"
69'-8"
74'-8"

Special features

- Cheerful sun room is surrounded with windows for added openness
- Double-door entry into the den keeps this space private
- A sink and extra counter space extends to dining room entrance for entertaining ease
- 4 bedrooms, 2 1/2 baths, 3-car side entry garage
- Basement foundation

TO ORDER BLUEPRINTS USE THE FORM ON PAGE 15 OR CALL TOLL-FREE 1-877-671-6036

View thousands more home plans online at www.familyhandyman.com/homeplans

The Family Handyman

Plan #708-0491

Covered Porch Highlights This Home

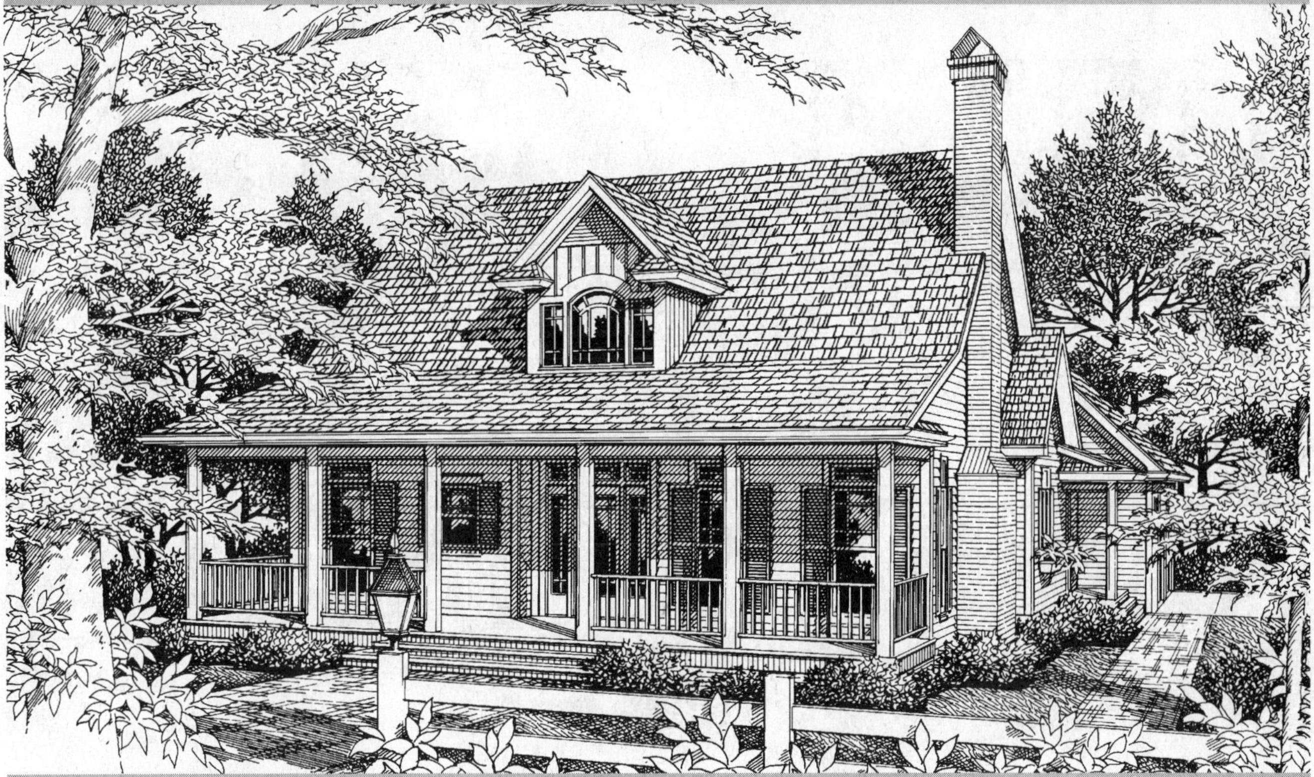

1,808 total square feet of living area

Price Code C

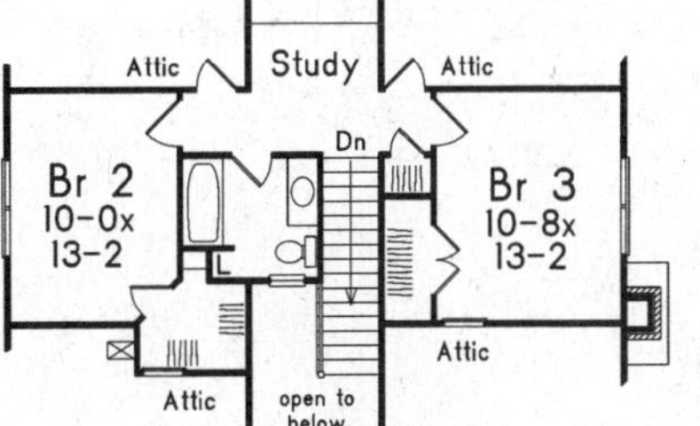

Attic
Study
Attic
Dn
Br 2
10-0x
13-2
Br 3
10-8x
13-2
Attic
Attic
open to
below

Second Floor
537 sq. ft.

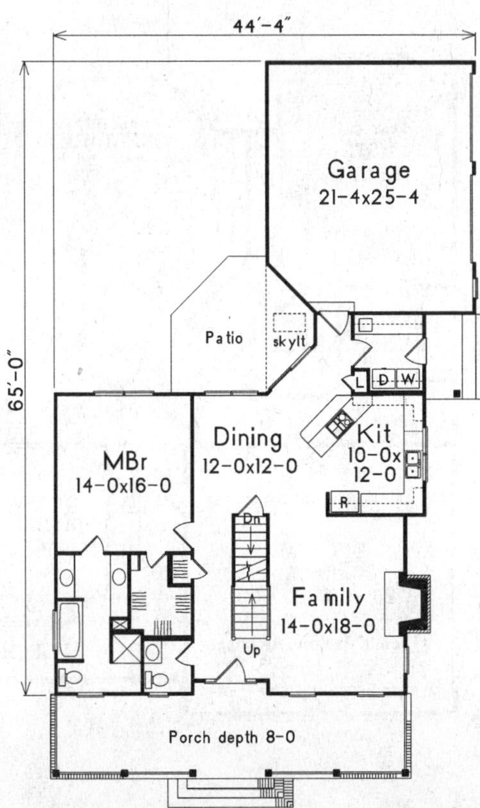

44'-4"
65'-0"
Garage
21-4x25-4
Patio
skylt
D W
L
Dining
12-0x12-0
Kit
10-0x
12-0
R
MBr
14-0x16-0
Dn
Family
14-0x18-0
Up
Porch depth 8-0

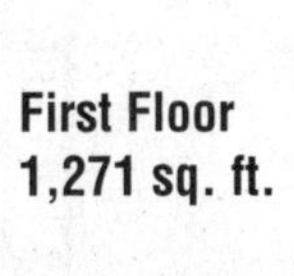

First Floor
1,271 sq. ft.

Special features

- Master bedroom has a walk-in closet, double vanities and separate tub and shower
- Two second floor bedrooms share a study area and full bath
- Partially covered patio is complete with a skylight
- Side entrance opens to utility room with convenient counterspace and laundry sink
- 3 bedrooms, 2 1/2 baths, 2-car side entry garage
- Basement foundation

TO ORDER BLUEPRINTS USE THE FORM ON PAGE 15 OR CALL TOLL-FREE 1-877-671-6036

Plan #708-AX-93304

Distinctive Ranch Home With A Columned Porch

1,860 total square feet of living area **Price Code D**

Special features

- Dining room has an 11' stepped ceiling with a bay window creating a pleasant dining experience
- Breakfast room has a 12' sloped ceiling with French doors leading to a covered porch
- Great room has a columned arched entrance, a built-in media center and a fireplace
- 3 bedrooms, 2 baths, 2-car side entry garage
- Basement, crawl space or slab foundation, please specify when ordering

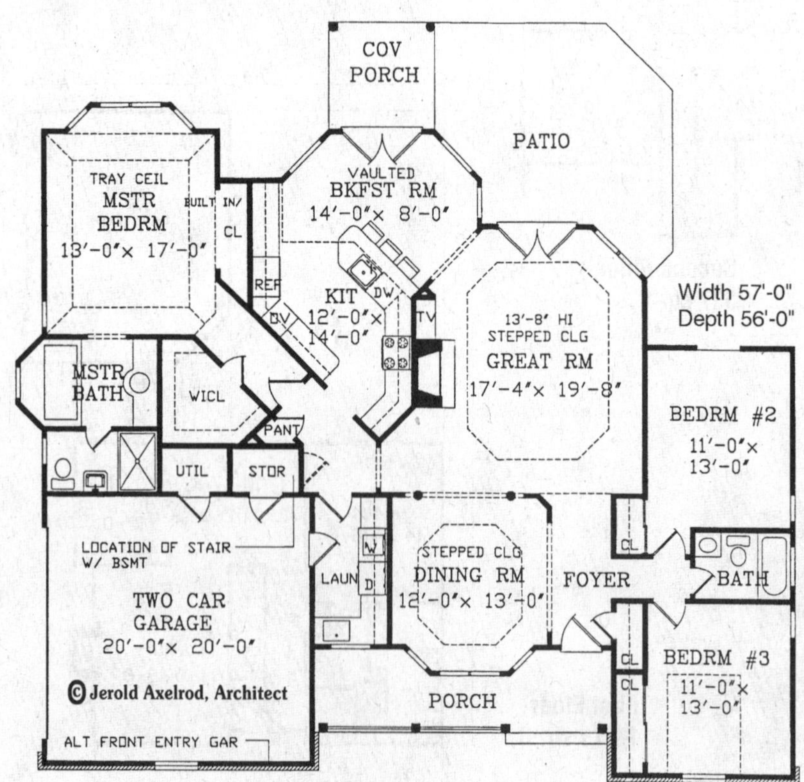
COV PORCH
PATIO
TRAY CEIL
MSTR BEDRM
13'-0"× 17'-0"
BUILT IN/
CL
VAULTED
BKFST RM
14'-0"× 8'-0"
REF
KIT
12'-0"× 14'-0"
DW
DV
TV
13'-8' HI STEPPED CLG
GREAT RM
17'-4"× 19'-8"
Width 57'-0"
Depth 56'-0"
MSTR BATH
WICL
PANT
BEDRM #2
11'-0"× 13'-0"
UTIL
STOR
LOCATION OF STAIR W/ BSMT
W
D
LAUN
STEPPED CLG
DINING RM
12'-0"× 13'-0"
FOYER
CL
BATH
TWO CAR GARAGE
20'-0"× 20'-0"
CL
CL
BEDRM #3
11'-0"× 13'-0"
© Jerold Axelrod, Architect
PORCH
ALT FRONT ENTRY GAR

TO ORDER BLUEPRINTS USE THE FORM ON PAGE 15 OR CALL TOLL-FREE 1-877-671-6036

View thousands more home plans online at www.familyhandyman.com/homeplans

The Family
Handyman

Plan #708-0372

Striking, Covered Arched Entry

1,859 total square feet of living area **Price Code D**

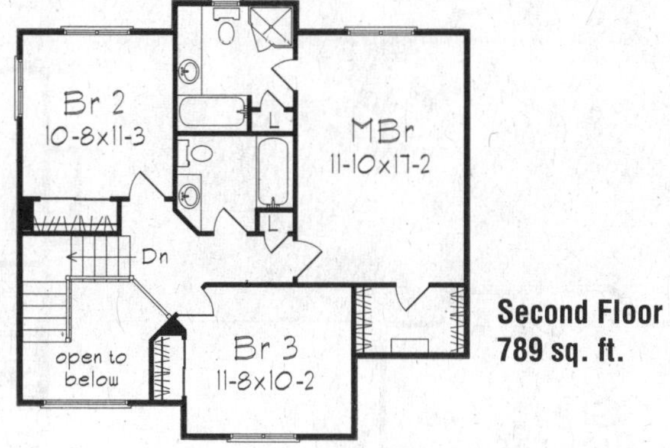
Br 2
10-8x11-3
MBr
11-10x17-2
Dn
open to below
Br 3
11-8x10-2

Second Floor
789 sq. ft.

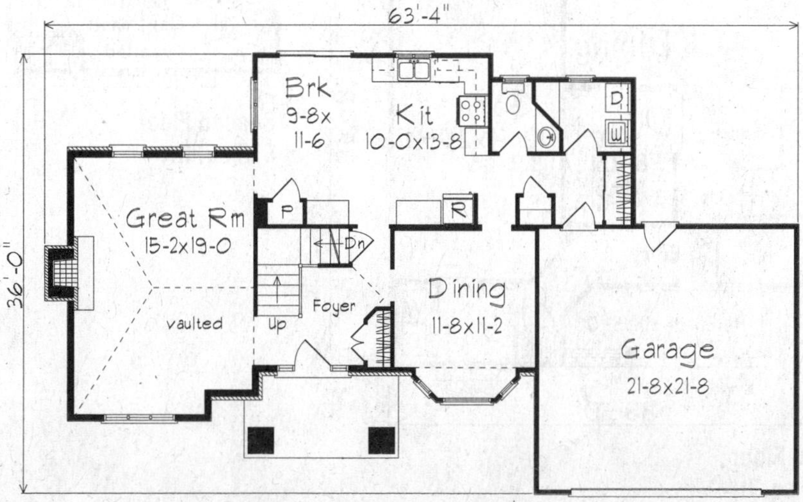

63'-4"

36'-0"

First Floor
1,070 sq. ft.

Special features

- Fireplace highlights vaulted great room
- Master suite includes large closet and private bath
- Kitchen adjoins breakfast room providing easy access to the outdoors
- 3 bedrooms, 2 1/2 baths, 2-car garage
- Basement foundation

TO ORDER BLUEPRINTS USE THE FORM ON PAGE 15 OR CALL TOLL-FREE 1-877-671-6036

View thousands more home plans online at www.familyhandyman.com/homeplans

Plan #708-0479

Trendsetting Appeal For A Narrow Lot

1,294 total square feet of living area **Price Code A**

Special features

- Great room features fireplace and large bay with windows and patio doors
- Enjoy a laundry room immersed in light with large windows, arched transom and attractive planter box
- Vaulted master bedroom with bay window and walk-in closets
- Bedroom #2 boasts a vaulted ceiling, plant shelf and half bath, perfect for a studio
- 2 bedrooms, 1 full bath, 2 half baths, 1-car rear entry garage
- Basement foundation

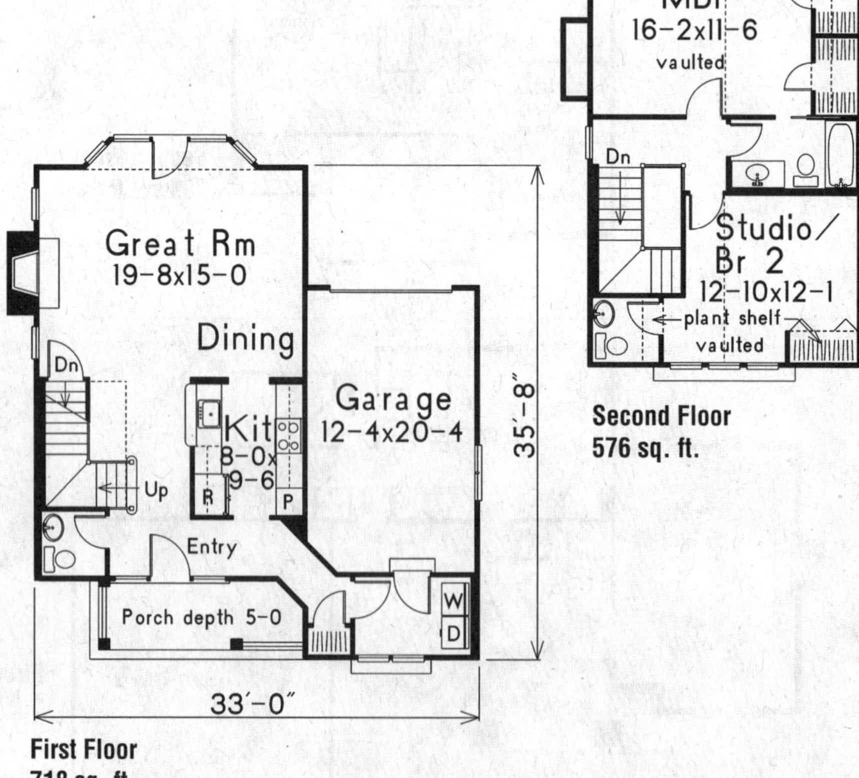
Great Rm
19-8x15-0
Dining
Dn
Kit
8-0x
9-6
R
P
Garage
12-4x20-4
Up
Entry
Porch depth 5-0
W
D
35'-8"
33'-0"
plant
shelf
MBr
16-2x11-6
vaulted
Dn
Studio/
Br 2
12-10x12-1
plant shelf
vaulted

First Floor
718 sq. ft.

Second Floor
576 sq. ft.

The Family
Handyman

Plan #708-GM-1842

Cedar Shakes Create A Charming Feel

COPYRIGHTED 1997
GREG MARQUIS

1,842 total square feet of living area **Price Code C**

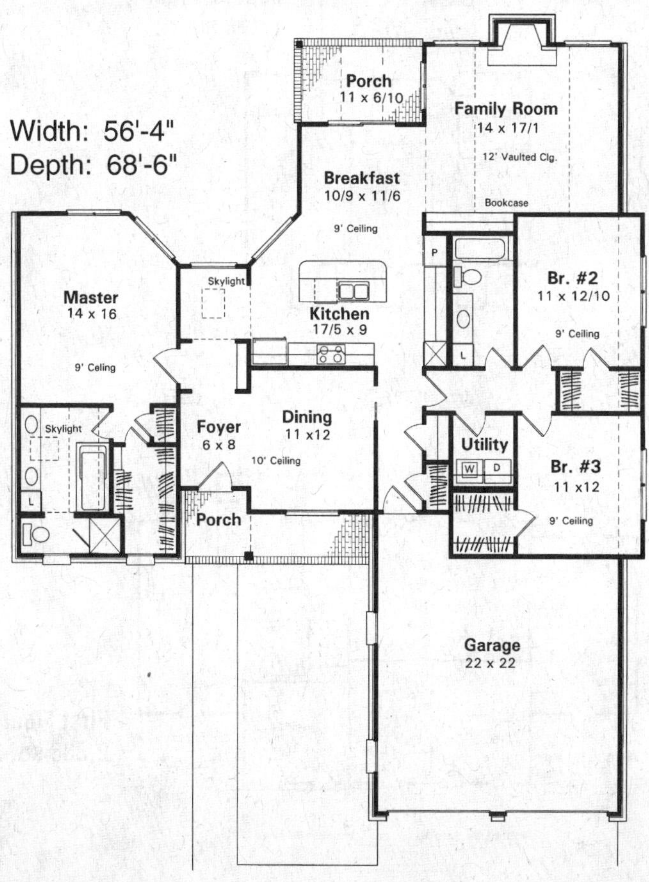

Width: 56'-4"
Depth: 68'-6"
Porch
11 x 6/10
Family Room
14 x 17/1
12' Vaulted Clg.
Bookcase
Breakfast
10/9 x 11/6
9' Ceiling
Skylight
Master
14 x 16
9' Ceiling
Kitchen
17/5 x 9
Br. #2
11 x 12/10
9' Ceiling
Skylight
Foyer
6 x 8
Dining
11 x12
10' Ceiling
Utility
Br. #3
11 x12
9' Ceiling
Porch
Garage
22 x 22

Special features

- Vaulted family room features fireplace and elegant bookcase
- Island countertop in kitchen makes cooking convenient
- Rear facade has intimate porch area ideal for relaxing
- 3 bedrooms, 2 baths, 2-car garage
- Slab or crawl space foundation, please specify when ordering

The Family
Handyman

Plan #708-0429

Outdoor Living Created By Decks And Porches

3,149 total square feet of living area **Price Code E**

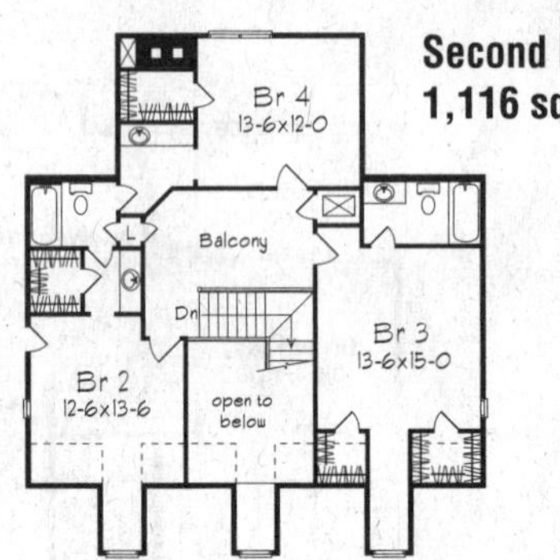
Br 4
13-6x12-0
Balcony
L
Dn
Br 3
13-6x15-0
Br 2
12-6x13-6
open to below

Second Floor
1,116 sq. ft.

Special features

- 10' ceiling on the first floor and 9' ceiling on the second floor
- All bedrooms include walk-in closets
- Formal living and dining rooms flank two-story foyer
- 4 bedrooms, 3 1/2 baths, 2-car detached garage
- Slab foundation, drawings also include crawl space foundation

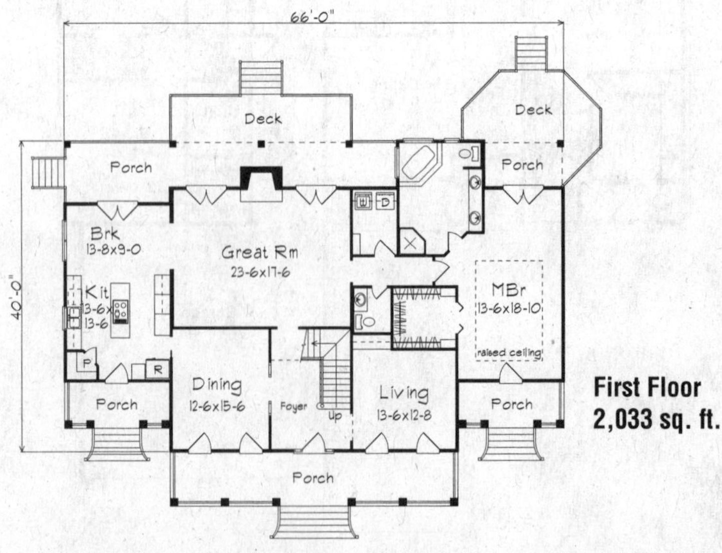
66'-0"
Deck
Deck
Porch
Porch
Brk
13-8x9-0
Great Rm
23-6x17-6
MBr
13-6x18-10
raised ceiling
Kit
13-6x
13-6
40'-0"
P
R
Dining
12-6x15-6
Foyer
Up
Living
13-6x12-8
Porch
Porch
Porch

First Floor
2,033 sq. ft.

TO ORDER BLUEPRINTS USE THE FORM ON PAGE 15 OR CALL TOLL-FREE 1-877-671-6036

View thousands more home plans online at www.familyhandyman.com/homeplans

The Family
Handyman

Plan #708-NDG-517

Wonderful Master Suite

1,989 total square feet of living area **Price Code C**

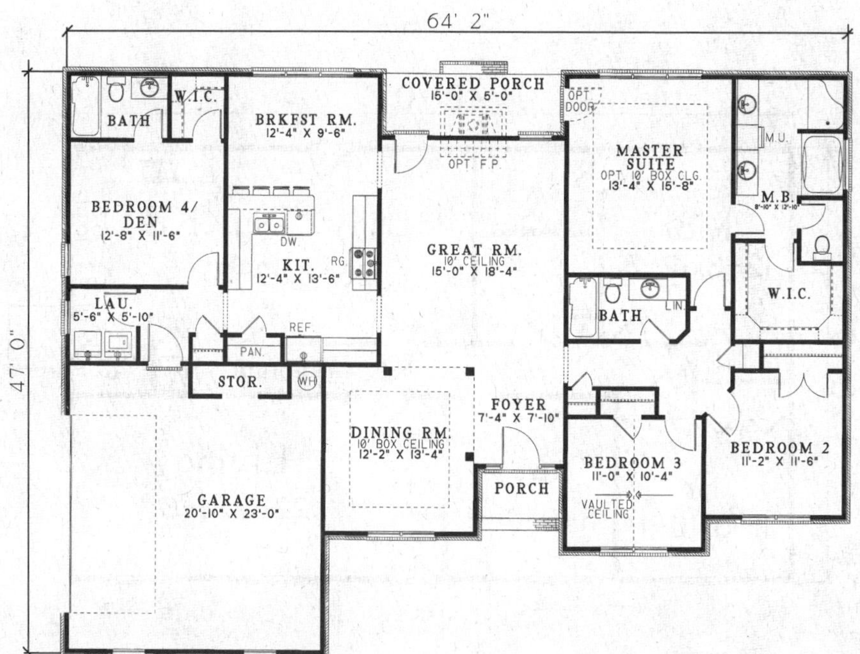

64' 2"
47' 0"
COVERED PORCH
15'-0" X 5'-0"
OPT. F.P.
OPT. DOOR
BATH
W.I.C.
BRKFST RM.
12'-4" X 9'-6"
MASTER SUITE
OPT. 10' BOX CLG.
13'-4" X 15'-8"
M.U.
M.B.
BEDROOM 4/ DEN
12'-8" X 11'-6"
DW.
KIT.
12'-4" X 13'-6"
RG.
GREAT RM.
10' CEILING
15'-0" X 18'-4"
W.I.C.
BATH
LIN.
LAU.
5'-6" X 5'-10"
REF.
PAN.
STOR.
WH
DINING RM.
10' BOX CEILING
12'-2" X 13'-4"
FOYER
7'-4" X 7'-10"
BEDROOM 3
11'-0" X 10'-4"
VAULTED CEILING
BEDROOM 2
11'-2" X 11'-6"
PORCH
GARAGE
20'-10" X 23'-0"

Special features

- Dining room has 8" decorative columns
- Master suite has optional door to rear covered porch
- Laundry area is convenient to kitchen and garage
- 4 bedrooms, 3 baths, 2-car side entry garage
- Crawl space or slab foundation, please specify when ordering

The Family
Handyman

Plan #708-0585

All The Essentials For Comfortable Living

1,344 total square feet of living area **Price Code A**

Special features

- Kitchen has side entry, laundry area, pantry and joins family/dining area
- Master bedroom includes private bath
- Linen and storage closets in hall
- Covered porch opens to spacious living room with handy coat closet
- 3 bedrooms, 2 baths
- Crawl space foundation, drawings also include basement and slab foundations

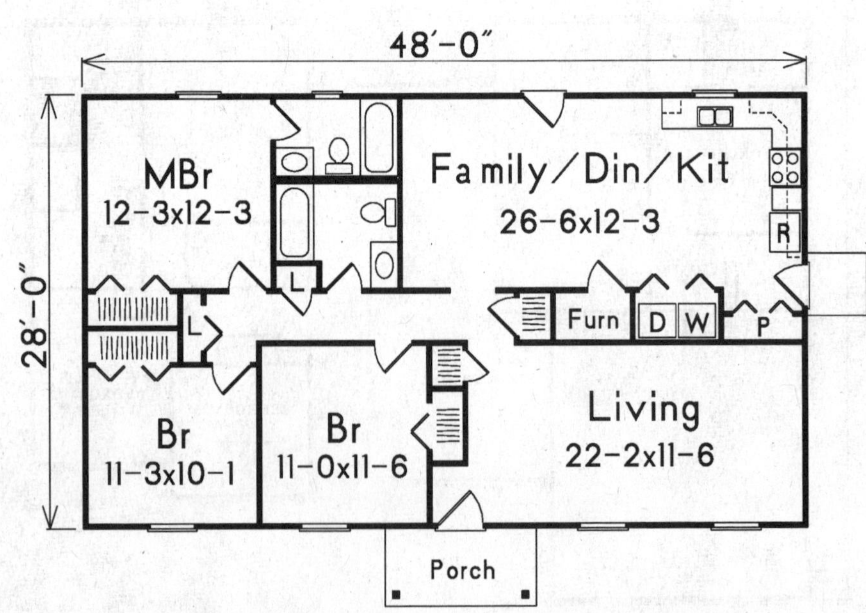
48′-0″
28′-0″
MBr
12-3x12-3
Family/Din/Kit
26-6x12-3
R
L
L
Furn
D
W
P
Br
11-3x10-1
Br
11-0x11-6
Living
22-2x11-6
Porch

TO ORDER BLUEPRINTS USE THE FORM ON PAGE 15 OR CALL TOLL-FREE 1-877-671-6036

View thousands more home plans online at www.familyhandyman.com/homeplans

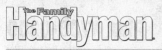

Plan #708-FDG-9035

Study Off Main Entrance

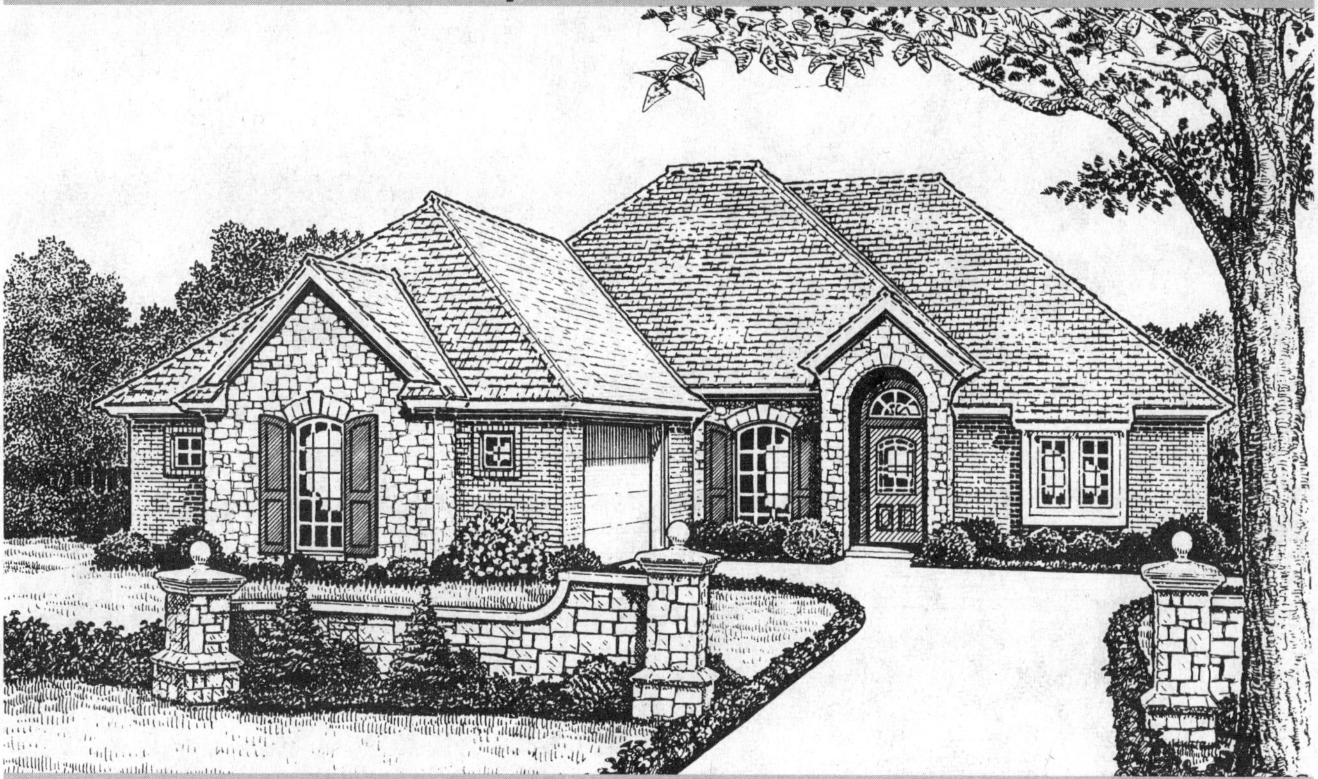

1,760 total square feet of living area **Price Code B**

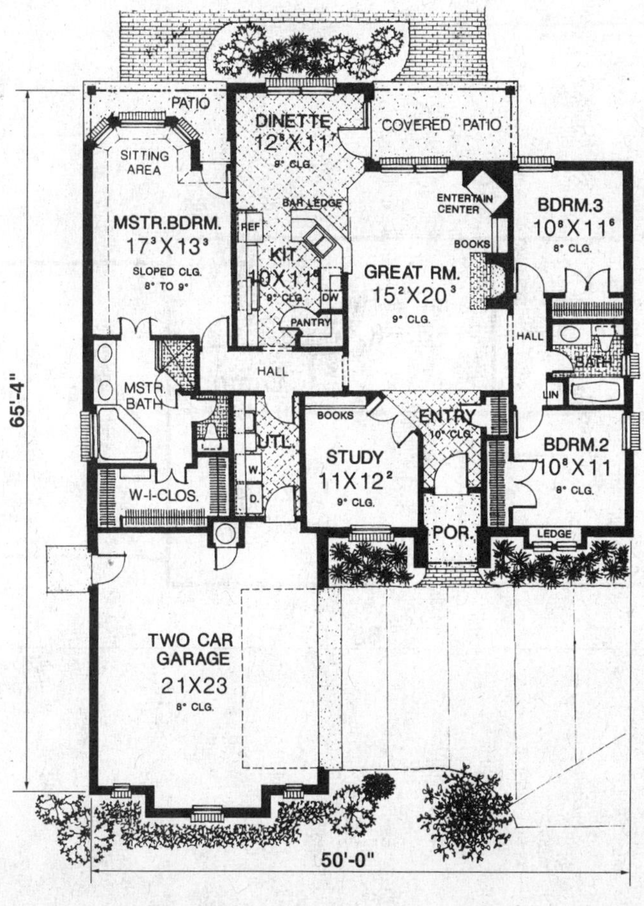
PATIO
DINETTE
12^8X11^7
9' CLG.
COVERED PATIO
SITTING AREA
MSTR.BDRM.
17^3X13^3
SLOPED CLG.
8' TO 9'
BAR LEDGE
ENTERTAIN CENTER
BDRM.3
10^8X11^6
8' CLG.
REF
KIT
BOOKS
GREAT RM.
15^2X20^3
9' CLG.
DW
PANTRY
HALL
HALL
MSTR. BATH
BATH
LIN
BOOKS
ENTRY
10' CLG.
UTL
STUDY
11X12^2
9' CLG.
BDRM.2
10^8X11
8' CLG.
W-I-CLOS.
W.
D.
POR.
LEDGE
TWO CAR GARAGE
21X23
8' CLG.
65'-4"
50'-0"

Special features

- Stone and brick exterior has old world charm
- Master bedroom includes a sitting area and is situated away from other bedrooms for privacy
- Kitchen and dinette access the outdoors
- Great room includes fireplace, built-in bookshelves and entertainment center
- 3 bedrooms, 2 baths, 2-car side entry garage
- Slab foundation

Roomy Ranch For Easy Living

1,343 total square feet of living area **Price Code A**

Special features

- Separate and convenient family and living/dining areas
- Nice-sized master bedroom suite with large closet and private bath
- Foyer with convenient coat closet opens into combined living and dining rooms
- Kitchen has access to the outdoors through sliding glass doors
- 3 bedrooms, 2 baths, 2-car garage
- Crawl space foundation, drawings also include basement foundation

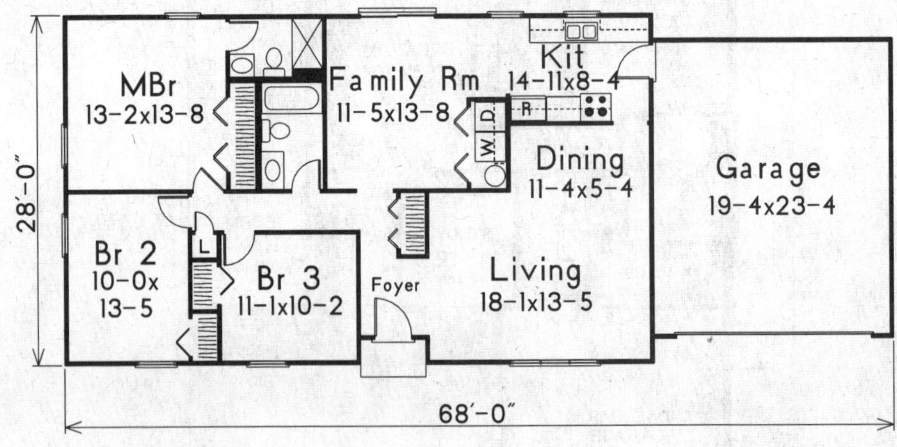
MBr
13-2x13-8
Family Rm
11-5x13-8
Kit
14-11x8-4
R
W
D
Dining
11-4x5-4
Garage
19-4x23-4
Br 2
10-0x
13-5
L
Br 3
11-1x10-2
Foyer
Living
18-1x13-5
28'-0"
68'-0"

The Family
Handyman

Plan #708-0319

Spectacular View From The Great Room

3,796 total square feet of living area

Price Code F

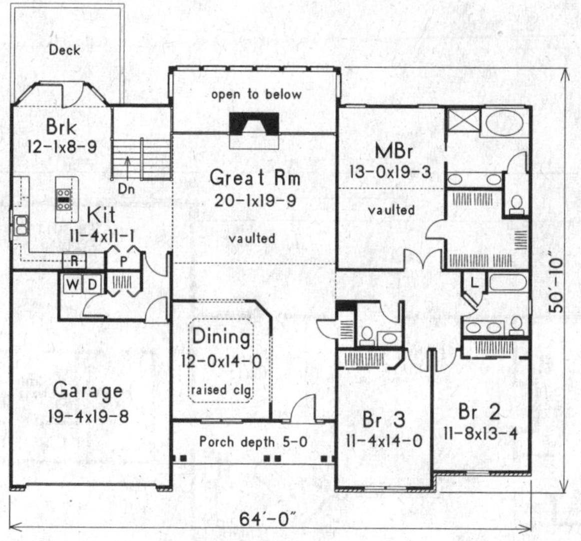

Deck
open to below
Brk
12-1x8-9
Dn
Great Rm
20-1x19-9
vaulted
Kit
11-4x11-1
R
P
W D
MBr
13-0x19-3
vaulted
L
50'-10"
Dining
12-0x14-0
raised clg
Garage
19-4x19-8
Porch depth 5-0
Br 3
11-4x14-0
Br 2
11-8x13-4
64'-0"

First Floor
2,436 sq. ft.

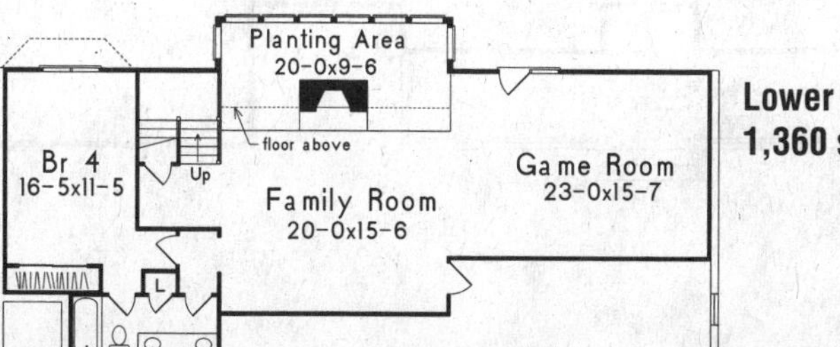

Planting Area
20-0x9-6
floor above
Up
Br 4
16-5x11-5
Family Room
20-0x15-6
Game Room
23-0x15-7
L
Unfinished Basement
Unexcavated

Lower Level
1,360 sq. ft.

Special features

- Entry foyer leads directly to great room with fireplace and wonderful view through wall of windows
- Kitchen and breakfast room feature large island cooktop, pantry and easy access outdoors
- Master bedroom includes vaulted ceiling and pocket door entrance into master bath that features double-bowl vanity and large tub
- 4 bedrooms, 3 1/2 baths, 2-car garage
- Basement foundation

TO ORDER BLUEPRINTS USE THE FORM ON PAGE 15 OR CALL TOLL-FREE 1-877-671-6036

View thousands more home plans online at www.familyhandyman.com/homeplans

The Family
Handyman

Plan #708-VL-1926

Optimal Family Living Layout

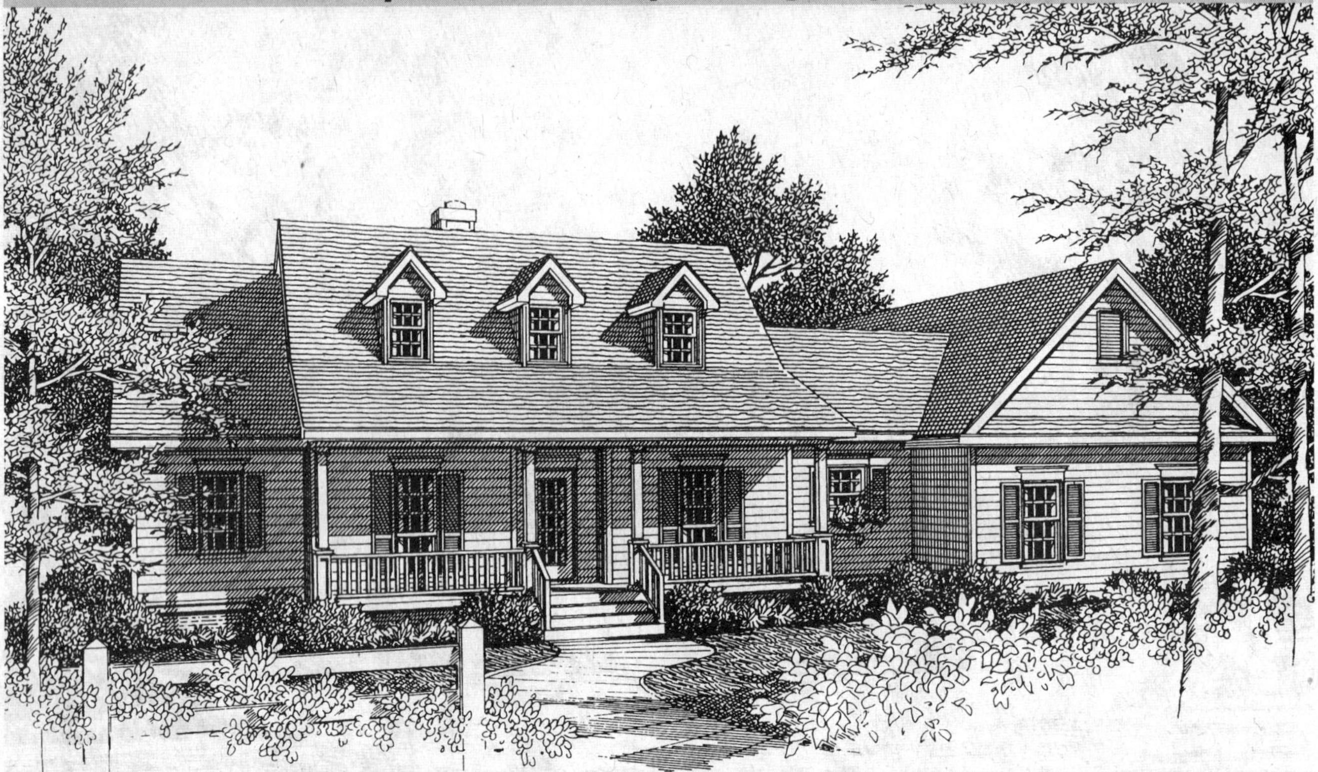

1,926 total square feet of living area **Price Code C**

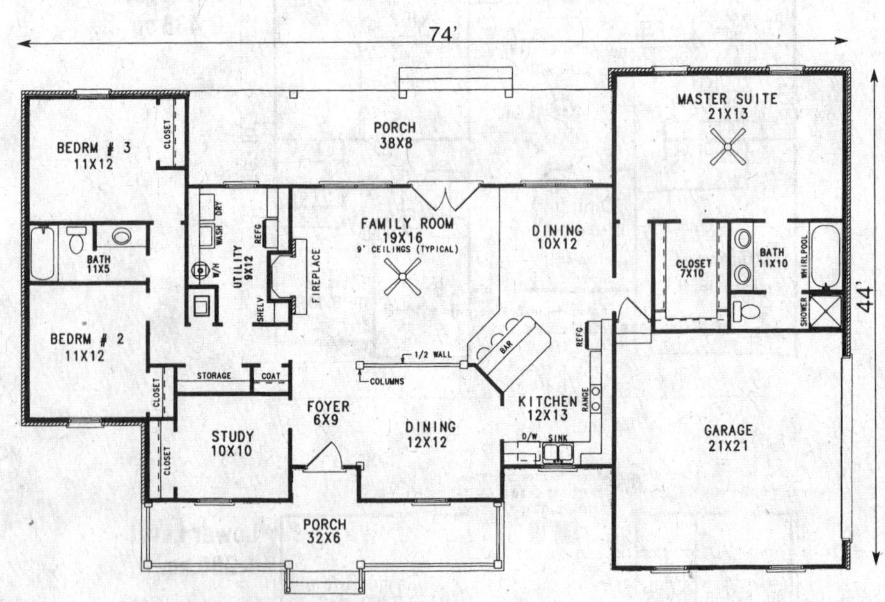
74'
44'
PORCH
38X8
BEDRM # 3
11X12
CLOSET
MASTER SUITE
21X13
FAMILY ROOM
19X16
9' CEILINGS (TYPICAL)
DINING
10X12
BATH
11X5
WASH
DRY
W/H
REFG
UTILITY
9X12
SHELV
FIREPLACE
CLOSET
7X10
BATH
11X10
WHIRLPOOL
SHOWER
BEDRM # 2
11X12
1/2 WALL
COLUMNS
BAR
REFG
KITCHEN
12X13
RANGE
STORAGE
COAT
CLOSET
FOYER
6X9
STUDY
10X10
CLOSET
DINING
12X12
D/W
SINK
GARAGE
21X21
PORCH
32X6

Special features

- Large covered rear porch is spacious enough for entertaining
- L-shaped kitchen is compact yet efficient and includes a snack bar for extra dining
- Oversized utility room has counterspace, extra shelves and space for a second refridgerator
- Secluded master suite has a private bath and a large walk-in closet
- 3 bedrooms, 2 baths, 2-car side entry garage
- Slab or crawl space foundation, please specify when ordering

Plan #708-0736

Two-Story Atrium For Great Views

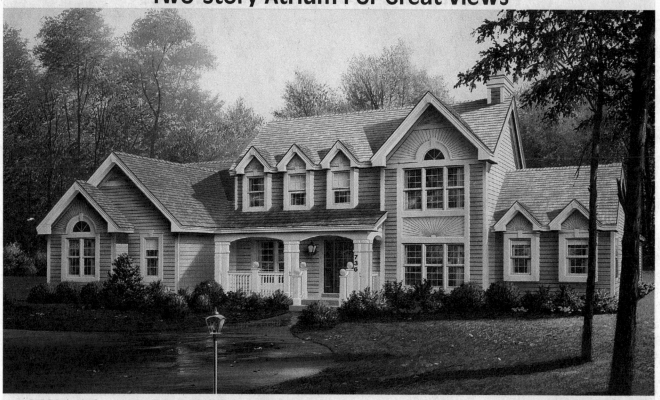

2,900 total square feet of living area

Price Code E

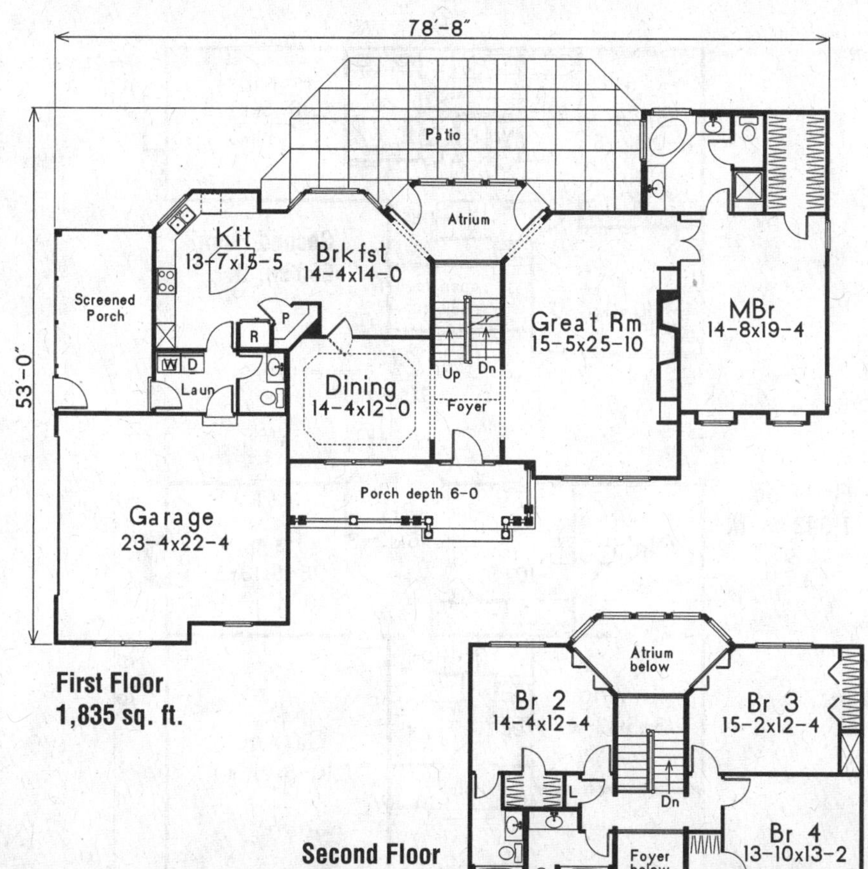
78'-8"
53'-0"
Patio
Atrium
Kit
13-7x15-5
Brk fst
14-4x14-0
Screened Porch
P
R
W D
Laun
Dining
14-4x12-0
Up
Dn
Foyer
Great Rm
15-5x25-10
MBr
14-8x19-4
Porch depth 6-0
Garage
23-4x22-4
Atrium below
Br 2
14-4x12-4
Br 3
15-2x12-4
L
Dn
Foyer below
Br 4
13-10x13-2

First Floor
1,835 sq. ft.

Second Floor
1,065 sq. ft.

Special features

- Elegant entry foyer leads to balcony overlook of vaulted two-story atrium
- Spacious kitchen features an island breakfast bar, walk-in pantry, bayed breakfast room and adjoining screened porch
- Two large second floor bedrooms and stair balconies overlook a sun drenched two-story vaulted atrium
- 4 bedrooms, 3 1/2 baths, 2-car side entry garage
- Basement foundation

TO ORDER BLUEPRINTS USE THE FORM ON PAGE 15 OR CALL TOLL-FREE 1-877-671-6036
View thousands more home plans online at www.familyhandyman.com/homeplans

The Family
Handyman

Plan #708-0171

Practical Two-Story, Full Of Features

2,058 total square feet of living area **Price Code C**

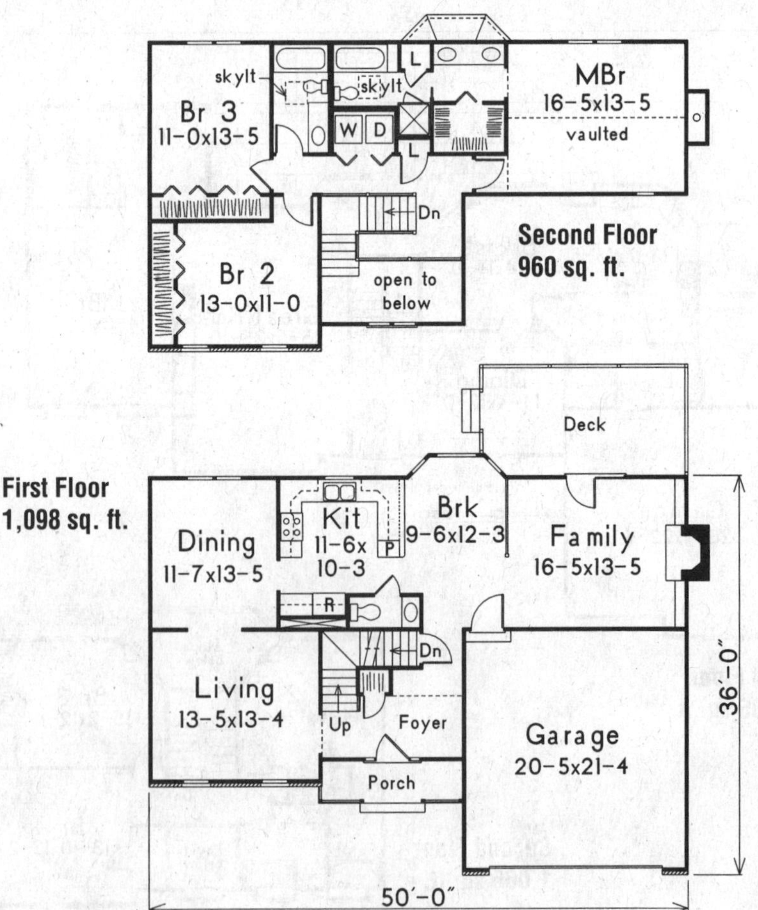
skylt
skylt
Br 3
11-0x13-5
W D
L
L
MBr
16-5x13-5
vaulted
Dn
Second Floor
960 sq. ft.
Br 2
13-0x11-0
open to
below
Deck
First Floor
1,098 sq. ft.
Dining
11-7x13-5
Kit
11-6x
10-3
P
Brk
9-6x12-3
Family
16-5x13-5
R
Dn
Living
13-5x13-4
Up
Foyer
Porch
Garage
20-5x21-4
36'-0"
50'-0"

Special features

- Handsome two-story foyer with balcony creates a spacious entrance area
- Vaulted ceiling in the master bedroom with private dressing area and large walk-in closet
- Skylights furnish natural lighting in the hall and master bath
- Conveniently located second floor laundry near bedrooms
- 3 bedrooms, 2 1/2 baths, 2-car garage
- Basement foundation, drawings also include slab and crawl space foundations

TO ORDER BLUEPRINTS USE THE FORM ON PAGE 15 OR CALL TOLL-FREE 1-877-671-6036

View thousands more home plans online at www.familyhandyman.com/homeplans

Plan #708-NDG-148

Bayed Dining Room

1,538 total square feet of living area

Price Code B

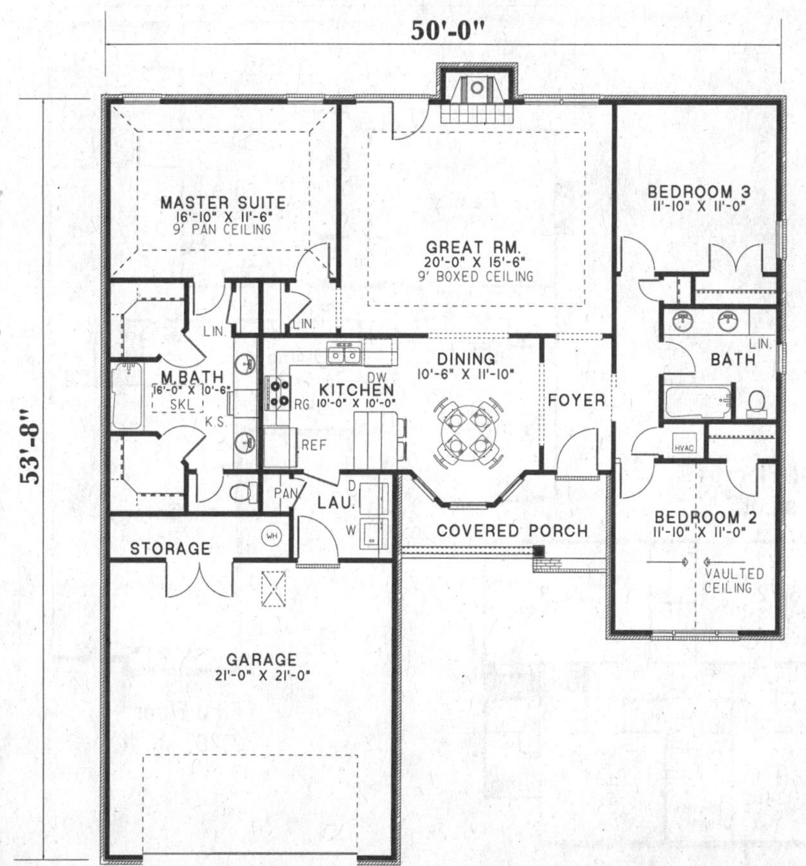

50'-0"
53'-8"
MASTER SUITE
16'-10" X 11'-6"
9' PAN CEILING
GREAT RM.
20'-0" X 15'-6"
9' BOXED CEILING
BEDROOM 3
11'-10" X 11'-0"
LIN.
LIN.
M.BATH
16'-0" X 10'-6"
SKL
K.S.
KITCHEN
10'-0" X 10'-0"
RG
DW
REF
DINING
10'-6" X 11'-10"
FOYER
BATH
LIN.
HVAC
PAN
LAU.
D
W
COVERED PORCH
BEDROOM 2
11'-10" X 11'-0"
VAULTED
CEILING
WH
STORAGE
GARAGE
21'-0" X 21'-0"

Special features

- Dining and great rooms highlighted in this design
- Master suite has many amenities
- Kitchen and laundry are accessible from any room in the house
- 3 bedrooms, 2 baths, 2-car garage
- Basement, walk-out basement, crawl space or slab foundation, please specify when ordering

TO ORDER BLUEPRINTS USE THE FORM ON PAGE 15 OR CALL TOLL-FREE 1-877-671-6036

View thousands more home plans online at www.familyhandyman.com/homeplans

Stately Elegance

3,657 total square feet of living area **Price Code F**

Special features

- Dramatic two-story foyer has a stylish niche, a convenient powder room and French doors leading to parlor
- State-of-the-art kitchen includes a large walk-in pantry, breakfast island, computer center and 40' vista through family room with walk-in wet bar
- Vaulted master bath features marble steps and Roman columns that lead to a majestic-sized whirlpool tub with marble deck surround and grandscale palladian window
- A jack and jill bath, hall bath, loft area and huge bedrooms comprise the second floor
- 4 bedrooms, 3 1/2 baths, 3-car side entry garage
- Basement foundation

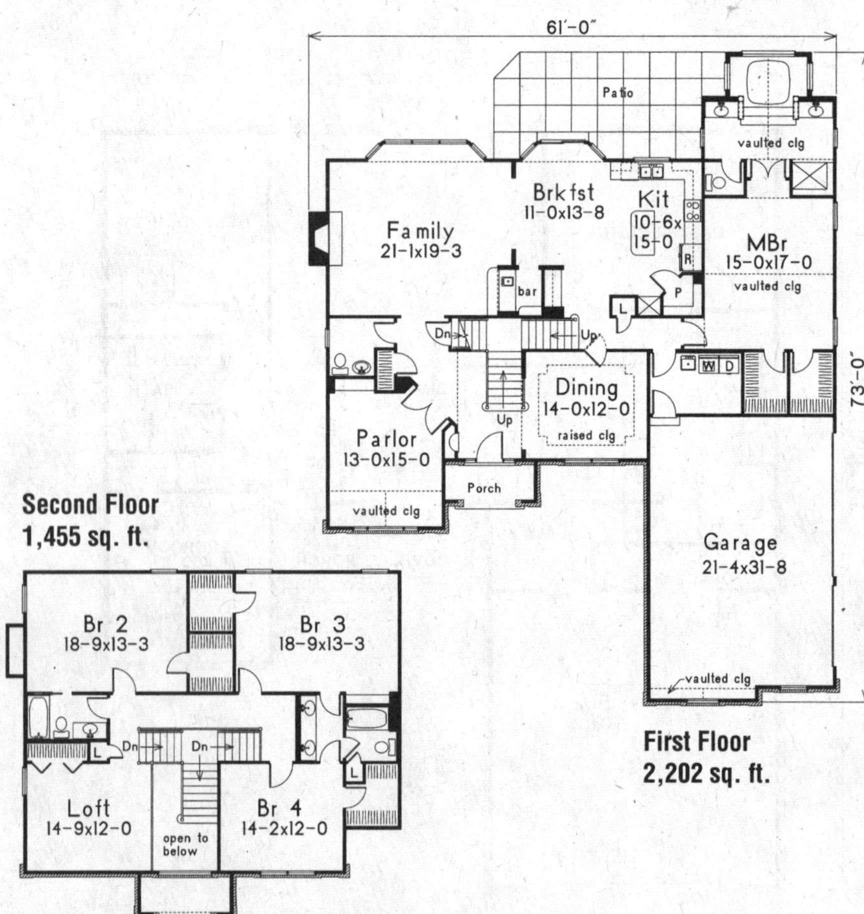
61'-0"
Patio
vaulted clg
Brkfst
11-0x13-8
Kit
10-6x
15-0
Family
21-1x19-3
MBr
15-0x17-0
vaulted clg
bar
Dn
Up
Dining
14-0x12-0
raised clg
Up
Parlor
13-0x15-0
vaulted clg
Porch
73'-0"
Garage
21-4x31-8
vaulted clg
Br 2
18-9x13-3
Br 3
18-9x13-3
Dn
Dn
Loft
14-9x12-0
open to
below
Br 4
14-2x12-0

Second Floor
1,455 sq. ft.

First Floor
2,202 sq. ft.

TO ORDER BLUEPRINTS USE THE FORM ON PAGE 15 OR CALL TOLL-FREE 1-877-671-6036
View thousands more home plans online at www.familyhandyman.com/homeplans

Plan #708-UD-D164

Optimum Style For Family Living

2,431 total square feet of living area **Price Code D**

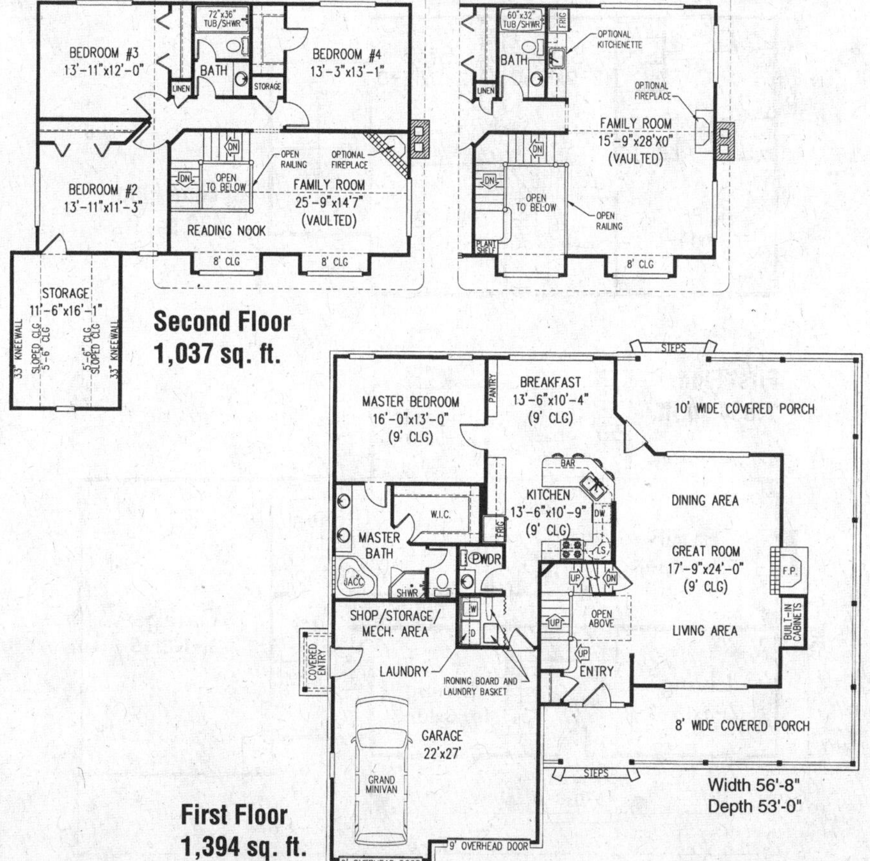
BEDROOM #3
13'-11"x12'-0"
72"x36" TUB/SHWR
BATH
LINEN
STORAGE
BEDROOM #4
13'-3"x13'-1"
BEDROOM #2
13'-11"x11'-3"
OPEN RAILING
OPTIONAL FIREPLACE
OPEN TO BELOW
FAMILY ROOM
25'-9"x14'7"
(VAULTED)
READING NOOK
8' CLG
STORAGE
11'-6"x16'-1"
60"x32" TUB/SHWR
OPTIONAL KITCHENETTE
OPTIONAL FIREPLACE
FAMILY ROOM
15'-9"x28'X0"
(VAULTED)
OPEN RAILING
PLANT SHELF
Second Floor
1,037 sq. ft.
STEPS
MASTER BEDROOM
16'-0"x13'-0"
(9' CLG)
PANTRY
BREAKFAST
13'-6"x10'-4"
(9' CLG)
10' WIDE COVERED PORCH
BAR
KITCHEN
13'-6"x10'-9"
(9' CLG)
W.I.C.
MASTER BATH
DINING AREA
PWDR
GREAT ROOM
17'-9"x24'-0"
(9' CLG)
F.P.
SHOP/STORAGE/
MECH. AREA
OPEN ABOVE
LIVING AREA
BUILT-IN CABINETS
COVERED ENTRY
LAUNDRY
IRONING BOARD AND LAUNDRY BASKET
ENTRY
GARAGE
22'x27'
GRAND MINIVAN
8' WIDE COVERED PORCH
9' OVERHEAD DOOR
Width 56'-8"
Depth 53'-0"
First Floor
1,394 sq. ft.

Special features

- Second floor includes a wonderful casual family room with corner fireplace and reading nook
- The great room, living and dining areas all combine to create one large space ideal for entertaining or family gatherings
- Built-in pantry in breakfast area
- 4 bedrooms, 2 1/2 baths, 2-car garage with shop/storage area
- Basement, crawl space or slab foundation, please specify when ordering

TO ORDER BLUEPRINTS USE THE FORM ON PAGE 15 OR CALL TOLL-FREE 1-877-671-6036

View thousands more home plans online at www.familyhandyman.com/homeplans

Plan #708-0298

Columns And Dormers Grace Stylish Exterior

3,216 total square feet of living area **Price Code F**

<u>*Special features*</u>

- All bedrooms include private full baths
- Hearth room and combination kitchen/breakfast area create large informal gathering area
- Oversized family room boasts fireplace, wet bar and bay window
- Master bath with double walk-in closets and luxurious bath
- 4 bedrooms, 4 1/2 baths, 3-car side entry garage
- Basement foundation

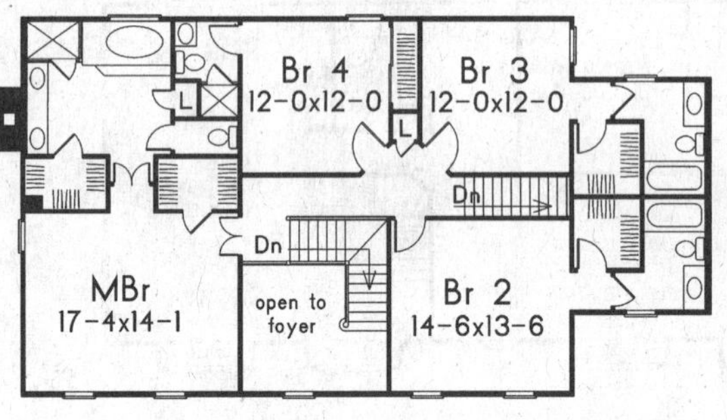
Br 4
12-0x12-0
Br 3
12-0x12-0
L
L
Dn
Dn
MBr
17-4x14-1
open to
foyer
Br 2
14-6x13-6

Second Floor
1,382 sq. ft.

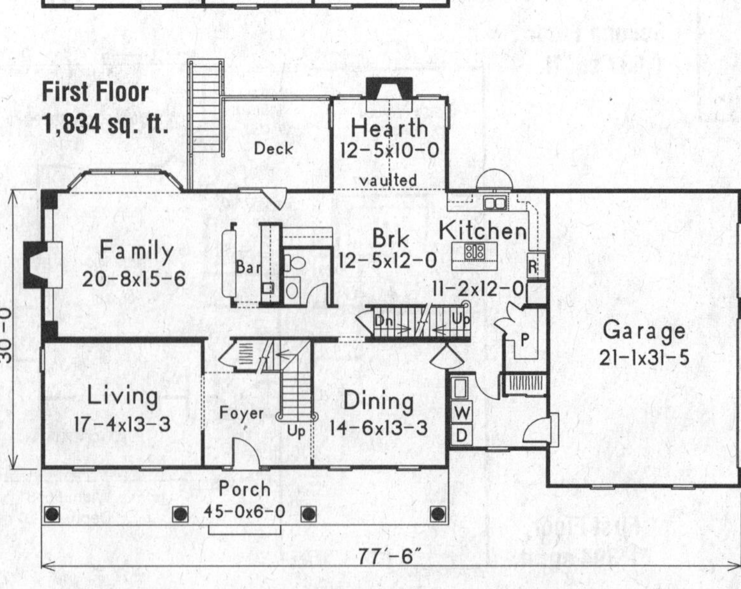
First Floor
1,834 sq. ft.
Deck
Hearth
12-5x10-0
vaulted
Family
20-8x15-6
Bar
Brk
12-5x12-0
Kitchen
11-2x12-0
R
Dn
Up
P
Garage
21-1x31-5
30'-0"
Living
17-4x13-3
Foyer
Up
Dining
14-6x13-3
W
D
Porch
45-0x6-0
77'-6"

TO ORDER BLUEPRINTS USE THE FORM ON PAGE 15 OR CALL TOLL-FREE 1-877-671-6036

View thousands more home plans online at www.familyhandyman.com/homeplans

The Family
Handyman

Plan #708-DR-2891

Majestic European Traditional

2,310 total square feet of living area

Price Code D

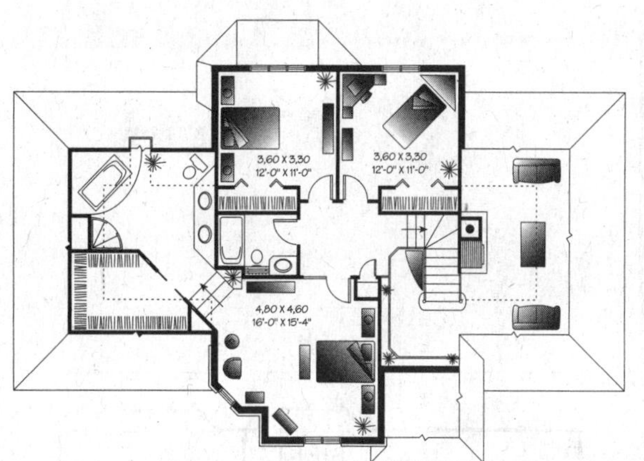
3,60 X 3,30
12'-0" X 11'-0"
3,60 X 3,30
12'-0" X 11'-0"
4,80 X 4,60
16'-0" X 15'-4"

Second Floor
1,074 sq. ft.

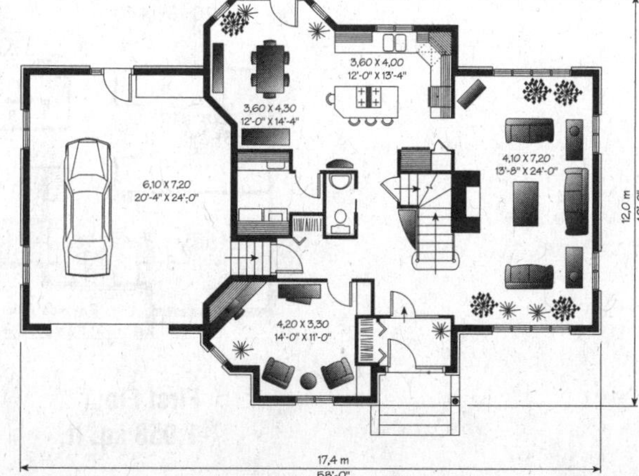
3,60 X 4,00
12'-0" X 13'-4"
3,60 X 4,30
12'-0" X 14'-4"
4,10 X 7,20
13'-8" X 24'-0"
6,10 X 7,20
20'-4" X 24'-0"
4,20 X 3,30
14'-0" X 11'-0"
12,0 m
40'-0"
17,4 m
58'-0"

First Floor
1,236 sq. ft.

Special features

- Snack bar in kitchen for eat-in dining
- Cathedral ceiling in living room
- Energy efficient home with 2" x 6" exterior walls
- 3 bedrooms, 2 1/2 baths, 2-car garage
- Basement foundation

TO ORDER BLUEPRINTS USE THE FORM ON PAGE 15 OR CALL TOLL-FREE 1-877-671-6036

View thousands more home plans online at www.familyhandyman.com/homeplans

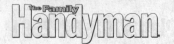

Distinctive Two-Level Living

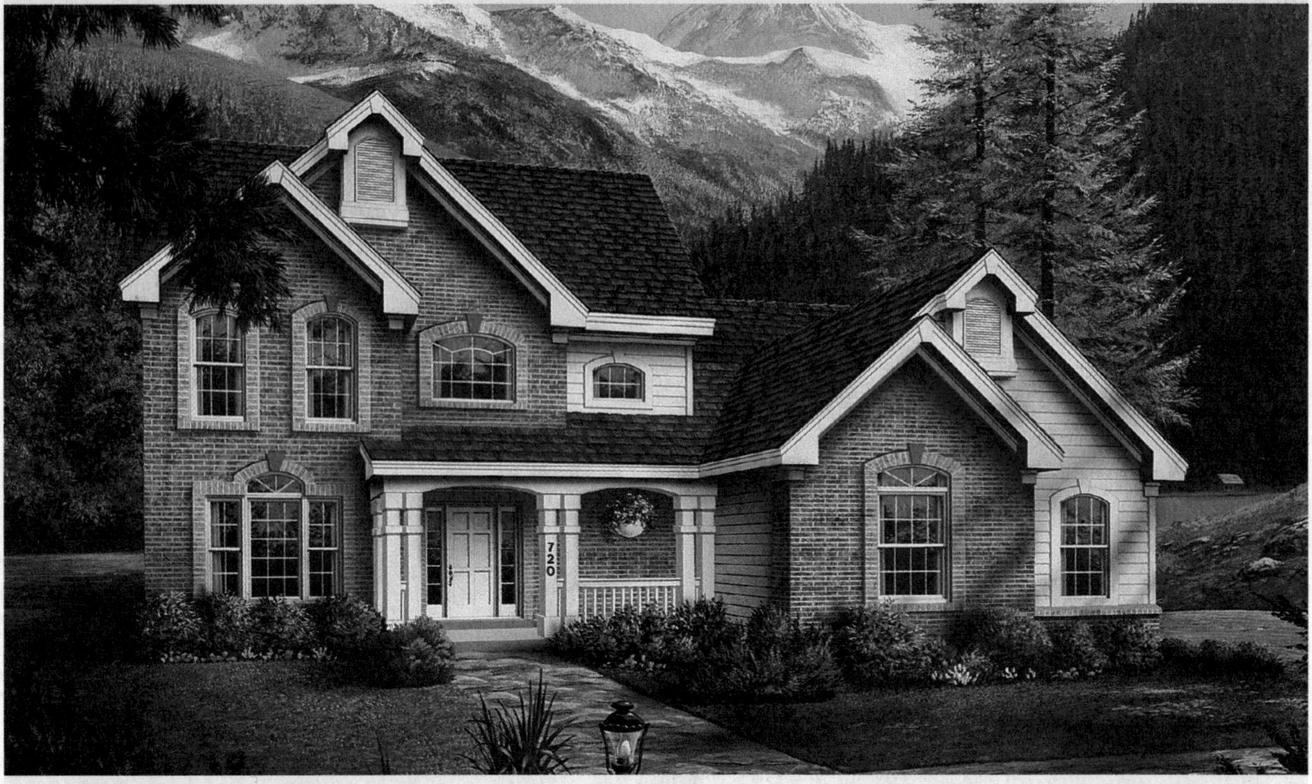

3,138 total square feet of living area | **Price Code E**

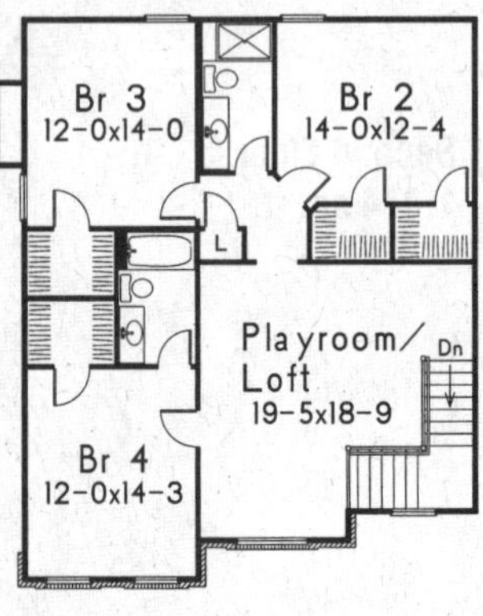
Br 3
12-0x14-0
Br 2
14-0x12-4
L
Playroom/
Loft
19-5x18-9
Dn
Br 4
12-0x14-3

Second Floor
1,180 sq. ft.

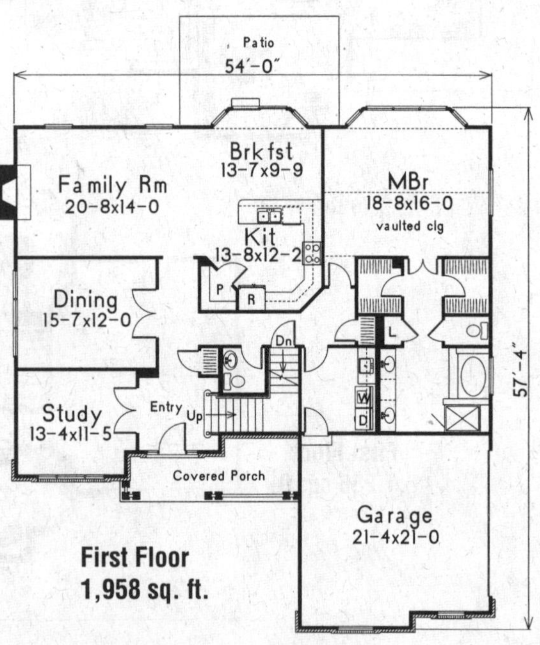
Patio
54'-0"
Brkfst
13-7x9-9
Family Rm
20-8x14-0
MBr
18-8x16-0
vaulted clg
Kit
13-8x12-2
P
R
Dining
15-7x12-0
Dn
L
W
D
57'-4"
Study
13-4x11-5
Entry
Up
Covered Porch
Garage
21-4x21-0

First Floor
1,958 sq. ft.

Special features

- Impressive stair descends into large entry and study through double-doors
- Private dining is spacious and secluded
- Family room, master suite and laundry are among the many generously-sized rooms
- Three large bedrooms, two baths and four walk-in closets compose the second floor
- 4 bedrooms, 3 1/2 baths, 2-car side entry garage
- Basement foundation

Elegant Entrance

3,357 total square feet of living area **Price Code F**

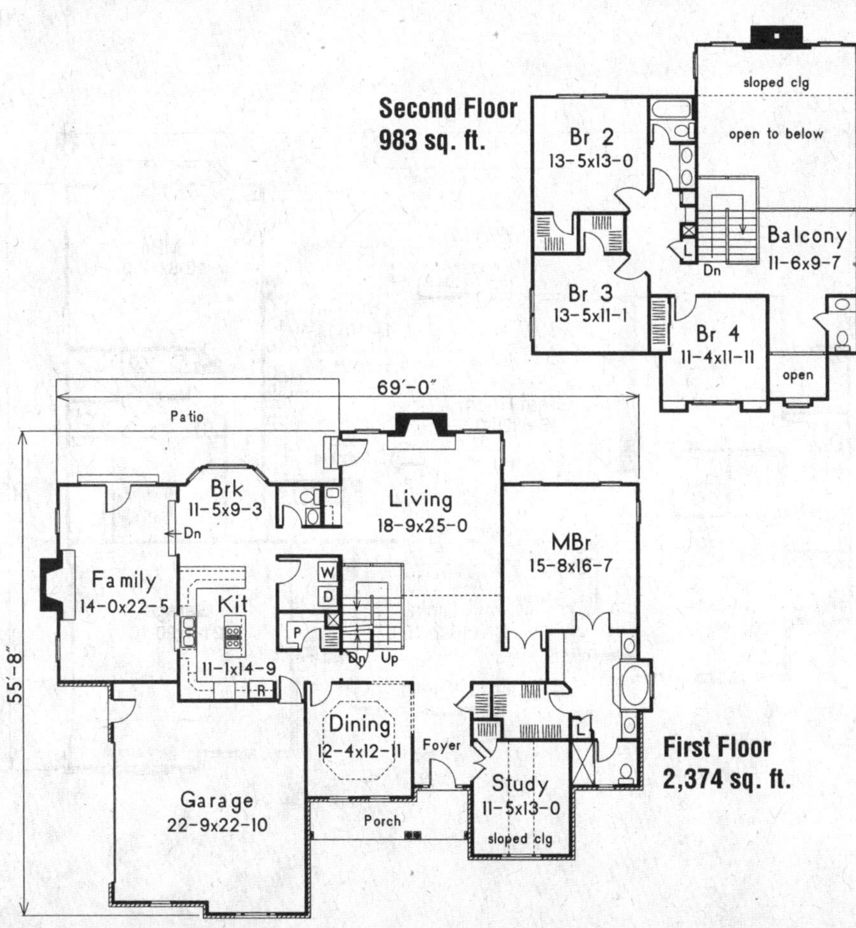
Second Floor
983 sq. ft.
sloped clg
open to below
Br 2
13-5x13-0
Balcony
11-6x9-7
Dn
L
Br 3
13-5x11-1
Br 4
11-4x11-11
open
69′-0″
Patio
Brk
11-5x9-3
Dn
Living
18-9x25-0
MBr
15-8x16-7
Family
14-0x22-5
Kit
11-1x14-9
W
D
P
R
Dn
Up
55′-8″
Dining
12-4x12-11
Foyer
L
Study
11-5x13-0
sloped clg
Garage
22-9x22-10
Porch
First Floor
2,374 sq. ft.

Special features

- Attractive balcony overlooks entry foyer and living area
- Balcony area could easily convert to a fifth bedroom
- Spacious kitchen also opens into sunken family room with a fireplace
- First floor master suite boasts large walk-in closet and dressing area
- Central laundry room with laundry chute from second floor
- 4 bedrooms, 2 full baths, 2 half baths, 2-car side entry garage
- Basement foundation, drawings also include crawl space and slab foundations

The Family
Handyman

Plan #708-0821

Spacious One-Story With French Country Flavor

2,695 total square feet of living area **Price Code E**

Special features

- A grandscale great room features a fireplace with flanking shelves, handsome entry foyer with staircase and opens to large kitchen and breakfast room
- Roomy master bedroom has a bay window, huge walk-in closet and bath with a shower built for two
- Bedrooms #2 and #3 are generously oversized with walk-in closets and a jack and jill style bath
- 3 bedrooms, 2 1/2 baths, 2-car side entry garage
- Basement foundation

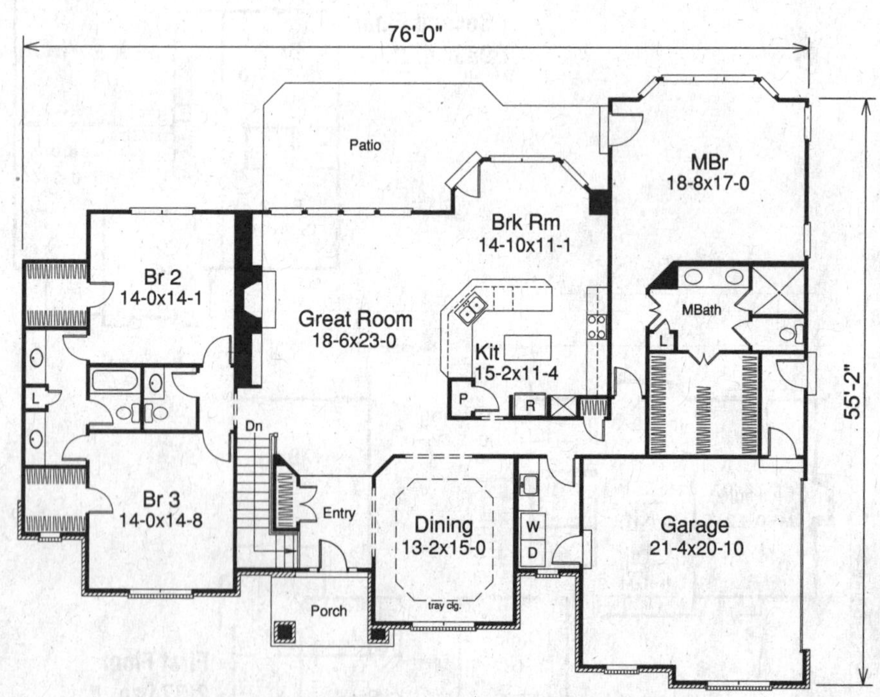
76'-0"
55'-2"
Patio
MBr
18-8x17-0
Brk Rm
14-10x11-1
Br 2
14-0x14-1
Great Room
18-6x23-0
MBath
Kit
15-2x11-4
Dn
Br 3
14-0x14-8
Entry
Dining
13-2x15-0
Garage
21-4x20-10
Porch
tray clg.

TO ORDER BLUEPRINTS USE THE FORM ON PAGE 15 OR CALL TOLL-FREE 1-877-671-6036

View thousands more home plans online at www.familyhandyman.com/homeplans

Refined Features Throughout

1,660 total square feet of living area

Price Code B

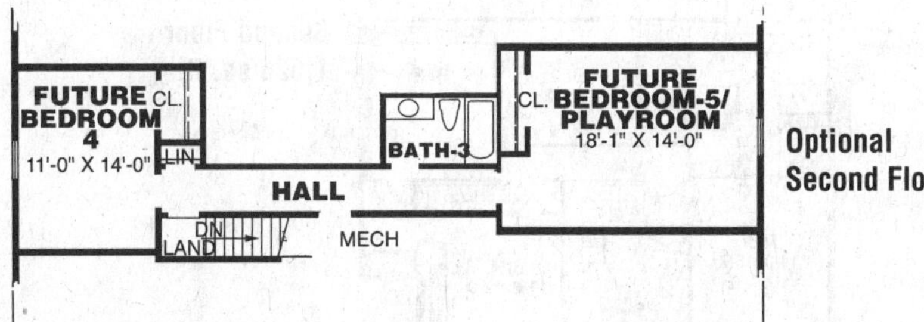
FUTURE BEDROOM 4
11'-0" X 14'-0"
CL.
LIN
BATH-3
CL.
FUTURE BEDROOM-5/ PLAYROOM
18'-1" X 14'-0"
HALL
DN
LAND
MECH

Optional Second Floor

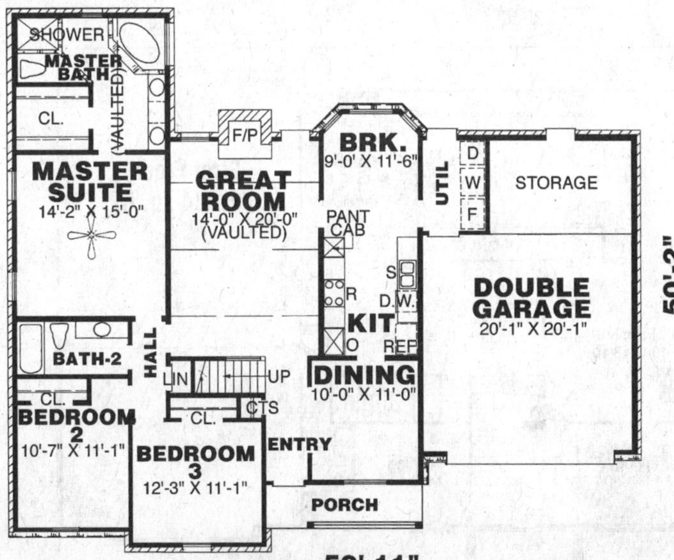
SHOWER
MASTER BATH
(VAULTED)
CL.
MASTER SUITE
14'-2" X 15'-0"
F/P
GREAT ROOM
14'-0" X 20'-0"
(VAULTED)
BRK.
9'-0' X 11'-6"
PANT
CAB
UTIL
D
W
F
STORAGE
R
S
D.W.
KIT
O
REF
DOUBLE GARAGE
20'-1" X 20'-1"
50'-2"
BATH-2
HALL
LIN
UP
DINING
10'-0" X 11'-0"
CL.
CL.
CTS
BEDROOM 2
10'-7" X 11'-1"
BEDROOM 3
12'-3" X 11'-1"
ENTRY
PORCH
59'-11"

First Floor
1,660 sq. ft.

Special features

- Vaulted great room with fireplace has a feeling of luxury
- Bayed breakfast room is a sunny dining area
- Large storage area in garage could easily be converted to a work shop
- Future area on the second floor has an additional 678 square feet of living area
- 3 bedrooms, 2 baths, 2-car garage
- Slab foundation

Plan #708-0754

Prestigious And Family Oriented

3,420 total square feet of living area **Price Code F**

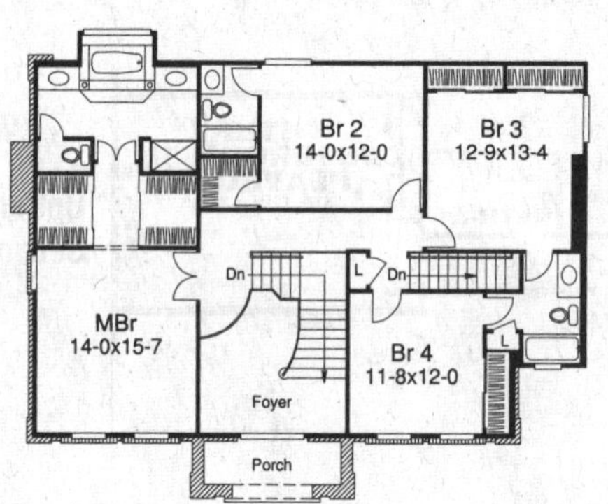
Br 2
14-0x12-0
Br 3
12-9x13-4
Dn
L
Dn
MBr
14-0x15-7
Br 4
11-8x12-0
L
Foyer
Porch

Second Floor
1,526 sq. ft.

Special features

- Hip roofs, elliptical windows and brick facade with quoins emphasize stylish sophisticated living
- Grand foyer has flared staircase in addition to secondary stair from kitchen
- Enormous kitchen features a cooktop island, walk-in pantry, angled breakfast bar and computer desk
- Splendid gallery connects family room and wet bar with vaulted hearth room
- Master bedroom has a coffered ceiling, double walk-in closets and a lavish bath
- 4 bedrooms, 3 1/2 baths, 3-car garage
- Walk-out basement foundation

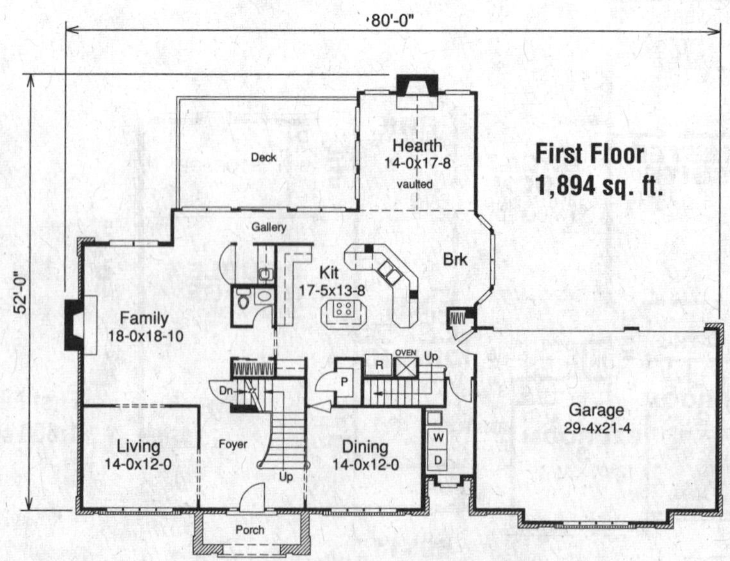
80'-0"
52'-0"
Deck
Hearth
14-0x17-8
vaulted
Gallery
Kit
17-5x13-8
Brk
Family
18-0x18-10
R
OVEN
Up
P
Dn
Living
14-0x12-0
Foyer
Dining
14-0x12-0
W
D
Up
Garage
29-4x21-4
Porch

First Floor
1,894 sq. ft.

TO ORDER BLUEPRINTS USE THE FORM ON PAGE 15 OR CALL TOLL-FREE 1-877-671-6036

View thousands more home plans online at www.familyhandyman.com/homeplans

Plan #708-0827

Affordable Two-Story Has It All

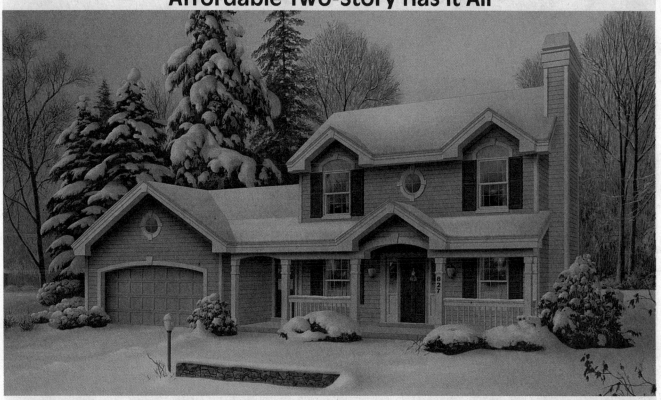

1,308 total square feet of living area

Price Code A

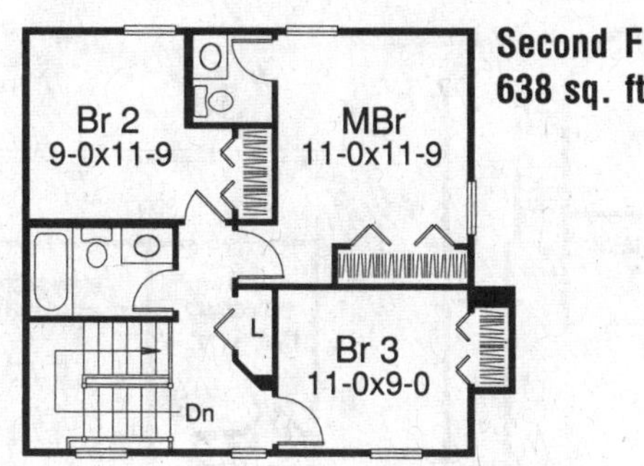
Br 2
9-0x11-9
MBr
11-0x11-9
L
Br 3
11-0x9-0
Dn

Second Floor
638 sq. ft.

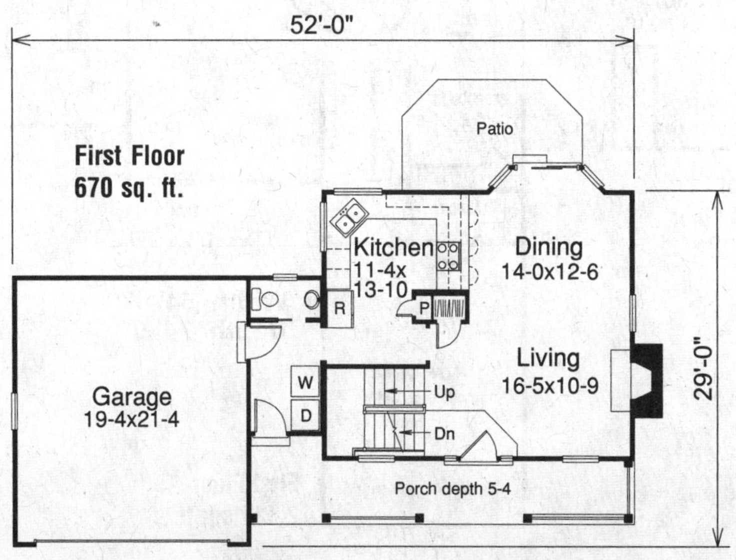
52'-0"
Patio
Kitchen
11-4x
13-10
Dining
14-0x12-6
R
P
Living
16-5x10-9
W
D
Up
Dn
Garage
19-4x21-4
Porch depth 5-4
29'-0"

First Floor
670 sq. ft.

Special features

- Multi-gabled facade and elongated porch create a pleasing country appeal
- Large dining room with bay window and view to rear patio opens to a full-functional kitchen with snack bar
- An attractive U-shaped stair with hall overlook leads to the second floor
- 3 bedrooms, 1 full bath, 2 half baths, 2-car garage
- Basement foundation

TO ORDER BLUEPRINTS USE THE FORM ON PAGE 15 OR CALL TOLL-FREE 1-877-671-6036

View thousands more home plans online at www.familyhandyman.com/homeplans

The Family
Handyman

Plan #708-MG-02120

Open And Airy Grand Room

© 2003, Garrell Associates, Inc.

Christine Canova 2/02

2,111 total square feet of living area **Price Code H**

<u>*Special features*</u>

- 9' ceilings throughout first floor
- Formal dining room has columns separating it from other areas while allowing it to maintain an open feel
- Master bedroom has privacy from other bedrooms
- Bonus room on the second floor has an additional 345 square feet of living area
- 3 bedrooms, 2 baths, 2-car side entry garage
- Basement foundation

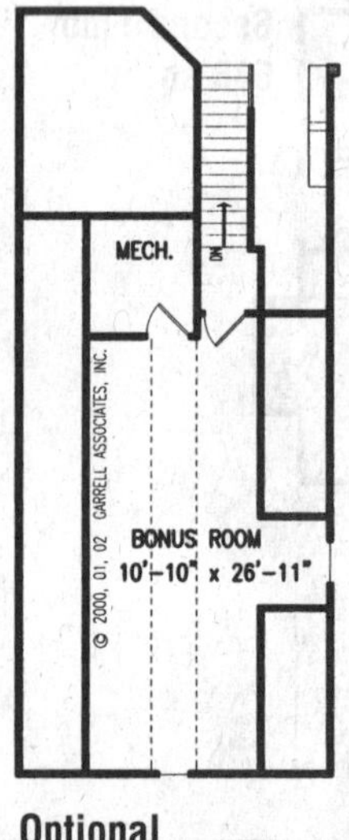
MECH.
BONUS ROOM
10'-10" x 26'-11"
© 2000, 01, 02 GARRELL ASSOCIATES, INC.

Optional Second Floor

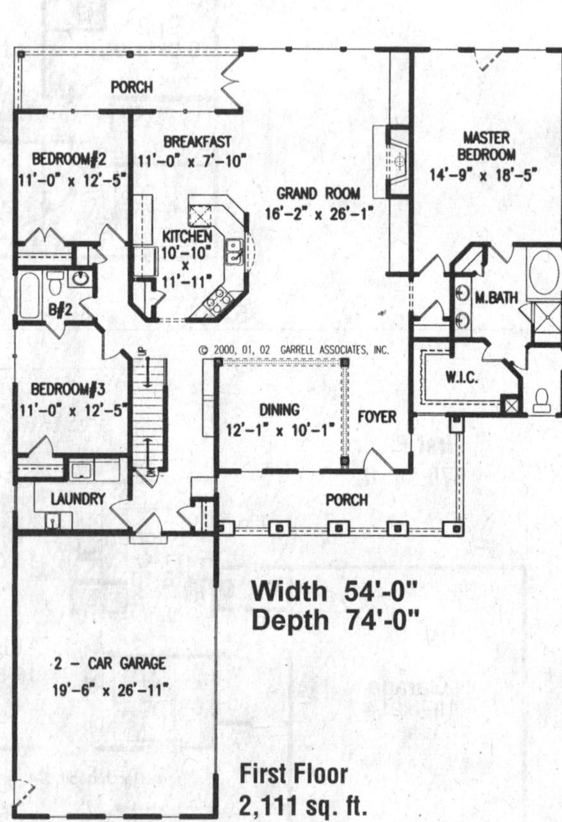
PORCH
BEDROOM #2
11'-0" x 12'-5"
BREAKFAST
11'-0" x 7'-10"
KITCHEN
10'-10" x 11'-11"
GRAND ROOM
16'-2" x 26'-1"
MASTER BEDROOM
14'-9" x 18'-5"
M.BATH
W.I.C.
B#2
BEDROOM #3
11'-0" x 12'-5"
© 2000, 01, 02 GARRELL ASSOCIATES, INC.
DINING
12'-1" x 10'-1"
FOYER
LAUNDRY
PORCH
2 - CAR GARAGE
19'-6" x 26'-11"

Width 54'-0"
Depth 74'-0"

First Floor
2,111 sq. ft.

TO ORDER BLUEPRINTS USE THE FORM ON PAGE 15 OR CALL TOLL-FREE 1-877-671-6036

View thousands more home plans online at www.familyhandyman.com/homeplans

The Family
Handyman

Plan #708-0224

Great Traffic Flow On Both Floors

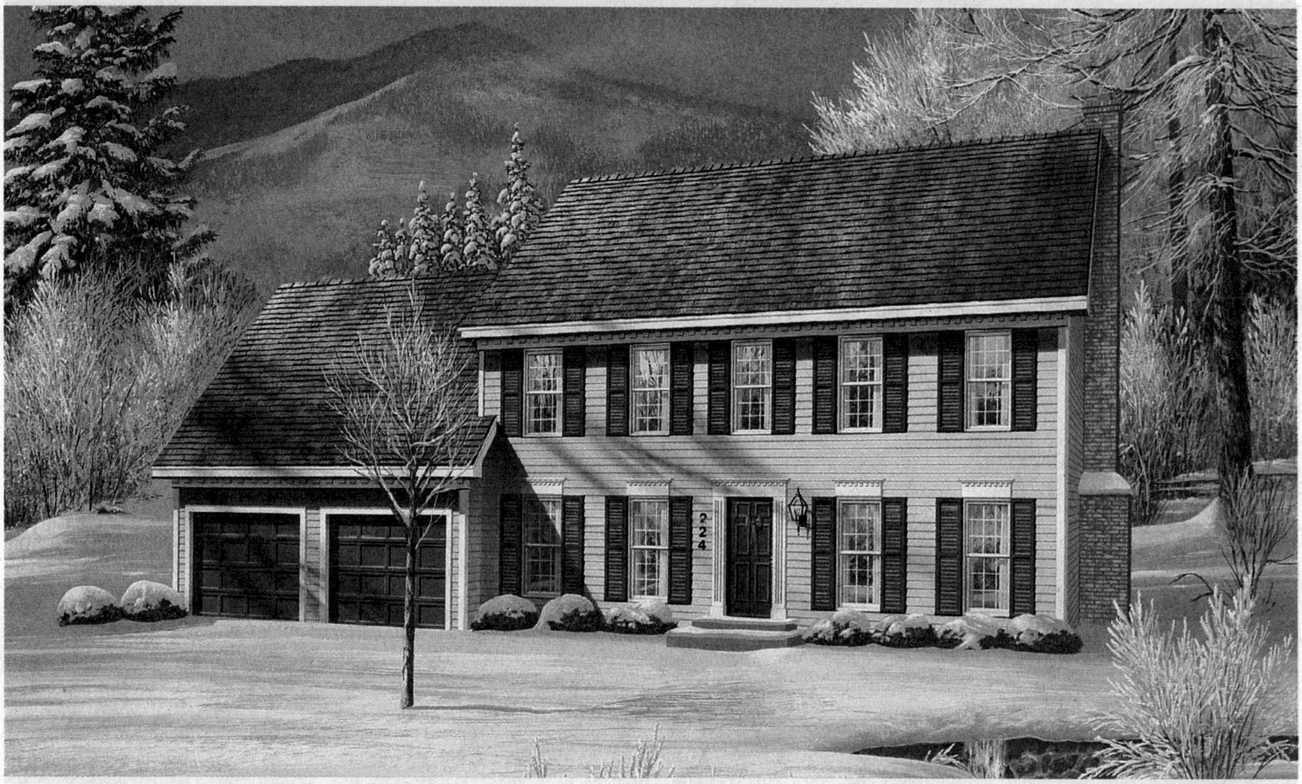

2,461 total square feet of living area

Price Code D

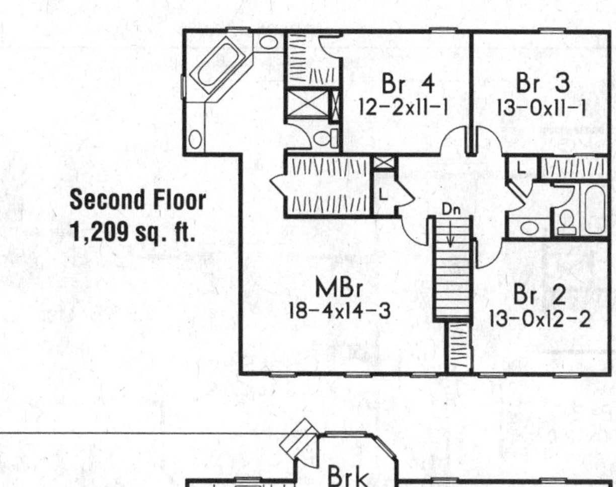
Second Floor
1,209 sq. ft.
Br 4
12-2x11-1
Br 3
13-0x11-1
L
L
Dn
MBr
18-4x14-3
Br 2
13-0x12-2

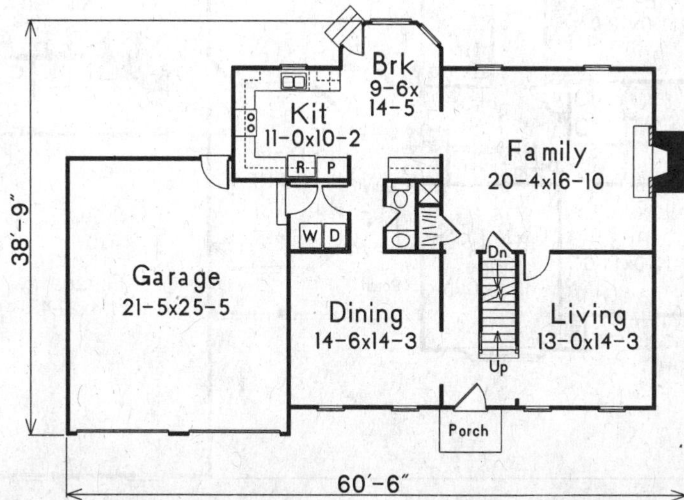
Brk
9-6x
14-5
Kit
11-0x10-2
R
P
Family
20-4x16-10
W
D
Dn
38′-9″
Garage
21-5x25-5
Dining
14-6x14-3
Living
13-0x14-3
Up
Porch
60′-6″

First Floor
1,252 sq. ft.

Special features

- Unique corner tub, double vanities and walk-in closet enhance the large master bedroom
- Fireplace provides focus in the spacious family room
- Centrally located half bath for guests
- 4 bedrooms, 2 1/2 baths, 2-car garage
- Basement foundation, drawings also include slab and crawl space foundations

The Family
Handyman

Country Home Focused On Patio Views

2,547 total square feet of living area **Price Code D**

Special features

- Grand-sized great room features a 12' volume ceiling, fireplace with built-in wrap-around shelving and patio doors with sidelights and transom windows
- The walk-in pantry, computer desk, large breakfast island for seven and bayed breakfast area are the many features of this outstanding kitchen
- The master bedroom suite enjoys a luxurious bath, large walk-in closets and patio access
- 4 bedrooms, 2 1/2 baths, 3-car side entry garage
- Basement foundation

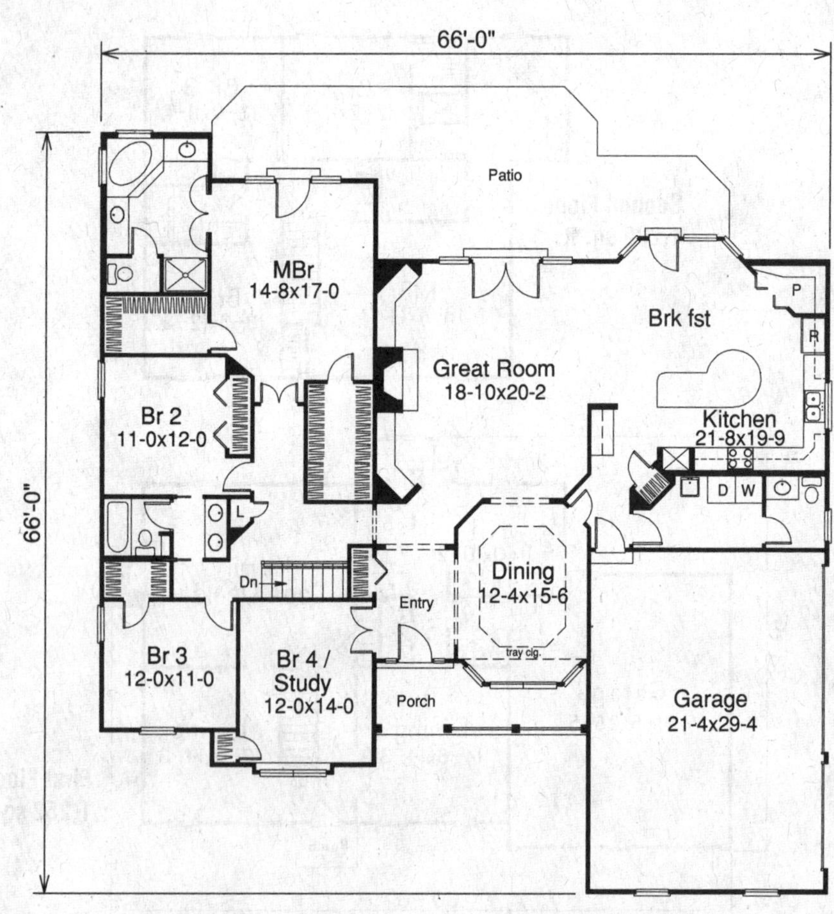
66'-0"
66'-0"
Patio
MBr
14-8x17-0
Brk fst
P
R
Great Room
18-10x20-2
Br 2
11-0x12-0
Kitchen
21-8x19-9
D
W
L
Dining
12-4x15-6
tray clg.
Dn
Entry
Br 3
12-0x11-0
Br 4 /
Study
12-0x14-0
Porch
Garage
21-4x29-4

TO ORDER BLUEPRINTS USE THE FORM ON PAGE 15 OR CALL TOLL-FREE 1-877-671-6036

View thousands more home plans online at www.familyhandyman.com/homeplans

The Family
Handyman

Plan #708-0485

Vaulted Ceiling Frames Circle-Top Window

1,195 total square feet of living area **Price Code AA**

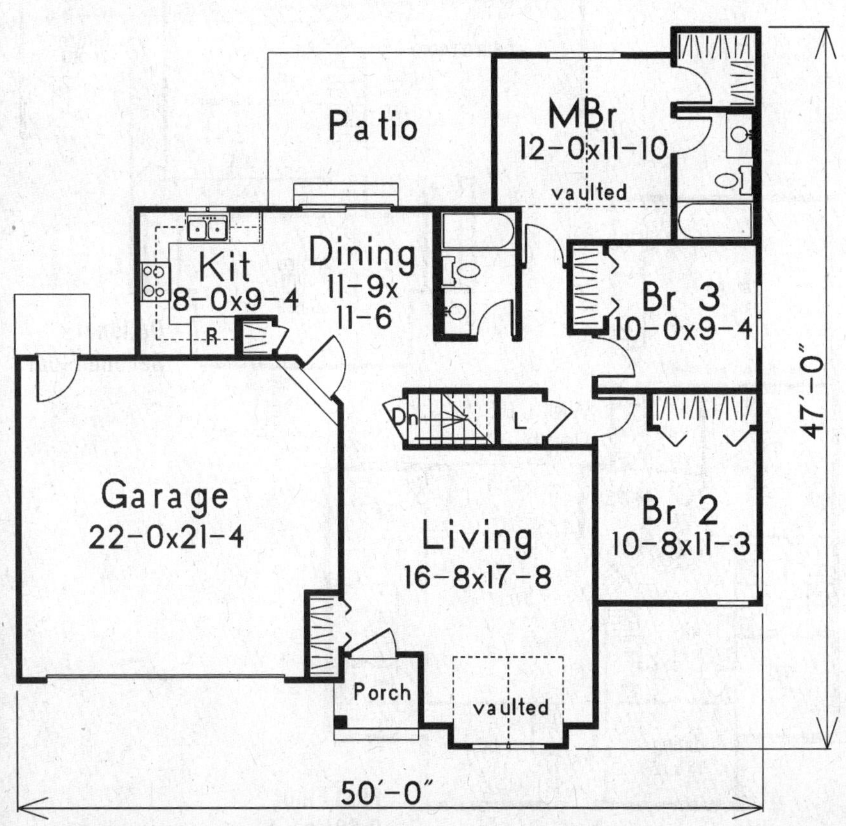

Patio
MBr
12-0x11-10
vaulted
Kit
8-0x9-4
Dining
11-9x
11-6
Br 3
10-0x9-4
R
Dn
L
Garage
22-0x21-4
Living
16-8x17-8
Br 2
10-8x11-3
Porch
vaulted
47'-0"
50'-0"

Special features

- Dining room opens onto the patio
- Master bedroom features vaulted ceiling, private bath and walk-in closet
- Coat closets located by both the entrances
- Convenient secondary entrance at the back of the garage
- 3 bedrooms, 2 baths, 2-car garage
- Basement foundation

TO ORDER BLUEPRINTS USE THE FORM ON PAGE 15 OR CALL TOLL-FREE 1-877-671-6036

The Family
Handyman

Plan #708-BF-2610

Private Master Suite

2,684 total square feet of living area

Price Code E

Special features

- Formal dining room off kitchen
- Enormous master bedroom with private bath and walk-in closet
- Optional second floor has an additional 926 square feet of living area
- 3 bedrooms, 2 1/2 baths, 2-car side entry garage
- Slab or crawl space foundation, please specify when ordering

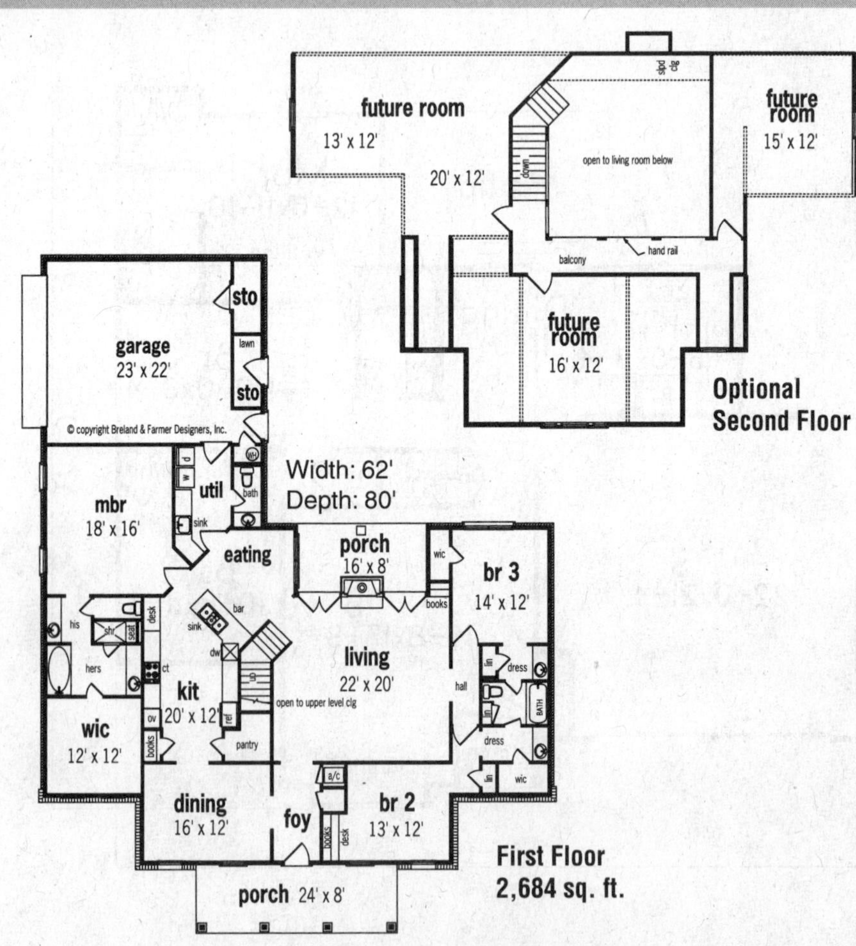
future room
13' x 12'
20' x 12'
open to living room below
future room
15' x 12'
down
balcony
hand rail
future room
16' x 12'
Optional
Second Floor
sto
lawn
garage
23' x 22'
sto
© copyright Breland & Farmer Designers, Inc.
util
bath
sink
mbr
18' x 16'
eating
Width: 62'
Depth: 80'
porch
16' x 8'
wic
br 3
14' x 12'
books
his
hers
desk
bar
sink
dw
living
22' x 20'
open to upper level clg
hall
dress
dress
wic
kit
20' x 12'
ref
pantry
wic
12' x 12'
ov
books
a/c
dining
16' x 12'
foy
books
desk
br 2
13' x 12'
porch 24' x 8'
First Floor
2,684 sq. ft.

Plan #708-0427

Lower Level, Great For Entertaining

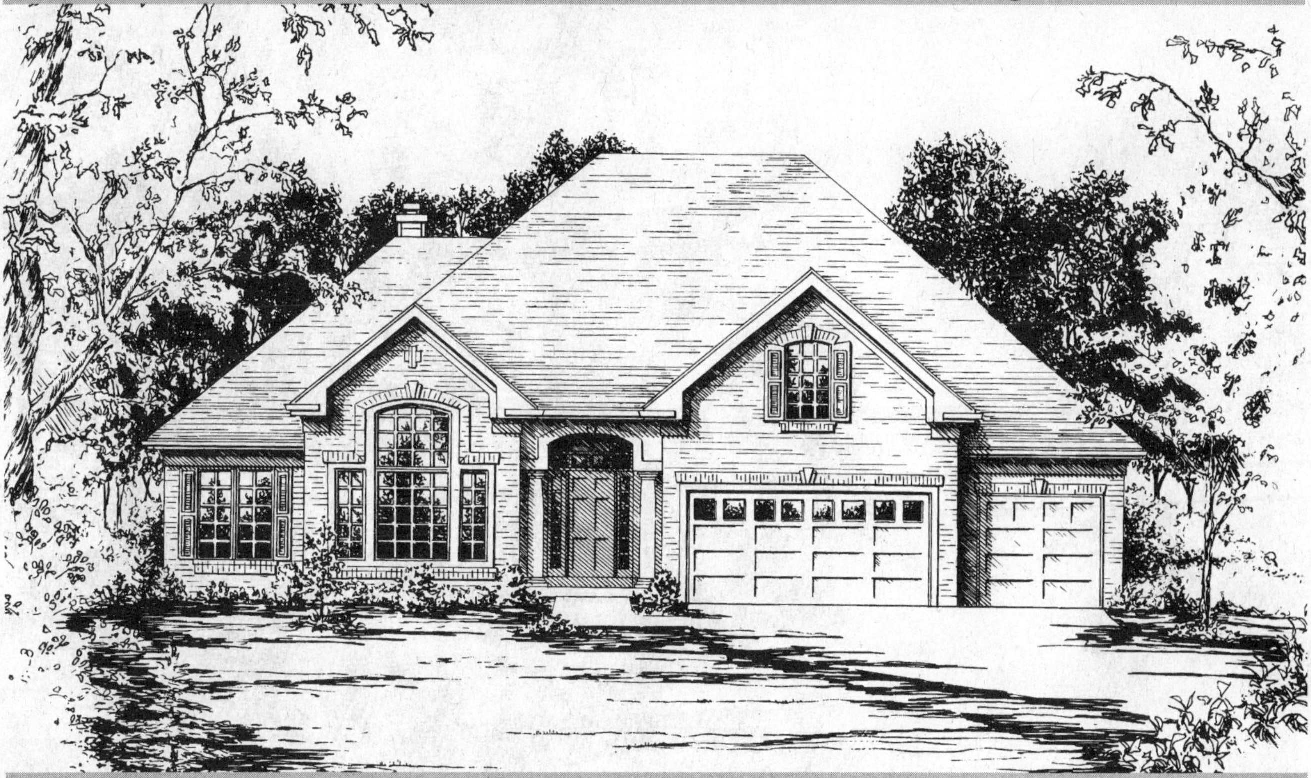

3,411 total square feet of living area **Price Code F**

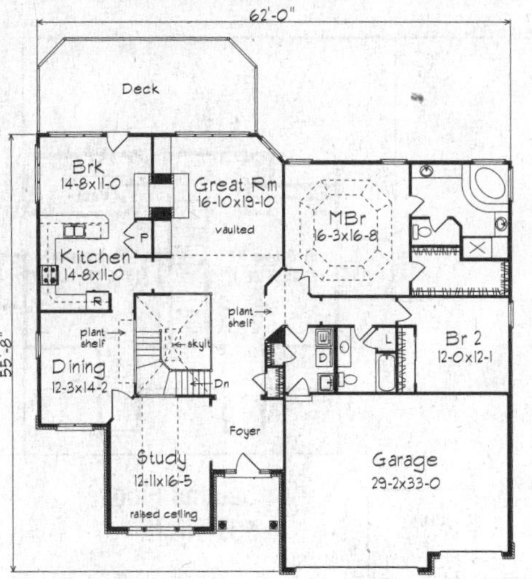
62'-0"
Deck
Brk
14-8x11-0
Great Rm
16-10x19-10
vaulted
MBr
16-3x16-8
Kitchen
14-8x11-0
plant shelf
plant shelf
skylt
Dining
12-3x14-2
Dn
Br 2
12-0x12-1
Foyer
Study
12-11x16-5
raised ceiling
Garage
29-2x33-0
55'-8"

First Floor
2,182 sq. ft.

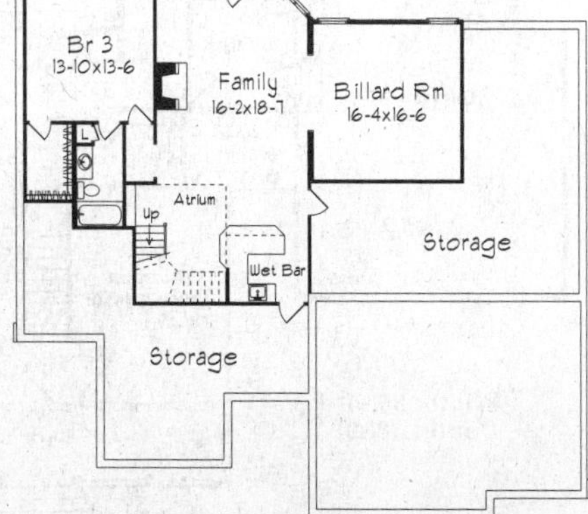
Br 3
13-10x13-6
Family
16-2x18-7
Billard Rm
16-4x16-6
Atrium
Up
Wet Bar
Storage
Storage

Lower Level
1,229 sq. ft.

Special features

- Foyer opens to large study with raised ceiling
- Master suite features octagon-shaped raised ceiling and private bath with double vanity and corner whirlpool tub
- Expansive windows and a two-way fireplace in great room
- 3 bedrooms, 3 baths, 3-car garage
- Basement foundation

Plan #708-CHP-1633-A-25

Efficient Floor Plan

1,609 total square feet of living area **Price Code B**

Special features

- Sunny bay window in breakfast room
- U-shaped kitchen with pantry
- Spacious utility room
- Bedrooms on second floor feature dormers
- Family room includes plenty of space for entertaining
- 3 bedrooms, 2 1/2 baths, 2-car garage
- Slab foundation

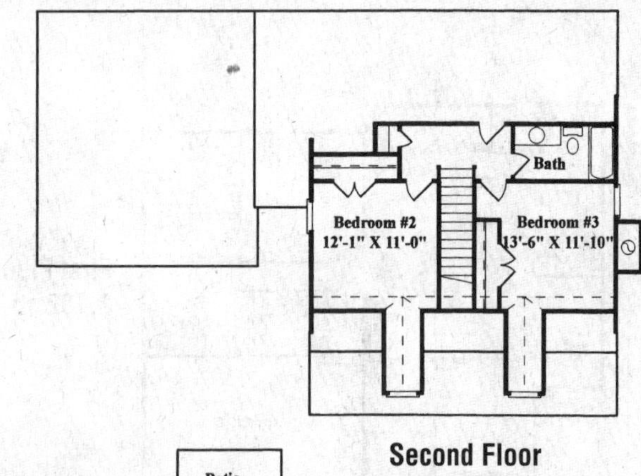
Bath
Bedroom #2
12'-1" X 11'-0"
Bedroom #3
13'-6" X 11'-10"

Second Floor
537 sq. ft.

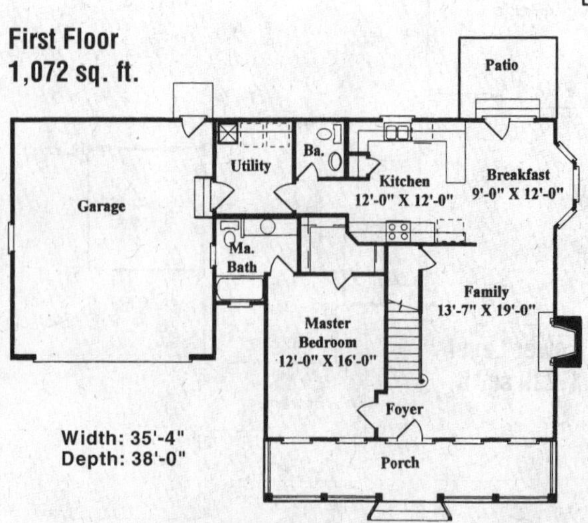
Patio
Utility
Ba.
Kitchen
12'-0" X 12'-0"
Breakfast
9'-0" X 12'-0"
Garage
Ma. Bath
Family
13'-7" X 19'-0"
Master Bedroom
12'-0" X 16'-0"
Foyer
Porch

First Floor
1,072 sq. ft.

Width: 35'-4"
Depth: 38'-0"

TO ORDER BLUEPRINTS USE THE FORM ON PAGE 15 OR CALL TOLL-FREE 1-877-671-6036

View thousands more home plans online at www.familyhandyman.com/homeplans

The Family
Handyman

Plan #708-0296

Compact Home With Functional Design

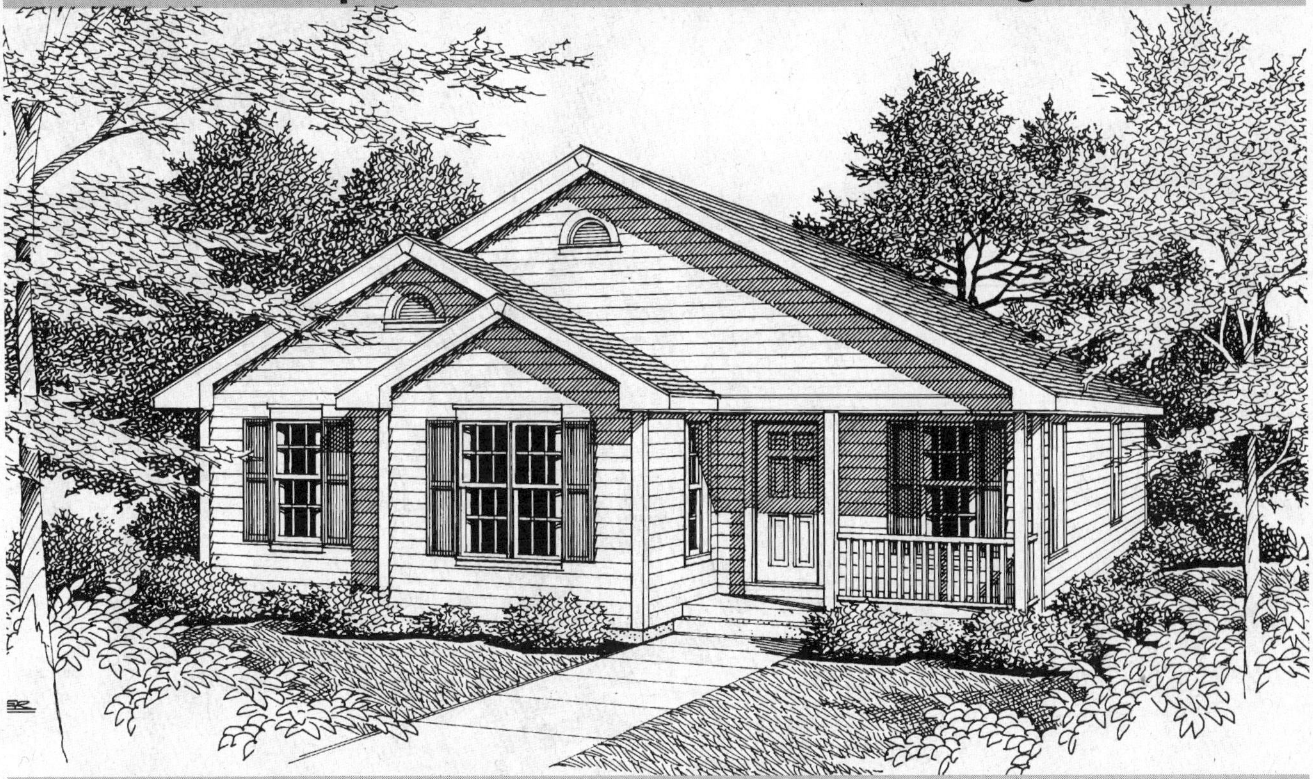

1,396 total square feet of living area **Price Code A**

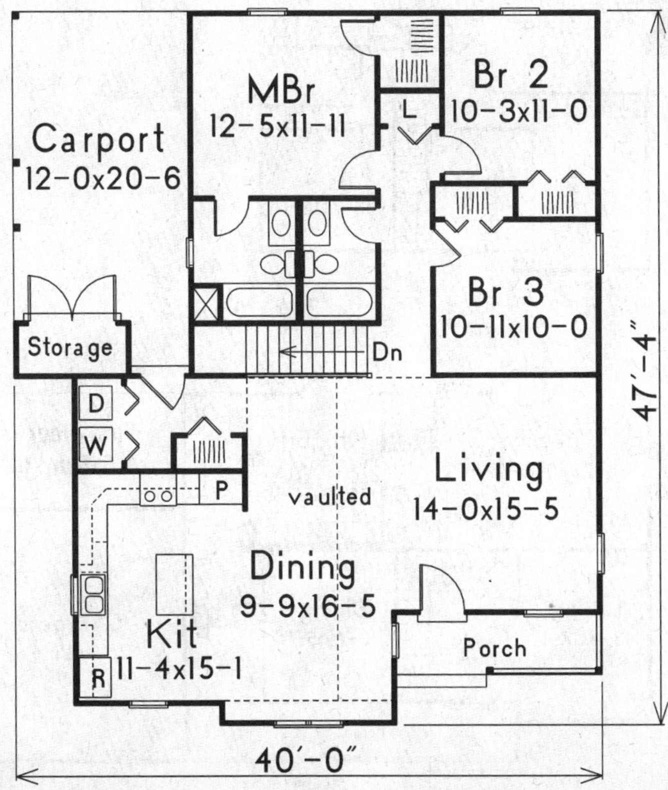
MBr
12-5x11-11
Br 2
10-3x11-0
L
Carport
12-0x20-6
Br 3
10-11x10-0
Storage
Dn
D
W
P
vaulted
Living
14-0x15-5
Dining
9-9x16-5
Kit
11-4x15-1
R
Porch
47′-4″
40′-0″

Special features

- Gabled front adds interest to facade
- Living and dining rooms share a vaulted ceiling
- Master bedroom features a walk-in closet and private bath
- Functional kitchen with a center work island and convenient pantry
- 3 bedrooms, 2 baths, 1-car carport
- Basement foundation; drawings also include crawl space foundation

TO ORDER BLUEPRINTS USE THE FORM ON PAGE 15 OR CALL TOLL-FREE 1-877-671-6036

The Family
Handyman

Plan #708-0152

Charming Victorian Has Unexpected Pleasures

2,935 total square feet of living area **Price Code E**

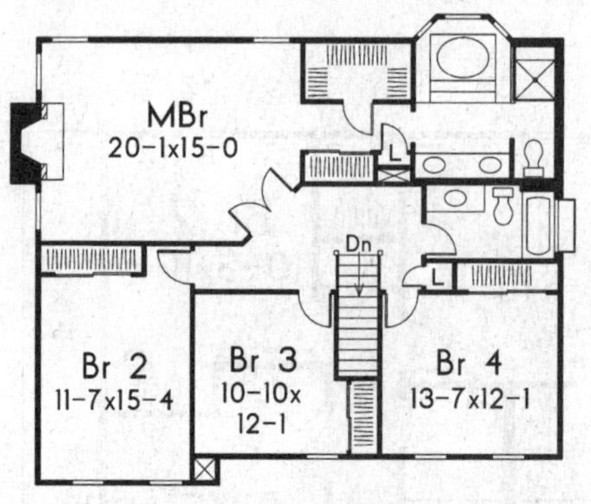
MBr
20-1x15-0
L
Dn
L
Br 2
11-7x15-4
Br 3
10-10x
12-1
Br 4
13-7x12-1

Second Floor
1,320 sq. ft.

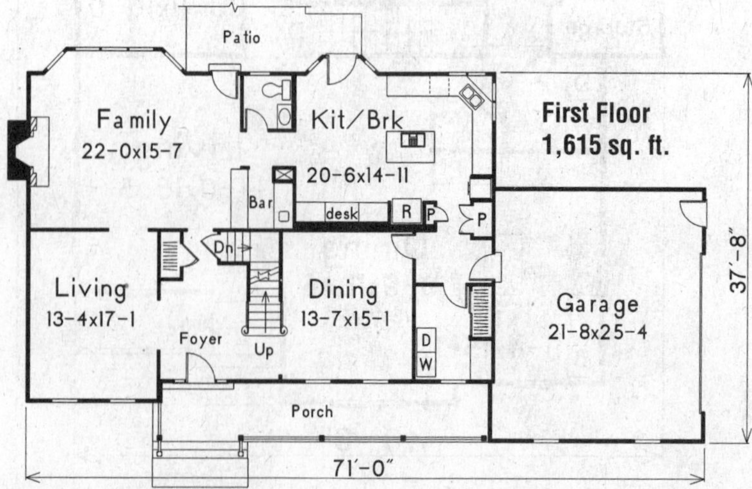
Patio
Family
22-0x15-7
Kit/Brk
20-6x14-11
Bar
desk
R
P
P
Dn
Living
13-4x17-1
Foyer
Up
Dining
13-7x15-1
D
W
Garage
21-8x25-4
Porch
71'-0"
37'-8"
First Floor
1,615 sq. ft.

Special features

- Gracious entry foyer with handsome stairway opens to separate living and dining rooms
- Kitchen has vaulted ceiling and skylight, island worktop, breakfast area with bay window and two separate pantries
- Large second floor master bedroom suite with fireplace, raised tub, dressing area with vaulted ceiling and skylight
- 4 bedrooms, 2 1/2 baths, 2-car side entry garage
- Basement foundation

TO ORDER BLUEPRINTS USE THE FORM ON PAGE 15 OR CALL TOLL-FREE 1-877-671-6036

View thousands more home plans online at www.familyhandyman.com/homeplans

The Family
Handyman

Plan #708-DDI-93-102

A Lovely Ranch Style

1,288 total square feet of living area

Price Code A

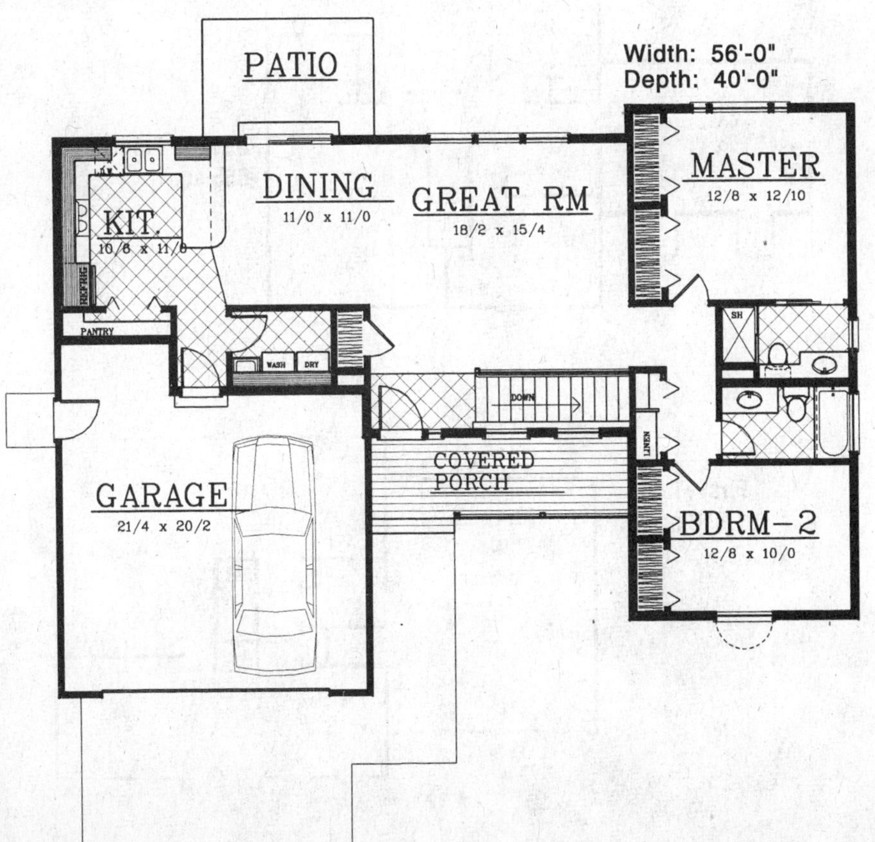
PATIO
DINING
11/0 x 11/0
GREAT RM
18/2 x 15/4
KIT.
10/8 x 11/0
PANTRY
WASH
DRY
DOWN
MASTER
12/8 x 12/10
SH
LINEN
COVERED
PORCH
GARAGE
21/4 x 20/2
BDRM–2
12/8 x 10/0

Width: 56'-0"
Depth: 40'-0"

Special features

- Energy efficient home with 2" x 6" exterior walls
- 9' ceilings throughout this home
- 2 bedrooms, 2 baths, 2-car garage
- Basement, crawl space or slab foundation, please specify when ordering

TO ORDER BLUEPRINTS USE THE FORM ON PAGE 15 OR CALL TOLL-FREE 1-877-671-6036

View thousands more home plans online at www.familyhandyman.com/homeplans

The Family
Handyman

Plan #708-AP-1908

Perfect Two-Story Traditional

1,998 total square feet of living area | **Price Code C**

Special features

- Large open living areas have enough space for gathering
- All bedrooms on the second floor for peace and quiet from living areas
- Formal dining space has direct access to the kitchen
- Bonus room on the second floor has an additional 320 square feet of living area
- 4 bedrooms, 2 1/2 baths, 2-car garage
- Crawl space foundation

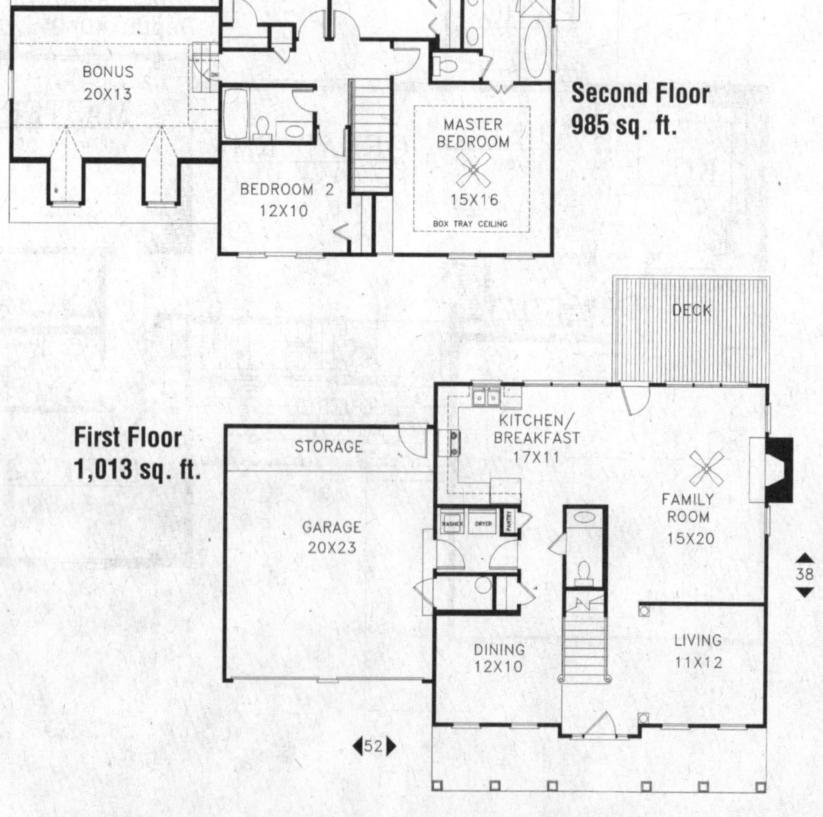
BEDROOM 4
10X10
BEDROOM 3
10X11
BONUS
20X13
MASTER
BEDROOM
15X16
BOX TRAY CEILING
BEDROOM 2
12X10
Second Floor
985 sq. ft.
DECK
KITCHEN/
BREAKFAST
17X11
STORAGE
FAMILY
ROOM
15X20
GARAGE
20X23
DINING
12X10
LIVING
11X12
38
52
First Floor
1,013 sq. ft.

TO ORDER BLUEPRINTS USE THE FORM ON PAGE 15 OR CALL TOLL-FREE 1-877-671-6036

View thousands more home plans online at www.familyhandyman.com/homeplans

Formal Living Room Greets Guests

2,380 total square feet of living area | **Price Code D**

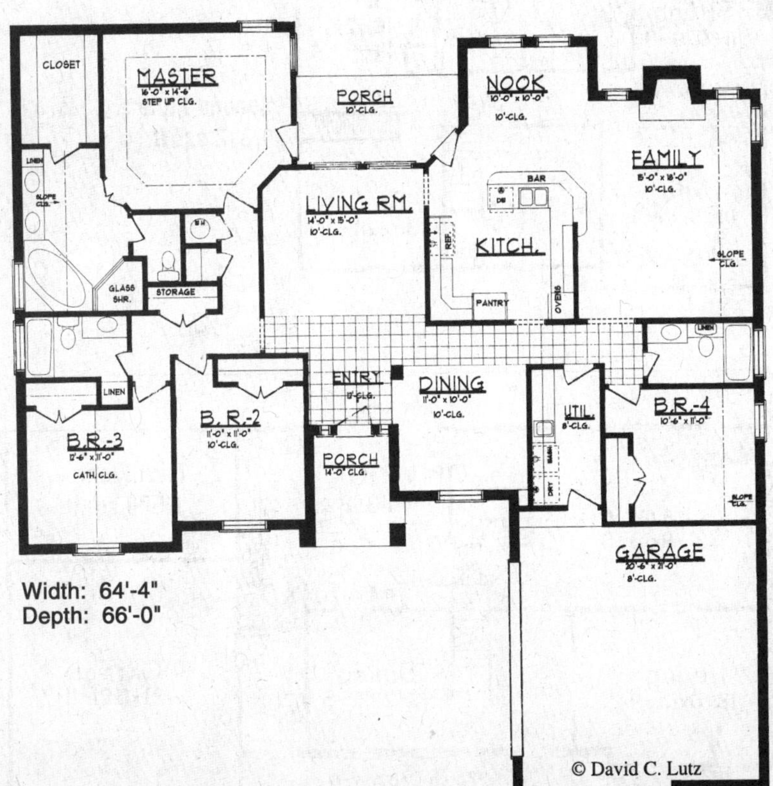
CLOSET
MASTER
PORCH
NOOK
FAMILY
LIVING RM.
KITCH.
BAR
PANTRY
STORAGE
GLASS SHR.
LINEN
ENTRY
DINING
UTIL.
B.R.-4
B.R.-3
B.R.-2
PORCH
GARAGE
Width: 64'-4"
Depth: 66'-0"
© David C. Lutz

Special features

- Unique master bedroom walks out to back porch
- Well-designed kitchen has plenty of counterspace
- Open dining room perfect for formal entertaining
- 4 bedrooms, 3 baths, 2-car side entry garage
- Slab foundation

The Family
Handyman

Plan #708-0147

A Substantial Home With Luxurious Touches

2,820 total square feet of living area **Price Code E**

Special features

- Convenient wet bar located between kitchen and family room
- Kitchen, breakfast room and large family room flow together for informal entertaining
- Luxurious master bedroom suite with fireplace and generous closet
- Oversized foyer leads to private living and dining rooms
- 4 bedrooms, 2 1/2 baths, 2-car garage
- Basement foundation, drawings also include slab and crawl space foundations

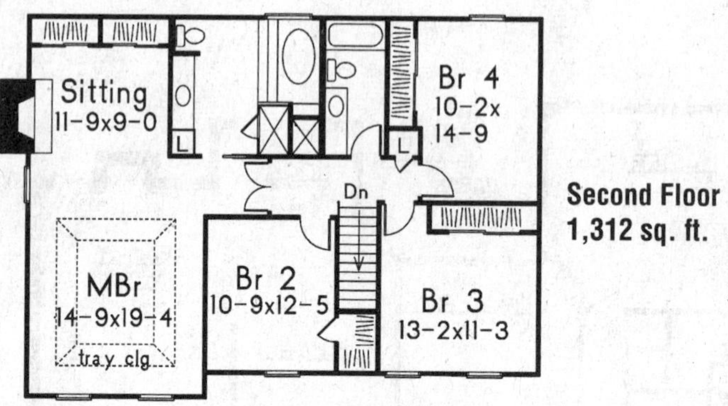
Sitting
11-9x9-0
L
Br 4
10-2x
14-9
L
Dn
MBr
14-9x19-4
tray clg
Br 2
10-9x12-5
Br 3
13-2x11-3

Second Floor
1,312 sq. ft.

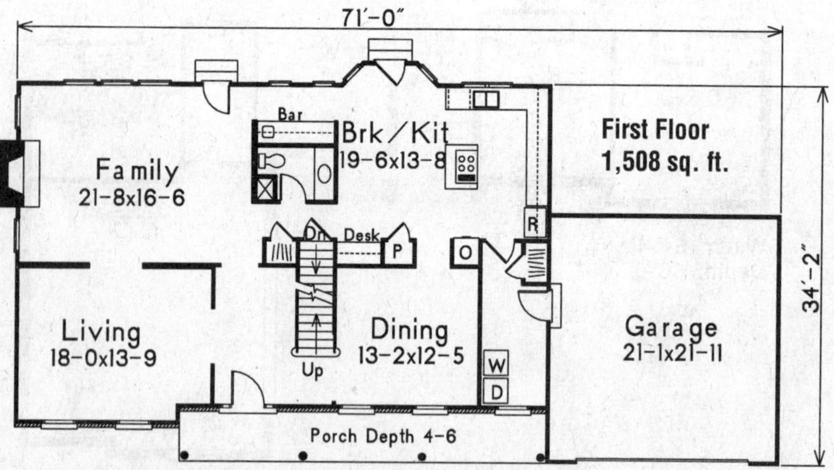
71'-0"
Bar
Brk/Kit
19-6x13-8
Family
21-8x16-6
R
Dn
Desk
P
O
Living
18-0x13-9
Up
Dining
13-2x12-5
W
D
Garage
21-1x21-11
34'-2"
Porch Depth 4-6

First Floor
1,508 sq. ft.

TO ORDER BLUEPRINTS USE THE FORM ON PAGE 15 OR CALL TOLL-FREE 1-877-671-6036

View thousands more home plans online at www.familyhandyman.com/homeplans

The Family
Handyman

Plan #708-SH-SEA-058

Fireplaces In Family And Living Rooms

2,170 total square feet of living area **Price Code C**

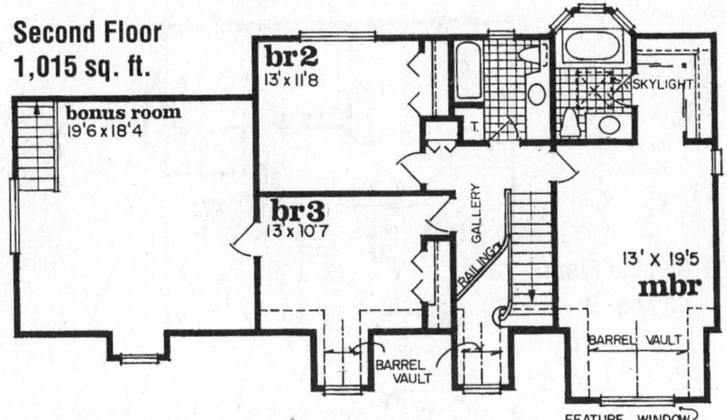
br2
13'x11'8
bonus room
19'6x18'4
T.
br3
13'x10'7
GALLERY
RAILING
SKYLIGHT
13' x 19'5
mbr
BARREL VAULT
BARREL
VAULT
FEATURE WINDOW

Second Floor
1,015 sq. ft.

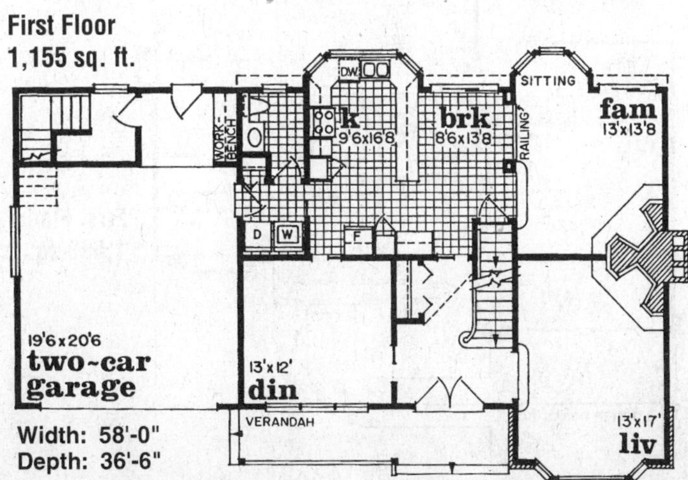
DW
WORK-BENCH
k
9'6x16'8
brk
8'6x13'8
RAILING
SITTING
fam
13'x13'8
D W
F
19'6x20'6
two-car
garage
13'x12'
din
VERANDAH
13'x17'
liv

First Floor
1,155 sq. ft.

Width: 58'-0"
Depth: 36'-6"

Special features

- Energy efficient home with 2" x 6" exterior walls
- Barrel vaulted two-story entrance foyer leads to an angled gallery
- Kitchen features a sunny bay window
- Bonus room with private staircase has an additional 390 square feet of living area
- 3 bedrooms, 2 1/2 baths, 2-car garage
- Basement foundation

TO ORDER BLUEPRINTS USE THE FORM ON PAGE 15 OR CALL TOLL-FREE 1-877-671-6036

View thousands more home plans online at www.familyhandyman.com/homeplans

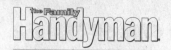

Large Utility Room

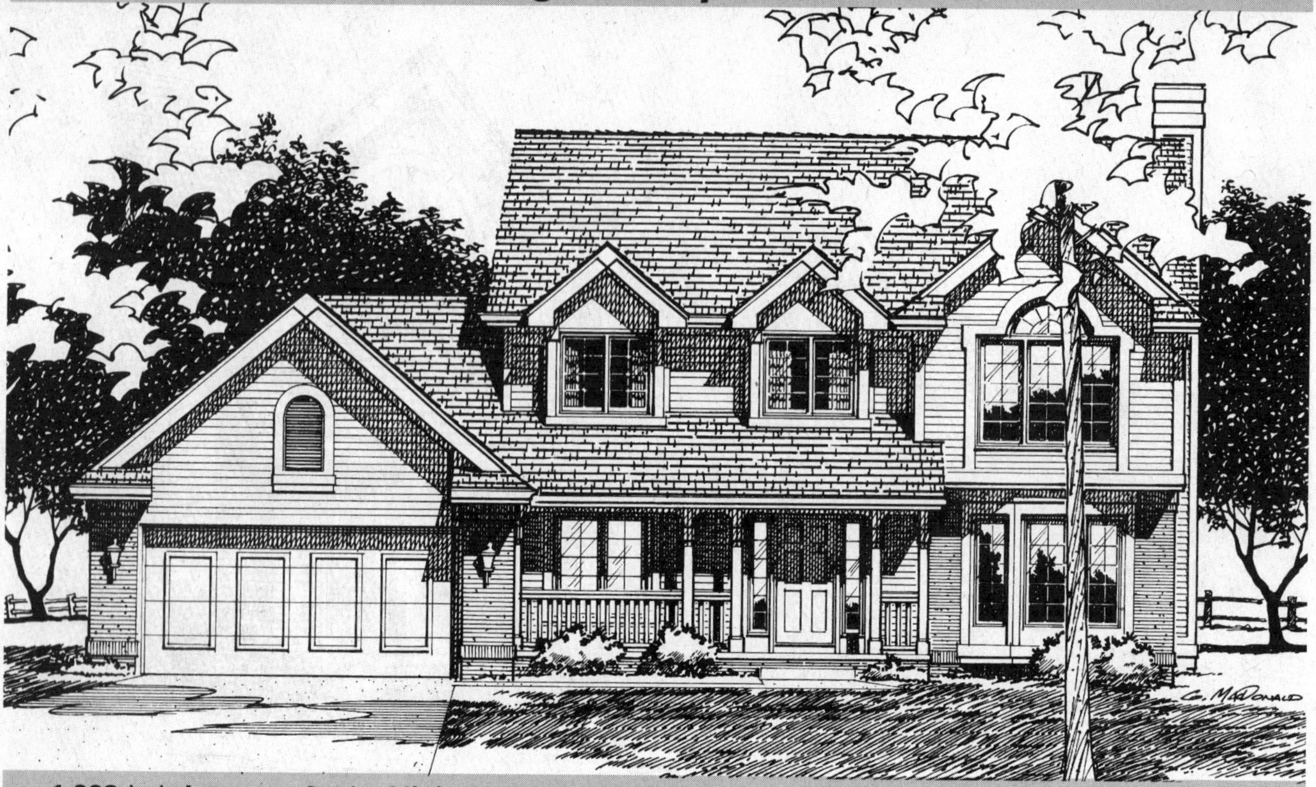

1,998 total square feet of living area

Price Code C

Special features

- Lovely designed family room offers double-door entrance into living area
- Roomy kitchen with breakfast area is a natural gathering place
- 10' ceiling in master bedroom
- 3 bedrooms, 2 1/2 baths, 2-car garage
- Basement foundation

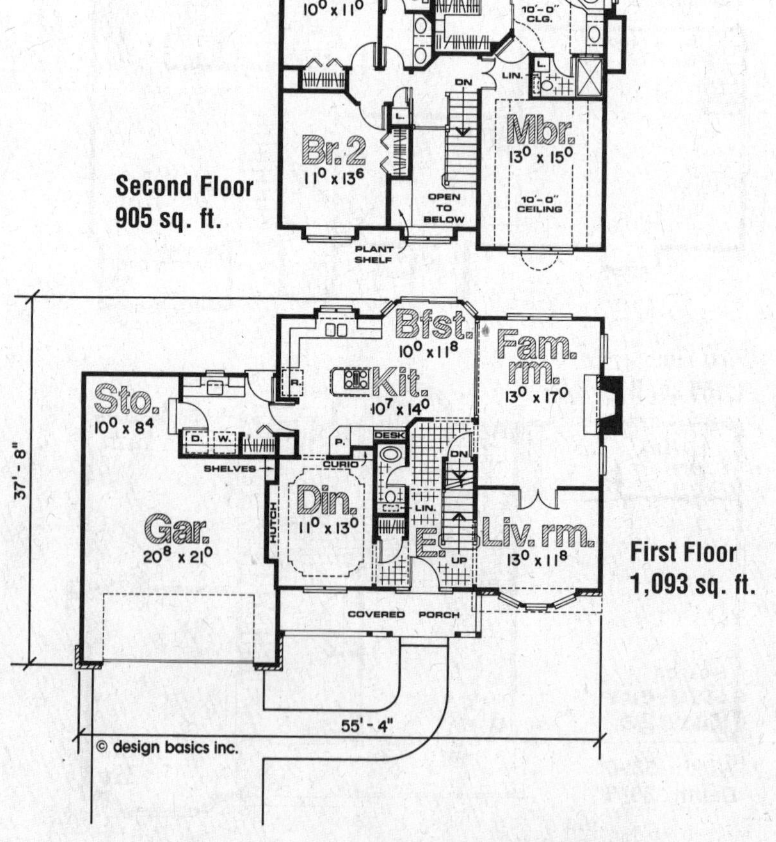

WHIRLPOOL
Br.3
10⁰ x 11⁰
10'-0" CLG.
LIN.
DN
Mbr.
13⁰ x 15⁰
10'-0" CEILING
Br.2
11⁰ x 13⁶
OPEN TO BELOW
PLANT SHELF
Bfst.
10⁰ x 11⁸
Fam. rm.
13⁰ x 17⁰
Kit.
10⁷ x 14⁰
Sto.
10⁰ x 8⁴
D. W.
DESK
P.
SHELVES
CURIO
HUTCH
Din.
11⁰ x 13⁰
Gar.
20⁸ x 21⁰
LIN.
Liv. rm.
13⁰ x 11⁸
UP
COVERED PORCH
37' - 8"
55' - 4"
© design basics inc.

Second Floor
905 sq. ft.

First Floor
1,093 sq. ft.

The Family
Handyman

Plan #708-AX-301

Country Ranch With Open Interior

1,783 total square feet of living area **Price Code D**

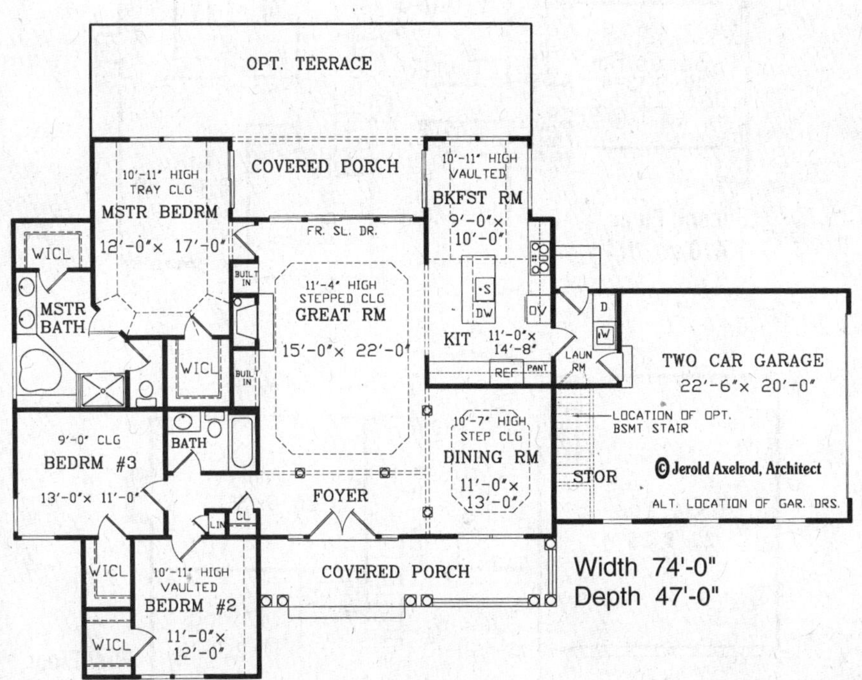
OPT. TERRACE
COVERED PORCH
10'-11" HIGH TRAY CLG
MSTR BEDRM
12'-0" x 17'-0"
10'-11" HIGH VAULTED
BKFST RM
9'-0" x 10'-0"
WICL
MSTR BATH
FR. SL. DR.
11'-4" HIGH STEPPED CLG
GREAT RM
15'-0" x 22'-0"
BUILT IN
KIT 11'-0" x 14'-8"
DW
DV
REF
PANT
LAUN RM
TWO CAR GARAGE
22'-6" x 20'-0"
WICL
9'-0" CLG
BEDRM #3
13'-0" x 11'-0"
BATH
10'-7" HIGH STEP CLG
DINING RM
11'-0" x 13'-0"
LOCATION OF OPT. BSMT STAIR
STOR
© Jerold Axelrod, Architect
FOYER
LIN
CL
ALT. LOCATION OF GAR. DRS.
WICL
10'-11" HIGH VAULTED
BEDRM #2
11'-0" x 12'-0"
WICL
COVERED PORCH

Width 74'-0"
Depth 47'-0"

Special features

- The front to rear flow of the great room, with built-ins on one side is a furnishing delight
- Bedrooms are all quietly zoned on one side
- The master bedroom is separated for privacy
- Every bedroom features walk-in closets
- 3 bedrooms, 2 baths, 2-car side entry garage
- Basement, crawl space or slab foundation, please specify when ordering

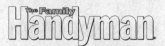

Handsome Traditional With Gabled Entrance

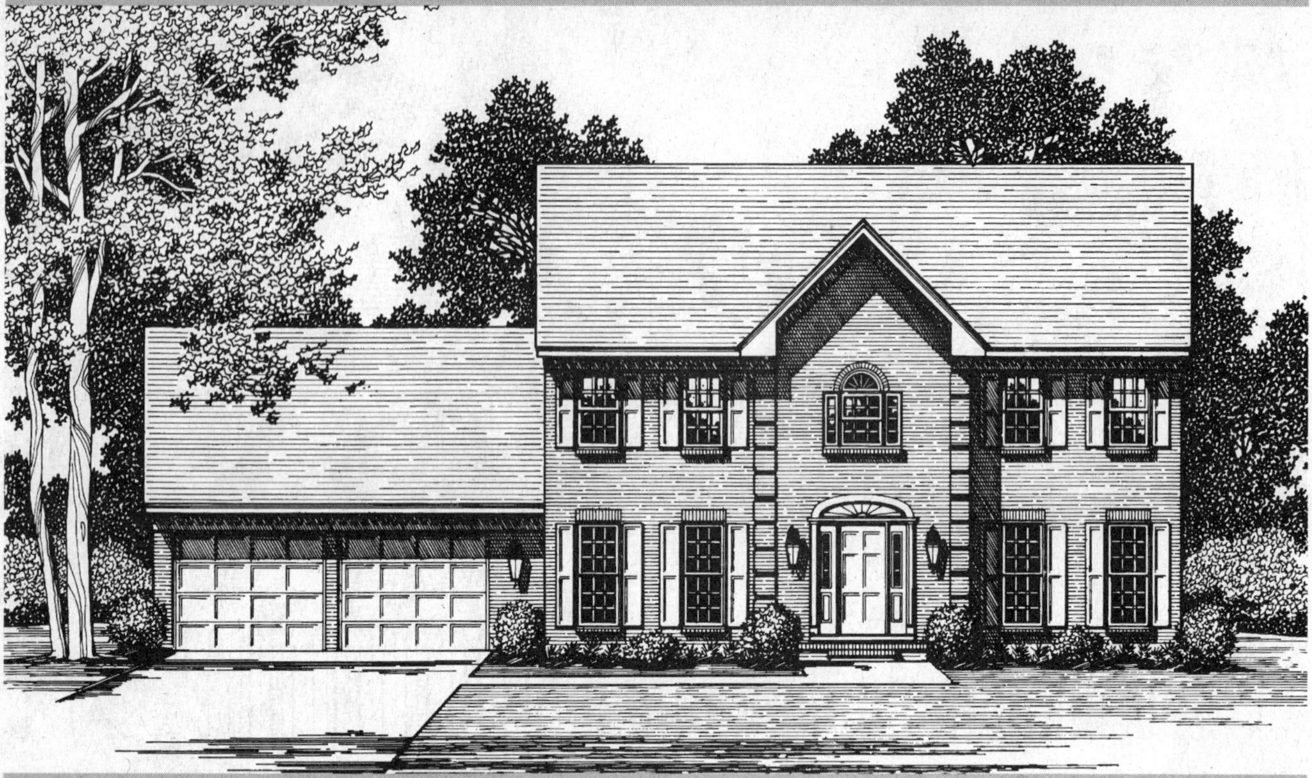

2,529 total square feet of living area

Price Code E

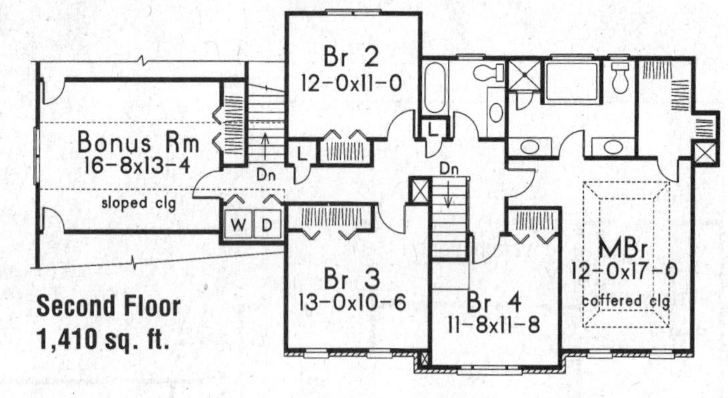
Br 2
12-0x11-0
Bonus Rm
16-8x13-4
sloped clg
Dn
L
L
Dn
W D
Br 3
13-0x10-6
Br 4
11-8x11-8
MBr
12-0x17-0
coffered clg

Second Floor
1,410 sq. ft.

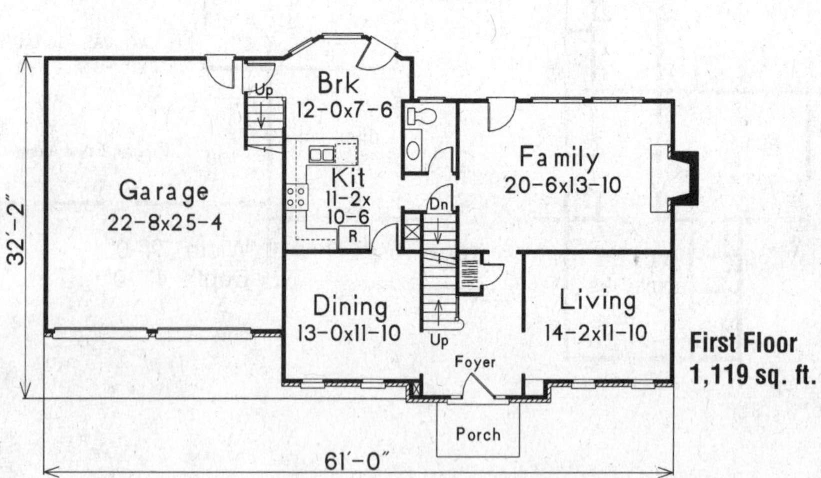
Up
Brk
12-0x7-6
Garage
22-8x25-4
Kit
11-2x
10-6
R
Family
20-6x13-10
Dn
Dining
13-0x11-10
Up
Living
14-2x11-10
Foyer
Porch
32'-2"
61'-0"

First Floor
1,119 sq. ft.

Special features

- Distinguished appearance enhances this home's classic interior arrangement
- Bonus room over the garage is included in the square footage and has direct access from the attic and the second floor hall
- Garden tub, walk-in closet and coffered ceiling enhance the master bedroom suite
- 4 bedrooms, 2 1/2 baths, 2-car garage
- Basement foundation

Plan #708-JA-62401

Inviting Covered Porch Entry

2,034 total square feet of living area **Price Code F**

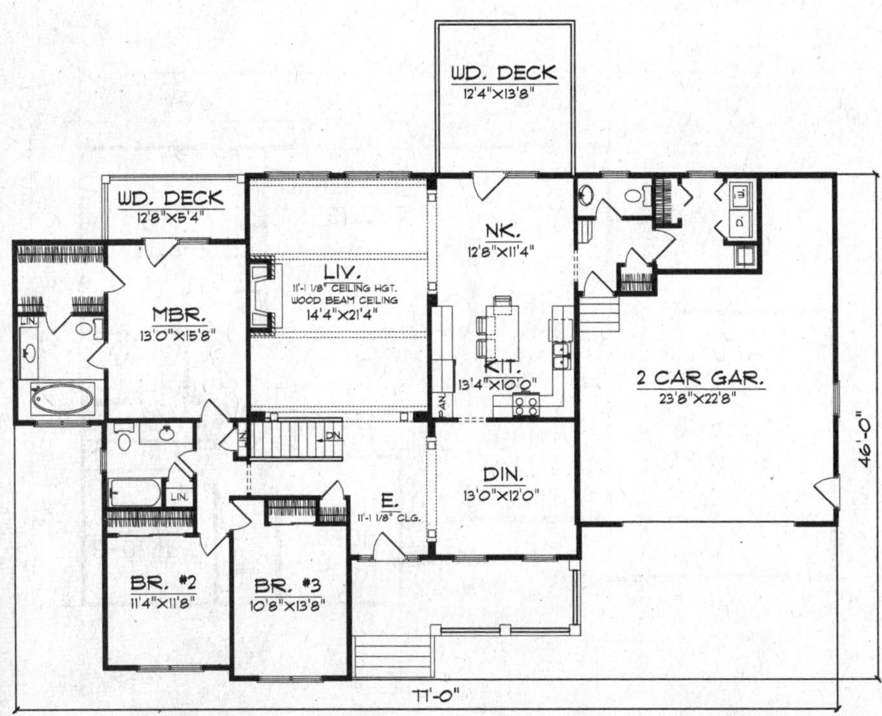

WD. DECK
12'4"X13'8"
WD. DECK
12'8"X5'4"
NK.
12'8"X11'4"
LIV.
11'-1 1/8" CEILING HGT.
WOOD BEAM CEILING
14'4"X21'4"
MBR.
13'0"X15'8"
KIT.
13'4"X10'0"
PAN.
2 CAR GAR.
23'8"X22'8"
DIN.
13'0"X12'0"
E.
11'-1 1/8" CLG.
DN
LIN.
LIN.
BR. #2
11'4"X11'8"
BR. #3
10'8"X13'8"
77'-0"
46'-0"

Special features

- Oversized tub in master bath adds luxury
- Rustic touches are present in the great room which features a beamed ceiling and a large brick fireplace
- Center island in kitchen features extra seating
- 3 bedrooms, 2 1/2 baths, 2-car garage
- Basement foundation

The Family
Handyman

Plan #708-0110

Vaulted Ceilings Create Spacious Feeling

1,605 total square feet of living area **Price Code B**

Special features

- Vaulted ceilings in great room, kitchen and breakfast area
- Spacious great room features large bay window, fireplace, built-in bookshelves and a convenient wet bar
- Dine in formal dining room or breakfast area overlooking rear yard, perfect for entertaining or everyday living
- Master bedroom has a spacious private bath with oval tub and separate shower
- 3 bedrooms, 2 baths, 2-car garage
- Basement foundation, drawings also include slab and crawl space foundations

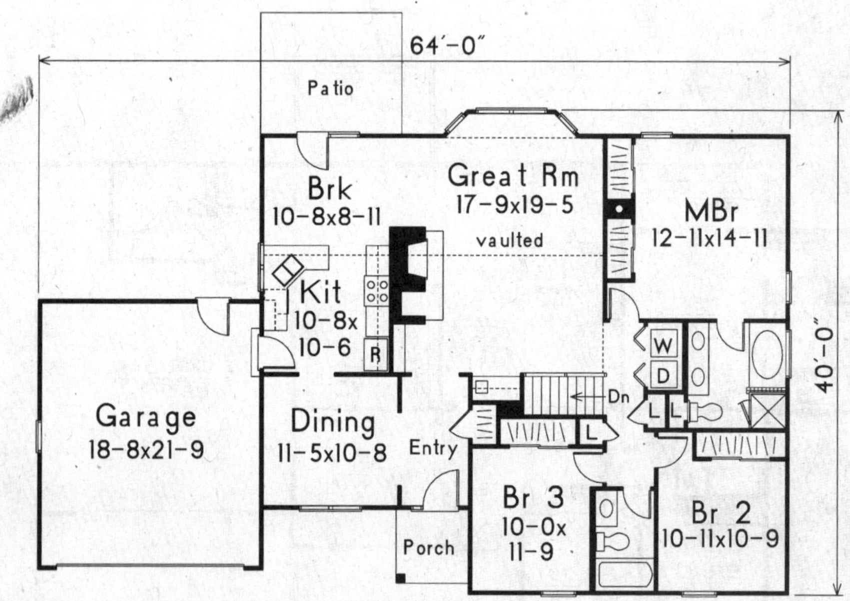
64'-0"
Patio
Brk
10-8x8-11
Great Rm
17-9x19-5
vaulted
MBr
12-11x14-11
Kit
10-8x
10-6
R
W
D
Dn
L
Garage
18-8x21-9
Dining
11-5x10-8
Entry
Br 3
10-0x
11-9
Br 2
10-11x10-9
Porch
40'-0"

TO ORDER BLUEPRINTS USE THE FORM ON PAGE 15 OR CALL TOLL-FREE 1-877-671-6036

View thousands more home plans online at www.familyhandyman.com/homeplans